Marriage

MARRIAGE

SECOND EDITION

Robert O. Blood, Jr.

ASSOCIATE PROFESSOR OF SOCIOLOGY, UNIVERSITY OF MICHIGAN

The Free Press, New York   Collier-Macmillan Limited, London

Preface to the Second Edition

This new edition of *Marriage* reflects the rapid pace of technological and social change in the intervening years. "The pill" and intrauterine devices have come into widespread use in family planning. The computer has become a new tool in dating and mate-selection. The civil rights movement has given interracial marriages a new urgency. These changes require new definitions and interpretations if we are to keep pace with the world in which we live and the people who live in it with us.

Research on marriage is constantly expanding, and the latest knowledge has been incorporated in this new edition. Masters and Johnson, in their book *Human Sexual Response*, have so greatly enlarged our understanding of sexual relations that the chapter on sex had to be extensively rewritten. Recent studies of mixed marriages have refined and altered our understanding of this phenomenon. Altogether, information from more than 100 new research articles and monographs has been added to this edition, each reference carefully selected to reflect something new in our understanding of marriage.

All the material, both new and old, has been extensively reorganized. Previously scattered information has been brought together for more cohesive treatment. Editorial polishing has generally improved the book's readability and has produced a more balanced treatment of such controversial topics as premarital intercourse and marital disenchantment. New diagrams have been prepared by staff members of the University of Michigan Department of Medical Illustration. Finally, the scope of the book has been widened to include such diverse topics as premarital counseling, interethnic marriages, boundary problems between nuclear family and kin networks, the effects of divorce and remarriage on children, artificial insemination and adoption, and premature births and congenital handicaps.

And, perhaps most importantly, a new emphasis has been placed on the role of commitment in marriage.

More than either of its predecessors, this new edition offers a comprehensive and practical distillation of the scientific knowledge relevant to marriage.

Robert O. Blood, Jr.

Tokyo, Japan
January, 1969

Preface to the
First Edition

This book is a successor to *Anticipating Your Marriage,* published by the Free Press in 1955. Though some case materials and illustrations are the same, the text itself has been almost completely rewritten to meet the eagerness of today's students for a mature and sophisticated treatment of a subject vitally important to them.

Specifically this book is:

Scientific. The best available scientific evidence about human behavior, its causes and consequences, has been drawn from more than 250 books and articles. Key data are presented in lucid charts and graphs, often simplified from the original sources for clarity of understanding. Where the evidence is conflicting, I have drawn the most probable generalizations from it. Where the evidence is lacking, I have drawn on the best available theories. Though the original sources are often highly technical, I have written for students without particular prerequisites (those with previous training should find this a useful synthesis of the scientific literature).

Idealistic. The book is concerned with more than mere description of what is. It is interested in what marriage can be like at its best and in how that ideal can be achieved. This does not contradict the scientific approach, for science can tell us not only what the *average* family does but also what *unusual* families do—the kind of families that achieve the most satisfaction, produce the most effectively socialized children, and attain other widely shared goals in life. Values, to be sure, differ from reader to reader. But this book spells out the means by which particular values may be achieved.

Integrated. The concept of "personal relationships" is the central theme of this book—how they develop in courtship, are maintained in marriage, and are extended to children. Similarities are spelled out between analogous situations at different stages of the family life cycle and between analogous facets of experience at any one time. The book searches for patterns amid conflicting data and for comprehensive generalizations from the subject as a whole. Scattered materials from sociology, psychology, biology, medicine, economics, religion, and elsewhere are synthesized into an integrated unit.

Focused. In a complicated and many-faceted world, this book is intentionally focused on those experiences that most Western (and especially American) young people can expect to encounter as they progress from dating to marriage and family living. Within Western society the experiences of the middle class generally, and of college students in particular, are emphasized, since they are my chief audience. Such readers can understand their own experiences and opportunities better against occasional references to differing groups and other societies. Always, however, the intention is to mobilize information and ideas that bear upon the practical experiences and choices the reader is likely to face in his roles as husband and father or wife and mother.

Robert O. Blood, Jr.

Ann Arbor, Michigan
March, 1962

Contents

6 Readiness for Marriage

7 Rites of Passage: I. Engagement

13 Religion in Family Living 270

14 Companionship in Leisure 279

15 Sex: The Most Intimate Relationship 293

20 The Advent of Children 426

List of Illustrations

Introduction: The Meaning of Marriage

Life consists of a combination of roles played in various settings—religious in the church, political in the community, economic in the corporation, marital in the family, and a few others. Of these roles, only two involve major segments of life for the average person: (1) A job takes 40 hours a week, more or less; a career spreads over 40 or 50 years. "What do you do?" is one of the most revealing questions a man can answer. (2) A woman who is "just a housewife" may deprecate her role, but marriage embraces most of her life. If she works also, she has two major responsibilities in life, as does her husband.

Even if we evaluate a man primarily as an employee rather than as a husband, the latter role still counts. Marriage means something special because it is so different from work. Work emphasizes the product. The people who work for a company are means to an end. To be sure, marriage has products too, in the shape of children, but the primary emphasis is not on reproduction but on the personal relationship between husband and wife. Regardless, therefore, of the time a married man or woman invests in his marriage as opposed to his job, marriage has special significance.

In recent years, the gap between the values emphasized by men and by women has narrowed. As more women enter the labor force, they are less home-oriented than before. With the maturing of the American economy, men are less production-minded and more interested in enjoying the good things of life, especially the companionship of wife and children. For at least some American men at some stages in life, family values have eclipsed occupational values in importance (see Table 1). In any case, family relationships rank high for contemporary Americans of both sexes.

1

Table 1. Expected Source of Greatest Satisfaction in Life Reported by College Men and Women

Expected Source of Greatest Satisfaction in Life	Men	Women
Family relations	60%	87%
Career	31	6
Leisure-time recreational activities	4	2
Religious beliefs and activities	3	4
Participation as a citizen in community affairs	1	*
Participation in activities directed toward national or international betterment	1	1
Total	100%	100%
Number of cases	629*	407

* Less than ½ of 1%.
Adapted from Goldsen, 1960: 210, and from unpublished data on women students kindly furnished by Dr. Goldsen. *Source:* Cornell University undergraduates, 1952.

Marriage as a Personal Relationship

The essence of marriage is the personal relationship between the partners. To use a more technical term, marriage is a *primary relationship*. As such, it falls (along with friendship) in a small class that contrasts with the majority of relationships. Typical secondary relationships involve employer and employee, politician and voter, salesman and customer, or bus driver and passenger—impersonal, official relationships. Officeholders are treated in certain ways because of the positions they hold, not because of who they are. A proper clerk treats every customer the same, regardless of who he is. His task is to sell his product, not to get involved in the customer's personal life, which is "none of his business." So clerk and customer limit their behavior to the transaction at hand. The rest of their personalities, problems, and interests remain hidden.

Personal relations, by contrast, are all-embracing. They involve the total personality in a face-to-face, person-to-person experience. Through extensive and intensive contact, people develop strong feelings—negative as well as positive.

Personal relations are ends in themselves, not means to ends. Because the emphasis is on the partner's total personality, and because every person is unique, personal relations are particularistic, glorying in the partner's distinctive characteristics. It matters little which clerk waits on me in a big store, but it makes all the difference in the world whom I marry. One clerk should be as good as another, but not just any wife will do. Marriage is too complex and too intimate for random interchangeability.

To say that personal relations are noninstrumental doesn't mean they yield no dividends. Rather, the benefits are not the focus of attention. The focus is on the encounter between the two persons, between what Martin Buber called the *I and Thou*. Awareness, sensitivity, and responsiveness are the dominant moods. Spontaneity and generosity characterize the inter-action. Love is the motivating force.

In contrast, the world of business consists of deals. *Quid pro quo*: A fair exchange. Justice arrived at by bargaining. Contractual arrangements—if you do this for me, I will pay you so much. Be sure to read the fine print! Watch out that you don't pay too much or sell too cheaply! Look out for your own interests!

Business relations are typically limited, standardized, unemotional, utili-tarian, and contractual. Conversely, personal relations are essentially un-limited, particularistic, emotionally involved, altruistic, and spontaneous (Parsons, 1959).*

The Functions of Personal Relations

Even though personal relations are nonutilitarian, they have practical consequences. Whereas business relations are designed to benefit the participants, personal relations are not; yet benefits occur nevertheless. Not bargained for, not claimed as rights, not agreed upon in writing, the benefits of personal relations are nevertheless visible. They may be classified under two headings: need gratification and social control.

NEED GRATIFICATION. The human animal has many needs. In many societies, the *biological* needs for food, clothing, and shelter have been met only through families. Modern urban society still provides most of these physical services through the family, even though purchasable substitutes are available in restaurants, laundries, and hotels. Personal relations are no longer the only possible source of gratification for physical needs even though they may still be the preferred source.

Another biological need—sex—is more ambiguous. Superficially it is pur-chasable, although only on the black market. However, sexual gratification is more than tension-release, and in this fuller sense it is available only in the context of personal relations. Indeed, I will suggest that sexual inter-course is the quintessence of personal relationship. Hence, a distinctive function of marriage is to gratify the partners' sexual needs.

Certain *psychological* needs are satisfied only through personal relations. Among these is the *need for affiliation*, that is, the need to be related to other people. By definition, a need for relationship requires personal rela-

* For details of references, see the alphabetical List of References at the back of the book.

tions. Although differing in strength and salience from person to person, it is a universal need.

Perhaps in simpler societies with stable communities and complex households it could be assumed that everyone's need for affiliation would be satisfied. The individual was embedded in a network of personal relations from which there was no escape. Life itself could not go on in solitude, and there were no crowds to get lost in. Today, however, "the lonely crowd" is the symbol of our civilization (Riesman, 1954). We are lonely in the midst of the crowd as long as our relationships with others are restricted and segmented. Only when we are able to establish personal relationships with other individuals do we escape the sense of estrangement that so often afflicts modern man. The need for affiliation is therefore met by personal relations in marriage (and in friendship).

In personal relations we achieve a sense of belonging, of being accepted for what we are, of being at home in the world. Personal relations are good for the ego because they provide someone who cares, an audience for our jokes and our troubles. No longer do we have to wonder whether anybody will listen to what we have to say. We can count on the attention and the response of our partner.

SOCIAL CONTROL. Because personal relations are reciprocal, the benefits I receive in gratifying my own needs are matched by my partner's claim to equal benefits. This is a moral claim, not a legal one. Indeed, my colleague G. E. Swanson believes that personal relations are the primary source of morality and ethics.

As I enter into a personal relationship, I become aware of my partner's needs, feelings, and desires. The intimacy of the relationship confronts me with my partner's expectations of me. The more I become involved, the greater my availability to care for my partner as I am cared for, to listen to my partner as I am listened to, to put myself out for my partner as is done for me.

Spontaneously and inevitably, a personal relationship becomes not only a source of satisfaction but a claim upon my energies. In a sense, the bachelor is quite right who calls marriage a ball-and-chain affair. A personal relation is always limiting. It limits my freedom to be irresponsible, to lead a gay, self-indulgent life without a care in the world. As soon as I enter into a personal relationship, I become responsible to and for another person. I am no longer free to ignore his needs.

Immature persons recoil before responsibilities; but learning to accept them is one of the benefits of personal relations. Responsibilities help us grow, lure us out of our protective shells, humanize us from the egotism of our infantile beginnings. Friendship and love complete our transformation into humane beings.

The Distinctiveness of Marriage

So far we have discussed personal relations in general, whether informal friendships or formal marriages. Friendship and marriage share many characteristics. However, the meaning of marriage lies partly in its distinctiveness as a sexual relationship, a comprehensive relationship, and a permanent relationship.

A SEXUAL RELATIONSHIP. I have already suggested that the sexual aspect of marriage reveals how personal it is. Marriage is the only *legitimate* personal relation that is sexual in nature. Our culture generally and our religions in particular teach that marriage is the only proper locus of sexual intercourse. This teaching is often violated; yet the violations are usually fleeting and irregular in comparison to the long-term regularity of intercourse in marriage. In this crucial sense marriage is more intimate than any other relationship.

Because of sex, marriage also uniquely involves child-rearing. Conception and reproduction may occur outside of marriage, it is true; but illegitimacy is not only stigmatized by society but generally unwanted by the unmarried themselves. Only within marriage are children both a natural and intended consequence of sexual intercourse. And any parent can testify to the pervasive repercussions of children on those who care for them.

A COMPREHENSIVE RELATIONSHIP. Marriage is not only uniquely sexual but uniquely comprehensive. Sexual activities may occur under other auspices. Even child-rearing may be approximated by an institutional housemother. But only marriage combines sex and parenthood and companionship and housekeeping "under one roof." Even though every personal relationship embraces many aspects of life, the most humdrum marriage eclipses all but the most extraordinary friendships in the breadth of the relationship. All facets of life—physical, mental, social, spiritual, financial —contribute to the comprehensiveness of married living.

A PERMANENT RELATIONSHIP. Despite the rising American divorce rate, divorce is still exceptional both statistically and normatively. The reasons are many. Partly it is a consequence of the features just mentioned. Because of the possibility of conception, women tend to cling to their sexual partner. When conception occurs, the long dependence of the human child requires a stable nurturing framework. Society's concern for the socialization of children creates social pressure for marital stability and corresponding disapproval of divorce.

In our technological society geographical mobility is increasingly common. As people move from town to town, their network of primary relationships is torn to shreds—all save one, their marriage. Friends must be left behind on moving day, but marriage partners are not. The permanence of marriage thus takes on new significance as the rest of life becomes more transient.

The Increasing Personalization of Marriage

There was a time when the personal aspect of marriage mattered less than it does today. Under primitive conditions such as the American frontier the harsh realities of life left little time for love-making. When the family was factory, farm, church, and school, it was an instrumental agency focused on jobs to be done. Similarly, in feudal societies, the household was a complex, three-generation affair, subordinating the personal relation of husband and wife even more. The wife typically found personal satisfaction in her children, and the husband with a concubine.

By stripping away utilitarian functions and restricting the household to the husband–wife–children nucleus, urban society has freed the family from its institutional, intergenerational shackles. Encumbered by fewer duties and obligations, the members of the family are able to appreciate each other more as persons. With increased leisure, they can enjoy each other's company.

Today's family specializes, as never before, in personal relationships. The "lost" functions of the family have been taken over by specialized economic, political, educational, and religious institutions. What remains is an opportunity for families to specialize in an area where no other social institution can. Perhaps in the past marriage was not a personal relationship. Now, however, that is the essence of marriage (Parsons, 1955).

The Prerequisites of Personal Relations

Perhaps few would question what has been said so far; the broad sweep of history is not easily overlooked. When we turn from social analysis to particular cases, however, we encounter tremendous variability. Although the average marriage is more personal today, there are countless exceptions. A man and woman may live in the same house, even sleep in the same bed, and ignore each other. They may carry on the pragmatic routines of keeping house together, but fail to look at each other, listen to each other, and give themselves to each other.

If we asked such couples how they feel about their marriages, they would undoubtedly express disappointment. Merely existing together leaves too many needs unsatisfied. Expectations for marriage have risen. We are no longer satisfied with the perfunctory functional relations that were once the rule. We hope to continue indefinitely the intense personal involvement we experience when love is new. We look askance at husbands so occupationally involved and wives so burdened with children that they have no time for each other.

Perhaps we expect too much. Perhaps one reason there are so many divorces is that we expect the impossible. Yet some couples do have good marriages—not perfect, perhaps, but good enough to excite the envy of those who don't. Are these people merely lucky or could others do as well if they knew how?

Some social scientists are fatalistic about this question. They point to deep-seated, irrational factors that plague unhappy marriages and to the way divorce infects the same families from generation to generation. Human personality is largely shaped in childhood, they say, and character defects are likely to plague a person for the rest of his life. There is some truth in this point of view. Human behavior *is* largely determined. Yet, within limits, every man has some freedom of choice. The man in the street may be clearer about this than the social scientist. The world is full of advice to the lovelorn, advice given and sought on the assumption that it will be useful. The world is full of books on how to be happily married (of which this is one) based on the premise that the die is not entirely cast at birth.

Perhaps the inappropriateness of marital fatalism can be seen more clearly by analogy. In the world of work, we don't give IQ all the credit for a job well done. Congratulatory speakers praise the leader's hard work, his untiring efforts, his willingness to overcome obstacles. Nor need the opposite of fatalism be Pollyanna's optimism. Success in marriage is no easier than on the job. But fatalism is unduly pessimistic. Effort can pay off.

If divorce were simply inevitable, the same people would go on having divorces all their lives. A few do—playboys, movie stars, and misfits. But the majority of divorced people do better the second time; their second marriage succeeds where the first one failed. This means that they either married the wrong person the first time, learned something in the meantime, or tried harder or were less distracted the second time. These are precisely the prerequisites of success in any marriage (not just in second marriages). To choose the right partner, to know how to treat him, to take the trouble to do so year in and year out, and to be supported by others in doing so—these are the prerequisites of a good marriage. In shorthand, they are (a) compatibility, (b) skill, (c) effort, (d) commitment, and (e) support.

Compatibility

Compatibility in this book has a restricted meaning. It does not refer to the adjustment a couple achieve after marriage by giving a little here and compromising there. Rather, it means the goodness of fit between the partners' intrinsic characteristics. Compatibility between two people, therefore, is a given. I am more compatible with this girl than with that one. In this sense, compatibility can be discovered between people. When sufficient compatibility is found, it provides the basis for the first choice in marriage—whom to marry.

Even though compatibility is primarily determined in the childhood socialization of the two individuals, it is not completely unchangeable. Observing a group of adults over a twenty-year period, Kelly (1955) discovered that they changed considerably. Moreover, his married couples did not grow any more like each other. They grew apart in as many ways as they grew together. This means that the average couple encounter new incompatibilities as new interests and attitudes arise. Unfortunately for the sake of young eligibles, future changes cannot be predicted; so one must choose on the basis of present compatibility.

Vocational counselors match the man to the occupation. The individual's aptitudes and interests need to fit the job. With many different jobs available, the task is to find the best fit. "Square pegs in round holes" lead to failure. Choosing the right vocation doesn't guarantee success, but makes it possible.

Similarly, compatibility between marriage partners determines how easily a personal relationship can be established. For a highly compatible couple, love blossoms easily. The less compatible they are, the harder it is to achieve success. Yet compatibility is not the only factor involved. A lazy man can be fired from the "right" job, and a compatible couple can let their marriage go to seed. Conversely, "hiring the handicapped is good business" if the handicapped are specially trained to compensate for their difficulties. And a couple can overcome substantial handicaps if they tackle them energetically.

Compatibility, then, provides only the potentiality for a good marriage. It is a necessary but not a sufficient condition. The more compatible two people are, the better, but potentiality must be translated into actuality.

Skill

The next step beyond vocational choice is vocational training. Ph.D., M.D., LL.B., B.D.—these are the admission tickets to professional practice. The skills of marriage are less clearly defined and less easily programed. In Japan they were traditionally flower arrangement, tea ceremony, and sewing for girls—none for boys. In America they were cooking and sewing for girls—again none for boys. The increased personalization of marriage, however, creates new standards of performance. These standards are expressed more often in terms of results than of methods, but greater finesse is clearly required to achieve those results.

For instance, for wives to be sexually satisfied requires finesse in foreplay. The therapeutic function of marriage requires skill in solacing hurt feelings. Shared decision-making demands skill in expressing needs and reciprocal skill in listening and empathizing with the partner. When conflicting preferences are expressed, skill in deadlock-breaking comes into play.

Few Americans realize that such skills exist. There are no road tests for getting a marriage license. Yet marital casualties result from clumsiness in human relations:

> I know now that I was too young when I got married. I forced myself on Arlene and didn't pay enough attention to her desires. Perhaps if we had waited a little longer, I would have treated her better.*

I won't attempt in this preview to discuss whether this husband's diagnosis was correct, whether, that is, expertise can be acquired simply by waiting. My point is that marriages differ tremendously in the skillfulness of the partners and the more skillful they are, the better their marriage will be.

For those unskilled in human relations, courses may provide significant training for marriage. One concern of this book is to describe some of the skills involved, especially in resolving conflicts.

Effort

In careers we take for granted that success depends on effort as well as on skill and aptitude. But experts disagree on the relevance of effort in marriage. Some people boil at the suggestion, feeling that marriage is the one place in life where they should be able to relax and enjoy themselves. Love, they say, cannot be forced. It is the spontaneity of love that makes it delightful.

To be sure, spontaneity does enliven the best human relationships. Especially at the beginning of a love affair, a remarkable momentum develops from discovering a compatible, skillful partner. The romantic enthusiasm generated by what Erich Fromm (1956) calls "the collapsing of the walls" between two people propels them into increasing mutual involvement. Buoyed up by the joy of discovering each other, they revel in acts of thoughtfulness and expressions of affection. Hence, a personal relationship between lovers often blossoms effortlessly.

However, the less compatible a couple are, the more problems they must resolve. The less skillful they are, the lower their spontaneous achievement will be. The greater the handicaps, the more appropriate it is to "turn on the steam" rather than to be satisfied with spontaneous mediocrity. Effort means taking the trouble to listen when the partner is talking, to rub her

---

* Case materials are adapted from a wide variety of sources. All names used are pseudonyms.

back when it hurts, to be nice to his mother even when she's crabby. It means doing more than "what comes naturally." It means extending the limits of patience, tenderness, and appreciation.

Is this possible? Can people act better than they feel? Can they transcend irritation and boredom to treat others as they would like to be treated? Certainly there are limits to what can be expected of human nature. But, whereas man cannot add a "cubit" to his physical stature, the saints of all ages have demonstrated that he can add to his moral stature if he tries hard enough. While few readers of this book will be canonized for marital excellence, altruism is needed to produce excellence in personal relations.

Effort may not be greatly needed by well-matched couples, at least in the beginning. Marital careers, however, rarely flourish indefinitely on mere spontaneity. The initial impetus of love tends to falter. As new discoveries cease, partners are taken for granted. Simultaneous with this weakening of mutual fascination is the declining impetus to interaction that results from aging. Gerontologists focus on men and women older than sixty, but aging is a gradual process that undermines spontaneous vitality continuously. Some of the declining pace of marriage is inevitable. Nevertheless, habituation and aging can be countered by extra effort. Declining averages don't mean that every marriage must decline. But this decline tends to happen "if you don't watch out."

Effort, therefore, can compensate for the corrosion of time in every marriage as well as for the special problems faced by incompatible and unskillful couples. Other things being equal, a marriage is better off with effort than without it, both in the short run and especially in the long run. With effort a couple may not only hold the line against deterioration but develop their relationship from year to year. If a man's career line can show progressively greater productivity and responsibility, why can't his marriage? It all depends on a willingness to try.

Commitment

The vows of marriage traditionally end with the phrase, "till death do us part." Many marriages fall short of that goal. Yet the intent of marrying for life is crucial to a successful outcome. Those who marry only "for better," unprepared to cope with the inevitable "for worse," are less apt to make the effort necessary to resolve those troubles. Divorce and remarriage may seem easier than the hard work of resolving conflicts. Commitment adds a time dimension to marriage—a long-term perspective which underscores the value of putting forth effort and improving skill. Given wholehearted commitment to spending their lives together, a couple are more apt to develop a virtuoso marriage.

Commitment is dangerous. It can be exploited. If my wife takes my commitment for granted, she may rest too easily on her laurels. Perhaps commitment should be not simply to each other as we are but to the highest potentialities we can achieve together. Commitment then would be to marriage not simply as a status but as a dynamic process. Let me commit myself to a lifelong adventure, the adventure of living with this woman. The route of this adventure has been only dimly charted by those who have gone before. Because I am unique and my partner is unique, our marriage will also be unique. We commit ourselves to undertaking this adventure together, and to following wherever it may lead. Part of the excitement of marriage is not knowing in advance what either the joys or the sorrows will be. We can be sure, however, that we will be confronted with countless challenges. Commitment provides the momentum for going forward in the face of those challenges.

Support

Although success in marriage depends primarily on the compatibility, skill, effort, and commitment of the partners themselves, marriages are not impervious to outside influence. Hence, external support makes an additional contribution. Support may come from both people and institutions. Significant people include relatives and friends. Parents may offer resources of money and personal service or they may pit husband against wife through destructive criticism or conflicting demands. Friends may provide models of marital stability and creativity, or they may tear a marriage apart through extramarital involvements.

Institutional support comes partly through joint participation in the same organizations, providing opportunities for companionship and a sense of common values. (Conversely, conflicting institutional demands strain interfaith marriages.) Support for marriages in trouble may be provided through community services, such as family-life discussion groups and marriage counseling facilities.

In particular cases positive or negative external forces may make or break a marriage.

Marriage in Context

The meaning of marriage can be found primarily within marriage itself —in the relationship between husband and wife. That, however, is not the whole story. Families do not live in a vacuum. Society sustains, shapes, and controls family life in ways too important to ignore. Moreover, each member of the family, as an individual, participates in social relations outside the family that affect his behavior within it. Thus, collectively and individually the external environment of the family impinges upon it.

The Social Environment of the Family

Over the past century, the setting for family living has been revolutionized. The physical environment is part of the transformation. Cities are bigger, churches bigger, supermarkets bigger. Houses may not be as big as they once were, but they are more adequately heated, easier to keep clean, and filled with noisier machinery. The outside world has been piped into our homes via television and is more accessible through improved transportation. The social environment keeps changing too, in pace with technical changes. Increased premarital and extramarital intimacy challenge the exclusiveness of marriage. Divorce and remarriage are more accepted, challenging the permanence of marriage. On the other hand, family-life education reaches more people.

It would be difficult to say whether the world has become a better or worse environment for families. The only thing we can be sure of is that it has changed and that the pace of change is accelerating. Our children will live in a world far different from our own. But the world never has been and never will be uniform. We can generalize about trends to suburban living but need to remember that there are still families living in slums, in apartment houses, in small towns (and even on farms) whose circumstances are significantly different.

Our primary concern in this book is to search for generalizations. To support those generalizations, we will draw upon the best available data from scientific research. We must remember, however, that research is seldom conclusive. The couples studied are usually too few, too localized, and too unrepresentative to offer the last word. Yet even fragmentary studies are better than none at all, better than sheer speculation. So we will exploit them for all they are worth. To any generalization, however, no matter how firmly supported, there are always exceptions. Generalizations apply to groups of marriages. They may not apply to a particular marriage. The burden of proof is on those who think they are exceptional. Our initial working assumption must always be that general tendencies apply to us insofar as we are ordinary, everyday people. But because every marriage is unique, we must be ready to be surprised whenever we shift from the simplicity of generalizations to the complexities of particular cases.

The External Roles of Family Members

If marriage were the full-time business of every man and woman, it would be simpler. But every man has "full-time" work to do as well as his family to attend to. He has duties and loyalties to his employer as well as to his wife. Since he is both husband and employee, he is subject to potential cross-pressures. The average man can't be an outstanding family man and an outstanding company man at the same time. The more time he puts in at the office, the less he has for his family, and vice versa. Perhaps, too, the more effort he devotes to one, the less energy he has for the other.

Yet being a good husband means earning a good income as well as responding to his wife. So every man must strike a balance between his occupational and marital roles. That balance is not easily found. It depends on how ambitious both partners are and on the requirements of the husband's job. The balance often shifts at different points in the family cycle and the career line. In general, the husband's involvement in the occupational system has extensive repercussions on his behavior as husband and father. Ditto the working wife's on her family roles. Ditto the other external roles of modern man: citizen, churchman, clubwoman, or whatever.

Although this pattern of life is more complicated than rural isolation, it isn't necessarily worse. Stresses from conflicting roles are offset by new rewards. Multiple group memberships provide variety in life. Outside the family, valuable resources may be acquired for the family's use.

To understand marriage fully, therefore, it is necessary to see husbands and wives functioning outside as well as inside the home, playing their nonmarital as well as their marital roles. Marriage is a major part of life. But it isn't the whole. Marriage is, or ought to be, a personal relationship. But other primary relationships in life supplement the rewards of marriage —or replace them for those who never marry. And, married or single, the secondary relations of business and government are equally essential. Marriage can mean wonderful things, but it is not the boundary of human existence. The meaning of marriage is only part of the meaning of life.

PART ONE

Courtship

Courtship is the entire process that leads up to marriage. Chapter 1 analyzes casual dating, which may provide a wealth of experience in personal relations and paves the way for the later stages of courtship. As set forth in two chapters on choosing a marriage partner, we know a good deal about the social characteristics of married couples and an increasing amount about personality needs in marriage. Traditionally undefinable, the feelings of love which characterize American courtship nevertheless deserve our fullest understanding (Chapter 4). Since love is seldom platonic, the question of sexual attraction and expression inevitably follows. However, love and sexual attraction by themselves do not guarantee readiness for marriage (Chapter 6). Once that readiness is achieved, most couples move swiftly through the transitional stages of engagement, wedding, and honeymoon into marriage (Chapters 7 and 8).

Together, these chapters portray the process of awakening interest in the opposite sex, gradual involvement and increasing intimacy with a few partners, and the final decision of two people to undertake the adventure of marriage together.

1 Dating: Practice for Marriage

In the eyes of many foreigners the American dating system is shocking. To date dozens of partners seems emotionally promiscuous. To disavow any thought of marrying most of them seems like callous exploitation. In many countries dating is either completely taboo or serious business. If taboo, "blind mates" may be arranged by doting parents or selected hardly less blindly from written reports and perhaps a formal interview with prospective applicants (Blood, 1967). If serious business, one normally marries his first date, or at least expects to marry her unless unexpected obstacles are encountered.

In the United States the connection between dating and marriage is less direct. Nobody infers that because John has a date with Suzy, he is likely to marry her. To be sure, he will eventually marry somebody he dates, but the chances for any one dating partner are slim.

The fact that Americans date more than others is no accident; our circumstances demand it. In a simple society almost any marriage partner will do, so mate selection can be casual. In a feudal society the emphasis on vertical relationships means that the bride is more a mother's daughter-in-law than her son's wife, so mate selection becomes highly formalized. In the United States mate selection is neither casual nor formal but highly personalized. Our society is complex and highly differentiated. Not only is it stratified into social classes, but within each class there are differences in temperament, tastes, and values from person to person. As a result, potential marital combinations differ in compatibility.

To some extent individual differences exist in every society, but Americans are less prepared to ignore them. In many countries, clashes between husband and wife are settled automatically by the rule of male dominance. Divergent recreational interests do not matter where leisure is not supposed to be spent together. Contrastingly, American patterns of shared decision-making and joint recreation require careful pairing. Dating provides an opportunity for trial-and-error selection. In our affluent, consumption-oriented society so much is expected of marriage that consummate skill in personal interaction is required to fulfil those expectations. Dating also provides opportunities to develop marital skills. So, in more ways than one, the American system of dating is a necessary foundation for our system of marriage.

Dating as Preparation for Marriage

Conscious motives for dating are seldom marriage-oriented, at least in early adolescence. Reasons for dating may be as diverse as self-improvement, group pressure, or to gain admission to a couples-only affair (Lowrie, 1951). Perhaps one should not think about marriage too soon if the full range of values is to be derived from dating:

> Dating for me began about the beginning of seventh grade. This dating took the form of steady relationships very early. My dominant motive was for close relationships to satisfy my emotional needs. I looked forward to marriage as a goal from my earliest experiences. As I look back on this time I see that my parents were right about this early dating being rushed too much, but what neither they nor I realized was that it was serving a vital need they were neglecting.
>
> The great error in my dating was that it became marriage-oriented at an unrealistic age. I considered qualities in dates on the basis of my marriage ideals almost from the very beginning. This orientation pushed me into involvement at too early an age. As a result, my dating partner variety has been less numerous and my dating span was cut short by early marriage.

The American dating system works well as an end in itself, as pure recreation. But regardless of the motives of the participants, dating has significant consequences for marriage: (1) knowledge of the opposite sex, and (2) development of interpersonal skills.

Knowledge of the Opposite Sex

Dating is not the only way of getting to know the opposite sex. Coeducation provides classroom and extracurricular contact. Aside from dating, however, these contacts tend to be platonic, unemotional, and uninvolved. Dating provides an opportunity for intimate, personal acquaintance. This acquaintance helps the individual understand the opposite sex as a group and as individuals.

As a Group. In some respects men and women are different, in others the same. Good marriages depend on understanding both the similarities and the differences. The grosser misconceptions about the opposite sex normally dissolve early in adolescence—the feeling that boys are rough and girls scatterbrained. However, few bachelors really know all there is to know about women, or vice versa. Dating provides continuing opportunities for analyzing the subtleties of masculinity and femininity.

As Individuals. All members of the opposite sex are not alike. The problem is to discover what sort of partner is best for me. Each new date provides an experiment in match-making, a chance to discover what makes compatibility and incompatibility. No matter how bad a date turns out, it adds to the participants' wisdom about their own requirements. Without realizing it, they sharpen their ability to discriminate between good combinations and poor ones.

Many years ago Willard Waller (1937) deplored the discontinuity between dating and marriage. The popular man at Penn State belonged to a fraternity, owned a car and a raccoon coat, and had plenty of money to spend—characteristics hardly related to compatibility in marriage. Since then, the discrepancies between dating popularity and marriage eligibility have diminished. Dating was a frivolous game one had to leave to get serious; today it leads more smoothly toward marriage. No longer is one kind of person preferred for dating and a different kind for marriage. Rather, premarital and marital preferences are largely identical. For example, a cross-section of University of Michigan students almost unanimously preferred the same qualities in both casual and serious partners:

1. Pleasant and cheerful.
2. Sense of humor.
3. A good sport.
4. Natural.
5. Considerate.
6. Neat in appearance. (Blood, 1956)

Not only has the gap between casual and serious preferences narrowed but the focus has changed to qualities that foster good personal relations both before and after marriage. When couples pair off on the basis of personal compatibility (rather than external qualities), dating provides better preparation for mate selection.

Development of Interpersonal Skills

Since dating corresponds so closely to marriage, it provides opportunities to develop interpersonal skills that are useful after marriage. Such lessons are learned on casual dates as well as serious ones. Even a "bad date" with a person one wouldn't think of marrying tests one's maturity in coping with frustration. This does not mean that people should go out of their way to date difficult partners for practice. It does mean that whenever they run into problems their response trains them for marriage—for better or for worse.

If marital lessons can be learned from casual dating, even more can be gained from serious dating. The longer a couple date, the more their interaction pattern reveals and shapes their subsequent behavior in marriage to each other or to someone else. Since the continuity between casual dating and marriage is less obvious, it may be useful to illustrate how casual dates provide opportunities for learning skills relevant to marriage.

SELF-EXPRESSION. One of the biggest problems in early dating is difficulty in communication. A shy girl or boy may be adept in talking to his own sex but afraid on a date of saying the wrong thing, or making a bad impression, or boring the partner. To date means to take responsibility for holding up one end of the conversation—an appalling responsibility for the uninitiated. But with experience comes relief from being tongue-tied. Self-confidence grows with conversational expertise. The opposite sex turns out to be hardly more difficult to talk to than one's own and may even offer new topics of conversation as each tells the other the mysteries of the private world of men or women he or she inhabits.

EMPATHY. Communication is a two-way process. It begins with self-expression but is completed only if the partner receives the message. Empathy is the ability to perceive the partner's attitudes and feelings. It differs from sympathy because it doesn't necessarily involve agreement or fellow-feeling with the partner. Empathy is a skill that can be acquired and developed through practice. Dating provides repeated opportunities for practice.

Lack of empathy impedes true self-expression. If I am afraid I'll "put my foot in my mouth" when I open it, I am too much concerned about myself and too little about my partner. If dating is to work best, both partners must express their own needs and be sensitive to the other's. Dating thrives on empathy in sensing the partner's moods in little things such as when she wants to go home and what she really wants to eat. Skill depends not only on listening to what she says but on sensitivity to nonverbal clues in facial expression. A skillful empathizer sees through verbal pretenses to the real feelings within.

DECISION-MAKING. The expressed needs of two persons often conflict. When choices must be made between mutually exclusive preferences, new skills are called upon. Altruism under these circumstances is no solution. If I want to go swimming when she would rather go to a concert, it doesn't help for both of us to say, "After you, Alphonse." Such dilemmas provide practice for settling problems after marriage.

COMMITMENT. We ordinarily think of commitment as a once-and-for-all lifetime affair which occurs at marriage. But commitment, too, takes practice. To jump all at once from self-involvement to marital commitment is perhaps impossible. The growth of love creates progressive commitment. Even before loves strikes, dating provides opportunities for tentative commitments. But those opportunities are not always exploited. Students in two Florida universities complained that lack of commitment by the partner was the chief obstacle to enjoying a date. They had several words for the same thing: "the date's lack of interest, uncooperativeness, or being in a bad mood." (Connor and Hall, 1952)

> I prefer casual friendships and dating a number of different men rather than going out exclusively with one. For this reason I like group activities more than spending an evening entirely with one person. I seldom share my inner thoughts and feelings. I feel that this leads to a greater involvement with the person in whom I might confide; and this is the type of relationship I am trying to avoid. If I get the impression that a boy I am dating is becoming serious, I quickly end the relationship.

This girl needed to commit herself to her partner, not irrevocably as in marriage but temporarily for the duration of the date. In a rudimentary way this resembles a willingness to love, not in the sense of "falling for" each new date that comes along but of participating fully in the relationship as long as it lasts.

Sociologists used to note an American predilection for "dallying." Young people, Waller suggested, "are careful not to allow their affairs to exceed a certain pitch of emotional intensity, if they can prevent it." (1938:230) One of the popular techniques for preventing emotional involvement was reliance upon a conventionalized conversational "line." Many words were expressed but they were just a game, masking true thoughts and feelings. Today's young people, however, commit themselves more easily than their predecessors did. They are less afraid of emotional involvement. This is another way (besides similar preferences for casual and serious partners) in which dating provides better preparation for marriage than it used to. Every date is an opportunity to commit oneself tentatively to another.

Self-expression, empathy, decision-making and commitment are only a few of the skills that can be learned in dating. They are sufficient, however, to illustrate the opportunities for developing interpersonal skills. The more they are developed in dating, the greater the preparation for marriage. Other benefits from dating are so closely related to readiness for marriage that they will be saved for that chapter—emotional weaning from parents and a sense of having "been around" enough to settle down with a lifetime partner.

Obstacles to Learning

Although dating provides opportunities, they are not always utilized. One condition that interferes with learning relationship skills is exploitation. When a girl is used for sexual purposes or a boy for financial purposes, free communication and rational decision-making cannot be expected. The criteria that a personal relationship should be an end in itself and should involve the *whole* person are violated. Exploitation frequently occurs when high-status boys date low-status girls (Ehrmann, 1955). Given the impetus of the male sex drive and the female wish for a "good" marriage, exploitation is understandable, but it is more likely to result in mislearning than useful learning.

Opportunities to learn are partly contingent on the activities engaged in. A campus is an ideal place for meeting compatible partners, but college facilities often inhibit the development of personal relationships (see Table 1-1). Parties, dancing, and other group activities are the chief ingredients of organized campus life. They are too public to enable dating

Table 1-1. Actual and Preferred Dating Activities

Activity	Actually Do Most Frequently on a Date	Like Best to Do on a Date
Go someplace to dance	51%	*
Go someplace to drink	34	12%
Chance to be alone	34	65
Go places where you "can be seen"	30	9
Outdoor activities, picnics, hiking, etc.	24	74
Relax in someone's house, talk, listen to radio, read	18	59
Go to concerts, lectures, discussions	9	28

* Not asked.

Adapted from Goldsen, 1960: 68. *Source:* 1,514 Cornell University men in 1950. Totals add to more than 100% due to multiple responses.

couples to get to know each other well. The preferred but less easily obtained informal outdoor recreation, indoor relaxation, and privacy are
more conducive to personalized interaction.

In recent years, administrative policies at many universities have shifted
away from *in loco parentis* to freedom for men and even women to live
off-campus. Apartment living has made the Cornell students' desire for a
place to relax and a place to be alone more attainable than before. Indeed,
the traditional Coke date is now challenged by the dinner date where the
meal is cooked by the girl responsive to the adage about the way to a man's
heart.

As Tom generally has dinner with us and sometimes lunch also, Joan
is eager to prepare what he likes. Having Tom in mind as a future husband, she has taken over about two-thirds of the cooking (which was
originally divided equally between the two of us) so as to be able to cook
Tom's "favorites" while impressing him with her domestic abilities. Since
Tom is pretty much of a permanent fixture in this scene, Joan's rating as
a potential housekeeper is also important. Here again she is considerably
more active in keeping mirrors polished, furniture dusted, floors clean,
and so on, than I am.

All three of us play pseudo-family roles. Joan plays the wife and mother
roles. She types Tom's papers, irons his shirts, and takes care of his business correspondence. Since I am barely five feet tall, I am jokingly known
as the "daughter" of this "family." Since I am not dating any one boy
in particular, I frequently consult "Mommy" and especially "Daddy"
about my dates. Sometimes my "parents" even tell my dates when to
have me back. Luckily these guys also have a good sense of humor. Tom
also partakes in the "family" jokes. He sits at the head of the table at all
meals and expects both of us, especially Joan, to serve him. He often goes
grocery shopping with us and carries the purchases for us. Also he does
the minor repair jobs around the apartment and usually takes the rubbish
and old newspapers downstairs to the incinerator. Occasionally he does
some light cooking and helps with the dishes if we are particularly busy.

At first Tom seemed to feel somewhat uncomfortable about eating and
spending a lot of time in the apartment because he did not know me very
well. But after a few weeks we became much more friendly and he began
to feel quite at home. In fact the three of us have become such pals now
that we often play cards together, have discussions, study together and
sometimes go out together.

Dating Career Patterns

Most Americans begin dating in junior high school and marry in their
early twenties, so their dating career normally covers six to eight years.

Since college students marry later than average, their dating careers may span a whole decade.

Extensity

More significant than the number of years from first to last date is the number of dating partners.

Table 1-2. Number of Partners Ever Dated by College Men and Women

Number Ever Dated	Men	Women
0–10	8%	12%
11–20	23	20
21–30	22	18
31–50	25	21
Over 50	23	28
Total	101%	99%
Number of cases	160	174

Source: Students enrolled in the University of Michigan marriage course (Sophomores-Seniors) in 1956.

The college students in Table 1-2 had typically dated twenty-one to thirty members of the opposite sex, but the number varied widely. It may be no accident that variation is more extreme among women than men. Because girls are handicapped in initiating dates, they are more apt to be limited to less than ten partners. At the other extreme the most popular girls date an unusually large number of boys. With the initiative in their hands, boys tend to have a more moderate number of partners. Presumably those who date less than a dozen partners have less perspective for choosing a marriage partner. There is little danger of dating too many persons unless it gets in the way of cultivating intensive relationships with anyone.

Intensity

Dating a broad range of partners is no substitute for getting thoroughly acquainted with a few. Intensive relationships are not necessarily serious (in the sense of being oriented toward marriage), but they do focus on one partner for the time being. Dating the same person repeatedly month after month requires a tentative commitment which offers new depths of understanding. Steady dating fosters the growth of a more personal relationship. In some ways it provides better preparation for marriage than

playing the field. It generally allows more opportunity to practice interpersonal skills.

Going steady often involves greater sexual intimacy for girls but less for
boys (Ehrmann, 1959). The quality of intimacy changes from casual
exploitation: "In random dating an individual is allowed to move from
one partner to another, rarely establishing any personal attachments; there
is less inhibition, possibly, to the *using* of dating partners as instruments
for one's own selfish gratification. It may be that going steady, by virtue
of its being less temporary, impersonal, and competitive, is capable of
inhibiting or reducing the motivations for the exploitation of one person
by his partner." (Herman, 1955)

Steady dating offers intensified doses of the marriage-preparation values
provided by dating in general.

> I took dating very seriously and never went with a girl I truly was not
> interested in. From each new girl I learned something more about the
> members of the opposite sex as well as more about myself. I learned what
> it felt like to be stood up, made a fool of, dominated, thrown over, and
> strung along; as well as being loved, cared for, admired, respected, trusted,
> and made secure. I dated each girl long enough to learn her good and bad
> points, my mistakes, how they treated me, and how they expected me to
> treat them.

Extensity plus Intensity

It would be easy to assume that extensive and intensive dating are
mutually incompatible. Probably, in extreme cases, they are. One can
imagine a girl dating so many boys that she never has time to date the
same one twice. When dating remains so superficial, neither compatibility
testing, emotional weaning, nor interpersonal skill mastery is likely to
progress very far.

The opposite extreme is a college senior who dated only one person in
his life:

> I didn't get around to dating in high school. When I got to college I
> met Alice in my Freshman English class and we started going together.
> We've been going together ever since and get along pretty well. But now
> that we're scheduled to get married in August, I'm suddenly full of
> doubts. I feel as though I didn't know for sure if she's the right one for
> me. She wouldn't like it one bit, but I sometimes wonder whether I
> shouldn't start dating some other girls just to help me make up my mind.

Table 1-3 shows, however, that steady dating is not generally incompatible with a wide variety of partners. Quite the opposite: those with the

Table 1-3. Steady Dating and Total Number of Dating Partners

	NUMBER OF STEADY RELATIONSHIPS					
	None	One	Two	Three	Four	Total
Median number of individuals ever dated	18	22	34	35	44	30
Percentage of total cases	15%	26%	28%	16%	15%	100%

Source: 264 men and women students enrolled in University of Michigan marriage course, 1960–61.

most steady partners have the most casual partners. Turned around the other way, the larger the number of casual partners, the greater the chances of going steady with some of them.

Initiating Dating

Getting started in dating is a serious problem for those who rarely or never date anyone. It also concerns the larger number who break up with old partners and must start over again. One deterrent to ending unsatisfactory relationships is reluctance to face the task of resuming dating "on the open market."

First dates have an extra excitement that reflects underlying tensions and anxieties. The chief source of anxiety between new partners is uncertainty whether they will be compatible. Both hope the occasion will go well. Perhaps the new partner will fulfil their dreams. When dreams are disappointed, it is not easy to dismiss the mismatch as "one of those things." It tends to be felt as personal failure. Besides being disappointed with the partner, each is painfully aware of the other's disappointment with him. Hence first dates take place under strain. Each partner strives to impress the other. The first impression has to be good or there won't be a second chance.

Sometimes anxiety is so intense that it paralyzes both partners. So great is the fear of saying the wrong thing that nothing is said. Later, reliance shifts from the safety of saying nothing to the safety of saying the expected. If I say the same things everyone else does, I can't go far wrong. The relationship will not become very personal as long as it is so undistinctive, but the conventional pattern provides a secure framework until the relationship can grow of its own accord.

Ways of Reducing Initial Strain

Certain types of dates create less strain. Structuring the dating situation to take the emphasis off the weak, unformed pair-relationship reduces anxiety. This can be achieved in group parties and double-dating. If one couple's morale suffers from incompatible pairing, the group offers distraction and compensation. Strain is thus diffused over a larger set of relationships.

Strain is limited when the first date offers a chance to get acquainted over coffee rather than plunging blind into a whole evening or weekend of paired activities. Tension is reduced by guaranteeing in advance as much compatibility as possible. Anxiety about the unknown vanishes when dates are chosen from old friends and acquaintances. If dating must be arranged, the ideal matchmaker knows both partners well and can predict their compatibility. Least satisfactory of all is a truly "blind" date where nothing more than chance brings two people together.

Besides providing a shock-absorbing group environment, parties and dances provide programed activities. Movies, concerts, and ballgames do, too. When something goes on around the couple, the conversational resources of the two individuals are only marginally tested. Instead of having to entertain each other all the time, they need to only during intermission. There is thus a certain wisdom in conventional coffee-and-movies patterns for first dates. Informal, private dates can come later. After a couple get to know each other, they can explore their special preferences. Better not to test unknown decision-making skills by arguing about where to go and what to do on the first date. Better to let the fellow decide, according to custom. Questions about paying for dates, similarly, can be raised later— if ever. For the beginning, the expected is the path of least resistance.

Once a date begins, a useful strategy can be derived from knowing that uncertainty about compatibility creates anxiety. The sooner I receive feedback of reassuring information, the better. The end of a date is a long time to wait to learn that the partner enjoyed the occasion. Some feedback comes from facial expressions and other nonverbal cues. But the sooner compliments can be expressed, the sooner we will be able to relax, knowing each of us is accepted. Mere flattery sounds hollow or produces a false sense of compatibility from which the couple may later have to extricate themselves. But genuine appreciation puts the partner at ease.

Male Initiative

Custom dictates that the initiative for dates should come from the man. While this gives him treasured freedom of action, it also imposes responsibility. Boys often wish girls would share this burden, but girls are just as glad not to have to. In one study of high-school students a majority of the boys thought "it would be a good thing if girls could be as free" as boys in asking for dates, but two-thirds of the girls disagreed (Christensen, 1952). People of all ages wish the other sex were friendlier and more easily accessible.

It takes self-confidence to ask a new girl for a date. Those most lacking self-confidence are also, unfortunately, those whose egos suffer most from rejection. For the fearful few, methods of tension-reduction are especially useful. However, an extremely shy boy may not even know a girl he could ask for a date. This condition arises most often among students confined to men's colleges or to fields of study where women are rare. For the very shy, a blind date may be unduly frightening. Better to make platonic friendships first. Church groups, hobbies, and clubs allow familiarity to grow up around common interests. Personal friendship among the members of such groups provide a basis for eventual dating and love, even though the love may be neither flashy nor spectacular. For those rare individuals who never marry, interest-group friendships provide alternative personal relationships.

For some, the inhibitions to dating go deep into past emotional conditioning and only professional therapy seems likely to overcome them. The following case happens to be a girl, but similar fears are not uncommon among boys (though the dynamics may be different):

> I am the youngest of three children and the only girl. I never played with my brothers though they often teased me. I played by myself except when my cousin Carole and I were together. I was very shy, afraid of people in general but particularly of boys who were rough. They were always running, not caring who they ran into, yelling, fighting, and I was afraid of getting hurt. I never had any real dates until I was out of high school. I think I was asked a couple of times but I didn't care for the boys who asked me. It is strange that though I wanted very much to have dates, I was more scared to have them. I never spoke to boys unless I had to—I was afraid of them.

Although boys don't have to worry about the roughness of girls, they sometimes fear their seductiveness. Because of negative parental attitudes toward sex, anything remotely sexual in nature may be disgusting. So the nondater plays it safe by avoiding social contacts that might expose his inadequacies and arouse his unconscious fears.

> My mother always taught me, "Never kiss a girl until you are almost engaged." Therefore, my general attitudes were very prudish. As a result of this I developed a brotherly attitude and have had this relationship with most girls. They tell me their troubles and ask my advice. Most of the time I am satisfied with this.

An emotionally inhibited person is often tied to his parents' apron strings. Dominated or overprotected by his parents, he is unable to grow to maturity. The parents may actively discourage dating. More corrosively, they undermine the child's self-confidence and self-respect.

The nondater may claim he's not interested in "that stuff." He may throw himself into other activities—studies, athletics, extracurricular organizations. Perhaps he claims he prefers platonic friendships with the opposite sex, pure camaraderie where sex makes no difference. This is apt to be a rationalization for inner inadequacies.

In early adolescence inhibitions are common. If they persist into the later teens, they deserve professional help to release normal desires for personal relations with the opposite sex.

Female Initiative

In view of the cultural ban on female initiative, unpopular girls are seriously handicapped. They are largely at the mercy of boys and must wait and hope that someone will be interested enough to make the first move. If their physical appearance is unattractive, they are additionally handicapped since first impressions are difficult to overcome. Dieting, exercise, and plastic surgery can sometimes reduce this barrier, but adolescent skin difficulties may have to be waited out.

Unpopularity can seldom be blamed entirely on male disinterest, though the temptation is beguiling. It's easy to rationalize situations in which the other sex is supposed to carry the responsibility. Nevertheless, girls can make themselves available and can even take initiative within limits.

Availability is partly a question of propinquity, that is, going where the men are. Unbalanced sex ratios occur on certain campuses, in occupations like teaching and in certain communities (Wallace, 1960). Vacation cruises may offer concentrated doses of contact with men, but marriage-oriented dating is more apt to emerge from friendships born of long-term association. Coeducational schools, jobs, organizations, and communities offer longer-term availability.

Besides sheer propinquity, availability reflects attitudes and behavior. Passivity does not invite dates. For boys who hesitate to initiate contacts, girls can pave the way by being warm, outgoing, and friendly:

> In high school I was pretty lonely. Finally in college I came to my senses—perhaps because I knew that time was short. Only one or two more years and I would be a career woman or, to put it brutally, an old maid. In the university were men galore. I began to see that to make myself more available I had to do more than sit by the telephone and wait for a call. I had to learn to go halfway in being friendly, to be genuinely interested in these boys, to care enough about their interests, to show a little warmth and enthusiasm. Perhaps I was learning to treat them as human beings. As I warmed up, they reciprocated.

Even though girls are generally forbidden to initiate dates, there are exceptions. In some circles a girl can say to a fellow (as casually as possible!), "I have two tickets to a play tomorrow night and my roommate is sick. Would you like to go in her place?" The boy may accept even though he suspects the whole story is a fabrication. His face is saved as long as the girl discreetly avoids pursuing him openly.

Another feminine problem is how to secure a "rain check" when a first invitation can't be accepted. Because unwanted dates are normally declined with polite excuses, a legitimate excuse is liable to be misinterpreted as a rebuff. Hence, a new inquirer needs to be explicitly encouraged to call again. Awareness of a girl's receptivity after (or before) a first inquiry can sometimes be spread by the grapevine. With discretion so necessary in initiating dating, the chief area for feminine initiative is the friendliness out of which more intimate relationships grow.

Organizational Sponsorship

In some countries, matchmakers are called upon to promote new dating relationships. In the United States blind dates are informally matched too. But, more formally, campus organizations serve this purpose when they schedule mixers, ski trips, and picnics. It matters little whether the organization has members of both sexes as long as the event is planned for both. Indeed the most legitimate opportunity for female initiative is a party given by girls who can invite whomever they wish.

On many campuses, fraternities and sororities are the chief agencies sponsoring organized dating. With a busy calendar of social occasions and group pressure for all members to participate, Greek houses are the scene of the most active dating on campus (see Table 1-4).

Table 1-4. Effect of Fraternity Membership on Dating Frequency

Dating Frequency	Fraternity Members	Independent Men
None	7%	20%
Less than once a month	22	28
Once or twice a month	36	26
At least once a week	35	26
Total	100%	100%
Number of cases	704	650

Adapted from Goldsen, 1960: 70–71. *Source:* Cornell University, 1950.

The most striking effect of fraternity membership is to reduce the percentage who don't date at all. Organized social life may not provide the most intimate setting for dating, but it almost guarantees a minimal amount. Members who lack the initiative to secure their own dates can have matches arranged by the house social chairman. Exchange dinners between fraternities and sororities also provide an organized framework for dating.

Computer Dating

For students who don't belong to sociable organizations and who attend large universities or commuter campuses where acquaintance is difficult, computer dating offers an entree. Especially when students arrive on campus as strangers in the lonely crowd, the computer offers something better than random selection of dating partners. The effectiveness of computer pairing depends on (1) the meaningfulness of the questionnaire used; (2) the honesty with which the questions are answered; and (3) the diversity of the pool of potential partners who have fed their data into the machine.

As in communities with skewed sex ratios, whichever sex is in short supply has the selective advantage. For both sexes, however, the computer rules out the most obviously ineligible partners and selects eligibles who are at least minimally compatible. (Computers sometimes demonstrate their competence by incestuously pairing brothers and sisters because their family backgrounds are so similar!) Knowing that the prospective partner is interested in dating someone new and has been machine-selected for similarity of interests makes computer dating more comfortable than stab-in-the-dark dating.

Iowa State University students were generally enthusiastic about their computer-selected dance partners. Of the men 52 per cent (versus 43 per cent of the women) felt the computer had matched them "quite successfully." Although a successful one-night stand seldom generates long-term relationships, half a year later 20 per cent of the men and 13 per cent of the women still felt that they would enjoy additional dates "a great deal" or "quite a bit." (Coombs and Kendall, 1966) Although I know of no comparative evaluation of the effectiveness of ordinary mixers, the computer has clearly proven itself a useful link between lonely individuals in our increasingly anonymous society. It is likely to be even more useful off-campus than on. College graduates who go to work in a large metropolis find the computer particularly strategic for beginning dating in a new environment.

Sex Roles in Dating

We have already dealt with one difference in the dating roles of men and women in discussing initiative. The sexes differ less about who should pay for dates. Only a small minority believe in "dutch-dating," and payment by the girl alone is particularly frowned upon (Christensen, 1952). Willingness to spend money symbolizes a man's affection for his girl. Sharing expenses seems like unwillingness to give on his part and unwillingness to receive on hers, reciprocal resistances to mutual involvement.

Affluence makes money less of a problem in dating. As long as the man has plenty of money, there is no reason why he shouldn't spend it. Girls generally spend enough on clothes, cosmetics, and hairdressers to balance the money the boys spend on dates. Perhaps the financial role of women is to attract men in the first place. Once attracted, men take over the operating costs.

Difficulties arise under marginal circumstances. If a date isn't exactly a date, what norm should apply? If a boy and a girl "just happen" to sit together at the lunch counter, his obligation to pay for her coffee depends on whether they think of it as a date. When her view differs from his, misunderstandings arise:

> I happened to bump into a girl from my psych class at the Sugar Bowl last week so we had Cokes together. We've never dated and she's only a vague acquaintance. Just to be courteous I picked up her check and went over to pay for it. But she came along and said, "You shouldn't do that. I can perfectly well pay for it." Sure she could. But I'd have been a lot happier if she'd just thanked me instead of creating a scene.

What if the man's financial resources are limited? Then conventional dating may be difficult but inexpensive activities are possible. Better to stroll in the moonlight than not date at all—affection is more important than the money that symbolizes it.

After couples have dated long enough to accept each other as persons, they become more "realistic" about money. The longer they go together, the less likely they are to let tradition stand in the way of a good time. Sharing or even total financing by the girl may be the best way of collectively using their resources. However, public face-saving may require her to slip the money to him in private.

Less directly, girls contribute through gifts. Koller (1951) found that although women in every generation received more than they gave, the balance was approaching equality. Indeed, more recently "the young women were in many cases giving more gifts to the men than they received in turn."

Dating Formalities

More than most circumstances, dating calls into play the niceties of social behavior: male chivalry—opening the door for the girl, walking on the street side of the sidewalk, rising when girls enter the room—and table manners for both sexes. Like money, these are symbolic means of showing consideration. Breaches of etiquette early in dating are liable to be interpreted as signs of displeasure or at least of not caring about the partner. Dates with a new partner rely on fulfilling social expectations in the absence of knowledge about the individual. As acquaintance increases, behavior becomes more individuated.

> On her first date with John, Marcia played the very innocent, feminine role. He at the same time acted the detached male, trying to display an air of being interested yet not overly impressed. Neither wanted to show his emotions for fear of leaving himself vulnerable to manipulation or rejection by the other.
>
> For the next few weeks, they saw each other steadily at least three or four times a week. John became a very understanding, very congenial boy friend who conformed to all the reasonable requests Marcia placed upon him. She began to be more her natural self—noisier, wilder, and more dominant. She even could finally permit herself to laugh at off-color jokes. Now that she no longer had to strive to impress him, she was able to allow her true personality to show through her facade of feminine naïveté.

As a relationship develops, both partners adapt their behavior to the other's needs. Such adaptation may modify traditional sex roles considerably. The danger in unconventional conduct, however, is that it may abandon the spirit of considerateness along with the form. Courtesy involves going out of one's way to be nice. The fact that the male tends to be rough and unfeeling is one reason why chivalry focuses on him. The essence of a personal relationship lies in concern and sympathy for the partner. Conventional behavior guarantees that the man will at least appear to be concerned pending the time when real concern develops. Another reason why chivalry is a masculine code is because it is the man who classically pursues the reluctant female, persuading her by his politeness that he would make her a loving and faithful husband.

It would be wrong to assume that social conventions and personal needs necessarily conflict. For well-socialized people they usually coincide. But, if one partner needs to be unconventional and the other to be conventional, it is difficult to satisfy both. Then, at least one partner must adapt his behavior to the other's counter-need if the relationship is to develop satisfactorily:

> Alan wanted to be chivalrous to me but I didn't want to accept it. For example, one evening when we went to a movie, I ran out of the house and jumped into the car. He was very irritated and said so. After several such episodes we finally talked it over. I told him it embarrassed me to act the clinging vine. I confessed that because of my size, most boys had not

felt particularly protective toward me, so I had assumed the facade of a happily independent girl as a defense. Alan explained to me that he had learned most of his social graces the hard way since his family didn't have them. Once the truth was out, we knew a greater closeness as I learned the pleasure of leaning a little and he had the satisfaction of showing off his social accomplishments to an admiring audience.

Masculine Dominance

Conventional sex roles call for men to dominate and women to submit. We would expect couples to adhere to this pattern in early dating but to conform less as they get to know each other better. At the University of Connecticut 46 per cent of casual couples exhibited traditional role behavior but only 33 per cent of serious couples and 10 per cent of committed couples (Heiss, 1962). However, some couples did not abandon male dominance. Men and women who believed in male dominance were *more* apt to be male-dominated after their relationship became more committed. Only couples who believed in equalitarianism became less male-dominated as marriage neared (see Table 1-5).

Table 1-5. Male Dominance, by Marital Philosophy and Degree of Commitment

Percentage of Male-Dominated Couples by Respondent's Marital Philosophy	DEGREE OF COMMITMENT		
	Casual	Serious	Committed
Husband-Dominant Philosophy			
Men Students	53%	57%	56%
Women Students	54	67	75
Equalitarian Philosophy			
Men Students	80	67	36
Women Students	64	50	37

Adapted from Heiss, 1962: 207. *Source:* Juniors and Seniors at the University of Connecticut.

Measures: To be classified as completely husband-dominant in philosophy, students had to agree with the following items:
  a. By and large, the husband ought to have the main say-so in family matters.
  b. A wife usually respects a strong and dominating husband.
  c. I respect a husband whose word is law in the family.
  d. If a man makes the money for the family, he should make most of the decisions about how it will be spent.
  e. The husband should usually have the last word when there is a disagreement.

Couples were asked to fill out a Family Opinion Inventory independently and then to resolve their disagreements on particular issues. The statistics in the table represent the percentage of couples where the man dominated the discussion by making 55% or more of the suggestions about how the disagreement should be resolved. Caution: the number of couples studied was small, ranging between 3 and 19 couples per cell.

Masculine dominance and feminine submissiveness are often adopted as a pose in early dating. The longer couples date, however, the more they replace that pose with behavior that expresses their personal value system. The more committed they become, the more they dare to be themselves. Perhaps also, the more honest they are with each other, the more meaningful the relationship becomes. In any case, early dating involves a good deal of culturally prescribed pretense which is gradually abandoned as couples lay aside their masks of conventionality.

Feminine Intellectuality

College women of superior ability are sometimes torn between their femininity and their intellectuality. This role conflict seems to be decreasing with the spread of an equalitarian philosophy. Nevertheless, some girls still worry about the impact of their academic prowess on their dating eligibility and at Cornell a few girls with high grades actually dated comparatively seldom (Goldsen, 1960).

Superior brains deprive girls of the opportunity to date boys less intelligent than themselves. On the other hand, that is part of the process of mate-selection. Were they to marry inferior men, intellectual incompatibility would result. Being natural about intelligence is one prerequisite for developing full person-to-person relationships. Although less capable men may be repelled, equally capable ones will not.

How then do we explain the fact that smart women have more difficulty in dating (and marrying) anyone? Some are the victims of circumstances. Enough men date down the intelligence scale to leave their feminine equals stranded. (Scott, 1965, calls this "the Brahmin problem.") In other cases the dynamics of intellectual unpopularity are different. Academic achievement (like social mobility) is sometimes a compensation for inadequacy in personal relations. Girls unskilled in personal relationships may seek substitute gratification in a career (Ellis, 1952). Their lack of dates is more nearly cause than consequence of high achievement. Sometimes intellectuality is their defense against emotional involvement or their weapon in the "battle of the sexes." In such cases popularity with the opposite sex understandably suffers. Provided this is not the case, there is no marriage-oriented reason for women to pretend to be dumb.

2 Choosing a Marriage Partner

To Choose or Not To Choose

From the romantic point of view marriages are "made in heaven." People are "destined" to marry each other, brought together by "fate," "mysteriously attracted to each other," and marry even if families, friends, and their own minds demur. It does not occur to romanticists that marriage partners need qualifications to be suitable for each other. Choosing a mate sounds too cold and calculating, evoking images of impersonal checklists fed into a heartless computer.

In practice more couples are thrown together by accident than by either the magic of romance or the strategy of intelligence. The typical young adult drifts along assuming that sooner or later he will get married. He dates, will-o-the-wisp, whoever attracts his fancy. Chance largely determines whom he dates. And, as expected, sooner or later he marries someone. To some extent both emotion and chance influence every marriage. The question remains, however, whether an individual can guide his own destiny by rational thought and whether deliberate choice works better than romantic fatalism or blind drifting.

Marriage is one of the three great events in life—along with birth and death. Birth just happens, and death too is largely beyond our control. Marriage, however, we can influence more actively. We decide whom to marry and when to marry. The crucial decision is the first.

In a society where so many marriages fail, marriage counselors often feel that they see troubled couples too late. If they had never married in the first place, much grief would have been spared. If they had been better matched, they would have experienced a richer life. The marriage die is largely cast in the process of mate-selection. Not with respect to skill and effort but by definition as far as compatibility is concerned, a couple's destiny is settled when the partnership is committed.

The Nature of Compatibility

In the Introduction I defined compatibility as the extent to which a couple's intrinsic characteristics fit together. Countless dimensions of compatibility could be discussed. I have selected *personal* compatibility in temperament, needs, role-conceptions, and values. Reserved for Chapter 3 are questions of *social* compatibility.

Temperamental Compatibility

By temperament I mean the physiological activity level and response pattern of the individual. Little research has been done on constitutional factors in mate-selection and marital success. However, Wallace (1960) pointed out that the behavior-controlling glands of one normal individual may be five to ten times as active as those of another healthy individual. He believes that "such biological differences help to explain many of the common problems and conflicts in mating and marriage: why one spouse is always active—bubbling with excess energy—and the other is inactive, quiet, and phlegmatic; why one spouse can't get going until late afternoon and doesn't want to go to bed before midnight, and the other works best in the morning and likes to go to bed early; why one partner wants sexual intercourse daily, or twice daily, and the other finds weekly or even monthly intercourse adequate."

Differences in energy level are predictable in marriages between partners of different ages. The older partner is likely to have less energy—to be less interested in mountain climbing, tennis, or having children than his younger spouse. Individuals of the same age may also differ in their responsiveness to stimulation. Some people are nervous and excitable, irritated by the slightest discomfort or distraction. Others are calm and even-tempered under provocation. Some lash out angrily at their environment while others retreat into sulking silence that lasts for days.

My hypothesis is that temperamental compatibility requires similarity between the husband and wife. Despite the young couples who claim his calmness is "good for" her excitability, such an exchange is likely to cause resentment in both partners. Temperamental differences create problems, test the individuals' ability to empathize, and are bridged only by substantial effort. If special effort is required, that is a sure sign of incompatibility.

Compatibility of Needs

All animals have physical needs, especially for food and sex. The original goal of both is tension-reduction, assuaging hunger pangs and releasing sexual tension. But psychological conditioning endows even these physical drives with secondary emotional pleasures and anticipations. In growing up, human beings acquire other needs which have nothing to do with their biological requirements. Through reward and punishment they come to value persons and activities as sources of psychological pleasure and anxiety-reduction. Because parents are the chief agents of reward and punishment, they are the primary sources of social needs.

Much of this learning occurs so early in childhood that these needs are unconscious (the individual is not aware of them). Sometimes they can be raised to consciousness by developing insight. Presumably, the more aware an individual is of his needs, the more intelligently he can choose a marriage partner. Hidden needs are difficult to recognize when masked by reaction formations. The son of an overprotective mother may need to be submissive. Males, however, are not supposed to be submissive, so he may react in the opposite direction with strenuous attempts to dominate others. Similarly, a girl with an underlying need to dominate may react with studied submissiveness.

When conscious needs camouflage unconscious ones, mate-selection is difficult. For example, a reactively domineering male is likely to choose a submissive wife who will fail to meet his hidden dependency needs. Psychotherapy may enable such an individual to accept his underlying motives rather than hide them.

Having noted the complexities caused by unconscious needs and reaction formations, I will proceed to ignore them from now on. For the sake of simplicity I will deal with needs as if they were always conscious and direct.

Two seemingly contradictory combinations of social needs are equally satisfactory in marriage. Some needs must be complementary in order to be compatible. Others must not be opposite but parallel. In both cases, the act of fulfilling the partner's needs meets the individual's own needs.

COMPLEMENTARY NEEDS. In complementary areas, opposites attract. The most important complementary needs involve *dominance* and *submissiveness* (Winch, 1958). If I need to dominate, I will tend to marry and be gratified by someone who needs to be submissive. The more dominant I am, the more submissive my partner should be.

> I need someone to check my impulsiveness. I can never say no or refuse a favor. Besides, I overestimate my physical capacities. Consequently, I

am always trying to do too many things at one time, and I end up running around in circles, not knowing which way to turn. Bob is always able to straighten me out and help me find the right direction. I depend on his ability to extricate me from my own maneuverings. I wouldn't be surprised if he gets a kick out of straightening me out too.

This wife's submissiveness got her into outside-the-family troubles which her husband resolved through his own forcefulness. He got a sense of accomplishment from her dependence on him. This combination of dominant husband and submissive wife was once the prescribed social pattern. It still meets the partners' personal needs in a socially acceptable fashion.

What about a man who, on the contrary, needs to be submissive? As an individual he needs a domineering wife. Yet if he marries such a woman he will be called "henpecked." When personal needs and social pressures conflict, marriages are less happy than when personal needs fit social expectations (Blood and Wolfe, 1960). Nevertheless, compatible needs may be more important than social pressure for those forced to choose:

> Mom in a sense rules the roost in our home. She produces an atmosphere that is quite secure in comparison to the outside world. She reacts in reliably similar ways to situations of stress or happiness and seems to produce a place of refuge for Daddy when he gets tired of the outside world.

As long as the wife's dominance is confined to the home, social repercussions are minimized.

If both marriage partners need to dominate, the result is explosive. As each seeks to dominate the other, competition breaks into open conflict. Instead of meeting each other's needs, the partners vie for top position. Perennial conflict results.

> I wish my wife would leave the store alone. She keeps coming over and acting like she owns the place. Unfortunately right now the business is incorporated in both our names which she uses as an excuse to meddle in it. When I suggested that it be put in my name only, she accused me of trying to put something over on her. I've tried to get her to sign an agreement that she won't come over to the store any more, but she won't do that either.

When both partners need to be submissive, the relationship may be equally frustrating, though less dramatic. If neither partner is able to make decisions or to provide warmth and reassurance, the marriage will be hollow and disquieting.

Regardless of whether both partners are dominant or both submissive, each partner seeks what the other cannot give. Hence competitive marriages frustrate the participants' basic needs.

So far I have assumed that people are either dominant or submissive. But most people are neither. The average American falls midway between. Rather than wishing to dominate or be dominated, he prefers to give and take in a fifty-fifty relationship. Hence he needs a similarly equalitarian spouse:

> Fran and I have been married ten years now and we really have a good time together. She's a very capable girl and I have a lot of respect for her. She gives a lot of leadership in community affairs just as I do—not necessarily in the same organizations but just as significant. It means a lot to both of us to be able to talk things over with each other, to share our achievements and troubles with someone else. When one of us is down in the dumps, the other cheers him up. All in all it's been a good marriage.

Is an equalitarian marriage an exception to the general rule that authority needs should be complementary? At first glance yes, but on closer examination it fits the same general scheme. Figure 2-1 presents a hypothetical distribution of submissive, dominant and equalitarian persons in the United States.

To simplify our task, we will ignore the possibility that sex differences in socialization make the average woman more submissive than the average man. Let us assume, rather, that the distributions for men and women are mirror images (see Figure 2-2). The ideal wife for dominant man C is submissive woman a. Similarly B-b and A-c are compatible marriages based on complementary needs. B-b is simply a special case of complementarity in which the husband and wife happen to be identical in their needs. Conversely, the competitive combinations in Figure 2-2 are A-a and C-c.

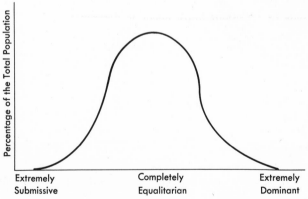

Figure 2-1. Hypothetical Distribution of Authority Need in the American Population

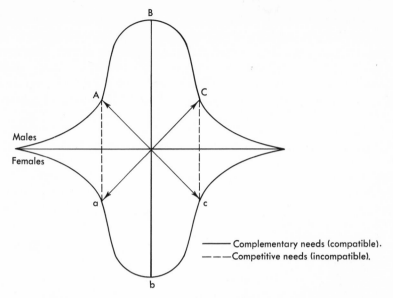

Figure 2-2. Complementary and Competitive Mate-Selection

Complementarity works like a pinwheel. The farther one partner is off-center, the farther must one go in the opposite direction to find the complementary partner. The pinwheel principle applies to several other needs: for instance, *nurturance* and *succorance.* Some individuals need to nurture others, "to give sympathy and aid to a weak, helpless, ill or dejected person." (Winch, 1958) Others have the complementary need for succorance, "to be helped by a sympathetic person; to be nursed, loved, protected, indulged." A man with a strong need to nurture would be compatible with a wife with a corresponding need to receive succorance. However, the average man and woman are intermediate types, capable of both nurturing and being nurtured in turn.

A third pair of complementary needs is *deference* and *recognition.* An individual who needs to admire and praise others would enjoy being married to someone with a corresponding need to "excite the admiration and approval of others." (Winch, 1958) Perhaps because of the masking effect of conventional roles in early dating, Kerckhoff and Davis (1962) find that complementary needs do not affect couples in their first 18 months of dating. However, those couples subsequently moved closer to marriage who were most complementary in their needs (a) to control versus to be controlled, (b) to include others versus to be included in activities, and (c) to give affection versus to receive affection. After marriage, masks drop aside further, allowing full play to complementary needs.

Complementarity must be distinguished from contradiction. Some couples seize the label of complementarity and pin it on any difference between them. But if she is sociable and I am solitary, our needs are not complementary but conflicting. If she is obsessively thrifty and I am extravagantly generous, our needs will clash head-on. If she is idealistic and I am realistic, we may manage to compromise on some middle ground, but it won't be a *happy* medium. Such differences may be resolvable, but they take energy to resolve. In contrast, complementary needs fit so beautifully that they require no compromise. They are reciprocally and simultaneously satisfied.

PARALLEL NEEDS. If all needs were complementary, there would be only one type of compatibility. However other needs function differently.

Complementary needs determine how two partners treat each other. If marriage were the whole of life, these needs would be the only kind. But husbands (and some wives) also participate in the occupational system. Activities outside the family provide alternative sources of gratification. Needs that are not gratified by the wife can be met at work. Indeed, some needs are more easily gratified outside the family than inside. *Achievement* in our technological society, for example, is measured in money earned, in power and prestige. Hence the need to achieve can be satisfied only outside the home.

To be successful in the outside world, a man must invest time and energy there. As a result his family roles tend to be neglected. What kind of wife would be ideal for an ambitious man? Are there women who would welcome his success rather than feeling neglected? Are there women who would prefer an ambitious husband to one who spent his spare time relaxing around the house? The wife of an ambitious man must be success-oriented herself. She doesn't have to engage in public affairs herself, but she must get vicarious satisfaction from her husband's triumphs. A special achievement need is what Winch calls *status* aspiration or status striving. Again, both partners need to be equally ambitious. Otherwise the mobile partner is likely to become disgusted with the stable one, or vice versa.

The opposite of achievement need is the need for *affiliation* (the need to be close to other persons). Sexual and love-making activities are valued by affiliative couples. They prize each other's company and would feel neglected by an externally oriented spouse. Parallel needs are concerned with orientation inward or outward. Are the partners primarily concerned with their relationship to one another or with getting ahead in the outside world? To be compatible they must be oriented in the same direction.

MULTIPLE NEEDS. So far I have discussed only one need at a time. But people have a variety of needs, and this variety complicates match-making. For example, a woman who needs to dominate and also desires upward mobility faces a quandary. Any husband dependent enough to satisfy her need to dominate is not likely to be a successful breadwinner. So she must choose between her contradictory needs or compromise both of them.

Such choices are affected by the intensity of the various needs. The stronger the need, the more emphasis it deserves. On the other hand, marital compatibility may be less crucial for externally oriented needs than for marriage-oriented ones. The chief problem for an ambitious man is to choose the right corporation, not the right wife. So the stronger the need and the more marriage-oriented its satisfaction, the greater the importance of marital compatibility.

Since marriage is a reciprocal affair, compatibility has dual advantages. If my partner's needs are compatible with mine, not only will she be able to satisfy more of my needs, but I will be able to satisfy more of hers. If our marriage is to succeed, each of us must be able to meet the other's needs. The more compatible our needs, the more rewarding our relationship will be with the same effort or the less effort we will need to produce the same results. The beauty of compatible needs is that the very process of gratifying my partner's needs intrinsically satisfies my own needs. Marriage sometimes calls for selfless sacrifice, but insofar as needs are compatibly matched, the services given are inherently rewarding.

Role Compatibility

Role conflicts after marriage can be minimized by marrying someone whose role conceptions and expectations mesh well with mine. Whereas needs are psychogenic in origin, roles are culturally defined. A role is a collection of rights and duties expected of an incumbent of a particular position in a system of relationships. Every husband has his own role conception—the patterned ways he thinks he ought to act as a husband. At the same time he has corresponding role expectations for his wife— ways he expects her to behave because she is a married woman. Compatibility requires that the husband's conceptions about how he should behave coincide with his wife's expectations of how he will behave, and vice versa. In an incompatible marriage the husband expects his wife to behave in ways she doesn't feel she should, or he feels he has a right to behave in ways she doesn't think he should.

SEX ROLES IN MARRIAGE. In every society there is some consensus about what makes a good husband and a good wife. In feudal societies a good husband is strong and protective, a good wife dependent and nurturant. (These terms sound like the ones used for needs—and they are. The difference is that a man may need to be submissive while society expects him to play a dominant role—needs and roles may not mesh.) In contemporary America the differences between the preferred characteristics of a husband and preferences for a wife reflect the cultural prescriptions for marital roles (see Table 2-1).

Table 2-1 presents typical role conceptions held by young people. In addition to greater responsibility for housekeeping, the wife's role requires an appearance attractive enough to satisfy masculine sexual needs. The husband's role emphasizes his responsibility to support his family financially and give it a respectable position in the community. This he achieves partly through inherited social status but mostly through skill and effort (by putting his education to good use through industrious work).

These differences in marital roles follow the traditional division of labor between the sexes. In recent years, however, the relative salience of these characteristics has decreased. McGinnis found that between 1939 and 1956 every one of the six items in Table 2-1 decreased significantly in importance for both men and women. During the same interval the emphasis on companionship increased. Greater stress was given to similarity in religion and education, love, dependable character, and the husband's desire for home and children.

If the whole American population changed its ideas simultaneously, role definitions might change without creating incompatibilities. The trouble is that contradictory conceptions exist simultaneously. Some people emphasize traditional role conceptions and others prefer modern ones. Moreover, traditional and modern conceptions don't come in neat packages, clearly labeled. Every shade can be found from ultra-conservative to ultra-modern. Nor is this a single dimension along which people can be placed. A given individual may have inconsistent ideas in different areas. He may be emancipated about sexual behavior and conservative about working wives—or vice versa.

Although role conceptions differ in many ways, differences about authority are clearest. The historical trend has been away from patriarchal ideas toward equalitarian ones.

Table 2-1. Relative Importance of Sex-Differentiated Features of Wife's versus Husband's Role

Characteristic	Wife's Role (male respondents)	Husband's Role (female respondents)
Good cook and housekeeper	2.09	.84
Ambition and industriousness	2.08	2.74
Education and intelligence	1.81	2.40
Good looks	1.41	.85
Favorable social status	.94	1.45
Good financial prospect	.63	1.60

Adapted from McGinnis, 1958. *Source:* Representative sample of University of Wisconsin students in 1956. The higher the number, the greater the emphasis.

PATRIARCHAL IDEAS. The word *patriarchal* means literally that the father is the authority in the family. Although to modern ears the word has an alarming ring, the traditional family pattern was not necessarily unpleasant. When both husband and wife believe in patriarchy, it can operate smoothly. In a completely patriarchal marriage the husband has the authority. He may delegate some of it to his wife. Indeed, to make every decision would be too time-consuming. But the wife has only delegated power. The husband can veto anything she decides and can revoke what he has delegated any time he wishes. A patriarchal husband may, if he chooses, consult his wife before making decisions. But when the chips are down, his voice counts.

The Old Testament Hebrew family was patriarchal. Nor did the New Testament challenge this system. Paul's words to the Ephesians are often quoted by modern patriarchs:

> Wives, submit yourselves unto your own husbands, as unto the Lord. For the husband is the head of the wife, even as Christ is the head of the church; and he is the savior of the body.
>
> Therefore, as the church is subject unto Christ, so let the wives be to their husbands in everything. Husbands, love your wives, even as Christ also loved the church, and gave himself for it.
>
> *Ephesians 5:22-25*

The wife's obligation to obey her husband is matched by his obligation to love her in return. Although patriarchal husbands sometimes abuse their authority, rights and duties are supposed to be reciprocal.

EQUALITARIAN IDEAS. At the opposite extreme from patriarchal monarchy is equalitarian democracy. Husband and wife are equally important, neither having the right to dictate to the other. The widespread deletion from the wedding vows of the wife's promise to obey reflects an equalitarian point of view.

The rise of this philosophy can be traced to social influences that have improved the status of women. The Industrial Revolution gave women a chance to work for outside employers. Education familiarized them with the outside world. Philosophical concepts such as democracy and individualism contributed to the emancipation of women from an inferior position. Emancipation outside the home brought increasing equality within the home.

MIXED IDEAS. Patriarchalism and equalitarianism represent "ideal types." They are logical extremes that seldom exist in pure form. Frontier conditions gave pioneer American women an importance impossible under pure patriarchy. And few contemporary families pursue pure equalitarianism. Most marriages fall somewhere between the poles.

The following case illustrates the combination of patriarchal and equalitarian elements:

> Mac is quite modern about letting me work when I want to and letting me express my ideas in conversations. He respects my ideas and lets me handle certain aspects of things that other women don't. For example, I handle my own finances. And he isn't always checking up on me. On the other hand, I have a sense of security about him. I know he will take care of me—he'll come and get me if the car gets stuck. And he doesn't hold it against me when I get in a jam. In some ways, he's old-fashioned. He expects obedience to him as the head of the house. He thinks the wife's job is to wait on the husband hand and foot.

PARENTAL MODELS. Where do differences in role conceptions come from? Normally they are learned in growing up. Role conceptions are one aspect of the cultural heritage transmitted to the child by his parents. Mostly this happens automatically. At the time the child doesn't realize he is learning a role, nor his parents that they are teaching him. But this educational process inevitably does go on in the family. Children grow up in a family role structure. They watch their fathers and mothers play the roles of husband and wife. Unconsciously they learn their parents' ways.

Usually children take their parents as role models. At three their favorite game is playing "Daddy and Mommy." By the time they are ready for marriage, they have absorbed their parents' patterns and learned the repertoire of behavior that was played before their eyes. If parents are unhappy or the child dislikes the way they treat him, he may reject their example and choose a different role. A rebel's ideas about roles may be more explicit because they have been chosen out of conflicting possibilities:

> My Dad never had any time to do things with Mother. Even on weekends he was always thinking up new schemes for his business. Mother used to gripe about how Dad never took her out and hardly had any time to talk to her. I decided when I grew up, I was going to treat my wife nicer than he did.

Children from happy families not only take their same-sex parent as role models for themselves but take their opposite-sex parent as the model for their marriage partner. One study of University of Minnesota alumni (Luckey, 1961) found a particularly close resemblance between the personality characteristics which happily married women saw in their fathers and in their husbands. Similarly, the men with the best marriages more often saw their mothers reflected in their wives' personalities. Conversely, the poorer marriages less often continued the role patterns learned in childhood.

Because equalitarianism is the American mode, children who accept their parents' role model normally have equalitarian marriages. However, children who rebel against their parents are assertive enough to dominate their marriage partner (provided that the partner conformed to, rather than rebelled against, his own parents). Among Burgess and Wallin's couples, boys who conflicted with either their father or mother became dominant husbands, whereas girls who rebelled against their mothers and other authorities, who got their own way as children or disliked the discipline to which they were subjected, became dominant wives (Lu, 1952). Thus childhood assertiveness toward adults carries over into marital assertiveness toward the spouse.

As brothers and sisters, children also develop patterns of interaction which are re-enacted in marriage. A study of business executives found that those with the happiest marriages had chosen wives who duplicated their childhood sibling structure: oldest sons married to youngest daughters or youngest sons married to eldest daughters. Contrastingly, oldest sons married to oldest daughters apparently fought for top position while youngest sons paired with youngest daughters were reciprocally disappointed with the other's spinelessness (Kemper, 1966).

Toman (1961) formulated a general hypothesis about the consequences of duplicating early childhood relationships as follows: "The closer the new relationships come in kind to old ones . . . , the better will the person be prepared for the new ones, and the greater their likelihood to last and be happy and successful." Other things being equal, sibling complementarity is yet another form of compatibility.

Compatibility of Values

A value is a hierarchically ordered preference that affects choices among alternative possibilities. Values come into play especially in allocating scarce resources. If my wife's values are the same as mine, we can easily decide how to spend our money and leisure time. But if she values mink stoles and sport cars while I value rare books and stereo records, we will have a hard time stretching our budget to fit, unless our resources are extraordinarily large. On the other hand, with modest tastes and reasonably adequate funds perhaps each of us can fulfil some of his preferences even if we don't like the same things.

Value consensus is rewarding because it makes one feel accepted by the other person. Conversation flows more easily between people with similar values because of the comfortable feeling created by common attitudes. Encounter across value divergences may be stimulating and challenging once in a while, but perpetual debate is too strenuous to be long sustained without relief and too dissonant with the solidarity expected of marriage.

As a major instance, people differ in the importance they attach to conformity. For some individuals, the only way to feel right is to be impeccably dressed and to mirror the opinions of the Establishment. For others, it is equally important to stand out from the crowd, to be proud of one's independence and nonconformity. Such diametrically opposite values clash so violently that the man in the gray flannel suit and the hipster are unlikely to date, much less marry. As a negative example, however, they illustrate the importance of compatibility in values.

Value consensus makes relationships more enjoyable from the very first date. After the computer-arranged dance at Iowa State discussed in Chapter 1, couples who saw eye to eye on the importance (or unimportance) of dancing ability, campus popularity, fraternity membership, stylish clothes, and good looks (a) were most satisfied with each other, and (b) found it easiest to talk to each other (Coombs, 1966).

Similarly, during the first 18 months of dating, Duke University students who held the same values about standards of family success moved closer to marriage (Kerckhoff and Davis, 1962). Value consensus this time lay in ranking in the same order such indices of family success as a respected place in the community, husband–wife companionship, healthy and happy children, and economic security.

The role of compatible values in promoting friendship can be seen not only in cross-sex but in same-sex friendships. Newcomb (1961) found that men students develop the closest friendships with colleagues who shared the same evaluations of the attractiveness of other house members and the same opinions about sex, politics, religion, race, and other controversial issues. The greater the agreement on values, the more students were attracted to one another as they got better acquainted.

It is not necessary, of course, for husbands and wives to agree on everything. No two people ever hold identical values or have identical interests. In their leisure time, husband and wife can go their separate ways in pursuit of divergent interests, provided the values involved are not antithetical.

INCOMPATIBLE VALUES. To be incompatible, values must conflict where differences are not allowable. For example, a church that calls itself the only true church creates value conflicts for members who enter mixed marriages (see Chapter 3). In contrast, religious differences between groups that tolerate each other cause less difficulty. Philosophies of life may also be antithetical:

> I am an optimist, a romanticist, and an idealist. I'm always willing to give people the benefit of the doubt. Thus I would be completely incompatible with a cynic or someone who is embittered and disillusioned with life. That's why I broke up with Frank. In the beginning I accepted his extreme cynicism with a grain of salt. I felt it was probably a result of some disillusioning experience and that through example I could change

his views. However, I came to realize that this wouldn't work because his cynicism touched on areas where I could exert no appreciable influence (for example, his business dealings). At first his attitude angered me (How could he be so jaded?). But gradually I began to feel sorry for him, in that I was in love with life and he wasn't. Pity, I came to realize, is no basis for love or marriage.

Marital strain may arise not only from irreconcilable beliefs but from unilateral preferences for pair-structured activities. Thus, mixed marriages involve not only different beliefs but different institutional memberships. My wife and I might have identical beliefs, but if she went to the First Church and I to the Second of the same denomination, we would both be frustrated.

Similarly, if one partner wants to go camping, it is not easy to go alone—especially if it is she who is interested rather than he. Even worse is the plight of the man who wants to entertain at home but whose wife abhors the idea, or the wife who likes to dance but who is married to a man with no sense of rhythm. In the latter case, the husband can try to learn, but it would be naïve to pretend that effort alone can produce compatibility in all areas. Couples are fortunate whose chief interests and values coincide.

Testing for Compatibility

How can a given couple know whether they are compatible short of consulting a marriage counselor? Can they find out for themselves how compatible they are? For couples who grow up together from childhood the answer is easy:

> Shirley's and my parents lived within three blocks of each other and our mothers wheeled their baby carriages together. (There is just one month's difference in our ages.) Both families attended the same church so that the two of us came up through Sunday school, catechism, and Luther League together. We also went to the same schools. Our families and friends took our courtship very much for granted and I guess maybe we did, too.

Childhood friends know each other so well that no special testing is needed. Strangers, however, may imagine compatibility where none really exists.

Self-Deception

Finding the right person is complicated by the human penchant for wishful thinking. If a date seems attractive at first glance, imagination tends to fill in the missing details. Perhaps this is the "girl of my dreams." The less I know her, the easier it is to believe she is "the one."

The more insecure the individual, the greater his need for idealizing his partner. Insecure people crave security so much that they "find" it in every date. While this illusion normally shatters with better acquaintance, it sometimes persists remarkably long. One girl talked herself into believing her fiancé was about to set the wedding date whereas in fact he was on the verge of breaking the engagement:

> I know I'm constantly engaging in wishful thinking. I keep thinking things are going to be rosy again. Maybe the reason is because I was so much happier last year when we first fell in love than I am now. It felt real good to have someone who loved me and whom I loved.

Among students living in an off-campus house at the University of Michigan, facing reality was easier for some than for others (Newcomb, 1961). Those with nonauthoritarian personalities were able to recognize value discrepancies when they encountered them and to change friends accordingly. But authoritarian students clung desperately to their first friends even after discovering that they were basically incompatible. They resolved this strain by self-deception, overestimating their value consensus in order to salvage their relationships. The problem for marital compatibility testers is to decide *whether* to commit themselves to a permanent relationship. To resolve cognitive dissonance by self-deception is to beg the question.

Studies of friendship show that it normally grows between people whose encounters are self-validating (Chambliss, 1965). Congruence between partners requires each to see the other the way the other sees himself. To be significantly overrated by the partner is uncomfortable. To have to live up to exaggerated expectations may be good for one's character but is too strenuous for friendship. The proverbial rose-colored glasses may create an illusion of love in the wearer but they are likely to scare off the partner. How then can self-deception be prevented and cured? That is the task of compatibility testing.

The Elements of Compatibility Testing

The more varied a couple's dating activities, the more thorough their discussions, and the more intimate their acquaintance with each others' families and friends, the better they can foresee what marriage to one another would be like.

VARIED DATING ACTIVITIES. Variety can be found in participant as well as spectator activities. Some couples rely on movies, concerts, and football games where entertainment is provided by the management. But this is too easy. Any two people should be able to enjoy themselves when they don't have to depend on their own resources. Television makes such stimulation possible after marriage too. But it takes more than television to hold a marriage together. Only by doing things that require no admission ticket can people discover how much they enjoy each other.

Dates also vary in physical setting. Traditionally dating is catalyzed by starlight, perfume, and alcohol. Does the relationship fall flat when these props are removed? Or does companionship survive in levis, chill winds, or dripping sweat?

Group activities yield different perspectives from pair-dating. Young lovers prefer their own company: "Two's company, three's a crowd." Yet married couples more often entertain friends and participate in organizations. Double-dating and partying with friends anticipates later sociability. Avoiding group activities to prevent being embarrassed by the partner is a bad omen.

> Karla and I don't like to go to parties. Maybe it's because of her deafness. She tends to lean toward the person she's listening to and grimaces with the strain of hearing. I know it's uncomfortable for her to have to mingle with a lot of people so I feel tense too. We just prefer to date by ourselves.

Maybe "we just prefer" to date alone. But maybe this is an escape from facing inner doubts.

Dating is also an opportunity to try out each other's hobbies—the unshared ones—to see whether they offer potential common interests.

> Dan is a bird watcher. When he first told me I thought it was silly. And when Spring came I began to resent the time he put in on it that he could have spent with me. Finally one day he persuaded me to go along with him. I was surprised how much fun it was! He started telling me about how the birds migrate and a lot of other stuff I never knew before and I got quite fascinated. Before I know it I'll turn into a bird watcher too.

Acquaintance with idiosyncratic interests doesn't always produce conversion. But if the effect is short of toleration, trouble lies ahead. When the result of trying out his interest in boxing matches or hers in church services is disgust that anyone could spend his time so foolishly, friction can be predicted.

Few marriage-minded couples need to be encouraged to include affectionate behavior in their dating. Suffice it to note here that loving belongs in the total range of dating activities.

There is no reason why every couple must try all the activities discussed here. The crucial task is to experience those activities which are most salient to the value systems of the particular individuals. Since value systems differ from couple to couple, relevant activities will differ accordingly.

DISCUSSION. Simple as it may seem, talk is also a step toward better understanding. Of course people usually talk on dates, but what do they talk about? The weather, the news, the music, how you look tonight—seldom do they let down the barriers and talk about themselves, about what makes them tick: their feelings, aspirations, ideas. When dates begin to share their thoughts as they would with their closest friends, mutual understanding results:

> My fiancée and I went together for a long time before we ever got to know each other. We went places and did things—had a lot of fun. But one evening when we sat down in front of an open fire and let our hair down, we began to feel as though we were really meant for each other. We talked about the things that meant the most to us, what we wanted to get out of life, and a lot of other things we'd never mentioned before. After that I had a different feeling toward her.

Whereas activities provide opportunities to explore contemporary pleasures and problems, conversations can probe the past and the future. Knowing each other's past makes it easier to understand the other's reactions and to foresee the future. If I know how my partner got to be the way she is, my empathy for her should increase.

Occasionally the question whether to confess past "sins" arises. Do individuals embarrassed about their past have an obligation to talk about it? This is not information one shares with casual friends. On the other hand, if it is to be shared at all, it deserves to be part of compatibility testing rather than delayed until the proverbial "final confession" before marriage.

Whether to confess delinquencies depends on whether they are likely to affect the partner. If she is likely to hear about it from others, better to hear it from me. If suspicion is already in the air, better to present the facts than allow uncertainty to threaten the relationship. On the other hand, if a brush with the law, with a homosexual or with a prostitute was a transitory episode not likely to be repeated, there is less reason to risk introducing unnecessary anxiety and misunderstanding into an otherwise good relationship.

Since marriage is an exclusive relationship, the details of previous involvements are emotionally threatening. Like extra-marital affairs, previous premarital affairs which went all the way to marriage-like sexual intimacy shatter what Waller and Hill (1951) called the "fiction of solidarity" so important to a dyadic relationship. To confront the partner with information about past intimacies is to strain his faith severely. Burgess and Wallin

(1953) found that talk about former friends of the opposite sex provoked more "reticence, tension, or emotion" during engagement than any other topic of conversation. When men confessed some or all of their previous sexual involvements to their fiancées, the latters' reactions were more often unfavorable than favorable (39 per cent versus 12 per cent, the remainder being at least ostensibly neutral). Because lovers rarely appreciate being told about their predecessors, conversations about the past should pass lightly over previous involvements unless they have serious implications for the new partner.

Many aspects of marriage can't be tested practically ahead of time but can be discussed. Even before engagement, ideas about preferred family size or ways of raising children can be explored.

Table 2-2 shows how many more topics were discussed in modern courtships than a generation or two before. One-fourth of the grandmothers never discussed any of these topics before marriage but reticence dwindled to 11 per cent among the mothers and almost disappeared (1.5 per cent) among the daughters.

Such conversations involve a search for areas of agreement. It's fun to find she has the same ideas I do. Yet if talking is to do more than contribute to an illusion of bliss, there must be a willingness to differ too. Not that dates must turn into debates, but being frank with oneself and one's partner requires expressing unique views as well as hugging the common ground.

SOLVING PROBLEMS. The ability to arrive at mutually satisfactory decisions is vital to marriage. Dating couples inevitably have decisions to make—about where to go and what to do. Sometimes decisions are passed

Table 2-2. Premarital Discussion of Marital Topics, in Three Successive Generations

	GENERATION		
Topic Discussed	Grandmothers	Mothers	College Alumnae
Having Children	19%	55%	85%
Place to Live	60	73	80
Husband's Occupation	29	45	76
Wife Working	8	30	74
Religion	33	46	73
Handling Money in Marriage	19	39	63
Average Number Discussed	1.7	2.9	4.5
Number of Cases	200	200	200

Adapted from Koller, 1951: 369. *Source:* Recent alumnae of Ohio State University, their mothers, and grandmothers. Their modal ages in 1949 were 23, 48, and 78 respectively. Reciprocal percentages did not discuss the particular topic before marriage.

over too lightly. The girl is apt to allow the boy to make decisions on dates that she would be unwilling to let him make after marriage. Before engagement is the time to test one's problem-solving ability with married-couple seriousness:

> Al always wants to get his own way. I used to let him get away with it, but I don't any more. Then I thought maybe I'd lose him if I disagreed with him because I didn't believe he was in love with me. Now that I know he is, I stand up more for my own rights. He's begun to have more respect for my opinion as a result.

In addition to capitalizing on current decision-making opportunities, couples can work toward tentative solutions to problems they anticipate in marriage. Detailed plans may have to wait until after engagement, but agreement in principle about what church to attend or whether the wife should work may significantly affect whether a couple will get engaged in the first place.

MEETING FRIENDS. Sometimes a person can be understood better by looking at his friends. Guilt by association may be poor politics but good psychology. The company one keeps is seldom accidental; rather, common interests and backgrounds draw cliques together. If a date looks attractive but her friends seem odd, they suggest hidden aspects of her personality.

> We got pinned last summer but somehow things haven't been going the way they should. We have very compatible personalities, but I think her friends have a bad influence on her. She's a music major and she hangs around with a bunch of long hairs who I think are nuts. She even admits herself that she lives a dual life—one where she's always acting, trying to impress people; the other when she's around me which is more settled, more domestic. The trouble is I can't get her to quit playing around with her arty friends.

This student overestimates his compatibility with his girl. If he were to take a closer look he might discover that her "nutty" friends meet needs in her personality that he doesn't. His revulsion to her friends is a warning that she may be a poor match for him.

VISITING EACH OTHER'S HOMES. Getting acquainted with the partner's family has some of the same advantages. People usually resemble their parents. Her mother previews what a "sweet young thing" may look like 25 years and 25 pounds later. The mother's behavior previews the mother the partner is likely to become, indeed the person she is likely to be in middle age.

Is it fair to judge a person by his family? Isn't there some justice in the remark that "I chose my friends but I couldn't choose my family"? Is it fair either to hold a person's family against him or to give him credit for them? A young person may reject his family. He may disagree on political and social issues, adopt new values, and make his own way in the world. Yet the very fact of rebelling instead of growing up with parental support and encouragement makes a difference:

> I don't think I really understood John until I met his father. His dad rules his family with a heavy hand. When he opens his mouth, everyone is supposed to jump. John's mother has put up with it all these years, but I never would. And John didn't either. He used to argue with his father about the race problem and tried to puncture his father's stereotypes. But it didn't do any good. Now I can appreciate better why John is so touchy about some things and why he's so enthusiastic about "the group process."

When a person reacts against his parents he is extra sensitive. Understanding the family background permits making allowances for bizarre reactions to seemingly innocuous situations. By visiting the family it is possible to anticipate overreactions.

Most people do not rebel against their parents. When feelings are positive, parents provide more direct insights into the partner's personality. Attractive qualities of the fiancée will usually be visible in her parents, for example. As her partner gets acquainted with them he is apt to find his good impression of her reinforced.

More important, however, than just meeting the partner's parents is seeing how he gets along with them. This adds depth to compatibility testing since it reflects the parents' influence during his formative years. A student may have learned to control his childish reactions since getting away from home, but they tend to reappear on visits home. Sometimes the picture isn't very pretty:

> I've never seen Nancy so down in the dumps as the week we spent at her home during spring vacation. Everything her folks said seemed to rub her the wrong way. When her mother asked her to do something, she would do it, but begrudgingly and with the least possible effort. I've never seen her so irritable before either.

Why can a visit home bring out the worst in a person? Because growing up is seldom smooth. Childhood is often a time of tension, anxiety, and conflict. Going home reactivates old feelings of resentment, jealousy, and rebelliousness.

According to an old saying, when you see how a man treats his mother, you know how he will treat his wife. Like most folk wisdom this contains both truth and falsehood. The hot temper, lethargy, or sullenness used as weapons against parents are firmly embedded in his personality. But most behavior is *situation-specific:* situations must be similar to produce the same reaction. Structurally, mother and wife occupy very different positions. My mother had controlling, authoritative, disciplinary responsibility for me whereas my wife is less threatening, more an equal partner. Hence, my wife can expect the treatment my mother received only when she acts enough like my mother to trigger off my old reaction. This can happen, however, without either partner realizing it.

> My mother has always dominated me. She's very precise and always wants things her way. She's always checking up on the way I spend my money and whether I'm eating the right things. I usually do what she tells me to, but only when I get good and ready. . . . In some ways Ruth dominates me too, but I don't react to her the same way. I think the difference is that my mother's demands are unreasonable, whereas I usually agree with Ruth's suggestions.

This illustrates how close courtship and marriage can come to childhood situations without touching off old reactions. Yet occasional transferences of old reactions to new situations do occur. One young bride who resented the way her family used to show her off when company came found that even as an adult she felt like "crawling in a hole" when guests arrived. Somehow she always managed to be busy in the kitchen, leaving her husband to greet them at the door.

If behavior is situation-specific, child-parent behavior patterns may not be transferred into marriage. A look at early family relations, however, shows what repertoire of behavior is potentially available. If the look is too frightening, the love affair may end. If it is inviting, it enhances the attractions of marriage. Midway, there may be a sobering recognition that the partner is very human but could be lived with comfortably if treated decently.

Other ends are also served by such a visit. Prospective in-laws provide a preview of in-law relationships. Moreover, the home setting enables the couple to participate in domestic activities. They can see what it's like to do the dishes together, take care of the baby sister, and rake the lawn. If prosaic chores are fun together, marriage becomes more attractive. A visit home also discloses the proverbial way she looks on the "morning-after-the-night-before." A day or two—better yet, a week—visiting each family is, therefore, a multiple means of compatibility testing.

TAKING TIME. With so many time-consuming activities already proposed, it is hardly necessary to suggest taking time for its own sake. Nevertheless, time serves a useful purpose. If by some magic it were possible to complete the other tests instantaneously, length of relationship would become important in its own right. Time tests the wearing qualities of a relationship. As the months go by do we still get along or do we get on each other's nerves?

> I need a man who is dominant, and at first Carl seemed just right for me. But as time progressed I began to notice aspects of our relationship that didn't bode well for the future. He had such a domineering personality that at times I felt my own individuality was being stifled. In a discussion of some controversial matter he would assert his views, but never really give mine a fair trial. Often the only retort he could think of was to say that my ideas were naïve—what could I say except that his were cynical? After a while we began to reach so many stalemates that rather than go through the frustration all over again, we started to avoid certain topics—religion, child-raising, fidelity. Because of his domineering attitude, much of our problem-solving was unsuccessful too. He would listen to my ideas, but then go right ahead and do what he originally intended. I finally realized that the kind of dominance I wanted was not that extreme. I'm glad now I didn't rush into a quick engagement the way he wanted to.

Some couples lose interest as the relationship becomes "old hat." Half the excitement may have been due to sheer novelty, while the fact that they weren't sure of each other whetted desires for conquest.

Marriage is designed to last a long time. When the wedding vows promise "till death," it is fitting that time be spent in pretesting the relationship. How much time is enough? One study showed the average New Haven couple dating for a year and a half before getting engaged (Hollingshead, 1952). Is eighteen months enough?

Table 2-3 shows that the longer the prior acquaintance, the greater the chances an engagement will last into marriage. Conversely, the shorter the dating span, the more likely an engagement is to be broken. Since a major decrease in broken engagements comes after 18 months, that seems to be a useful minimum for the average couple. The number of months needed

Table 2-3. Outcome of Engagement, by Length of Acquaintance

Outcome of Engagement	LENGTH OF ACQUAINTANCE BEFORE ENGAGEMENT		
	Under 18 Months	18-35 Months	36 Months or More
Broken	18%	12%	9%
Unbroken	82	88	91
Total	100%	100%	100%
Number of couples	356	290	354

Adapted from Burgess and Wallin, 1953: 286. *Source:* 1,000 college-educated engaged couples in Chicago, 1937–1939.

for compatibility testing, however, depends on several factors. The older and more mature the couple, the sounder will be their judgments. The more intensive and varied their dating with each other, the greater the value of the passing months. Conversely, young and inexperienced couples who seldom see each other need extra months to be sure.

Is separation a good test? Wealthy fathers proverbially send an eligible daughter to Europe before allowing her to marry. They do this mostly, however, when they dislike the fiancé. Though claiming the trip is a test of love, they really hope it will be an antidote. Short separations are not likely to dissolve well-established relationships, so compatible couples have little to fear. For immature couples clinging together or incompatible couples blinded by emotional involvement, intervals apart may provide detachment, an opportunity for reflection and better perspective. When forced by parents, separations often boomerang in rebellious resolves to preserve doubtful relationships or in defiant elopements. Voluntarily undertaken, however, separating may benefit couples too deeply involved to be objective.

Long separations, on the other hand, can destroy even *sound* relationships. Just as friendships wane when friends move away, love tends to fade when unreplenished by contact. Long separations allow old ties to be replaced by new ones. Separating does test relationships, but the longer the separation the harder the test. Even the best potential mate may be lost if tested too severely.

Living Together? If it is useful to visit each other's homes and try one's hands at household chores, why doesn't it test marriage even better to try living together? Then, presumably, one would get the most realistic picture of marriage. One trouble is that marriage requires a crucial element that would be missing—commitment. The purpose of compatibility testing is to provide a basis for deciding whether to make that commitment. To live together without commitment is to confuse the test program with the action program. It is to blur the distinction between being married and not being married. It is to drift into marriage so imperceptibly that marriage loses its meaning.

At some point, testing needs to end and commitment to begin. That turning point is at engagement. To get engaged to be married means to replace the possibility of test failure with an affirmation that the tests have been passed and that soon the partners will irrevocably commit themselves to living together.

Professional Testing

Up to this point I have described activities which every couple may undertake as amateurs. Although amateur testing may suffice for the average case, professional assistance may be useful in special cases.

COMPUTER SELECTION. Like computer dating, computer match-making has all the virtues and all the limitations of the scientific and human resources invested in the computer's memory bank. If the information fed into the computer is relevant to marriage and if the applicants are a cross-section of the eligible market, the machine will recommend matches which are worth considering. The joker is the second *if*. While a computer-dance on a college campus may attract applicants by the hundreds, professional introduction services attract mostly the dregs of the marriage market: (1) women culturally forbidden to take the initiative in finding marriage partners and (2) individuals past the normal age of marrying. The net result is that men who seek computer assistance have a wide range to choose from, but the older a woman gets, the less likely she is to find it useful. On the other hand, the older she gets, the less her competitive strength on the "outside," too. So even a badly skewed computer pool may be worth trying if she seriously wants to marry.

SCIENTIFIC TESTS OF COMPATIBILITY. Social scientists have devised a number of tests which predict the likelihood of success in marriage. Most of the items used are not concerned with compatibility but with the skill component of success in marriage. For example, items deal with happiness of family background, personal intelligence, education, income, religiosity, and sociability. These contribute to an individual's marital success, to be sure, but they affect his chances of success in marrying anyone. They fail to measure the compatibility of the particular couple. Some day, scientific tests of interpersonal compatibility will be improved. For the present, the tests available through commercial testing services are more likely to be suggestive than conclusive.

PREMARITAL COUNSELING. If today's tests require careful interpretation to be meaningful, the key professional resource is the counselor who administers them, not the tests themselves. With or without paper-and-pencil tests, a skillful clergyman or other premarital counselor can be helpful to couples of doubtful compatibility. Any man and woman who find themselves caught between conflicting views (a) within themselves, (b) between partners, or (c) between themselves and their parents would do well to seek professional counsel. Parents can usually be counted on for detached feedback, but a professional man is even more dependable. Parents have little knowledge to go on save their own marriage and those of their immediate circle. Counselors have the double advantage of scientific knowledge about marriage and experience in counseling other couples, so their perspective is broad. Quite apart from any professional judgment the counselor may render, the very act of discussing their situation with a neutral party is likely to yield new insight and objectivity for the couple themselves.

Increasing Compatibility

Compatibility testing reveals whether couples are compatible or incompatible. When incompatibility is discovered, couples usually break up. But sometimes people feel that compatibility could be increased by changing the partner's personality. Is this possible?

Human personality is not static. No matter how old they are, people keep changing their interests, attitudes, and reactions. Moreover, behavior depends a good deal on how one is treated. With proper handling could the partner behave better? The possibility of change is often dismissed with a sneer—"You can't change a leopard's spots." Personalities seldom change very much, to be sure, but that doesn't mean they don't change at all. The easiest change is to develop latent potentialities. Before going together, one partner may never have been exposed to the other's church, sport, or hobby. Common interests could develop spontaneously once the novice is introduced to them.

More difficult are changes in old ways of doing things, especially in temperament and need-feeding habits. Even such attempts don't always fail, however:

> I think Esther's pressures have been good for me. I used to put off studying until the last minute, but now I'd rather study first and play afterward so I can enjoy the playing more. Esther's changed, too, since we started going together. She has a pretty sharp temper and she used to jump on me and not care. But we've talked it over so that now she tries to keep it down to a minimum and she apologizes afterward when she does blow off at me.

Several aspects of this couple's approach contributed to their success:

1. The reform program was not one-sided but based on the premise that both partners had deficiencies.
2. Changes were pursued openly with no attempt to "put something over" on anyone. By frankly talking out their critical reactions to (and positive aspirations for) one another, a feeling of mutual respect was created.
3. As a result of this process of persuasion each partner accepted the other's desires as a goal for himself and felt supported by the other's respect and love. Under these circumstances the critical partner was not putting pressure on a reluctant person but helping in the attainment of shared goals.

4. The changes were pursued early in the relationship rather than hoped for in the future. If improved compatibility is necessary to marital satisfaction, it should be achieved before getting engaged.

BEFORE ENGAGEMENT. There are two reasons why desired changes should be tried out before deciding whether to get married. The main one is that personal effort or even professional therapy may not succeed. It is seldom possible to predict how much a person will change. Marriage is too serious to enter on faith that the partner will "come around" eventually. It can safely be undertaken only when each partner accepts the other as he is.

The second value in pursuing change early is that courtship is one of the most plastic times in life. When there is hope of winning someone's affection, the incentive to change is strong. This may provide the impetus without which therapy is useless and reform impossible:

> I had tried for years to give up smoking for the sake of my health and never succeeded. When I fell in love with Vic I was surprised to find how easy it was to stop. He didn't smoke and I believed he would respect me more if I didn't.

There is always a risk that changes will be only temporary. After marriage old patterns may reassert themselves with the waning of romantic ardor. But pessimism is not necessarily realistic. A new personal relationship reinforces courtship-induced changes, reducing the danger of "back-sliding." In any case lovers feel such risks are worth taking.

Assuming that change will occur after marriage is foolhardy. To marry the proverbial drunkard in order to reform him is likely to result only in martyrdom. Better not to marry at all or to postpone engagement than to plunge in before compatibility is established.

The Final Choice

As compatibility testing proceeds, the time comes when the results must be assessed and acted upon. Either one must get engaged, break up, or postpone the decision still longer. In case of doubt, parental opinions are often helpful. But in the last analysis every individual must make his own decision.

Parental Roles in Mate-Selection

In feudal societies parents traditionally chose their children's partners for them. In industrial societies parents lose this authority. Nevertheless,

Table 2-4. Parental Participation in Mate-Selection of Sons and Daughters

	Father	Mother
Son's choice of mate	49%	79%
Daughter's choice of mate	69	97

Adapted from Bates, 1942. *Source:* 136 young married persons. Reciprocal percentages of parents were not active in the mate-selection of the specified child.

modern parents are interested in their children's mate-selection and eager to help them choose wisely.

Table 2-4 shows the large proportion of parents who influenced their children's mate-selection overtly enough to be remembered by the children themselves. Mothers were more active than fathers (as in most aspects of child-rearing), and parents were more concerned with daughters' than sons' marriages. Mate-selection is a female specialty.

Parents typically give advice, make comments about dating partners, and talk over marriage plans in family conferences. The emphasis is on consultation and guidance, not on pressure and directives. Parents express their opinions about dating partners, and children in turn consult them for advice. In most cases parents' and children's reactions are similar since successful socialization inculcates the parents' standards in the child:

> My parents have never forbidden me to go out with anyone, but they always let me know if they don't like my date, either by ridicule or by not saying anything about him. If they do like someone I go out with, they tell me so and what they like about him, and I find that I always have a much better time when I am out with someone I know my parents like.

When parents and child disagree, the child tends to discount their opinions. Parents belong to another generation with different ideas and different experiences. Their acquaintance with the partner is superficial. No matter how much the parents go out of their way to talk to the partner their contact is slight compared to the time the couple spend together. Besides, parents stress values other than the tenderness, companionship, and love that matter most to the couple. Men students at the University of Wisconsin's Milwaukee campus, for example were advised by their parents to find a wife (1) of the same religious faith, (2) who would be a good wife and homemaker, (3) from a good family background, and— only lastly—(4) with a pleasing disposition and personality (Prince, 1961). The advice for girls was similar except the man's financial prospects were deemed even more important than his religion. Commented one coed:

> My mother has told me to be sure to select a mate of the same religion, one who has a good job, and who is dependable. However, I feel that she

is too interested in having me marry someone with money rather than someone I love. In this way, I don't feel she is regarding me. She only wants prestige for herself.

Despite such limitations parental opinion is usually helpful. Parents are less involved in the affair. As outsiders they can look at the couple more objectively or at least from a different perspective. From the outside in, it may be easier to see aspects of the relationship the participants have overlooked:

> Six months before I finally came to my senses and broke our engagement, my family was up in arms about it. My brother told me I was getting a raw deal and my folks were dead set against the marriage because of the way Don was treating me. They thought it was rude and inconsiderate of him to keep breaking dates at the last minute the way he did. But I kept hoping for the best.

Parents have a useful time perspective, too. As members of an older generation, they can see farther ahead than young daters care to look. The latter focus on the near future—engagement, wedding, and honeymoon. But parents realize the importance of establishing a home and raising children. Their long-range view throws new light on the present relationship: "Sure she's a nice kid, but could she ever settle down to keeping house?"

Parents are also apt to have a keen appreciation of their child's needs. Having lived with him so many years, they may know him even better than he knows himself:

> Dad said I'd never be happy with Ray because he was selfish. At the time I couldn't understand what he meant. Ray spent money so lavishly on me that he seemed the most generous person I had ever known. In fact, I thought some of Dad's relatives were the stingy ones because they were so tight with their money. . . . But now that I've been married to Ray a few months I've discovered that the only person he's really interested in is himself. He never gives either his time or his love to anyone else. I guess Dad knew better than I that Ray wasn't the one for me.

Parents have so many bases for judgment that their opposition is a harbinger of doom. Table 2-5 shows that twice as many affairs terminated short of marriage or early in marriage when both parents were opposed as when both approved. Given the greater concern for daughters, the girl's parents were more crucial than the man's.

Table 2-5 suggests how seriously parental opposition deserves to be taken. Nevertheless, a majority of the parent-opposed marriages did survive at least three years. Parents are sometimes wrong and the couple right. The question is how to tell the difference.

Table 2-5. Duration of Relationship, by Attitude of Girl's Parents

| | ATTITUDE OF GIRL'S PARENTS | | |
| | Both | One | Both |
Duration of Relationship	Approved	Disapproved	Disapproved
Broken before marriage	13%	16%	32%
Broken after marriage (separation or divorce)	4	7	4
Married three years or more	83	78	64
Total	100%	101%	100%
Number of couples	660	45	91

Adapted from Burgess and Wallin, 1953: 561.

IRRELEVANT OPPOSITION. Some parents are irrational, more concerned with their own emotional needs than with the child's welfare. A widowed or divorced mother or even an unhappily married one may be so emotionally dependent on her son that she cannot let him go. A woman who dreads the loss of her child-rearing role may hang on to her last child. Such a parent may criticize *any* marriage prospect, no matter how suitable.

Other parents may use criteria rejected by the child. A Baptist mother may wish her daughter-in-law belonged to the same church; but, if her son is an agnostic, that preference means little. Similarly, a businessman's objections to his daughter's "impractical" fiancé is not likely to override their shared interest in theatrical careers. Parental advice is inappropriate when the child has been upwardly mobile. A higher social status involves new tastes and values difficult for parents to understand. One study, for example, of women students at Temple University in Philadelphia found that their mothers had only 11.7 years of education on the average. Faced with upward educational mobility, a majority of the mothers and even more of the daughters (55 per cent and 77 per cent) felt that a girl should marry the man she loves even if her mother "strongly objects" to him (Bell and Buerkle, 1962).

A third criterion is the structure of the family. If parent-child ties are close, opposition is more serious. In an aristocratic or wealthy family the older generation carries more weight. Especially if father and son are to be associated in business, parents may veto an unsuitable daughter-in-law. Conversely, if parent-child relationships are remote, opposition matters less.

Although marrying in the face of parental opposition inevitably strains parent-child relationships, anguish can be minimized by considerateness. Elopements are an easy way of by-passing hostile parents but antagonize them even more. Most parents want to attend the wedding even if they aren't enthusiastic about the match. They appreciate being kept informed of plans, even when they disagree with them. Sensitive handling of parental opposition may not dissolve it immediately but will pave the way to better relationships after marriage.

Occasionally, match-making instead of match-breaking needs thwarting. Children of immigrant families sometimes face this problem in acute form:

> My parents were very anxious to have me marry someone from their part of Italy. They picked a mate for me about five years ago and held an engagement party for me. I felt trapped because I didn't care for this man. Finally, I left home a month before the wedding was to take place —otherwise I would have been forced into it.

Other parents apply less drastic pressure yet urge their children into unsuitable marriages. Since parents are not going to live with the person, they should not make the decision. Parents serve best as consultants.

Friends play similar roles in mate-selection. They are more likely to share the individual's values than parents. Through double-dating they may get to know the partner well. They, however, less often express their doubts openly because they lack the authority of parents (Mayer, 1957). If friends fail to express disapproval, it doesn't mean they necessarily approve. Reticence can usually be interpreted as disapproval. In those rare cases where disapproval is actually expressed (especially to the girl), their doubts spell future trouble (Burgess and Wallin, 1953).

Standards of Compatibility

Some couples worry about too much compatibility. They fear that similarity of interests may lead to boredom. But the changing tasks of family life and the challenges of occupational and community roles guarantee that no couple need ever stagnate. The problem for most couples is not "too much" compatibility but whether they have enough. Since no two people are completely alike, no two are ever completely compatible.

How much compatibility does it take for a good marriage? The answer lies in the balance between costs and rewards of the relationship. For couples who quarrel often or feel chronically insecure and dissatisfied, marriage would drain their emotional resources. Marriage can never be all reward and no cost, but the effort expended should result in meeting the other's needs. A couple's own doubts are a sign of incompatibility. Doubts are relatively rare among engaged men. Their fiancées, however, tend to be less confident. Uncertainty often foretells a broken engagment or divorce (see Table 2-6).

Basic uncertainty frequently means something is wrong with the rela-

Table 2-6. Duration of Relationship, by Confidence of Engaged Woman

	WOMAN'S CONFIDENCE OF SUCCESS IN MARRIAGE		
Duration of Relationship	Very Confident	Confident	Uncertain
Broken before marriage	13%	20%	31%
Broken after marriage (separation or divorce)	3	4	15
Married three years or more	84	76	54
Total	100%	100%	100%
Number of couples	571	209	48

Adapted from Burgess and Wallin, 1953: 565.

tionship or at least with the readiness of the partners to get married. Therefore, it is premature to marry as long as either partner has serious doubts.

The Necessity of Commitment

If mate-selection involved choosing the best of all eligible partners, it would be simpler. A choice between visible alternatives is relatively easy. Unfortunately, the choice must often be made between a visible prospect and invisible alternatives. If the current prospect meets minimum standards, marrying him might be better than marrying no one. Indeed, he may be the best one to come along. What a pity, however, to marry him today and discover someone better tomorrow!

Whether to wait for somebody better depends on how good the chances are. Do more compatible people really exist, or is this just daydreaming? How eligible am I? If better partners exist, what are their chances of being interested in me? This is partly a question of time. For teenage girls the chances of encountering more compatible partners in the future are excellent. Past the age of thirty, the chances of marrying *anybody* dwindle to less than fifty-fifty. Somewhere in their late twenties, most people must quit waiting for something better and marry whoever meets their minimal standards—if they want to marry at all. Up to that age, waiting often pays off:

> When I was a Senior, I fell in love with a boy who wanted a wife to cook, to entertain, and to make babies—nothing else. I was tempted to marry him, but after a struggle I came to the conclusion that I couldn't surrender my intellectual interests. I gradually became more sure that there would be other loves—that life *could* go on without him!
>
> I met my husband a year later. I had never met anyone so interesting to talk to nor with so bright a mind. I was drawn to someone with so

wide a range of interests, someone gentle and considerate, yet who knew who and what he was, and someone with a wonderful sense of perspective. To him I was one person who could be everything—friend and mistress and wife and mother. We both wanted *everything* from one person, and we still think we got it.

Regardless of whether one marries gloriously or settles for a satisfactory minimum, marriage always involves commitment. It means committing oneself to this person, even if a more intriguing one turns up later. It also means creating a marital relationship by applying skill and effort. Choosing a partner is only the beginning of marriage.

3 Mixed and Unmixed Marriages

The preceding chapter focused on the personal characteristics of potential marriage partners. This chapter considers their social involvements. People are not just individuals; they are also members of groups. They belong to churches, are citizens of particular countries and members of more-or-less distinguishable ethnic groups and social classes. Whether they marry someone from the same group makes a difference in married living. Most people do "marry in" (that is, "homogamously"). The exceptional "heterogamous" cases encounter extra problems which require extra compatibility testing. Though focused on the option whether to marry homogamously, this chapter anticipates problems and solutions for those who marry out.

Like Marries Like

Chapter 2 showed that "opposites attract" in some aspects of personality. However, in terms of groups, the general rule is "like marries like."

Reasons for Homogamy

PROPINQUITY. In part, homogamy results from propinquity (geographical proximity). People who live, worship, work or study in the same place get acquainted with one another, date, and get married. Propinquity produces homogamy because people from the same groups have the most contact with each other. Cities are segregated into nationality, religious, class and racial areas. So like meets like within the neighborhood.

68

The typical American marries someone who lives only a score of blocks away. The higher one goes in the social scale, the greater the distance between home addresses. Nevertheless, propinquity still operates, though the foci may be different (Katz and Hill, 1958). Instead of the neighborhood, middle-class couples may meet in church, at work, or at college, making them homogamous in religion, occupation, or education. The segregation of American life makes the members of most groups share not just one but several characteristics. For example, members of a given church tend to be of the same race, class, and ethnic background also.

Quite apart from deliberate strategy or special motivation, homogamy results from like *meeting* like. Groups provide an institutional framework that brings members together regularly so they can get acquainted. Because interaction produces sentiment, marriage choices tend to be made between people who meet repeatedly in the same social contexts.

Table 3-1 shows that marriages are more homogamous than chance alone can explain. Twice as many marry within their religious group as would be expected if people were randomly paired off. The discrepancy between expected and actual homogamy is especially great for Jews and Catholics, suggesting correspondingly greater pressure to marry in. Protestants, however, are so large and diverse a group that they have less consciousness of kind and less pressure for homogamy. (This may explain why Heiss, 1961, found in midtown Manhattan that Catholics and Jews generally suffer negative consequences when they marry out but fewer Protestants report such troubles.)

Religious homogamy in the United States is partly caused by the fact that propinquitous contacts are segregated along religious lines, but social pressure, personal prejudice, and rational considerations also determine which one of the many persons we meet, we finally marry.

SOCIAL PRESSURE. Organization leaders usually discourage mixed marriages. Occasionally college officials or employers invoke their authority,

Table 3-1. Religious Homogamy, by Religious Group

| | RELIGIOUS GROUP | | | |
	Protestant	Catholic	Jewish	Total
Percentage of U.S. Population	66%	26%	3%	95%*
Expected homogamy due to chance	53	16	2	42
Actual homogamy	91	78	93	88
Ratio of actual/expected	1.7X	4.9X	46.5X	2.1X

* Plus 1% other religion, 3% none, 1% no answer.
Adapted from Glick, 1960. *Source:* Representative sample of 35,000 U.S. households (Bureau of the Census). Certain methodological problems may mean that the above figures overestimate the amount of actual homogamy (Rodman, 1965). However, our primary interest is in the differential between groups.

especially against interracial couples. More pervasively, social pressure comes from parents and friends. Friends may make disapproving remarks or shun mixed couples. Parents are even more apt to intervene on behalf of their children's "best interests." Favorite techniques include withdrawing children (especially daughters) from college or sending them abroad. A student going steady with a Venezuelan boy reported:

> When I told my mother I was thinking of marrying Rafael she was very upset. She says I'm blind and don't know what I'm doing. Since then she has avoided any mention of the subject because it makes her feel so badly. But I found out that she wrote a letter to Rafael and asked him not to marry me. All my girl friends except one think it's terrible—and she's going to marry a South American too!

Sometimes pressure backfires, making the individual more determined to get married. Frequently, however, it succeeds in breaking up the relationship.

The success of parental pressures for homogamy can be seen among student marriages at the University of Utah. Students who lived at home during courtship were significantly more apt to marry homogamously than students who lived away from home (see Table 3-2).

PERSONAL PREJUDICE. The average person is drawn to those with whom he has the most in common. Shared values, interests, and rituals contribute to feelings of congeniality. A common history of persecution creates a special unity within minority groups. Members of the same church or social class feel more at ease with one another than with outsiders. This feeling results not only from sharing a common culture but from belief in the superiority of that culture. Ethnocentrism is inculcated during the child-rearing process. Hence, most young people have deep-seated preferences for friends and mates from their own group.

Table 3-2. Premarital Residence and Marital Homogamy

	PREMARITAL RESIDENCE AT HOME		
	Neither Partner	One Partner	Both Partners
Marital homogamy			
Religious homogamy	64%	80%	88%
Status homogamy	61	72	83
Minimum number of cases	22	46	36

Adapted from Coombs, 1962: 156–57. *Source:* Married student couples at the University of Utah. Religious homogamy was defined as Catholic versus Protestant versus Mormon. Status homogamy was measured by Warner's Index of Status Characteristics. Reciprocal percentages of couples married heterogamously (e.g., 36% of the couples where neither partner lived at home married someone of a different religious faith).

RATIONAL CHOICE. Homogamous marriages may be sought in order to improve marital compatibility. Recognizing that mixed marriages encounter extra problems, conscious planners may limit their selection to their own kind.

To summarize, factors both within and outside the individual make mixed marriages the exception rather than the rule.

The Consequences of Homogamy

Homogamy guarantees compatibility of certain interests and values. In addition it provides a supporting framework of social relationships. Membership in the same organizations and social circles buttresses the relationship between the partners. Homogamous partners have a solidifying environment to support them. Mixed couples, by contrast, find their internal difficulties magnified by the counterpulls of their separate "tribal" involvements. The social pressures and personal preferences that cause homogamy in the first place help to cement homogamous marriages. Approving parents and friends lend support and encouragement. Churches, clubs, and ethnic organizations provide opportunities for joint leisure-time activities. The identification of husband and wife with the same groups gives them a feeling of common destiny.

Mixed Marriages

Despite the pressures for homogamy, mixed marriages do occur. Marriages may be mixed along only one dimension or along several. Because of the pressures toward homogamy most mixtures are unidimensional. For example, American soldiers who married Filipino girls after World War II usually chose those with similar education and social status (Hunt and Coller, 1957). Since unidimensional mixtures are most common, they will be the focus of the remainder of this chapter. Where mixtures are multidimensional, problems are correspondingly multiplied.

The degree of mixture also depends on the degree of identification of each partner with his own group. In some cases the tie is so residual that the marriage is mixed only externally, not internally; that is, the social involvements of the partners may conflict, while their personal values and interests do not.

Residual Mixtures

The chief external complication in residual mixtures is that parents feel rejected by the child. Rejection may take the form either of loss of identification or of transfer of identification to the partner's group.

Loss of Identification. Second-generation Americans are a classic example of lost identity. Whereas first-generation immigrants cling to the language and customs of the old country, subsequent generations are increasingly identified with American culture (Campisi, 1948). As a result, the rate of intermarriage between nationality backgrounds rises from generation to generation.

America is such a mobile society that people desert all sorts of groups, not just old-fashioned ones:

> I was brought up Catholic and my mother is pretty religious now. But since I came to college I've gotten away from the Church. I still go occasionally when I'm home, more out of respect for my mother than anything else. But I don't accept the official beliefs any more. I'm beginning to wonder whether I should list myself Catholic at registration time.

To call this student Catholic would be misleading. When group identification is so attenuated, it loses most of its meaning. Were he to marry a Protestant it could hardly be called a Catholic-Protestant marriage. Yet even in such cases there are potential problems. A devout Catholic mother is likely to want her son's children baptized and raised in the Church. And even the son may discover he wants his children baptized and confirmed as he was. Nevertheless, his marriage would be considerably less mixed than if he were a "good" Catholic.

Children of mixed marriages are more apt to enter mixed marriages. (For example, in Detroit, children of interfaith marriages were roughly twice as likely to marry out as children of homogamously Protestant or homogamously Catholic parents [Besanceney, 1962]). Children of mixed marriages are likely to have identity problems, and their parents before them may have contracted their own mixed marriages as a result of initially weak religious identification. Weak identities and mixed marriages go hand in hand in such families.

Transfer of Identification. A second residual mixture involves persons who have actively joined another group. Religious converts and social climbers are good examples. Rabbi Richard Rubenstein (1963) concluded that many Gentile students marrying Jews were also "marrying" the Jewish community (i.e., converting to Judaism). He felt they wanted to "join the community of the alienated" or were attracted to an intellectual or artistically sensitive way of life they had encountered among Jewish friends.

In one Nebraska city, a large proportion of interfaith mixtures became residual because one partner changed religions at marriage, resolving the background difference and bringing the couple into religious homogamy. Typically this change was made after the couple became committed to marriage but before they had children. Otherwise, it was made before the first child was old enough to know the difference. These converts attended chuch even oftener than ordinary members of the faith but became church leaders less often (Babchuk, 1967). Religious mobility presumably minimized potential strain in these marriages.

McGuire (1950) estimated that one-fourth of all Americans move up the social scale. Social climbing requires learning the behavior patterns of the new group and unlearning the patterns of the old. A lower-class boy must avoid swearing, "dirty" jokes, and sexual promiscuity to enter the middle class. He must learn how to study hard, save money, and dress neatly. Then he may become sufficiently identified with the middle class to be able to marry a schoolteacher with only mild "mixing." She might notice occasional slips in grammar and etiquette but otherwise encounter few internal problems. His parents' reaction would depend on whether they felt bereft or proud of their son. In either case, they are likely to feel uncomfortable with a high-status daughter-in-law. Her parents, on the other hand, are apt to doubt that he is good enough for their daughter. So in-law relationships are not likely to be easy in either direction.

The greater the difference between groups, the greater the in-law difficulties. For parents, however, it may be a toss-up whether it is worse for one's child to lose interest in their values or for him to join the "enemy camp." For parents who take their own religion seriously, a switch to an alien faith may be less disappointing than abandoning religion altogether. Yet conversion from one loyalty to another may be consciously wholehearted without wiping out the last unconscious traces of childhood socialization. In times of emotional stress—whether negative or positive—an individual is liable to "forget himself" and slip back into old patterns, to the dismay of both partners. For example, foreign partners may find their native language more useful than English when they lose their tempers.

When loss of identification persists for generations, "pseudo-mixture" might be a better term than "residual mixture." In Manhattan intermarried "Catholics" often came from homes where religion was unimportant, and intermarried "Jews" often had parents who never attended religious services (Heiss, 1960). Under these circumstances even the residual consequences of intermarriage are less likely to occur.

Residual mixtures are halfway between homogamous marriages and the genuine mixtures in which we are mainly interested. In genuine mixed marriages each partner retains his identification with his separate group, holds differing beliefs and values, and follows a different way of life.

Motives for Mixing

Because mixed marriages are exceptional, their motivation may be unusual. Sometimes the individual is attracted to difference for its own sake.

FORCED MARRIAGE. A good many couples enter mixed marriages unintentionally. Indeed, Mayer has written a whole book on this subject, *Jewish-Gentile Courtships*. He examines courtships which culminated in marriage in spite of the initial reluctance of one or both partners to marry out. Many of his subjects drifted into marriage without fully realizing what was happening to them, either interpersonally or subjectively. Interaction led them to become so involved with one another that their scruples against intermarriage were overcome.

In other cases, the pressure to get married is more drastic. Substantially more interfaith than homogamous marriages in Detroit involved premarital pregnancies (32 per cent of mixed couples versus 17 per cent for Protestants and 20 per cent for Catholics). Pratt (1965) suggested, "a plausible interpretation here is that interfaith marriages are quite frequently brought about by the fact of pregnancy where a marriage might not otherwise have occurred." We cannot assume that all mixed marriages are deliberately contracted. Some couples are forced to marry despite their differences. Some, I will suggest below, *choose* to marry despite their differences. But many couples find their differences appealing in one way or another.

SELF-HATE. The most neurotic motive for intentional out-marriage is to degrade oneself by marrying an inferior. Rubenstein (1963) described a Radcliffe girl of Protestant background who became pregnant by two successive Jewish boys. He noted that she was strongly ambivalent toward Jews:

> Women frequently enter such relationships in order to degrade themselves and their families. Similar mechanisms are often at work in liaisons between white women and Negro men. As the need for self-degradation wore out, resentment against the husband as the imagined source of degradation could create a host of thoroughly unpleasant situations (p. 126).

REBELLION. An individual who dislikes his parents may marry an outsider in order to hurt them or to assert his independence.

> In high school I dated a boy against mother's wishes (not behind her back, however). His brother had gotten a girl into trouble and I guess mother thought it ran in the family or something. He was the son of a fireman in our town, which was another thing mother had against him.

She thought Dick and I wouldn't have much in common, and now that I think about it, we didn't. But I was feeling rebellious at the time, and I thought I was pretty fond of him. I met his friends who seemed very different from the boys I had known and sometimes not as nice. Sometimes it was very dull, and when we both got bored we would neck, which I discovered was an excellent antidote for boredom. . . . The main attraction was, I suppose, that mother didn't approve of him.

The vindictive satisfaction of defying parents temporarily offsets the strains of incompatibility. In the long run, however, parents die and the marriage partner must be lived with for his own sake.

In other cases intermarriage reflects estrangement from one's ethnic group. Among intermarrying and mixed-dating students at the University of Hawaii, childhood feelings of rejection and social isolation were common (Freeman, 1955). Such feelings evoke sympathy for the person whom one's own group despises.

SOCIAL REFORM. Marrying for social reform intrigues sensitive members of majority groups. Embarrassed by the discrimination their fellows inflict on minorities, they are tempted to demonstrate their liberalism by marrying out. Articles on race relations sometimes suggest that intermarriage is the ultimate solution. For some young people the opportunity to contribute to this solution through their own marriages seems too good to pass up.

FASCINATION BY THE EXOTIC. The notion that "opposites attract" motivates still other marriages. Glamor, mystery, and sex appeal surround the stranger, whereas the boy next door seems dull and commonplace. One coed felt that going halfway around the world to marry an Egyptian would be an "adventure" she wouldn't want to miss. Fascination with the unusual may be felt between Americans as well as internationally. A rabbi fell in love with a divorcee whom a friend described as "a woman unconventional to the point of bohemianism, an artist and dancer who resents convention to her very core." Because she was nominally Jewish, the match was not mixed ethnically but occupationally. When couples answer the call of the mysterious, the mystery fades as they get better acquainted. As the Egyptian's fiancée recognized, "even life with him could become humdrum after ten or twenty years." The lure of the exotic is likely to be ephemeral.

PERSONAL GAIN. Finally, prudential motives produce mixed marriages for social and economic gain. Social inferiors strive to "marry up." The stenographer who marries her boss, the Jew who marries a Gentile, the war bride who marries a Yankee soldier may hope to profit socially from their "good" marriages. Since the man confers his social position on his family, women are more apt to "marry up." But if the benefits were only one-way, aspiring women would find fewer takers. Foreign brides may seem more traditionally feminine and more appreciative of the husband's income. Perhaps the husband's ego benefits as much as the wife's social position. Similarly, men uncomfortable with equalitarianism often marry down in order to be more patriarchal.

Scott (1965) pointed out that low-status women expect less from marriage and are therefore less expensive. High-status men discover that ". . . the favors, including the prospect of marriage, of low-status women can be had for a smaller investment of their own scarce time, money, and emotion." Time-short medical students were especially apt to find low-status girls attractive for this reason. This is hardly the path to a productive relationship, but it is certainly the path to an inexpensive one for men more interested in their careers than in their marriages.

Marriage *because* of difference undermines one prerequisite for personal relationships, since the partner is treated as means rather than end. The acid test is whether the marriage would occur if the out-group character of the partner disappeared. If not, the attraction is categorical rather than personal.

BASIC SIMILARITY. By contrast, most mixed marriages are undertaken in spite of the differences. They are motivated by love of the individual for his own sake. The partners are attracted because they meet each other's needs and share many common interests. These marriages would be even more likely to occur if the group difference disappeared. They are homogamous in enough respects to provide a basis for coping with the stresses created by their mixture. For minority groups too small to offer more compatible alternatives, marginal mixtures may be the only alternative to celibacy.

Problems of Mixed Marriages

Contrasting backgrounds create potential problems. Not all problems will arise in every mixed marriage, but possible trouble spots should be explored in contemplating such a marriage. Some problems are characteristic of all mixed marriages, while others occur only in specific mixtures.

Between Husband and Wife

At the very beginning of marriage, mixed religious couples face the problem of choosing one partner's wedding ceremony over the other's.

Some by-pass the choice by resorting to a civil ceremony (Chancellor and Burchinall, 1962). Though both sides "lose out" this way, there may be advantages in losing equally. But if one partner is reluctant to marry out of his faith and the other doesn't care, the amenable partner is usually willing to use the reluctant partner's ceremony. (Out of sixteen Jewish-Gentile couples in New York where one partner was reluctant to marry out, only two chose civil ceremonies. All the rest were married in the reluctant partner's ritual [Mayer, 1961].)

Mixed couples bring conflicting cultures into their marriages. For instance, domestic rituals may differ. Dietary differences complicate menus for the cook and flood the house with "strange odors." The church calendar differs for Christians and Jews, with such key festivals as Christmas and Easter as unfamiliar to the Jew as Hanukkah and Yom Kippur are to the Christian. Decisions whether to put up a Christmas tree can be surprisingly difficult.

Marriage roles may differ between cultures. A second-generation Syrian-American reports that when men of his nationality background marry "old" Americans, trouble ensues because the wife's "aggressiveness and independence" clash with the husband's expectations. By contrast, girls from "back home" are properly submissive. The role conflicts of international marriages are intensified when the wife's nationality has more prestige than the husband's. For example, a Brazilian man married to an American girl wrote:

> Having been brought up in an authoritarian society, I often manifest elements of this orientation that are usually resented by Laura who has been reared in a middle-class American family. I have complained about her being bossy, but she probably feels that she has as much reason to call me bossy, too.

DIFFERENTIAL IDENTIFICATION. Quite apart from conflicting values and cultures, a mixed marriage is "a house divided against itself." Husband and wife have their roots in contrasting traditions which create a sense of estrangement. A Protestant wife writing in a Catholic magazine concluded thus:

> I have never had occasion to alter my original opinion that my husband is the finest man I have ever met. . . . But even so there is still that intangible consciousness of effort that is always with us, always standing as a barrier. We must live with this as with a stranger in the house. And no one relaxes when there are strangers in the house.

People from contrasting backgrounds can take less for granted—fewer common assumptions, common values, common habits. Hence they have to work harder at communicating with each other. When trouble arises, the sense of difference is magnified. Most men and women unconsciously share the prejudices that exist between groups—prejudices held by minorities as well as majorities. Traditional stereotypes become painful epithets in domestic quarrels.

DIFFERENTIAL PARTICIPATION. Insofar as mixed partners participate separately in their own groups, their solidarity is weakened. Finding common friends is difficult since cliques tend to be segregated the same way marriages are. Sometimes other mixed couples are available. For instance, World War II veterans with Japanese wives associated almost exclusively with similar couples in Chicago (Strauss, 1954). Small communities rarely offer a mixed clique, so separate friends or few friends may be the only choices available in the face of social ostracism.

If each partner participates in his own group, the couple are deprived of what could otherwise be a binding element. At worst, this causes open conflict. Where other couples go to church together, interfaith couples go their separate ways. Though during courtship they may attend both churches every Sunday, the complications of parenthood tend to terminate that luxury.

Between Parents and Children

When children come, a decision has to be made as to which group they shall be reared in, participate in, identify with. This is the most difficult and pervasive problem in interfaith marriages. Where one parent belongs to a persecuted group, identification is extra baffling for the child:

> There was only one major conflict in our family. Owing to the religious faction (my mother is a Quaker and my father Jewish Reform) neither parent had fully conceded to the other. The problem was not one of conflicting theologies, because these two religions are about as similar as any two, but rather one of frame of reference. This is exemplified by the fact that before marriage my parents decided any boys would be trained in the synagogue and any girls would go to the Friends Meeting. Luckily there are no boys because that would have emphasized the already existing conflict. Although there were no arguments or even discussions about this topic, the conflict was conveyed subliminally to me, making my parental attachments, identifications, and so forth, unusually difficult by creating a sense of conflicting loyalties. This problem has existed for me as far back as I can remember, even in grammar school where I was first exposed to anti-Semitism in the form of ridicule from playmates. My identification and ultimate participation in Jewish or non-Jewish groups is still unresolved and probably will remain so until I marry. This remains a problem because I have long since discovered that in realistic

adult situations (as contrasted with university life) participation in and vacillation between both groups is practically impossible from the standpoint of acceptance and the resulting rewards of group identity. I think I prefer to marry a Jewish man mainly because I perceive the great security derived from functioning entirely in what appears to me to be a more clearly defined and more highly integrated group than the non-Jewish groups.

If one partner's group identity is more meaningful than the other's, the latter will usually hesitate to intervene. (This concession resolves much of the conflict between the parents, though it does not prevent the children from being exposed to the split identity of their parents.) Among 20 Jewish-Gentile couples in New York City where one partner hesitated to marry out but the other didn't care, four couples were unable to agree how to raise the children but the other 16 raised them in the faith of the reluctant parent (Mayer, 1961). Where both partners are equally committed or equally uncommitted, the question is less easily resolved.

Conflict between mixed-marriage husbands and wives over how to raise their children involves the children most directly. But children are remarkably sensitive to *any* problems which disturb their parents. Any husband-wife or kinship conflict in a mixed marriage is likely to be felt by them. Some children "act out" their inner disturbances in delinquent behavior (see Table 3-3).

Table 3-3 shows that juvenile delinquency was two to eight times as common in mixed marriages as in unmixed ones. The negative effect on children increased the greater the barriers to intermarriage. Protestants are generally least disturbed by intermarriage and Jews most disturbed. Table 3-3 suggests that their children's behavior problems reflect parental difficulties correspondingly.

One consequence of the difficulty of raising children in a split house-

Table 3-3. Arrests for Juvenile Delinquency, in Children of Religiously Mixed and Unmixed Marriages

	PERCENTAGE OF CHILDREN EVER ARRESTED BY RELIGIOUS HOMOGAMY OF PARENTS		
Religious Identity of Father	Unmixed Marriage	Mixed Marriage	Ratio
Protestant	5.8%	11.1%	1.9X
Catholic	4.0	9.8	2.5
Jewish	5.1	41.1	8.0

Adapted from Zimmerman and Cervantes, 1960: 158–59. *Source:* Families of high school seniors and of friends of their families. For simplicity, this table is limited to St. Louis but similar results were obtained in Boston, Denver, New Orleans, and Omaha. The total number of cases for the three religious groups combined was about 9,600 unmixed marriages and 1,100 mixed marriages.

hold is a tendency to have fewer children. Among white families in Manhattan the interreligious birth rate fell the farthest for Catholic individuals compared to homogamously Catholic couples carefully matched in other respects. For Jewish and Protestant individuals who married out, the number of children also decreased, though not as much. Specifically, the birth rate was reduced .34 child for intermarried Catholics, .25 for Jews, and .19 for Protestants (Heiss, 1961). Even when religion is held constant, international couples have fewer children. For example, Catholics married to Catholics averaged fewer children when one parent was foreign-born than when both were Americans. Similarly, in Protestant marriages, fertility was lower in international marriages than in domestic marriages (see Table 3-4).

External Problems

No matter how cohesive a couple may be internally, mixed marriages encounter external stress. Pressure is greatest when group ties are easily identifiable to outsiders (as in interracial marriages) and when the two groups have hostile feelings toward each other.

ALIENATION FROM FAMILIES. Family opposition to mixed marriages is most acute before the wedding. If opposition is strong enough, it leads mixed couples to get married "behind their parents' backs." Though not all out-of-state weddings are elopements, mixed marriages ceremonialized away from home symbolize the girl's estrangement from her parents. In Iowa in the mid-1950's, for example, only 12 per cent of intrafaith weddings involved brides from other states compared to 28 per cent of interfaith weddings (Chancellor and Burchinall, 1962).

Most mixtures produce in-law difficulties. To mixed couples, in-laws appeared aloof (Duvall, 1954). A foreign husband described his relationship with his American in-laws thus:

Table 3-4. Number of Living Children in Unmixed and Mixed Nationality Marriages, by Religion

	AVERAGE NUMBER OF LIVING CHILDREN BY NATIONALITY OF PARENTS	
Religion of Parents	Unmixed Nationality (Both Americans)	Mixed Nationalities (One American, one Foreign)
Both Protestant	2.49	2.38
Both Catholic	2.76	2.42

Adapted from Bresler, 1961: 17. Source: Parents of students at Brown University, Providence, Rhode Island.

I often thought of my in-laws as being distant toward me, especially when I remember that they objected to our marriage at first. But as I got to know them better, I gradually changed this impression about them. Nevertheless I still feel tense and uneasy whenever they visit us or when we visit them.

Whereas in-law problems are relatively rare in unmixed marriages, they are almost universal in mixed marriages (see Table 3-5).

Mixed marriages not only have more difficulties but fewer "patterned intergenerational family activities," such as financial help, visiting, and joint vacations (Sussman, 1953). Though aloof from the son-in-law or daughter-in-law, older couples put pressure on their child to keep him in line with family traditions. Such pressure focuses on the grandchildren. Interfaith marriages occasionally provoke a veritable tug-of-war between the two sets of grandparents for the souls of their grandchildren. At the very least, in-law pressures make the losing parent feel worse:

I come from a devout Catholic family and my wife from a very strong Protestant one. She raised all the children Protestant. My family still condemns me for it, but Martha put her foot down on this before we were married. I still feel guilty about the whole situation even though I'm not a practicing Catholic and don't believe in much Catholic dogma myself. Needless to say, due to factors other than the distance, Martha and I have never been very close to the relatives on either side.

Alienation from in-laws is a natural corollary of mixed marriages motivated by rebellion or by loose family ties. Where the family of orientation had disintegrated through death or voluntary separation, the usual family pressures for homogamy were diminished and the postmarital sanctions on heterogamy were correspondingly less (Hunt and Coller, 1957).

FRIENDSHIP PROBLEMS. In the Manhattan study I have cited before, Heiss found that intermarried couples had fewer close friends than

Table 3-5. Intergenerational Difficulties in Religiously Unmixed and Mixed Marriages

Intergenerational Difficulties	TYPE OF MARRIAGE	
	Religiously Unmixed	Religiously Mixed
Yes	18%	90%
No	82	10
Total	100%	100%
Number of cases	156	39

Adapted from Sussman, 1953. *Source:* Interviews with middle-class New Haven parents of married children.

homogamous couples. Protestant partners were not bothered by this, but the loss was felt strongly by Jewish outmarryers (for whom sensitivity to social discrimination was most acute). Catholics in mixed marriages were also more apt than their unmixed confreres to say they wanted more friends. Apparently friendship problems are created generally for Catholic/ Protestant or Jewish/Gentile couples, but the stress caused by social isolation varies with one's sensitivity to potential social discrimination.

OCCUPATIONAL PROBLEMS. A majority-group partner may experience the same discrimination as ordinary members of the minority group to which he is attached by marriage. In some cases his fate is worse. In sensitive positions or sensitive communities, marrying into a minority group is worse than being born into it. The latter can't be helped, but intermarriage is unforgivable. However, social discrimination by friends and strangers and institutional pressures from one or both groups vary greatly from one locale to another.

Decreasing Problems

Most kinds of mixed marriages are becoming more common in the United States, especially Catholic-Protestant, Jewish-Gentile, and Negro-white marriages. The gradual integration of Catholics, Jews and Negroes into American society has increased contact between groups and decreased the social and economic barriers which previously separated them. The ecumenical movement stimulated by the Vatican Council has stimulated interfaith dialogue and mutual respect between Catholics and Protestants. Anti-Semitism is on the wane and race prejudice has been publicly defined as illegitimate.

Increased contact and acceptance between groups have triple effects. Not only do they (1) increase the rate of mixed marriages but they (2) increase the likelihood of conversion and (3) decrease the problems created. As problems decrease, the number of intermarriages increases still further.

One illustration of decreasing problems comes from the Jewish community in Providence, Rhode Island. Whereas in an earlier generation Gentile wives of actively Jewish husbands retained their separate identity, more recently they often converted to Judaism. Before, Gentile wives of Jewish men bore 30 per cent fewer children than Jewish wives. In a more recent generation, the gap narrowed to 10 per cent. And whereas earlier mixed marriages were delayed by the obstacles involved ("mixed" husbands and wives were older than usual), the age lag subsequently disappeared (Goldstein and Goldscheider, 1966). Internal and external strains cannot be expected to disappear altogether, but our shrinking planet promises to become a more viable home for mixed marriages.

Difference as Opportunity

The statistics cited in this chapter suggest that the average mixed couple react negatively to their differences. But exceptional cases can be found. The extraordinary people whom Maslow (1954) called "self-actualizing" were less afraid of differences, better able to tolerate them, sometimes able even to appreciate them. For broad-minded people, mixed marriages are another opportunity for mind-stretching. The adventure of sharing another culture and discovering first-hand how "the other half" lives, enlarges their capacity for empathy and their understanding of mankind.

> You ask me if I would marry Joan again if I had my life to live over again, and my answer is yes. It isn't easy for a rabbi to have a Gentile wife. Some people raise their eyebrows, you know. But since much of my counseling is with students considering intermarriage, my own experience helps me to understand the situation they're in. Raising our own children has been hard work but rewarding as we've tried to introduce them to the best of both our religious traditions. But the main reason I'm glad I married Joan is because she's been a good wife and we still love each other so deeply after all these years.

Perhaps it is fair to assume that extraordinary people rarely intermarry just for the sake of broadening themselves. Probably their primary motive is basic similarity and person-to-person love. But once they find themselves in a mixed relationship, they transform it into an opportunity for mutual enrichment. Mixed marriages in this sense are risky. But high-risk games have high payoffs—for those who win. For extraordinary people, mixed marriages may pay off in extraordinary excitement and creativity. But for ordinary people, the low-risk sureness of modest returns from a homogamous marriage is a safer bet.

Catholic–Protestant Marriages

Differences in religious faith present obstacles to personal relationships, especially for church members who believe they have the only true faith. Under such circumstances couples lack not only spiritual unity but also the respect for each other's convictions that makes it possible to live and let live. Marriages between "good" Catholics and "good" Protestants tend to experience these tensions. If couples do not feel them spontaneously, devout relatives and friends and clergymen may create them.

Interfaith marriages are vulnerable to the usual in-law problems but rarely have occupational difficulties. Religious training of children is particularly difficult if their church affiliation is considered a matter of eternal concern. Differences in values between Catholic and Protestant partners are most acute over birth control, though they may also occur over politics, civil liberties, parochial schooling, and the like. If both partners attend their own churches, they are separated at times that are normally family-oriented.

Valid and Invalid Catholic Mixed Marriages

In 1966, the Catholic Church relaxed some of its regulations governing marriages between Catholics and other Christians. The non-Catholic partner is no longer required to promise in writing that he will allow his children to be raised Catholic, but he is still expected to make this promise orally. The written obligation now falls on the Catholic partner only. For the marriage to be valid in the eyes of the Church, the wedding must still be performed by a priest. However, non-Catholic clergymen are now allowed to play subsidiary roles in the ceremony. The former restriction of the elaborate nuptial mass to unmixed Catholic couples has been lifted, so mixed couples may use any Catholic rite they wish.

These new regulations reflect the liberalizing influence of the ecumenical movement and are sometimes symbolized by designating mixed marriages as "ecumenical marriages." Elements of a new bilateralism include encouragement of mixed couples to receive instruction in both partners' faiths before marriage and to attend both partners' churches every Sunday. However, the requirement that the Catholic partner wholeheartedly practice his own faith imposes on the couple a moral obligation to practice Catholic teaching about birth control and to attempt to raise all children in the Catholic faith.

Invalid mixed marriages are contracted by American Catholics almost as often as valid ones. Frequently they are undertaken by nominal Catholics to whom church affiliation is relatively meaningless. In other cases they reflect unwillingness of the non-Catholic partner to accept the Catholic conditions or the fact that one party is divorced and therefore ineligible to contract a valid Catholic marriage.

Consequences of Interfaith Marriages

Anticipating negative consequences, a considerable proportion of interfaith couples break up before marriage. In Burgess and Wallin's sample

(1953), 19 per cent of the engaged couples of differing faiths broke their engagements compared to 11 per cent of those of the same faith. Because of this higher drop-out rate before marriage, mixed couples who do marry represent a select group with somewhat better prospects. Despite this selectivity they still have more than their share of troubles.

MARITAL FAILURE. We have already seen that interfaith couples bear fewer children than religiously homogamous couples. We should not be surprised to learn that the strains which depress the fertility of mixed marriages sometimes destroy those marriages altogether (see Table 3-6).

The divorce rates in Table 3-6 are relatively low because they are limited (1) to high status couples (2) in the early years of marriage. Our main interest, however, is not in the absolute rates but in the differences between unmixed and mixed marriages. For both Catholic and Protestant women, the divorce rate in interfaith marriages was several times the rate for intra-faith marriages. This Iowa study found that denominational affiliation made little difference when one Protestant married another. Interdenominational marriages had roughly the same divorce rates as intradenominational marriages. However, when Catholics married Protestants, the more alike the two churches, the less the strain. When Catholics married members of "high" churches (Lutherans and Presbyterians) the divorce rate was only two and a half times the Catholic norm. When they married members of "low" churches (Methodists and Baptists), it was four and a half times as high. The worst rate of all, however, occurred in marriages to "unspecified Protestants" belonging to no church at all (almost twenty times the normal Catholic divorce rate). This reflects the marital instability of nonreligious persons (see Chapter 13). However, it is also more difficult for a person who holds religious values to get along with someone who rejects that whole orientation to life than to marry someone with a *different* religious orientation. To be equally serious about religion gives an

Table 3-6. Divorces of Catholic and Protestant Women in Religiously Un-mixed and Mixed Marriages

	PERCENTAGE DIVORCED BY RELIGIOUS HOMOGAMY		
	Religiously	*Religiously*	
Faith of Wife	Unmixed	Mixed	Ratio
Catholic	1.4%	10.6%	7.6X
Protestant	5.1	12.1	2.4X

Adapted from Burchinal and Chancellor, 1963: 357. *Source:* All high-status couples (professional and managerial husbands) married in the state of Iowa between 1953 and 1959 who were divorced by the end of 1959. Reciprocal percentages were still married. The number of divorces represented by each of the above percentages were respectively:

	225	111	
	2,227	125	

interfaith couple a common value, whereas a devout believer is doubly estranged from an unbeliever of another religious background.

RELIGIOUS CONSEQUENCES. Partners in mixed marriages attend church less often than unmixed couples. It is not clear, however, how much this religious casualness is effect and how much is cause of the mixed marriage. In any case, it is understandable that interfaith couples should deemphasize religious practices as a means of avoiding issues that divide them. If parents in mixed marriages are initially and/or subsequently irreligious, it follows that their children will also be irreligious. Many receive little or no religious education and identity with neither parent's church (Thomas, 1956). The remainder most often adopt the faith of the mother, especially in the case of daughters. (In Landis' study, 75 per cent of the daughters and 65 per cent of the sons followed the mother's faith, regardless of whether she was Catholic or Protestant.)

So far we have seen that interfaith marriages fail more often and interfere with the faith of both parents and children. Chapter 19 will show that they also involve compromises in contraceptive practice for both the Catholic and the non-Catholic partner.

Jewish–Gentile Marriages

Despite the fact that the Jewish community is much smaller than the Catholic, its mixed-marriage rate is lower. Residential and social segregation, both voluntary and discriminatory, reduce opportunities for Jews and Gentiles to fall in love. Centuries of persecution have produced strong in-group preferences, particularly for those who identify with Judaism or Zionism as religious and ethnic faiths. Nevertheless, the assimilation of Jews into American life is producing more intermarriages based on propinquity. For the United States as a whole, only seven per cent of all Jewish *marriages* involved a Gentile partner (Glick, 1960). However, in states such as Iowa where the Jewish population is very small, the intermarriage rate may reach 20 per cent or more (Chancellor and Monahan, 1955).

Intermarriages are more often undertaken by Reform Jews than by Conservative or Orthodox Jews whose culture patterns are more distinctive and whose lives more segregated (Bigman, 1957). For Orthodox Jews, a child who married a Gentile was traditionally considered dead. His name was no longer mentioned. He was shunned personally and stricken from the parents' will. More recently, says Gordon (1964), "this is seldom the case." Yet Gentile partners unfamiliar with Jewish attitudes are often surprised to discover "how strongly Jews feel about intermarriage." (Mayer, 1961)

More Jewish men than women marry Gentiles (Goldstein and Gold-scheider, 1966). This may be because of (1) the greater integration of males into the life of the larger community through their occupations and (2) their greater emancipation from parental control. Mixed marriages of Jewish men with Gentile wives are no more successful than mixed marriages of Catholic or Protestant women (some of whom marry Jewish men).

Table 3-7 shows a 70 per cent higher rate of failure for mixed marriages in New Orleans and five times as many failures in each of the other cities. Since the methods used in this study are different from those used in the Iowa study of interfaith marriages, it would not be appropriate to compare the rates in the two tables. The point is that both kinds of mixed marriages fail substantially more often than homogamous marriages. However, we *can* compare the pattern portrayed in Table 3-7 with Zimmerman and Cervantes' own data for Protestant husbands and Catholic husbands. In every case, St. Louis is the typical (median) city in the ratio of divorce-and-desertion failures in mixed as against unmixed marriages. For Protestant husbands in St. Louis, the failure rate doubled, for Catholics it tripled, and for Jews, as we have seen, it is five times the homogamous rate (1.9X, 2.9X, and 5.2X, respectively). This pattern suggests that Jewish-Gentile marriages are more hazardous than Catholic-Protestant marriages.

One reason for the extra hazardousness of Jewish-Gentile marriages may be that most American Christians are fairly religious whereas most American Jews are not. For Protestants and Catholics, church ties tend to be important, whereas for Jews, communal bonds are strongest (Lenski, 1961). This is illustrated by student responses to the question, "To whom do you owe your greatest loyalty?" The most popular answers were "God" or "family." But whereas Catholics placed God above family (74 per cent to 24 per cent), Jews rarely named God first (11 per cent to 74 per cent for

Table 3-7. Desertions and Divorces of Jewish Men in Communally Unmixed and Mixed Marriages

PERCENTAGE OF DESERTIONS AND
DIVORCES BY COMMUNAL HOMOGAMY

City	Communally Unmixed	Communally Mixed	Ratio
New Orleans	33.4%	57.4%	1.7X
Omaha	12.6	62.2	4.9X
St. Louis	8.6	44.4	5.2X
Boston	4.7	25.4	5.4X
Denver	8.4	48.3	5.8X

Adapted from Zimmerman and Cervantes, 1960: 153–54. *Source:* Families of high school seniors and of friends of their families. In the five cities combined the total number of cases studied was about 1420 intracommunal marriages and 450 intercommunal marriages.

family loyalty). Protestants fell in between but closer to the Catholic pattern (Maier and Spinrad, 1958). This strong sense of family feeling among Jews tends to reinforce their endogamous (marrying-in) norm and leave the Gentile partner viewed askance as an outsider.

In most American homes, the mother is primarily responsible for religious rituals. Jewish-Gentile marriages are no exception. In Washington, D.C. 59 per cent of intermarried Jewish mothers had conducted Passover services in their homes at least once, but only 19 per cent of intermarried Jewish fathers had ever done so (Bigman, 1957). The children of these marriages generally identified with the mother's faith and chose marriage partners of her faith.

Illustrative of the mother's influence is the experience of Gentile mothers in mixed families belonging to the 20,000-member Jewish community in Providence, Rhode Island. Children in these families were subjected to many forces influencing them toward a Jewish identity—fathers, neighbors, friends, and community institutions. If the mothers converted to Judaism, all of the children considered themselves Jewish. But if the mother did not convert, only 58 per cent of the children became Jewish despite the family's public identification with the Jewish community (Goldstein and Goldscheider, 1966). We can easily imagine how many more children would identify with a Gentile mother if the family were not embedded in the ethnic community.

We can generalize, for both Catholic-Protestant marriages and Jewish-Gentile marriages, that children tend to follow in their mother's footsteps. Child-rearing is primarily the mother's responsibility and religious and cultural training are her special province; as a result, her values are transmitted to the children more often than her husband's.

In the Washington study, most families reared all their children either as Gentiles or as Jews. Less than one-tenth compromised by raising some children one way and some the other. Gordon (1964) comments that in the latter families "the likelihood of marginality and personal insecurity for the children is further increased." It is difficult enough to have parents with differential identities, but it is an even greater strain to split brother from sister. We have already quoted a student who was not sure whether to identify with the Jewish community. The fact that persecution has so often been the Jewish fate gives the question of group identification strong emotional overtones. Gentiles marrying Jewish partners may encounter prejudice and discrimination. In some parts of the United States anti-Semitism is virulent and Jews are excluded from clubs and resorts and subjected to college admission quotas. How much the Gentile partner and the couple's children feel the brunt of such practices depends on where they live and on the extent to which the family is identified as Jewish. The very existence of such variation adds to the tension.

International Marriages

International marriages require a drastic change of residence for one partner, usually the woman. It is often said that women make most of the adjustments in marriage, but this is especially true when they move to another country. The partner who moves geographically must make a drastic social move as well. The problems of any immigrant confront the foreign spouse—learning to speak and write a new language, to like new foods and sports, to master new customs and values. Adapting to the new homeland is aided by the spouse and his family. Strauss (1954) found that the husband's parents "generally greeted their Japanese daughters-in-law warmly . . . and played an important part in the acculturation of the bride, teaching her about shopping, about kitchen equipment and the like." Parents in old countries may be less helpful:

> I was rather shocked when I received a letter from my husband's parents one week before our wedding saying in no uncertain terms that marriages engineered by young couples themselves would not and could not work out. They demanded that we drop our "childish fantasies," and told my husband to return to Pakistan where they would arrange a marriage for him. Fortunately, a short while afterwards we received their blessing.

Facilities and equipment are mastered more easily than the subtleties of language. For Japanese war brides language was perhaps the greatest single difficulty. "The difficulty was greatest in times of crisis or emotional excitement and in such situations as the discussion of technical matters or joking." (Schnepp and Yui, 1955) The strain of having to speak a foreign language creates a longing to mingle socially with fellow compatriots so the native tongue can be enjoyed again.

In Filipino-American marriages the sharpest conflicts involved child-care practices, housekeeping practices, and sexual attitudes and practices (Hunt and Coller, 1957). The first two were moderated by the American husband's tendency to think of them as in the wife's domain, even if he disapproved of the way she handled them. The Filipino wives were sexually modest and passive by American middle-class standards (in much the same way as lower-class American wives), which disappointed and frustrated the husbands.

To change lifelong habits may seem worthwhile for a foreign spouse rewarded with the high American standard of living. But an American woman who emigrates finds fewer compensating advantages unless she genuinely enjoys the foreign culture. Some couples disagree about which country to settle in. One American veteran wanted to go back to Japan, whereas his Japanese wife wanted to stay here. How much cultural retraining is required depends on the culture. Mates from English-speaking countries have fewer problems than those who must learn a new language. Western Europeans are more like Americans than Orientals or Arabs. Recruits to high-status marriages have often had a cosmopolitan upbringing that provides the tools for assimilation.

We cannot assume, however, that the best international marriages always involve the greatest cultural similarity. If that were the case, the best marriage for a Japanese war bride would be to a Japanese-American man. Yet Kimura (1957) found that in Hawaii fewer of these marriages were as well adjusted as when Japanese women married men of other nationality backgrounds (39 per cent versus 75 per cent). The trouble with the Japanese/Japanese-American marriages was that the wives thought they were marrying an emancipated American man, whereas the husband's family maintained traditionally authoritarian Japanese ways that she had hoped to escape. The Japanese-American culture was not different enough from what she had left behind to give her the new values she sought. In this case ethnic homogamy created value incompatibility, making matters worse rather than better. Conversely, Japanese wives of non-Japanese-American men were treated with more respect by the latters' families and were allowed to work out their desired marriage patterns with less interference.

International marriages occur more often between American men and foreign women than between American women and foreign men. Which partner is American and which country the couple settle in are crucial determinants of the problems involved. International marriages are so rare that it is difficult to find data on their success. Probably they fail more often than homogamous marriages. But Strauss' study (1954) of surviving marriages of Japanese war brides in this country showed them coping to their own satisfaction with the difficulties involved.

Interethnic Marriages

Combining some features of international marriages, interclass marriages, and interracial marriages are marriages between persons whose families immigrated recently from different foreign countries. Hawaii is an excellent place to study the effects of ethnic intermarriages because so many national backgrounds are represented there. By comparing divorces granted with marriages contracted in the late 1950's Lind (1964) was able to compute divorce rates for various ethnic groups. For homogamous marriages, these fell in three main categories:

1. Stable groups (Japanese or Chinese—15 to 18 per cent divorced).
2. Intermediate (Caucasians—35 per cent divorced).
3. Unstable (Filipino or Puerto Rican—46 per cent divorced).

Unlike Catholic-Protestant marriages (whose divorce rates are higher than either group taken alone), most interethnic marriages produced divorce rates between the rates for the two groups involved. For 19 out of 29 interethnic combinations, the divorce rate fell between the rates for the separate ethnic backgrounds. This suggests that for most marriages, interethnicity is no more of a problem than is interdenominationalism for American Protestants. However, the remaining ten ethnic combinations were exceptions to this general rule. Four had divorce rates higher than either partner's group and six had fewer divorces than would be expected. Caucasian women were involved in the two "worst" combinations, and Caucasian men in two of the three "best" mixtures (see Table 3-8).

The most detrimental combinations involved Caucasian women married to Japanese or Chinese men whose ethnic groups normally have the lowest divorce rates in the entire islands. Perhaps the very stability of these groups is the source of trouble. We have already seen that Japanese war brides married to Japanese-American men had conspicuously unhappy marriages.

Table 3-8. Detrimental and Beneficial Ethnic Mixtures in Hawaii, by Ratio of Divorce Rates in Unmixed and Mixed Marriages

| | DIVORCE RATE BY ETHNIC HOMOGAMY | | |
Detrimental Mixtures	Ethnically Unmixed	Ethnically Mixed	Ratio
Japanese man	14.7%	57.5%	3.9X
Caucasian woman	35.4		1.6X
Chinese man	17.7	43.2	2.4X
Caucasian woman	35.4		1.2X
Beneficial Mixtures			
Filipino man	46.0	32.4	0.7X
Puerto Rican woman	46.0		0.7X
Caucasian man	35.4	24.4	0.7X
Filipino woman	46.0		0.5X
Caucasian man	35.4	20.1	0.6X
Puerto Rican woman	46.0		0.4X

Adapted from Lind, 1964: 22. *Source:* Divorces granted 1958–62 per 100 marriages contracted 1956–60 for the entire State of Hawaii.

Apparently the same solidarity of family structure which oppressed those emancipation-seeking women also annoyed the already-emancipated Caucasian women. I assume that the Japanese/Chinese husbands and their extended families sought to assert their traditional authority over these wives—without success. A Caucasian-American wife is too assertive to submit to patriarchy. She would rather get a divorce. Caught in a power struggle with a domineering husband-and-family, a wife accustomed to equality opts out.

At the opposite extreme, the most beneficial marriages in Hawaii paired Caucasian men with Puerto Rican or Filipino women. Here the converse situation existed. Caucasian men are accustomed to equality but women from Spanish cultures expect to be submissive. More importantly, perhaps, the relatively low status of their island economies probably made the wife look up to her "American" husband and feel grateful to and dependent on him. For her this was an unusually "good" marriage which she would be reluctant to leave. Such marriages are not necessarily the most satisfying from the standpoint of the interpersonal criteria used in this book. They may be deficient in companionship and empathy. But they are extraordinarily stable.

Prospects for a successful marriage in the following case are not entirely clear. However, an Anglo-Saxon woman marrying an Italian-American man seems likely to encounter sharp challenges after marriage:

> During the early stages of our relationship, Angelo purposely overemphasized the things that were closest to his heart in order to elicit my most violent reactions. The men in his family are engaged in a series of entrepreneurial activities which have been extremely lucrative. Angelo's choice of an occupation is almost entirely dependent upon his prospects for making money—in large quantity. This attitude was distasteful to me. I have lived modestly all my life, and never been inclined to regard money as an index of status or prestige. I was rather amazed when he interrogated me about the material arrangements I would require of a prospective husband—i.e., the kind of house, the type of vacation, etc. It seemed almost as though he was offering me a dowry, and I was taken aback by the businesslike quality of the transaction. However, I slowly came to reconcile myself to these and other aspects of his thinking as I saw them more within the context of his family's expectations.
>
> When we had been seeing one another steadily for about six months, Angelo introduced me to a good friend of his—a middle-aged contractor who drove a white Cadillac. I had very little in common with this man, but I recognized the event as a challenge to my sociability and attempted to make the most of it. A week later the friend appeared again and I was obliged to invite him to join us at a large party given by a classmate of mine. This time the three of us were together for a whole evening, drinking, dancing, learning how to shoot pool, etc. Several weeks elapsed before I learned the true identity of this mysterious friend—he was

Angelo's brother (an emissary from the other camp) scrutinizing my behavior under "normal conditions."

I was being groomed—in numerous subtle ways—for marriage into a style of life essentially foreign to my own, and, in a sense, the older brother was performing as the first (and probably most sympathetic) judge of my progress. The experience made me more consciously aware of what might be my major difficulty in adjusting: I had become accustomed to a kinship system which was based upon limited communication, tacit understanding and psychological rather than emotional closeness—very much in contrast to the active mutuality and interdependence which marked many facets of Angelo's familial responsibility.

Interclass Marriages

By interclass marriages I mean couples who differ markedly in education or whose fathers differ significantly in social status as measured by occupation, income, and/or education. I will exclude residual mixtures where one partner has been upwardly mobile to the other partner's class level in order to concentrate on genuine mixed marriages where the partners' class statuses differ at marriage.

Husband-High Marriages

Just as international and interethnic marriages differ according to the sex of the partners, so do interclass marriages. Usually it is the woman who marries up. From her point of view, this makes a "good marriage" since the husband's social status is normally conferred on his wife and children. By marrying "well" she can hope to share his prestige as well as his standard of living. For the husband this match is no better than marrying at his own class level unless he prefers a dependent wife. But some feminine qualities such as good looks are not confined to the middle class. He may find a low-status girl physically attractive and overlook her lack of social amenities. Or he may prefer her old-fashioned interest in children, religion, and sociability to a college-educated girl's interest in community affairs (Feldman, 1966).

Nevertheless, husband-high marriages are less successful than homogamous ones (see Table 3-9). This is not to say that an upward-marrying wife regrets her choice, but her satisfactions are financial and social rather than marital. Likewise, the husband may be glad he married her, yet find she commits enough *faux pas* to impair their sense of companionship. For Feldman's differentially educated couples, both partners reported feeling

Table 3-9. Marriage Adjustment, by Comparative Class Status of Husband and Wife

| | COMPARATIVE CLASS STATUS | | |
Marriage Adjustment	Same	Husband Higher	Wife Higher
Good	53%	35%	28%
Fair	26	33	31
Poor	21	32	41
Total	100%	100%	100%
Number of cases	215	116	65

Adapted from Roth and Peck, 1951. *Source:* Burgess and Cottrell's 526 married couples in Chicago, 1931–33.

less close after conversations—apparently because talking exposed their differences.

Wife-High Marriages

The problems of husband-high marriages are mild compared to husband-low marriages. The latter are difficult for the wife if the husband's income provides less than her accustomed standard of living. To be sure, most couples start with less than their parents have attained, but husband and wife are usually "in the same boat." What bothers a "poor little rich girl" is that her comedown is greater than her husband's. What hurts even more is seeing her children deprived of luxuries she enjoyed in childhood. The fiancée of a modestly paid high school teacher expressed her anxiety thus:

> Bruce will probably earn less than half what my father pays in income tax. This won't bother me too much because my family has never lived on a showy plane. But I'm afraid that when my children are old enough to demand things, I won't be able to give them all the money they want. I don't want them to have to pinch pennies when they get to college but to be able to splurge and eat out whenever they want to. I don't want them to have to worry about money or even think about it.

A man who marries up has problems too. He is touchy about finances. Gifts from the wife's family are insulting reminders of his lower income. His wife pressures him to get ahead. Such sensitivities do not make for easy husband-wife or in-law relations. The problems of wife-high marriages are not only financial. The husband's lower status tends to pull the wife down to his level of reputation and participation in the community. Moreover, the male ego is undermined by the wife's disappointment over his occupational "inadequacy." Feldman discovered that such couples spend less time in conversation, presumably because of their mutual alienation.

While all husband-low marriages tend to suffer from psychological strains, the most disastrous marriages involve women who have been upwardly mobile past their husbands' position (Roth and Peck, 1951). Such wives are most concerned about their social status and suffer from their husbands' inadequacies. The men in turn feel degraded by their wives' successes.

Marriages which start off handicapped by educational differences are less trapped with that discrepancy today. Expanding facilities for adult education for both sexes and the new emphasis on "continuing education" for women offer opportunities for removing educational deficiencies. Even in middle age, mothers and fathers of growing children may restore their self-confidence and revitalize their marriages by going (back) to college.

Interracial Marriages

Nothing would infuriate the average white American more than his daughter's marrying a Negro. No other mixture touches off such widespread condemnation as race mixing. And no combination of races epitomizes miscegenation as dramatically as Negro-white marriages. The problems of any other race mixture are mild by comparison. American hostility to interracial marriages is illustrated both by their extraordinary rarity and by nearly unanimous opposition in opinion polls. For example, 80 per cent of the students questioned in 40 American colleges and universities labeled interracial marriage the most difficult type of mixed marriage (compared to 9 per cent for interfaith or intereducational marriage, 4 per cent for international marriage and 3 per cent for interclass marriage as measured by economic background [Gordon, 1964]).

Paradoxically if one looks simply at the characteristics of the two individuals, no type of mixed marriage involves less intrinsic incompatibility. Negroes and whites are citizens of the same country. If they are also members of the same faith and students at the same college, what is there to differentiate them except their physical appearance? Despite the efforts of black nationalists to cultivate "soul music, soul food, and soul religion," Negro culture is hardly a full-fledged entity. Those who make a fetish of blackness are not likely to find a white spouse attractive anyway. So individuals color-blind enough to cross the color bar are unlikely to find that "bar" dividing them, provided they are homogamous in other respects.

Trouble for interracial marriages comes chiefly from without. The segregation, discrimination, and prejudice-proneness of American society can hardly fail to affect those who defy the "rules." If the Negro partner is recognizably Negro, the couple will be the perennial target of astonishment and curiosity, if not of ostracism and abuse. The white partner must expect to share the discrimination and segregation to which Negroes are usually subjected. Both partners must expect stares from strangers, interrogation by new friends, and occasional beatings by new enemies (Smith, 1966). Forceful intervention by unofficial strangers is rare, however, compared to the "rather common" experience of Smith's middle-class New York couples being stopped by strange officials on the highways. Policemen can hardly imagine that a black-and-white couple might be married. The woman is assumed to be either a prostitute or maid, the man either a rapist or chauffeur. To minimize hostile reactions from the community, interracial couples often hide their relationship from public view. (Smith's couples rarely announced their engagements publicly, rationalizing that "society would do a rather thorough job of 'publicizing' their marriage anyway.")

In most communities, a mixed family becomes Negro socially—except in those rare metropolises where interracial couples form their own subcommunity. Rejection by relatives is most severe from the "superior" side (as usual in mixed-level marriages). For the Negro relatives, a mixed marriage may be a "good" marriage, and in any case may tap the sympathy acquired through generations of persecution. Alienation from parents is the most difficult emotional problem reported by white partners (Smith, 1966).

For the children of an interracial marriage, life is not greatly different from the normal Negro pattern. The identity problem facing children of interfaith marriages does not arise since the community classifies them as Negro. In appearance they may be indistinguishable from peers whose so-called "Negro" parents contributed just as many white genes acquired in earlier generations.

The main question for the white partner, therefore, is whether he or she (usually she) is prepared to join the Negro race. If so, Smith reported that external persecution sometimes drew husband and wife closer together. However, outside pressures had at least occasional inside repercussions. The Negro partner tended to be supersensitized by his experiences. The original establishment of the interracial relationship usually depended on overtures from the white partner since most Negroes were afraid of being rejected if they made any advances. After marriage, the Negro partner tended to be touchy about seeming racial slurs and to insist on the white partner's need to learn to "understand" Negroes. Interracial marriage is never easy in contemporary America—even in cosmopolitan New York City.

Evaluating the Prospects for a Mixed Marriage

The hazards of mixed marriages are clear from the preceding pages. Nevertheless, *some* mixed marriages turn out well. What makes the difference between those that succeed and those that fail? The answer depends on each couple's ingredients for marriage.

Prerequisites for Success

For mixed marriages the prerequisites are the same as for other marriages —compatibility, skill, effort, commitment and support—but they are more important than usual.

COMPATIBILITY. Greater compatibility in other respects is needed to offset the mixture. The amount of incompatibility involved in the "mix" differs. There is less to fear from a residual mixture than a genuine one. Even genuine mixtures vary in their strain-potential. A "High-Church" Episcopalian or Lutheran feels more kinship for Catholic liturgy, a Unitarian for Reform Judaism, an Asia expert for a Chinese wife. In interclass marriages, Roth and Peck find that the wider the class difference, the more the marriage suffers. This can be extended to all mixed marriages—the greater the difference between groups, the greater the problems.

SKILL. Given a certain problem, the wisdom of marrying depends partly on the couple's coping-ability. The more skillful they are, the better they should be able to resolve their differences. They can be sure that a mixed marriage will test their problem-solving skills to the utmost. Maslow's "self-actualizing people" were unusually skillful. They were more confident of their ability to cope with the stresses of mixed marriages and even found them stimulating:

> In the more external and superficial characteristics, e.g., income, class status, education, religion, national background, appearance, the extent of homogamy seems to be significantly less than in average people. Self-actualizing people are not threatened by differences nor by strangeness. Indeed, they are rather intrigued than otherwise. They need familiar accents, clothes, food, customs and ceremonies much less than do average people (1954: 259).

For average people, skillfulness is crucial. If rational problem-solving is hard, if one partner (or both) is easily provoked to rage or moodiness, if they are short on patience and sympathy, one prerequisite for successful mixing is missing.

EFFORT. Mixed marriages require more effort than unmixed ones. For couples unwilling to make the extra effort, mixing produces frustration and bitterness. With effort they can work to "make the best of a bad situation."

Willingness to keep trying is related to one's motives for mixing. For individuals rebelling against parents or fascinated by the exotic, effort is likely to wane with the passing of parents or of the novelty. Social reform and personal gain are more persistent goals yet they interfere with mutual love. The stress of mixed backgrounds requires an extra measure of love, willingness to sacrifice, and concern for the partner's walfare.

COMMITMENT. The very anxiety created by the prospect of a mixed marriage, the warnings of others, and the soul-searching deliberations guarantee that once the commitment to marriage is finally made, it is likely to be a firm one. To marry in the face of contrary advice is to make a public commitment which is unusually humiliating to break. Not only to outsiders but to oneself and to each other, the resolve to make a go of it is unusually explicit—and unusually necessary. Firm commitment will not guarantee success, but it helps mixed couples get through the crises they are bound to encounter.

SUPPORT. Even hostile parents or friends are likely to switch from opposition to support once they lose the battle to prevent a mixed marriage and are faced with a *fait accompli*. In exceptional cases where hostility persists, it may be advisable to move away. Couples faced with strong community opposition also may flee to safer ground. Perhaps flight is cowardly, but a safe haven may make the difference between social support and social disruption. Mixed marriages can seldom afford less than the best social circumstances.

Procedures for Deciding

To determine whether they meet the prerequisites for success, mixed couples need all the usual compatibility testing, and then some.

DISCUSSION. Discussion can inform the partner of the hidden world at hand:

> Coming from a subsistence economy, I gave first consideration to the question of differences in our level of living. I tried my best to inform Diane as accurately as I could about living conditions in Chile—discussed them in detail, gave her materials to read, and cautioned her against forming impressions from tourist advertisements. In addition, I suggested that she should talk to other people—Americans as well as Chileans—who could give her a more detached evaluation of my country. One of these was a missionary who spent about five years in my country, and he had a lot to tell Diane.
>
> Second was the question of the trustworthiness of an American wife.

This question kept coming to my mind because of the stereotype (probably gained from the movies) that the people at home have about American wives, especially those married to racial minorities, which is not very complimentary. I also informed Diane about this. In my effort to resolve this question, I took into consideration the following items: (a) Diane's family background which was furnished to me by a townmate of hers; (b) the judgment of a friend of mine with whom I arranged a double date so that he could see Diane for himself; (c) my own evaluation compared to the comments of other people whose judgment I respected.

SOLVING PROBLEMS. Mixed couples need to do more than develop their general problem-solving skills. They need to resolve their *specific* problems before deciding whether to marry. Preliminary plans may not work when the time comes, but they are the best available preview of the ability to solve critical issues. When people are in love, facing problems is not easy. It seems a shame to "spoil" a romance by bringing up troublesome questions. It's more fun to dream in the moonlight than to quarrel about non-existent children:

> Jack and I are sitting on top of the world this week. We had some rough times during the last few weeks but now that we've finally agreed to be married by the priest but to use contraceptives until he's settled in his job, we're really enjoying life again. We've decided to postpone trying to decide about the faith of our children because we don't want to shatter this wonderful feeling.

Anticipatory decision-making is practiced successfully by many mixed couples. McLean (1953) found that well-educated Protestant-Catholic couples did considerable problem-solving before getting married. A third of his couples discussed their religious differences extensively before marriage and nearly all the rest did to some degree. Most of the couples planned what church(es) they would attend and agreed on the religious training of children. However, only a minority decided in advance about birth control.

VISITING EACH OTHER'S HOMES. Visiting each other's families previews whether the prospective in-laws will accept or reject the "outsider." Although rejection is common in mixed marriages, it is by no means universal. One Jewish-Gentile couple found a warm welcome from both families:

> My mother is crazy about her because she's just the age my sister would have been if she had lived. Our mothers got together during Thanksgiving vacation and hit it off real well. Our families seem to have a great deal in common. After we decided to get married, her mother wrote me a grand letter welcoming me into their family.

Negative reactions to prospective mixed marriages may not be expressed directly by parents afraid of seeming prejudiced. Almost one third of Mayer's Jewish-Gentile couples suspected that their parents were more unhappy than they let on. Many parents translated their opposition to the prospect's ethnicity into criticism of his/her personality, appearance, occupation—"everything except the fact that she was Gentile." Contacts with the prospective child-in-law tended to be cold, reserved, and distant more often than explicitly hostile (Mayer, 1961).

The indirectness of parental opposition sometimes results from the couple's delay in visiting each other's homes. The greater the fear of the parents' reactions, the longer couples tend to put off the confrontation or to disguise it by not telling parents the "awful truth." When parents finally have a chance to react, they may be confronted with a *fait accompli* in a relationship too committed to be undone. When compatibility testing is so long delayed, it hardly deserves the name. Early confrontation not only gives young people a chance to assess their parents' reactions but gives parents time to recover from the shock. Table 3-10 shows how violently parents react when first confronted with a mixed involvement. But among couples who eventually marry, parents usually come to appreciate the prospective partner as a person, or at least decided to make the best of the situation.

In assessing Table 3-10 we need to remember that it does not tell us how many other couples broke off their relationship because their parents remained adamantly critical. To begin testing family reactions early is urgent precisely because parents can be expected to be initially hostile and time must elapse before one can discover whether they will gradually become more supportive. Just as repeated contacts are necessary for young couples to fall in love, so repeated visits to parents are necessary for positive feelings to develop. The greater the resistance, the greater the contact

Table 3-10. Parental Opposition to Jewish-Gentile Marriages at Two Stages of Courtship

Degree of Parental Opposition	On Learning the Relationship Was Serious	At Time of Marriage
Strong	70%	27%
Moderate	20	17
Mild	10	41
None	0	15
Total	100%	100%
Number of cases	29	29

Adapted from Mayer, 1961: 170. Source: Jewish-Gentile couples in New York City who were initially opposed to intermarriage but who eventually married across communal lines.

required to overcome it. On that acceptance—or continued rejection—hinges the outcome of this testing.

GETTING FEEDBACK FROM FRIENDS. Many mixed couples were brought together initially by a common friend. Mutual friends played an important supportive role in bridging the gap created by conflicting group identities. They provided a social base on which the new love could be erected (Mayer, 1961). For mixed couples with no antecedent common friends, the situation was more ambiguous. Peers were more apt than parents to share the individual's values and therefore to be less hostile to the prospective partner. However, friends who did have negative reactions rarely expressed them because they did not feel they had the right to volunteer their opinions unless they were asked (Mayer). This means that no news cannot be assumed to be good news. If individuals really want to know, they must ask their friends and must emphasize that they want their opinions honestly expressed. When friends do react critically, the individual is in a dilemma. He must drop either his friend or his lover. Since love is by definition stronger than friendship, the usual casualty is the friend. At least for Mayer's Jewish-Gentile couples who eventually married, hostile friends usually ceased to be friends.

Yet this is the easy way out—the path of least resistance. The challenge for mixed couples is to take the hard way and confront both family and friends before becoming inextricably involved. If a good relationship can be worked out with both family and friends, the couple can count on a well-supported marriage. But if either family or friends feel the marriage is unwise, the courtship should at least be slowed down if not actually ended.

VISITING THE "OUTGROUP." A distinctive step for mixed couples is participating in the activities of both groups in order to understand each other's backgrounds. Most interfaith couples attend services at both churches. One white girl went to live in Harlem to help decide whether to marry a Negro boy. Immersing herself in an impersonal mass of strangers of her boy friend's race gave her fresh insight into the social complications of an interracial marriage (Karpf, 1951).

Other mixed couples are usually glad to report their own experience. Caution is needed, however, in interpreting the experience of any particular couple. Some couples are miserable and others are blissful. Couples already divorced have disappeared from public view. Nobody else's experience guarantees what will happen in one's own case. Nevertheless, such conversations reveal potential problem areas and potential solutions.

GETTING EXPERT HELP. For couples whose pre-engagement attempts to solve problems end in failure, the future is ominous. Both partners might visit a marriage counselor for "trouble-shooting" interviews. These may clarify thinking and lead to sounder conclusions. If the decision is affirmative, the counseling may also help resolve the problems in the relationship.

Making the Final Decision

The final decision whether to marry out depends on the attractiveness of the particular prospect and of the available alternatives. A mixed marriage may seem advisable if there is little chance of a homogamous one because homogamous partners are scarce or because one's bargaining power is low. Overall compatibility with a mixed partner may be greater than with the best homogamous partner met so far or likely to appear in the future. These relative balances must be weighed.

Because they involve special problems, mixed marriages require extra testing in advance. If the tests are passed with flying colors, there is little reason to fear heterogamy. Although mixed couples have a higher casualty rate than unmixed ones (both in broken engagements and broken marriages), most mixed marriages succeed. The risks may be greater, but they aren't necessarily overwhelming. Some mixed marriages aren't much different from unmixed ones. And some mixed couples find in diversity a breadth of experience which they prize. In the last analysis each couple must decide for themselves. If the criteria and procedures suggested in this chapter are followed, a better decision will be made.

Avoiding Mixed Marriages

Other things being equal, mixed marriages are more difficult than unmixed ones. So it may be useful to take steps to avoid getting involved with mixed partners and to locate homogamous partners.

Avoiding Mixed Involvements

Most dating is homogamous. At the University of Florida, for example, three-fifths of the casual couples and nine-tenths of the steady couples were homogamous by social class (Ehrmann, 1959). The reasons for homogamy in dating are the same as for homogamy in marriage: propinquity, pressure, and preference. Only one-tenth of the students at 40 American colleges and universities, however, followed a policy of never dating outside their religion, whereas 21 per cent did so rarely, 39 per cent sometimes, 20 per cent frequently, and 9 per cent almost always (Gordon, 1964). A conservative approach would shun mixed dating altogether.

People with more confidence in their own maturity may draw the line between casual and serious dating:

> I would rather not date a boy excessively who is not of the same religion since I am not a believer in mixed marriages. This does not mean that I will not date a person of different religion, but I would prefer to keep such dating to a minimum as I realize I might fall in love with such a person and this I would rather not do.

What is a safe minimum? Where is the dividing line between noninvolvement and involvement? Mayer (1961) interviewed 25 Jewish-Gentile couples in New York City, who started their relationships with at least one of the partners initially opposed to intermarriage. One man thought interdating was "safe" because he was too young to marry at age 16, a widow because she wasn't interested in remarriage, another man because he was only interested in sex. All three eventually married "dangerously" the dating partners they hadn't intended to fall in love with. Some couples did not discover each other's ethnic identity until after they had already become emotionally involved. Early inquiry presumably would have led them to break up. But even early knowledge of the partner's ethnic incompatibility might not have prevented intermarriages where couples were thrown together involuntarily. If they worked in the same office or were lab partners in a biology course or lived in the same neighborhood, propinquity produced heterogamy despite initial antipathy.

Mayer's study suggests how difficult it is for *some* couples to avoid getting involved. Many of his young people were especially vulnerable to new involvements because they had just lost a parent or were unhappy at home or were lonely or unattractive. They needed to fall in love so badly that they responded uncritically to the nearest available partner.

Though problem-laden people may find it difficult to govern their behavior rationally, normal people are more capable of choosing homogamously. For instance, Duke University coeds' serious involvements were increasingly homogamous in religion, education, and class background as they moved from high school to college dating to engagement (Kerckhoff, 1964). For most, the shift from home town to college campus inevitably narrowed the field of eligibles. But the abandonment of relatively mixed "last previous serious partners" in favor of more homogamous fiancés can only be credited to selectivity. In so doing, they drew the line at the last possible place—between serious dating and marriage.

Finding Homogamous Partners

There is a saying that "it's just as easy to fall in love with the right person as the wrong person," but this depends on the availability of the right kind of person. For members of small nationality and religious groups, special efforts are required.

> There were only two other Armenian families in our town and neither had any daughters old enough for me to be interested in. For a long time my parents opposed my desires to date American girls. They kept talking about the importance of preserving our culture and even suggested that I should go all the way to Boston to date "some nice Armenian girl." But finally they had to give in because I wanted to take part in our high school activities so badly.

Casual dating in high school doesn't necessarily lead to marriage. But once an individual grows old enough to marry, homogamous partners become important. In an earlier generation, marriage-brokers scoured the small towns of the South and Midwest, bringing isolated Jewish men and women together. Today the responsibility rests on the young person himself.

Where are homogamous partners likely to be found? Church colleges and denominational student groups offer sustained opportunities for contact. The larger and more complex the community, the more its component parts tend to be segregated ecologically and organizationally. By strategic ecological location and organizational commitment, the chances of homogamous marriage may be enhanced. For example, at the College of William and Mary, the Greek half of the student body was socially segregated from the independent half. Particularly for members of the top-rated fraternities and sororities, serious dating tended to develop within organizational boundaries (see Table 3-11).

The organizational segregation of campus dating promoted homogamous mate-selection because Greeks differed from independents in family origin and personal characteristics. Even at a generally high-status college like

Table 3-11. Organizational Segregation of Serious Dating Relationships, for Fraternity and Independent Men

	MEN'S ORGANIZATIONAL MEMBERSHIP		
Partner's Organizational Membership	Top Fraternities	Bottom Fraternities	Independent
Top sororities	63%	14%	0%
Bottom sororities	12	19	9
Independent or off-campus	25	67	91
Total	100%	100%	100%
Number of cases	60	52	11

Adapted from Reiss, 1965: 198–99. *Source:* College of William and Mary, Williamsburg, Virginia, a coeducational, liberal arts college with 1800 students, half of whom belong to fraternities and sororities.

William and Mary, fraternity and sorority members came more often than independent students from professional and executive families. Moreover, members of a campus subgroup tend to hold common values. The Greek students at William and Mary were more sociability oriented (valuing clothes, manners, parties, dancing ability and physical appearance) whereas independents were more academically oriented. Even the Greek world may be further subdivided into Gentile, Jewish, and Negro segments (Scott, 1965) as well as into the prestige rankings portrayed in Table 3-11. Hence fraternity/sorority pairings are likely to be unusually homogamous.

Ethnic summer resorts, summer projects and conferences provide briefer opportunities after graduation. Some communities and some companies offer more chances for finding a homogamous partner. Marriage is such an important aspect of life that extra effort spent in mate-selection may bring major dividends.

4 Love: Developing a
Personal Relationship

Love is the word that best captures the meaning of marriage in America. Before marriage it is the *sine qua non* of courtship. Dating leads to love affairs, great and small. Mate-selection depends on the growth of love.

The Nature of Love

There are many kinds of love. The kind we are concerned with is love between a man and a woman. It may be defined as *an intense emotional attachment between two people of the opposite sex.* Intensity is a matter of degree—despite the romantic myth that it is an all-or-none affair. The minimum intensity of love cannot be precisely defined—many couples cannot pinpoint precisely when their friendship changed to love. All we can say is that love is more intense than "mere" friendship.

The emotionality of love signifies its dynamic characteristic. Love is a yearning to be together, an urge for oneness, a desire to please the partner. Love enlarges one's emotional capacity. Each time the heart is stretched a bit, the individual becomes more perceptive and aware than before. The more people learn to feel, the more they can express the qualities in human life that civilization values—compassion and creativity. Because love is emotional, it is a favorite theme of those connoisseurs of emotion—the poets. For the same reason it is not easily pigeon-holed by academicians. Nevertheless, analyze it we must because it is central to courtship and marriage, the authenticating stamp without which they are empty forms.

Love is an attachment between people, not a "free-floating" feeling. It is a cathexis to an object, a personal object. One might call it an attraction, since sexual attraction is one of its ingredients. But attraction can be unreciprocated, and one-sided love is only a crush. Attachment is a better word than attraction because it symbolizes the solidarity of the relationship between the partners. They are involved with each other, related by ties of interdependence. Whether married or not, they are functional relatives of one another.

But attachment can be too close. The love which grows into a lasting marriage needs both attachment and release. After the partners learn to be close, to be companions, and to care for each other, release is an expression of trust, respect, and acceptance. Can the partners allow each other freedom to grow as individuals? A man who delights in his wife's separate blooming will find her more closely his own because he released her. The woman who encourages her husband's personal fulfillment will sense his gratitude and satisfaction. If one partner is afraid to let go and tries to control the growth and creativity of the other, love will be strangled.

Elements of Love

Love is a blend of many elements—sexual attraction, companionship, care, and affirmation.

Sexual Attraction

Love between a man and a woman is not platonic; it is a desire for proximity. It means enjoying each other's presence, being quickened by the sight and touch of the other, being physically impelled toward each other. The intensity of love is part of one's lifetime sexual education. Slowly the body awakens to its potentialities. Accepting oneself as male or female is easier when walking hand in hand. Lovers find their awakened sexuality responding to the sexual identity of the other in a delicious blend of masculine/feminine complementarity.

Heterosexual love means literally "otherness-love." An intriguing quality of love between the sexes is that it penetrates the barriers which still separate the sexes even in our relatively integrated society (Krain, 1966). Biological differences, emotional differences, and social role differences make each sex mysterious and challenging to the other. Love bridges the gap between the sexes—without dissolving the tension created by the differences.

Companionship

This is the social element in love: the enjoyment of doing things together. It is the basic element in friendship and is intensified in love. Companionship in leisure is the organizing framework of the dating from which love springs. In marriage, the scope of companionship enlarges to embrace more of the practical aspects of life. So basic is companionship to love that it hardly needs extended discussion.

Care

> I enjoy being with Bert unless he's in a bad mood, though I've found a good deal of pleasure in helping him snap out of those moods. Even if he gets mad at me, I like the evidence it gives that he cares about me. I'm happy when I'm with him and enjoy doing things with him and trying to make him happy.

Both sex and companionship can be exploited. But care is by definition altruistic. It involves concern for the partner, interest in his welfare, and effort to meet his needs. Caring is intensely personal. The ministry of care is carried on joyously. He who truly cares never considers himself a martyr or deserving of special praise. Awareness of the partner's needs is enough to bring response.

Caring rewards not only the recipient but the giver. To meet the partner's needs is to be needed oneself. To be useful is to be alive and growing. Love is like water: dammed up it become stagnant; only when it flows is it fresh. My partner not only meets my needs but in depending on me allows me to give myself to her. In the words of Erich Fromm (1956: 23).

> Giving is the highest expression of potency. In the very act of giving, I experience my strength, my wealth, my power. This experience of heightened vitality and potency fills me with joy. I experience myself as overflowing, spending, alive, hence as joyous. Giving is more joyous than receiving, not because it is a deprivation, but because in the act of giving lies the expression of my aliveness.

Affirmation

Beyond the reciprocal attractiveness of sex and companionship, beyond caring responsiveness to the needs of the other, lies affirmation of the other as a person. Perhaps the chief danger in mate-selection is premature affirmation. Yet once the commitment has been made, it needs to go beyond appreciation of the elements that bind the couple together to acceptance of even the elements that divide them. One who feels loved is able to love another. The process begins when a baby is cared for by his parents. Their warmth helps to create an adult who can trust and accept others. Affirmation can carry the couple over difficult moments; for it includes acceptance of the physical functions and needs of human beings as well as their moments of anger, irrationality and aggression.

Affirmation at its climax becomes gratitude for the other's existence and all his differences. This is the point at which love transcends mere coziness. Without surrendering one's own individuality, to be able to recognize and accept the other's differentness is to rise above the narrow confines of the ego. This is the point at which love becomes most mature.

Love Is a Synthesis

There are many ingredients of love; sex, companionship, care, and affirmation are simply the most prominent. Unlike a recipe there are no fixed proportions. Love differs from couple to couple in the balance of the ingredients. For some the physical element is prominent; in others it is below the level of consciousness. Love also changes over time. For example, the caring element grows as partners come to understand each other's needs.

In love the various elements are blended. Love differs from friendship most in the strength of the sexual element. But it is not so much composed of unique ingredients as a unique combination of ordinarily scattered elements into an intensive relationship with a particular person.

Conditions for Love

The conditions under which love arises can be stated very simply: *love is the sentiment that men and women feel who have a fully personal relationship with another.* Their relationship provides the framework within which love catches fire.

Interaction

To say that love occurs within personal relations emphasizes that it does not occur in a vacuum. A pin-up picture or a star's image on the movie screen may be enough for a "crush." But a crush is only a daydream, not the real thing. Love depends on coming to grips with one another, not just dreaming about the other. It requires mutual involvement and interdependence.

Autonomy

Interaction is a necessary but not a sufficient condition for love. The other condition is autonomy. Even after marriage, the partners are still separate human beings. The two may become "one flesh" sexually but they do not lose their separate existence. Autonomy requires respect for the other's right to differ in his life goals and his immediate concerns. It requires freedom of expression, freedom to make demands. More subtly, it requires recognition that the other person is the only one who knows his own feelings and needs:

> Roger makes me furious. Just because he is a psychologist he thinks he knows better than I do how I feel. He never accepts what I say but twists it around into his own jargon. But I know enough about psychology myself to be able to recognize that the things he says about how I "really" feel are just projections of his own imagination. I wish he could see the difference between his feelings about me and my own feelings about myself.

When husband and wife respect one another as individuals, love becomes a creative, releasing force. Without respect, it becomes a prison. If autonomy is missing, love turns into mutual exploitation. The mere satisfaction of needs is no guarantee of love:

> We've broken up many times but we just can't stay apart. I'm sure we both would get along better with others, but whenever we break up she always comes running back to me. We've had three really bad fights. She cries and says she hates the way I push her around. I'm terribly involved with her and I just don't have the strength to stay away from her.

Love must be given and received freely—not compulsively. Each partner must respect the dignity of the other. Even after the wedding ceremony there must be no possessiveness, no treating the other as property. The other must always be seen as an individual.

Some Pseudo-Loves

When any condition for love or element of love is missing, the remainder is correspondingly distorted. Although the participants may think they are in love, they are deluded. The resemblance to love is more apparent than real.

Infatuation

An affair based on sexual attraction to the exclusion of companionship and care is an infatuation. The dictionary defines infatuation as "an extravagant or foolish passion." The folly of infatuation stems from the madness of passion. Human beings can be attracted physically by countless persons. But sex appeal is no proof of love. When excitement is merely sexual, passion is a better word:

> Usually we make up by a kiss—it's sort of sex. I think Sam's manhandling is sex too. I considered breaking up with him but I can't stay away from him when he lives so close and we have classes together. He's real fierce when he's mushy. He grabs me passionately and says, "Would you ever let another man do this to you?" I can't reason with him. I can't keep saying, no, no, no! I'd miss him too much to be able to drop him now.

The fact that two people are passionately involved with each other does not prove that they are merely infatuated. But if sex holds them together against their better judgment, it is pretty sure to be pseudo-love. Care and companionship are missing. If they marry, only a lucky coincidence would produce the other elements of love. Without those elements, marriage would become repugnant as the sexual impulse ebbs with age.

Infatuations are dangerous but not inevitably disastrous. Just because an affair starts out as an infatuation does not mean it is doomed. Initial interest in face and figure does not prohibit the growth of other facets of love. But whether infatuation turns into love depends on whether the relationship broadens to embrace the entire personality of the partner—not just the body.

Idealization

Infatuation responds to a limited object; idealization to an imaginary one. Although the beloved is not invented, she is seen through the proverbial rose-colored glasses. Enthusiasm outstrips what she really is. Idealization projects into the partner my own ideals of what she *should* be. If the process is unconscious, the illusion of perfection appears where the actuality does not exist.

Lack of compatibility is masked when both partners engage in idealization simultaneously. This frequently happens in love at first sight (though occasionally the latter is caused by the sudden discovery of unusual compatibility). The boost to the ego from being idealized by another provides an illusion of compatibility without the substance. An image of destined choice balloons from the interplay of separate enthusiasms (Solomon, 1955). After an excited beginning it is hard to admit failure, especially if one's need for love is great. Unfortunately, the very persons most prone to idealization are least capable of recognizing it.

Idealization thrives in the absence of interaction. It is most prominent in love at first sight. As interaction increases, knowledge converts the dream image into awareness of the real partner. Awareness punctures the dream bubble and brings the relationship down to earth. That earthy reality is frequently less attractive than the idealized image.

Men are particularly prone to idealization. For instance in that computer dance at Iowa State referred to earlier, the men were more enthusiastic than the women about their new partners: they felt more romantic attraction, liked their partner's personality and appearance more, and were more apt to feel a happy marriage was possible—after just one date! Six months later, both the men and the women had generally revised their estimates downward. Presumably the still-enthusiastic relationships were by then past idealization and more solidly grounded (Coombs and Kenkel, 1966).

Only those too immature to accept any shortcomings in the partner go on indefinitely living in a dream world. Indeed, one characteristic of real love is that both partners drop their defenses and reveal themselves, no longer hiding their faults and weaknesses (Maslow, 1953).

Provided that compatibility is eventually tested and proved before engagement, initial idealization does no harm. At the beginning of a new romance, idealization is natural and enjoyable. Life would be poorer if dreaming were taboo. Wishes may be disappointed, but the anticipation of love is part of the fun. Even after commitment, there is room for idealization. Husband and wife need not concentrate on the partner's unattractive features as much as on the attractive ones. Life is pleasanter if both partners exaggerate each other's virtues and minimize their deficiencies. For example, Levinger and Breedlove (1966) found that the higher the *assumed* agreement between husbands and wives on their marriage goals and on the relative importance of various communication topics, the greater their marital satisfaction. Not total realism but basic compatibility is what marriage requires.

THE SPICE OF LIFE. By themselves infatuation and idealization are respectively a snare and a delusion. But as parts of the total experience of courtship, they may serve useful functions. Fascination with the other weans the individual from his parents. Even the elusive attraction of idealization helps one break out of the accustomed security of family and friends. Moreover, the pseudo-loves add spice to life, even if only temporarily. As long as they don't trap people in incompatible marriages, they are harmless enough games, enjoyable in their own right.

Infatuation and idealization add spice not only as substitutes for love but as elements in love. Infatuation overemphasizes the sexual element. In due proportion sexual attraction adds strength to love. Similarly, an idealized image of a partner may become a self-fulfilling prophecy if she responds to my hopes by becoming the kind of person I want her to be.

Sexual attraction and idealization are welcome when they occur between individuals who are well matched. Indeed, the American ideal of courtship combines physical attraction and idealized intensity with companionship love.

Varieties of Love

The difference between pseudo-loves and varieties of love is that the former are partial and ephemeral whereas the latter involve enduring differences in emphasis and intensity.

Variations in Emphasis

Because love combines many elements, the proportions cannot be standardized. Every marriage partner combines the roles of parent, sibling, and lover in the ways he treats his spouse. This means that marriage taps and carries forward childhood family relationships and is not an entirely new role. Love experienced from parents, siblings, and friends is not abandoned at marriage but incorporated into the repertoire of marital behavior.

PARENT-CHILD TYPE OF LOVE. The caring element in love corresponds to the responsibility parents assume for their children's welfare. The ultimate in tenderness is symbolized by a mother holding her baby. In marriage, husbands and wives care for each other just as earlier they were cared for by their parents. They are no longer as helpless as infants (except in sickness and death), but no one is ever too old to appreciate kindness, cheering up, or soothing down.

In every marriage there are times when each partner nurtures the other. In some, however, nurturance flows mostly one way. Where one partner's need for succorance is complemented by the other's need to nurture, love takes on a parent-child emphasis. The "parent" may be of either sex. There are "mother-son" marriages and "father-daughter" marriages. Because they emphasize care and protection, they tend to neglect the other elements of love. As long as that neglect is not complete, they are normal variations of love.

BROTHER-SISTER TYPE OF LOVE. To those reared in families racked by sibling rivalry, it may seem strange to suggest that siblings might love each other. Yet they provide an analogy for love that emphasizes companionship.

Historically, love has evolved from father-daughter type love to companionship love. This corresponds to the trend from patriarchalism to equalitarianism. As girls became better educated and more emancipated, the feeling tone of love shifted from protectiveness and dependence to mutual sharing. But historical trends seldom embrace a whole population —so companionship love is not the only kind to be found today.

LOVER TYPE OF LOVE. This is the love of adults who have come to terms with their sexual feelings, and can express them, enjoy them, and treat one another in an emotionally responsible manner.

Families differ in intimacy. Some are reserved and distant, with little kissing good-by or good night. Families which demonstrate their affection more freely prepare their children to accept their sexual feelings as they mature. Styles of loving vary accordingly in their physical demonstrativeness.

Variations in Intensity

Although love is by definition intense, its strength varies considerably. Among Burgess and Wallin's engaged couples, 24 per cent described themselves as "head over heels" in love, 70 per cent "very much" in love, and 7 per cent only "somewhat" or "mildly" in love (1953). What causes such differences?

FEVER-PITCH INTENSITY. Although some people dismiss feverish romance, it can happen—not as often in real life as in Hollywood movies nor as often as people wish, but in some cases.

1. The greater the impact of a love affair on the individuals involved, the greater the emotional intensity. This is partly a question of speed. Sudden and unexpected changes in life arouse more emotion than gradual, long-term transitions. This makes summer romances exciting. A stranger comes suddenly into my life—and if I am vacationing with nothing else to do, intrudes intensively. Impact also reflects the attractiveness of the partner. The greater the compatibility, the more exciting the discovery. Finally, impact reflects the individual's needs. Those who are insecure and lonely with no one to love (or be loved by) respond most eagerly.

2. The more insecure the relationship, the greater the excitement. To discover gold and not know whether one can keep it is maddening. The danger may be the partner's unsureness. Or the danger may come from outside the relationship. Summer romances are intensified by the knowledge that autumn will bring inevitable separation. Though separation may not test compatibility, it often heightens feeling, at least as long as there is hope of reunion. Parental opposition also may increase desire.
3. The more temperamental a person, the higher his temperature rises in love. Some individuals are more sensitive than others. Their feelings are volatile and easily stirred. For them love is a more searching experience than for matter-of-fact dullards or carefully controlled sophisticates.

In medicine, fever is symptomatic of illness, and at least one social scientist has suggested the same for love:

> All societies recognize that there are occasional violent emotional attachments between persons of opposite sex. . . . Their rarity in most societies suggests that they are psychological abnormalities. . . . The hero of the modern American movie is always a romantic lover just as the hero of the old Arab epic is always an epileptic (Linton, 1936: 175).

But this is cynicism not science. Fever-pitch love is abnormal statistically but not psychologically. It seldom occurs and rarely lasts long. Perhaps it is just as well, or its "victims" might become exhausted. But they are victims only in the sense of being gripped by a profound experience. The experience is enviable not tragic. These are the fortunate few who achieve the modern ideal.

Difficulties are not inherent in excitement itself but only in the assumption that excitement is proof of love or that without it there can be no love.

LOW INTENSITY. According to the romantic myth, true love can be recognized by its intensity. Indoctrinated with this idea, those who don't have cardiac-respiratory symptoms fear something is wrong:

> Other boys have given me more of a rose-colored feeling than Louie. Does this show that I don't have the proper basis for marrying him? Or am I just getting too old at twenty-five for such an adolescent reaction to any man? We're engaged because I think being married to such a fine guy would be a very rewarding experience. But being engaged is not nearly as exciting as I expected it to be.

Failure to feel as strongly as expected is disappointing. Skepticism deserves extra testing to be sure the lack of enthusiasm does not result from incompatability. But a distinction must be drawn between doubts about the soundness of a relationship and calm, unruffled certainty.

Certainty, indeed, is one cause of calmness. The more secure a relationship, the calmer the couple. In long courtships and long engagements, love may pass its peak intensity. The more gradual the involvement, the less earth-shaking it is, especially for couples who were casual friends long before falling in love. For lifelong acquaintances, years of preadolescent companionship or disinterest make sudden excitement unlikely. For instance, young people who grow up in the same collective community in Israel (*kibbutz*) rarely fall in love with each other and, if they do, rarely love passionately. They know each other too well for that:

> "We are like an open book to each other. We have read the story in the book over and over again and know all about it." . . . They refer to the curiosity, excitement and anticipation that unfamiliar people evoke in them and to the exhilarating sense of discovery and triumph they get when they establish a relationship with them. They describe the unfolding of their affair as an exchange of confidences and emphasize the importance of relating and comparing different life histories. The affair with the outsider is experienced as an *overcoming of distance between persons* and as a growth of a newly won and unfamiliar sense of intimacy (Talmon, 1964).

Some loves are fated by circumstance to be calm. Others reflect the dispositions of the participants. People who never get ruffled in crises or triumphs are not likely to get excited in love. While some people are predisposed to be easygoing from birth, the average person becomes more philosophical as he grows older. The insecurity of adolescence gives early loves an urgency that later ones lack. As young adults grow in self-acceptance and emotional independence, they become more dispassionate. Hence the girl quoted above may have been right in thinking that she was too old for the excitability of adolescence. For reasons of maturity, then, or temperament or long acquaintance, low intensity is sometimes inevitable.

The Course of Love

So far I have discussed the emotional aspects of love. From here on I will deal with the rise and fall of love relationships.

Starting Points

According to mythology, love explodes full-blown at first sight. No preparation is needed, no previous acquaintance. If people are destined for each other, they will "recognize" each other immediately.

To become interested in another person means far less than falling in love. Yet Table 4-1 shows that even such minimal attraction didn't happen at first sight for most of Burgess and Wallin's respondents. Most couples get acquainted first and only gradually become interested in each other. Love seldom begins at first sight. It usually emerges within the context of a growing personal relationship.

A social context for personal interest is especially necessary for women. They are less apt to fall for brand-new acquaintances and more apt to get serious about developed friendships. One reason is that it takes time to analyze a man's occupational prospects whereas a girl's appearance can be appraised at a glance. The fact that men have more freedom of choice in mate-selection also makes them less cautious about involvements that can be terminated if they turn out badly. Finally, the choice of marriage partner is more crucial for women, affecting a larger proportion of their total life.

The starting point for love varies from couple to couple and even between partners in a single relationship. The typical (median) couple in Table 4-1 became interested after becoming acquainted, but for some the experience began earlier and for others much later. Normally, love grows by intensification from mildly positive experiences or at least neutral contacts. Occasionally, however, the first encounter is inauspicious:

> June and I first met on a blind date. I wasn't much impressed. She looked gawky to me. However, I was hard up for a date to the house dance the next weekend, so I asked her to go with me. She didn't exactly bowl me over that time either, but we had a good time and I began to appreciate her sense of humor. It got so we were seeing each other fairly regularly after that and we gradually discovered that we were in love.

MULTIPLE RELATIONSHIPS. Can a person love more than one person at a time? Traditionally, no. Love is supposed to be so absorbing that one "doesn't even notice" others. It is said that anyone who claims to be in love with two people simultaneously is *ipso facto* not in love at all; he just thinks he is. One study of college girls showed, however, that one fourth

Table 4-1. Degree of Acquaintance at First Becoming Interested in the Partner, by Sex

Degree of Acquaintance	Male	Female
On first meeting	46%	34%
After becoming acquainted	34	37
After becoming friends	20	29
Total	100%	100%
Number of cases	226	226

Adapted from Burgess and Wallin, 1953: 160.

had already been in love with multiple partners simultaneously (Ellis, 1949).

Women get involved with multiple partners more often than men because of our system of mate-selection. Because men have the initiative, they pursue their favorite date of the moment, abandoning lesser interests along the way. What happens though if two men court the same girl? Short of engagement there is no reason she must choose between them. Though no two men are exactly alike, they can be equally compatible (in different ways). Personal relationships and emotional attachments can develop with both as long as she dates both.

Whether both attachments can be intensive enough to be called love is the crux of the problem. I would say yes, it can be love, even though simultaneous involvement in two personal relationships is so demanding that it limits the ultimate possibilities for either one.

If a girl is equally attracted to two men, her feelings are no help in deciding which one she should marry. If she is equally compatible with both, she will have to choose one and drop the other, recognizing that the rejected suitor could have been a good husband, too.

The Pace of Development

Love seldom develops suddenly. In most cases acquaintance comes gradually, relationships develop slowly, and love grows apace. It takes effort and interaction to build a solid relationship. Except in cases of idealization, love takes time to develop:

> My first date with Sandra was the night before Christmas vacation. We were pushing a taxi out of a snowdrift in front of the Administration building and the man asked us if we wanted a free ride downtown for the work. Naturally we accepted and went down to a show. This was the start of a friendship that has grown into companionship and finally love. We talked together some that spring and did many things, but it was purely on a friendly basis and actually we didn't mean much to each other. We began to talk more about religion and our philosophy of life. As we talked we found we were drawn closer together. It wasn't until this fall that we found we were sure of our love for each other. It has not been a "falling" in love but "growing" in love.

THE SEXUAL ELEMENT. Just as love deepens within a growing relationship, its sexual component develops gradually too. Affairs that begin as infatuations are unusual. The usual sequence is to get acquainted first and be sexually attracted later.

Table 4-2 is a sequel to Table 4-1. After becoming interested in the other partner (typically after becoming acquainted), there is a further lapse of several months before being strongly attracted. This period is typically two months for men and three for women, illustrating anew the tendency for men to get involved faster than women.

COMPANIONSHIP. Since dates are joint recreation, companionship tends to grow fastest. The partner's presence is increasingly prized as more experiences and more of the self are shared.

CARING. Caring often lags behind the other components of love. One basis for caring is empathy—understanding the partner's point of view. Empathy presupposes knowledge which can only be acquired through continuing interaction. As time goes by, couples improve their ability to judge the partner's satisfaction with various aspects of their relationship. The more they date each other and the more committed they become, the more accurately they assess the partner's satisfaction (Vernon and Stewart, 1957). Similarly, knowledge of the partner's views about marriage roles increases as couples progress from casual dating to going steady and into engagement (Hobart, 1956). With increasing empathy come opportunities to respond to the partner's needs and to assume responsibility for them. By the time a sense of responsibility develops, love has been established.

COMMITMENT. Commitment sounds like a once-and-for-all affair, but it isn't. Its gradual development is portrayed in the movement from casual to steady dating and on into engagement, which is supposedly a definite commitment to marry. The "final" commitment comes in the wedding vows. Yet, according to Farber (1964), even after marriage many Americans feel "permanently available" for a change of partners. Such people never commit themselves totally but only tentatively. Commitment, therefore, tends to be progressive prior to marriage and variable after marriage. For some it develops subconsciously. Others consciously decide to commit themselves to the partner and even renew that commitment at Catholic Cana Conferences or similar ceremonies.

Table 4-2. Interval between First Interest in Partner and First Strong Physical Attraction, by Sex

Interval	Male	Female
Less than one month	28%	26%
One or two months	25	16
Three to five months	14	20
More than five months	33	37
Total	100%	99%
Number of cases	226	226

Adapted from Burgess and Wallin, 1953: 161.

Presumably, commitment is the last element of love to develop. Attraction comes first—then commitment. But the relationship between commitment and the other elements of love is reciprocal. Once a commitment is made, it provides a basis for the further growth of the other elements.

The pace of love is usually slow and uneven. Relationships reach plateaus and then break through to greater intimacy. Love, like marriage, has moments for better and for worse.

Spontaneity and Effort in Love

Love cannot be commanded. As Southern whites protest, they may be forced to sit with Negroes but they cannot be forced to like them. Loving must be voluntary. But does this mean one cannot resolve to love? Must it be completely spontaneous?

To be sure, spontaneous love is the most delightful. An effortless response to the discovery of compatibility is pure joy. The faster love develops and the higher its intensity, the more the emotional capacities of the partners are mobilized in the cause of intimacy. But not all loves begin so enthusiastically or maintain momentum indefinitely. These other loves suggest the value of conscious effort in supplementing the natural momentum of love. The following case shows how one may deliberately deepen a relationship:

> I dated Dave on and off for a year. We had good times folk dancing, going to concerts, talking politics. I was sure he was the man for me. Though he liked me, it didn't look like love since he never told me how he felt about me. Soon school would be over and we would go our separate ways. Dared I be the one to speak first? I became a "scheming woman," planning when and how it might be done. The right moment came and I found courage to protest that despite all the fun we'd had he really didn't know or care about "me." He agreed—and by morning the stars were in his eyes too. If I had waited for him to start things moving I probably would be waiting still!

Once love is mutual, it achieves its spontaneous potential without effort. Beyond that its potentialities remain untapped unless effort is expended. Couples do not have to transcend spontaneity. But those who don't are not likely to experience love to its fullest.

Erich Fromm writes persuasively of "the art of loving," an art capable of being perfected with practice. The requirements, he believes, are self-discipline, concentration on the task at hand, patience with the slowness of achieving mastery, and supreme concern to achieve that mastery (1956). Love is enhanced the more people concentrate on meeting each other's needs. The more rewarding activities a couple undertake together and the more thoughtfully each ministers to the other, the greater their love will grow. The great achievements in life require sacrifice and work, and love is no exception. Casual affairs may be nice, but those who wish to experience the deepest relationships must be more than dilettantes.

A Loving Personal Relationship

The course of love leads ultimately to a solid personal relationship which provides the foundation of marriage. Gradually the relationship grows in strength and comprehensiveness. The richer the relationship is before marriage, the richer it will be after marriage.

For example, among young middle-class married couples in Tokyo, I found marked continuity between pre-engagement interaction patterns and marital interaction patterns. Couples who tell each other their troubles before engagement rely most often on each other for therapeutic relief after marriage. Those who share more of their personal news with each other early in their relationship are more open with each other in later years (Blood, 1967). Such continuity from premarital to marital love is not surprising. Human beings are creatures of habit. Vital interpersonal relationships grow from year to year; weak ones tend to shrivel.

Like the married years themselves, the months before marriage provide opportunities to create a mutually rewarding relationship or to destroy it. The climax of love is a personal relationship which will flourish through all the changes of later years.

The Death of Love

So far we have assumed that love progresses more or less evenly toward marriage. But often it ends short of marriage. When love dies, the empty shell sometimes remains.

Deterrents to Dissolving a Relationship

Once people get involved in a personal relationship, breaking up may be more easily said than done. Indeed, Bolton suggests that couples may be just as addicted to one another as a drug addict to his heroin: " . . . the individual seeks to perpetuate a relationship in order to avoid the psychological withdrawal symptoms accompanying cessation of sexual, affectional, or prestigeful relations." (1961)

LETHARGY. For one thing it's difficult to part with a known partner since hard work may be necessary to capture a potential partner:

> I hate to think about dropping her just when I was all set and secure. I never did like that game of idle chit-chat that you have to carry on with a new date. It would be awful to have to go through the rigors of that again.

For girls, restricted dating initiative provides another reason for clinging to the existing partner.

RAPPORT. New prospects may look singularly unattractive by comparison to the empathic responsiveness of a partner dated for a long time:

> I still have a strong feeling for Andy in spite of his faults. I've never met anyone who was so warm and understanding as he is. Other people never seem to be able to appreciate my moods and bolster my ego the way he does.

Maybe Andy *is* special. More likely others would yield as much rapport as soon as they were dated as long. Often what seem to be unique virtues in the partner reflect instead unique familiarity with him.

PHYSICAL INTIMACY. Sexual involvement may make breaking up difficult because of reluctance to lose a source of sexual gratification or because of guilt feelings about "loving her and leaving her."

> I realize that Laura and I should never get married, but right now I just can't resist her. I'm not proud of being so wishy-washy, but when Saturday night rolls around I make a beeline for her apartment. Then at church on Sunday morning I could kick myself for having so little self-control.

EMOTIONAL DEPENDENCE. Reluctance to break up stems not only from egocentric but altruistic motives. When breaking up would hurt the partner as much as me, distaste multiplies. No one likes to inflict pain on others:

> We've gone together so long that I know Roger would be awfully hurt if I returned his ring. He's just gotten used to my being around. In fact the way he takes me for granted is one thing that gripes me about him. I'm afraid leaving him now would demoralize him completely.

When emotional dependence is one-sided, the more mature person tires of the relationship first. Yet knowing how much his partner gains emotional support from the relationship, he may hesitate to pull the props out from under her:

How do I explain to Jill that I want to do more dating with others before I say she's the right one (especially since I've been dating her for three years and still am not happy). She's happy no matter what I do, as long as I decide on her in the end. I don't think I will, but she looks so sad when I mention any doubt, it breaks my heart.

When the partner is emotionally unstable, continuing the relationship may seem the only way to prevent a nervous breakdown or even suicide. Though the risks may be great under such circumstances, the responsibility for preserving mental health should be transferred from romantic to psychiatric facilities.

SOCIAL PRESSURE. Family and friends used to seeing a couple together may pressure them to stay together.

I lived just a block away from Gretchen and our families were close friends. We went together all through high school and junior college. Then I went away to the university and fell in love with the girl who is now my wife. When they heard about it, my family and Gretchen's were both shocked, and Gretchen came close to having a nervous breakdown. The whole gang at home accused me of being unchivalrous in letting her down this way. But we weren't engaged and I couldn't see why everybody kicked up such a fuss.

PUBLIC COMMITMENTS. An engagement is always difficult to break off—it entails a public acknowledgment of personal failure, a ring to return, and so forth. It is harder yet for couples who don't change their minds until after the wedding date is set, invitations sent, travel reservations made, and the gifts have begun to arrive. If family and friends thought it was a good match, disengagement is all the more difficult.

No matter how painful breaking an engagement may be, breaking a marriage or living incompatibly is worse. Many people come to regret their marriages, but few who break up in advance ever regret it. Usually, they recognize how narrowly they escaped a trap:

When I returned from Vietnam, I needed a romance regardless of the personality. I found a childhood friend who had been sick for six months with mononucleosis and she too needed a date. So, unfortunately, we kept on dating, and because we wanted to be in love we thought we were. The consequences were an engagement ring and wedding plans. Our parents were very good friends; we attended the same church and were superficially very compatible. But our interests and approaches to situations and goals in life were very different. We weren't really in love even, and as soon as I woke up enough to realize it, it was a month before the wedding. It was an unfortunate experience in some ways, but breaking the engagement was the only answer, and I'm certainly relieved that I was able to do so.

Aids to Dissolving a Relationship

Though poignantly felt, the barriers to terminating unsatisfactory relationships are seldom insuperable. Often they crumble of their own accord. If not, a strategic attack with reinforcements can vanquish them.

Loss of Interest. Affairs frequently end through the evaporation of attraction for one or both partners. When disinterest is mutual, the relationship ends unmourned by either partner. For the students reported in Table 4-3, nearly half their love affairs died bilaterally. No "breaking up" was necessary because the partners simply drifted apart.

If one partner falls out of love before the other, it is twice as apt to be the girl as the boy. Girls have little opportunity to initiate new relationships, but they can more often choose between competing attractions. As we shall see with sexual intimacy, so in love as a whole, the boy initiates and the girl controls. Her chief power is to say no.

Table 4-3 suggests that for both sexes disillusionment is ordinarily mutual or else the dissatisfied individual already has a more attractive partner to turn to. Under such circumstances leaving the old partner is not so difficult.

The Example of Others. Knowing that others change partners takes the onus off abandoning one's own. Repeated serious involvements are a growing feature of modern dating, which means that experience in dissolving relationships is equally widespread. I have already reported that the typical Michigan undergraduate has gone steady with two partners, and Kirkpatrick and Caplow's Minnesota undergraduates similarly had at least two "important love affairs." Broken engagements, though less common than discontinued uncommitted loves, are by no means rare. Among Bur-

Table 4-3. Cause of Termination of Love Affairs, by Sex

Cause of Termination	Male	Female
Mutual loss of interest	47%	38%
Subject's interest in another person	15	32
Partner's interest in another person	30	15
External pressure (parents, friends)	8	14
Total	100%	99%
Number of respondents	230	414

Adapted from Kirkpatrick and Caplow, 1945: 123. *Source:* University of Minnesota sociology students reporting on their previous love affairs.

gess and Wallin's engaged couples, 24 per cent of the men and 36 per cent of the women had broken at least one previous engagement, and 15 per cent of the current engagements subsequently ended.

STRATEGIC WITHDRAWAL. When emotional involvement has been intense, individuals may fear they will lack courage. Those who can't face the partner's disappointment sometimes employ "go-betweens" or the U.S. mails to carry the fateful message. Those who don't trust their ability to resist the partner's persuasiveness may schedule the break just before leaving town. When one's own dependence is the problem, filling the vacuum with new dating bridges the gap between loves (though it also creates the danger of rebounding into love).

A clean break is usually easier than gradual withdrawal. To back out gradually prolongs the agony for both partners. "Now you have it, now you don't" is as disconcerting for a lover as for a half-weaned baby or an addict with an undependable supply of narcotics. Once the decision has been made to terminate a relationship, quick surgery is more effective.

MORAL SUPPORT. It is not necessary to go through crises alone. Telling friends of the decision is one way of burning one's bridges to prevent retreat:

> The first few times I refused more dates with Shep were the hardest. After that it wasn't so bad. My friends were skeptical at first because I had sworn off him so many times before. I finally convinced them that I really meant business this time and needed their help. They were grand too. They fixed me up with blind dates to help me get my mind off him. My roommate would grab the phone and tell Shep I wasn't in. That really made the break a lot easier.

A sympathetic counselor can provide similar encouragement to the fainthearted. A firm commitment to any outsider bolsters emotional resources for the ordeal. Most people, however, need no maneuvering to end their old loves. They are capable of making up their own minds and expressing their thoughts directly to the old partner.

Recuperating from "Bereavement"

Knowing how often dissolution reflects mutual disinterest or growing interest in an alternative partner, we should not expect many individuals to feel shattered. Only those who are dropped when they still wish to continue a relationship are likely to be hurt.

Table 4-4 shows that negative reactions are far from universal. Almost

Table 4-4. Feeling after Termination of Love Affairs, by Sex

Feeling	Male	Female
Crushed, hurt	12%	19%
Angry, bitter	9	8
Remorseful	7	7
Mixed regret and relief	22	21
Indifferent	19	16
Satisfied	12	8
Relieved	15	17
Happy	4	4
Total	100%	100%
Number of respondents	230	414

Adapted from Kirkpatrick and Caplow, 1945: 124.

as many are pleased the affair has ended. Most typical, however, are those who feel neutral, either because they are indifferent or because they are ambivalent.

Further confirmation of the untraumatic nature of most break-ups is found in the report that half the Minnesota students required no recuperation period while less than a fourth took more than a few weeks. Rarely is breaking up as awful in retrospect as it sometimes appears in prospect.

Love and Marriage

In choosing a marriage partner, love is a useful criterion. The pseudo-loves are no help and may lure the individual away from more marriageable persons. Infatuation or idealization may grow into love but don't necessarily. Regardless of how deviantly a love affair begins, whenever it develops into genuine love, it points the way toward marriage. Love provides the dynamic force that makes compatible couples want to marry and leads them through the bittersweet experiences of life together.

5 The Sexual Expression of Love

Loving draws people together, at first in small ways and gradually in more intense ways. Communication between lovers is more complete and sensitive than in ordinary human relationships. They have broken the usual restraints between people and can use the full range of sensual experience. The possible joys of intense experience are accompanied by the danger of hurting one another just as acutely. Yet love is not the only motive that draws men and women together sexually—in marriage and out. So the whole panorama of motives must be examined if we are to understand not only what sexual love is but also what it is not.

The Impulse to Intimacy

"Intimacy" is used in this chapter as a variable. It includes physical contact from the simplest kiss to the heaviest petting and complete sexual relations. Not that the degree of intimacy does not matter, but many of the causes and consequences of various levels in intimacy differ in degree rather than kind. For the sake of brevity, I will often discuss intimacy generally, subdividing my discussion only where necessary.

The Momentum of Love

As people grow in love, it embraces more and more of their lives. Although their relationship may have been platonic at first, they are increasingly attracted physically. It is pleasant not only to do things together but to be together—close together. A kiss tangibly expresses their feelings.

127

Other expressions take the form of words or traditional symbols: flowers, candy, and valentines. But physical contact is one of the most meaningful ways to express feeling. A kiss and embrace speak eloquently of how much people love each other. Indeed the physical dimension is a distinguishing feature of love.

The last chapter noted that most love affairs begin platonically and develop sexual feelings as time goes on. The longer people go together, the stronger their love becomes; and the stronger their love, the greater the impulse to intimacy. This is why I classify sex as one of the components of love. The growth of sexual attraction between lovers is natural and inevitable.

ANTICIPATING MARRIAGE. As marriage approaches, a new factor emerges. Commitment to be married brings complete intimacy onto the horizon. As plans for the wedding, honeymoon, and married living are worked out, as more and more aspects of life are shared in anticipation, the temptation grows to "jump the gun."

> First and foremost among my reasons for having intercourse with Joy was that I loved her very much. In the heat of my love—and I have no doubt that some of it was passion—I felt that to have this experience with love in my heart would be all right. I had begun to doubt whether the wedding ceremony made the sex act more sacred or satisfying. I concluded that in the light of our love for one another we were already married anyway.

TESTING FOR COMPATIBILITY. With all the emphasis that has been placed on choosing a suitable marriage partner, is premarital intercourse a useful means of discovering whether people are right for each other? If sexual compatibility were primarily a question of physique, such evidence might be useful. However this is not the case. Despite adolescent speculations to the contrary, human beings of almost any shape and size are able to mate successfully. For this reason it is not necessary to "try each other out for size."

The crucial factors in sexual compatibility are psychological, not anatomical or physiological. But the psychologies of premarital and marital intercourse are not the same. Premarital intercourse suffers from the handicaps of a less secure relationship devoid of social and religious sanctions. Yet couples who feel guilt-stricken or anxious in intercourse before marriage might function quite satisfactorily after marriage.

Compatibility testing is a doubtful argument for premarital intercourse. What matters is whether the couple share common attitudes toward sex. If their philosophy about its importance or unimportance and their emotional responsiveness to one another are similar, they can count on developing a satisfactory sexual relationship in marriage.

STRENGTHENING THE RELATIONSHIP. I will discuss later whether intimacy actually strengthens relationships. In any case a girl may make herself available in the hope of intensifying the boy's interest. Recognizing that sex means a great deal to him, she may give herself to him:

> I gave in to Bill because I knew he wanted me to and that it would keep him coming back. The first few times we petted, and many times after that, I myself did not experience any satisfaction at all, something Bill knew and that I did not care about as long as it strengthened our relationship.

Sometimes the motive is exploitive, especially if the girl feels that sex is all she has to offer a desirable male. Kirkendall (1961) found that lower-class girls were often sexually aggressive with middle-class boys, hoping through intercourse or pregnancy to be able to make a "good" marriage. Even if marriage is out of the question, sexual experience may offer an emotionally gratifying substitute for love:

> I had the misfortune of maturing ahead of the rest of my class. When one boy repeatedly tried to touch my breasts, there quickened in me doubts, fears, and a sense of ugliness about sex. Later, in junior high school, I tried to be friends with two very popular class leaders. Both were dating skinny, flat-chested girls and wanted only an opportunity to pet. As long as they kept saying "I love you" I gave in out of a hunger for affection and pride in catching these popular boys. It never went beyond light petting, but at the time I hated myself for it. I learned then that sex can be cold and meaningless if it isn't an expression of real love.

Here the impulse to intimacy was only pseudo-love. Yet, for an emotionally starved girl, pseudo-love may seem better than no love at all.

Even though girls are more inclined to use sex as a means to love, men are not altogether immune. They may take a girl's willingness to surrender as proof of their own desirability. And since everyone likes to be loved, this incentive is very appealing.

Sexual Desire

In the preceding section, I described impulses to intimacy that were not primarily sexual. Sexual motives as such include sexual desire and sex drive. By sexual desire I mean the desire for sexual experience with a particular person; by sex drive, the physiological force that seeks release in sexual expression.

Sexual desire is aroused by the sex appeal of the partner. It is the excitement created by a girl's face and figure, by a man's handsome features and physical vigor. Although the primary components are physical, sexual attractiveness is also affected by speech, manner, and subtle nuances of behavior. And even though the focus of desire is on the partner, one's mood and the setting affect one's response. (Hence the traditional soft lights, background music, food-and-drink setting for seduction.)

As I have already mentioned, sexual desire is not the usual starting point of courtship but tends to follow the development of friendship and affection. Of course, attractions that are initially altogether sexual may subsequently develop the remaining components of love. But they do not always. Sometimes sex remains the entire basis of a relationship or especially of a single episode between people.

This is one reason why summer romances so often have a sexual emphasis. It takes time for friendship to grow and for the whole range of shared interests in a fully personal relationship to develop. Sexual desire, on the other hand, can be aroused instantaneously. Indeed, the greatest intensity of sexual desire often occurs under circumstances where the participants do not have to worry about long-term complications or what their friends will think:

> Worrying about how far to go when you hardly know someone seems ridiculous. However, I have found that most fellows will spend as little as possible and try to squeeze payment from you. When I asked him why he had given me such a hard time, one fellow told me he felt that, since he would never see me again, it wouldn't matter what he tried. "Who knows, maybe you would have been one of those real easy ones."

If this man thought he might want to see her again, he would have been less aggressive for fear of ruining his chances. Or if he thought she would see him again, he might hesitate to acquire an aggressive reputation among her friends. But when the network of primary relationships among friends and between partners is severed by geographical mobility, the mechanisms of social control break down and exploitive behavior becomes more ruthless.

Sometimes the intimacy achieved in casual circumstances exceeds what the aggressor had expected. As in the case above, a man may not expect a girl to allow very much but feel impelled to test the limits. Like children with a new baby sitter or substitute teacher, there is a compulsion to discover how much one can get away with, partly for the thrill of forbidden experience, partly to find out what sort of person she is.

Sexual desire is accentuated by novelty, which accounts for the notion that men are "naturally polygamous." Physically, a new partner may have no more to offer than the old one. But sexual desire responds to psychological factors, not the least of which is the excitement of a new prospect. Although girls are not entirely exempt from the attractions of novelty, the feminine mind tends to operate differently. The classic phrase is not that human beings are polygamous but men are. Men tend to "love 'em and leave 'em." As a result, girls are afraid of being abandoned (especially, abandoned with a baby). They emphasize love and marriage, so only males are apt to experience sexual desire in a social vacuum. This does not mean that girls have no sexual desire, but that they usually experience it within a context of love and interpersonal security. For men sexual desire tends to be stronger and arises under more varying circumstances. So great is the contrast between the sexes that Ehrmann summarized his research with the epigram: males are erotic; females are romantic (1959).

Sex Drive

I have defined sex drive as physiological pressure for sexual expression—the biological aspect of sexual motivation. The dynamic force behind the impulse to intimacy comes from hormones secreted into the bloodstream and from semen accumulating in the male gonads. The latter process produces nocturnal emissions periodically if no other occasion for ejaculation occurs. Experimental evidence of the physiological component in sexual behavior includes the discovery that "the administration of male hormones (androgens) to either humans or animals may increase the general level of sexual response." (Kirkendall, 1961a) The precise balance between the physiological and psychological components of sexual motivation is difficult to determine. Ford and Beach (1951) emphasized that one of the main differences between the sexual behavior of humans and other mammals is the lesser influence of hormones over humans. We are less at the mercy of our body chemistry. Nevertheless, the biological underpinnings of sexual motivation are important in understanding human behavior.

SEX DIFFERENCES IN SEX DRIVE. One of the myths of modern man is that males and females do not differ in sex drive. Women, it is said, are only restrained by conditioning. Daughters are raised more conservatively than sons. Taboos on promiscuity are greater for girls than for boys. Hence, women are more sexually restrained than men in our society. But this is a cultural artifact. If only women could be emancipated from the handicaps of more restrictive socialization, it is concluded, they would be just as sexually aware as men. I have labeled this argument a "myth" because I believe it is false. It is difficult to disentangle the physiological and nonphysiological components of sexual behavior. Nevertheless, a number of facts suggest that sex drive is intrinsically stronger in men than in women.

For instance, whereas the administration of hormones increases male sexual responsiveness, there is no corresponding increase for females. The fact that males produce seminal fluids wheras females have no equivalent fluid is a second difference. Shuttleworth (1959) concluded that "males behave as if they were under rather constant physiological pressures, strong in some individuals and weak in others, to obtain an orgasm which will release accumulated seminal fluids." The occurrence of ejaculation only in males suggests greater biological urgency. A third differentiating factor is the larger size and external location of the male sex organ. Whereas the penis is a prominent feature of the little boy's awareness of himself, the clitoris is so rudimentary in size and so hidden in location that many girls are unaware of it. In short, males are driven by hormonal chemistry, by seminal pressures, and by genital awareness. As a result, the average male is more sex-conscious and sex-motivated.

Data on sexual *behavior* cannot be taken as a direct measure of *sex drive* since behavior depends on the accessibility of partners. Nevertheless, Kinsey's data on frequency of orgasm from all sources including masturbation are an indirect index of the nature and magnitude of age and sex differences.

Figure 5-1 pictures the total sexual activity of single males. For females the data underestimate sexual activity, since young women may engage in sexual behavior without reaching a climax. The wide discrepancy between the two curves, however, presumably reflects in part underlying differences in sex drive. Since we are dealing in averages, it is well to remember that in particular cases, the man may be less sex driven than his partner. Especially when we add the psychosocial components to sexual motivation, the role of the sexes may be reversed. But not in general.

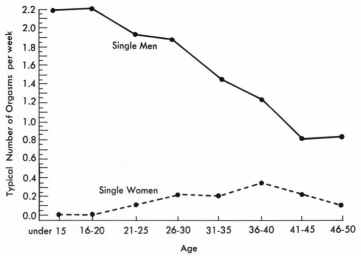

Median number of orgasms per week among single men and women. Based on Kinsey, 1949: 226; and 1953: 549.

Figure 5-1. Frequency of Orgasm in Single Men and Women, by Age

AGE DIFFERENCES IN SEX DRIVE. If sex drive is biologically defined, it depends on the vigor of the human organism. Just as a baseball player is old at thirty, a sexual athlete's capacity wanes in middle age. Kinsey (1949) stated that male aging "sets in soon after the initiation of growth." Sex drive in males is strongest during the premarital years. In females, sex drive as such may not increase in middle age so much as the capacity to achieve orgasm increases. The rising frequency of orgasm among single women is probably due more to learned sexual responsiveness than to increased physiological drive. Figure 5-1, however, and Kinsey's discussion of sex differences in hormonal factors imply that females begin sexual aging later. Probably this is correlated with women's greater life span.

Social Pressures

It is important not to overemphasize the physiological factors in sexual behavior. Sometimes the motive is neither sexual nor personal. When teenage boys use prostitutes, "a desire for sheer physical release [is] one of the least important of the several motivations." (Kirkendall, 1960) Instead "the desire to be a part of a group and to participate in a group experience [is] a major motivation." Often groups of teenagers invade a house of prostitution on a dare, the main concern of every participant being to prove that he is not "chicken." With less deviant partners, social pressure is usually less direct. Bull sessions about sex create an atmosphere that stimulates experimentation. Individual curiosity is aroused and prestige offered to those who boast of conquests.

So far I have discussed positive pressures for sexual activity. For girls the peer group more often expects sexual restraint. However, the fact that girls are taught *not* to engage in sexual intimacies creates the hazard that a deviant few will rebel. If parents are authoritarian, sexual delinquency is an effective way of retaliation (consciously or unconsciously). Such girls may get no physical pleasure from their sexual adventures but great emotional gratification from forbidden activities. Similarly, in "hippy" circles, sexual freedom may be part of a general rebellion against middle-class society.

The Course of Sexual Involvement

Regardless of their motives, how far do American young people go before marriage? And what circumstances determine how far they go?

Sources of Sexual Restraint

Given the many impulses to sexual involvement, perhaps the most remarkable feature of American life is that there are any young people who practice restraint. In some societies, premarital intimacy is universal. In ours it is not. What makes some people more restrained than others?

RELIGIOUS TRAINING. The religions of America are concerned with ethical behavior. Indeed, "immorality" often means precisely *sexual* immorality, especially nonmarital intercourse. We therefore may expect intercourse to be less common among individuals subject to a church's ethical teaching, group support, and supernatural sanction for conforming behavior. Studies by Burgess and Wallin, Ehrmann, Kanin, and Kinsey support this generalization.

Figure 5-2 shows that premarital intercourse decreases as church attendance rises. In a study of married students at Indiana University, Kanin (1958) found an even closer correlation between church attendance and

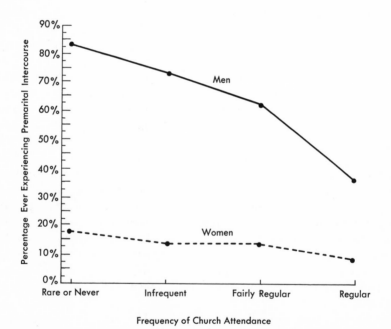

Adapted from Ehrmann, 1959: 93. *Source:* University of Florida students (Gainesville). Reciprocal percentages have never experienced intercourse.

Figure 5-2. Premarital Intercourse, by Frequency of Church Attendance, for College Men and Women

lack of intercourse *between* the two partners before marriage. Where both partners attended church regularly, only 28 per cent of the couples had premarital intercourse. By contrast, if only one partner attended regularly, 48 per cent had intercourse, and if neither was regular, 61 per cent. Such data suggest that religion is a major source of sexual restraint.

PARENTAL TRAINING. Most parents advocate sexual restraint for their children (regardless of whether they practiced it themselves when they were young). The more explicitly they encourage restraint and the more influential their general relationship to their children, the greater the reduction in premarital intimacy. Children generously supplied with care and affection by their parents acquire stronger consciences incorporating parental norms. Conversely, those whose training is either neglected or harshly overdone, are respectively underexposed to the norms of restraint or prodded into rebellious rejection.

The contribution of satisfactory family environments to sexual restraint is demonstrated in various studies. English women whose parents were happily married, for example, were more restrained than those from unhappy homes or who lost their mother through death or lost either parent through separation or divorce (Chesser, 1957). In happy homes, parents collaborate in socializing their children more successfully. Restraint was also greater among women who got along well with both parents than among those who had trouble. (Even boys, who are generally less influenced by their parents than girls, were more sexually restrained if they got on well with their mothers than if they rebelled against them [Schofield, 1965].) Also notably unrestrained were women reared by anyone other than the parents (Chesser), especially those who grew up in foster homes or in impersonal institutions (Illsley and Thompson, 1961). Such children notably lack the teaching influence of parents.

Divorced men and women are not only handicapped in raising their children unaided but have different sexual philosophies. In his national sample of adults, Reiss (1967) found that separated and divorced parents were three times as apt to be highly permissive sexually as married parents (40 per cent versus 13 per cent). Their permissiveness presumably reflected their eagerness to remarry. Such parents are (like college students) actively engaged in courtship and correspondingly interested in sexual freedom for themselves. Hence the premarital intimacy of children from broken homes reflects the example and perhaps even the implicit teaching of the remaining parent.

In Chapter 21 we will find that certain child-rearing methods produce strong consciences. The same methods produce sexual restraint. Chesser (1957) found that women whose parents exercised moderate discipline (neither too weak nor too strong) and rarely punished them physically were less apt to have premarital intercourse. Similarly, Ehrmann (1959) found that regular discipline induced restraint among his women students. Consistency, moderation, and nonpunitiveness of discipline produce the most successfully socialized children generally and the most sexually restrained girls. (Evidence for boys is less clear since their behavior is largely controlled by their partners.)

SELF-ACCEPTANCE. One consequence of happy families and effective child-rearing is emotional health for the child. We would expect, from what has already been discussed, that premarital restraint would be associated with mental health. The evidence to support this generalization is indirect but suggestive. Chesser found that girls who felt their own childhood was happy were less apt to have premarital intercourse. At Cornell University, self-confident American girls were more restrained when dating foreign students. Conversely, girls who were hard up for dates because they were unattractive and overweight tended to go farther and faster sexually. (Freeman and Freeman, 1966).

At Vassar, the most sexually active girls scored high on an "impulse expression" scale which included needs for dominance, recognition, aggression, autonomy, acquisition, exhibition, change, and excitance (Freedman, 1965). Such needs are more characteristic of men in our society, and may reflect rejection of the traditional feminine role. Those girls were considered ideal students by their professors because of their self-assertive academic achievement. Presumably they go on to successful careers in graduate school and the occupational world. We have no reason to assume that they are unattractive. Rather their sexual involvement seems likely to reflect a rebellious emancipation from conventional femininity. The most promiscuous men, correspondingly, are psychiatrically judged to be engaged in a desperate attempt to drown unconscious doubts about their masculinity beneath a flood of hyper-masculine behavior.

Restraint is easier, then, for those who accept their sexual identity. The more self-accepting the person, the less his/her need to use sex as a substitute for affection or a means to affection. Self-confidence and emotional balance enable the individual to be patient and discriminating in progressing toward long-range goals. When both partners are emotionally mature, they can deal openly with each other, take their convictions seriously, and work out a pattern of sexual expression appropriate to those convictions:

> Paul had considerable experience with premarital sex, while I had relatively no experience at all. Although Paul felt that if two people really cared for one another, sex was entirely appropriate, I was set against it. For eighteen years it has been instilled in me that premarital sex was immoral, and I could not conceive of it in any other sense. Fortunately Paul has respected my wishes in all matters dealing with sexual intimacy. This was one matter on which I had to have the final word or there

could be no relationship. By the end of the first three months, my worries about "how far" to go ceased, because he had proven to me that he could be trusted and that he would never do anything which could hurt me physically or psychologically. It is natural that when there is a strong emotional tie between any two people, their expressions of love get more intense. But intercourse is out of bounds until marriage. I have asserted myself in this instance, and Paul has shown his respect, love, and masculine control to suppress his drives for my wishes and happiness. Interestingly enough, he does not seem to feel his masculinity threatened or lessened in any way by my dominance and control in this instance. It is one way in which he can prove his love and admiration for me, and he does not feel that this makes him any the less masculine.

THE PARTNERS' SOCIAL STATUS. The three sources of restraint already mentioned affect the individual's ability to control his own sexual impulses. The comparative social status of the partners also affects their sexual relationship. The higher the girl's status, the more the man respects her, and the less aggressive he is with her sexually. Conversely the average girl is more sexually responsive with a high status man (hoping thereby that she may secure his temporary or permanent attention) but more restrained with a man who seems her inferior.

Nursing students at Presbyterian St. Luke's Hospital in the slums of Chicago had great difficulty finding dates who would not give them a hard time sexually (Skipper and Nass, 1966). Usually, their home town friends were too far away to date. Their slum neighbors were high school drop-outs who might have treated them deferentially but were too far beneath them socially to be attractive dates. The only other men available—college students and medical students—were too far above them to be sexually restrained. The college men looked down on the nursing students' technical training devoid of liberal arts. They also thought of nurses as sexually knowledgeable (due to their study of anatomy and their occupational contact with the bodies of male patients). They inferred that sex knowledge produces sexual eagerness (a *non sequitur* as we shall see in discussing sex education in Chapter 22). The girls, on the other hand, were so eager to hold the interest of these superior boys (and hopefully to marry them) that they often surrendered to the boys' sexual advances. The social and perceptual asymmetry of the situation made these dates primarily sexual in character. Needless to say, they seldom culminated in marriage. (Men who had dated three different kinds of partners reported that college girls were most restrained, nursing students least restrained, and working girls intermediate.)

With the medical students, interns, and residents at St. Luke's, the students were at even more of a disadvantage. (1) The doctors had even greater educational superiority than the college students. (2) They were correspondingly older. (3) They were the girls' bosses at the hospital and were reputed to take reprisals at work against girls who were "uncoopera-tive" on dates. The familiar cartoons of secretaries sitting on the boss' lap reflect status differentials similar to those which undermine restraint be-tween doctor and nurse.

Among men students at the University of Florida, sexual restraint was greatest with girls from higher family backgrounds, least when dating town girls from low-status families (see Table 5-1).

Similarly, among married men at an Indiana university, 69 per cent had refrained from premarital intercourse if the wife was from an upper-middle-class family, compared to 58 per cent for lower-middle-class girls and only 17 per cent if she was from a working-class family (Kanin, 1958).

In the two previous studies, the college men were usually of middle-class origin themselves. A third study by Lindenfeld (1960) showed college men from lower-class backgrounds more restrained than their nonmobile middle-class colleagues. Of his upward mobile men, 64 per cent had never had intercourse versus 55 per cent of the men who had grown up in the middle class. The extraordinary restraint of men from the lower class contrasts with the lack of restraint of the friends they left behind. That restraint presum-ably reflects deference toward dating partners of higher origin, plus concen-tration on career aspirations. Just to master college courses when one's parents never went to college (to say nothing of working one's way through college) requires time and energy which socially secure boys can afford to spend in heterosexual recreation. Finally, to be upward mobile requires stricter adherence to the norms of the class of destination than is necessary for men who inherit their class position. Since sexual restraint is one char-acteristic of high-status Americans, it is practiced more assiduously by socially ambitious men.

In general, then, both sexes are restrained when the man encounters a higher status partner. Conversely when the woman's status is inferior, she is more receptive and the man more aggressive than usual.

Table 5-1. Maximum Intimacy of College Men, by Comparative Class of Companion

	COMPARATIVE CLASS OF COMPANION		
Maximum Intimacy	*Female Higher*	*Same*	*Female Lower*
Holding hands	20%	6%	6%
Necking, light petting	47	39	13
Heavy petting	16	26	16
Sexual intercourse	18	30	66
Total	101%	101%	101%
Number of cases	107	531	154

Adapted from Ehrmann, 1959: 147. The total numbers of cases are not mutually ex-clusive. 338 men dated companions at the same class level only, 39 at the same and higher levels, 86 at the same and lower levels, and 68 at all three levels. *Source:* University of Florida (Gainesville).

HOMOGAMY. Restraint is also produced by many kinds of homogamy. For instance, Italian-American boys in a Boston slum respected the neighborhood girls whom they eventually married but sought out non-Italian girls when they wanted sexual fun (Whyte, 1955). Similarly, foreign men at Cornell told the Freemans they dated American girls primarily for fun and sex. These international dates involved more sexual intimacy than either the domestic dating of the American girls or the back-home dating of the foreign men. The sexual aggressiveness of men while they are overseas corresponds to the notorious behavior of traveling salesmen while they are away from home.

This is not to say that sexual intimacy prior to marriage always presents a sorry picture. As usual in the social sciences I am discussing shades of gray rather than black and white differences. However, the background factors in sexual intimacy are generally several shades darker than the picture presented by those who are more restrained before marriage:

> My sex education from my parents was very limited. When I was in high school I used to read all the sexy novels I could get hold of so that I could find out all about it. The first time a fellow tried to make out with me I thought he must be insane, but as time went by and I gained knowledge and experience in the field of sex, I became less frightened of any type of experience along that line. I had no guilt feelings because of my actions and desires. Before I actually participated in any sexual activities I had lost my religion and broken all ideological ties with my family.

Circumstances of Sexual Involvement

So far we have noted the kinds of people who become intimate before marriage but have paid relatively little attention to the circumstances under which they do so. While our interest is primarily in circumstances that lead directly to marriage (that is, serious courtship), casual experiences affect the sexual aspect of marriage just as casual dating is relevant to marriage.

CASUAL VERSUS SERIOUS LIAISONS. Middle-class men and women differ sharply in the extent to which they require a serious relationship before they are prepared to become sexually involved. For women, the greater their affectional involvement, the more intimate they are willing to become. Many men, however, do not restrict their sexual behavior to serious affairs. Indeed, some men are more willing to have intercourse with women they would never consider marrying than with eligible women.

Table 5-2 shows that roughly 45 per cent of Burgess and Wallin's couples had premarital intercourse with each other. The men and women differed sharply in their previous sexual experience. Half the men but only one eighth of the women had intercourse with anyone else. If the women had intercourse at all before marriage, it was usually confined to the fiancé. The men, however, were more apt to be sexually polygamous.

The appreciable number of men in Table 5-2 who had intercourse only with women whom they did not marry reflects the "double standard" which tolerates sexual relations with low-status women but not with the fiancée. In some cases the "other" person may have been a temporary fiancée (one third of Burgess and Wallin's individuals had been engaged before). This accounts for some of the women who had intercourse with "other" men. It does not explain the net difference between men and women.

Table 5-2. Premarital Intercourse with Fiancé(e) and Others, by Sex

Partner in Premarital Intercourse	Men	Women
None	32%	53%
Fiancé(e) only	17	36
Fiancé(e) and others	28	10
Others only	22	2
Total	99%	101%
Number of cases	580	604

Adapted from Burgess and Wallin, 1953: 330. *Source:* College-educated couples in Chicago, 1940–43.

The tendency of men to be more intimate with casual partners while women are more intimate with serious ones can be seen more clearly in Table 5-3. Men become more restrained with the women they love than with those for whom they have little feeling. By contrast, women are more intimate with those they love.

Who are the nonfiancées with whom college men have intercourse? Kirkendall (1961) reported on 200 sexually experienced Oregon State men who were typically 20 years old when interviewed. On the average they had

Table 5-3. Maximum Intimacy of College Men and Women with Friends and Lovers

Maximum Intimacy	MEN With Friends	MEN With Lovers	WOMEN With Friends	WOMEN With Lovers
Necking, light petting	22%	36%	82%	42%
Heavy petting	18	40	12	41
Sexual intercourse	60	24	6	17
Total	100%	100%	100%	100%
Number of cases	50	45	50	42

Adapted from Ehrmann, 1959, 179. *Source:* University of Florida (Gainesville).

already had more than three partners apiece (either before or during college). The bottom row of Table 5-4 shows that 14 per cent of their partners were prostitutes and 18 per cent were picked up exclusively for sexual purposes. The largest category I have labeled "exploitive dates." These dates were purely means to the end of obtaining intercourse, (the man reported no feeling for the girl as such). In "friendly dates," the possibility of intercourse arose after dating began with acquaintances or friends. Serious dates involved "considerable emotional attachment." The small proportion of fiancées reflects the fact that many of these men had not yet been engaged at all, or engaged long enough to have reached complete intimacy. If the same men were reinterviewed at marriage, fiancées would loom considerably larger in their total sexual experience.

Most of the sexual experience of the men in Table 5-4 seems to have been motivated by sexual desire to the exclusion of love and affection. The difference in length of acquaintance between types of partner is highly correlated with the definitions of the types. Nevertheless, it illustrates how widely knowledge of one another varies under these contrasting circumstances. Only in serious dating and engagement does enough time elapse to build genuinely personal relationships.

Kirkendall's research suggests a qualitative hierarchy of premarital intercourse. In terms of the time allowed to develop a personal relationship (portrayed in Table 5-4) as well as the amount of communication, responsibility, mutuality, etc., prostitution falls at the bottom and engagement at the top of this hierarchy. Although much of this chapter focuses on the advantages of premarital abstinence, the higher the threshold at which premarital intercourse occurs, the more nearly ideal the circumstances. Table 5-4 demonstrates the enormous differences between alternative settings for premarital intercourse.

Closely correlated with the casualness of most male experience is a lack of communication prior to intercourse about marriage, possible pregnancy, or even whether to have intercourse itself. The man's approach is usually indirect, and both partners rely heavily on nonverbal gestures and symbols:

> I remember many first dates when I would try constantly to figure out what the girl was thinking of me. What did different signs mean? Why did she leave her arm waving by her side? This meant it was all right to hold hands. I would cautiously start swinging at exactly 180 degrees out of phase with hers. Sooner or later there would be a delightful collision of hands and thus the first step toward a physical love was achieved.

One "advantage" in nonverbal communication is that it is more ambiguous. The man is able to seduce the girl by easy stages, sometimes without her realizing what is happening. To speak of sex would seem too blatant and invite a rebuff. Subtlety allows progressive intimacy without

Table 5-4. Interval to Intercourse, by Type of Partner, for College Men

			TYPE OF PARTNER			
Time Prior to Intercourse	Prostitute	Pick-up	Exploitative Date	Friendly Date	Serious Date	Fiancee
Less than one week	100%	96%	32%	7%	0%	0%
One week to two months	0	3	43	17	2	0
Two to twelve months	0	1	18	56	36	20
Over one year	0	0	7	20	62	80
Total	100%	100%	100%	100%	100%	100%
Number of cases	91	116	219	112	93	25
Per cent of total liaisons	14%	18%	33%	17%	14%	4%

Adapted from Kirkendall, 1961: 258. Source: 200 men students at Oregon State College, (Corvallis), 1952 ff, reporting on all the sex partners they had ever had anywhere.

an explicit mutual decision. Kirkendall concluded that "communication about sex is very difficult. Generally speaking it seems easier to engage in actual intercourse than it is to refer openly to it."

There are exceptions, however, particularly after engagement. In Kirkendall's sample nearly half the sexually experienced engaged couples had communicated extensively before having intercouse. Most of their talk was understanding in nature rather than argumentative or persuasive. The more serious the relationship, the higher the quality of interaction between the partners as measured by the amount and kind of communication and by willingness to assume responsibility for potential consequences (such as pregnancy).

DURATION OF THE RELATIONSHIP. Although many men are less intimate with serious partners than with casual ones, any given relationship tends to become more intimate the longer it exists. This is especially true within engagement. For example, only 39 per cent of Burgess and Wallin's couples with short engagements (under nine months) went all the way versus 50 per cent of those who were engaged more than 15 months. Intimacy tends to be progressive anyway, and waiting becomes correspondingly difficult the more remote the wedding date seems.

FIRST VERSUS SUBSEQUENT INTERCOURSE. The first experience is the hardest—for an individual or for a couple. Fear of inadequacy, fear of being hurt, or anxiety about the unknown, are most acute the first time around. Uncertainty about the partner's response and the need to persuade her to cooperate or to involve her by nonverbal means make the first experience of complete intimacy a major event. Once the barrier is broken, restraint tends to diminish.

For couples who have intercouse often, it may become almost as routine as a good night kiss, hardly needing persuasion any more. Presumably, the more frequent the experience, the less elaborate it is liable to become. A girl's first experience requires substantial foreplay if she is to be physiologically prepared to participate (see Chapter 15). Perhaps this is one reason why Kinsey found premarital intercourse (by definition, early intercourse) more time-consuming than marital intercourse.

PHYSICAL CIRCUMSTANCES. According to popular mythology, the chief locale of premarital intercourse is the back seat of a car. For Kinsey's women, however, the usual place was the family home of either partner or his or her apartment (once they had left home). To be sure, couples occasionally took advantage of more notorious locations—motels, hotels, woods, and cars—but the typical location was domestic. Fear of discovery was not a major problem at home since most intercourse occurred when parents were away.

The Consequences of Premarital Intimacy

We have seen that premarital intimacy varies enormously in degree and quality. Its consequences are equally diverse. Even when discussion is limited to a single type of intimacy, the consequences are affected by many situational variables. For simplicity I will concentrate on complete intimacy rather than lesser degrees.

Physical Consequences

The physical consequences of complete sexual relations are relatively unique. Short of genital apposition, conception is impossible and venereal infection unlikely.

VENEREAL DISEASE. In an earlier era when prostitutes were the usual partners in nonmarital intercourse, they were a prime vehicle for spreading venereal disease. Since World War II, two things have happened. (1) Premarital sexual activity has shifted from commercial to noncommercial partners. (2) The discovery of better methods of curing venereal disease has led to the belief that the risk of infection has largely disappeared and to a corresponding reduction of treatment programs. The net result has been what public health officials call an "alarming increase" in venereal disease among American young people (Deschin, 1961). As a result, venereal disease may be a greater hazard in premarital intercourse than it used to be.

PREMARITAL PREGNANCY. Premarital conception is an even more common consequence. Almost one-fifth of the sexually experienced women in Kinsey's sample had at least one premarital pregnancy. As with the discovery of penicillin for syphilis, the invention of improved contraceptives has not solved the practical problem of preventing premarital conceptions. Many of the most effective methods of contraception require a prescription which unmarried girls are reluctant to request and doctors reluctant to give. Moreover the unpredictable, uncommunicative, and irresponsible character of most premarital intercouse is not conducive to the regular practice of the methods which are available. Consequently many couples take chances. And the more chances they take, the more apt they are to "get caught" with an unwanted pregnancy.

Once a pregnancy occurs, the secondary consequences are not entirely physical but may be discussed here for the sake of simplicity. The alternatives are abortion, illegitimacy, or premature marriage.

ABORTION. In Kinsey's sample the most common outcome of premarital pregnancy was an induced abortion, usually performed secretly by an M.D. This was the fate of three-fourths of the premarital pregnancies reported to Kinsey (Gebhard, 1958). These induced abortions were illegal. The average cost was several hundred dollars, depending on the patient's ability to pay and the doctor's risk of arrest. Subsequently, fees of more than a thousand dollars became commonplace for high-status patients (Bates and Zawadzki, 1964). As a result, traveling overseas to secure a legal abortion in such countries as Japan became financially competitive as well as medically safer than illegal abortions at home.

Two-thirds of the unmarried women interviewed by Kinsey about their abortions reported no unfavorable consequences. However, 18 per cent reported postoperative physical complications, 14 per cent negative emotional reactions, and 4 per cent social repercussions such as gossip.

ILLEGITIMACY. Though a premaritally pregnant middle-class girl may choose to bear her child out of wedlock, she is unlikely to raise it herself. Rather, she will try to place it for adoption. In earlier years, adoptive placement was easier. More recently the rising illegitimacy rate has increased the supply of adoptable children and the increased ability of the medical profession to cure infertility has decreased the demand from childless couples. Hence, easy adoption can no longer be taken for granted.

PREMATURE MARRIAGE. Nineteen per cent of Kinsey's premaritally pregnant couples got married. A few of them also secured abortions but most of them had live births. Many of these couples planned to marry eventually anyway; however, an unwanted pregnancy raises problems. Early marriage disrupts the compatibility testing process, so that couples of doubtful compatibility get married who otherwise might have broken up. Doubt whether her husband married her because he loved her rather than just because she was pregnant may plague such a wife the rest of her life. For him it may be an excuse to shirk his marital responsibilities or abandon them altogether. Forced marriages are often so rushed and so embarrassing that they by-pass religious ceremonies in favor of civil weddings. In Detroit, almost half of all civil ceremonies involved couples who were already pregnant versus less than one-sixth of the religious weddings (Pratt, 1965).

When undergraduates become pregnant, premature marriage and parenthood frequently terminates their education. (Pratt found that 13 per cent of all Detroit marriages where both partners were college drop-outs were premaritally pregnant compared to only 4 per cent of marriages in which both partners finished college.)

The husband-wife relationship is strained when the complications of pregnancy and parenthood are added to the crucial first year of marriage.

Such problems almost doubled the divorce rate for premaritally pregnant couples. Moreover, their divorces were obtained unusually fast (Christensen and Meissner, 1953). The more immature the couple and the less compatible they are, the greater the likelihood of divorce. To me, all this suggests that relinquishing an illegitimate child for adoption may have fewer negative repercussions than marrying prematurely.

HEIGHTENED FEMALE SEXUALITY. Chapter 15 describes how female sexual responsiveness awakens gradually through marital sexual experience. Whether it is good or bad for this awakening to happen before marriage depends on one's values. That it is one of the physical consequences of premarital intimacy is suggested in the following case:

> When we first started going together, Sarah was rather cold and I could tell that she was a virgin. I told her the "facts of life" which were all pretty new to her. At first she was against petting, but I gradually worked around to it. After a while she discovered that she enjoyed it too, and now she's even more eager than I am.

When sexual feelings are aroused, the physiological tendency is toward release through climax. Most petting, however, stops short of this point. Only a third of the men and women who engage in petting *ever* experience orgasm as a result (Kinsey, 1953). Hence premarital petting usually means stimulation without release. Some individuals are impelled by this heightened tension to sexual intercourse. Others find release through masturbation. For the rest there remains the problem of living under tension. A few men and women experience localized pain in the genital region (Kinsey). Far more common are simple frustration and preoccupation with this frustration. When sexually aroused, it's difficult to think of anything else. If arousal is intense, the frustration may be acute. After enough time elapses (perhaps in such traditional distractions as cold showers, or vigorous exercise), passions may cool. The physical effects of petting are, keynoted, however, in the word "frustration":

> We've done so much petting that it's become a natural part of our life. But it's been quite frustrating for both of us. Petting gets you all worked up but then you have to stop. I don't like it but I do.

"I don't like it but I do." Along with negative feelings of frustration go positive sensations—the pleasures of sensual stimulation. In fact frustration implies not simply a negative but an ambivalent situation. Petting short of climax means an appetite whetted but unfed, a thirsty man given salt tablets instead of water.

Psychological Consequences

In comparison to such tangible effects as pregnancy, abortion, and disease, the emotional consequences of intimacy are harder to measure. Feelings don't come in all-or-none doses, and research results must be treated cautiously. Comments depend on the wording of questions and the context in which they are asked.

How many of those who are sexually intimate regret it later? When Kinsey asked adult women how they felt about the premarital intercourse they had had in earlier years, relatively few reported any regrets. However, when college students were asked about their current behavior, more qualms appeared.

Table 5-5 shows that the greater the intimacy, the greater the proportion who felt guilty. (More than twice as many women as men reported guilt feelings, but patterns were similar for the two sexes.) More important than degree of intimacy, however, were the individual's own sexual standards. Guilt was experienced universally in this sample by those whose behavior violated their own standards. It was rarest among those who stopped short of going as far as their standards would allow. Curiously, however, guilt was relatively widespread among those who were moderately to extremely intimate and yet said they believed it was all right. Apparently student sexual philosophies often masked latent inhibitions which rose up to plague those who engaged in petting or intercourse. Freedman (1965) attributed the widespread opposition of Vassar students to premarital intercourse "to deep-lying and complex sentiments that were dimly comprehended." These subconscious feelings seemed to involve "caution, control, and inhibition." Perhaps if one violates such scruples often enough, they

Table 5-5. Guilt Feelings of College Students about Current Sexual Intimacy, by Sexual Standard

	CURRENT DEGREE OF SEXUAL INTIMACY		
Sexual Standard	Necking	Petting	Intercourse
Necking is permissible	25%	100%	100%
Petting is permissible	5	63	100
Intercourse is permissible	0	42	56

Adapted from Reiss, 1967, 116. Source: Men and women students in certain classes at the State University of Iowa (Iowa City). Reciprocal percentages of students reported no guilt feelings about their sexual behavior. The number of cases on which each percentage was based is as follows:

16	8	1
21	105	7
4	26	54

eventually disappear. But during the college years, even "believing" in the rightness of sexual intimacy is no guarantee against feeling guilty afterwards.

> Through attending discussions on boy–girl relations, I had heard that petting was not wise. Until I was eighteen I didn't know what petting really was. I found out the hard way. During the course of an evening my date and I talked a lot about our attitudes toward sex and I told him I did not believe in petting. Before I got home that night I knew what petting meant. The experience was a terrific emotional shock which took me a couple of weeks to get over.

This girl recoiled from the suddenness of betrayal into forbidden experience. Given the more conservative views of women and the fact that they are more often seduced against their better judgment, the guilt hazard is greater for women than for men. When religious devoutness and the strict moral teaching of the Roman Catholic Church are added to these general factors, guilt is even more common. Although few of Kinsey's devout Catholic women violated their taboo on premarital intercourse, fully half of those who did subsequently regretted it. Similarly, Christensen and Carpenter found sharp differences between Mormon, mid-Western, and Danish students in the pleasantness or unpleasantness of feelings the day after first intercourse (see Table 5-6). The Mormon faith is similar to Catholicism in its stringent opposition to premarital intimacy. Scandinavia, on the other hand, is conspicuously secular and correspondingly permissive. The stronger the cultural ban on premarital intercourse, the more widespread the negative reactions.

Table 5-6. Feelings of Unmarried Men and Women at Three Universities on Day After First Intercourse

Feelings	UNIDENTIFIED MORMON UNIVERSITY		PURDUE UNIVERSITY (INDIANA)		UNIVERSITY OF COPENHAGEN (DENMARK)	
	Men	Women	Men	Women	Men	Women
Pleasant	33%	14%	45%	35%	71%	73%
Unpleasant	67	86	55	65	29	27
Total	100%	100%	100%	100%	100%	100%
Number of experienced students	37	7	107	29	93	49
Per cent of total students who had ever had intercourse	39%	10%	51%	21%	64%	60%

Adapted from Christensen and Carpenter, 1962: 68–69. Pleasant feelings included happiness, relaxation, and sense of conquest. Unpleasant feelings included tenseness, remorse, guilt, disgust, fear of others knowing, fear of religious punishment, fear of pregnancy, and fear of venereal disease.

Table 5-7. College Students' Feelings of Having Gone Too Far in Sexual Intimacy, by Stage in Courtship

	Degree of Intimacy			
	PETTING		INTERCOURSE	
Stage in Courtship	Men	Women	Men	Women
Casual dating	25%	54%	44%	65%
Going steady	32	37	44	61
Engagement	32	26	41	41

Adapted from Bell and Blumberg, 1960: 62. *Source:* 160 men and 250 women students at Temple University (Philadelphia). Reciprocal percentages of students never felt they had gone too far.

Table 5-6 also shows that the more unusual the behavior was statistically, the more unpleasant the reactions. For both men and women, the smaller the proportion of students who ever had premarital intercourse, the larger the proportion with negative reactions. This suggests the profound influence of peer behavior on the meaning of sexual experience.

Qualms about intimacy depend on three factors: the strength of one's scruples; the degree of intimacy; and the crudity or sensitivity with which intimacy occurs. If the relationship is exploitive or merely casual, regrets are more likely than when the participants love and cherish each other.

Table 5-7 shows how the last two factors interact. Regret was felt more often by those who had intercourse than by those who confined themselves to petting. It was also more common when intimacy occurred prematurely. The less committed the couple, the more regrettable petting or intercourse seemed, especially to the woman. Only when intimacy occurs within a context of love and mutual commitment is regret likely to be avoided.

At Vassar, similarly, the few students who had intercourse in casual relationships were usually dissatisfied with their experience (Freedman, 1965). Vassar students generally considered love and serious involvement crucial as a basis for physical intimacy. Necking and petting were typically welcomed within a deeply affectional context but not sought for their own sake. The 22 per cent who experienced intercourse prior to graduation almost always confined it to serious relationships (especially to engagement).

When doubts arise about the partner's commitment, intimate behavior correspondingly palls—at least for the girl:

I've been going with Hal for two years now and during most of that time we've been living together on weekends. At first it seemed to me to be all right, but lately I've been so depressed that I can't concentrate on my school work. Hal says he won't have enough money to marry me for another two years, so I'm afraid our present relationship is going to continue for a long time to come. I don't see how I can go on feeling so guilty this way. I've made up my mind that either he marries me in

June when I graduate or else I'm going to get a job so far away that I don't have to see him any more.

In Kinsey's sample, if intercourse occurred with the fiancé at all, it was usually limited to the last year before marriage. (The reaction to intercourse hinges on the certainty with which the couple are moving toward marriage. The less committed they are, the more regret.) Similarly, regret was twice as common for women who had intercourse with men they did not marry as for those who restricted intercourse to engagements which culminated in marriage.

However, even women who had no personal regrets preferred that their children refrain from premarital intercourse (Chesser, 1957). Apparently, complete intimacy is seldom traumatic enough to make it regrettable for those uninhibited enough to engage in it. On the other hand, it isn't sufficiently rewarding (at least for the female partner) to make it positively commendable. The psychological consequences of premarital intimacy are therefore not generally negative for women who choose it but not positive enough to make them recommend that others follow their example.

Interpersonal Consequences

Crucial to a book on marriage is the effect of intimate behavior on the relationship between partners. The short-range question is whether intimacy strengthens or weakens the relationship; does it increase or decrease the likelihood that couples will marry? In the long run, how is premarital intimacy related to marital sexual adjustment and to marital satisfaction?

We have already seen that premarital intercourse (a) sometimes results in pregnancy which (b) sometimes results in marriages which (c) sometimes would not have occurred otherwise. Indeed, Kirkendall (1961) reports that some girls try to become pregnant in the hope that this will persuade the partner to marry them.

PREMARITAL CONSEQUENCES. Except for occasional "shot-gun" marriages, intimacy produces more broken relationships than strengthened ones. More engagements were broken by Burgess and Wallin's couples who had intercourse than by those who did not (18.2 per cent versus 10.9 per cent), and the more frequent the intercourse the larger the proportion of rings returned. The instability of intimate relationships is surprising in view of the feminine tendency to cling to a man with whom one has had sexual relations. Especially with the first sexual partner, a girl feels that she has more to lose if they break up. If they quarrel, she feels, "How could you, when I have given you so much?" If he threatens to leave, she feels betrayed. Nevertheless, the facts show that couples who have intercourse are more apt to break up. Sometimes, the split is mutual. After intercourse, the relationship has changed from attraction to fulfillment, from the appeal of the unknown to familiarity with the known. Daydreams built on anticipation and desire are suddenly destroyed in confrontation with a reality possibly quite different from what had been fantasied.

More often, it is the man who severs the relationship. His reasons may be either sexual or psychological. For most men, inaccessibility heightens the partner's sex appeal and increases his desire to pursue her. Once she gives in, his interest may diminish. If he believes in the double standard, her surrender automatically disqualifies her for marriage. Unjust though it seems from an equalitarian viewpoint, such men lose respect for the girls they succeed in seducing. The more secure the relationship, the less the likelihood that intercourse either within or outside the context of the relationship will disrupt it. Intercourse is least able to destroy a relationship secured by marriage, but even married couples are not immune to the external temptation to abandon familiar partners for more exciting new ones. After marriage, however, the social sanctions of the wedding ceremony, the economic interdependency of the common household, and responsibility for children buffer the relationship against the acids of disillusionment.

Prior to marriage the greatest security is found in engagement to marry, especially when the engagement period is short, the wedding date set, and compatibility high. The effect of intimacy depends on the balance of forces leading toward marriage and away from it.

The preceding paragraphs describe observable differences between characteristic male and female reactions to premarital intercourse. To emphasize how great the variations are in the quality of such experiences and their effects on the couple's relationship, here is a case characterized by unusual mutuality of understanding:

> Until the eighth month of our engagement, the limit of our physical intimacy was a deep kiss. From that point forward, we progressed gradually through light petting to heavy petting, and, finally, nine months later, to intercourse. Neither of us had had prior sexual experience other than kissing, and, in retrospect, we have enjoyed learning together.
>
> Generally, I took the lead, but we had a tacit agreement that we would make progress slowly, mixing discussion with discovery. Before and after progressing to the next level, we both freely gave our views concerning the implications of the act, our questions about each other's physiology, and our attitudes toward what we were doing. This process of mutual learning and mutual understanding was, and is, both a very valuable and a very cherished experience to us.

When premarital intercourse is based on such a foundation of intimate acquaintance, mature love, and complete commitment to marriage, it may increase the couple's feeling of closeness. Kirkendall (1956) pointed out, however, that other couples gain a similar feeling of unity from cooperative sexual restraint. Kirkendall's case histories indicate that "in the great majority of situations, premarital intercourse has negative consequences for personal interrelationships." Very few of his couples were able to prepare the way for intercourse by full and free discussion, to "place the importance of their total relationship ahead of sex," and to be motivated primarily by love for each other. Only under these rare circumstances, Kirkendall believed, did couples "have a chance to engage in premarital intercourse without damaging results to their interrelationships."

In lesser degrees of intimacy, different factors apply. No anxiety about pregnancy provokes desperate attachment for the girl. Nor does sexual fulfillment affect the man. Intimacy short of the ultimate generally increases the sexual appetite. When people have little else in common, petting may intensify an infatuation:

> I don't understand exactly why I didn't leave Sally alone from the time we first started petting, but for some reason I couldn't. I knew it wasn't good for me because I was constantly in a state of nervous excitement when she was in sight. The worst part was that she attracted me even while I wished she wouldn't excite me so. But I knew she didn't care about me except as a means of sexual gratification. I tried several times to lift the relationship above the level of petting, but my good resolutions always broke down.

What happens when one partner pushes toward intimacy before the other is ready? Such premature initiatives are almost exclusively masculine (not that girls never initiate sexual activity, but their partners are seldom unready for it). Kirkpatrick and Kanin (1957) found that Indiana coeds who had been offended by an aggressive partner most often felt angry with him. They frequently felt disgusted or disillusioned with him, afraid of further aggressiveness, or guilty about their own involvement. After being offended once, they often refused to date the aggressor again and warned their girl friends about him. If a couple were already going steady or were engaged before the sexual offense, they were less likely to break up. But even engagements collapse when men push their sexual desires to the point of violence.

This study dramatizes the difference between intimacy that expresses mutual love and that which pushes a girl farther and faster than she is prepared to go. Loving intimacy may strengthen a relationship, but the same action expressed aggressively can ruin it.

MARITAL CONSEQUENCES. On the whole, premarital intimacy (especially if premature in timing or unlimited in degree) tends to destroy relationships. This disorganization remains visible after marriage, although subsequent events gradually obscure the impact of premarital events.

Locke (1951) found that more divorced men and women than happily married couples had had premarital intercourse. The differences between the two groups were especially great for promiscuous behavior—more divorced people had intercourse with several people before marriage, not just the future spouse. Terman (1938) similarly found the greatest marital happiness among couples who postponed intercourse until marriage, next where it was restricted to engagement, and least where multiple partners were involved. Burgess and Wallin (1953) found that the more frequently a couple had premarital relations with each other, the lower their marital happiness, mutual satisfaction, love for one another, and confidence in the permanence of their marriage.

In general, then, people who engage in premarital intercourse have less happy marriages and more divorces. Premarital intercourse contributes to marital difficulties by paving the way to extramarital intercourse. In Kinsey's female sample, those with premarital intercourse were more than twice as apt to engage in extramarital intercourse (29 per cent versus 13 per cent for the premaritally restrained). Those who do not consider wedding vows necessary to intercourse before marriage are less likely to do so after marriage.

Premarital intimacy may not be the only cause of these marital problems. It is partly a symptom of personality characteristics and values which undermine personal relationships before and during marriage. The more rapid the involvement and the more promiscuous the circumstances, the more premarital intimacy violates the attitudes and behavior patterns necessary for success in marriage.

These generalizations seem warranted in spite of the fact that the *sexual* satisfaction of sexually experienced wives excels that of novices. For example, Kanin and Howard found that experienced women were more satisfied with intercourse during the first two weeks of marriage. In fact, the greater their prior intimacy, the greater their sexual satisfaction on the honeymoon (1958). Although Chesser's experienced women reported the same sexual advantage on the honeymoon, their margin diminished within the first few months of marriage and disappeared altogether after that (1957).

These findings reflect heightened female sexuality as a consequence of intimacy. The sooner a woman begins to be sexually active, the sooner she becomes sexually responsive. This does not mean that the sooner one begins, the more satisfactory the initial experiences, even from a purely sexual point of view. If there is any difference at all in physical satisfaction between initial intercourse before marriage and initial intercourse after marriage, I would expect the latter to benefit from the security and legitimacy of marriage. Given the same *amount* of sexual experience, women who wait for the fullness of time are probably at least as responsive as those who rush into sexual intimacies. We will see later that the happiest married couples and the warmest mothers are those who delay those experiences until they are fully ready. Probably the quality of sexual experience also rises with increased readiness.

In summary, the main interpersonal consequence of premarital intimacy seems to be instability before and after marriage. The greater the intimacy, the larger the number of partners, and the more exploitive and irresponsible the circumstances, the more destabilizing the effect. Conversely, the more closely sex is integrated with love, responsibility and marriage, the greater its contribution to the solidarity of a faithful relationship.

The Control of Premarital Intimacy

So far my discussion of premarital intimacy has focused on what people do, why they do it, and what the consequences are. I come now to the question of codes or standards, what people feel they ought to do, and how they can (and actually do) control their behavior in line with their norms.

Contemporary Philosophies

Four main philosophies about premarital intimacy exist in the United States, one double standard and three single standards—conservative, conditional liberal, and unconditional liberal. Under the *double standard*, premarital intercourse is acceptable for men but not for women. This means that only prostitutes or other low-status women may have intercourse (and thereby render themselves ineligible for marriage). The *conservative single standard* advocates abstinence for both sexes. The *conditional liberal standard* permits intercourse within engagement or between people who are in love. The *unconditional liberal standard* allows sexual intimacy under any circumstances, regardless of whether the partners are in love.

The distribution of these standards on several college campuses is given in Table 5-8.

The most striking feature of Table 5-8 is the contrast between men and women. Despite the divergence between colleges, more women at every institution favored sexual restraint. Indeed, if we combine those who advocated abstinence for both sexes with those who advocated it for women only (in the double standard), a majority of women at every institution favored restraint for their collective selves. Conversely, a majority of men at all four colleges advocated sexual freedom for themselves. Thus, the

Table 5-8. Premarital Sexual Standards of Men and Women in Four American Colleges and Universities

Premarital Sexual Standard	COLLEGE OF WILLIAM & MARY (VIRGINIA)		UNIVERSITY OF MICHIGAN (ANN ARBOR)		UNIDENTIFIED NEGRO COLLEGE (VIRGINIA)		BARD COLLEGE (NEW YORK)	
	Men	Women	Men	Women	Men	Women	Men	Women
Conservative single standard	45%	77%	28%	45%	15%	39%	14%	24%
Double standard	34	19	9	15	37	37	26	36
Conditional liberal standard	15	3	54	39	33	23	36	35
Unconditional liberal standard	5	1	9	1	16	2	24	6
Total	99%	100%	100%	100%	101%	101%	100%	101%
Number of students	110	147	127	199	70	80	86	84

Source: University of Michigan data from students enrolled in the marriage course in 1962–63 (mostly seniors, many of them engaged to be married). Data for the remaining colleges represented cross-sections of each student body in 1959. They were adapted from Reiss (1967: 26) by the elimination of erroneous "reverse double standard" responses.

two sexes who must cooperate in heterosexual relationships typically start from incompatible assumptions.

I have arrayed the colleges from left to right in Table 5-8 in terms of increasing liberalism. (1) William and Mary is a high status, Ivy-League type, liberal arts college located in the South (the most conservative region of the United States according to Reiss' national sample of adults). (2) Permissiveness with affection at the University of Michigan may be sub-divided between those who required engagement as a condition and those who required simply love (love was enough for 31 per cent of the men and 24 per cent of the women). The popularity of conditional liberalism in the Michigan sample was at least partly due to the fact that many students enrolled in a functional course on preparation for marriage met the conditions which they prescribed. They were either in love or already engaged and advocated sexual freedom for people in their situation. (Reiss found that the more often students had been in love and the more exclu-sive their current dating relationship, the more they advocated sexual freedom.) (3) The liberalism of students at the Virginia Negro college reflected a general split between blacks and whites in sexual philosophy which survived even when racial groups were matched on many status characteristics (Reiss). (4) Bard is a small progressive college in the God-dard-Antioch tradition located near New York City in the most liberal region of the United States. It was described by Reiss as having "a long-standing reputation for being an extremely liberal school in terms of sexual beliefs."

In an earlier work, Reiss (1960) predicted that the coming years "will witness an increasing acceptance of person-centered coitus and petting." In an increasingly affluent and urbanized society, increasing liberalization of American sexual attitudes seems inevitable. Reiss (1967) found, for example, that the larger the home town, the more permissive students were (39 per cent "highly permissive" for towns under 10,000 versus 61 per cent for cities of 1,000,000 or more). Whether liberalization is prog-ress or regress depends on one's evaluation of sexual philosophies.

An Evaluation of Sexual Philosophies. From the standpoint of marriage, can such philosophies be ranked as "better" or "worse"? This is a controversial question, a matter of judgment. Before I became a sociolo-gist, I was temperamentally inclined to rebel against sexual conservatism. However, the longer I have studied the evidence from scientific research, the more I have been forced to recognize the positive consequences of restraint.

From the data cited in this chapter and from both a "personal relation-ships" and a broader sociological frame of reference, I have come to the following conclusions. I rank the double standard lowest because it exploits low-status women, accustoming the male to disdain his sexual partner. Unconditional liberalism seems one notch above it, having at least the virtue of mutuality. However, both standards separate sex from love, whereas ideally sex expresses love. Sex without love views the partner too narrowly. The relationship is merely sexual rather than fully personal. Love guarantees a personalized relationship.

The conditional liberal and conservative standards agree that love is prerequisite for intimacy. They differ on whether marriage is also necessary. Here I think the choice must be made in terms of long-range consequences. From the standpoint of the quality of the immediate experience (mutual giving, person-centeredness, understanding, and communication), there may be no difference between love and marriage. But waiting has two long-range advantages: (1) it provides a secure setting for children conceived from sexual intercourse; (2) drawing a sexual distinction between "not-marriage" and marriage accentuates the importance of marriage and contributes to its stability.

For society at large, both illegitimacy and divorce are problems. Premarital chastity prevents illegitimacy and reduces divorce. I have already presented data on the marital instability and adultery associated with premarital intercourse. Here, I wish to make a new point: *the sharper the boundary between one social status and another and the more elaborate the ceremonies marking the transition, the greater the solidarity of a social group.* Premarital intercourse blurs the distinction between courtship and marriage. One consequence of this vagueness is that couples who have already had intercourse are less apt to take a honeymoon. (Only 47 per cent of Kanin and Howard's sexually experienced student couples took a honeymoon compared to 87 per cent of the restrained couples.) If one already feels married, what is there to celebrate?

Hence my conclusion: The integration of love and sex enhances the immediate quality of a sexual relationship. Limiting intercourse to marriage contributes to the stability of marriage. Therefore, the conservative single standard is the ideal sexual philosophy, and the conditional liberal standard next best.

Implementation of the Ideal

It is one thing to have an ideal and another to carry it out. For instance, Karen (1959) found widespread inconsistency between ideals and practices among students at San Diego Junior College. Violations of their own ideals occurred most often in casual dating when the male "predatory-recreational orientation" was untamed by interest in the partner's welfare. Though women less often violate their own standards, they are not immune to the temptation, especially when faced with what Burgess and Wallin described as the "frequent and intensive erotic stimulation" that usually precedes final breakthroughs in intimacy. Many couples find it difficult to adhere to their ideals. What practical steps may make it easier to limit premarital intimacy? First, the standard needs to be clear-cut. Second, motivation to violate the standard can be reduced. Third, the ideal can be given external support. And fourth, the premarital period can perhaps be shortened.

CLARIFICATION OF THE IDEAL. An ambiguous norm invites infractions. A vague situation invites the aggressive partner to test the limits. Since most of the sexual initiative in campus dating is taken by the man (Ehrmann, 1952), and the girl usually has higher ideals, the chief responsibility falls on her to express her convictions when pressed to go farther than she wants. Instead of simply saying no, she can contribute to the emotional growth of the relationship by discussing her ideals:

> The most successful method I found was not just to say "no" and drop the matter, but to stop the fellow and, before he had an opportunity to get mad or feel guilty, to engage him in a serious discussion of the situation. This usually meant finding out his reasons for his undesirable action, telling him frankly and kindly my reasons for not desiring such conduct, and ending the discussion with a mutual revealing of ideals concerning sex and its ultimate relation to marriage. By this time most fellows would realize that they were acting contrary to what they ultimately desired, and usually this ended the trouble. Often they seemed grateful for the opportunity of serious discussion of what was a problem to them as well as to me. I found that quite frequently the fellow merely was seeking to find out what kind of companion he had. More than one fellow told me that if I had been willing to cooperate without any limitations, he wouldn't have known what to do because that wasn't what he really wanted.

Not all men could say that intimacy was not "what they ultimately desired," but an honest statement of conviction commands respect. At the University of Florida, most men accepted the girl's control:

> This type of control represented usually an equilibrium point that was acceptable to both parties. The male did not try to go beyond it because he knew that the girl would not go farther or because he felt that he ought not to try to go farther in consideration for her moral attitudes (Ehrmann, 1952).

Once a standard is clarified, it is more easily respected. Discussion, however, often reveals conflicting norms—the boy's liberal one and the girl's conservative one. In such circumstances sexual intimacy must be limited to the least common denominator if the conservative partner is not to be offended.

Some girls wonder whether they should ignore their own convictions in order to express their love. Does the fact that it would be personally distasteful make such sacrifice unselfish? Affirmative answers to this question cause trouble. In the long run the only way to preserve one's self-respect and personal integrity is by sticking to one's own beliefs. If the partner is not willing to respect this moral integrity, he is not the kind of person to marry. Better to lose one's fiancé than one's self-respect. Norm-clarification is therefore the first step not only for the partner but for oneself.

REDUCTION OF MOTIVATION. How well a norm can be observed depends not only on its strength and clarity but also the forces that seek to break it. If a norm is strong enough, and if it is held by both partners, few situations would seriously tempt a couple. But if a norm is weak or held by only one partner, the difference between adherence and nonadherence may depend on the temptations that are encountered. Couples who wish to reduce their sexual "temperature" may hold a tighter line on their sex play. Girls may avoid the game of sex-tease. Men may reduce their sex drive by sexual release through masturbation (which Kinsey concluded was the most practical alternative to premarital intercourse [1949]).

SOCIAL SUPPORT. Informal chaperonage by parents present in the house or by double-dating may provide external support for personal norms. Whether double-dating is supportive, however, depends on the other couple's norms. Otherwise the effect can be quite the opposite:

> Our problems, such as they were, seemed to be caused by the gang of kids we were with continually. My girl and I were seldom by ourselves in the evening. So the conversation usually was between the three or four couples, and when that became quieted down there was probably more necking than if each couple had been alone, because it is extremely difficult to carry on a private conversation when others are with you. Besides, when in Rome . . . !

REDUCTION OF THE ENGAGEMENT PERIOD. Maintaining restraint is increasingly difficult the longer couples go together and the closer they come to marriage. Especially after engagement, holding the line becomes difficult. The longer the engagement, the worse the problem. Hence, it may help to hold off engagement until the wedding date is set.

The Place of Intimacy in Courtship

Every couple needs to keep sex under some kind of control. Going too far too soon endangers courtship. Preoccupation with sex may produce individual guilt feelings, disrupt a promising courtship, or fixate it on a precarious foundation. The contributions of sex to courtship are not all negative, however. For couples deeply in love, the physical dimension may enrich their total relationship and increase their mutual enjoyment.

The sexual side of courtship usually develops spontaneously. Anyone from an affectionate family finds it natural to be affectionate. If one's parents have been undemonstrative, one function of courtship may be to cultivate more affectionate ways. Gradually the individual can develop toward sexual maturity:

> My girlish ideas about love and sex have changed a lot in the last few years. I used to abhor any demonstration of affection. In high school I seldom kissed a date and always felt awkward when I did. As far as sex went, I was really mixed up. About the time I was seven or eight I decided I never wanted to hear anything about sex. When my brother asked my parents about it I would plug my ears and sing songs so I couldn't hear anything. Later in my teens I got in on hen-sessions so I wasn't entirely naïve. Fortunately for my mental health I met a boy in college who was able to help me overcome these attitudes. It wasn't an easy or sudden change, and Dick has admitted to me that he almost gave up in his attempts to convert me into being able to express myself more completely in a love relationship. However, I progressed slowly as he subtly laid the groundwork until I was gradually able to take the next step. In each case he waited patiently for me to be ready to make the first move.

This fiancé patiently and skillfully nurtured his girl as only a psychotherapist might otherwise have done.

Sexual maturity depends not only on freedom to respond but on ability to interact with another person on an adult level. Facing up to the challenge of this complex area can strengthen the total partnership. The crux of the matter is each couple's willingness to share their thoughts and arrive at a mutual agreement about the sexual expression of their love.

6 Readiness for Marriage

Finding the right partner and developing a personal relationship are the first two steps toward marriage. But a couple may be thoroughly compatible, very much in love, and still not ready for marriage—yet. Are they mature enough to take on the responsibilities of marriage? This is primarily a question of age and experience, though in special cases other problems are unresolved. Some problems are internal residues of unhappy family backgrounds or inadequate child-rearing. Some are external obstacles that delay engagement and marriage.

Personal Readiness for Marriage

Couples who function well on dates may nevertheless lack the added resources necessary for married living. Marriage embraces more aspects of life and requires taking more responsibility for one another. Hence, marriage requires special skills and resources.

Emotional Maturity

Emotional maturity is a normative concept in developmental psychology which means that the individual has arrived at adulthood. He is no longer a helpless infant, a naïve child, or a rebellious adolescent. Emotional maturity is tested in the crises of life. Faced with frustration, a mature person makes the best of the situation, adapting his course of action to surmount obstacles or accepting the inevitable with reasonable grace. To an immature person frustration is an occasion for a tantrum. Overwhelmed by feelings of rage, persecution, or defeat, he charges blindly at the nearest target or runs away from his problem into self-pity.

A mature person has *the ability to establish and maintain personal relationships.* Infants lack this ability. They depend on those who gratify their needs without being able to give in return. Adolescents, on the other hand, are too eager to demonstrate their independence to be secure in their relations with others. Maturity involves both the ability to give (which infants lack) and the ability to receive (which adolescents distrust). In other words a mature person has the ability to love.

Empathy is the ability to perceive the feelings of others. Immature individuals are so wrapped up in their own needs that they can't understand how others feel. Babies are egocentric and take years to learn to recognize the feelings of others. This does not mean they surrender their own identity in the process. But it does involve learning to recognize the identity of others.

Beyond merely recognizing others' needs is willingness to assume *responsibility* for meeting them. An immature person may have moments of altruism, but he shies away from long-term commitments that might interfere with his shifting interests. Getting married means taking on a lifetime responsibility, entering into a contract to meet the partner's needs to the best of one's ability. Having children is an even greater responsibility because of their utter dependence. Besides these moral obligations of personal relationships, there are the instrumental responsibilities for men of supporting the family and for women of keeping it fed and clothed. To the immature such responsibilities are disconcerting. To the mature, they are a challenge:

> There is a lot more to being ready for marriage than just being able to handle your own problems. Part of mature love is being able to support and help your husband when he has problems and not depend on him to always be your emotional support. It is being able to stand on your own and being able to help him even when you are already carrying a load of your own.

Lifelong commitment is one feature of the responsibility of marriage. It is also related to the *stability* that comes with maturity. Adolescents are volatile and impulsive; their values and interests change unpredictably. Mature adults have settled down enough to know what they want out of life. Though life is never static, the pace of their fluctuations has slowed so other persons can hope to keep up with them.

All human relationships require maturity, but marriage requires more than most. Married couples live so close together for such a long time that immaturity is disastrous. Egocentrism provokes defensive counterattack in vicious cycles. In the intimacy of marriage, behavior cycles generate rapidly and ramify in many directions. Marriage affords few opportunities for cooling down, for detachment, for breaking cycles once they begin. To prevent negative cycles one mature person is enough. He can see beneath the partner's demands to his underlying needs, meet them responsibly, and tolerate attacks that would irritate a lesser man beyond forgiveness. The more immature the partner, the greater the strain on one's emotional resources. Although one mature participant may be able to hold a marriage together, two can cope more easily with the burdens of children and external reverses.

The modern family imposes greater demands on the partners' emotional resourcefulness. In the old days wives were primarily housekeepers and husbands primarily farmers. Their success did not depend on their personalities. An egocentric person can make good pies or crops, but he cannot be a good companion, confidant, sexual partner, or emotional therapist in marriage.

Today, marriage is no longer an economic necessity. Its success depends on the partners' ability to devote themselves to one another. The new emphasis on the quality of interaction involves higher expectations. This tests the maturity of every husband and wife. Relieved of old economic pressures, each partner's ego is exposed to full view of the other. If the ego flunks inspection, the marriage loses its *sine qua non*.

OLD ENOUGH TO GET MARRIED. For the average person maturity comes automatically with growing up. It is produced by socialization in the family, dating, school, and work. It is accelerated by service overseas, in the Peace Corps or in the military. But regardless of experience, age is a rough index of maturity.

How old must a person be to be ready for marriage? This question is answered by the legislatures of the American states. Typically the legal age is 18 for boys and 16 for girls with written permission from their parents. Only when the boy reaches 21 and the girl 18 are they ordinarily allowed to decide for themselves. Are these legal specifications adequate definitions of maturity? The fact that divorce rates are highest for those just barely meeting them suggests that they are not.

The later people marry, the lower the divorce rate, especially after age 21. Figure 6-1 suggests that chronological maturity is especially valuable for men (since they mature later). Despite the hazards, the general trend is toward earlier marriage in the United States. In 1962 the median age for all first marriages was 19.9 for wives and 22.9 for husbands (N.C.H.S., 1967). College graduates married later than the general population. Wives who finished college were almost 24 when they married, and male graduates typically 26 (Glick and Carter, 1958).

Although younger-than-average marriages do not automatically fail, they

Adapted from Monahan, 1953. Source: 52,722 first marriages and 8,040 first divorces, 1945–47, Iowa.

Figure 6-1. Ratio of Divorces to Marriages, by Age at Marriage of Men and Women

face extra hazards which make extra maturity imperative. Couples marrying earlier than usual need to be more precociously mature than their contemporaries if their marriages are to survive.

Social Maturity

A person may be emotionally mature and yet not have experienced enough of the social life of adolescence to be ready for marriage. "Social maturity" stems from fulfillment of one's quota of premarital living.

Enough Dating. One of the delights of youth is getting acquainted with new dating partners. Often at this age new partners look more interesting than existing ones. As long as marriage is postponed, no legal commitment prevents pursuing new interests. Individuals who never date more than a handful of persons may feel later that they missed something and wonder what others are like. Such curiosity leads middle-aged neo-adolescents on extramarital sprees. Fortunate are those who get their fill of variety before settling down to monogamy:

> I'm not getting any younger, but I still have a lot of experiencing to do in my relations with men. I don't think I'll be ready to get married for several years yet. My feelings haven't crystallized enough about the kind of man I want. I'm enjoying this freedom from being involved and the chance to flirt with so many men. Right now variety is the spice of life for me!

Sooner or later, the average person discovers that new pastures are not likely to be any greener than those he's already visited. Instead of exploring further, he wants to settle down. How many partners it takes to satisfy a given person cannot be predicted—maybe a dozen, maybe 50 members of the opposite sex. In any case one characteristic of social maturity is one's willingness to disregard unknown potential marriage partners and commit oneself to building a relationship with one particular person. Dating must be "enough" not only in number of partners but in frequency. Few college students wish to miss out on campus life. In the following case even a tentative commitment back home did not warrant by-passing it:

> In my Freshman year, there was a strong pull between campus dating and Gene, my high school steady. It was a very distressing situation for both of us, because neither of us wanted me to be deprived of this once-in-a-lifetime opportunity yet Gene was afraid to lose me, and I was a little afraid to relax completely for fear that I might decide to like someone else. At the time, although I liked Gene intensely, thought I loved him, surely did not want to hurt him, the thrill of campus dating was far too wonderful to give up for any mortal man. At this point I can look back with satisfaction and say that I went to enough campus functions to get it out of my system, and I am very happy and content to settle down with the boy who was wonderful and kind and patient enough to wait for me while I had my fling.

Once an individual tires of the superficiality and insecurity of dating, he is ready for marriage. Anyone who has had a diversified dating pattern is less likely to feel later that he was short-changed in his social life. Having dated widely enough for new partners to lose their fascination, he can concentrate henceforth on the one who interests him most.

Enough Single Life. Besides dating enough, it is important to be independent for a while. Having just become emancipated from parents, it's too soon to take on the bonds of matrimony. Single life has advantages. Spare time can be used as one sees fit. Jobs can be changed. Travel is limited only by the time and money available. Nobody else's wishes have to be consulted nor moods catered to.

Girls may feel challenged to prove to themselves, their parents, and the opposite sex—that they are capable of supporting themselves and managing their own destinies. Supervised more closely than boys are by parents in childhood and by housemothers in college, they have yet to achieve a full sense of personal identity:

> Sure I want to get married and have kids eventually. But right now, I'm having too good a time going to parties, singing in operettas, and being foot-loose and fancy free. I want to prove to myself that I'm as good as the next person before I settle down to marrying him.

People are ready for marriage only after they have tasted freedom and found it good. Then it is time for something more permanent.

Emotional Health

The dividing line between emotional immaturity and emotional disturbance is a fine one. Maturity normally comes with age. When it doesn't, the individual may be permanently disqualified from marriage unless he gets help. Human personality is so complex that emotional problems take many forms. Among the signs of emotional maladjustment are moodiness, anxiety, insecurity, and suspiciousness. Every person has such feelings occasionally. But when they are constant, they ruin interpersonal relations. They may plague the individual with imaginary difficulties. A jealous suitor whose girl actually is devoted to him is a typical emotional aberration:

> Clyde has done a funny thing this winter. He's a good dancer and we used to go to all the big dances and have a lot of fun. But lately I can't get him to take me any more. He mentions something about being afraid the other fellows will steal me away from him and suggests we go to the movies instead.

Marriage to such a man would be a nightmare of harassment: Who came to the door today? Who was that on the phone? Why did you talk to that man at the party?

Emotional problems usually bear the trademarks of immaturity: possessiveness, irresponsibility, and unpredictability. Occasionally, however, they take the opposite form—"overmaturity" or excessive rigidity. An oversocialized person may be unable to tolerate the frailties of others:

> I don't think Janie realizes how often she criticizes me. She couldn't understand why I ran out of money last semester and accused me of being irresponsible and lacking in foresight. She tells me I don't study hard enough and could get better grades if I only wanted to. After we've been to a party she tells me all the things I did wrong.

Perfectionism may be applied not only to the partner but to oneself, producing masochistic overaltruism. Though an excellent giver, such a person may be unable to accept love in his anxiety to avoid any hint of selfishness.

Emotional problems can usually be traced to the parent-child relationship. Where that relationship was twisted and tense, the grown child's negative reactions are often transferred to the spouse:

When I go home I get a tight feeling in my abdomen because of the way my mother harangues me. She infuriates me so much that I just have to get up and leave the table. I'm afraid that when I get married I'll be oversensitive to my wife and react the same way if she ever is even the least bit critical of me.

DESENSITIZATION. Because emotional maladjustment can wreck a marriage, such persons are not ready for marriage. Should they therefore be written off as "unmarriageable"? Some people's problems *are* so difficult that no help is enough. For many, however, change is possible. Emotional disturbance is not likely to diminish simply with the passage of time. Nor do problems often yield to self-help through self-analysis. If one's emotional response system is out of kilter, the services of a skillful counselor are required. Fortunately, most colleges offer such services to their students and most communities to their citizens. Counseling is indispensable to marriage preparation for those who have such problems.

Role Preparation

Most people learn how to be good husbands and wives in the process of growing up. They learn what it means to be a husband and a wife by observing their father and mother. When parents set a good example, this readiness can be taken for granted. When they do not, children are not prepared for marriage roles. The parents' faults tend to haunt the next generation. Old patterns are either blindly repeated or desperately rejected, leaving a strained clumsiness:

Tony's father is from the old country and he still has a lot of old-country ideas about husband-wife relations. He has pretty bad temper tantrums every once in a while during which he beats his wife and once he even threatened her with a gun. I never realized it before but, you know, Tony really treats me pretty much the same way. When he shoves me around and gets mad at me for having my own ideas it's just like his father and mother all over again.

This son unconsciously imitated his father. Others reject the unhappy example of their parents. But they lack a better model. Moreover, they are apt to lean over backwards in their anxiety to avoid their parents' mistakes. They try too hard in marriage—feeling so anxious about parental trouble spots that they overreact to problems. Events that would cause only minor irritation in an ordinary marriage plunge others into terror and despair by recalling dreaded foibles of the older generation:

All I did was take a little nip at the office party, but she really told me off when we got home. She said I was so tipsy I made a fool of myself with the stenographers. Well, it just wasn't so. I was only enjoying the spirit of the occasion. Just because her old man was a drunkard and a philanderer doesn't mean I'm going to turn into one!

Those whose parents were unhappy lack perspective in sensitive areas. Their overeagerness to avoid their parents' difficulties boomerangs. The very attempt to prevent difficulty causes trouble:

Unfortunately, my mother-in-law had an affair with a roomer and my husband has never been able to forget it. He seems to have lost faith in women as a result and is afraid I'll go off and leave him for someone else. To prevent that he keeps me home all the time except when he can go out with me. It's begun to get on my nerves so much that if he keeps on chaperoning me he'll drive me away himself.

These cases suggest one reason why children from unhappy homes are poor marriage risks. Conflict and divorce churn on from generation to generation.

REMODELING FOR MARRIAGE. Should children from unhappy homes, then, never get married? No more than emotionally immature or maladjusted individuals. Initial unreadiness doesn't necessarily disqualify people permanently. What can be done to break the spell of the parental model and provide a substitute model?

Anyone who reacts against his parents' example is apt to think he has broken away from their influence. However, rebellion is itself a sign of continuing concern. To replace either apprehensive rejection of the parents' behavior or unconscious identification with it, insight into both parents and self is needed. If I understand why my parents behaved as they did and how their actions influenced me, I will be able to marry more confidently. Insight makes it possible to accept residual sensitivity. It may even produce a sense of humor about inherited trouble spots. Premarital counseling provides a setting for talking out bitter memories and fearful anticipations.

To break the spell of the past, however, creates a vacuum. A new marriage model is needed. Reading and study may help. Better yet is the opportunity to observe and participate in a smooth-running family:

My folks had so much trouble getting along that it was no fun going home to hear them quarrel. Ever since Lesley and I have been going together I've spent most of my vacations at her house and it's been a real eye-opener for me. Her Mother and Dad are really wonderful people—friendly, easygoing—everything my parents aren't. They've just taken me in as practically a member of the family. I know it's been good for me to be able to live for a while in a house where the air isn't blue all the time.

For other people it may not be prospective in-laws but married friends who provide the desired example. Fiction and biography may fill the gap. Alternative models help erase the memory of trouble at home. In such ways handicapped persons can prepare themselves to take on the role of husband or wife.

Circumstantial Readiness

External circumstances are less important than personal readiness. Couples can undergo almost any physical hardship and come out stronger, *provided* they don't blame each other. (Geiger [1955] found Russian family solidarity increased by political persecution blamed on the government but lowered by financial problems blamed on the husband.)

The unforeseeable tragedies of marriage cannot, by definition, affect the decision when to marry. The relevant question is whether people are prepared to cope with foreseeable problems. If hardships clearly lie ahead, are both partners ready to tackle them as challenges to be surmounted jointly rather than as grudges to be borne against each other? When handicaps are assumed voluntarily, they need not threaten a relationship. Nevertheless, circumstances are sometimes so inauspicious that they affect the timing of the wedding.

Financial Resources

What is the minimum income a couple must have to get along? The answer varies from couple to couple, depending on their values. Some people "just couldn't survive" on less than $10,000 a year and would rather stay single than try. For others, rock bottom is a good deal lower. Every couple has a minimum standard below which life would be too barren. Realistic budgeting (see Chapter 11) can determine what that minimum is.

Few couples begin at the level their parents have reached. Except when upward mobility is unusually fast, the husband's first pay check is drastically lower than either his father's or hers. Consequently the accustomed standard of living of both partners is slashed.

The fact that both suffer similarly is a saving grace. If eating hamburger and making do with second-hand furniture in a one-room apartment is an equal comedown for both, neither is likely to feel bitter. Stretching dollars can even be challenging.

In earlier generations, money in the bank proved one's readiness for marriage. Today's couples depend more on their current income potential. With both partners working, total family income may be higher initially than it will be again for many years. However, dual incomes depend on postponing children. Sooner or later the earning power of the husband alone will be tested by the wife's retirement coincident with the addition of extra dependents.

What if the couple's financial resources are not adequate? Does this mean they are categorically unready for marriage, or may parents legitimately help them?

PARENTAL SUBSIDY. To some young people help from parents would be unthinkable. It would sacrifice bitterly won adulthood or threaten precarious masculinity. Financial dependence, after all, is still dependence, and supportive relatives are likely to be influential relatives. Nevertheless, for people sure of their own abilities, aid from the older generation need not create anxiety:

> In our family there is a regular tradition of helping each new generation get started in marriage. The old folks are glad to do it because they don't need the money themselves. The young couple aren't supposed to repay the parents but are expected to pass the money on to their own children when they get ready to be married. This way each generation gets the help when they need it the most.

From a financial point of view this policy makes sense. When a man is in his twenties and thirties, his income is low but his child-rearing and house-buying expenses are high. The result is heavy pressure on the budget. At the same time his father's earning power has reached its peak while his expenses have dropped with the launching of his children (and possible completion of his mortgage payments). The senior family has a financial surplus precisely when the junior family has a shortage.

Many middle-class parents help their children financially. Sussman (1953a) found that more than three-fourths of his New Haven families gave regular financial help to their married children. The following is a typical parent's attitude:

> At today's prices and costs of housing you can't expect children who have just finished school to be able to build or buy a house or even live decently in an apartment without help from the family. It might have been all right in my day to say, "You are 21, you are on your own." Today it is different. Our feeling is that we have enough money now that

we really don't need, and after all, our desires are very few at our age. So why not help the children?

Parents can proffer their help diplomatically. Wedding gifts like a home, an automobile, or a substantial check are more acceptable than a regular stipend. Christmas and birthdays provide customary occasions for presents. Sussman found that help that met genuine needs did not create friction between generations. Only where the parent-child relationship has been chronically tense is difficulty likely to arise. Normally, parental aid provides a workable alternative to postponing an otherwise impecunious marriage.

Resources of Time

The next chapter describes the planning necessary for the wedding, honeymoon, and first year of marriage. To rush through this planning means going into marriage unprepared, risking miscalculations which get things off to a bad start, and causing worry during what should be a delightful period of anticipation. A generous interval is needed to pave the way to the wedding day.

After the wedding comes the honeymoon—which time-pressed couples are tempted to omit or defer. The value of a week or more for this activity is suggested in Chapter 8.

Here I wish to discuss time for living together during the first year of marriage. If a couple know they will be separated after the wedding, should they wait for a more auspicious time? The answer depends both on the length of the separation and the length of the interval between the wedding and the date of departure. Long separations create problems that threaten new marriages.

DIFFERENTIAL SOCIALIZATION DURING SEPARATION. Both partners change while they are apart. This is not due to separation alone, for personalities change constantly. When people are together, however, changes are adjusted to as they occur. New interests and behavior patterns develop so gradually that people hardly realize what is happening. But if the same people are apart, the cumulative effect of the same changes is conspicuous. (Parents are never so startled by their children's growth as relatives who don't see them for a whole year.)

Personality changes not only pile up during separation but are accentuated by it. When couples are together they are exposed to similar influences. Separation introduces differential influences. In military separation this change of environment is especially marked:

When I was drafted into the Army, I began an entirely new phase of my relationships and views of the opposite sex. Broadmindedness was the only asset I acquired in regard to women due to the service. I found that the average serviceman was interested in one main object in women —sex. After getting out of basic training, I was transformed by my environment from a "good little boy" to one of their kind, which consisted of wine, women, and sex. In the service I learned through actual experience about the "good" girls and the "bad" girls. To the common serviceman the latter were preferred. In my wandering from Chicago to Germany, Hawaii, and Vietnam, I acquired a knowledge of "worldly" women. I met many women in the service, but maybe because I was a soldier I didn't meet many "nice" ones. By the time I returned to America I had obtained a disgust for womanhood.

Personality changes result from the contrasting experience of separated partners. The greater the contrast, the more they are liable to grow apart in philosophy of life or recreational interests. The shock effect of these changes can be reduced and the nature of pending readjustments anticipated by adequate communication. The principal vehicle for this must be correspondence. Letters are a poor substitute for face-to-face conversations, yet they can convey emerging aspirations and interests, disillusionments and problems. Reluctance to communicate these changes may stem from fear that they will be misunderstood because their meaning will not be adequately conveyed. The inevitable slowness of question and answer in letter-writing is nerve-racking. But misunderstandings can be clarified in later letters. The long-run interests of any couple are best served by frankness.

MAINTAINING A SEPARATED RELATIONSHIP. Chapter 4 lists interaction as a condition for love. Separation weakens love by preventing interaction. The longer the separation, the more the relationship atrophies. The weaker the relationship in the first place, the less its ability to survive.

Separation is a major cause of severed engagements (Burgess and Wallin, 1953). Even couples who avoid new involvements find rapport dwindles and divergences grow. However, new involvements are the greatest threat. The greater the interaction with new partners, the greater the likelihood a new love will supersede the old. Even the commitment of engagement or marriage may be revoked if new relationships eclipse them. Only the timely interruption of a college separation salvaged the following relationship from disaster:

When I saw Sunny again during vacation, I realized that my doubts about her had been due to the fact that she wasn't with me at college. Last fall I had a strong need for feminine companionship and felt a considerable tug in the direction of a girl in my Poli Sci class. Although

I was attracted to her, I felt guilty when I dated her because I was engaged. I'm glad now to discover that Sunny really is the one for me after all.

Separation after marriage is less apt to terminate the entire relationship. But if it comes during the early months, it disrupts a crucial period of adjustment. If the adjustment process is interrupted before satisfactory performance levels have been achieved, each partner may worry about the durability of a half-built marriage:

> Max and I only had two weeks together before he was shipped out. In general we had a grand time but not sexually. I hadn't been able to get prepared through premarital medical treatment with the result that sexual relations weren't satisfactory for either of us. I feel very guilty about not having been able to fulfill my marriage vows to Max in this way and I'm afraid that he resents it.

Marriages are best timed when they allow both advance preparation and a solid year of post-wedding interaction before any extensive separation. If this much time is not available, I believe a marriage is better deferred.

ADJUSTMENT TO REUNION. Change during separation necessitates readjustment on return. Although few people think of reunion as a crisis, Hill (1949) found it would be better if we did. If couples recognize that growing apart is normal, they will be less disturbed. If they approach reunion determined to work out a new relationship with this partial stranger, they are more apt to succeed. For already married couples, a second honeymoon provides an opportunity for getting reacquainted and dramatizes the fact that married life is not continuing an old relationship but making a new start.

Even if no observable divergences arise, a relationship is inevitably weakened by the dearth of interaction. Married or not, the courtship must begin again. Even though it is likely to be telescoped this time, a feeling of intimacy must be rebuilt. Since the time necessary for rekindling love cannot be predicted in advance, separated couples should leave their relationships open-ended rather than predetermine a post-separation wedding date. Better to leave the date-setting for a time when they feel psychologically ready than to ration too meagerly their time resources after a long separation.

Student Marriages

Student marriages present few new problems beyond those already discussed. Studying is an unpaid occupation; hence most students lack financial resources. Heavy schedules limit the time a couple can devote to one another. New, however, is the threat to educational plans presented by marriage, especially for the girl.

FINANCING STUDENT MARRIAGES. A 1959–60 study of a national sample of families showed that 61 per cent of the college expenses of the average student came from parents, 23 per cent from earnings, 8 per cent from scholarships, and 8 per cent from other sources (Lansing, 1960). How are these resources altered when students marry?

Since two can live together as cheaply as two alone, marriage may affect total expenses relatively little (as long as there are only two). However, the specific allocation of expenses changes with marriage. At Michigan State University, married students spent less on clothes, perhaps because they no longer needed to dress up to impress the opposite sex (Shaffer, 1963).

As for income, the chief question is whether parents will continue to subsidize their children after marriage. We have already described the widespread practice of subsidizing young families generally. For married students some parents favor assistance even more to insure that their education will be completed. College savings are thought of as "belonging" to the child, regardless of whether he happens to be married or not. Parents of both partners may continue paying tuition and other educational expenses after marriage.

Table 6-1 shows that in actual practice, married students receive far less parental subsidy than the single students reported above. Much of the difference results from the fact that married students are not a typical cross-section of the student body. They are older and more advanced in

Table 6-1. Financial Support of Married Students, by Role of Wife

| | Role of Wife | | | |
| | NONSTUDENT | | STUDENT | |
Source of Income	Childless	Mother	Childless	Mother
Husband's current earnings	11%	35%	27 %	29%
Wife's current earnings	62	15	19	7
Couple's savings	4	13	8	15
Parental subsidy	3	7	24	28
Scholarships	17	20	13	19
Miscellaneous	2	12	8	0
Total income	99%	102%	99%	98%
Number of couples	84	66	35	11

Source: Unpublished study under the author's direction by Rex Richards and Barry Stulberg of married students at the University of Michigan, 1955–56. Two-thirds of the husbands involved were graduate students. Percentages are the proportion of total income derived from the particular source. Most couples relied on more than one source.

their studies. Hence they are more self-sufficient than most undergraduates. Even when both partners are in school, parents provide less than half as much support as usual.

The gap is filled primarily by the couple's own earnings. Frequently the wife works to finance her husband's education. Under such circumstances marriage may be a financial gain to the husband, enabling him to complete his education faster than if he were self-supporting. However, if he acquires a student wife or if they have children, he usually has to work harder than when he was single.

In general, financing a student marriage imposes burdens unless the wife has already completed her education and the couple postpone children longer than usual. The other exception is when parents continue to finance their children's education after marriage—but this is not the general practice in student marriages.

SCHEDULING MULTIPLE RESPONSIBILITIES. If neither partner works full-time, marriage may be no more time-consuming than single life. Extra time spent cooking and keeping house may be offset by not dating any more.

But if either partner combines work and study, the pressure on time is severe. Something has to give. At Michigan State University it was recreation not studying that was cut (Thorpe, 1951). For individuals who are socially mature, this is no great shock. For the immature, or for the stay-at-home wife of a hard-working student, the slash in recreation can be painful:

> My wife isn't romantically involved with anyone else but she keeps wanting to step out with anyone she can pick up because she says it's too boring here at home. She seems to have decided she just doesn't want to be tied down any more. She likes to dance and I don't, but anyway I just have to stay home nights and study.

Another consequence of the time shortage is pressure for sharing housework. If the wife is going to school, the husband is pressed to help out with housekeeping and baby-sitting. Nevertheless, in student marriages (as in nonstudent marriages), wives carry the major share of the burden. At Syracuse, student husbands spent one hour a day in housework, student wives three hours a day (Chilman and Meyer, 1963). Perhaps that explains why wives studied less than unmarried girls. If only the husband is a student, the average wife tries extra hard to protect his study time from household burdens (Christopherson *et al.*, 1960).

Given the multiple demands of studying plus working plus keeping house, time becomes a precious commodity that must be carefully rationed. A schedule of daily and weekly routines guarantees that time is allocated to crucial activities:

We have a very strict schedule in which every five minutes of our day is utilized to the utmost. We have a full schedule of classes from eight to noon and work from one until about six. Then we hurry home, hurry through dinner and dishes, and go straight to studying until about 11 every night. Saturday is spent doing housework and washing and ironing. We work together on everything. About every other Saturday night we take off from our studies if we see we can both afford to, and we relax. Sunday mornings are spent at church. Sunday afternoon we try to spend about an hour visiting one of our families, and the remaining time we study. Our matched schedule leaves a lot of time when we are both working together and can talk. Even though we probably work harder than any couple on this campus, we believe our marriage is the happiest one there has ever been.

If, to all these responsibilities, children are added, full-time education becomes almost impossible. The wife's college career is usually impeded if not terminated altogether. Moreover, her difficulty in continuing work once she has a child increases the husband's financial responsibilities. Hence, young fathers are less apt than childless married students to go to school full time. (In the Michigan study, only 52 per cent of the graduate-student fathers were going to school full-time compared to 79 per cent of the childless graduate students.) Moreover, couples burdened with children have less satisfactory marriages than childless couples. Indeed, the larger the number of children, the worse the marriage (Christensen and Philbrick, 1952).

Foreseeing such complexities, most married students hope to postpone child-bearing until after graduation, or until the latter part of graduate study. Conversely, students who do not believe in contraception shy away from marrying. But belief in contraception is not enough to guarantee success. Many of the children born to married students are unplanned. (At Western Michigan University two-thirds of all the babies born to married students in the late 1950's were unplanned [Eshleman and Hunt, 1967].) Unexpected children are one of the major hazards facing college marriages.

PROTECTING EDUCATIONAL GOALS. I have already described children as a threat to the college career of both husband and wife. For students who avoid having children, how does marriage itself affect their education?

At Florida State University, married students earned better grades the term after marriage than the term before, but so did comparable non-marrying students (Cohen *et al.*, 1963). Some studies show greater gains for married students than for single students. At Stanford and San Jose City College, married men majoring in political science, economics, and education gained significantly more than single men; physics and English majors improved at the same rate, regardless of marriage; but chemistry majors who married fell behind those who stayed single (Schroder, 1963). These findings suggest that marriage may increase the academic efforts of men who are not already working up to their capacity.

However, these studies do not tell us how often marriage disrupts education completely. It seems likely that a substantial proportion of women drop out of college after getting married. Not known is how many men also fail to finish their education because they "temporarily" drop out to support their dependents, never to return.

It is not clear whether men who marry early are less academically or vocationally oriented than those who postpone marriage. However, marriage seems to increase their seriousness of purpose (Foreman, 1957). Student husbands are apt to be from families of lower social status (whose nonstudent friends are marrying at the same age [Marshall and King, 1966]). Perhaps one reason they marry young is because early marriage is customary in their social background.

For women, the decision whether to stay in school after marriage or drop out depends on how academically ambitious they are. At Syracuse University, wives who stayed in school were achievement-oriented and "masculine" in their interests. Wives who dropped out were traditionally "feminine," devoid of educational striving and interested in creating a warm, sociable, orderly home (Chilman and Meyer, 1960). Presumably drop-out wives get what they want in the short run. But two questions might be raised. (1) What will happen to their marriages as their husbands outstrip them educationally? (2) What kind of jobs will they be prepared to assume after their children grow up? In the short run, these women don't care about educational goals. In the long run, they are liable to regret it.

The fact that married students who manage to stay in college do all right in their studies shows that college and marriage are not inevitably incompatible. However, this discussion suggests that educational goals can best be achieved under the following conditions: (a) parental subsidy or other financial assistance; (b) postponement of child-bearing; and (c) postponement of marriage itself until the wife at least has almost finished her education.

LIVING WITH EDUCATION-INDUCED TENSIONS. Like salesmen on commission, athletes in competition, and entertainers before the public, life for students is full of tension. Grades for a whole term may hinge on an all too brief final examination. Term paper deadlines must be met. Graduate students face comprehensive examinations covering vast fields of knowledge. And finally there are the agonies of grinding out a doctoral dissertation. Even for those who manage to cross every hurdle without stumbling, there is anxiety enough to cause sparks to fly in marriage. Irritability, tenseness, and critical reactions make university counselors talk about a "graduate school syndrome" of marital difficulty.

For those who fail academically, there are tougher problems. Some lash out at their partner in displaced retaliation. Others sink into depression. Spouses in academic difficulty are hard to live with. Few of these problems are unique to student marriages. But they are predictable enough to test the maturity, the patience, and the compatibility of those who marry on campus.

Deciding When to Get Married

A rational decision about when to marry is often complicated. Timing for college students is restricted by the difficulties of marrying in midterm. Summer, Christmas, and between semesters are the chief periods when honeymoons are possible. After graduation, vacations from jobs are a determining factor. Most of the issues are long-range ones. Becoming socially and emotionally mature are gradual processes which don't change much from month to month but do change over longer periods. Such considerations determine whether this year or next is the right time to get married.

Most couples set the date by mutual discussion, though one partner may be more eager than the other. The final decision should be voluntary, since force produces an uncooperative spouse. Eager as one partner may be, it is better for the other to be sure he is ready. Though less crucial than choosing the right person, deciding when to marry indicates that an engagement is in order.

7 Rites of Passage: I-Engagement

In most primitive societies elaborate ceremonies mark the transition from one stage of life to the next. Especially when later stages involve heavy responsibilities, rites of passage emphasize the seriousness of the change. The most widespread initiation ceremonies are puberty rites for adolescent boys which mark the assumption of the adult role on which the economic and military survival of the society depends.

Closely analogous are the rituals that signal the initiation of marriage. In any society ritualization of the transition from single youthfulness to married adulthood adds strength and stability to the institution of marriage. The wedding ceremony is the central feature of modern rites. However, the preceding engagement period and the following honeymoon trip are other ritualized elements in the transition.

Engagement as a Ritualized Transition

The engagement period lasts so long that we rarely think of it as a ceremony. However, the girl's ring on her finger, her picture in the paper, and the round of showers deserve the term, even though the man is marginal to the process. (Getting married is the crucial transition in life for women whereas it has to compete for central importance with occupational changes for men.)

The Engagement Ring

Almost every engaged girl in the United States wears an engagement ring. In New Haven, only six per cent failed to get one (Hollingshead,

1952). Usually the traditional diamond is the stone, but for ceremonial purposes any ring on the third finger, left hand will do. If a diamond is beyond the man's resources or if ceremonial expenditures are low in the couple's scale of values, an inexpensive substitute may function equally well psychologically and socially. However, to have no ring at all may leave the girl feeling only half engaged. She knows that marriage is impending, but the public is less informed, so she gets less recognition of her role transition.

The Newspaper Announcement

Less universal than engagement rings is the engagement announcement in the local newspaper. Although the initiative comes from the girl and her family, the society page editor may veto it. In large cities, only elite couples are newsworthy. But when such news does appear in print, it further ceremonializes the engagement process.

Parties and Showers

Less standardized are customs governing group celebrations of the engagement. In some segments of society they include teas or cocktail parties to introduce the prospect to the partner's family's social set. On college campuses fraternity and sorority serenades celebrate the step. As the wedding draws closer, friends shower the bride with household goods whose practical value may be considerable and whose symbolic meaning is to mark her impending exodus into the world of married women. The excitement of these occasions reinforces her awareness that she is about to become a true adult and impresses the couple's parents with the impending "launching" of their children.

Timing the Transition

If engagement is a transition, it should not last indefinitely. Couples should not get engaged until they know when the wedding will be (what month or at least what season). To be engaged with no end in sight is too stagnant. It destroys the transitional meaning of the rite. Engagement is not an end in itself but a commitment to get married. Its meaning is distorted unless the goal is calendared.

Conceivably a couple could plan to marry in June two years hence. In practice most engagements run less than one year. In New Haven the average for the whole city was ten months (Hollingshead). Among Ohio

State University graduates the median was only six months and growing shorter from generation to generation (Koller, 1951).

There are several advantages in putting the engagement off until the wedding day is decided upon. Engagements of more than a year tend to lose their momentum. A sense of anticipation can be sustained through one cycle of seasons but hardly more than that. The ambiguousness of long engagements tempts couples to blur the sexual distinctiveness of marriage.

Although a year seems a workable maximum, the minimum is less easily determined. Suffice it to say that at least several months are needed if the functions of engagement are to be carried out successfully, even if we assume complete readiness for marriage.

The Functions of Engagement

Implicit in my comments on the meaning of engagement have been the functions it is designed to serve: public notice of serious intent, the last chance for compatibility testing, and time to make plans for getting married.

Public Announcement

In some churches publishing the banns theoretically makes possible the last minute intervention of anyone who feels a couple are not suited for marriage. Engagement serves the same function. It notifies families and friends that the couple intend to get married. The effect of such notice on interested parties varies. Parents who had misgivings from the start but hadn't taken the affair seriously may belatedly intervene, hoping to head off the marriage. On the other hand, parents who wished their child had found a better mate may now resign themselves to the inevitable. More positively, they may try to establish a better relationship with their prospective son- or daughter-in-law.

In any case a secret engagement is a contradiction in terms. Publicity gives the couple a chance to discover how it feels to be officially committed. Formal engagement serves notice that other eligibles have been dropped and the future is to be concentrated on the "one and only" who remains.

Compatibility Testing

No matter how long a couple have gone together, engagement introduces a new twist. They may have seen a great deal of each other, yet have been uncommitted to spending the rest of their lives together. The responsibilities of making a home and having children may not even have entered their heads. Engagement brings a sobering realization of the closeness and seriousness of marriage. In unexpected ways it alters the tone of the relationship:

> Before I got engaged, I was very romantic about Dick. We were both trying to impress each other with our best behavior. After we got engaged and began to plan for a future together, I was shocked at my practicality. Where I used to be impressed at his extravagant gifts and flowers, I now began to worry. I suddenly became analytical. Before we were engaged, if we would argue neither one of us was too upset, but now we take our disagreements very seriously and try to understand the cause. We feel very secure in our love for each other, but we realize that we have many problems to solve. Both of us have spent two years playing games—now that we are facing reality, we run into many conflicts. We probably would have been better off if we had been more objective two years ago. However, I suppose neither one of us was interested in marriage at the time.

In this case, engagement improved the relationship. But sometimes the opposite effect occurs. Sometimes the fact that the chase is over and the partner won takes the momentum out of love. If romantic attraction stemmed from the inaccessibility of the object, the security of engagement may be too dull. Or perhaps the fiancé becomes possessive and inconsiderate after the pact is sealed.

Although tested relationships seldom encounter new sources of incompatibility, the prospective mate may be seen in a new and unpleasant light as the wedding draws near. Broken engagements are therefore occasionally to be expected. They embarrass all concerned because engagement is so public. Yet the complications are mild compared to divorce. One virtue of engagement is that it is a revokable commitment. It is an opportunity to see what it feels like to be almost married, but not quite—partly committed but not completely. It's the last chance to pretest the marriage.

Planning for Marriage

Although nothing prevents couples from talking about marriage beforehand, once they are engaged they must begin planning in earnest. Plans must be made not only for the wedding and honeymoon but also for the first year of marriage.

PLANNING THE WEDDING. The wedding itself requires many decisions. If the girl is away at school, communicating with her mother through correspondence is painfully slow. If the man and his family are actively interested, negotiations become more complex. Fortunate are couples who begin planning months in advance. Organizing and administering a wedding is hectic enough without trying to make last-minute decisions.

Setting the date for the wedding requires balancing many factors. The ideal date allows ample preparation time and honeymoon time. It takes account of the bride's menstrual cycle to prevent interference with the sexual side of the honeymoon (unless pharmaceuticals are used to postpone menstruation). It enables relatives and friends to make plans for attendance. And it utilizes the desired clergyman, caterer, and facilities for the wedding and reception (often committed months in advance for the crowded June calendar). Booking the honeymoon may take less advance notice but still must be planned.

PROFESSIONAL PREPARATION FOR MARRIAGE. Most states require a blood test for syphilis before issuing a marriage license. An increasing number of couples use their doctor's professional skill more comprehensively to prepare them for marriage. This is an opportunity for a complete physical examination to detect physical conditions that could be remedied by medical or surgical treatment. For the first time, the reproductive system becomes important. Anatomical and physiological irregularities may be discovered. Most defects lend themselves to remedial measures. In those few cases where the doctor discovers that a couple could never have children, stock-taking is inevitable. Some couples decide to go ahead with marriage, hoping to adopt children or willing to risk doing without children for the sake of their love. Other couples part regretfully. A woman who has anticipated the day when she would bear children may abandon a sterile man. A man too may feel he wants children who are "flesh of my flesh and bone of my bone." In any case, having the information before marriage helps couples know what to expect.

Medical preparation for sexual intercourse includes dilating the vaginal opening (by the doctor or by the girl herself following the doctor's instructions). Dr. Lovett Dewees reported in 1947 that only ten per cent of his patients had hymens elastic enough to make intercourse comfortable without dilation. For couples who intend to use contraceptives, engagement is the time to secure instructions and materials from a physician or Planned Parenthood Clinic. Some doctors also counsel the bride and groom about the sexual side of marriage. Couples who desire this preparation should choose one with this special competence.

Just as doctors provide premarital medical treatment, clergymen provide premarital counseling. Some refuse to marry anyone who has not been instructed in marriage. Their methods vary from didactic instruction to nondirective counseling. Interest focuses on the "spiritual" aspects of marriage, but this may be broadly defined. Couples who take their religion seriously often consult their pastor about marriage generally and not just the wedding.

PLANNING FOR MARRIED LIVING. As soon as the honeymoon is over, the newlyweds will settle into a new way of life. In earlier generations this life was left to chance or entered on faith, but the trend has been to make more plans ahead of time. We saw in Table 2-2 that typical topics of engagement conversation are handling money, having children, where to live, religion, the wife working, and the husband's occupation. Over the past three generations the number of Koller's engaged couples who never discussed any of these issues dropped from one-fourth practically to zero, whereas the number discussing all of them rose from 5 per cent to 50 per cent.

Not only discussing how to handle money but preparing a detailed budget for the first year of marriage is advisable. Agreement is also needed on whether to practice birth control (for those who have doubts). Setting up housekeeping involves finding a place to live and choosing such things as tableware and furniture. Planning is not only important but enjoyable. As with a round-the-world cruise, half the fun of being engaged is anticipating the experiences ahead.

Interaction during Engagement

The imminence of marriage is welcome but often raises new issues.

Conflicts

Couples who can't get along with each other gradually drop out during courtship, but those who get engaged are not immune to conflict. Burgess and Wallin's couples (1953) typically disagreed in several areas. Their biggest problems were how to deal with families, how to dress and act in public, and personal friendships. Kirkpatrick and Hobart's Indiana University couples (1954) quarreled about neatness, in-laws, and economic roles.

These conflicts reflect the engagement situation. Couples close to marriage seldom quarrel about such familiar matters as dating (the *rarest* source of conflict in the Burgess-Wallin study). Rather, they have trouble over their external relations with family and friends, their public appearance as a committed couple, and the economic roles that will support them after marriage. These areas could have been explored before but engagement brings them to the fore. Some disagreements between any two people—no matter how compatible—are inevitable. The question is not whether a couple have disagreements so much as how well they resolve them.

Deepened Relationships

Conflicts, though widespread, are seldom chronic. The overwhelming feeling of engaged couples is not anxiety but euphoria and elation. Shorn of the insecurity of uncommitted dating and excited by the imminence of the marital adventure, they glow with love. As the wedding day approaches, the momentum of courtship accelerates into a flood of festivities crowning the remaining days of not-quite-marriedness.

8 Rites of Passage: II–Wedding and Honeymoon

If engagement is properly labeled a rite of passage, the wedding and honeymoon are even more so. All three stages in the transition to marriage strengthen it as a social institution. The more ritualized the ceremonies, the sharper the realization of the significance of the step. The great event toward which courtship points is the wedding ceremony. This is the culmination of planning, the fulfillment of childhood dreams, the high point in many a girl's life (rivaled chiefly when she gives birth to her first child). Though the man is handicapped by traditions of masculine unemotionalism, he, too, is apt to find the occasion deeply moving.

Members of the Wedding

Who cares whether a couple get married? Who is the wedding for—the bride and groom, the parents, or the spectators? When there are conflicts between parties, how can they be reconciled?

The Couple

The central participants are the bride and groom. This statement seems trite, yet it needs emphasis because sometimes the couple's wishes are ignored in the complexities of organizing the ceremony. There is no one more pathetic than the bride who stands by helplessly while her parents run away with the wedding. Such a situation usually reflects the dominating personalities or social ambitions of the parents. Exploiting the wedding to

186

serve their own needs is facilitated when the bride's parents pay the wedding expenses:

> I'm very much afraid my father is going to dominate the wedding plans. He's already begun talking enthusiastically about his favorite processional music (which I detest) and he even wants to hire someone to sing "Oh Promise Me." He seems to think that since he's going to pay for the wedding he can buy just the kind he wants. Sometimes I feel so disappointed I'd rather junk the whole church wedding, but I'll probably make the best of the situation when the time comes.

Resentment at being left out of wedding plans is natural. It tempts couples to elope, running away to be married in a strange community, bereft of family and friends. Elopement is a deviant solution to a difficult situation. Like a child who runs away from home, an eloping couple signify that something has gone wrong in parent-child relations. Sometimes parents have opposed the marriage as such. If they did not oppose the marriage but drove the couple to desperation by disregarding their wedding preferences, an elopement shows that the members of the wedding were out of balance.

For the couple the ceremony marks the beginning of a new way of life. The consequences of the wedding are so far-reaching that their desires deserve high priority. Traditionally, the bride is in the middle of wedding preparations while the groom remains on the periphery, the butt of jokes about being trapped by a female conspiracy and failing to show up at the church. Left out of the planning, he is the victim of circumstances beyond his control. This contrast in involvement reflects the greater change in the status of women. Yet with the development of shared marriages, grooms become as interested as brides. So, traditions aside, they share in planning the wedding. Presumably, the more they participate, the more meaningful the occasion becomes.

The Parents

The wedding marks a turning point for parents as well. When their first child is married, they enter the launching phase of the family life cycle. With their last child, the postparental stage begins. In-between marriages mark off inexorable steps toward old age and death.

A son's or daughter's marriage is a bereavement. There is joy, of course, in the child's happiness. But when he leaves home forever, a void is left behind. Going away to college or work paves the way for this bereavement, but family ties are still unbroken. Home is still the place to go when in trouble and during vacations. At the point of marriage, however, the child transfers his loyalty, his dependence, and his home base. As a result, life never looks the same again to his parents.

The impact of the wedding depends on the parents' personalities. For a mother whose life for a quarter century has been wrapped up in her children, the effect is drastic (as her tears bear witness). Parents feel deeply involved with the child they've nourished, enjoyed, and worried about for twenty years or more.

The wedding is also a major social event. For elite families it rates a splash on the society page. For many families it is a chance to make an impression in the right places. Parents differ in the extent to which they care what others think of the wedding. Those who are socially secure may care little. Those who are socially conscious may be anxious to avoid mistakes in etiquette. The ambitious may treasure the opportunity to lure "the right people" into the church and reception hall. To most brides and grooms such ambitions appear irrelevant and selfish. Yet feelings that mean a great deal to parents cannot be disregarded without offense.

Important as the wedding may be to them personally and socially, most parents are not preoccupied with their own interests so much as eager to launch their children successfully. They want the wedding to be attractive and memorable primarily for the sake of the bride and groom. Though generations may differ in taste, their goals are essentially the same—a good wedding.

The Clans

Weddings are joyous occasions for the gathering of the clan, matched in importance only by the somber occasion of funerals. Particularly for recently immigrated ethnic groups, weddings are a family reunion for aunts, uncles, and cousins who otherwise seldom see each other. Weddings are an excuse to abandon everyday cares and fly halfway across the United States. For a few hours, the bride and groom may hold the center of the stage, but for the rest of the weekend the kin group dominates the scene as it celebrates the marriage of one of its offspring. Brother and sister kiss and embrace, tears flow, old stories are told, and for a while the hands of the clock are pushed back.

For such clans, a wedding is not so much planned by the couple for their guests as staged by the clan for their protégé. For a clan member not to be invited would be unthinkable. Even members who are not ordinarily on speaking terms are duty bound to be invited and duty bound to attend. Indeed, one of the miracles of wedding feasts is the transformation of disunity into reunion.

For young people who have always belonged to such a kin group, a clan wedding is taken for granted. For those who marry into one, the prospect may seem overwhelming. But if one is to become a clan member, the time to join is on one's wedding day.

Friends

Less involved but still interested are friends of both families. Numerous, sometimes innumerable, they pile up on invitation lists at an astonishing rate. If both partners come from the same community, the pressure of this "cloud of witnesses" on the wedding budget becomes insistent.

The friends of the bride and groom—classmates and favorite teachers—are obvious participants. From among them are recruited the bridal party, the best man, and the ushers. They bring joy to the couple.

But what about the parents' friends and business associates? Mostly members of an older generation, these people seem like excess baggage, destroying the intimacy of the occasion. Do they have a right to "barge in" on so sacred an occasion? Even though few of these people know the couple well, they want to join in the festivities. For old married couples each wedding brings back memories. Since "all the world loves a lover," weddings give all but the cynic a lift. But friends of the family are attracted to more than weddings in general. They are specifically interested in *this* couple, even if that interest isn't reciprocated. When the child of an employee or bridge partner gets married, they want to see how the bride and groom look and share a bit of their happiness, and the happiness of the parents. Being present may not be indispensable, but they appreciate being invited—and feel left out if they are not. As friends of the marrying families, they feel that they deserve to be members of the wedding.

Professionals

Weddings are not just family affairs. To be legal they require a representative of the state: a clergyman or judicial official. Most weddings are concerned not only with the legalization but the sanctification of the new family. Hence, the clergyman represents not only the state but God. Slater (1963) called the clergyman "the central person in the proceedings." Having performed so many weddings before, he is the ceremonial expert on whom families rely amid the uncertainties of their first few weddings. His very expertise, however, makes him resist innovation, even where it is allowed by church law. The busier he is, the less time and energy he can devote to exploring idiosyncratic preferences. Nevertheless, he is a key figure in the wedding planning.

The larger the wedding and reception, the larger the number of secular functionaries who join the team of planners. Caterers, florists, and photographers also get carried away by their expertise. Florists have standard arrangements that they supply to "every" wedding. Photographers have package deals which call for particular shots. To secure them, the man with the camera may interrupt the wedding and reception to ask people to assume the customary poses. He may even infringe on the wedding ceremony itself unless carefully supervised. Caterers are accustomed to managing receptions. For couples who don't care how theirs goes, caterers are a blessed relief. For those who do, they are another source of conflict:

> We didn't have a very big wedding but the caterer had big ideas, nevertheless. He insisted on providing his usual multitiered wedding cake. When we asked him to make a different kind, he said he couldn't—his baker was too busy. When we got another cake elsewhere, he was so mad he refused to cut and serve it so we had to do it ourselves while he stood there glowering. I almost cried!

Professionals have vested interests which must be taken into consideration. Whether the bride and groom think of these "outsiders" as members of the wedding or not, professionals see themselves as indispensable.

Conflict of Interests

With so many different people involved, it would be miraculous if everyone had the same ideas. What the wider circle thinks doesn't matter much. But two parties are apt to clash—the couple and the girl's parents. They are the four people on whom the responsibility for the wedding falls most directly. Because of differences in age and in the nature of their involvement, these two couples are likely to disagree.

The commonest conflict is over the size and cost of the wedding. The younger generation often want to restrict invitations to their personal acquaintances, whereas the older generation want a wider circle of guests. Paradoxically, parents often want to spend more on the wedding, while the bride wants them to save their money or give her a bigger wedding present instead.

As a general rule, the parties most concerned with the particular issue should have the most influence. If the details of the wedding ceremony or the members of the bridal party are at issue, these affect primarily the bride and groom. But adding relatives and family friends to the invitation list is the parents' concern. Hence, conflicts over wedding size should normally be resolved on the large side. If parents want to spend their money, it should be their privilege. Young people who worry lest a large congregation spoil their sense of intimacy can take comfort in realizing that they will be so absorbed in the ceremony that they will be oblivious to extra faces:

> Greta and I had a wonderful wedding. The weather was perfect, Father O'Brien performed the ceremony, and we were deeply moved by it. There's only one thing I would do differently if I were doing it over again. We felt that we wanted to limit the invitations to the very closest friends and relatives. So we ruthlessly crossed off the list an awful lot of people who would have liked to be there. I realize now that it really wouldn't have made any difference at the time to us and I've regretted ever since that we were so exclusive.

In recommending that conflicts be settled on the large side, I do not mean to advocate a particular number. Bowman (1960: 255) suggested, "A wedding, like a garment, should fit. . . . As is true of a garment, there is no point in having the largest one possible." A fitting size reflects the number of relatives of both families and friends of both generations who are geographically accessible.

Conflicts with professionals may be minimized by careful selection (where choice is possible) of those whose approaches correspond with the family's preferences. If the family presents its preferences early, the professional will be properly oriented. Ultimately, conflict resolution usually requires concessions from both sides. Successful conflict resolution meets the needs of all interested parties. With conflicts settled, the wedding can be appropriately solemn and the reception appropriately joyous.

The Wedding Ceremony

Solemnity befits the lifelong commitment undertaken by the two partners. It is best provided under religious auspices. Hollingshead (1952) found over 80 per cent of all New Haven weddings in church settings, with most of the remainder conducted by clergymen at the bride's home. Religious weddings add supernatural sanction to the solidarity of the new family: "What God hath joined, let no man put asunder." The sanctuary brings together the religious community to support the new subcommunity.

Churches have customary wedding rituals. Some allow no leeway, but most of the "free churches" permit couples to modify the ceremony. Some couples prefer to speak their own vows instead of relying on the clergyman for coaching. Some alter the vows, for example omitting the bride's promise to obey. Alterations are more apt to be improvements than mere deletions. Lester Kirkendall's family substituted the following postscript to the wedding ceremony for the traditional "giving away" of the bride:

Marriage brings into being a new family. This is the meaning of the ceremony you have just witnessed. But no family stands of itself alone. It exists in a fabric of other families, and draws strength from and gives support to others as it becomes a part of the community of families. The most important ties for either a new or an established family are the ones which unite those of one flesh and blood.

As a token and as acknowledgment of those ties and of their mutual interdependence, this husband and wife and their parents have expressed a wish. It is their desire to give visible expression of their purpose to support and sustain each other in the life before them.

Mr. and Mrs. _____ (the groom's parents), will you take a place by the side of your new daughter? Mr. and Mrs. _____ (the bride's parents), will you take a place by the side of your new son?

As a pledge to your intention will you unite by the joining of hands?

I now pronounce you a new family. Your unity will be established and your outreach will extend as you show each other forbearance and understanding and offer one another appreciation and solace in good times and in bad.

In order to give the congregation a chance to participate, there may be congregational hymn-singing, the reading of collective prayers, or opportunities to offer a prayer or message. To make the ceremony meaningful to the bride and groom, their favorite music may be played on the organ or a phonograph and their favorite passages read from the Bible or poetry. The variants are many. The larger the number of treasured elements the couple can incorporate, the more meaningful the occasion will be for them. The rewards are rich for those who create a ceremony that expresses their ideals for their new life together:

We wish all of our friends might have been with us, for it was an experience both glad and solemn, fulfilling for both of us the dream of a ceremony beautiful with lovely simplicity and depth of feeling.

By contrast, other churches and couples prize the age-old symbols and would be uncomfortable with the slightest innovation. For them the familiarity of rituals enhances their beauty. Moreover, clergymen, organists, and other church officials develop habits even about matters not prescribed by church law. These organizational functionaries have had so much experience that they think they know best what is needed (perhaps even, what is wanted). Hence they may be reluctant to modify accustomed procedures to meet idiosyncratic requests.

Nevertheless, idiosyncrasy is another word for personal meaningfulness. For a once-in-a-lifetime wedding, arduous negotiation is worthwhile if it produces an event of peculiar significance. What matters is that the ceremony fit the couple's values, affirming their aspirations and pledging their commitment in terms that are meaningful to them.

The Reception

The reception allows each member of the wedding to congratulate the bride and groom individually by handshake or kiss. It is also a party celebrating the wedding. The wedding breakfast or wedding cake represents symbolically the first meal together of the couple as husband and wife.

The reception is the most expensive part of most weddings. The party may be a gala affair with dancing until the early hours. Liquid refreshments may be costly. Families with limited means may have to choose between limiting the guests at the reception or limiting the cost per person. Etiquette allows the former discrimination to be made between those invited to the wedding alone or to the reception also. However, guests don't like to be discriminated against, so it may be preferable to stretch the budget to fit the people. If people are more important than refreshments, champagne can be dispensed with. True friends are not offended by simplicity, and merriment does not have to be stimulated.

In New Haven most families invite all the wedding guests to the reception. (The median attrition from wedding to reception was a mere 18 from the typical 177 guests at the church, according to special computations Hollingshead made for me.)

Wedding Finances

Table 8-1 portrays the range of variation in wedding costs to the families involved.

Both families furnish their own clothes, the ring to be given away, and gifts and flowers (corsages or boutonnieres) for their own attendants. The

Table 8-1. Reception Costs, by Size of Wedding

| | | SIZE OF WEDDING | |
Conditions	Small	Average	Large
Attendants	2	6	11
Guests	Family	150	300
Reception location	Home	Church	Country Club
Costs			
Bride's family	$188	$761	$3,002
Groom's family	50	183	507
Total	$238	$944	$3,509

Adapted from United Press news release, July 20, 1956. Source: Study by University of Cincinnati students of Professor Margaret Jane Snydam.

bride's family normally pays for invitations and announcements, church expenses, and the reception. The groom's family provides flowers for the bride and both sets of mothers and grandmothers, the marriage license, and a gift for the officiating clergyman.

Though custom discriminates financially against the family of the bride, the groom's family can redress the balance by generous wedding gifts, especially of honeymoon expenses. If an impecunious girl marries a wealthy boy, wedding costs can be shifted, but delicate negotiations will be needed to avoid hurt feelings.

Money spent on the wedding is indirectly returned to the bride and groom in the form of presents—the larger the wedding, the larger the number of gifts received. In New Haven, the gifts received were worth well over half the entire cost of the wedding and reception. Gifts provide the new family with equipment for their new household and symbolize the good wishes of relatives and friends.

The Honeymoon

Occasional magazine articles warn that honeymoons are dangerous, so exaggerated in their reputation that they are bound to be disappointing. Admittedly, one can expect too much from anything and thereby be disappointed. Nevertheless, the fault lies with the expectations, not the practice. Apparently most people's expectations are not unattainably high (three-quarters of the women interviewed by Brav [1947] reported they were completely satisfied with their honeymoons).

The Functions of the Honeymoon

In festive tone the honeymoon resembles the reception, but in exclusiveness it marks a literal departure. Leaving the reception before it ends, the couple embark on their private celebration.

CELEBRATION. Were they to remain at the reception instead of taking a honeymoon, the couple might prolong their celebration by a few hours. But the other celebrants would soon tire of celebrating someone else's wedding or would have to leave to return to their own concerns. One's own wedding, however, deserves more than that. For marriages destined to continue "till death us do part," a day's observance is not enough. So, long after the other members of the wedding resume their ordinary tasks, newlyweds continue their celebration. This symbolizes the depth of their gratitude for one another and heightens their sense of the contrast between their earlier separateness and their new togetherness. The honeymoon in this sense is the final rite of passage.

INTIMACY. Unlike the preceding ceremonies, all of which were distinctively public, the honeymoon is strictly private. If receptions lasted indefinitely, they could perform the celebration function, but the new dyad needs celebrating as a separate unit. The honeymoon provides the first chance to be alone as a married couple. With nothing to divert their attention they become aware that they are really married at last.

Discovering what it means to be married involves new revelations. After all the compatibility testing that has been advocated, it may seem doubtful that people could get any better acquainted. Yet marriage is different from even the most intimate courtship. No matter how long the courtship, hidden facets of the personality emerge during the honeymoon: he likes his eggs "practically raw" and she requires a fantastic number of blankets to keep warm. Then there are the new experiences of marriage to encounter: the first breakfast together (no matter how many meals have been shared before); the first church service as man and wife; the first dance. Marriage will bring new experiences with each passing year, but they never crowd together as intriguingly as on the honeymoon.

Central to the intimacy function of the honeymoon is sexual intimacy. Those who have already been completely intimate often dispense with a honeymoon (Kanin, 1958). But for the uninitiated, the first intercourse represents the consummation of the marriage. It completes the "joining together" proclaimed in the wedding ceremony.

For some, however, intimacy is so frightening that they cut their honeymoon short and hurry back home:

> . . . the desire to return early seemed related to anxiety about the intimacy situation. If there is a lot of anxiety about being involved in an intimate two-person situation, one may expect a corresponding sense of relief or even eagerness at the prospect of returning to a more diffuse pattern of relationships (Rapoport and Rapoport, 1964).

It is not necessary to take a honeymoon trip in order to have intercourse. Nevertheless, the leisureliness of a vacation enables honeymooners to indulge their sexual desires more freely and flexibly. For many couples the honeymoon is the peak period of sexual activity of their entire married lives.

Criteria for the Honeymoon

If the marriage is to be celebrated and intimacies are to be enjoyed, what conditions must be present?

PRIVACY. Achieving a sense of identity as a married couple requires leaving the reception behind. However, newlyweds are classically not allowed to escape unnoticed. Ambivalence about letting them go is expressed toward the departing couple in the customary jokes, which

> . . . have the covert purpose of hindering the couple's departure. These include tampering with the couple's automobile, hiding their luggage, etc. Furthermore, a number of devices, such as signs, streamers, or tin cans fastened to the automobile, stones placed in the hubcaps, and, again, the confetti, serve to make the couple conspicuous, and thus have the sense of minimizing or negating the sense of privacy which has been granted to them (Slater, 1963).

Most couples hope to escape the seemingly watchful eyes of others. However, newlyweds are notoriously conspicuous in their radiance and self-consciousness. Try as they may to disguise their honeymooning, they are apt to give themselves away:

> When we drove up to the Norwich Inn, we were determined to act so calmly and naturally that no one would know we'd just gotten married. Jan went in first to pick up the reservations and I followed with the suitcases. Despite my efforts to appear blasé, the guests in the lobby seemed to be looking at me and nodding their heads knowingly. While I was disconcertedly trying to figure out how they guessed our secret, Jan turned around and burst out laughing. I had perched one of her little hats on my head while unloading the trunk and it was still there!

After a day or two it is less embarrassing to be seen in public, but unself-conscious enjoyment of sexual intimacy requires being able to withdraw behind closed doors, undisturbed by visitors or phone calls. Guaranteeing privacy is one reason for traveling away from friends and relatives. Privacy doesn't require fleeing to the North woods but simply to an anonymous environment. One peculiarly American custom is the honeymoon hotel at Niagara Falls or Miami Beach where honeymooning couples are seated together at long tables (men on one side, women on the other) or paired off at tables for four. The Rapoports (1964) commented that "Europeans tend to be astonished by this custom, noting that they would wish to get away from other people at such a time, certainly from others in the same situation." Presumably organized sociability is as reassuring for newlyweds unsure of their ability to sustain a dyadic relationship as is double-dating for shy teenagers. The question is, however, whether joint honeymoons with either strangers or friends are sufficiently private to allow full-fledged marital intimacy. I doubt it.

LEISURE. Leaving home is necessary to get away not only from social obligations but from occupational ones. Even without going back to work, moving immediately into a new apartment would be too practical to make it possible to concentrate on each other as persons. A honeymoon is, therefore, a type of vacation. Like all vacations, honeymoons take time. Some people call a weekend a honeymoon but they would hardly call it a vacation. Most people, fortunately, manage the week or two which celebrating minimally deserves. (Hollingshead found the New Haven average was nine days.)

But a honeymoon is not an ordinary vacation. The only one of its kind, it deserves to be extraordinary. Whatever the couple deem most enjoyable should be the criterion for choosing the proper locale. Since tastes differ, appropriate locations vary accordingly. For some couples it is the bright lights of the city. For others nothing could be less attractive. In either case the honeymoon deserves to be as enjoyable as possible. If ever a vacation is to be special, this is it.

ECONOMY. The enjoyment of leisure is affected by the cost. If the honeymoon costs so much that the first year of marriage will be financially undermined, its attractiveness diminishes. Only if the cost is borne by the parents is it irrelevant to honeymoon enjoyment. On the other hand, if the occasion is to be memorable, it must cost something. Fortunate but rare are couples whose friends offer cottages free of charge. For the rest, the uniqueness of the honeymoon makes it worth more than the usual vacation allotment.

IMMEDIACY. The only absolute criterion for the honeymoon is that it follow the wedding immediately. This is one of the few now-or-never situations in marriage. It is not absolutely necessary to take a honeymoon, but to postpone one is to turn it into a mere vacation. The special functions of the honeymoon can hardly be reproduced later. Even a brief delay dulls the edge of enjoyment. To celebrate a marriage and savor its intimacy, the honeymoon must be taken at once.

Usually it is (honeymoons were skipped by only 6 per cent of Hollingshead's New Haven couples). For married students, however, limited money and time more often bar the way. Thirty per cent of Kanin's married students failed to take a honeymoon. This was one of the sacrifices exacted by marrying before the husband was occupationally launched. Similarly, Hollingshead's individuals who had been married before felt less need to repeat with a new partner what they had been through before.

From such data the following conclusions emerge. Ideally every couple making the transition into marriage should take a honeymoon trip of at least a week's duration if they can possibly afford the time and money. The honeymoon means most if it represents their first experience of complete sexual intimacy, though its meaning is not altogether lost upon those who have already had intercourse. In any case, the honeymoon is indispensable to the full-fledged celebration of the rites of passage into marriage.

There is a very dismal aura to the thought of getting married on Wednesday and going to work on Thursday. It is almost as if someone could ask you, "What did you do yesterday?" and you could answer, "Oh, nothing much. I just got married!"

PART TWO

Marriage

Once the couple return from their honeymoon, they begin married living in earnest. The first year of marriage is an initiation period which profoundly affects whether the marriage ultimately succeeds or fails (Chapter 9). Chapters 10 and 11 are concerned with the practical matters of earning and spending money, Chapters 12 and 13 with the couple's external involvement in kin networks and religious institutions, and Chapters 14 and 15 with their internal relationship in leisure generally and sexual activity in particular.

Every couple face the challenge of maintaining a vital relationship over time (Chapter 16) nor can they escape the necessity of conflict resolution (Chapter 17). If these processes do not succeed, many couples turn to divorce (and hopefully remarriage) in the search for marital happiness (Chapter 18).

9 Initiating Marriage Roles

This chapter is concerned with organizing the new family. This requires working out reciprocal patterns of husbandly and wifely behavior, especially in making decisions and doing housework.

Marriage as a System of Roles

Chapter 2 emphasized the value of choosing a partner with similar role conceptions and expectations. Marriage is a miniature social system which must be kept in equilibrium if it is to function smoothly. The equilibration of marriage requires meshing each partner's behavior with the other's expectations.

There is a second sense in which marriage is a social system. As a relatively independent social unit, every marriage is more or less self-sufficient. To maintain a household and manage the family finances (to say nothing of less tangible services) requires that essential tasks be performed. Since there are only two members of the household, whatever functions are not performed by one partner must be done by the other, or else the system breaks down. It does not matter much whether the husband or the wife carries out the trash, but it matters a great deal that someone does it.

By and large, role differentiation is expected to follow sex lines. Our society says not only that the lawn should be mowed but that the husband should be the one to do it. Role expectations brought into marriage not only predict what the husband or wife will do but are "evaluative standards applied to an incumbent of a position." (Gross, 1958) They are beliefs about what the spouse *ought* to do. Were our society completely standard-

201

ized, the partners' sets of role expectations would coincide. The fact that it is not means that no two people have identical expectations, no matter how carefully they have chosen each other.

Enacting Marriage Roles

The acid test of role compatibility comes in the first year. After the limits on premarital interaction are removed, husband and wife begin acting out their roles in full.

PRECONCEPTIONS OF ROLE BEHAVIOR. Each partner wants to be a good husband or wife and begins acting out his own preconceptions. Few of these conceptions are conscious; they are largely the residue of childhood observations of the parents' example. When the behavior of husband and wife turns out to be complementary, it commands no attention and hence no awareness. Except for unusually incompatible couples the bulk of marriage-role behavior happens automatically.

Nevertheless, over half the national sample studied by Gurin, Veroff, and Feld (1960) felt personally inadequate as a marriage partner. They criticized themselves most often for inadequacies in the division of labor (as provider or housekeeper) and secondarily for dominating the spouse or not being protective or considerate enough. To feel inadequate means to be aware of a gap between one's role conceptions and one's role enactments. The higher the standards one sets for oneself, the greater the likelihood of feeling inadequate. Such idealism is especially characteristic of young couples (whom Blood and Wolfe [1960] report are also the best role performers).

NEEDS AFFECT ROLE BEHAVIOR. So far we have pretended that role behavior is influenced entirely by ideology. Yet role enactments are also influenced by personality factors such as needs and drives. Each individual seeks to satisfy his needs through a socially acceptable role. However, if his needs run counter to the prescribed role, his behavior may respond more to the needs than to the expectations. If both partners have unconventional needs, role reversal may work well internally (even though it is likely to incur public censure). However, if competing needs produce begrudging submission on the part of the loser, discontent is magnified when the conflict is resolved contrary to social norms:

> Mother definitely dominates our family. Dad has withdrawn from the family circle and lets her make most of the decisions. He hasn't submitted wholeheartedly, however. There is a strong undercurrent of resentment and rebellion within him which my mother is a little afraid of.

Even when the wife needs to dominate and the husband needs to submit, both are likely to feel ambivalent about a role structure which is not
socially approved.

CIRCUMSTANCES AFFECT ROLE BEHAVIOR. External circumstances also
shape role enactments. A man may believe in being the breadwinner, and
psychologically need to be, yet have no opportunity. He may be unemploy-
able due to illness or discrimination, or temporarily unemployed by a
strike or recession. Deprived of the chance to play his preferred role, he
may even be forced into role reversal if his wife supports the family while
he keeps house. The fact that one has no choice but to violate one's own
conceptions does not make the experience less demoralizing.

Role Conflicts

Discrepancies between one's role conceptions and enactments might be
called a kind of "role conflict"—intrapersonal conflict. But since marriage
is a social system, we are primarily interested in conflicts when one partner's enactments violate the other's expectations, that is, in interpersonal
conflict.

All new couples find that the partner falls short somewhere. Two types
of noncomplementary behavior occur. (1) Both partners may compete for
the same role. For example, each expects to decide which family to visit
at Christmas time. If each has always been home for Christmas, both may
assume that marriage enlarges rather than alters this pattern. Each partner's
unconscious assumption contradicts what the other takes for granted, without either one knowing it. (2) Both partners may avoid a disliked task.
Each may expect the other to carry out the trash and find no place for
doing it in his conceptions of his own role. The husband may feel it is
women's work because it is connected with keeping house, while the wife
feels it is men's work because the trash can is outdoors.

As soon as role discrepancies are discovered, there is a practical urgency
about getting them resolved. Married living is strained until they are. Most
couples realign their expectations and enactments sooner or later. If not,
the stress on the marital bond is severe. For example, take incompatibility
in decision-making. Since women tend to be more feminist than men, it is
rare to find a woman whose husband is more equalitarian than she. When
this combination occurs, it causes little conflict. If the husband prefers to
give the wife more equality than she wants to assume, he may be disappointed, but there is no struggle for power. The opposite combination
(an equalitarian wife and a patriarchal husband) is explosive. If the
wife wants to be independent and the husband objects, friction is inevit-

able. If she is denied the voice she wants, she is liable to become a nagging wife.

The combination of patriarchal husband and equalitarian wife is so disastrous that it is found chiefly among divorced couples. In a study of the role ideas of married and divorced couples in Chillicothe, Ohio, Jacobson (1952) found that the divorced couples characteristically held these conflicting views, but still-married couples seldom did.

Among married students, Ort (1950) found that the larger the number of conflict areas, the less happy the marriage. Wives were typically disappointed by the husband's failure to continue to be an affectionate lover, while husbands were unhappy about the wife's failure to be more active sexually. Husbands at Brigham Young University similarly complained most about their wives' sexual apathy, while the wives complained most about their husbands' failure to spend enough time at home (see Table 9-1). Perhaps the fact that all the husbands were enrolled in a university whereas 30 per cent of the wives had never been to college made it hard for the wives to empathize with their husbands' preoccupation with their studies.

Also noteworthy in Table 9-1 is the larger total number of complaints made by wives. In every area of marriage except the sexual, more wives than husbands had grievances. The reasons for the large number of feminine complaints are undoubtedly many and complex. We will see again and again, however, that wives are more grievance-conscious than husbands. (Nor is this a uniquely American phenomenon. In my study of Japanese marriages, I found the wives less satisfied than their husbands with their marriages [Blood, 1967].)

Table 9-1. Complaints of Role Expectation Violations, by Husbands and Wives, in Campus Marriages

Behavior	PARTNER COMPLAINING OF ROLE EXPECTATION VIOLATION BY SPOUSE	
	Husband	Wife
Verbal expression of affection	20%	19%
Frequency of sexual intercourse	23	15
Care of the home	17	19
Sharing of ideas	16	14
Spending family income	12	11
Spending time at home	3	14
Personal neatness and appearance	9	8
Total	100%	100%
Number of complaints	94	134
Number of respondents	60	60

Adapted from Cutter and Dyer, 1965: 198. *Source:* Campus marriages at Brigham Young University (Utah) in which the husband was under 23 years of age.

The Moralistic Dimension of Role Conflicts

Role conflicts are difficult to cope with because they are laden with value judgments. Role expectations are "evaluative standards," so any husband who violates his wife's expectations is shirking his duty or infringing on her rights. This is more than a personal affront. He has transgressed against what the whole society expected of him. Not that everybody really holds the same view. But the unconscious acquisition of role expectations in childhood lends them an appearance of absolutism. This gives role contenders a sense of self-righteousness and of moral indignation which is infuriating to the spouse since he feels equally strongly in return.

Though partners with incongruent role expectations each tend to feel that "I am right and you are wrong," the surrounding world is not likely to be divided so evenly. An immigrant husband, for example, is likely to discover that Old World expectations are not reinforced but condemned by popular opinion. As a result, his role enactments are censured not only by those within but also by others outside the family:

> Occasionally my father has tried to be authoritarian. But his authoritarian attitude is in conflict with the democratic currents of our time. My father is vaguely aware of it and has sometimes seemed bewildered when his sporadic attempts to rule the family have not been successful. He tries to get his friends to sympathize with him but even they tell us just to humor him when he gets Napoleonic.

In Chapter 17 I will explore the processes of resolving role conflicts. Meanwhile, I will turn to an examination of the structural patterns assumed by American marriages.

The Power Structure of American Marriages

"Power structure" refers to the partners' influence in allocating resources of time, energy, money, and facilities. It includes both their influence over each other as persons and their unilateral areas of influence in family operations.

Power may be wielded equally or unequally in marriage. Equality involves either sharing all decisions ("syncratic" power) or making an equal number of separate decisions ("autonomic" power). Inequality traditionally yields dominance to the husband, but wives also sometimes dominate.

American marriages are highly equalitarian (Blood and Wolfe, 1960). Especially at first, couples tend to be syncratic, talking over major decisions and arriving at joint solutions. Even then, however, some aspects of marriage are controlled autonomously, especially decisions linked to sex roles in the division of labor. For instance, husbands usually make the final decision about their own jobs since that's "his own business," while wives make food purchasing and petty housekeeping decisions.

The longer a marriage exists, the greater the tendency to make decisions separately. This is one form of estrangement in marriage. Just as husbands and wives talk less about the day's events, they talk less about decisions, leaving power in the hands of the partner with the greater interest. Since family affairs are the wife's specialty, this means shifting not only from syncratic to autonomic decision-making but toward wife-dominance. Wives seldom seize power, but husbands often abdicate it.

Decision-Making Pattern and Marital Satisfaction

Because newlyweds enjoy doing things together, syncratic power structures should be the most satisfactory. Table 9-2 shows that this is indeed the case.

In general, the more husbands and wives share in making decisions, the healthier the marriage. Unilateral decision-making may be quick and easy, but it is liable to allocate resources contrary to the wishes of the unconsulted partner. At the same time failure to maintain communication with the partner leaves him feeling alienated.

> Unlike most of our neighbors, ours was a definitely patriarchal family. For example, social invitations were always referred to Daddy before the reply was given, final permission for our going places was granted by him, and it was he who took care of the serious disciplining. A few years ago, he decided he wanted to move, and with very little family discussion and despite our criticism, he bought a new house. Once he had made up his mind, Mother accepted the fact without more ado since she knew it was hopeless to oppose him.

However, the unhappiest women are not the unconsulted wives of dominant husbands but "deserted" wives left with the burden of making decisions

Table 9-2. Wife's Marital Satisfaction, by Decision-making Pattern

| | DECISION-MAKING PATTERN | | | |
	Syncratic	Autonomic	Husband Dominant	Wife Dominant
Wife's marital satisfaction	5.06	4.70	4.64	4.40
Number of families	120	187	120	91

Adapted from Blood and Wolfe, 1960: 258. *Source:* Representative sample of Detroit wives, 1955.

alone. Decision-making at its best is not only equalitarian and shared but mutually deferent. Altruistic partners are willing to go more than halfway in meeting each other's wishes. Buerkle (1961) finds that well-adjusted wives have "deference and respect for the husband's judgment," and well-adjusted husbands show "respect and deference for the personal feelings of the wife." Their final decision is often a fifty-fifty compromise, but the willingness of both partners to concede more than half the battle means that solutions are arrived at generously rather than grudgingly.

Sources of Power in Marriage

The balance of power between husband and wife is influenced to some extent by their philosophy about marriage roles. Especially at the beginning, their behavior is shaped by preconceptions about how decision-making ought to be handled. In the long run, however, pragmatic factors affect power more. The partners bring some resources to marriage from prior experience. The remainder are determined after marriage as the partners go out into the community to tap resources relevant to the decision-making process.

MATE-SELECTION AND THE BALANCE OF POWER. In Chapter 2, I described individuals who need to dominate and others who need to be submissive. When such people enter complementary marriages, the balance of power is determined by their combined personality characteristics. How dominant a given individual is depends on the situation. A man who would be equalitarian with a vigorous wife might dominate a clinging vine. Hence the balance of power in a given marriage cannot be predicted from the personality characteristics of either partner alone but only in combination.

Blood and Wolfe reported two background characteristics that affect the balance of power: whichever partner is (1) better educated and (2) older tends to wield the most power. Formal schooling provides knowledge and communication skills rarely equaled by those who quit school early. As a result, better-educated wives tend to dominate their husbands, and better-educated husbands to dominate their wives. Where one partner has been to college and the other has not, the latter is likely to feel inferior. As a result he is more deferent in decision-making.

Table 9-3 is an example of deference to better-educated partners. These would have been religiously mixed marriages but one partner converted to the other's faith. Note how often the better-educated partner won the decision. Presumably he both dominates the marriage and offers social mobility rewards as well (assuming that his denomination has greater social prestige).

Table 9-3. Change in Religious Affiliation, by Comparative Education of Husband and Wife

Direction of Change in Religious Affiliation	COMPARATIVE EDUCATION		
	Husband More	Equal	Wife More
Wife changed to husband's affiliation	74%	50%	27%
Husband changed to wife's affiliation	26	50	73
Total	100%	100%	100%
Number of couples	19	26	11

Adapted from Babchuk et al., 1967: 555. Source: Parents of sixth-grade public school boys in a Nebraska city. Limited to couples in which one partner changed to the religious affiliation of the other. (In 19 additional cases, religious heterogamy was resolved by changing to a third faith.)

Although differences in education of as little as a year or two noticeably alter the balance of power, differences in age must be bigger to be significant. Since the average husband is several years older, influential age differences are correspondingly skewed. In the Blood-Wolfe study, husbands 11 or more years older and wives four or more years older had significantly more power than those in between. In extreme cases older husbands have a father-daughter relationship with their wives. Having lived longer, they have more savoir-faire and sophistication, so their wives look up to them and depend on them. Conversely, older wives tend to mother young husbands, taking care of them and supplying the main strength in marriage.

In general, any previous experience or training that gives one partner greater knowledge, skill, or self-confidence, tips the balance of power in his favor.

EXTERNAL PARTICIPATION AND THE BALANCE OF POWER. The die is not entirely cast at the beginning of marriage. The husband's and wife's participation in the outside world also increases the resources they bring to the "bargaining table." The most tangible resource is money. If only the husband works, the higher his income, the greater his influence in major economic decisions. Decisions about investments, real estate, and employment become so complex and delicate that wives leave them up to the husband's judgment (Blood and Wolfe).

Where income is earned by both partners, the balance of power shifts correspondingly. The more the balance of participation in the economic system tips away from the husband, the more his power declines (see Table 9-4).

It would be a mistake to assume that shifts in the balance of power reflect explicit economic bargaining. Occasionally husbands or wives say, "It's my money, so I can do with it what I want." But only at great cost to marital solidarity. Normally, family income, whatever its origin, goes into the family exchequer to be distributed according to need.

Economic productivity heightens family influence chiefly in psychological and social ways. Psychologically, a successful man or woman gains self-confidence and skill in managing affairs. As the community recognizes his success, he gains prestige in the eyes of the partner. The crucial evidence that the balance of power is not determined purely economically comes from noneconomic forms of external participation. Blood and Wolfe found that the balance of power also reflects whichever partner belongs to more organizations or goes to church more often. Thus, power can be derived from voluntary community activities as much as from paid employment. Conversely, stay-at-home wives (or husbands) are relatively inactive in major decisions.

Emphasizing *major* decisions is necessary because routine household decisions are often delegated to the stay-at-home partner. Influence over housekeeping actually decreases for wives who go to work (Blood, 1962). In general, the balance of power reflects not only the resources but the practical interest of the two partners.

The Division of Labor in the Home

The division of labor in the home involves the allocation of responsibility for running the home. In contrast to the generally shared decision-making in American marriages is the highly specialized task-performance which makes "division" of labor an apt label. Despite cartoons of aproned husbands, little change has occurred in the traditional split between men's work and women's work (Blood and Wolfe, 1960). Men still do the heavy outside tasks like shoveling snow, mowing lawns, and juggling storm windows and screens. They do simple repairs around the house and wash the

Table 9-4. Husband's Power, by Comparative Work Participation of Husband and Wife

	WIFE NOT EMPLOYED			WIFE EMPLOYED		
	Husband Overtime	Husband Full Time	Husband None	Husband Overtime	Husband Full Time	Husband None
Husband's mean power	5.62	5.28	4.88	4.50	4.46	2.67
Number of families	195	218	25	44	57	3

From Blood and Wolfe, 1960: 40. Copyright © 1960 by The Free Press, A Corporation; used by permission. *Source:* Representative sample of Detroit wives, 1955. A higher figure represents a larger share of marital decisions made by husbands.

car. Women do almost everything else: cooking, table-setting, and dish-washing; dusting, vacuuming, and mopping; washing, ironing, and mending clothes; making beds and picking up the house.

Many masculine tasks are seasonal or intermittent whereas most feminine ones occur every day. As a result, the division of time is very uneven. Wives do most of the work, husbands only a small fraction. A national survey found housewives working five and a half hours every day at home compared to 25 minutes for their husbands (Converse, 1966). Fifteen minutes was all it took the average man to fix things around the house. For ten minutes more he helped his wife. Apparently this was enough to satisfy most wives (only one-fourth expressed a desire for more help).

The biggest daily chore for wives was cleaning the house (2.2 hours), followed by 1.7 hours cooking and washing dishes, and 1.4 hours doing the laundry. The main reason for this one-sidedness is that the husband's chief assignment is away from home. The 40 hours he spends on the job prevent him from doing more housework. Conversely a nonworking wife has ample time for housework.

The tasks allocated to men and women are affected by human biology. Intermittent child-bearing correlates nicely with child-rearing and house-keeping, leaving the man to earn money away from home. The few tasks men do around the house reflect their larger muscles and mechanical apti-tude (Scheinfeld, 1943). Car-washing, for example, fits masculine mechan-ical interests and away-from-home traveling.

Many middle-class women report that their husbands are a net loss as far as housework is concerned: they create so much untidiness around the house that their modest help is only partial compensation. One-half of all the middle-class housewives in a Manhattan study complained about their husband's messiness—his commonest fault (Mayer, 1966):

> When my husband comes home from work, he takes off his coat and drops it, then he pulls off his shoes and throws them about. He lets his clothes lie about instead of putting them in the hamper.

And another Mayer case:

> He's untidy. When he eats in the living room, he leaves his plate right there. He doesn't throw his mail away after looking at it—he just leaves it lying around.

Most husbands perform the traditional masculine tasks. On the border-line between masculine and feminine are some tasks that are harder to classify, such as shopping and paying bills. Either sex is physically capable of doing them, and they are ambiguously linked to other roles, for ex-ample, to the husband's earning money and daily exodus from the home versus the wife's spending money for food, clothing, and interior-decorating. As a result, many couples share these responsibilities, while others may assign them to either the husband or the wife.

Keeping track of money and bills is an administrative task closely associated with the family power structure and with the size of the husband's income. The higher his income, the greater the likelihood that he will control the outflow of money by paying bills and figuring accounts (Blood and Wolfe).

Specialization in Task Performance

The specialized nature of the division of labor in the business world increases productivity. Is specialization in the home equally efficient? Probably it is for complicated tasks like making pies. But most housekeeping tasks are so simple that peak efficiency is soon reached. Hence specialized family activities may be more a psychological than a practical necessity:

> Each of us likes to be autonomous in our own roles. Tom worked for a summer as a camp cook and knows plenty about cooking and yet never criticizes or offers any suggestions about my cooking unless I ask him. Once when I cooked pizza I found out by asking him that he knew a lot more about it than I did. He told me that he wouldn't have said anything and let me use my own method if I had not asked him. Likewise when we bought an outboard motor and he had trouble working it, I didn't offer to help him, even though I knew something about it, because I felt that it was his role and prerogative and that unless he asked me to help I would not say or do anything.

Figure 9-1 shows that couples tend to specialize more as they move through the family life cycle. One reason for increased specialization is the partners' declining interest in togetherness. At first, keeping house is fun—especially when lovers can do it together. After a while, however, the partners drift apart. The path of least resistance is to work separately, each at his own task. Then there are no arguments about whose turn it is to take out the garbage or when they should do the dishes. Each can work at his own pace at his own convenience, unhampered by the partner's whims.

Modern marriages do not require that *all* housework be done jointly for maximum satisfaction. The most satisfied wives in Blood and Wolfe's study shared less than half their tasks. Nevertheless, husbands who *never* shared any tasks had the least satisfactory marriages, no matter how well they may have done their own jobs.

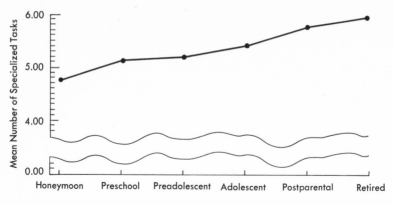

Stage in Family Life Cycle

Adapted from Blood and Wolfe, 1960: 70. Average number out of a total of eight
tasks which are performed unilaterally by the husband and/or the wife.

Figure 9-1. Task Specialization, by Stage in Family Cycle

Adaptability to Special Circumstances

The normal pattern is for the wife to do most of the housework. However, this takes ample time and energy. If she contracts away her time to an
employer or loses her vitality through illness, the housekeeping suffers
unless husband, children, or servants come to the rescue. Most husbands
respond to such crises, so the balance of housekeeping shifts with the
amount of time at the husband and wife's disposal.

The one reversal in Table 9-5 involves retired husbands whose wives are
also at home. Retired husbands do no more housework than those who are
employed full-time. The reason is:

> If the wife is home all the time, she can do her traditional tasks without
> much help from the husband. Even if he's home full time (as when
> neither partner works), he is not likely to invade her sphere as long as
> she is capable of doing her own traditional work (Blood and Wolfe,
> 1960: 63).

Provided that both partners have enough time to do their own tasks,
the relative time at their disposal doesn't matter. But when time gets short,
both partners are pressed into service to the extent of their availability.
Particularly when the wife goes to work, the division of labor must be
revised. Then, the wife's time is cut so severely that something has to give.
Housekeeping standards may sag, efficiency increase, and some of the burden be shifted to others. In the United States as a whole, wives slashed
their housework time by two hours or 36 per cent when they went to work

Table 9-5. Wife's Household Task Performance, by Comparative Work Participation of Husband and Wife

	Comparative Work Participation					
	WIFE NOT EMPLOYED			WIFE EMPLOYED		
	Husband Overtime	Husband Full Time	Husband None	Husband Overtime	Husband Full Time	Husband None
Wife's mean household task performance	5.81	5.57	5.64	4.66	3.40	2.33
Number of families	198	218	28	50	58	3

Adapted from Blood and Wolfe, 1960: 62. *Source:* Representative sample of Detroit wives. A higher figure represents a larger share of the housework done by wives.

(Converse). How much the husband can take up the slack depends on how much he is home. That most men don't help very much is suggested by a study of Blood and Hamblin (1958) in which husbands of working wives did 25 per cent of the housework, only slightly more than the normal 15 per cent.

Illness for the wife similarly shifts the division of labor in the husband's direction. Conversely, if the husband takes on extra vocational or community responsibility, the wife must forego his help and take over his tasks. Such adaptability maintains the balance between the husband's and wife's total roles in life, inside and outside the home.

Support for the Wife's Role

Lest it be thought that keeping house is an unattractive role thrust upon married women by tradition and circumstance, note the following description of its advantages as an occupation:

> Relatively speaking, the homemaker's job is more varied both during each day and from day to day. . . . The variety of tasks should relieve not only the monotony but also the fatigue and strain. The homemaker, furthermore, since she is both manager and worker, is able to plan her own tasks and is free to lay them aside or to take them up in the order she chooses. She has no boss except the exigencies of the work itself; she need punch no time clock; she can arrange her own rest periods and vacations. . . . Furthermore, the housewife works in her own home with working conditions in the way of light, air, cleanliness, and layout of workroom under her own control. She need spend no time going to and returning from her work. The fact too that the work is for herself and for her family should augment its interest and relieve its tedium. . . . The order, harmony, cleanliness, beauty, healthfulness, and restfulness that

she achieves are the product of her labors and hers alone. They are not lost in the contributions of scores of others (Kyrk, 1953: 278).

Despite these advantages, housework has liabilities. The more challenging the prehousekeeping role, the starker the contrast:

> I had to give up a lot when I got married—sorority life, not worrying about meals, the rah-rah of going to games with a bunch of kids, talking with people about subjects you can get worked up about. Those things are more glamorous than a kitchen. Housework was a comedown after the excitement and stimulation of college.

The most objectionable features of housework are isolation and lack of recognition. Childless housewives spend their working hours alone. Radio and TV are poor substitutes for live companions. Somewhat better are telephone calls to girl friends. Most satisfying are friends and relatives who drop in for midmorning coffee or collaborate on major chores. Even when exploited to the full, these remedies fail to match the interpersonal stimulation of most jobs.

Isolation is physical as well as social. The converse of not having to commute is being confined to the same four walls day in and day out. Not only is isolation monotonous during working hours, but the fact that most leisure is spent in the same location creates the housewife's proverbial sense of never getting her work done. With no boundary between work place and leisure place, complete relaxation is difficult.

Recognition for housework comes naturally from empathic husbands. It doesn't take much effort to reward one's wife with compliments. In any case, she has the satisfaction of knowing she is meeting basic needs as she cooks, presses and spruces things up:

> For me the challenges of housekeeping are to keep a supply of clean clothes available, to get meals ready on time and to keep the house neat, all within the limits of my husband's income. The test of my success is that my husband and children would rather be home than elsewhere. It's not that I do all the work. George puts the children to bed at night, and on Saturday or Sunday he takes over the family completely so I can go out by myself. The children want to "help" me with my tasks which slows me down now but will be a real help when they are older. I feel both George and the children are happier if they have certain jobs to do at home. In the last analysis, though, I am the one who ultimately makes this house into a home.

10 *Occupational Roles and Marriage*

The husband's and wife's employment profoundly affect their marriage. The financial consequences are obvious, and we have seen how their work affects the power structure and division of labor in marriage. Occupational involvement affects marriages in many other ways, depending on the nature of the job and the degree of commitment to it.

The Husband's Occupation

The husband's occupation affects his family *via:* (1) resources provided for family living; (2) conflicts between occupational and family roles; (3) new experiences to which he is exposed which socialize him differentially; and (4) external demands imposed on family living patterns.

Resources for Family Living

The husband's work produces both income and social prestige for the family.

MONEY. Despite the increased number of working wives, husbands are still the main source of sustenance. The family's standard of living depends primarily on the money he earns. In general, the higher his income, the more satisfied his dependents are with their standard of living. Exceptions arise, however, when the husband earns less than his reference group. If the wife's standard of comparison is unusually high, she may be disappointed even though he earns more than the national average. For instance, Blood and Wolfe found that Jewish wives in Detroit were not satisfied with Detroit-average incomes but only with Jewish-average incomes (several thousand dollars higher). Most American wives, however, are satisfied with their standard of living. Most husbands provide economic security for their families and are rewarded with their dependents' appreciation.

SOCIAL STATUS. Money cannot buy everything. Even though respect in the eyes of the community is generally related to income, there are exceptions. Money earned by disreputable means seldom buys access to better social circles, although inherited wealth tends to become respectable in subsequent generations. Conversely, families with little income may enjoy a fine reputation in the community if the husband is a professional. An unscrupulous businessman may have ten times a clergyman's income but only one-tenth the social standing.

If a man doesn't like his work, this affects his relationship to his wife and children. Family relations are undermined when the husband ranks low in community esteem. By contrast, if he holds a high-prestige job, his family respects him too.

Conflicting Roles: Occupation Versus Family

The resources provided by the husband's occupation do not come free of charge. They must be earned by investing time and energy. Since most husbands work away from home, this is time and energy taken away from the family. As long as the husband invests no more than everybody else, he isn't perceived as depriving his family. Customary expenditures are taken for granted. But when a man spends more time or different time than other husbands, family living is altered. Then the husband is caught between the demands of his job and of his family.

A QUESTION OF VALUES. When occupational roles and family roles collide, a couple's hierarchy of values is tested. If they hold the same values, the dilemma is easily resolved. Even if the family role is subordinated, family solidarity is preserved when the choice is mutual.

In recent years the American value system has shifted away from occupational values toward family values. More college students expect family roles to be their chief source of satisfaction in life than give priority to their occupation (Goldsen, 1960). Perhaps, then, role conflicts will often be resolved in favor of the family:

I purposely chose a job with a company that I felt would not hold the tension and continuous pushing that the big corporations hold. I don't want to come home to my family in the evenings tense from the day's work and preoccupied with my job. Both my wife and I feel that the family should be of first-place importance before my job. I intend to do my very best in the engineering field and to strive to progress but not to the point of sacrificing my time and relationship with my family. For example, I will take a lesser salary if it means being able to spend more time with my family or living in a territory where the children are most happy with school and friends and my wife and I are most happy.

On the other hand, if both husband and wife are eager to rise to the top, family sacrifices seem petty:

> I must admit that I am jealous of the fact that Mel has the luxury of an expense account and travels a good deal, and I do get irritated when he fails to call me and say he'll be late for dinner. But I realize that if he is to progress up the ladder of success, he will have to relinquish some extra time at home in favor of the office. If he gets so engrossed in his work that he forgets to call me, it's a sign he's really putting his whole heart and soul into his work.

What if husband and wife disagree? Then the husband's devotion (or lack of it) to his work becomes a source of contention. Pressure to work harder may come from either partner. Normally, the husband devotes more time to his job than the wife thinks he should. As a participant in the occupational system he is constantly exposed to its incentives and competition. Successful business executives reach the top precisely through their willingness to subordinate other roles to the demands of the job. When Henry (1949) described the successful executive as "a man who has left home," he meant the parental home, but he could just as well have meant the marital one:

> All the successful executives have strong mobility drives. They feel the necessity to move continually upward and to accumulate the rewards of increased accomplishment. . . . All show high drive and achievement desire. They conceive of themselves as hard-working and achieving people who must accomplish in order to be happy. . . . The executive is essentially an active, striving, aggressive person. His underlying personality motivations are active and aggressive. . . . This constant motivator unfortunately cannot be shut off. It may be part of the reason why so many executives find themselves unable to take vacations leisurely or to stop worrying about already solved problems.

Whether achievement drive is "good" or "bad" depends on the context. To a corporation it is a priceless asset. To a wife it may be a source of pride and vicarious gratification. Nevertheless, it also means that her husband is home relatively little and even then his thoughts are liable to be elsewhere. LeMasters (1957) reported, for example, that General Motors provided its chief executive with complete living facilities near his office so he wouldn't have to go home except on weekends. A major study of Protestant ministers in the United States found that half of them had not taken a single day off for recreation with their wives during the preceding month (Douglas, 1965). Many of the neglected wives felt alienated from their husbands. For a wife with high affiliation needs and low mobility aspirations, such occupational devotion is horrifying. She feels rejected and unloved. She pressures her husband to stay home and take longer vacations. To accede to her values, he must sacrifice his own ambitions. If he doesn't she feels sacrificed to the corporation. In neither case are both partners likely to be happy.

Sometimes, the ambitious partner is the wife and the familistic one the husband. One study of young couples found more wives than husbands willing to make sacrifices so the husband could get ahead. Specifically, more wives were willing to move to a strange part of the country, leave friends behind, send the children to a poorer school, and even postpone having the next child. The biggest difference was in the partners' willingness to have the husband spend less time with the wife and children. Two-thirds of the wives but less than one-third of the husbands were willing to sacrifice family companionship to vocational ambition (Westoff, 1961).

Perhaps this willingness of wives to make sacrifices should be interpreted as an altruistic deference to what they think the husband wants. When wives push the husband beyond his own ambitions, however, the result is conspicuously unhappy. Such a man escapes into fishing expeditions or fraternal lodges to be safe from his wife's nagging. Sometimes he makes half-hearted attempts to please, but since her values are not his, these efforts are not likely to last long enough to pay off. Even if they did, the compensation in prestige and promotion might not seem worthwhile to him. Indeed, since promotion brings increased responsibility, it only makes such a man feel trapped. Conflicting values never have easy solutions. Such couples are poorly matched. Theoretically they never should have married in the first place. They must endure continuing conflict up to the very day the husband retires from the outside world.

A QUESTION OF OCCUPATIONS. Sometimes the trouble comes from the job itself. It's not that the husband voluntarily spends too much time at work but he is required to do so. Some jobs compel him to be away from home long hours or irregular hours, whether he likes it or not. Occupations that serve the public's leisure, for example, upset the normal schedule of family living. Although the wife can adjust her schedule accordingly, the children's school hours prevent them from having much contact with their father. Even for the parents, not being able to entertain restricts their social life as a couple. Still more difficult to adjust to is employment on a "swing shift" where family life constantly changes because one week the husband works days and the next, nights (Mott, 1965).

Other occupations require emergency duty outside regular hours. A doctor's plans must often be tentative, subject to last-minute interference. In some organizations, simulated emergencies remind both sexes that potential conflict between job and family is inherent in the contract:

> The commanding officer at one air base organized a duty night, which after two hours of work, turned into a stag party till 3:00 A.M. There were later objections from the wives of officers present, about which the commanding officer said. . . . "I called that duty night because that's exactly what it was. There's too much of this dashing for the gate right after a man's shift is over to get home. . . . I wanted to take this means of informing my men that radar comes first, family . . . second. If I, as their CO, want them to stay till three in the morning to work they'll do it. If I want them to play poker till three, they'll do it, because I said so. Let the wives gripe. It's time they found out their husbands are in the Air Force." (Gross, 1953: 372)

Another source of strain is the distance between home and work. As cities grow in size, commuting time devours family time:

> Being in a relatively suburban residential commuting town, the pace of family living was swift. My father left at seven every morning and returned dead-tired from commuting at seven. The business pressures on him were great and much of his time home was spent with business reports. There was occasional conflict when my brother and I interrupted him with our noise and wrestling. Even when he was home, he seldom had time or energy to be a father to us.

The sharpest conflict is between family roles and traveling jobs. Jokes about traveling salesmen testify to the unsettling consequences. Just as separation disrupts engagement, travel undermines husband-wife relationships and creates opportunities for competing personal involvements. Figure 10-1 shows that traveling salesmen's marriages were the least happy of white-collar occupations.

Traveling salesmen get into trouble because they are emancipated from social controls in strange communities away from family and friends. The difference between clergymen and traveling salesmen is partly a question of social support. Clergymen face the strictest social control because their behavior is expected to be exemplary. Similarly, teachers and professors are public employees expected to set good examples. Clergymen and professors also have flexible schedules so they can spend time with their families. Yet even traveling men can choose how to spend their time when they are home. In Nagasaki, I met a Japanese woman who saw little of her merchant marine husband during his annual shore leaves because he hobnobbed with friends. Contrast this with the following case:

> One of the pleasantest memories of my childhood was the Saturday noon luncheon. Because my father's work took him out of town a lot, we saw very little of him during the week. However, he always arranged to eat lunch with us on Saturdays and then do something special together for the afternoon. This weekly reunion was one of the things my mother, brother and I always looked forward to. We gained a greater feeling of closeness by being with my father under completely relaxed conditions for a few hours. We also worked harder all week so we could make him happy with our accomplishments.

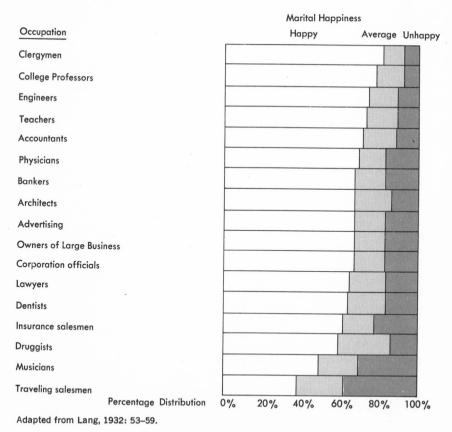

Figure 10-1. Marital Happiness, by Husband's Occupation

Differential Adult Socialization

The husband's work may reshape his outlook on life. If the partners fail to share these experiences, they are differentially affected. As a consequence, an originally compatible relationship may be strained.

Differential socialization is especially likely when the husband is socially mobile. Upward mobility doesn't necessarily mean that husband and wife grow apart, but it takes effort to enable the lagging partner to keep up with the leader. If this effort is not made, disengagement may be rapid:

> Father started out at the very bottom of the company ladder and has worked his way up to his present position as branch manager. He has never stopped learning, thinking, and developing new interests. Materially, this has contributed to harmony in that my mother has more luxuries than she possessed as a girl. On the other hand, it has contributed to discord in that she ceased development at marriage. While he began moving in new circles, she clung to a small circle of friends and a few outside activities.

Jobs offer mobility channels for working wives just as for working husbands. In either case, if only one partner forges ahead, a gap opens between the partners:

> Mother and Dad both started out at the same place since neither of them went to college. But Mother has actively striven for self-improvement, spending her earnings carefully, and taking full advantage of the contacts she makes in her work. As a result she has gained higher status than Dad and puts pressure on him to keep up with her (which he fails to do). Because of the uneasy feeling between them, both parents avoid entering into outside activities together and rarely do any entertaining at home.

Downward mobility creates even more strain. Not only do the partners grow apart but the standard of living falls. Hence economic deprivation is added to differential socialization. Roth and Peck (1951) found that both downward mobile and unilaterally mobile marriages suffer. If the wife moves upward occupationally, the marriage suffers because she can't confer her new status on her husband the way masculine mobility almost automatically benefits the wife. Differential mobility creates mixed marriages out of what were initially homogamous ones. Just as couples from different social backgrounds have difficulty in marriage (especially if the wife's status is higher), so do couples who move into different social circles. Although moving up together is never easy, it can be achieved if both partners will make the effort. Husbands resocialized on the job can tutor receptive wives (and vice versa).

Occupational Pressures on Family Living

Some occupations require the whole family to adopt certain styles of living or to live in special places.

CONFORMITY PRESSURES. Families in the public eye feel the influence of social expectations. The President's family know no privacy and must consider what others will think of every move. A minister's wife and children are supposed to behave well:

> We always had to keep the living room in order because Daddy was so particular that it be in perfect condition for anyone who might drop in. Whenever my parents were invited to a member's home for dinner, my brother and I felt that we were greatly wronged to have to always go along. My parents couldn't very well say to the hostess, "My children are very bored eating at your place so we got a baby sitter for them." When this type of conflict was at its peak, Fred and I were very angry with our parents, begrudgingly spoke to them on the day of the engagement, and shattered their nerves by shutting up like clams in obvious disgust when visiting.

Whyte (1952) noted that many corporations regulated social competition among their executives by creating detailed norms of family behavior for each level in the organization chart:

> One rule transcends all others: *Don't be too good.* Keeping up with the Joneses is still important. But where in pushier and more primitive times it implied going substantially ahead of the Joneses, today keeping up means just that: keeping up. . . . The good corporation wife . . . does not make friends uncomfortable by clothes too blatantly chic, by references to illustrious forebears, or by excessive good breeding. And she avoids intellectual pretensions like the plague.

Corporations differ, however. Some say explicitly that it is none of their business how their executive families live. In academia, the larger the institution the more likely it is to give faculty families free rein in their private lives. Similarly, established denominations allow their ministers more latitude for family life than new sects which demand priority for vocational roles (see Table 10-1).

The sharp differences between sectarian couples and church couples in their responses to conflicts between family and vocation demonstrate that, even in a given field, the demands of the occupation vary enormously.

Although Table 10-1 deals with hypothetical situations, the wives' actual responsibilities as "assistant pastors" infringed correspondingly on their companionship with their husbands and children. Only 19 per cent of the church wives reported such interference compared with 82 per cent of the sect wives.

Wives may become instruments of social mobility by making the right impression on the right people. In some occupations the right people are clients—actual or potential. In others they are superiors with the power to advance or hold back a man's career. In either case occupation-derived norms influence the family's style of life.

RESIDENCE REQUIREMENTS. Corporations also typically expect junior executives to climb the company ladder via the national circuit of branch offices. This requires men to move every few years. The main burden of moving falls on the wife:

> . . . it is she, who has only one life in contrast to her husband's two, who is called upon to do most of the adjusting. The move at once obsoletes most of her community friendships, severs her local business relationships with the bank and the stores, takes her from the house and the garden on which she worked so long, and if the move takes her to a large city it probably drops her living standards also (Whyte, 1951).

The central adjustment for the wife is transferring her housekeeping operation from one house to another. Modern vans make this less difficult than it once was, but the husband's briefcase or filing cabinet is still moved more easily than a houseful of furniture and children. Nevertheless, cor-

Table 10-1. Priority of Occupational or Family Role, for Ministers Employed by Churches versus Sects

A definite time had been previously scheduled for the husband to be with the family simply for the sake of companionship	TYPE OF EMPLOYER	
	Church	Sect
1. Husband would leave the family to call a meeting of the church board on request of an important church official	0	73%
2. Husband would leave the family to give counsel on a religious or moral matter	4%	88%
Number of husbands and wives	26	36

Adapted from Scanzoni, 1965: 398–400. *Source:* Sample of Protestant ministers in an unidentified metropolitan area. A church was defined as a denomination that "accepts" the social environment, whereas a sect "rejects" it. Reciprocal percentages of respondents said the husband should either postpone the occupational activity or decide on the basis of the urgency of the request.

poration wives find the moving itself less difficult than its unpredictability. Neither they nor their husbands determine *when* the next transfer will come, so life is uncertain. The corporation not only prescribes where they will live but changes the prescription at irregular intervals, requiring the family to be highly adaptable.

Families in international service encounter more exotic locales. For government officials and businessmen the destinations are usually the capitals of the world, though even capitals may seem strange when they are named Kabul or Lagos. For missionaries and other pioneers, home may be on primitive frontiers amid alien ways which tax the adaptability of wives in keeping house and raising children. Remote locations require shipping older children to distant boarding schools, and even wives must leave when conditions become revolutionary. Marriage ties and parent-child ties in such circumstances are subordinated to vocational commitment. As long as partners share that commitment, the balance is counted as gain rather than loss; the wife's sacrifices are her contribution to the husband's occupational role in the family division of labor. But the vocation's gain is the family's loss in face-to-face interaction.

The Wife's Occupation

An increasing number of wives are employed outside the home. Less than half the Detroit women married before World War I ever worked after marriage versus more than three-fourths of those married after World War II (Blood and Wolfe). The proportion of wives working at any one time has risen even more dramatically because married women today work longer than they used to. Between 1940 and 1961, the percentage of American wives currently employed more than doubled from 15 to 33 per cent (U.S. Women's Bureau). Nor was this the total who worked at some time during the year. For example, 31 per cent of all wives were working in March 1959, but an additional 11 per cent had worked some-time during the previous year (U.S. Bureau of Labor Statistics).

The time is approaching when paid employment will be an almost universal experience for wives at one point or another after marriage. The old taboo on work for married women has been thoroughly demolished. Even wives who don't work nowadays feel they could if they wanted to.

Conditions for Employment

Employment for married women may have become socially acceptable, but it depends on the balance of needs inside and outside the home more than on the aspirations of the mother.

ECONOMIC NECESSITY. "Need" is a slippery term, subject to both Madison Avenue manipulation and neighborhood example. The proverbial Joneses set the consumption pace. Wives are especially sensitive to neighborhood influence, since this is the world they inhabit:

> I'm afraid my wife is too ambitious. She never seems to be satisfied with what she has in life. If a neighbor buys a new car, she wants one too; if another changes the wallpaper she must do the same; if a third buys color television, she must have a better set. So she keeps wanting more and more money to spend every year.

Pressure to imitate is especially strong with objects that are externally visible like new cars or aluminum storm windows. After World War II television aerials spread from house to house like the flu, and Whyte (1954) found that window-ledge air conditioners were equally contagious.

Some families' needs are more basic. The easiest source of extra money is a second pay check. So the lower the husband's income, the higher the proportion of working wives (see Figure 10-2).

For low-income families, extra money goes for elemental necessities— food, clothing, and shelter. The higher the husband's income, the more choice couples have about the use of the wife's income and the more relative the question of need. Blood and Wolfe reported two ways in which relativity influenced the wife's decision to go to work. (1) If the husband had less education than the wife, she was apt to work to make up for his low-income potential. (2) If the husband was downward mobile in comparison to his father (that is, held a worse job), the wife responded to their mutual disappointment by going to work. In other words, if the husband could not provide the standard of living the wife expected, she filled the gap.

FREEDOM FROM CHILD-REARING RESPONSIBILITY. However, the wife's freedom to work depends on whether there are children at home. The younger the children, the greater her supervisory responsibility. For the first few months of life, babies are unable to tell the difference between their mother and other caretakers. However, the year between six months and 18 months appears to be a critical period in the child's development. (The Associated Press quoted psychiatrist Carl Stern as saying that mothers who are absent [or worried or distracted] at those ages are liable to cause depressions which scar children for life. "There are many exceptions, of course, but that age is the danger zone.")

If the husband's income is adequate and the children are young, wives

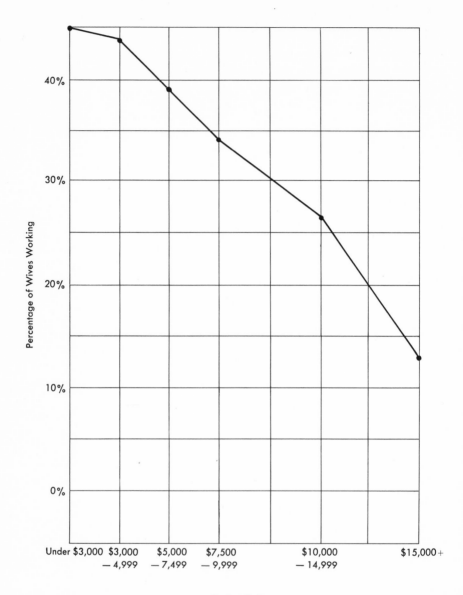

Adapted from Morgan et al., 1962: 114. Source: National sample, 1959. Wives who worked at any time in the year.

Figure 10-2. Proportion of Wives Working, by Husband's Income

have double reason to stay home. Conversely, low-income families without children have the highest proportion of working wives (see Figure 10-3).

The reversal of the usual relationship between income levels at the "unlaunched" stage (where children over 18 years of age are still at home) reflects the low-income tendency for older children to work and bring their pay check home, relieving economic pressure on the mother. At higher income levels "adult" children are more apt to be college students whose educational expenses are paid from the mother's earnings.

After the honeymoon peak, the proportion of working wives crests again between age 45 and 50 (Metropolitan Life Insurance Company, 1963). This led Blood and Wolfe to make the following predictions about the emerging life-cycle pattern of the employment of married women:

1. Nearly all wives are likely to work after marriage until their first pregnancy.
2. Very few mothers of preschool children (mostly hardship cases of severe economic necessity) will work even part-time away from their children.
3. When the last child enters first grade, employment will rise sharply

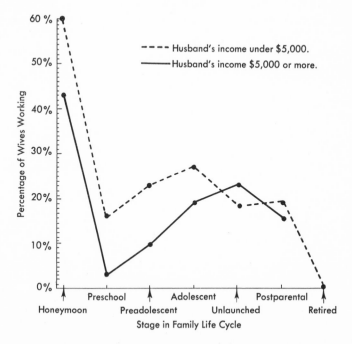

Adapted from Blood and Wolfe, 1960: 105. *Source:* Detroit wives working in 1955/husband's 1954 income.

Figure 10-3. Percentages of Wives Working, by Stage in Family Life Cycle by Husband's Income

and continue to increase until the last child leaves home or reaches adulthood, when employment will reach a second peak. This figure may not equal the pre-child-bearing starting point, since by this time most families have purchased a house and accumulated the major capital goods, diminishing their economic need. However, the increasing proportion of American children seeking increasingly expensive college educations provide a new financial incentive for mothers to work in the early postparental years.

Economic Consequences of the Wife's Employment

Some of the money earned by working wives disappears in income taxes. Some goes to meet the costs of working: meals out, working clothes, transportation (two cars instead of one), laundry, and baby sitters. Despite the increased expenses, however, most working wives appreciably increase their family's disposable income.

What do two-income families do with their extra income? Nonacademic employee families at the University of Illinois (married five to 16 years) spent more on recreational activities and equipment, clubs, education, books, magazines, records, and liquor. On the other hand, they spent less on vacations and weekend trips, perhaps because they could less easily spare large blocks of time from their busy schedules (Hafstrom and Dunsing, 1965). These families spent substantially more on expensive, durable purchases (20 per cent more on houses, 23 per cent more on large appliances, and 26 per cent more on furniture). They bought more furnishings and new rather than second-hand cars and replaced them faster. Indeed they bought new things so fast they went deeper in debt than housewife families. Presumably they felt more confident about repaying installment credit with their double incomes. Finally, they spent 27 per cent more on insurance premiums (their chief form of investment). Most of the extra insurance was taken on the life of the wife. Presumably families which depend on the wife's earnings to repay installment indebtedness are wise to cushion themselves against the accidental loss of her income.

The Impact of the Wife's Employment on Marital Satisfaction

We have already noted that the wife's employment alters both the balance of power and the division of labor between husband and wife. The wife participates more in major economic decisions and less in household tasks and decisions. What do these structural changes in marriage do to the partners' feelings for each other?

Unfortunately, we know relatively little about how men feel. When wives, regardless of economic need, were taken together, working and non-working wives were about equally satisfied with their marriages. However, when need was taken into consideration, differences emerged. In low-income homes, working wives were more satisfied with their marriages. Conversely, in high-income homes, they were less satisfied than stay-at-home wives. The two most satisfied groups of wives were those who responded to the need to work and those who stayed home when there was no need to work (Blood, 1962).

The causal relations between the wife's employment status and her marital satisfaction are not clear. I infer, however, that when wives go to work under economic pressure, their pay check reduces the strain on the family finances and is appreciated. By contrast, when a wife "needlessly" works, her absence is resented. Family members dislike the loss of her housekeeping services and of her time generally, since her income has little marginal utility. The husband resents having to share her housekeeping responsibilities. Hence, if the husband's income is adequate, few wives work unless they are dissatisfied with their marriages. Though employment may be personally rewarding, it further strains the marriage.

My guess is, therefore, that husbands of working wives are even more sensitive than wives to economic need. I know that Japanese husbands feel relieved when their wives rescue them from financial distress (Blood, 1967). Conversely, high-income American husbands probably resent the loss of the wife's personal services when she goes to work and welcome her companionship in leisure when she quits. If the wife's freedom from child-rearing responsibilities were added to this equation, these differential evaluations should be accentuated. A working mother of young children is likely to experience personal guilt feelings and husbandly accusations of neglect unless her income makes the difference between starvation and plenty. Only if her pay check more than compensates for the loss of her daytime presence can her work be appreciated and family solidarity strengthened.

The impact of the wife's employment on marital satisfaction depends on the balance between gains and losses. Do increased resources for family living outweigh the strains on the division of labor and the loss of leisure? If so, employment is a net gain. But if there is a net loss, even a career-minded wife must weigh her personal rewards against the costs to her family.

OCCUPATIONAL SATISFACTIONS. The value of the wife's employment depends not only on the money she brings home but on the work she does. If she and her family believe her work is important, they will appreciate it more (and resent it less). For example, ministers' wives who taught school derived satisfaction from enriching their pupils' lives whereas those who worked in offices found their work less satisfying (Douglas, 1965).

In order to qualify for professional work, many mothers return to college to secure advanced training or take refresher courses which will bring their previous training up to date. Some take one course a term as soon as their last child reaches nursery school age, gradually expanding their load as their children become more independent. They are then ready for meaningful work when the time comes.

ROLE-COMPATIBLE ARRANGEMENTS. Some jobs mesh with family responsibilities better than others. For instance, wives with light housekeeping responsibilities may be able to work part-time without asking the husband for domestic assistance. Similarly, school teaching is uniquely compatible with school-age children since mother and children have similar "working" hours and identical vacations.

Highly paid wives may be able to employ full-time housekeepers. Those whose talents are unusual may feel that the family's loss is society's gain. (Who can say whether family or society should take precedence?)

Some wives assist their husbands: nurses with doctor-husbands, colleagues in research or writing, family businesses or family farms. Though seldom paid a salary, they save the husband from hiring someone else and may increase his productivity. Their sense of companionship in work more than offsets the loss of companionship in leisure (since spare time must be devoted to catching up on housework). In the Protestant ministry, for example, the happiest wives were those who saw themselves as "team workers" with their husbands. They found fulfillment in their semiprofessional "vocation" and felt close to their husbands through their joint involvement in the same organization (Douglas, 1965).

Circumstances vary. Yet the general pattern is for wives to play a sequence of roles, externally oriented at the beginning and end of marriage, but inwardly focused during the child-rearing years.

The Impact of the Mother's Employment on Children

Most middle-class mothers stay home while their children are young. Barring financial extremity, work is attempted earliest by those who dislike housework:

> I had a good job before I got married, and the company was good enough to give me a maternity leave. Three months after the baby was born, I went back to the office. My days are busy ones, it is true, and I am often tired. But at least the fatigue comes from accomplishing something instead of the dull tiredness of the woman who has her child under foot all day. When I come home I feel glad to see my child and he is to see me. Yet because he is used to my working, he never raises a fuss when

I leave. I firmly believe that doing what makes me most contented can only bring greater happiness and security to my family.

For working mothers, the chief problem is finding enough time to spend with their children. They often make a deliberate effort to give their children concentrated attention. Mothers who worked because they enjoyed it felt so guilty about neglecting their children that they tended to overindulge them when they were home (Hoffman, 1961).

The older the children become, the more appropriate it is for them to be independent. Indeed, by the time they reach adolescence, they may benefit from having their mother away from home part of the time. Daughters of part-time working mothers "show an independence of thought and values generally rare among girls" (Douvan and Adelson, 1966). Ordinarily middle-class girls are liable to be oversocialized. If the mother works, this danger is minimized. If she works part-time when her daughter is an adolescent, a nice balance is struck between family and vocation (see Table 10-2, items 9 and 10).

Just as mothers who work part-time are able to balance work roles and leisure roles, so their daughters engage in an unusual number of leisure-time activities. Nor is this time taken away from their families. They are even more apt to spend their leisure with their families than girls whose mothers are always home.

If the mother works full-time, however, the daughter is inducted into precocious maturity—going steady earlier, holding an outside job and carrying major responsibility within the home, all at the expense of time for recreational activities with her family or anyone else (except, perhaps, her steady date). Douvan and Adelson suggested that girls "form these

Table 10-2. Effects of Maternal Employment on Adolescent Girls

		MATERNAL EMPLOYMENT		
	Daughter's Activities	None	Part-time	Full-time
1.	Major household responsibility	5%	17%	22%
2.	Holds a part-time job	70	74	81
3.	Goes steady at ages 17–18	27	38	45
4.	Belongs to extracurricular groups	75	84	69
5.	Highly active in leisure activities	39	49	35
6.	Spends leisure with her family	47	52	38
7.	Mother is her adult ideal	31	43	42
8.	Rated highly feminine in traditional sense	27	15	19
9.	Resists peer pressure to break a promise to her parents	13	28	16
10.	Tends to reject adult authority	5	16	6
	Number of cases	769	158	235

Selected from Douvan, 1963: 145, 150–51. *Source:* National sample of girls 11–18 years old. Reciprocal percentages of girls did not report the specified activities.

extra family involvements in order to supply emotional needs which have not been met at home, perhaps because their mothers are overextended in their own commitments outside the home."

So far I have mentioned only daughters. Many effects of maternal employment on sons are the opposite of effects on daughters. Girls benefit from their mother's employment by her example of feminine achievement. As a result, daughters of working mothers more often choose them as their ideal. However, the improved morale of the employed woman reflects adversely on her sons insofar as they see their father losing power relative to her. Sons of working mothers were more dependent and obedient than sons of nonworking mothers whereas daughters were more independent and disobedient (Siegel, 1959).

Like their fathers, both sons and daughters of working mothers are pressed into domestic service. However, the sexes differ again with respect to taking part-time jobs. Girls followed their working mother into employment whereas boys reactively worked less outside the home (Roy, 1961). One might almost say the boys seemed to nurse a grudge against their absent mothers.

Perhaps such factors lie back of the increased juvenile delinquency of sons of middle-class working mothers in Flint, Michigan (Gold, 1961). Just as middle-class wives' marriages often suffer when they go to work, so their sons' socialization suffers. The less necessary the mother's employment, the more it is liable to boomerang on the male members of her family.

These studies suggest that significant questions to be considered by a mother in deciding whether to work are (1) how old are my children? (2) what sex are they? and (3) how many hours a week will I be away? The older the children, the larger the proportion of girls, and the fewer the hours worked, the more likely the repercussions are to be positive.

Unpaid Equivalents

Paid employment is not the only alternative to housekeeping. If income is adequate, volunteer positions have advantages. Whereas part-time employment is difficult to find, volunteers have more flexible working hours. Not only may they choose almost any degree of involvement, but they are freer to be absent when children fall sick or other emergencies arise. Moreover, many organizational responsibilities subside during summer holidays when family needs are high. In short, volunteer work can more easily be integrated with the role of wife and mother than most paid jobs.

Even in personal satisfaction, volunteer work may match paid work. To be sure, lack of pay means the rewards are less tangible. But the work itself *may* be more challenging. Many a secretarial job is as routine as washing dishes, whereas political campaigning and social service involve rigorous responsibilities and fascinating insights. The comparison depends, of course, on the kind of work done (either for pay or for free). But some of the most provocative and important tasks are available only without pay.

Nor should we forget that the supportive role of middle-class wives in their husbands' advancement is also a volunteer role. Working wives are too busy to entertain much. And the outside contacts that win clients for young business and professional men come primarily through community activities.

In short, the middle-class wife who chooses not to work during the child-rearing years need not be confined to her home. Though her children have priority, she can allocate an increasing share of her time to the community as they grow older. Given this "occupational" role, she may gain most of the rewards of paid employment with fewer penalties for her husband and children.

11 Family Finances

Despite the highest incomes in the world, Americans quarrel over money more than anything else. Perhaps that's just the trouble. Perhaps they have too much money. Poor people have no choice. Their money must go for bare necessities. But as income rises, options increase. Hence financial disagreements become more common. On the other hand, if people get rich enough, they no longer have to choose. Both partners can have what they want. So financial problems become less difficult. (Blood and Wolfe found financial disagreements most common among couples with incomes just above the median, where discretionary funds were available but not inexhaustible.)

Table 11-1 shows the conspicuousness of financial conflicts when American wives recalled the main disagreements they had ever had with their husbands. Other studies find the same thing: money is the most common bone of contention between husbands and wives.

Why so? (1) Families rely on money for the goods and services they consume. (2) Husbands earn most of the money but wives spend most of it, leaving husbands wondering where it went to. (3) American marriages are equalitarian enough to make both partners feel they should have a voice in major decisions. When discretionary funds are limited, decisions won by the other side deplete one's own chances for implementing one's values in a classic "zero-sum game." One-sided power structures may not produce happier marriages, but they prevent conflict because it takes two to quarrel. (4) Whereas in-law problems are concentrated at the beginning of marriage and child-rearing problems in the middle, financial conflicts spread over the whole life cycle, taking new forms as circumstances change.

(5) Financial problems are more tangible than most conflicts. If the husband impulsively buys a new car, it visibly reminds the wife that she was not consulted.

Current Expenses

How much does it cost a family to live? The answer varies over the life cycle and depends on how efficiently the family spends its money.

Life Cycle Crises

Newly married couples with both partners working are remarkably prosperous. Though they begin with little equipment, consumption needs are low with only two mouths to feed. The husband's income may be low, but their combined income often exceeds what he alone will be able to earn for many years. If his promotional prospects are dim, family income may never be as high again unless the wife goes back to work.

On the heels of this prosperity comes the deepest depression. Disagreements about money are commonest in families with children (see Figure 11-1). Children precipitate a major crisis. They remove the wife's income and add the baby's food, clothing, medicine, and housing expenses, creating the severest financial strain most families ever experience.

Financial disagreements jump from minimum to maximum in response to this squeeze. Liquid assets drop sharply, most families go in debt, and their satisfaction with their standard of living sags to low ebb (Lansing

Table 11-1. Areas of Disagreement in Urban Families

Area of Disagreement	PERCENTAGE OF WIVES MENTIONING	
	First	At All
Money	24%	42%
Recreation, companionship	16	30
Children	16	29
Personality characteristics	14	28
In-laws	6	10
Roles	4	7
Miscellaneous (religion, politics, sex)	3	5
None, or not ascertained	17	17
Total	100%	168%*
Number of families	731	731

* Total adds to more than 100% because wives could report more than one area of disagreement.
Adapted from Blood and Wolfe, 1960: 241.

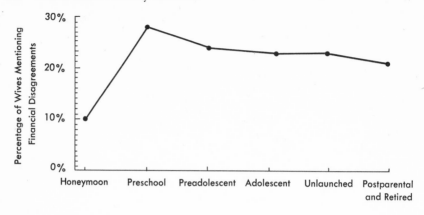

Stage in Family Life Cycle

Adapted from Blood and Wolfe, 1960: 247.

Figure 11-1. Financial Disagreements, by Stage in Family Life Cycle

and Morgan, 1955). The larger the number of children and the faster they arrive, the deeper the crisis.

Children are even more expensive as they get bigger, but most husbands' incomes rise with experience and seniority. Consequently, the strain eases gradually during the child-rearing years, save for the college crisis. Paradoxically, the average husband's peak earnings come around age 50, too late to benefit his children directly since the last child has normally left home. By then a sufficient inventory of family equipment has accumulated to reduce overhead expenses. Consequently, optional expenditures rise. Subsequently, retirement brings a second cut in income, the severity of which depends on retirement savings.

This life-cycle analysis discloses three critical intervals: the child-bearing years, college-education years, and retirement years. Conversely, there are two eras of plenty—at the beginning and just before the end. Each phase will command our attention, the first four in this chapter, the fifth in the next chapter on kinship.

Allocation of Financial Resources

How do families distribute their money among the expenses that confront them? The answer depends on three major factors: the amount of money at their disposal, the number of children, and their stage in life. The more money available, the larger the proportion they can spend on luxuries. Conversely, basic necessities consume a smaller proportion.

Table 11-2 compares college-educated men at three different income levels. As income rose, people didn't smoke much more, eat much more, get sick oftener, or get more haircuts, so fixed-cost-type items shrank percentage-wise. Transportation was a relatively standardized cost, provided it was confined to local travel. Housing and utility costs also declined proportionately.

On the other hand, allocations to discretionary areas increased. More money went to operate the household, buying services to relieve the parents in the division of labor: maids, baby sitters, and gardeners. More emphasis was placed on clothes, both in size of wardrobe and stylishness (versus the low-income concentration on multipurpose, durable clothes). Time freed from housework shifted to recreation and education. More money was saved in many forms, including personal insurance. The biggest change, however, was increased generosity to persons and organizations outside the family. Low-income families spent most of their resources on themselves. As income rose, gifts to relatives, friends, and worthy causes became more feasible.

Table 11-3 shows the effect of children on the standard of living when income was held constant. There were more mouths to feed, more bodies to bathe and clothe, and more dependents to provide for after death. Yet there was less money available for housing them. The old house, the old furniture, and the old car must do. Even the last visit to the doctor must suffice. Gifts and contributions declined with each added child except for

Table 11-2. Expenditures of College-Educated Families, by Family Income

	NET INCOME			RICH/POOR RATIO
Expenditures	$3,000–3,999	$6,000–7,499	$10,000+	
Mean Expenditures	$3,929	$6,689	$13,254	
1. Tobacco	1.6%	1.2%	0.9%	0.6X
2. Medical care	5.3	4.6	3.1	0.6X
3. Utilities	3.5	3.1	2.4	0.7X
4. Transportation	14.3	12.8	10.5	0.7X
5. Food and beverages	27.2	25.2	20.4	0.8X
6. Personal	2.1	1.9	1.6	0.8X
7. Housing	12.4	10.4	9.8	0.8X
8. Furnishings and equipment	6.7	6.4	6.5	1.0X
9. Recreation, reading, education	5.3	6.8	6.4	1.2X
10. Clothing	9.9	11.0	12.7	1.3X
11. Personal insurance	3.2	5.3	5.3	1.7X
12. Household operation	4.4	5.4	8.2	1.9X
13. Miscellaneous	0.9	1.4	2.2	2.4X
14. Gifts and contributions	3.2	4.7	10.0	3.1X
Total	100.0%	100.2%	100.0%	

Computed from U.S. Bureau of Labor Statistics (1957), 18: 74–75. Source: Urban family heads with 13 to 16 years of education (mean 15 years). 1950 income after taxes.

Table 11-3. Expenditures of Young High-Income Families, by Size of Family

Expenditures	SIZE OF FAMILY					LARGE/SMALL RATIO
	Two	Three	Four	Five	Six+	
1. Housing	11.4%	9.5%	9.0%	11.8%	5.0%	0.4X
2. Furnishings and equipment	10.4	6.9	8.7	7.4	6.4	0.6X
3. Transportation	15.2	13.3	14.5	15.7	9.8	0.6X
4. Recreation, reading, education	5.6	8.0	6.3	6.9	4.2	0.7X
5. Medical care	4.1	4.6	4.3	3.4	3.2	0.8X
6. Gifts and contributions	4.3	4.1	2.7	2.3	4.3	1.0X
7. Personal care	1.9	1.9	1.8	1.6	2.0	1.1X
8. Food and beverages	24.0	23.7	25.7	26.0	28.0	1.2X
9. Household operation	3.9	6.8	4.6	4.1	4.9	1.3X
10. Clothing	10.5	12.4	11.2	10.9	13.5	1.3X
11. Personal insurance	4.0	4.5	5.0	3.1	7.1	1.8X
12. Tobacco	1.4	1.3	1.7	1.0	2.6	1.9X
13. Utilities	1.8	2.3	3.3	4.4	4.6	2.6X
14. Miscellaneous	1.6	0.9	0.7	1.5	5.6	3.5X
Total	100.1%	100.2%	99.5%	100.1%	101.2%	

Computed from U.S. Bureau of Labor Statistics (1957) 18: 86–97. Source: Urban husbands age 25 to 35 with 1950 incomes of $6,000–7,499 after taxes.

the biggest families (who may have had such familistic values that they spent more on birthday and Christmas gifts for family and kin).

The next table is based on the assumption that income rises over the life cycle. I selected income levels and family sizes most representative of the college-educated population in order to hold values and life-styles constant. While Table 11-4 is not restricted to college-educated husbands, the *average* husband in every category went partway through college.

Childless couples made heavy down payments on cars and houses. The advent of children accentuated the need for household furnishings and equipment. The child-rearing years generally raised the costs of clothing, food, recreation, reading, education, medical care and insurance (provided there weren't too many children). As children got older, families spent more for transportation, perhaps on multiple automobiles for husband and wife and eventually for children old enough to drive.

The departure of the last child freed the budget for increased housekeeping services (extra-appreciated in old age) and contributions to the happiness and welfare of others. At 65 there was a last-minute spurt of insurance investment for the retirement and widowed years.

DECISION-MAKING ABOUT CONSUMPTION EXPENDITURES. Though groups of families differ only marginally in their allocation patterns, individual families vary widely. Transportation costs are sharply reduced for those who do not own a car. The cost of ownership increases with the car's expensiveness, newness, and frequency of replacement, since the trade-in value of model-changing brands depreciates rapidly when they are new. In clothing, style-consciousness and growing children produce rapid obsolescence. Housing costs rise to provide space for family recreation, hospitality for friends and strangers, or private offices for writing books like this.

Like other choices, financial decisions reflect personal values. In the nineteenth century, the American middle class was production-oriented, giving priority to financial reserves. Today, values have shifted toward consumption-orientation, symbolized by *You Can't Take It With You*. In both eras a minority of families have been neither production nor consumption but service-oriented. All three types necessarily spend most of their income on consumption, but their values lead them to emphasize respectively savings, consumption, or contributions. Although eras differ in their financial emphases, individual families in any era must find their own balance between physical consumables, aesthetic and intellectual sustenance, responsible savings for the family's future, and concerned service to others.

Values differ between husbands and wives as well as between families. When they do, the usual processes of decision-making and conflict-resolution come into play. Conflict may focus on a particular purchase or on the whole pattern of expenditures (for example, when couples feel their total expenses are too high or that too little money is available for a particular

Table 11-4. Expenditures of College-Educated Families, by Stage in Family Life Cycle

Husband's Age	Under 25	25–34	35–44	45–54	55–64	65–74	Old/Young Ratio
Children	0	2	2	1	0	0	
Family Income	$6,000–7,499	$7,500–9,999	$7,500–9,999	$10,000+	$10,000+	$10,000+	
Mean Expenditures	$5,988	$7,655	$7,946	$12,599	$12,031	$11,821	
Mean Number of Workers	1.6	1.1	1.2	1.4	1.0	0.9	
Expenditures							
1. Furnishings and equipment	6.5%	9.7%	6.8%	6.4%	3.9%	3.9%	0.6X
2. Transportation	23.9	8.7	11.9	15.5	11.5	14.5	0.6X
3. Clothing	11.0	12.0	10.5	12.4	9.7	7.2	0.7X
4. Housing	12.3	9.6	9.3	8.6	9.7	8.5	0.7X
5. Food and beverages	22.6	24.9	25.4	18.6	17.5	17.9	0.8X
6. Recreation, reading, etc.	5.8	7.9	6.7	7.3	4.8	4.6	0.8X
7. Personal care	1.7	2.0	1.6	1.7	1.6	1.6	0.9X
8. Medical care	2.1	4.1	4.2	5.3	3.9	2.2	1.0X
9. Tobacco	1.4	0.8	1.3	0.8	0.8	1.5	1.1X
10. Utilities	2.1	3.4	3.6	1.8	2.3	3.1	1.5X
11. Household operations	4.7	6.7	6.5	5.7	9.2	10.3	2.2X
12. Gifts and contributions	3.3	3.4	4.1	7.2	19.0	11.3	3.4X
13. Personal insurance	2.7	6.6	7.0	5.9	4.6	12.0	4.4X
14. Miscellaneous	0	0.4	1.1	2.7	2.5	1.4	—
Total	100.0%	100.2%	100.0%	99.9%	100.0%	100.0%	

Computed from U.S. Bureau of Labor Statistics, 1957, 18: 86–95. Net income after taxes for urban families in 1950.

240

purpose). When the whole pattern is questioned, budgeting offers a systematic method of decision-making.

BUDGETING. A budget is a plan for allocating financial resources. It records decisions about how to spend money during a forthcoming interval. Usually plans are made a year at a time, especially when salaries change yearly. Any period is appropriate during which income and expenses are reasonably stable or predictable. For couples whose income fluctuates wildly, a budget can chart the use of a conservative minimum, treating surpluses above that base as windfalls to be decided about later.

Only half the families in Morgan's 1965 representative Detroit sample were budgeting at that time. Somewhat more had budgeted or expected to budget at critical points in life. Leavitt and Hanson (1950) believed that "only two groups of persons of necessity should plan and keep a detailed budget: (1) newly wedded couples who have not yet had a chance to test their ability to live within their incomes; and (2) married couples . . . who find themselves in financial difficulties or who think they should save more of their incomes. . . . Budgets are to keep people out of trouble." I would add (3) newly divorced couples whose expenses suddenly rise as they establish two households and incur stiff legal fees. Budgeting is needed most by those in danger of bankruptcy, but is useful to anyone who wishes to allocate expenditures more rationally. Couples who want to get the most for their money (spending it in accordance with their needs and values) find budgeting a means of seeing their whole financial picture.

Budgeting strikes a balance between income and various possible expenditures. Fixed obligations such as mortgage payments determine budgetary allotments in advance. Whyte noted a trend toward "budgetism" which increased the proportion of expenditures which were contractually scheduled:

> This does not mean that they actually keep formal budgets. Quite the contrary; the beauty of budgetism is that one doesn't have to keep a budget at all. It's done automatically. . . . Just as young couples are now paying winter oil bills in equal monthly fractions through the year, so they seek to spread out all the other heavy seasonal obligations they can anticipate: Christmas presents, real-estate taxes, birthdays, spring cleaning, outfitting the children for school. If vendors will not oblige by accepting equal monthly installments, the purchasers will smooth out the load themselves by floating loans (Whyte, 1957: 356–57).

No matter how committed a couple are to fixed costs, they always have marginal areas that are discretionary: food, clothing, recreation, and charitable contributions, for example, can vary widely and hence are usefully planned in advance—not in terms of what is to be bought but what weight is to be given each category.

The first budget is the hardest. Planning the first year of marriage requires shooting in the dark. However, current expenses recur so regularly that experience is soon gained for future planning. What guidelines can engaged couples use in planning the first year? Previous expenditures for personal items may not change much with marriage. The new costs of keeping house can be learned better from newlyweds who've just set up housekeeping than from parents who've long since equipped their houses and moved into higher income brackets.

Even couples of the same age and income can hardly provide more than a point of departure. Each couple's values shape their distribution of money. No one need adhere to a precut financial plan. If they choose to sink money in a particular direction, that's their privilege as an independent married couple:

> Reg and I figure on spending over a hundred dollars a month on food. When I tell my friends about it they are horrified and say, "How can you afford it on a teacher's salary?" Of course, we have to give up some of the fancy clothes they go in for. But Reg has a huge appetite and both of us feel that a thick juicy steak is one of the really good things of life.

Every couple must work out their own financial destiny. Lists of "proper" percentages can be more hindrance than help if taken as inflexible rules rather than suggestive guides. Even the budget's categories should reflect personal predilections. Those with a passion for photography or music will need separate categories for their hobbies, while others can lump these costs under recreation. From year to year, as interests wane and new needs arise, categories should change accordingly. A good financial plan allocates (1) to such categories as are significant to the couple (2) those amounts of money that will yield the maximum mutual satisfaction.

Few budgets say just what the money in each category will be spent on. Rather, they guarantee that "X" dollars a month will be there to spend as the food-buyer sees fit. There is still freedom to decide whether to have chicken or pork chops tomorrow. A husband limited to $150 a year for clothes may still choose between a new summer suit or a winter one. The fact that he can't afford both reflects his income more than the budget. The budget just makes his "poverty" unmistakably plain.

Those who wish to maximize their freedom can specify a "miscellaneous" item or personal allowances monogrammed "his" and "hers" and splurge-able will-o-the-wisp:

> Sylvia is terribly frugal about records. She thinks it's wonderful the way you can borrow them from libraries. I like to buy lots of them and get a keen pleasure out of coming in the room and seeing that long shelf of LP's even though I may not play any one of them very regularly. Since I haven't been able to sell her yet on the value of buying records, we put

a fat $15 a month personal allowance in the budget which gives me a chance to go ahead and buy records whenever I want to.

Though plans are usually made a year in advance, revisions to meet new circumstances are always possible. Especially in the first year of budgeting, revisions must be expected. Beginning planners typically overlook Christmas and wedding presents, vacation trips, newspapers and magazines, dry cleaning and shoe repairs, lunches away from home, liquor and tobacco, entertaining, contributions, and savings for emergencies. These need not all be separate items, but the budget should provide somewhere for these "little" costs that add up to so much.

Although making a budget takes a good many conversations, it saves subsequent spats. To apply it requires keeping records to show where the money has gone so far. Tallying up the month's expenses takes time, but filling out an income tax "long form" is easier with complete records. Until couples get on their financial feet, the dividends of budgeting are likely to be worth the time invested. A budget is not a panacea. Couples who lack the prerequisites for rational problem-solving will probably violate it. Even for self-controlled couples, it is never more than a prediction of how money will be spent. Inevitably, actual expenditures differ from the prediction. But even crude forecasting is better than none, especially for people subject to impulse buying:

> When we first got married, Tom would cash his monthly pay check, pay the bills and buy things with very little thought of how we would meet the expenses of the last half of the month. We would eat quite well the first two weeks and skimp the last two. Even though I wanted him to be the head of the home, I would accuse him of being stupid when it came to handling money. I urged him to budget our money but he said he couldn't—it made him nervous. Finally we came to realize that he definitely is not a mathematician. So we agreed that I should take over the responsibility of budgeting our money to meet all the demands. This way he isn't frustrated by a task he isn't temperamentally suited for, and I have a free hand to use my skill for the benefit of the whole family.

With increased experience many couples gain a "feel" for financial allocation that requires less detailed control. The more rapidly their income rises, the less the danger of bankruptcy. Hence the need for systematic planning gradually decreases. In changing circumstances, however, and especially when change is for the worse, systematic decision-making via budgeting helps prevent disaster and maximize returns from limited resources.

SPECIFIC PLANS. Budgeting is the most comprehensive form of financial planning. Regardless of whether a couple budget their routine expenses, it is useful to plan unusual expenditures. When a major appliance or new car is to be bought or the house is to be redecorated, planning is more efficient.

In a study of three generations of families in the Twin Cities, Hill (1963) found that the larger the proportion of planned actions, the more efficient the financial decisions. Efficiency also rose with planning definitely for a particular time rather than vaguely for "sometime" in the future. Long-range planning frequently suffered from vagueness. Hence the most definite planning was geared to the short range—the next step to be taken, given the known facts of the present.

Although consumer satisfaction was promoted by all the above steps, it was enhanced most by efficient decision-making. This required four steps:

1. Securing information about costs of the desired object and of alternatives.
2. Considering the long-range consequences as well as the immediate effects of making the purchase.
3. Conferring with the family so that all affected persons' views were considered.
4. Creating a family policy to guide the action to be taken.

Families who took the time to prepare carefully for new expenditures were less likely to make costly mistakes.

Hill also found that the better educated the husband and the more communicative the marriage, the more effective "consumership" was. However, most couples got sloppier as time went on. At first, they took the time to shop around and plan together, but as the years went by, they bought more impulsively. Couples with high incomes also did less planning. They could afford to make mistakes and would rather save time than money.

In general, then, specific planning and comprehensive budgeting are efficient methods of financial management for couples with modest incomes who can hardly afford the spontaneity of planless buying.

Major Expenses

Budgeting and budgetism take care of routine expenses. Items too large for current income require special arrangements. We have already mentioned two of these items: college education and retirement expenses. The remaining one arises earlier—buying and equipping a house. Since couples usually buy their furniture and appliances first and their house later, we will consider them in that order.

Equipment for Family Living

Most newly married couples live in rented apartments. The easiest place to begin keeping house is in an apartment already equipped with major appliances and furniture. Renting furnished enables couples to concentrate on buying cars for access to their two jobs and their leisure-time recreation spots. Television and a hi-fi are other early purchases since they seldom come with furnished apartments. Many couples move next to an unfurnished apartment or house, buying furniture and perhaps a refrigerator, stove, washer and dryer. Few husbands earn enough to pay cash for expensive items, especially when several purchases come at once. Hence couples often resort to installment buying or rely on the wife's income.

INSTALLMENT BUYING. One element in Whyte's "budgetism" was buying on credit whenever possible. Most families used credit in buying houses and cars but only a minority did for smaller items. In general, of course, the more expensive the item, the fewer the families able to pay cash. Conversely, the higher the family income, the larger the proportion paying cash (Huntington, 1957). Some families use credit even for inexpensive items. But installment buying is a costly alternative to paying cash:

> A mythical couple we will call the Frugals decide to defer all but necessary purchases for enough months to accumulate an extra $500. They will then have a revolving fund of their own which they can use for cash purchases, and instead of paying a fixed amount each month in installment loans, they will use these sums to replenish the $500.
> Now let's take a normal couple. The Joneses, with precisely the same income, don't put off purchases but instead commit themselves to a combination of installment loans and revolving-credit plans. At the end of ten years the Joneses would have paid out somewhere around $800 in interest. The Frugals, by contrast, would have earned interest—roughly $150. Not counting the extra benefits they would have reaped by being able to buy for cash, they would be, in toto, almost a thousand dollars better off (Whyte, 1957: 360–61).

In these days of discount houses selling only for cash, the benefits to the Frugals are likely to be even greater.

In money terms, installment buying is expensive (see Table 11-5). Sometimes, as in buying a house, credit may be worth the cost. In every case the cost must be weighed against the loss suffered in deferring the purchase until cash could be accumulated. The lower the cost and the less urgent the purchase, the greater the advantage of waiting to pay cash.

USE OF THE WIFE'S INCOME. For newlyweds with dual incomes, waiting

Table 11-5. Stated and True Interest Rates, by Various Sources of Credit

Source of Credit	Typical Stated Rates	True Annual Rates
Home mortgages	5½–6% yearly	5½–6%
Credit Unions	⅔–1% monthly	8–12%
Bank personal loans	$4–$7 per $100	8–14%
F.H.A. home-improvement loans	$5 per $100	10%
Car finance charges (new cars)	$6–$7.50 per $100	12–15%
Bank charge, check credit plans	1–1½% monthly	12–18%
Revolving charge accounts	1–1¾% monthly	12–21%
Retail installment credit	1–2% monthly	12–24%
Car finance charges (used cars)	$9–$18 per $100	18–36%
Small loan companies	1½–3½% monthly	18–42%

Adapted from *Coronet*, September, 1961: 125.

for cash doesn't take long—provided the wife's income is not squandered in riotous living. There are good reasons for allocating to special purposes the wife's net income (after taxes and her extra expenses). When her income is spent on current expenses, living standards are raised spectacularly. Hamburger is converted into filet mignon and beer into champagne. But the shock when she quits work is terrific:

> We were living pretty well until Lorraine quit work in September and stopped bringing home her $345 a month. We used to go out quite a bit but we can't afford to now. Both of us have begun to worry now about the financial responsibility for the home and the baby.

Belt-tightening is painful. Living beyond the husband's means spells trouble ahead or else the wife feels pressured to keep working indefinitely:

> At first I worked out of necessity because a lawyer's income is so unpredictable when he first starts. But I never really felt I could quit. We got so accustomed to the "little extras" which came with the money I earned that I felt I had to keep at it. When I wanted to stop, the extra expense of the children kept me going.

If the wife is to stay home after the children arrive and her income isn't to be dissipated on "little extras," using her income for current expenses must be avoided. Only when the husband's income can be counted on to rise quickly (for example, on completing school or a medical internship), is it safe for the wife to contribute to everyday maintenance. No matter how meager the husband's salary, her income should ordinarily be earmarked for special purposes.

Diverting the wife's income to special purposes eases the impact of children in two ways. In addition to preventing the parents from getting accustomed to a level of living they must abandon, it reduces the burden on the husband's subsequent income. The larger the number of appliances and furniture items purchased while the wife is still working, the better equipped the couple will be for children. After cars and furnishings are paid for, her income can be turned toward buying a house.

Housing for Family Living

In recent years the U.S. Government has reduced the down payment on FHA mortgages so it is now possible to buy a house soon after marriage. Low down payments have one disadvantage, however. The lower the down payment, the higher the monthly payments. To ease the strain on the child-rearing years, it is desirable to have monthly payments as small as possible. Hence, it is valuable to make the largest possible down payment. This implies that dual-income couples should put off buying their first house until the wife is ready to quit working. Until then, she is too busy to take care of a family-size house anyway. When she is ready to change roles, a bigger down payment will be available. To protect such savings from disappearing in current expenditures, they need to be transferred from the regular checking account to a savings account (where they will have the added advantage of earning interest).

Higher Education for Children

College educations are becoming more difficult to pay for since costs are rising faster than American income. (In January 1961, *Coronet* estimated a five per cent per year increase which means costs will double by the time today's babies enter college.)

As early as the 1950's, almost half the parents of college students felt they were not helping their children enough (Lansing, 1960). The lower the family income and the larger the number of children, the larger the proportion of parents having difficulty. As long as current trends persist, family finances will be increasingly strained by this major expense.

For the academic year 1959–60, parents contributed 61 per cent of their children's total expenses, students earned 23 per cent, scholarships provided 9 per cent, and miscellaneous sources the remaining 7 per cent. Where did parents get their share?

Table 11-6 shows that less than half the families saved any money in advance. For those who did, the college years were less difficult. However, another reason they were easier was that only high-income families managed to save much in advance. (In 1959, Roper found that only 39 per cent of parents expecting to send children to college had begun saving. Median savings the previous year for this minority were almost $700 for high-income families but hardly more than $100 for average-income families.) Since families typically began saving only ten years before a child entered college, $100 per year would hardly finance a single college education, much less several.

Theoretically, borrowing money fits the life cycle better than saving it in advance. If the average family has a financial surplus *after* children go to college, it should be easier to repay borrowed funds than to set aside savings during the lean years while children are growing up. Most families could secure thousands of dollars by refinancing the mortgage on their home.

Table 11-6 shows, however, that borrowing was rare. Moreover, it was chiefly an act of desperation by those in the greatest financial difficulty. Extra work by the father or mother, similarly, was forced on those whose past or present incomes were not adequate for setting aside the necessary amounts.

Advance saving was the most popular method of financing. Where was it saved? Parents invested their college savings in the following places (in order of frequency): (1) bank savings accounts; (2) endowment insurance; (3) government bonds; and (4) common stock (interpolated from Lansing, 1960 and Roper, 1960).

SAVINGS ACCOUNTS. The most popular investment was in savings accounts in banks and other financial institutions. This relied on parental self-discipline to put money in the account, and even more on self-discipline to leave it there. Roper's respondents listed as one of the major "advantages" of a savings account the fact that it could "be used for other things" besides education. This liquidity means savings accounts are frequently multipurpose affairs, not restricted to educational purposes. They are often raided in family crises, leaving the children lucky if their educational funds survive intact.

Table 11-6. Parents' Sources of Funds for Children's College Expenses

Source of Funds	Percentage of All Parents of College Students
Saved money in advance	48%
Current income, reduced expenses	44
Mother worked more	19
Father worked more	8
Borrowed money	8
Total	127%

Adapted from Lansing, 1960: 52. *Source:* National sample of parents of students in college 1955–60. Total adds to more than 100% because some families used more than one method.

ENDOWMENT INSURANCE. An insurance policy designed to mature when the child reaches college age provides for regular, forced payment whenever the bill arrives. It insures against the premature death of the father, provided the policy is written on the life of the father with the child as beneficiary. (Unfortunately, the child's life is often insured, instead.)

Some form of insurance is necessary to protect the child against the death of the father before college funds have been accumulated. Families that invest their savings in more profitable directions should insure the father enough to cover the interval during which savings are accumulating. Decreasing term insurance (see below) is an especially appropriate form.

GOVERNMENT BONDS. "Safety" was the most distinctive appeal of government bonds. Where payroll-deduction, bond-a-month plans exist, they also have the forced payment advantages of endowment insurance. However, since they come in small denominations, there is more temptation to cash in "just one" bond than to liquidate a whole insurance policy. Like insurance policies, government bonds carry maturity dates which discourage the impulsive raiding to which savings accounts are subject.

COMMON STOCKS. Rarest of the four methods of investment is the purchase of common stocks, either directly or through mutual investment funds. Unlike the fixed return from the other three methods, stocks bring a fluctuating return correlated with the fate of the economy. When the economy declines, stocks do too. Conversely, they gain during inflationary periods. Indeed, investigation by James T. Sudol of the University of Michigan showed that the annual rate of return on 92 major industrial stocks purchased regularly between 1950 and 1961 was 13.5 per cent.

Common stock was especially lucrative when held long enough to amortize the broker's fees over a period of ten or more years. Like other piecemeal investments, it requires supplementary insurance. King (1954) also recommended conservatively that reliance not be placed exclusively on fluctuating investments but on a combination with fixed-return savings to provide a hedge against deflation. The long-run trends in the United States are inflationary. Hence families should investigate the higher returns and the hedge against inflation that Roper's stock-purchasers valued.

For a few American families real-estate investments serve the same purpose. Though a poor market situation may make it difficult to liquidate by selling out, real estate (like most forms of saving) can be used as collateral for borrowed funds.

Retirement Income

The problems of retirement income are similar to those involved in college expenses. In both cases many years are available for accumulating the necessary reserves. For retirement income, Social Security provides a useful cushion but must be supplemented. The investments discussed for college savings are also available. However, if college expenses 20 years hence are difficult to predict, retirement has the added enigma that death is even less predictable. The starting date for retirement can be planned in advance but the end cannot. It is necessary, therefore, to rely on annuities (insurance policies that will yield income as long as the beneficiary lives). Such policies spread the risk of longevity among a large enough group to be able to support even those who "survive to one-hundred-and-five." They guarantee support not only to the man after retirement but to his widow for the decade or more by which the typical American wife outlives her husband. Many companies have compulsory retirement programs. For families who have not previously saved enough, launching the last child is the signal to set aside a major portion of income.

Investment

Much of what has been said about investing savings toward special purposes applies to general investment as well. Once the major costs of family living have been met, affluent families have a margin to spare. By investing in stocks directly or through mutual funds, buying rental property, etc., such families augment their annual income (see Table 11-7).

Dividends, rents, and other investment income may be plowed back into a pyramiding estate or used to supplement earned income. The latter enables men to take risks in changing jobs or occupations. It frees them to go back to school, to travel, or to volunteer their services for the public welfare. Many a civil servant responded more easily to the call of public service because a lower salary could be offset by investment income.

Table 11-7. Major Investments, by Family Income

Percentage of Families Owning Each Type of Investment	FAMILY INCOME			
	$5,000–7,499	$7,500–9,999	$10,000–14,999	$15,000–24,999
Home	62%	74%	82%	84%
Life insurance, retirement plan	67	77	82	82
Stocks	16	21	36	52
Business or profession	17	19	23	29

Adapted from "Survey of Financial Characteristics of Consumers," *Federal Reserve Bulletin,* March 1964: 292. Based on a national sample of family income and assets in 1962. Reciprocal percentages of families did not own the specified investments.

Insurance Against Catastrophe

In rural societies, neighbors and kin rescue families from the economic consequences of fire, illness, and death. When a barn burns, they build another. When a farmer is ill, they harvest his crops. When he dies, they take in his widow and children. A network of personal obligations based on blood and community cushions each family against the blows of fate.

In urban societies these ties weaken. Geographical mobility undermines the sense of community and weakens the bonds of kinship. Urban housing offers less room for relatives, and few urban dwellers know how to rebuild a house. Money purchases the skills formerly commandeered by personal loyalties. So the modern resource for coping with catastrophe is insurance.

Property Insurance

Though the chief risk of losing a home is from fire, "extended coverage" for storms and other threats costs little more than fire insurance alone. Comprehensive home insurance policies cover liability for damages incurred on the property and theft of personal belongings. Package policies are less expensive than separate ones covering the same risks.

Cash buying, as usual, saves installment costs. Families thrifty enough to pay for several years' insurance win substantial discounts over the cost of annual (or worse yet quarterly) installments.

Automobile Insurance

The chief threat of economic disaster in owning an automobile is not what someone may do to my car but what I may do to him. To be sure, if I have a new or very expensive car, I may wish to protect myself against having to replace it. Indeed, if I don't own the car outright but am only buying it piece by piece, the financier may require me to protect *his* investment by carrying collision insurance.

Otherwise, it is more economical to bear the collision risk myself, especially for cars whose trade-in value has depreciated. Even for new cars, the insurance problem is how to pay for big bumps not little ones. It is cheaper to subscribe to deductible clauses that insure against damage above a certain amount (such as $100). Nondeductible insurance is exorbitant because rates must be high enough to cover the cost of processing petty claims.

Liability insurance is another matter. An automobile can wreak destruction on life and property totaling thousands of dollars in damage suits. Liability insurance protects me from bankruptcy should I have the misfortune to incur such a financial obligation to others.

Health Insurance

Like higher education, the cost of medical care has risen faster than the cost of living. As medical science becomes more specialized and medical equipment more elaborate, the possibility of disastrous medical bills multiplies. As with collision insurance there is little need to cover everyday medical expenses. These can be budgeted almost as predictably as other current expenses. The insurance problem involves the rare but catastrophic long illness or major surgery that costs thousands of dollars.

"Major medical insurance," has a thrifty deductible clause for bills under $100 or so per family member. But when bills run sky high, major medical insurance takes over. The purpose of any insurance is to protect against the worst disasters not the little ones, hence the value of major medical insurance.

Life Insurance

The worst thing that can happen to a family financially (as well as otherwise) is to lose the father while the children are young. This may mean losing hundreds of thousands of dollars of potential income, compared to which losses through illness, fire, or auto accidents are trifling. The chances of any given husband's premature death are small, but the consequences are so severe that this risk deserves to be spread through the community by means of insurance.

SOCIAL SECURITY. Thanks to Social Security, most American families have some protection against the husband's death. Although the monthly allotments to widows with dependent children are not sufficient to sustain an adequate standard of living, they help fill the gap and reduce the amount of personal insurance that needs to be carried.

LIFE-CYCLE CHANGES IN INSURANCE NEEDS. The purpose of insurance is to provide money for recouping economic losses or meeting expenses that could not otherwise be met.

To lose a child will not bankrupt a middle-class family. After burial expenses have been met, the burden on the family income is reduced by one less dependent. Hence, insurance need not be taken on the life of a child.

Losing a wife is more serious. To be sure, if there are no children, the husband could take care of himself again (just as the widow could support herself). Childless couples have no need for life insurance. However, a mother of young children is less easily dispensed with. The father cannot stay home to care for the children, so there would be baby-sitting and housekeeper expenses. If the husband's life were adequately insured, there might be some point in insuring the wife's too during the years when she has dependent children.

The trouble is that very few families insure the father adequately. As of 1950 the average American family carried enough insurance to replace the husband's income for only *one* year (Morgan, 1955). To be sure, Social Security provides almost half the average husband's income for the duration of the children's dependent years, but where is the other half to come from after the insured two half-years are used up? Social Security benefits are reduced if the wife works appreciably, so that resource is almost useless. The average American family would suffer at least a 50 per cent cut in its standard of living should the father die too soon. (The higher the family income, the greater the loss, since Social Security benefits are proportionately smaller.) To prevent this hardship, families need enough insurance to close the gap between Social Security and their normal living costs until the youngest child reaches maturity. If this gap were $5,000 per year and the youngest child had 20 years to maturity, a family would need $100,000 worth of insurance (disregarding the complexities of compound interest). Although $100,000 would be needed the first year, only $95,000 is necessary the next year, and so on, until nothing is needed after the last child leaves home.

The basic life insurance needed by a family begins at zero in the honeymoon phase but hits higher peaks with the birth of each succeeding child. After the last child is born, the need declines steadily to zero when he leaves home.

The most insurance is needed just when family economic resources are lowest. Hence the average family needs insurance that is as inexpensive as possible and that declines in value from year to year. Only one type of insurance offers these features.

Types of Life Insurance. The following list (adapted from Morgan, 1955: 163) shows the approximate cost per year for insurance with an initial value of $100,000 purchased at age thirty:

20-year endowment	$4,615
20-payment life	3,090
Ordinary life insurance (paid up at eighty-five)	1,940
20-year term insurance	735
20-year decreasing term insurance	390

"Decreasing term insurance" is the only form that most families can afford during the child-rearing years and the only one that decreases from maximum value at the beginning to zero at the end. Any form of term insurance is pure insurance with no investment. Like fire insurance which repays only in the event of fire, it pays off only if the owner dies during the life of the policy. Decreasing term comes under a variety of names, often called "mortgage protection" insurance since it decreases at a rate similar to a mortgage loan. Or it may be called "income protection" insurance. For pure insurance geared to the child-rearing phase of the family life cycle, decreasing term is the best buy. It must be supplemented, however, by other means of saving for educational and retirement expenses (in case the husband survives).

All other forms of insurance are so expensive that they limit most buyers to too little coverage in the early years when need is greatest. On the other hand, they provide more coverage than necessary in the later years if taken out in adequate amounts at the beginning of child-bearing. As a result, the middle class consists of young families with too little insurance and middle-aged couples with too much.

Other forms of insurance cost more because they return more—more than the minimum needs for protecting children against the premature death of their father. Families who can afford it may wish to buy these "extras." But extras should not take precedence over the basic requirement of providing enough pure insurance.

"Ordinary life insurance" is the commonest form. Premiums are paid as long as the individual lives (or up to a certain age, such as the 85 shown in the list). Whenever the individual dies, the beneficiary gets the face value of the policy. In the meantime, the policy gradually increases in loan value or cash surrender value, since it combines savings with death protection.

"Twenty-Payment Life" insurance is limited-payment insurance. At the end of 20 years the policy is completely paid for and remains in force for the life of the insured. If I wanted to buy insurance at age 45, I might choose this kind so my payments would be completed before retirement.

"Twenty-year Endowment" pays full value should the insured die during the 20-year interval. If he survives, the company pays the face amount to the beneficiary at that time. This is primarily a savings program with the insurance feature added. It is the most popular form of insured savings for children's college expenses.

Families who rely on insurance policies to cover both their protection and savings needs often combine different types of policies in varying amounts. Families seeking higher returns on their savings may use decreasing term insurance for maximum protection at lowest cost while they invest their savings in stocks and other equities.

One option in most forms of insurance is a disability waiver of premiums. If the husband is disabled and cannot work, the family is in a fix. The fix can be relieved slightly by policy provisions that waive the necessity of paying any further premiums in case the insured is unable to work. Such provisions cost slightly more but provide added protection.

Theoretically, it would be desirable to carry insurance that would provide family income in the event of the father's disability. Unfortunately, Morgan concluded that such insurance was too expensive and too hedged with limitations to be worthwhile (1955). This is one financial crisis which our society has not yet solved.

12 Kin Networks

Marriage is not just an individual affair. Parents and other relatives are vitally interested. Every partner acquired is a new recruit to the family. In some feudal societies the bride joins the husband's family (and leaves her own). But in our bilateral American system both partners join each others' families. Hence they participate in two kin networks, the husband's and the wife's.

The most important links in these networks are between parents and children, that is, between the husband and his parents, the wife and her parents. Prior to marriage these are one's closest ties, originating in the dependency of infants on parents and the long years of nurture to maturity.

When there is more than one child, parents become the focus for continued association among adult siblings. Children who grow up together feel closer to each other than to any other relative except their parents. Childhood ties with siblings and parents are the primary links in kin networks. Cousins who never live together have weaker bonds.

Marriage brings together individuals whose strongest ties are with their respective families of orientation. As they create a new family, there may be transitional problems, boundary problems, allocative problems, or problems of culture conflict. But almost always, beyond the problems, there are positive ties of sociability and mutual help.

Sources of Conflict

In America the word "in-law" is one to conjure with. "Mother-in-law" has particularly negative connotations. In a free association test, students

256

typically gave me such responses as "fight," "bother," "terrible," "ugh," "hatred," and "hell." Mother-in-law is the modern incarnation of ancient witchcraft, the butt of jokes and cartoons expressing the resentment of persecuted sons- and daughters-in-law.

Waller and Hill (1951) pointed out that "grandmother" is a far more positive word, even though mother-in-law and grandmother are the same person, once children arrive. Yet not quite. From *my* point of view, *my* grandmothers were those women two generations removed who were kind to me as a child. However, *my* mother-in-law is this stranger, only one generation older, whom I acquired by marriage. Whereas grandparents are part of my birthright, parents-in-law intrude later in life and require getting used to. Hence the transitional problems in interfamily relationships.

Transitional Problems

Though less prevalent than other problems, in-law problems are uniquely concentrated at the beginning of marriage. For example, Blood and Wolfe (1960) found disagreements over in-laws commonest in the honeymoon stage, declining steadily thereafter. Thomas (1956), similarly, found in-law problems prominent in Catholic marriages that broke up soonest, especially those that failed within the first year.

Marriage is a new relationship that develops during courtship as boy and girl gradually depend more on each other and less on their parents. Some parents resist the "loss" of their dependents, and some children feel ambivalent about the realignment. Then parent-child ties vie with husband-wife ties in conflicts of loyalty.

PARENTAL POSSESSIVENESS. When the source of difficulty is a parent's inability to allow children to grow up, the mother is especially likely to be the culprit. Men generally encourage independence (Rosen and d'Andrade, 1959). Women, however, are more apt to enjoy having others depend on them. If a woman's chief satisfaction lies in being a mother, the prospect of children leaving home is frightening. Sometimes the first child's marriage provokes the strongest resistance. Sometimes the last child is the last defense against an empty life. In either case mothers get most of the blame for "possessiveness" (Duvall, 1954).

The solution to possessiveness is to discover alternative roles to replace the mother role. A vital marriage is one alternative. Going to work and plunging into community activities are others.

CHILDISH OVERDEPENDENCE. Overpossessive mothers produce overdependent children. The wife's mother is the usual focus of conflict in cases of overdependence. Since daughters are sheltered more than sons, wives are more apt to figuratively or literally "go home to mother" when tension arises between husband and wife (Stryker, 1955). Overdependence is commonest among those who marry young. It is one expression of immaturity and incomplete preparation for marriage. The younger the bride, the greater the frequency of in-law disagreements (Blood and Wolfe). When youthfulness causes overdependence, time may solve the problem. In extreme cases attachment between wife and mother may need therapeutic intervention before it can be reduced to normal proportions.

Boundary Problems

Normally a couple establish their autonomy vis-à-vis the relatives with little difficulty. Their collective identity must be respected by both kin networks if their marriage is to remain intact. Generally speaking, this is no problem. However, a forthcoming paper of mine suggests that excessive contact with kin may threaten the autonomy of the nuclear family. For example, if relatives drop in unannounced, they invade the couple's privacy and lessen their marital solidarity.

Figure 12-1 suggests that contact with kin is consistent with marital

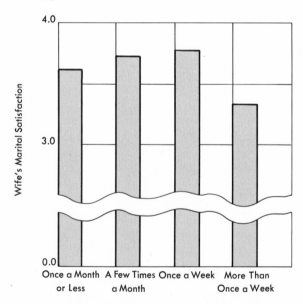

Adapted from Blood, forthcoming. Source: Detroit wives, 1955.

Figure 12-1. Kin Visiting and Marital Satisfaction

satisfaction up to a point of diminishing returns. In this sample, excessive contact involved getting together with relatives more than once a week. The same paper shows, incidentally, similar boundary problems when the whole clan gathers together more than once a month. Apparently, relatives are a supportive resource in moderation, but the nuclear family requires some autonomy to avoid being overwhelmed.

Allocational Problems

Transitional and boundary problems are exceptional rather than the rule. Every couple, however, must divide their time between two kin networks (every couple, that is, who have two networks available). For couples with only one network, allocational problems are minimized. They may still have to choose between different units of the network—which to visit when. But jealousy seems less likely within a given network than between networks.

In international marriages, bilateral kin are replaced by a single network. If the bride moves to the husband's side of the world, her family ties are so weakened that they cease having much functional significance. International marriages, therefore, may have better-than-average relations with the remaining network—at least this was true of many American soldiers with Japanese brides (Strauss, 1954).

Normally, however, both networks are accessible and make competing demands for time and attention. Both families may want simultaneous visits from their children. Especially at Christmas or High Holy Days, the custom of gathering together the children (plus their spouses and the grandchildren) is felt with equal urgency. Only a Solomon could find a solution that would not disappoint one family (or both):

> At every holiday we always get invited out by both our families. Michelle and I come from very close-knit families so, if we don't watch ourselves, we go right ahead and tell both, "Of course we'll be there." More than once we've separately committed the family to being in two places 100 miles apart for Thanksgiving dinner, and then there's general hair-tearing all around.

Both families may expect financial help in distress, constant letter-writing, visits from grandchildren, and other favors that tax the couple's resources. It would be a mistake to assume that all claims are initiated by the older generation. The fact that husband and wife grow up in separate families makes each identify with his own network and push its claims. Even if both partners could be neutral, no couple can be in two places at once. So when familistic occasions arise, choices must be made.

Problems of Culture Conflict

The most common complaint against in-laws generally and mothers-in-law in particular was meddlesomeness (Duvall, 1954). Parents have many reasons for intervening in the life of a young couple, but the most potent is a clash of cultures. Husbands and wives have enough trouble resolving their differences without reinforcements rushing in. Yet when matters of principle are at stake, restraint is difficult. Even in technical matters like cooking or keeping house, in-laws intervene all too easily, escalating the conflict and extending it beyond the issue at hand to questions of their right to get involved at all.

CONFLICTING FAMILY CULTURES. Every family has a culture of its own—distinctive ways of living that are deeply ingrained. One element is family ritual: "a prescribed procedure, arising out of family interaction, involving a pattern of defined behavior, which is directed toward some specific end or purpose, and acquires rigidity and a sense of rightness as a result of its continuing history" (Bossard and Boll, 1950). Ways of celebrating holidays, of spending Sundays, or of putting children to bed are brought to marriage along with peculiarities of etiquette, vocabulary, and the division of labor. Whose culture is to prevail? Usually the wife's, since she is the chief custodian of the children. Yet in the process, wife and mother-in-law may come to verbal blows:

> I have a problem with Van's mother. We never had any trouble until the baby was born, but we had a big argument over the formula. She thought I was making it all wrong, but my father's a doctor and I've been to prenatal classes so I figure I ought to know.

Conflict about how to raise the baby is common even between young mothers and their *own* parents. Yet when the trouble is with *his* mother, it snowballs into "in-law trouble." Whether string beans should be cooked with ham or without, whether to say "either" or "eyether," to dress four-year-olds in suits or playclothes—the possibilities of conflict are endless. In the first months of marriage both sets of parents unconsciously welcome decisions in favor of their own idiosyncrasies and bristle when their ways are snubbed. Probably the fact that women are the chief bearers of family culture explains why they are the chief contenders in in-law conflict.

Table 12-1 suggests three principles of in-law conflict: (1) parents cause more trouble than siblings; (2) female relatives cause more trouble than male relatives; (3) wives are involved more than husbands. All three coincide in the relationship between wife and mother-in-law, making it crisis-prone.

INTERGENERATIONAL CHANGE. Conflicts between family cultures tend to suck in the older generation. Parents normally enjoy seeing their traditions carried on in the next generation. But what if one's own son or daughter feels that familiar ways are not good ones but bad? Then battle lines are drawn, not neatly between networks, but complexly between parents and both child and child-in-law. Then junior couples struggle to rebel and senior couples to dominate in endless feuds. Then mutual respect and affection between young and old are replaced by bitterness.

Intergenerational conflict is not universal. It occurs when societies change so fast that a gulf opens between generations (as in postwar Japan). It occurs when immigrant families move to the United States—the older generation clinging to old-country customs and the younger generation to the new. (In Minnesota a whole generation of students rebelled against their rural Scandinavian background and strenuously avoided their kin networks [Dinkel, 1943].) It happens also when ambitious couples move up the social scale, leaving their parents behind (LeMasters, 1954). If the generations meet under such circumstances, they can expect to clash. To prevent trouble, they usually avoid each other, keeping their interaction to an obligatory minimum. In either case the warmth of kinship is chilled.

MIXED MARRIAGES. I discussed in Chapter 3 how in-laws become involved in the identification problems of children of mixed marriages and need add little more. Culture conflict in mixed marriages is more vivid but all couples have some trouble fitting two ways of life together. Even in mixed marriages, in-law problems diminish with time. Steadfast solidarity between husband and wife is contagious, winning respect and eventually affection for the alien spouse. At first an unusually strange stranger, eventually he or she is integrated into the kin network as an individual human being.

Table 12-1. In-Laws with Whom Husbands and Wives Experienced Friction

| | PERCENTAGE EXPERIENCING FRICTION | |
In-Law	Husbands	Wives
Mother-in-law	9.0%	14.7%
Sister-in-law	3.4	3.8
Father-in-law	3.2	3.2
Brother-in-law	0.6	1.8
Two or more of the above	5.1	5.9
Total	21.3%	29.4%

Adapted from a study by Judson T. Landis of 544 couples in the early years of marriage (Landis and Landis, 1958: 406). Reciprocal percentages had never experienced any friction with any in-laws.

Sociability with Kin

It would be unfortunate if the preceding discussion left the impression that most couples have trouble with their in-laws. The small percentages in Table 12-1 are reassuring. Most couples get along well with their relatives. Indeed they spend a great deal of time together, more than with neighbors or other friends.

According to Table 12-2 the typical married couple in Detroit saw at least one relative every week. In rural Michigan a companion study of mine showed that farm families got together with relatives even oftener (and with other friends less).

Visits occur primarily between senior couples and their children and grandchildren. It is an extension of the companionship parents and children enjoyed when they were living together.

Visits go in both directions—from older to younger and younger to older, depending on ease of movement and facilities for hospitality. If more than one child lives in the same community, the house they grew up in is the natural meeting place.

Some visits to parents are motivated by a sense of obligation. Parents invest so much in their children that they create a debt children can hardly repay. Nevertheless, most visiting seems to be voluntary. Most couples prefer their parents and siblings over other companions. They visit back and forth because they want to, not because they have to. In the process parents feel rewarded in affection, companionship, and attention for the money and effort they expended on their children.

American families normally visit as total units (Detroit Area Study). Husbands and wives rarely leave their children behind (and then mostly

Table 12-2. Contact with Relatives, Neighbors, Co-Workers, and Other Friends

| | GROUP CONTACTED | | | |
Frequency of Contact	Relatives	Neighbors	Co-Workers	Other Friends
Everyday or almost every day	29%	20%	1%	3%
Once or twice a week	38	25	8	22
Once or twice a month	20	17	20	43
Less often	13	14	30	24
Never	0	24	41	8
Total	100%	100%	100%	100%
Number of families	728	723	723	726

Adapted from Detroit Area Study, 1956. Source: Representative sample of Detroit Metropolitan area married women, 1955.

because of conflicts with bedtimes or other responsibilities, rather than by choice). One spouse is even more rarely left behind. Our bilateral system does not mean that the husband participates in his kin group and the wife in hers, but both participate in both. The norm is equilateral participation. If relatives are equally accessible, they expect equal contact. Otherwise, vacation visits to the distant family are expected to balance weekend visits to the close one.

Differential compatibility skews the frequency of visiting relatives. Nor are other factors equal. An only child should visit home more often than a many-siblinged partner. A widowed or ill parent needs more visits.

Visits between parents and married children are as ritualized as other aspects of family living. The most popular frequency in Table 12-2 was once or twice a week. Many families get together every weekend, going to church or eating dinner like clockwork year after year.

Although gatherings of the clan occur less often, they also tend to be ritualized (see Table 12-3). Special days on the calendar and familistic events like weddings and funerals bring kin together. Christmas is the favorite season for family visits in the United States:

Table 12-3. Occasions for Large Family Gatherings in City and Country

Occasion	FAMILY RESIDENCE	
	City	*Country*
Family ceremonial occasions		
Family reunions	10%	42%
Birthdays	25	31
Weddings and engagements	14	13
Mother's Day, Father's Day	3	18
Anniversaries	9	9
Funerals	8	9
Children's religious rituals, graduations	7	6
Holidays		
Christmas	34	37
Other religious holidays	7	37
National holidays	43	28
Social occasions	28	24
Total occasions	188	254
None	24	11
Total	212%	265%
Number of families	*724*	*178*

Adapted from Blood and Axelrod, 1955. Representative samples of married women in Detroit Metropolitan area and on Southeast Michigan farms. Totals add to more than 100% where families gathered on more than one occasion.

Daddy's family all got together nearly every holiday but especially at Christmas, at which time they just wouldn't allow anyone to be absent. Only Daddy liked the Swedish food: lute fish, potato sausage, and raisin pudding. This caused conflict every Christmas because no matter how much Mother and we children wanted to do something different, Daddy insisted that we not let his folks down.

This family quarreled over the diverse backgrounds of the parents. But if parents share the same ethnic tradition, clan rituals produce cohesiveness and give a sense of continuity between past and future.

Accessibility

Two types of accessibility affect kin sociability. Geographical distance is more obvious, but social distance may be just as significant.

RESIDENTIAL PROPINQUITY. Typically, people marry within the same community, so their networks overlap. The requirement that couples establish a new ("neolocal") residence does not mean they must go off to a new community but to a new dwelling unit. The chief exceptions are teenage couples so strapped financially that they take advantage of shelter offered by parents. When emergency living arrangements are necessary, couples are more apt to move in with the wife's parents than the husband's, thereby avoiding culture conflict between wife and mother-in-law (Glick, 1957).

Despite the high rate of geographical mobility in America, married couples typically live in the same community with their parents. (In one Indiana county, the median distance from both sets of parents was three miles [Locke, 1951].) Most couples prefer to live near their families and childhood friends. Moving away may improve vocational opportunities, but it reduces family sociability. The greater the distance, the greater the reduction.

If husband and wife come from different communities, where is the ideal place to live? At first glance equality suggests compromising midway. However, if the distance is great enough, sociability would be difficult with both families. More is gained by settling near one family (preferably the wife's) and devoting vacations to visiting the alternate community.

SOCIAL DISTANCE. Cultural diversity strains kin relations the same way it strains husband-wife relations. Sociability suffers when marriages link diverse networks. Mixed marriages create impediments to easy sociability between the extended family and the "outlaw." As a result visiting may be sharply reduced or may not occur at all.

Nine months after the wedding, Joe gave up his childhood Catholicism and joined the Episcopal church that I belong to. He was the first member of his entire blood relation to buck tradition and leave the Church of Rome. This hit his parents hard. For 11 months they would have nothing to do with their son. Not until the baby was born did they come around, acting as if nothing had happened. By that time, however, permanent damage had been done. Joe and I both still feel resentment toward his parents. To this day visits are very infrequent (not more than three or four a year), and we are not invited to any of the Mulligan family reunions.

Social distance is created by social mobility as well as by intermarriage. When children move up the social scale (even with the parents' blessing), visiting becomes less congenial. The more stratified the society, the greater the barrier created by mobility. In Britain, the consequences are particularly apparent (see Table 12-4).

Reduced contact due to social mobility is not unique to Great Britain. In LeMaster's study (1954) of parents of University of Wisconsin students, social mobility also produced "a deterioration of the relationship between the mobile nuclear group and other groups of relatives less mobile."

Reduced contact between divergent families is an adjustive mechanism. Were such families to attempt to associate intimately, they would experience tension and conflict. By avoiding one another, they reduce their difficulties and make it easier to maintain a minimum of positive contact.

Mutual Help in Kin Networks

The essence of kin contact is pure sociability. When emergencies arise, however, kin are the first people to whom most couples turn. Over the life

Table 12-4. Contact between Married Men and Their Fathers, by Occupational Mobility

	OCCUPATIONAL MOBILITY	
Contact with Father	*Stable*	*Mobile*
Within previous day	29%	13%
Within previous week	37	30
Not within previous week	34	57
Total	100%	100%
Number of families	49	76

Adapted from Willmott and Young, 1960: 83. *Source:* Middle-class London suburb, 1959.

cycle, help tends to balance out—as much given as received. Young parents, however, primarily receive.

Help, like sociability, is exchanged primarily between parents and children, and among married siblings—rarely among more distant kin. Nursing care is the commonest help. Presumably it is needed most when the wife is sick. It compensates for one weakness in neolocal families—no mother-substitute is available within the household. Young mothers also periodically depart to hospitals to have babies. Then again grandmothers rescue motherless households.

Even more frequent when children are small is mother-substituting for mothers who are *not* ill. Professional baby sitters cost more than most couples can afford as often as they wish. So nearby grandmothers release their daughters and daughters-in-law from bondage to young children.

Free baby-sitting does not come without complications, however. The child-rearing methods of mother and grandmother are seldom identical, especially when the grandmother is one's mother-in-law. Most grandparents indulge their grandchildren more than parents who are responsible for them all the time. Studies in various cultures suggest that this is a general human tendency: adjacent generations normally tense and alternate generations lax.

Children occasionally are confused by inconsistent handling or try to play their handlers off against each other. But the net effect for all concerned is usually positive. Indeed, free baby-sitting is a major argument for living near one's parents.

Housework is one of the few kinds of help supplied by siblings as often as by parents (Detroit Area Study, 1956). Perhaps the particular tasks are so strenuous that young women are better able to perform them. Again, it is young wives who receive the most help, since young children create the biggest messes.

The preceding types of help are personal services of woman to woman and therefore appropriately matrilateral (that is, concentrated in the wife's

Table 12-5. Help Exchanged in Primary Kin Networks

Type of Help	DIRECTION OF HELP			
	From Parents	To Parents	From Siblings	To Siblings
Help during illness	46%	47%	39%	42%
Financial aid	47	15	6	10
Child care	21	4	11	30
Advice (personal and business)	27	2	5	3
Valuable gifts	18	3	3	2
None	20	44	55	52

Adapted from Sussman, 1959: 336. *Source:* 53 middle-class and 27 working-class families in two areas of Cleveland. Totals add to more than 100% because many families received more than one type of help.

kin network). Table 12-6 shows that help when a child was born came in general four times as often from the wife's mother as from the husband's. Moreover, this matrilineal bias was greatest among high-status families of urban background (the vanguard segment of the American population). Only when the wife's mother lived elsewhere did the local husband's mother become the prime source of help, but even then some wives' mothers made the pilgrimage.

The services I have not discussed yet are largely economic and correlated with the masculine role. If the wife's family gives financial aid, it is liable to be interpreted as criticism of the husband's occupational ability. So, for sensitive egos aid comes better from the man's family. Nevertheless, mature egos can receive as well as give and do not suspect the motives of those who would be generous. As one husband put it:

> Because we travel this life but once, our pride and ego should not stand in the way of opportunities that are placed before us. No one is completely independent. Therefore, the husband should never prevent his family from accepting gifts bestowed upon them, no matter how small or how big. If he does object, he is denying them a life a little fuller, a little brighter.

More than any other type of help, financial aid comes from parents. This reflects the affluence of postparental couples. Given the highest income of a lifetime and lessened expenses, they can help precisely when their children are hardest pressed. In New Haven, financial aid rarely was

Table 12-6. Help After Childbirth, by Residence of Wife's and Husband's Mother

Percentage Receiving Help from Specified Source	Both Mothers	LOCAL RESIDENCE		Neither Mother
		Wife's Mother Only	Husband's Mother Only	
Both mothers	9%	2%	8%	4%
Wife's mother only	53	50	19	42
Husband's mother only	11	5	28	8
Other relatives only	4	15	15	12
Friends, employees only	3	2	4	6
No help	20	26	26	28
Total	100%	100%	100%	100%
Number of cases	210	58	53	50

Adapted from Siddiqui, 1962. *Source:* Representative sample of white wives in Detroit whose first, second or fourth child was born in July 1961. Families in the first three rows may have received help from other sources besides the specified mothers but those listed as "wife's mother only" were not aided by the husband's mother and vice versa.

a regular subsidy, unless the husband was still in training. Normally it provided extra resources for unusual costs like purchasing or building a home (Sussman, 1953a).

The only exception to the general pattern that help flows primarily to young couples occurred with valuable gifts. A large number were received by wives over 60 years old, suggesting that children often chose this means of expressing appreciation for help they had received. Repayment was seldom *expected* to be financial, however. In return for their financial assistance, parents expected children to provide them with affection, attention and personal services, and to include them in some of their activities (*ibid.*).

Some couples feel that help from relatives threatens their marriages. In extreme cases, it probably does. But my forthcoming paper shows that the larger the number of kinds of help ever received, the more satisfied Detroit wives were with their marriages. It seems that relatives usually strengthen those they aid rather than overwhelm them.

Care for Aged Parents

Through most of the life cycle, help flows primarily from parents to children. But when parents get old and feeble, they may need personal care and attention even if they are financially independent. After one parent dies, the survivor is apt to find living alone difficult or precarious. Dependent parents create a dilemma. Most Americans react negatively to the idea of having older people live with their children. (Specifically, almost two-thirds of a national sample were opposed [Morgan, *et al.*, 1962].) Indeed, the older they got, the more often people were unqualifiedly opposed. For both generations, merging households is a last resort to be postponed as long as possible. Moving to the same community, the same neighborhood, or even a separate apartment in the same building is preferred as long as it is feasible. Living nearby makes frequent contact possible without infringing on either family's integrity.

But eventually a surviving parent may need more care and attention than can be provided in an independent location. If grandmother can no longer safely cook her own meals, a separate apartment is no longer possible. The ultimate choice lies between placing her in a nursing home and bringing her into the home of one of her children. That choice depends on both practical and personal factors: (1) How satisfactory are the alternative facilities? Does the family have a room to spare? Is there an attractive institution which the family can afford? (2) How warm is the relationship between the grandmother and her children? For reasons which by now are familiar, mothers move in with daughters more than with sons (by a ratio of 55 to 45 [Glick, 1957]). The wife will have to provide most of the care and sociability, and this happens more spontaneously with one's mother than one's mother-in-law.

If and when an aged parent moves into a child's home, stress is minimized by mutual respect for the autonomy of the still separate "families." Grandmother's room needs even more to be her private castle when she no longer has a house of her own. Conversely, she must respect the integrity of the family whose guest she is (Duvall, 1954).

Should senility wreak its worst havoc, however, even favorite daughters find the strain too much. When mental deterioration means that an aged parent no longer recognizes who is taking care of her, a nursing home is no loss to her, but a relief to the family.

When help for the aged involves financial support, all the descendants deserve to share according to their ability. The kin network is one place for pure communism: from each according to his ability, to each according to his need.

13 *Religion in Family Living*

According to the billboards, "Families that pray together, stay together." According to researchers, the billboards are right.

Religious families have fewer divorces than nonreligious families. For example, couples whose marriages subsequently failed attended church less than those whose marriages were happy. Especially in the latter half of marriage, couples in trouble dropped out of church. However, even in the first half they attended less often (see Table 13-1).

In the second half of marriage, divorcing couples may quit going to church from embarrassment over their marital difficulty as well as decreased willingness to do anything together. Theoretically, churches are supposed to help people in trouble, but people often feel ashamed to face a seemingly judgmental congregation.

Table 13-1. Church Attendance of Happily Married and Divorced Men and Women during the First Half of Marriage

Attended Church per Month	MEN		WOMEN	
	Happily Married	Divorced	Happily Married	Divorced
Four or more times	31%	19%	44%	29%
Two or three times	23	12	14	13
One or less	28	35	30	28
None	18	34	12	30
Total	100%	100%	100%	100%
Number of cases	165	162	167	186

Adapted from Locke, 1951: 241. Source: Cross-sections of an Indiana County, 1939–44. For happily married couples, the "first half of marriage" refers to half the interval prior to being interviewed.

In the first half of marriage also, some of the nonattendance of divorce-prone couples probably results from incipient incompatibility. However, church attendance apparently fosters marital stability. This is illustrated by the fact that individuals who attended Sunday school and church before marriage had more successful marriages (Burgess and Cottrell, 1939).

Most factors that prevent divorce also promote success among nondivorcing couples. Hence, we should expect churchgoers to have more successful marriages.

Table 13-2 shows that church attendance was related to marital happiness for wives. Since religion matters less to the average man than to the average woman, the correlation for husbands was lower. Nevertheless, marital satisfaction for husbands too was associated with regular church attendance (Burchinal, 1957).

In Table 13-2, the unhappiest marriages were not the least religious but the religiously incompatible ones where one partner failed to share the other's religious interests. This suggests an important qualification: *religion contributes to marital stability and success when it is shared by husband and wife.* Sharing involves both identification with a common faith and participation in common activities. If either is missing, religion may be a disintegrative force.

However, as shown in Chapter 3, the highest divorce rates for interfaith marriages were not where a Catholic married a Protestant but where he married someone of no faith at all (or so loosely tied to Protestantism that no denomination could be specified). In that study, marriages between inactive Protestants had an extraordinarily high divorce rate despite their nonreligious homogamy. Moreover, the divorce rate was substantially reduced (from 65 per cent to 18 per cent) when inactive Protestants married denominationally affiliated Protestants (Burchinal and Chancellor, 1963).

From these two studies, it is not clear which is worse—no religion for either partner or no religion for just one. The only thing that is clear is

Table 13-2. Marital Happiness of Wife, by Husband's and Wife's Church Attendance

	CHURCH ATTENDANCE			
Wife's Evaluation of Marriage	Both Regular	Both Occasional	Both Never	Wife Occasional Husband Never
Exceptionally or very happy	91%	79%	62%	55%
Fairly happy	8	19	32	33
Unhappy or very unhappy	1	2	6	12
Total	100%	100%	100%	100%
Number of couples	120	479	269	170

Adapted from Chesser, 1957: 279. *Source:* Women patients of English physicians.

that two religious persons are better than one or none in producing marital stability and happiness.

Religious activity benefits not only adults but their children. For example, Morgan (1962) found that the children of parents who attended church at least twice a month stayed in school and college longer than those whose parents attended less often (even after holding constant parental education, income, and a dozen other intervening factors). Moreover, parents with no religious preference had especially unsatisfactory results. Morgan was puzzled but suggested that the educational achievement of children from religious families may have been "an indication of strongly held values such as family responsibility."

Similarly, in five American cities, arrest rates for juvenile delinquency were higher for children of parents with no religious affiliation than for homogamous marriages of any religious faith (Zimmerman and Cervantes, 1960).

Although causal relations cannot always be determined, religion is correlated with many indicators of family success and stability. At the very least, religious activity and family solidarity are elements in a common way of life.

One more qualification is necessary, however. Religion is important to Protestants and Catholics but not to Jews (Landis, 1960). American Jews generally have happy, stable marriages despite the fact that they seldom attend religious services. Within the Jewish community, the relationship between religious activity and family vitality is not clear. Apparently Jewish communalism—strong today despite the decline of Judaism—provides families with the support which religious associations supply to Christian families (Lenski, 1961).

With these important exceptions religion promotes marital success. How it does so is another question. Unfortunately, the answers have yet to be studied scientifically. Meanwhile, I suggest three contributions: religious rituals in the home, religious institutions in the community, and religious ethics.

Religious Rituals in the Home

Rituals of any kind—secular as well as religious—promote family integration and pride (Bossard and Boll, 1950). Religious rituals offer rich potentialities to family living. Less common in American homes today than in the past, religious rituals nevertheless give those who still practice them a sense of participating in a pattern of meaningful activity.

Grace at Meals

The most frequent religious ritual is grace before meals (Fairchild and Wynn, 1961). The form, of course, varies from faith to faith and family to family. For some, grace means silent meditation, holding hands around the table. For others, it means a chorus of singing together, a time-worn recital by a child, or a spontaneous prayer by a parent. The most tangible consequence is to coordinate family eating. To be sure, grace-less families may rule that eating is taboo until all are seated. However, grace requires coordination. When all eat together, the possibilities of conversation around the dinner table increase. Mothers, especially, are integrated into the family circle when others wait until she finishes serving before even the hungriest child may plunge in.

Family Worship

Family worship is more time-consuming than grace and more difficult to schedule. The gathering of the family around the table for meals is a logical occasion for worship. Extensive worship before meals is difficult for maidless mothers to share and taxes the patience of hungry children. After dinner in the evening offers greater leisure.

A major spread in children's ages may make separate worship necessary for older and younger children. As families move through the life cycle, new patterns become useful, so flexibility and a willingness to experiment are desirable.

Families who don't worship regularly may turn to group reflection in crises. The illness or death of a loved one, the loss of a job or a failed course in school can be an occasion for deepening ties if families pause to explore its meaning together.

Festival Rituals

Just as High Holy Days bring to synagogues those who otherwise never attend, so families that otherwise have no religious activities at home, ceremonialize the festive seasons. Family traditions for celebrating special days appeal especially to children. Sometimes they come down from previous generations through husband or wife. Sometimes they are borrowed from friends or mass media. Sometimes they are invented—intentionally or accidentally. No matter what their source, traditions for celebrating

Christmas and Easter or Hannukkah and Passover add interest and variety to family living.

Participation in Religious Organizations

Churches are composed of families. More than any other institution, they look upon families as their basic units. Families have their own pews. Husbands and wives are expected to attend services together. The clergyman calls on the family at home. As a result of such familistic emphases, church participation promotes family welfare.

External support comes in three ways: (1) participation is a joint family activity; (2) the church provides a supporting network of primary relations; (3) the clergyman is a therapeutic resource in time of trouble. (The last point will be discussed in Chapter 17.)

Church Attendance as a Family Activity

Any joint activity strengthens the family provided it is mutually rewarding. When families leave their home base (where each member has his separate distractions) and go out into the community together, they achieve a sense of group identity. The more regular and frequent the expeditions, the greater the benefit. Church activities aren't unique in this regard. Friday evening expeditions to the swimming pool have similar effects. Yet this is one by-product of church attendance—provided the whole family go together.

Church participation fluctuates over the life cycle. More couples participate after they have children, despite the mobility handicaps presented by small children. As children grow older, attendance by parents reaches a peak (Anders, 1955). Sometimes children themselves ("contaged" by playmates) drag their parents to church. More often parents take the initiative out of a sense of responsibility for their children. After children are "launched," some parents disengage themselves from church activities. Thus churches and families are most closely allied during the child-rearing years.

Institutional Support for Family Life

Church participation links families with similar values. In minority faiths and small, intimate congregations, family friends tend to be drawn from the church (Zimmerman and Cervantes, 1960). When friends interact throughout the week as well as on Sundays, they reinforce each other's values. Their network of primary relationships provides social control, encouraging good behavior and discouraging irresponsibility.

For mobile families "often the church constitutes the one familiar spot in an otherwise strange community." (Fairchild and Wynn) It provides an entree into the community for new families. This is especially true for Catholics, since the world is divided into parishes to which they are automatically assigned. For Protestants the problem is more complex if their old denomination does not exist in the new community. Most Protestants hold their denominational ties lightly, switching to the most accessible church with an attractive minister and a flourishing Sunday school. Indeed, many suburbs offer "united" churches which appeal to liberal Protestants from diverse backgrounds (Whyte, 1957). In any case, the church's latchstring is out, providing a quick means of integration into the community for newcomers.

Even large, impersonal congregations promote commitment to familistic values. Attendance produces a sense of identification with the institution and the values for which it stands. Hence, both informally and formally, as a group and as an institution, the church provides external support for families.

Religious Ethics

Religion is concerned with the way family members treat each other.

Norms of Family Behavior

Most of the ethical content of religion originated in family life. References to the fatherhood of God and the brotherhood of man use family analogies. Religion demands that one treat every man as if he were a member of one's family. Conversely, one should treat every member of one's family as he ought to be treated.

Religious ethics present ideals about human behavior. In the Old Testament they are codified into familistic commandments: "Honor your father and your mother," "You shalt not commit adultery." In the New Testament they are summarized in the great commandment: "Love your neighbor."

Love is the beginning of marriage. Yet it does not always last. The love of man for woman tends to fade, of brother for brother to sour. Family members need to be reminded that though we fail, we must try again. Religion is a reminder. The church is devoted to the propagation of love. Not family love alone, to be sure, but love within the family as much as anywhere else. In sermons and classes the church teaches love. The teachings spell out the requirements of personal relationships: Fidelity—"What God has joined, let no man put asunder." Responsibility—"Bear one another's burdens." Forgiveness—"First be reconciled to your brother." Things to do and things to avoid that heighten the quality of family living.

So high is the idealism of religion that no family ever attains it. Religion asks a "summit" experience of I-Thou relationships. Even though unattainable, lofty goals influence those who take them seriously. They encourage the effort to do better and chill the temptation to be irresponsible.

Besides teaching idealism, religion introduces a third Person into dyadic relationships. Just as a professional counselor has a reconciling influence on marital conflict, so awareness of God provides a new perspective. The change from dyad to triad depolarizes conflicts between husband and wife. From the divine-human relationship also comes grace to forgive and be healed. Then love is not just an ideal to be striven for but a gift strengthening the resolve and the ability to do right by those with whom we live most intimately.

The Family Is not an End in Itself

In the 1950's a Cleveland disc jockey who had accepted kickbacks from manufacturers for playing their records exonerated his behavior by saying he had done it for his family, not for himself. I suppose he was justified in feeling that family selfishness is less primitive than individual selfishness. Yet religion has a broader perspective—the whole human race, past, present, and future. This means that men have obligations beyond their families and that families too have obligations beyond themselves.

Religion makes claims upon money. The biblical minimum is ten per cent, though only the devout and the wealthy manage to share that much.

In Chapter 11 we saw that the average American family gives away less than five per cent of its income. Table 13-3 shows that most of these gifts go to relatives, a modest share to the family church, and only a tiny fraction farther afield. To be sure, some church funds go to benevolences, but most purchase consumer services for the family. In short, the average family in the United States—the richest and one of the most religious countries on earth—spend the bulk of their financial resources on themselves. However, the man (or the family) who "has everything" may not be the happiest.

Religion impels men and women to spend time away from their family in the service of others. Sometimes that time is devoted to local service. Sometimes it severs family ties for months or years under arduous

Table 13-3. Gifts and Contributions to Individuals and Organizations, by Family Income

	NET FAMILY INCOME AFTER TAXES			
	$5,000–5,999	$6,000–7,499	$7,500–9,999	$10,000+
Mean income	$5,447	$6,630	$8,350	$17,055
Contributions to individuals outside the household				
Gifts (Christmas, etc.)	$ 78	$ 88	$125	$ 303
Money for subsistence	40	57	117	454
Contributions to organizations				
Religious	68	81	108	215
Charitable	17	21	35	194
Educational, political, etc.	8	23	16	170
Total	$211	$270	$401	$1,336
Percentage of net income contributed to individuals and organizations	3.9%	4.1%	4.8%	7.8%

Adapted from U.S. Bureau of Labor Statistics, 11 (1957), 292. Source: Families living in large northern cities, 1950 (mean age of husband, 45–49).

circumstances (though the modernized world requires less separation than before). As long as family members share the same values, separation need not be divisive.

Not just parents but the whole family have something to give to others. The home can provide hospitality to those in need of friendship. The foreign student, the patient released from a mental hospital, the lonely widow—these are the people whom religion bids us befriend. "I was a stranger and you took me in. . . ."

14 *Companionship in Leisure*

Between 1900 and 1959 the average working week shrank from 60 hours to 40, and from six days to five (U.S. Bureau of Labor Statistics). Vacations lengthened. Labor-saving devices and prepared foods were invented. As a result, ordinary families have almost as much leisure today as Veblen's celebrated "leisure class" of a few generations ago. The new leisure poses new questions for marriage. How much time should be spent together and how much separately?

The Place of Companionship in Marriage

Elite marriages in feudal societies segregated the sexes so sharply that husband and wife rarely did anything together (except for sexual intercourse). Even sex in many feudal families was diverted to concubines and mistresses (Levy, 1949).

By contrast, companionship is the central feature of modern marriages. Given a choice of five aspects of marriage, urban and rural wives in Michigan overwhelmingly said companionship was the most valuable.

To be sure, the list of alternatives in Table 14-1 was not exhaustive. Nor do we know whether husbands prize companionship as much. (They probably emphasize sex more at the expense of other aspects of marriage.) Nevertheless, companionship is so prominent in Table 14-1 that it is probably the most valued aspect of marriage for both sexes. This emphasis on companionship results from our system of courtship. Couples marry after months and years of conpanionship in dating. One might say they get the companionship habit.

Table 14-1. The Most Valuable Aspect of Marriage, for Farm Wives and City Wives

Most Valuable Aspect of Marriage	Farm Wives	City Wives
Companionship in doing things together with the husband	55%	48%
The chance to have children	23	26
The husband's understanding of the wife's problems and feelings	11	13
The husband's expression of love and affection	9	10
The standard of living—house, clothes, car, etc.	2	3
Total	100%	100%
Number of families	173	724

Adapted from the author's 1955 Detroit Area Study and companion rural research project. Source: Representative samples of Metropolitan Detroit families and Southeast Michigan farm families.

Though Americans normally restrict the term "dating" to unmarried couples, Britishers apply it to married couples as well. When married couples leave their children behind and go out for a good time, they recapitulate premarital dating.

Dating after Marriage

Marriage slashes the proportion of a couple's time devoted to dating. Before marriage they seldom saw each other except on dates. Afterwards most of their time is devoted to routine activities such as eating, sleeping, and housework. Husband and wife may be in the same room but their attention is on the task at hand rather than on each other. Much of their leisure is spent in separate activities or in joint activities focused on the recreational task. Even if couples spent as much time dating after marriage as before, the proportion focused on each other as persons would be reduced.

Dating actually dwindles after marriage. Couples who spent every possible minute going places and doing things before marriage no longer find it necessary. Since they live together, they no longer have to date to be together. On the contrary, dating becomes an escape from everyday routine.

CONTRASTING ROLES. The need to escape varies with the partners' roles. Husbands and wives who have challenging or exhausting occupational or volunteer responsibilities enjoy being home for a change. But the usual division of labor gives the husband more outside experience than the wife. A man who has been in the bustle of business all day hopes for a quiet evening in front of the TV. But the lady of the house has seen too much of those four walls and is eager to go places and do things:

> After I've worked all day at home, I wish Floyd would take me to the symphony, ballet, or opera, but he never does. He says he likes to spend his evenings at home with me—at first I was flattered, but after four years I've had too much of a good thing!

Differential external participation creates conflicting recreational needs. The husband's need for rest is as real as the wife's need to escape. When needs conflict, what principle can be invoked? To compromise would mean going out half as often as the wife wishes. Few wives would expect their wishes to be met every time. Nevertheless, if the choice is between activity and passivity, between doing something and doing nothing, there is much to be said for doing something. Resolving conflicts in favor of activity produces a strenuous life, but in the original Latin, life is synonymous with vitality.

Given a choice between need for activity and need for rest, more effort is required to meet the former. The latter requires only self-control by the wife—and frustration. The net gain to a dated housewife in personal pleasure and to her husband in appreciation for his effort should outweigh the gain to an undisturbed husband in personal rest and to his wife in appreciation for not pressing her point. In extreme cases, to be sure, the husband's fatigue is so great and the wife's boredom so trivial that the balance tips the other way. Ordinarily, however, activity seems the better choice.

THE NEED FOR LOVE. A second reason for strenuous solutions is what it does for the marriage. Dating means doing something together, whereas staying home usually means doing nothing. Moreover, dating has special connotations. Before marriage it produced the intense love of courtship, so after marriage it revives memories of a treasured past. If this were all, however, it might only make married couples bitterly nostalgic. More importantly, dating revives and recreates love. When husband and wife go out to dinner or a movie, conditions are provided for the growth of love.

Before marriage couples are often criticized for being too wrapped up in each other. After marriage the chief danger is that other roles will prevent husband and wife from paying enough attention to each other. This is the disengagement that creates problems in maintaining personal relationships. Dating gives each partner a feeling of still being appreciated and loved:

> Although our recreational activities are fewer now than they were when we were engaged, we still find much companionship in folk-dancing,

canoeing, camping, and hiking together. We seem to enjoy these things even more than before we were married, because now we are less self-conscious and less intent on impressing each other, and can enjoy the sport and each other that much more.

Domesticated Leisure

Even though dating has a crucial role after marriage, it fills only a fraction of the total leisure. The balance of this chapter is devoted to the remainder—leisure together at home, leisure shared with friends, and leisure apart from each other.

Most marital companionship is found at home. Indeed, the happiest marriages depend least on dating-type activities. Table 14-2 ranks activities in terms of the proportion of couples engaging in them, roughly the proportion of time the typical couple devotes to them.

The data in Table 14-2 are fragmentary because of gaps in the available statistics. Nevertheless, they suggest patterns worth considering.

POPULAR ACTIVITIES. The three most popular activities were listening to the radio, music, and reading. Subsequently, television has replaced radio as the chief source of mutual enjoyment. Although music may be heard in various places, TV watching, radio listening, and reading are all fireside activities. None requires much attention to be paid to the partner. Rather, they are parallel activities couples engage in side by side, he reading his newspaper and she, her magazine. As long as both enjoy reading, these activities are harmless enough. Indeed, they may stimulate conversation. However, they are not very romantic.

I emphasize the contrast not because reading and TV should be abolished. They cost so little energy and money that they are understandably the basic stuff of married companionship. By contrast, dating, is the "frosting on the cake." The shift from face-to-face to parallel leisure activities underlies the qualitative transformation of relationships after marriage.

Though domestic leisure occupies first place, married couples don't stay home all the time. Movies, parties, and sports events were mutual attractions for more than half the happily married couples in Table 14-2 (and, in the case of movies, for divorce-prone couples too). Lest anyone think going to the movies increases the danger of divorce, I hasten to add that this difference is not statistically significant, although happily married couples *are* significantly more often *mutually indifferent* to movies.

The last four activities in Table 14-2 are less easily domesticated. For each of them mutual indifference was more auspicious than mutual enjoyment. Even so, a good many couples managed to integrate card-playing and dancing with successful marriage, so those activities need not be blacklisted altogether. They present hazards, however, for incompatible couples. Cards pit husband and wife against each other or, worse yet, team them up so that blunders cause trouble:

> I really enjoy playing bridge as long as I don't have to play with Art. I'm not really a bad player, but every once in a while I bid more conservatively than he thinks I should and he explodes. Any other partner he'll

Table 14-2. Mutual and Unilateral Leisure Activities of Happily Married versus Subsequently Divorced Men and Women

		PARTNER ENJOYING ACTIVITY		
Activity	Both	Husband Only	Wife Only	Neither
Listening to the radio				
Happily married couples	90%	3%*	6%†	2%*
Subsequently divorced couples	75	9*	12†	8*
Music				
Happily married couples	89	4*	1†	4†
Subsequently divorced couples	75	10*	22†	10†
Reading				
Happily married couples	72	9	12†	—
Subsequently divorced couples	46	20	38†	—
Movies				
Happily married couples	68	—	5	17*
Subsequently divorced couples	72	—	13	7*
Parties				
Happily married couples	57	1	4*	24†
Subsequently divorced couples	46	7	11*	45†
Sports				
Happily married couples	54	20*	3†	22†
Subsequently divorced couples	36	35*	15†	32†
Playing cards				
Happily married couples	39	8	—	36*
Subsequently divorced couples	45	21	—	24*
Dancing				
Happily married couples	25	2	7	45*
Subsequently divorced couples	38	9	21	24*
Drinking				
Happily married couples	7	10	1*	42
Subsequently divorced couples	19	38	8*	28
Gambling				
Happily married couples	2	10†	—	—
Subsequently divorced couples	3	40†	—	—

* Reported by husband.
† Reported by wife.
Unstarred percentages are averages for husbands' and wives' reports combined.
"Neither" column means that both partners were "indifferent" to the activity.
Adapted from Locke, 1951: 257–60.

forgive but he says I should know better because he's instructed me so many times.

Bad enough to lose points through the partner's incompetence; worse yet if every point costs money. In any case, scoring systems dramatize differential competence in competitive games, confronting losing couples with undodgeable evidence of their inadequacies. On the other hand, cross-couple doubles pit husband and wife against each other so that each partner's gain is the other's loss. For those whose recreation is deadly serious, this breeds hostility within marriage and positive feeling within the extramarital coalition (Young, 1964).

New coalitions may also be established in noncompetitive situations. As long as husband and wife dance together, *their* romance is promoted. Once they change partners, the new combination is potentially strengthened. If they dance old-style, cheek to cheek, sexual stimulation is added to the mixture. Drinking dissolves marital boundary lines by lowering inhibitions, releasing the power of attraction to new (and therefore more fascinating) partners.

Most gamblers lose more money than they win, their families suffering accordingly. Both gambling and drinking in Locke's study were primarily masculine activities rather than mutual interests.

COMPATIBILITY OF INTERESTS. A striking feature of Table 14-2 is that every comparison between divorced and happily married couples in the two middle columns shows more one-sided interests among the divorced. Some of this must be discounted because divorced people retrospectively exaggerate their differences. (For example, 56 per cent of Locke's divorced women said the husband alone enjoyed drinking, whereas only 20 per cent of the husbands confessed to this.) Nevertheless, the least we can say is that unilateral activities tended to become a focus of marital conflict. Beyond this, we can infer from the undomesticated items at the bottom of the table that while mutual interests in cards, dancing, drinking, or gambling were dangerous enough, unilateral interests were even more likely to lead to disaster. (In every case the percentage difference between divorced and happily married couples was greater when interest was one-sided than when it was mutual.)

Unilateral interest in the remaining areas probably has fewer negative repercussions. To be sure, unilateralism by definition contributes nothing directly to the relationship. On the other hand, separate interests are tolerable, provided they are not considered immoral and do not provoke jealousy or squander the family's resources. Undomesticated activities suffer on all these counts. Conservative moralists consider them inherently sinful; hence if only the partner enjoys them, he is liable to condemnation. More tangibly, financial resources are jeopardized by the cost of liquor and by the threat of alcoholism to the husband's wage-earning capacity. Gambling, with or without cards, is a similar financial hazard. Dancing, as I have already mentioned, threatens the marriage bond, especially if the wife goes dancing alone.

Compatibility of interests is always preferable to incompatibility. However, some activities reinforce marriage more than others. In particular cases Locke's findings may call more for restraint in the way an activity is pursued than for its elimination altogether. However, just as alcoholics must abstain because their defenses are weak, so weak marriages may have to abandon some pleasures to avoid destruction.

Sociability

People who make the best marriage partners also make friends most easily. Before marriage they have more friends of both sexes. After marriage they maintain old friendships not severed by mobility and make new ones. Marriage, therefore, is not exclusive in the sense that it terminates other friendships. Rather, it is the most intimate and durable of friendships. Just as marriage links two kin networks, it also links two sets of friends. Husbands and wives with the ability to establish good personal relations, gradually get to know each other's friends so that they become common friends.

During courtship, double dates with the man's friends are more common than with the woman's. Hence the common friends of newly married couples are more often husband-initiated than wife-initiated (Babchuk, 1965). Most friendships are initially man to man or woman to woman but for married couples they usually become couple to couple friendships. The closer a friendship is, the more likely it is eventually to include both partners in both couples. Despite this diffusion, however, friendships remain partly specialized along sex lines, the man interacting more with men and feeling closer to them, and the same for wives.

Babchuk found that half of his middle-class couples in Lincoln, Nebraska, shared all their closest friends, whereas the remainder had some separate close friends. Couples with the largest number of friends had both the most joint friends and the most separate friends, proving there is no necessary antagonism between these two types. Similarly, Locke's happily married couples had more common friends than those who later got divorced. Clearly, the same human relations skills underlie both marriage and friendship.

Unless opportunities to interact develop, friendship networks cannot coincide completely. Especially with his own sex, each partner moves in circles partially removed from the other. As a result of this segregation, men have more male than female friends, and vice versa.

Because of both the personal sociability and the mutual companionship of happily married couples, they have more friends of both their own sex and the opposite sex than unhappily married couples (see Table 14-3).

CROSS-SEX FRIENDSHIPS. Opposite-sex friends are often met through the spouse or with the spouse—couple to couple. Unanswered in Table 14-3 is how many opposite-sex friends are not shared with the spouse. I have already pointed out that happily married couples tend to share their friends with each other. They also tend to acquire opposite-sex friends jointly as they do things together. Nevertheless, I doubt that they make sharing a *sine qua non* of cross-sex friendships. Before marriage they made friends easily with the opposite sex, and they make new friends after marriage. Just as they were attracted to marry across sex lines, so they are attracted to friends of the opposite sex (as well as their own sex). Unlike "authoritarian personalities" they are not prejudiced against the opposite sex nor rigidly segregated in their social life (Adorno, 1950). They are not afraid of mixed company nor embarrassed to find themselves the only man in a group of women, or vice versa.

If people who make good marriages make friendships easily with persons of the opposite sex, does this mean there are no dangers in unshared cross-sex friendships? Triangular divorces show the potential dynamite. Even couples whose marriages never come close to divorce may be plagued by jealousy and tension when cross-sex friendships threaten to develop into love affairs. Just because one is married does not guarantee that friends will remain just friends. The forces which produce the momentum of love and the impulse to intimacy before marriage, generate increasing involvement outside marriage as well.

Husbands and wives face the same problems in limiting extramarital intimacy that they do premaritally (see Chapter 5). And the same arguments about the value of distinguishing between marriage and nonmar-

Table 14-3. Men Friends and Women Friends during Marriage, for Happily Married versus Divorced Men and Women

| | Men Friends | | | | Women Friends | | | |
| | HUSBAND'S | | WIFE'S | | HUSBAND'S | | WIFE'S | |
Number of Friends During Marriage	Married	Divorced	Married	Divorced	Married	Divorced	Married	Divorced
Many or several	87%	74%	56%	31%	64%	52%	86%	64%
A few or almost none	13	26	44	69	36	48	14	36
Total	100%	100%	100%	100%	100%	100%	100%	100%

Adapted from Locke, 1951: 232–34. *Source:* 200 happily married couples and 201 divorced couples plus additional one-partner-only reports.

riage apply here. Again the ideal is to avoid drifting into quasi-marital relationships with extramarital partners. Again the crucial distinction is in sexual intimacy. If cross-sex friendships are to be integrated successfully with marriage, they must be limited to something less than the total involvement of marriage.

The multiplicity of cross-sex friends for happily married individuals decreases the likelihood of overinvolvement with one friend. The greatest danger occurs when a special friend becomes an alternative resource, or worse yet an ally against the partner. When a man complains about his wife to another woman and seeks her sympathy, he is a long way down the road to remarriage. By his criticisms he destroys the "fiction of solidarity," revealing thereby what Waller and Hill (1951) believe is "a master symptom of alienation." By his plea for sympathy he flings open the door to a new affair. In both respects he crosses the boundary line between safe and hazardous cross-sex friendships.

The fiction of solidarity is also destroyed by those few men (and even fewer women) who remove their wedding rings to date unsuspecting partners. This pretense requires the anonymity of urban environments. In rural communities public knowledge of one's comings and goings minimizes deviant behavior. But even in suburban apartment complexes, the deadend courtyard has been described as "the greatest invention since the chastity belt":

> . . . it's almost impossible to philander without everyone's knowing about it. One's callers are observed, and if neighbors feel there is anything untoward, suburbia's phenomenal grapevine will speed the news. This is not mere venom; in a web of relationships as delicate as that of a court, an affair can harm not only two marriages, it can upset the whole court applecart (Whyte, 1957: 393–94).

A web of relationships buffers marital stability. Attempts to escape this web through secrecy are a sign of trouble. As long as cross-sex friendships are openly conducted, there is little to fear, save in those rare circles where the whole group engages in wife-swapping.

Ultimately, however, each person must limit his heterosexual friendships at the particular point where they threaten his spouse. This point will not be the same for every couple (except that it will be somewhere short of the uninhibited intimacy of marriage). The stronger the marriage and the more emotionally secure the partner, the deeper the friendships he or she will be able to tolerate. The deeper those friendships become, the more open the partners will need to be in order to maintain each other's confidence and to work out whatever anxieties arise. In short, the harder the partners work at their marriage, the richer both their marriage and their friendships can become.

Here, indeed, is a major distinction between the premarital and the extramarital situation. Before marriage, the impulse to involvement with the beloved is unchecked by any competing loyalty. After marriage, love for the partner and commitment to the partner limit the individual's freedom to become involved with others. Moreover, the other partner provides a social control similar to the neighbors. In sum, the individual's own commitment to the marriage partner and the partner's active concern impose dual restraints on extramarital friendships to keep them from overheating.

Before marriage the relationship between one man and one woman is uncomplicated by third parties. After marriage, cross-sex friends are by definition third parties. Indeed, if both friends are married, there are four parties involved. The complex social structure of the extramarital situation imposes limitations which the premarital dyad did not face in moving toward ultimate involvement in marriage. Before marriage the cross-sex task is to choose a marriage partner. After marriage it is to achieve meaningful human relationships short of marriage while being married to someone else. It is a complicated task, but for adults skilled in human relations it is not impossible. Indeed, both the person and the marriage may be enriched by this achievement. Just as the child learns how to love from his parents, the adult may enlarge his capacity to love through every deep friendship.

JOINT SOCIABILITY. One change from courtship is the increased popularity of double-dating. Whereas before marriage the most precious commodity is privacy, afterward the preference is for group activity. In elite circles business is mixed with pleasure as entertaining colleagues and clients becomes a major activity.

Families acquire friends who perform the same supportive function which Whyte described for the court groupings of Park Forest. In six American cities, Zimmerman and Cervantes (1960) found most families surrounded by an enduring cluster of families who shared their values. By associating together, they gained satisfaction from compatibility within the group and protective solidarity against outsiders with different values. Moreover, the more homogeneous the group (in class, religion, kinship, and region of origin), the lower the divorce rate. The same compatibilities that promote marital stability reinforce that stability when extended to a larger circle. If couples choose compatible friends, their leisure-time sociability can be a major reinforcement.

The Place of Individuality in Marriage

Perhaps everyone agrees that married couples need to spend some time together. But the obverse question is more difficult—should they spend *all* of it together?

The Romantic Ideal

In the full flush of romance, couples dream of merging their lives. "The twain shall become one flesh"—usually applied to sexual communion—is extended to singleness of mind and purpose: common attitudes, common interests, common thinking. This ideal has no room for lasting differences. Diverse interests and views should be worked at until common ground is established. Separate friends and separate activities must be abandoned with bachelorhood. Marriage should be a united front. "Marriage prediction tests" likewise imply that unification is desirable. To get the maximum score, couples must engage in all conventional activities together (Locke, 1951). Carried to its logical conclusion, however, the merging of personalities loses its attractiveness:

> Before her marriage, Charlotte was a person of many and varied interests. She loved music and read widely. In short, she was an interesting person. Then she married. She was very much in love with Tim, so when at first she started acting and thinking like him, it was "cute." But then the situation reached a point where it became heartbreaking to her friends and relatives. She no longer talked to them from her own point of view. She now said, "Tim thinks this" or "My husband says that," even in matters of the smallest importance. She seemed to lose the power to become angry in her own right. She no longer said, "I was so mad," as she had many times before, but now she said, "My husband was so mad." In short, she has reached a point where she no longer has any individuality.

Cooperative Individuality

An alternative ideal balances unity and individuality. This ideal was expressed by Gibran: *

> But let there be spaces in your togetherness,
> And let the winds of the heavens dance between you.
> Love one another, but make not a bond of love:
> Let it rather be a moving sea between the shores of your souls.
> Fill each other's cup but drink not from one cup.
> Give one another of your bread but eat not from the same loaf.

> Sing and dance together and be joyous, but let each one of you
> be alone,
> Even as the strings of a lute are alone though they quiver with
> the same music.

This poetry values the cooperation of interdependent persons in marriage, not their "blending" into one.

INDIVIDUAL FREEDOM. Continuing individuality requires mutual respect and personal privacy after marriage. This is symbolized by leaving the partner's mail to be opened by him rather than blithely assuming that now that we're married, all mail is for us. Similarly, marriage need not end all individual activities and friendships. Husbands obligated to give up their good times with "the boys" find marriage stifling instead of invigorating:

> I wanted to go to the office ball games on Wednesday nights, but my wife always manages to interfere so I never have any liberty. I'd like to go with the fellows to the fights too, but she complains about that. You can't go out together all the time!

If there were no differences between masculine and feminine interests, men interested in baseball and boxing might marry women with the same interests. Since the sexes differ, there aren't enough feminine ball and fight fans to go around. Nor are there enough hunters, football players, and poker players. To reverse the problem, too few males match female interests in art, music, poetry, and drama. To make matters worse, some organizations are closed to the opposite sex:

> We submit that tavern society is still basically a man's world. The world of the Elks Club, the American Legion, the Moose, are basically male worlds. Luncheon clubs, athletic clubs, veterans' organizations, hunting clubs—all these, within limits, illustrate a way of life that is essentially masculine in our society (LeMasters, 1957: 489).

Similarly, the League of Women Voters, the Garden Club, and the Junior League are off limits to even the most talented husbands.

Scrupulous adherence to the romantic ideal would eliminate many recreational activities. Most married men and women don't make these sacrifices. The only question is whether they should. If Gibran is right about spaces in togetherness, they shouldn't. Separate activities threaten marriage chiefly when they engulf a man's leisure, leaving none for his wife. Only when the husband's friends prohibit all marital companionship is the wife justifiably resentful:

All summer long Cliff has spent every Saturday afternoon playing golf with some of the other V.P.'s and it annoys me. Not that I want to take his fun away from him. It's just that I like to play too, and he never pays any attention to me. It makes me feel gypped and cheated. On our vacation last week, when he suggested a game to me I nearly fell over. I think we both had a whale of a good time. I know I did.

This wife didn't want to play golf with her husband all the time—only some of it. After he plays with her for a change, she should be able to accept the next separation more easily.

The choice is not between no freedom and complete freedom, but how to balance freedom and togetherness. Moderation was not inconsistent with marital happiness in Locke's research (1951): almost half of his happily married couples engaged in some but not all of their outside interests together. Moreover, I doubt the remaining couples' assertion of complete unity. Happy couples tend to overstate their togetherness because they are so satisfied with their marriages. When checked more precisely, they confess to interests engaged in separately without offending the partner (Benson, 1955). In short, they share enough common interests to be able to accept separate activities without anxiety. Only when companionship is insufficient or personal insecurity excessive do separate activities cause conflict.

Individual talents need not atrophy just because the spouse does not share them. If the husband is a crack shot with a rifle but his wife is afraid of guns, he doesn't have to stay glumly home nor must she drag herself around the countryside. If a musical wife is married to a tone-deaf husband, he doesn't have to attend quartet rehearsals in order to prevent her from wasting her talents. Instead he can relax at home with his mystery story while she fiddles away elsewhere—each of them unguiltily enjoying his favorite sport—provided there are other things they do together.

INDIVIDUAL GROWTH. The problem is not simply to retain talents brought into marriage. If husband and wife have a free relationship, they will cultivate new interests, even though the spouse may not join the effort. The challenge of marriage is to maintain love between continually growing and changing human beings. This challenge is more difficult but more rewarding than monolithic unity.

If husband and wife continue growing, they will grow apart as well as together. Common experiences will bring them closer together, but distinctive roles in life will stimulate divergent interests. The husband's professional growth may make his shop talk unintelligible to his wife. And even in equalitarian marriages, the wife is apt to develop more interest than the husband in child psychology. Besides, chance factors may spur one partner in new directions. Couples who originally saw eye to eye politically may find one partner suddenly enthusiastic about a candidate of the opposite party. The wife may catch the contagion of faith-healing while the husband's religious fervor cools. Such divergencies create problems in husband-wife understanding and empathy, but they also mean the partners have not stagnated.

INDIVIDUALITY VERSUS DISENGAGEMENT. In Chapter 16, I will describe "disengagement" as a major threat to marriage: drifting apart into separate ways. What is the difference between disengagement and individuality? How can the first be harmful and the second beneficial when they sound so much alike? I suspect the difference is not in what couples do when they are apart but in what happens when they come back together. Disengaged couples ignore each other. But couples still involved with each other bubble over with the events they have experienced apart. They have more to share because something has happened that the other doesn't know about. In communicating their private worlds, they enable the partner to share vicariously in their achievements. The horizons of life are stretched to cover the territory each has explored alone. Such couples fulfill Martin Buber's phrase: "All life is meeting." For them, the stimulus of autonomous experience revitalizes their encounter. Their individual activities harvest resources to be brought home. Their marriage becomes wealthier than it would have been if they had confined their explorations to paths they could walk together.

Freedom in marriage—yes. But there must be unity, too. Too much freedom ends in separation and divorce. Too much unity is smothering. Happy are those who maintain a flexible bond between growing personalities. For them, marriage is a liberating force and a creative achievement.

15 Sex: The Most Intimate Relationship

The theme of this book is the achievement of intimacy between men and women. Sexual intercourse can provide the ultimate intimacy—can but doesn't necessarily. Physically, to be sure, intercourse involves the greatest intimacy, the greatest revelation of the self, the maximum interaction of body with body. When it unites partners in love, they give themselves unreservedly to each other. As a profoundly sensual experience, it adds a new dimension to their relationship.

But sex is not necessarily intimate psychologically. When mental blocks exist between husband and wife, when he forces himself upon her, when she begrudges being "used," physical intimacy is shorn of emotional unity. Incongruity between the physical and psychological relationships of husband and wife may even widen the gap between them.

The challenge of marriage is to integrate the sexual and nonsexual aspects to produce a deeper oneness, expressing in new terms the language of love. Then husband and wife experience most profoundly the communion of one life with another. Then marriage becomes fully personal, relating the whole man and the whole woman. Then marriage is unique, transcending the closest friendship.

The Essence of Marriage

Many phrases equate marriage with sex. The "marriage bed" is not where couples sleep but where they have intercourse. Even "sleeping together" is synonymous with intercourse. The "wedding night" refers to sexual initiation. Intercourse is the "consummation" of marriage. Without it even the most conservative legal jurisdictions and religious communions consider couples not yet fully married, a so-called marriage can be annulled, and the partners are free to enter a true marriage with someone else. This may seem to overemphasize the place of sex, but these phrases symbolize the importance society attaches to the sexual aspect of marriage. Subjectively, many a wife feels that when she "goes to bed with" her husband, she is most truly being a wife:

> I didn't know much about sex before I got married. I didn't think much about it because I was so much in love. I was a little scared, too. Now? It's just about like it was when we first got married. *Any time he wants me for a wife*, it's O.K. with me. That's the way it should be. If you want to have a happy family you have to feel that way about each other. It's important to both of us; it makes us feel closer to each other. We both enjoy it equally (Rainwater, 1960: 105; italics added).

Sex and the Rest of Marriage

Though sex is the essence of marriage, success in marriage depends on more than that. Nor are other aspects of marriage so unimportant that sex is unaffected by them. Rather, cause and effect work both ways between sex and the rest of marriage.

This can be seen most clearly when things go wrong. Trouble in one area spreads to others. Sexual inadequacy leaves couples tense and grumpy, liable to flare up when other frustrations arise. Conversely, nonsexual problems create barriers to sexual satisfaction. Wives with grievances against their husbands often refuse to have sexual relations. If they have intercourse despite marital tensions, they can't relax and respond in intercourse. Though the husband's physical response is less affected, he cannot enjoy the experience when his wife is angry (unless he is a sadist).

Because of this reciprocal influence, most couples are either satisfied or dissatisfied with both the sexual and nonsexual aspects of their relationship. For example, Chesser (1957) found a close correlation between the wife's sexual satisfaction and her love for her husband. Similarly, Terman (1938) found positive correlations between both partners' marital happiness and their frequency of intercourse, their degree of physical release from intercourse, and the wife's frequency of orgasm.

The crucial test of influence comes in exceptional cases where the sexual and nonsexual aspects of marriage are temporarily out of kilter. If sexual adjustment is high and marital adjustment is low, will the marriage get better or sex deteriorate? For husbands in one follow-up study, the answer was fifty-fifty regardless of whether it was the sexual adjustment or the nonsexual that was initially poor (Dentler and Pineo, 1960).

Although we will see shortly that sexual responsiveness in wives generally increases with length of marriage, Table 15-1 shows that this was true chiefly for marriages which were consistently happy. By contrast, in marriages which were never very happy, the wife's sexual responsiveness fell even lower than it was originally. The sexual "temperature" of marriages which went sour understandably dropped most sharply. On the other hand, couples who got off to a bad start and subsequently improved their marital relationship failed to overcome their initial sexual handicap even though they wound up next to the top in sexual responsiveness. The table dramatizes the close relationship between the marriage as a whole and sexual adjustment in particular.

A QUESTION OF VALUES. Generally speaking, sexual difficulty affects the rest of marriage. This depends, however, on the importance the particular people attach to sex. For those who feel sex is unimportant, sexual difficulty is less disappointing.

When wives were divided into those with strong and weak sexual desires, sexual deprivation affected marriage the most for those whose desires were strongest (Wallin, 1957). Values differ between the sexes as well as between individuals. Men generally value sex more than women do. Therefore, sexual gratification affects marital satisfaction more for men than for women. Deprivation, after all, is relative, depending not so much on amount of sexual experience as on the relationship between actual and desired experience.

To summarize, sex is an essential part of marriage and in many respects the crux of the husband-wife relationship. However, couples and individuals differ in the importance they attach to sex. The penalties of sexual

Table 15-1. Women's Sexual Responsiveness, by Marital Happiness and Duration of Marriage

Marriage type	MARITAL HAPPINESS BY DURATION OF MARRIAGE		DURATION OF MARRIAGE PERCENTAGE SEXUALLY RESPONSIVE BY		NET CHANGE
	<3 years	5+ years	Under 3 years	5 or more years	
Happy	+	+	82%	88%	+6%
Disillusioned	+	−	78	61	−17
Late-blooming	−	+	71	67	−4
Unhappy	−	−	65	56	−9

Adapted from Clark and Wallin, 1965. Happy marriages were described by the wife as "very happy" (plus sign). Unhappy marriages were rated as "moderately happy, moderately unhappy or very unhappy" (minus sign). The numbers of cases for the four marriage types were 116, 67, 75, and 139 respectively. Sexual responsiveness was defined as "usually or always" achieving orgasm in intercourse. Reciprocal percentages achieved orgasm less often.

difficulties and the benefits of sexual achievement vary correspondingly.

COMPARATIVE DIFFICULTY. The uniqueness of the sexual aspect of marriage means it is less predictable than the rest of marriage. To be sure, those who begin sexual relations before marriage have a head start on working out their sexual adjustment (Kanin and Howard, 1958). Nevertheless, the initial phase—whenever it comes—more often discloses discrepancies and dissatisfaction than any other aspect of the interpersonal relationship. One study of parents of Michigan State University students showed fewer husbands and wives satisfied from the beginning with their sexual experiences than with any other aspect of marriage (Landis, 1947). Difficulties of initial sexual adjustment generally reflect differences between the sexes in the "equipment" they bring to marriage.

Sexual Equipment

Differences between the sexes in anatomy, physiology, and psychological processes affect sexual experience. These are the ingredients the partners bring to the marriage bed, out of which they face the task of fashioning a satisfying sexual relationship.

Sexual Anatomy

Married couples don't have to know as much anatomy and physiology as a physician in order to achieve satisfaction. Nevertheless, some facts have practical implications for marital sexual behavior, and a basic vocabulary aids communication. In both sexes clusters of nerve endings sensitive to touch provide the major sensations of sexual experience.

THE GENITAL AREA. In men these nerves center chiefly in the penis, especially in the head of the penis. In sexual excitement, spongy blood vessels become so engorged with blood that the penis almost doubles in length (to an average of six and one-quarter inches [Masters and Johnson, 1966] *). The length of the erect penis is not proportional to the flaccid size. Rather, there is some tendency for a short penis to lengthen more than a long one. Nor is there any correlation between the size of a man's body and the size of his penis. Rather, the length of the limp penis varies

* This chapter draws heavily on Masters and Johnson's intensive laboratory investigation of human sexual response. For simplicity, I will henceforth omit the date in referring to Masters and Johnson's 1966 book or use the abbreviation M/J.

widely between individuals of the same height. The enlarged penis is labeled "erect" because it stands out stiffly from the body, enabling penetration of the vagina. The erectile stretching of the skin covering the head of the penis increases its sensitivity to tactile stimulation (see Figure 15-1).

Technically speaking, the female analogue of the penis is the clitoris (see Figure 15-2). Much smaller than the penis, the clitoris is embedded in fleshy tissues so that many women are initially unaware of it. Nevertheless, like the penis, it enlarges when its spongy blood vessels expand in sexual arousal. With further sexual arousal, it retracts to become even less accessible than usual. The head of the clitoris is so sensitive that it is liable to become irritated if manipulated directly. Most women prefer indirect stimulation of the clitoris via manipulation of the mons pubis.

After the clitoris retracts, direct stimulation by manual manipulation or penile contact becomes practically impossible. However, indirect stimulation occurs "in every coital position where there is a full penetration of the vaginal barrel by the erect penis." (M/J) Some women achieve more rapid and intensive clitoral response in the female-superior position which allows them to control coital movement.

Most women enjoy indirect stimulation of the clitoris during orgasm. This comes with continued male thrusting. Because most males prefer to

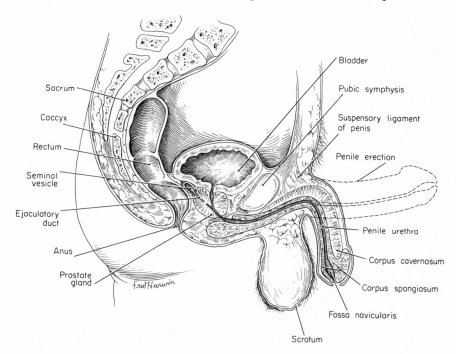

Figure 15-1. Male Genital Organs in Cross Section (Side View)

cease thrusting on reaching climax, this suggests that ideally the woman's climax should precede the man's.

The vagina has very few tactile nerve endings. Some of the tissues surrounding the vaginal entrance are highly sensitive, especially the small inner lips (or "labia minora") and the vestibule of the vagina. Since these surround the vaginal opening, they are stimulated by the rhythmic movements of the penis during intercourse and are a source of pleasure to the woman.

If the hymen is large enough to prevent easy entrance of the erect penis, it interferes with first intercourse, often tearing and bleeding in the process. This can be prevented by advance dilation or surgical cutting.

The vagina is elastic in both length and diameter and is equipped at the entrance with engorgable spongy tissues and a sphincter muscle which enable it to adapt to the penis. Even though individuals of both sexes differ considerably in the size of their genital organs, vaginal adaptability makes anatomical incompatibility rarely, if ever, a problem. Among Masters and Johnson's 400 women subjects, only two had vaginas small enough to create pain if intromission occurred prior to achieving high levels of sexual excitement with corresponding vaginal dilation. Under maximum stimulation even these women were able to accommodate a penis of any size. One has only to realize how much the vagina stretches during childbirth to appreciate its extraordinary flexibility.

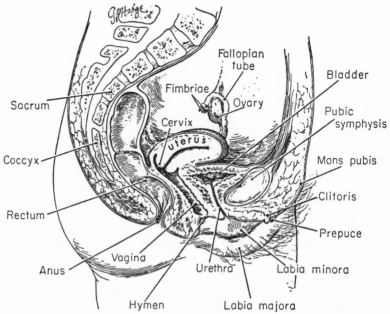

Figure 15-2. Female Genital Organs in Cross Section (Side View)

Torn muscles and loss of muscular tone after childbirth create the opposite problem of vaginal enlargement for some women. Their physical sensitivity in intercourse is reduced but they are usually sufficiently stimulated psychologically to find intercourse satisfying nevertheless.

Sexual Physiology

In both sexes, sexual stimulation produces two major responses: (1) vasocongestion (concentration of blood in particular locations) and (2) muscular tension.

Sexual Arousal. The initial physiological response of the male is erection of the penis due to vasocongestion of the spongy tissues. Its analogue in the female is lubrication of the vaginal walls by a process similar to sweating. Masters and Johnson report that both responses occur with equal ease under either physical or psychic stimulation.

During sexual arousal, muscular tension produces an erection of the nipples in three-fifths of all men and women (M/J). Blood flowing to the breasts enlarges them most extensively in women whose breasts have not yet been stretched to full size by milk produced after childbirth.

Blood flowing to the skin produces a measles-like rash known as a "sex flush" in a minority of males and a majority of females. This reaction is irregular but increases with the growing responsiveness produced by extensive sexual experience. A minority of men and women feel a cold sweat after the sex flush disappears at orgasm.

The Nature of Orgasm. Although preadolescent boys achieve climax without ejaculation, after puberty the two are essentially synonymous. Contractions of various fine muscles force the seminal fluid from the penis under such pressure that it may project one or two feet from the unencumbered penis. (In intercourse this deposits sperm deep in the vagina adjacent to the cervix.) The larger the volume of fluid ejected, the more pleasurable the sensation. Volume generally increases the longer the interval since the last ejaculation.

The focus of female orgasm is the outer third of the vagina. This anterior segment of the vaginal wall becomes congested with blood and responds during orgasm with a series of strong, rhythmic contractions approximately one second apart (the same interval as in male ejaculation). The larger the number of contractions, the more intense the orgasm. Masters and Johnson label three to five contractions "mild," six to eight "normal," and eight to fifteen "intense." They describe the sensations of orgasm as follows:

1. Orgasm has its onset with a sensation of suspension or stoppage. Lasting only an instant, the sensation is accompanied or followed immediately by an isolated thrust of intense sensual awareness, clitorally oriented, but radiating upward into the pelvis.
2. A simultaneous loss of overall sensory acuity. . . .
3. . . . a sensation of "suffusion of warmth" specifically pervading the pelvic area first and then spreading progressively throughout the body. . . .
4. . . . a feeling of involuntary contraction with a specific focus in the vagina or lower pelvis. . . . [The] sensation . . . of "pelvic throbbing" . . . though initially concentrated in the pelvis, was felt throughout the body . . . often . . . continuing until it became one with a sense of the pulse or heartbeat (1966: 135-136).

Although the penis and vagina are the focus of orgasm, many other parts of the body are also involved. Contractions of the vaginal "orgasmic platform" are paralleled by contractions of the uterus, especially in women whose uterine muscles have previously contracted in successive childbirths. Both sexes involuntarily breathe faster and more deeply, the heart beats faster, and the arms, legs, and neck may jerk in muscular spasms.

After orgasm, the blood which has engorged the penis, vaginal wall, clitoris, and breasts disperses more rapidly for men than for women. Consequently men relapse faster into relaxation and sleep.

ORGASM CAPACITY. Both sexes attain orgasm more easily in masturbation than in intercourse. Masturbation enables the individual to stimulate himself more effectively and to focus on his own sensations. It is the best measure of the maximum physiological capacity of the two sexes.

In Kinsey's research, men and women differed in their speed of attaining orgasm through masturbation. Although there was great variation among individuals of the same sex, the average woman required twice as long as the average man (see Table 15-2). Unfortunately, no comparable data are available for intercourse. However, the fact that climax in intercourse is less regular for women than for men suggests that the female time lag may be even greater there. In any case, a common task in marriage is to delay the husband's climax and hasten the wife's.

For most males, ejaculation dependably follows erection. If a man is capable of being sexually aroused, he can usually go all the way to climax. Women are more variable in their orgasm capacity, although their responsiveness has increased in recent decades.

Table 15-3 shows that American women have become progressively more responsive. We shall see later that similar progress occurs within the average marriage. Nevertheless, ten per cent of Kinsey's respondents never achieved an orgasm, no matter how long they were married, and many others were only occasionally successful.

The lesser dependability of the female capacity for orgasm is offset by

Table 15-2. Speed of Arousal to Orgasm in Males and Females

Number of Minutes	Males	Females
Under 1 minute	31% ⎫	
1 to 2 minutes	21 ⎬	45%
2 to 3 minutes	12 ⎭	
3 to 5 minutes	18	24
5 to 10 minutes	12	19
Over 10 minutes	6	12
Total	100%	100%
Median	1.9 minutes	4 minutes

Adapted from Kinsey, 1948: 178 and 1953: 626. *Sources:* Speed of orgasm in masturbation for preadolescent males and for females of all ages (including only those women eventually reaching orgasm).

Table 15-3. Responsiveness to Orgasm of Two Generations of American Wives Early in Marriage

Percentage of Marital Intercourse with Orgasm	DECADE OF BIRTH	
	Before 1900	1920–29
None	33%	22%
1–29%	9	8
30–59%	10	12
60–89%	11	15
90–100%	37	43
Total	100%	100%
Number of cases	331	484

Adapted from Kinsey, 1953: 403. Data for last six months of first year of marriage.

the capacity of many women (but few men) to achieve repeated orgasms within a few minutes. Moreover, successive orgasms are increasingly pleasurable for the female but decreasingly so for males as the volume of ejaculate decreases (M/J).

Orgasms are physiologically inevitable only for males. Accumulated semen must eventually be released through involuntary nocturnal emissions ("wet dreams") if in no other way. Women have no comparable inevitability.

Sexual Psychology

Men are erotic—women are romantic. This epigram poses a key challenge to marriage.

SOURCES OF SEXUAL AROUSAL. Men and women are sexually aroused by contrasting stimuli. For men erotic stimuli are most provocative, whereas women are stimulated by more romantic sources.

Table 15-4 shows that the sexes differed most in response to unambiguously erotic stimuli. To be sure, some of the female diffidence to erotic stimuli reflects the fact that floor shows and burlesque are largely designed for males. Nevertheless, equalization of the stimulus did not equalize the response. Masculine stimuli leave most women cold or even disgusted, whereas the more erotic the female stimulus, the more excited men become. The differences between the sexes diminished or were reversed in those areas ambiguous enough to allow the sexes to respond to different features of the situation. Women responded most distinctively to commercial movies and literature. I suspect that they differed sharply in the books and films which aroused them. Men prefer European movies and sexy paperbacks. Women prefer romantic movies and novels. Thus, even where the sexes seem most alike, they still differ.

SEX AND LOVE. These contrasts reflect the fact that sex and love are linked more closely for women than for men. To most women, sex apart from love is revolting. To most men sexual arousal apart from love happens frequently. The task of marriage is to link an erotic man with a romantic woman in a mutually satisfactory relationship. This is neither easy nor natural. Left to the free play of their impulses, men would be polygamous or at least promiscuous, to the dismay of their wives.

However, the restraining influence of civilization enables men and women to meet each other's contrasting needs. The more civilized, the better educated, and the more mature the individuals, the greater their success in integrating sex and love. In his study of mentally healthy people,

Table 15-4. Sources of Sexual Arousal for Males and Females

Stimulus	PERCENTAGE EVER SEXUALLY AROUSED BY PARTICULAR STIMULUS	
	Male	Female
Fantasies about the opposite sex	84%	69%
Portrayals of sexual activity	77	32
Observing the opposite sex	72	58
Burlesque and floor shows	62	14
Reading books	59	60
Nude photographs	54	12
Hearing erotic stories	47	14
Watching commercial movies	34	48

Adapted from Kinsey, 1953: 651–71. Reciprocal percentages had never been aroused by the particular stimulus. All percentages were based on those actually exposed to the stimulus.

Maslow (1953) found that "sex and love can be and most often are very perfectly fused with each other in healthy people. . . . Self-actualizing men and women tend on the whole not to seek sex for its own sake, or to be satisfied with it alone when it comes."

To fuse sex and love requires contrasting efforts by the husband and the wife. The wife must give herself physically to her husband and be willing to have sexual relations more often than her impulses dictate. The husband's strategy must be to seduce his wife romantically, to put her in the right frame of mind by words and settings that appeal to her. With such efforts men and women can bridge their differences in sexual psychology and synthesize sex with love and the rest of marriage. In middle-class marriages these efforts enable most wives to enjoy sex as much as their husbands (59 per cent of the wives in Rainwater, 1965). To be sure, if one partner enjoyed sex more than the other, it was almost always the husband rather than the wife (33 per cent versus 8 per cent). But one of the achievements of modern civilization is that marriage has become sufficiently equalitarian in power structure, desegregated in role structure, and emotionally close to enable wives to enjoy sex. Moreover, even where husbands enjoyed it more than their wives, both partners had essentially positive feelings. Most of those wives felt mildly positive, however, rather than strongly positive like their husbands. (Negative feelings were concentrated almost exclusively among wives of unskilled workers.)

Development of the Sexual Relationship

At least as much as any other aspect of marriage the sexual relationship is dynamic. Both its physical and social elements produce changes over time.

The First Experience

Like a first parachute jump or first childbirth, the first intercourse is an adventure never to be repeated. Whether it comes after marriage or before, whether with fiancée or stranger, curiosity and discovery are involved. Since no art can be perfected without practice, initial doubts and anxieties are understandable. The more secure the relationship, the more easily qualms can be shared and inadequacies forgiven.

The uncertainty of initial events can be reduced by advance education and orientation. Slater and Woodside reported that "Ignorance is remembered with regret, instruction with satisfaction. . . . Books on sex have helped, and create a mental background which favours attempts at a planned adaptation. . . ." The unhappiest women go into marriage naïve, never having heard or read about sex. Advance orientation may involve conversation between partners or reading the same books.

For most people, early intercourse does not function as well as more practiced occasions. This does not mean it is necessarily unpleasant but that it is less satisfactory than it will become later. The mutual love and consideration which benefit sexual relations under any circumstances are especially needed at the initiation:

> My husband's thoughtfulness on the first night of marriage was the key that unlocked the door to our happy marriage. We were both tired and in need of rest. He suggested that I get ready for bed while he unloaded the car. I felt this was an excuse to spare me embarrassment and I appreciated his thoughtfulness. Once in bed we tried to go to sleep in each other's arms. But despite our weariness, we could not sleep. Finally, I said, "Honey, you want to have intercourse, don't you?" He answered, "Only if you really want it. I don't want to ever have it unless you want it too." The unselfishness of his statement, in the face of his strong desire, caused me to love him in a way I never dreamed I could love anyone.

Considerateness is especially appreciated when embarking on an unknown and emotion-charged experience. In the 1920's, 21 per cent of the husbands and 35 per cent of the wives interviewed by Hamilton (1929) reported feeling reluctant, shy, fearful, or averse to first intercourse with the spouse. The percentages may have dwindled with intervening improvements in sex education, but underlying uncertainty in the face of new experience will always make sexual initiation deserve empathic cooperation.

Intercourse reveals the body to the opposite sex—often for the first time in life outside the family. It also reveals the person in a new light. Sexual skillfulness or clumsiness, responsiveness or coldness, and tenderness or ruthlessness are now manifested. For the man, there are hazards in achieving or maintaining an erection or in reaching a climax soon enough but not too soon—hazards encountered by 15 to 20 per cent of Hamilton's respondents at first intercourse with the spouse.

In the context of love, failures can be forgiven. The risk of well-intentioned clumsiness is the price paid by couples who choose to initiate sex together. Counterbalancing this risk is a sense of mutuality derived from adventuring together.

Even the worst initial difficulties rarely ruin a continuing relationship:

> Such experiences usually, but not always, sink into the past without serious after effects ("we often laugh about it now"). They are in any case productive of misery and embarrassment at the time, and a disturbance of harmony that needs to be surmounted: "There were difficulties in the beginning, but affection carried us through" is true of many (Slater and Woodside, p. 173).

THE WEDDING NIGHT. For inexperienced couples the wedding night is the usual occasion for initiation. Couples expect to climax their wedding ceremony this way. However, rules are made to be broken when they don't fit. In Hamilton's sample hardly more than half the inexperienced couples attempted intercourse on the wedding night, and less than half succeeded in achieving intromission. All sorts of reasons caused postponement: menstruation, contraceptive inadequacy, lack of opportunity, fatigue and reluctance.

> Following the wedding and reception, Rich and Peggy began their drive to Canada. Late the first night they checked into a hotel. After checking in she put on her peignoir, especially bought for the occasion, and went to bed to wait for him while he went out for some cigarettes. When he returned, he undressed and put on pajamas. They made . . . a few half-hearted attempts at love-making—kissing and caressing—but without much verbal communication; they both seemed to arrive at the conclusion that it would be best not to press to sexual relations this first night. They were both tired, they wished to start early in the morning, and neither felt like initiating an experience as complex as sexual intercourse appeared to them at this point. After watching TV for a while they went to bed (Rapoport and Rapoport 1964: 49).

The first experience deserves auspicious circumstances. If circumstances aren't right the first night, they are worth waiting for.

THE HONEYMOON. For the initiated and the uninitiated alike the honeymoon is a time of sexual enjoyment. Even couples who have had intercourse before find the circumstances changed. At the very least, the honeymoon provides more leisure than before.

With experimentation and practice, the inadequacies of the first marital experience are soon left behind. Table 15-5 shows that both inexperienced

Table 15-5. Wedding Night and Honeymoon Sexual Satisfaction of Sexually Inexperienced and Experienced Brides

Evaluation of Intercourse	SEXUALLY INEXPERIENCED BRIDES		SEXUALLY EXPERIENCED BRIDES	
	Wedding Night	Honeymoon Period	Wedding Night	Honeymoon Period
Very satisfying	18%	34%	33%	56%
Satisfying	29	42	39	36
Not satisfying	49	24	23	8
Very unsatisfactory	4	0	5	0
Total	100%	100%	100%	100%
Number of cases	100		77	

Adapted from Kanin and Howard, 1958. *Source:* Retrospective self-ratings of first marital experience and of first two weeks' experience by wives of married students at an Indiana university.

and experienced brides found the whole two weeks after the wedding more satisfying sexually than the first marital attempt. Experienced wives had a head start, to be sure, but by the end of a fortnight, the novices caught up with where the experienced ones were before. For both groups initial intercourse was less satisfactory, but diligent couples soon learned how to make it more meaningful, both during the honeymoon and after.

One problem which may be encountered is what Dr. John Gosling calls "honeymoon cystitis." Although the cause is not entirely certain, the frequent intercourse of the first weeks of marriage produces a bacterial infection of the female bladder (perhaps as a result of penile irritation of the bladder through the vaginal wall). The first symptoms are increased frequency of urination and a burning sensation during urination. Couples need not refrain from intercourse for fear of causing this problem, but if it arises the wife should seek medical treatment. Incidentally, even old married couples risk the same problem if they markedly increase their frequency of intercourse; so it plagues second honeymoons as well as the first.

Learning the Art of Sex

Marriage manuals offer preliminary instruction in the skills of lovemaking. However, the most important lessons are not found in books. Each individual must learn the meaning of sex for himself—and must learn from his partner how they can interact to best advantage.

STIMULATION. New facets of life must be explored together. The questions are both physiological and psychological, not only what parts of the body are most sensitive to touch but what parts the partner *wants* touched. Eventually, all the erogenous zones are likely to be explored, but at first one may not be ready for unusual contacts. Stimulating the wife is the main problem (since the husband is so easily stimulated). Caressing many parts of the body—the legs, the back, the neck, the ears—is likely to send shivers up and down her spine. As the husband experiments, the wife is the only one who can report the results. By her sighs of joy and her words of appreciation she can tell him what parts of her body thrill to his touch. This "feedback" of sensations is essential if he is to learn well.

A second task is to learn what type of caress is most desired. Is it a firm and masterful stroke or a light and airy brush? Perhaps a light touch pleases some parts of the body more than others. Or variation may be enjoyed. Again, learning depends on communicating reactions. Although the husband's responsiveness is rarely a problem, he too has preferences about his wife's caresses. So learning is reciprocal.

Foreplay is an enjoyable part of sexual experience. Words of love and tender caresses create in both partners a mood of anticipation and in the woman relax the ring of muscles surrounding the vaginal entrance and stimulate the internal lubrication of the vagina.

Although preliminary arousal may result from stimulating almost any part of the body, the peak is seldom reached by general petting. Masters and Johnson suggest that the intensive and uninterrupted physical stimulation of masturbation provides the best model. The mons pubis and labia minora are the primary focus of stimulation in feminine masturbation and are correspondingly important in intercourse.

How much foreplay is enough? For particular couples the answer varies considerably. In general, however, foreplay increases the wife's orgasm capacity—up to a point.

Figure 15-3 shows that the average woman reached her maximum responsiveness after some 20 minutes of foreplay. Beyond that point there was little further increment of responsiveness. This suggests on the one hand the value of sex play in moderation, but also that there is little to be gained by prolonging it indefinitely. Indeed fatigue becomes a new problem eventually.

RESPONSIVENESS. Men hardly have to learn to be sexually excited. Even the husband, however, must learn to react to the specific sensations of intercourse. Vaginal contact with the penis is different from masturbation, and it may take time for the husband to respond to the new sensations. Wives characteristically must learn responsiveness itself. To be sure, few brides have never known any sexual feeling. (Kinsey reported that the typical single girl experienced her first orgasm by age 20.) Nevertheless, responsiveness at first is slow and erratic. Only with cumulative experience does it become more rapid and regular.

Paralleling the rapid increase in satisfaction with intercourse in the first two weeks of marriage was a continued but decelerating increase in sexual responsiveness (see Figure 15-4). Almost half the wives in Kinsey's sample experienced their first climax from intercourse within the first month of marriage, and three-fourths within the first year. From then on, some wives each year learned to respond, until a maximum of 90 per cent was reached in the fifteenth year of marriage. For the remaining 10 per cent, orgasm never occurred, no matter how long they were married.

Increased experience also makes orgasm become more regular. The rising curve in the median wife's percentage of orgasm implies the gradually increased responsiveness the individual woman can expect. In striking contrast to other indices of marriage that decline over time, ability to respond sexually can be acquired only with experience.

Because the wife's sexual anatomy is diffuse, this learning process is subtle and complex. She must learn to relax, to let herself go, to abandon herself. She must become aware of new sensations. The requirements for responsiveness are diametrically opposed to the responsibility for control

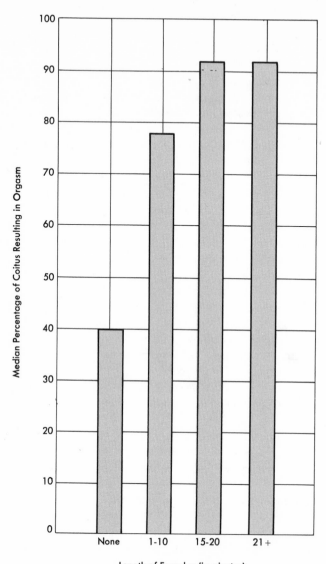

Length of Foreplay (in minutes)

Adapted from Gebhard, 1966. *Source:* 1,026 women in intact marriages (interviewed 1939–60).

Figure 15-3. Orgasmic Responsiveness, by Length of Foreplay

she bore before marriage. Little wonder, then, that the transition is not instantaneous.

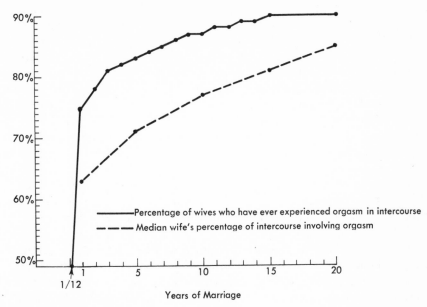

Percentage of wives who have ever experienced orgasm in intercourse

Median wife's percentage of intercourse involving orgasm

Years of Marriage

Adapted from Kinsey, 1953: 408.

Figure 15-4. Orgasm Experience for Wives, by Length of Marriage

Even though maximum responsiveness may be long in coming, the learning period need not be frustrating. It is a time of gradual progression from low-keyed sexuality to a higher pitch. Hence, there is a sense of accomplishment even in minor gains:

> Although it was about two years after our marriage that I experienced my first climax from intercourse, I had felt perfectly satisfied prior to that time. Perhaps a person doesn't miss what he hasn't had. Anyway, being together and learning about each other was pleasant in itself.

The goal for both husband and wife should be to make their sexual experience as rewarding as possible. With mutual love and skillful stimulation from the husband, more frequent orgasms for the wife can be hoped for. Wives who consistently fail to respond may try to make the best of the situation. But for the average wife (and her husband too), frequency of orgasm is positively correlated with both sexual satisfaction and marital satisfaction (Thomason, 1955). This works both ways. Not only does orgasm produce satisfaction, but other marital accomplishments enhance sexual responsiveness.

CONTROL. The converse problem for the husband is learning to control his responsiveness in order to be able to delay his ejaculation. At the beginning of marriage husbands often find foreplay so stimulating that they ejaculate before intromission. Since erection rapidly subsides, intercourse cannot be completed. Even more widespread is ejaculation so soon after intromission that the wife is not stimulated sufficiently to reach her climax. Ejaculation leaves the head of the penis so sensitive that the male ceases thrusting. Indeed Masters and Johnson report that further thrusts are painful for most men. This means that penile stimulation of the female can be continued only as long as ejaculation is postponed.

Control may be achieved through both physical and psychological measures. Frequent intercourse reduces the physiological pressure for ejaculation by decreasing the accumulation of semen. A condom to sheathe the penis or a topical anesthetic applied to the penis makes it less sensitive. By experimenting with the depth and rhythm of penetration, the man can learn what movements stimulate his wife without bringing himself to climax too soon. Certain coital positions may stimulate the wife more and the husband less.

In addition, the masculine susceptibility to psychological stimulation makes self-control easier. Whereas concentrating on his own sensations and fantasies speeds a man's orgasm, concentrating on the wife's reactions will delay it. By focusing on stimulating the wife, the husband will enhance his ability to sustain that stimulation. Then when she reaches her climax, he can readily achieve his.

The objective is not to prolong intercourse indefinitely. Terman (1938) found only the slightest correlation between length of intercourse and either partner's happiness. Gebhard (1966) similarly found the wife's frequency of orgasm significantly reduced if the husband ejaculated less than a minute after intromission. But orgasmic response attained a high level soon thereafter and rose barely perceptibly with prodigious feats of control lasting ten or 15 minutes or more. Gebhard noted that very few men were capable of sustaining intromission for more than seven minutes and his data suggested there was little reason why they should. The main task is to sustain intromission a relatively short time (once a longer period of foreplay has brought both partners to the threshold of orgasm).

The goal is to enable both partners to reach a climax and secondarily to time their orgasms fairly closely. Sexual and marital adjustment were appreciably higher for couples who usually reached climax together in contrast to those where one partner regularly got there first (Thomason, 1955). While ability to time orgasm is seldom so perfect that simultaneity can be engineered, self-controlled husbands increase the partners' sense of togetherness. When the wife's orgasm comes first, there is no control problem. In the converse situation, the husband may stimulate the wife manually so she can achieve orgasm.

With the passing years couples can look forward to less discrepancy in their sexual capacities. As the wife's responsiveness increases with experience, the husband's decreases with age, so that intentional and fortuitous simultaneity occur more often.

Varieties of Sexual Experience

The range of sexual experience in marriage has widened. The emancipation of women, the equalitarianization of marriage, and increased education for both sexes have encouraged experimentation. Most couples approach marriage with the attitude that they will try almost anything once. They may not enjoy it, and may never repeat it. Nevertheless, the best way to find out is to try. As a result of this willingness to experiment, manual-genital stimulation has become almost universal, especially for highly educated couples (Kinsey, 1953). Oral-genital contact was tried by more couples but by no means all. Indeed, one study of Philadelphia divorces granted between 1937 and 1950 showed that wife-initiated divorce suits involving sexual complaints frequently blamed the husband's desire for oral-genital contact (Kephart, 1954b). In short, some enjoy variety, but respect for the partner's feelings is fundamental.

Along with varied techniques of foreplay come varied positions in intercourse. Kinsey found that the female-above position was the chief alternative to the usual male-above position, followed by the side-by-side, rear entrance, sitting, and standing positions (1953). Entry from the rear was often used late in pregnancy. As with foreplay, unusual positions are often experimented with early in marriage but abandoned in favor of simpler or customary ones as time goes on. Variety is not the ultimate rule for all couples. All that matters is that they do what they want to do. But since at the beginning of marriage, two strangers come together with differing life histories, the only way they can both be satisfied is by communication, experimentation, and feedback.

Varied Circumstances

Variety is not limited to technique. The biological and psychological aspects of sex are too closely related for that. Variety comes as much by changing circumstances as by changing techniques. The way the husband and wife treat each other affects their sexual experience, especially the wife's:

> Our sex life has improved a lot now that there is less tension between us. Since I've been helping out more around the house, Karen isn't so tired either so she's able to enjoy intercourse more.

Few wives are able to enjoy intercourse when their marriage is in trouble. Love and sex must go together or sex turns bitter. Reconciliation must occur before sexual responsiveness can be released again.

Freedom to enjoy sexual intercourse reflects the way the day's routine has gone as well as the state of the marriage:

> I enjoy sexual relations the most when the day progresses favorably— if the children behave so my nerves don't get frayed. Similarly, George seems to be in a good mood after watching TV or after he's gotten a big job finished at the office.

In the happiest marriages, sex is fun:

> It is quite characteristic of self-actualizing people that they can enjoy themselves in love and in sex. Sex very frequently becomes a kind of a game in which laughter is quite as common as panting. . . . The sex life of healthy people, in spite of the fact that it frequently reaches great peaks of ecstasy, is nevertheless also easily compared to the games of children and puppies. It is cheerful, humorous, and playful (Maslow 1954: 251–52).

Marriage is never quite so boring as pessimists suppose. Nor marital intercourse. Even when confined to a single position, it is never the same. Differences in mood color the experience:

> Sometimes the pair will be close and affectionate. Tenderness will pass into a rather solemn passion, a confirmation of their abiding love for each other. At other times their mood will be wholly frivolous. Intercourse then will be just a rattling good time without deeper implications. Or the husband will seek protection and cuddling at his wife's breast. Or he will lie like a girl while she takes possession of his body. At times he will vulgarize the act with smutty words or take a fine pleasure in hurting his wife and forcing her to his will. Or the couple may play at an illicit relationship, acting out a little seduction farce for their own benefit. They will try out odd positions and experiment with unusual parts of the body. Often, too, intercourse will be a routine satisfaction of a bodily need about as romantic as orange juice, toast, and coffee for breakfast. Our uninhibited married couples will take all of these variations and find them good (Levy and Munroe, 1945: 129).

The changing flavor of sexual experience reflects the changing setting. As partners go through life, sharing parenthood, homemaking, and personality growth, intercourse mirrors the changing environment. The moon shining in the window one night and snow falling another create stage effects for the sexual drama. With changing moods and changing settings, intercourse is never completely routine. Even if it were always the same, it wouldn't be boring. Like a swim on a hot summer day, the tension and release of sexual communion is exhilarating.

Variations in Frequency

Couples differ enormously in frequency of intercourse, even those in similar circumstances (age, length of marriage, number of children, and the like). Although Kinsey's young married couples typically had sexual relations two or three times a week, one-fourth of them averaged once a week or less while another quarter averaged four to seven times a week (1953). For both men and women (though mostly for women) it is possible to have too much of a good thing. Happiness depends less on the absolute frequency of intercourse than on the relationship between actual and preferred frequencies. If both partners want intercourse often, happi-

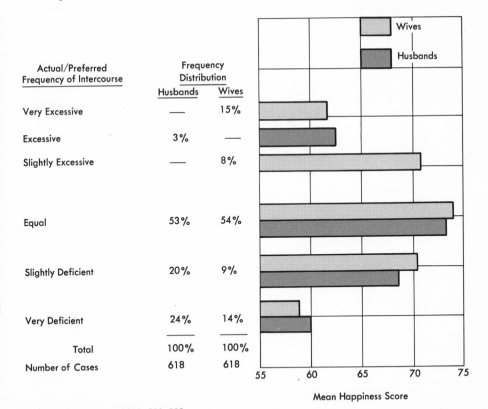

Adapted from Terman 1938: 281, 283.

Figure 15-5. Happiness of Husbands and Wives, by Relation of Actual to Preferred Frequency of Intercourse

ness increases. But if it comes more often than either partner prefers, it becomes a nuisance.

The percentages listed in Figure 15-5 show that few husbands had intercourse more often than they wanted to, but seven times as many wives did. Deficiencies are more common than excesses, since intercourse requires the cooperation of two partners and either can deprive the other. However, because the male sex drive is usually stronger, more husbands than wives complain of too little intercourse. Deficiencies result from the unwillingness of one partner to meet the other's demands. Unanswered in Figure 15-5 is the cause of the discrepancy. Does it result from unusually high preferences of the demanding partner or unusually low preferences of the uncooperative partner?

Table 15-6. Preferred and Actual Frequencies of Sexual Intercourse

Mean preferred and actual frequency per month as reported by	RATIO OF HUSBAND/WIFE PREFERRED FREQUENCIES			Total Preferred Frequency	Total "Actual" Frequency
	Husband Greater	More or Less Equal	Wife Greater		
Husband	13.1	6.7	7.4	9.3	7.0
Wife	6.5	6.6	14.7	7.8	7.8
Number of cases	23	28	9	60	60

Adapted from Levinger, 1966: 294. "More or less equal" couples differed by not more than two times per month in their preferred frequencies. *Source:* Middle-class couples in Cleveland, married 13.6 years on the average.

The data in Table 15-6 are drawn from a Cleveland sample where the biggest discrepancies resulted from the extraordinarily high preferences of some men and a few women. Their spouses could be expected to be reasonably cooperative (they had fairly typical preferences themselves). But trouble resulted if either sex pushed the other farther than he was willing to go. Despite the difference in average preferences, discrepancies produced almost identical effects on men and women. Deficient wives were just as unhappy as deficient husbands, and surfeited husbands just as unhappy as surfeited wives:

> Robert's appetite for sex and mine seem quite different. I seem to be impossible to appease while he seems disinterested very often. I have never reached a climax and feel destined to remain frustrated until this gap is breached. When I make overtures to him after three or four nights' waiting, he tells me to stop tickling him or pretends he is going to sleep. Several times I have told him the way I feel as openly as I can to which I get no response, no apology, and even worse no effort.

Terman (1938) found that the partners of dissatisfied individuals were almost as unhappy as they were. Hence even when one partner gets his way, the other's reluctance reduces the eager one's satisfaction. Fortunate then are couples able to match frequency and preference (either by changing their frequency or adapting their preferences).

OBSTACLES TO INTERCOURSE. The fact that deficiencies are more common than excesses reflects both a tendency for intercourse to be confined to the least common denominator of preferences and various practical problems.

Every month the wife's menstrual flow prompts a period of abstinence. Among Masters and Johnson's female subjects, only one-tenth felt that intercourse during menstruation was objectionable on either religious or aesthetic grounds. On the contrary, more than half expressed a desire for intercourse, especially during the latter half of the period. A substantial minority reported that masturbation to orgasm produced uterine contractions which expelled the menstrual fluid accumulated at the beginning of menstruation, thereby relieving cramps and backaches. The authors concluded that "from a purely physiologic point of view, there is no contraindication to coition or automanipulation during menstruation." Nevertheless, most couples don't.

In the last six weeks of pregnancy and the first six after childbirth, many physicians prescribe abstinence. However Masters and Johnson believe the latter prohibition is unnecessarily rigid. They sympathize with couples who violate it, especially nursing wives whose lactation experiences arouse sexual tension. They advocate resumption of intercourse as soon as the episiotomy and other vaginal traumas have healed. If the wife has a history of miscarriages, the ban may extend to the whole nine months of pregnancy, especially during the first three months when uterine contractions during orgasm are liable to provoke a spontaneous abortion. During such intervals couples may fall back on mutual or separate masturbation.

Once children arrive, they interfere more with the timing than the frequency of intercourse. Couples who experimented with intercourse at odd hours of the morning or afternoon must check their impulses until children are asleep. When children are ill or upset, undistracted time may never come. Children exhaust the wife. Husbands may be fatigued by work, making weekends (especially Saturday nights) more opportune. Illness in either partner diminishes enthusiasm for activity of any kind, sexual or otherwise.

Sometimes, housing facilities are inadequate. The privacy necessary to free abandonment is destroyed by noise conveyed in either direction—into or out of the bedroom. Fears that children may hear (in the next room or worse yet in the same room), that in-laws may hear (for families living doubled-up), or that neighbors may hear (through flimsy apartment walls) prevent unrestrained movement. Intruding noises prevent the concentrated attention needed to maintain sexual arousal. Nor is distraction a problem for women only. Masters and Johnson found that erection "may be impaired easily by the introduction of asexual stimuli" such as talking about an extraneous subject, a change in lighting or temperature, or a sudden loud noise.

Sexual Cooperation in Marriage

Couples whose motivation is similar have the fewest problems. Even for them, however, the partners' moods only occasionally coincide. When they have been to a party, movie, or dance, both may be eager for intercourse. After an exhausting weekend with the kids or when the wife is bulgingly pregnant, neither may be interested. But since moods are individual, the partners' ups and downs often differ. Sometimes the wife looks forward all afternoon to her husband's return and conveys her eagerness by a warm embrace. Or the husband was intrigued by a good-looking girl on the way home and is ready to go to bed early. When these moods fail to coincide, then what?

The first step is communication. Subtly or openly the interested partner expresses his interest, the reluctant partner his reluctance. From then on they must choose. Sometimes the reluctant partner cooperates for the sake of the other. On other occasions his reluctance is too great, and the eager partner backs down. In the long run, equalitarian couples strike a balance between decisions won by each spouse and between yeses and noes. Neither partner feels his wishes should automatically prevail. The toughest problems face couples whose wishes differ consistently. For them initiative and response are troublesome questions.

Initiative

Information is unfortunately unavailable on patterns of initiative. According to modern ideology wives are supposed to initiate sex as often as husbands. However, there are reasons for believing that they seldom do unless their sexual desire is stronger than their husband's. (1) Sexual initiative before marriage is predominantly male. (2) Often the husband's preferred frequency is higher than the wife's. [The characteristic sexual complaint of husbands suing for divorce was that their wives had too little interest in sex relations, whereas plaintiff-wives complained that their husbands had too much (Kephart, 1954b).] (3) The major difference between husbands and wives in unrealized role expectations is that many husbands are disappointed because their partners fail to initiate sexual activity half the time (Ort, 1950). These data suggest that husbands initiate intercourse more often than wives.

There is at least one biological factor in addition to the difference in sex

drive. Although husbands are often interested in intercourse, t
always capable of it. Most men cannot achieve immediately
ejaculations. The older they get, the longer the interval require
their potency. Wives, by contrast, are capable of intercourse at
time. Hence, intercourse depends on the husband's readiness fo
especially in the later years of marriage. As a result, husbands not only want
intercourse more insistently but want it when they are ready for it.

Since initiative comes primarily from the male, the wife must choose
whether to agree or to refuse. The husband can make her acceptance easier
and can reward her for cooperation. Ease of acceptance is symbolized by
the contrast between rape and seduction. Husbands who force their wives
to submit by insisting on "rights" or by economic or physical coercion gain
their sexual goal at the cost of alienating the wife. Seduction is a fine art,
the art of making a woman *want* to have sexual relations even though she
wasn't interested initially. In marriage this means sensitivity to the wife's
mood—choosing times when she is fresh, relaxed, and happy enough to be
agreeable. It means a person-centered, loving approach. It means respect-
ing her right to decline if she so desires. If she accepts, the husband can
make the experience more rewarding by stimulating her to climax and
expressing appreciation for her cooperation. If women are more romantic
than men, men have a responsibility to mobilize their romantic resources.

Response to Initiative

The corresponding responsibility of women is to mobilize themselves to
meet the husband's sexual needs. Under the significant title, *The Sexual
Responsibility of Woman*, Maxine Davis expressed herself vigorously:

> A woman should be willing to learn. She should not cooperate in any-
> thing that proves to be actually distasteful or unpleasant for her after she
> has attempted it for a time, for it would tarnish their love. But she should
> have an open mind and adventurous spirit and be willing to try anything
> that might make the relationship more flexible and gratifying to them
> both. . . .
> A woman has a profound responsibility in maintaining an active marital
> relationship. . . . A wife sometimes finds that her husband's spontane-
> ous desire for intercourse occurs more often than she is able actively to
> respond, no matter how much she would like to. . . . If she enjoys it
> most of the time she should certainly participate whenever he *needs* her
> (1956: 186–88).

The key word here is "needs." If the husband's needs are stronger than
the wife's, she should go out of her way to meet them as much as possible.
This expresses her love (just as he in return should meet her typically

feminine needs for affection, companionship, and religious fellowship). Where needs are not symmetrical, the more each partner goes out of his way to serve the other, the more meaningful the marriage becomes. This is the opposite of the least-common denominator to which marriage so easily sinks. It goes beyond compromising halfway between the husband's and wife's desires. The ideal is for the less interested partner to please the more interested one. This is not to say that a wife must never rebuff her husband. Some selectivity is inevitable. However, she should respond to her husband's overtures as often as possible.

Table 15-7. Frequency of Refusing Intercourse, by Husbands and Wives

Frequency of Refusing Intercourse	Husbands	Wives
Frequently or very frequently	1%	9%
Sometimes	2	27
Rarely	24	44
Never	73	20
Total	100%	100%
Number of cases	593	593

Adapted from Burgess and Wallin, 1953: 664. Source: As reported by spouse.

Table 15-7 shows that the typical wife rarely refused her husband (even though refusal was characteristically a feminine role—the converse of masculine initiative). Only unhappy husbands and wives refused intercourse very often (Terman, 1938). Uncooperative wives not only express their sexual disinterest but often punish the husband at the same time for non-sexual grievances. The fact that sex means so much to the average man makes the wife's power to say "no" or to bargain for concessions a potent weapon. However, the weapon is liable to backfire. When sex sinks to bargaining and contentiousness, love is rapidly destroyed.

Problems in Sexual Relationships

Sexual problems frequently take physical shape—an insufficiently relaxed vagina, an excessively relaxed penis, or the disappearance of sexual activity from a marriage. The causes of these physical problems are often emotional and relational.

Disengagement

The longer most people are married, the less often they have intercourse.

This is visible in declining frequencies by length of marriage, age of husband or age of wife (see Figure 15-6).

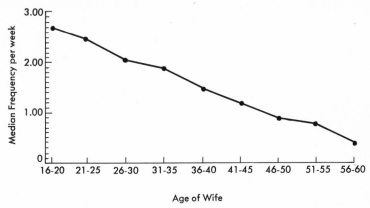

Age of Wife

Adapted from Kinsey, 1953: 394.

Figure 15-6. Frequency of Intercourse, by Age of Wife

Intercourse does not end abruptly when the wife reaches 60—Kinsey just ran out of cases. There is no age limit beyond which sex is universally impossible. Indeed, menopause brings increased enjoyment to women afraid of conception. However, both sexes avoid strenuous activity as they get older, not so much because they are incapable as because they are lazy.

Masters and Johnson reported that aging reduces the intensity of sexual responsiveness in both sexes. Vasocongestive and muscular spasmic reactions weaken or disappear, especially those involving parts of the body farthest removed from the genital focus (for example, the sex flush and spasms of the hands and feet). Vaginal lubrication decreases sharply about five years after menopause so that a lubricating jelly may have to be used. Another geriatric problem is thinning of the vaginal walls so that thrusting movements of the penis irritate the adjacent bladder. This may be minimized by adequate lubrication and early ejaculation but the wife is liable to need a postcoital trip to the bathroom.

After menopause, the normal uterine contractions in orgasm become painful for some women. This problem may be treated with hormones. Masters and Johnson advocated "endocrine replacement therapy" for both sexes to reduce attrition of the sexual organs and maintain capacity for sexual functioning.

However, the main problem is not medical.

1. For both sexes the best way to maintain sexual capacity is by exercising it. Unused, responsiveness wanes. Exercised at least once or twice a week, that capacity remains alive.

2. Sexual vitality requires physical vitality. Masters and Johnson observed with dismay that "rarely does the middle-aged male in our culture make any effort to maintain his physical being in good condition." Vigorous physical exercise keeps the body fit for intercourse.
3. A vital marriage provides a solid basis for sex. Masters and Johnson noted that many middle-class people became so preoccupied with outside activities that they had little time left for each other.
4. To revive the flagging interest of the husband, Masters and Johnson encouraged wives to maintain their sexual attractiveness by continued attention to their personal appearance and continued expression of sexual interest in the husband.
5. The less frequent intercourse becomes, the greater the value of scheduling it under the best possible conditions. Crises or distractions impair sexual functioning more than before since "sensitivity to mental fatigue is one of the greatest differences between the responsiveness of the middle-aged and the younger male." (M/J) Physical vigor is impaired by fatigue, overeating, or liquor. The tranquilizing effect of alcohol destroys the muscular tension necessary to erection. To put it positively, couples need to be emotionally and physically refreshed if intercourse is to be most successful—at any age!
6. Lastly, older couples must be willing to risk failure. Occasional failure is normal, even under the best of circumstances. The danger is that episodic failure will create fear of future failure. This makes anxious men discontinue intercourse with partners who remember their prior failures (even though they may be potent with a new partner). The problem, then, is the couple's ability to tolerate occasional failure. The wife can support the husband with understanding and empathy when he fails to achieve an ejaculation.

Masters and Johnson concluded their chapter on "The Aging Male" with an optimistic forecast:

> There is every reason to believe that maintained regularity of sexual expression coupled with adequate physical well-being and healthy mental orientation to the aging process will combine to provide a sexually stimulative climate within a marriage. This climate will, in turn, improve sexual tension and provide a capacity for sexual performance that frequently may extend to and beyond the 80-year level (M/J: 270).

Impotence

For a variety of reasons, impotence is an increasing problem as men grow older. Impotence was defined by Masters and Johnson as:

Disturbance of sexual function in the male that precludes satisfactory coitus. It varies from inability to attain or maintain full erection to total loss of erective powers (M/J: 341).

Impotence is not directly concerned with ability to ejaculate but only with the erection necessary to achieve intromission. It rises sharply in old age (see Figure 15-7).

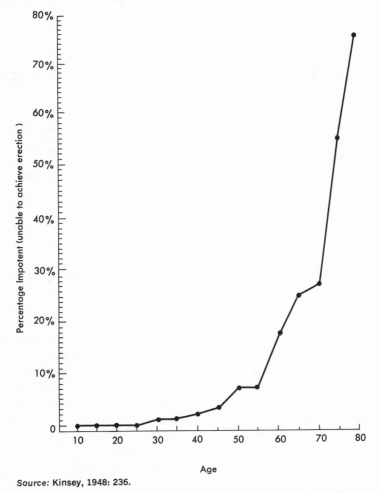

Source: Kinsey, 1948: 236.

Figure 15-7. Impotence, by Age of Man

Men who are impotent from the beginning of marriage usually need medical treatment with hormones, psychotherapy, etc. Secondary impotence, developing later in life, is more easily prevented and cured (as described above). Masters and Johnson found that secondary impotence began more often when men had drunk too much than under any other circumstance. Prevention requires either avoiding intoxicated intercourse or recognizing that impotence under the influence of alcohol means not that one is too old for sex but too relaxed for it. Impotence induced by alcohol need not recur when sober—unless one is paralyzed by fear that it will! Continued potency requires self-confidence more than anything else.

Although the usual task in marriage is to arouse the wife, impotence requires stimulating the husband. The wife can tantalize him psychologically by playing seductress. She can help him achieve a sustained erection by "long periods of manual stimulation in a sensitive, sexually undemanding, but physically relentless fashion." (Johnson and Masters, 1961) For many men, oral-genital contact is even more stimulating. In any case, an ingenious wife aided by a communicative husband will find whatever foreplay is most stimulating.

At least half of all men suffer from inflammation and enlargement of the prostate gland as they get older. This frequently interferes with their sexual functioning. Following surgical removal of the prostate gland, most patients return to normal sexual functioning. Among those who do not, Rubin (1965) suspects that the operation was more often excuse than cause of the subsequent impotence.

Female Unresponsiveness

Whereas male impotence is categorical (the husband either is or is not able to effect intromission on any particular occasion), female unresponsiveness is more diffuse and variable. The mildest problem is inability to have an orgasm or to have one regularly. We have seen that this is commonplace at the beginning of marriage, decreasing as responsiveness is learned.

Whenever a woman fails to experience orgasm, her physical pleasure is correspondingly reduced. She may still find satisfaction in being loved by her husband and in meeting his sexual needs. The sense of intimacy and mutual love expressed through intercourse may be undiminished. She may also enjoy the stimulation of intercourse, both in foreplay and in intercourse itself. Nevertheless, physical pleasure is never as intense without climax as with it. How frustrated she will feel depends on the wife's (and her husband's) expectations. If they recognize the unpredictability of feminine orgasm, they will be less disappointed. But disappointment is understandable. The choice for married couples lies between sympathetic and antagonistic handling of their disappointment:

> In all the years we've been married, Debby has never had an orgasm and this disturbs both of us greatly. She feels bitter about it and accuses me of using sex simply for self-gratification at an "animal" level. I feel frustrated too by my inability to produce an orgasm in her.

Frustration reduces the marital satisfaction of women who rarely have an orgasm. Gebhard (1966) found no variation in marital happiness in a broad middle range of orgasm capacities. But at the two extremes, women who seldom or never reached climax and those who almost always did found their marriages correspondingly less or more satisfactory. Perhaps the relationship can be turned around. Perhaps marital unhappiness depresses sexual responsiveness and happiness promotes it: "very unhappy" wives typically reached a climax in only 18 per cent of their intercourse, "moderately unhappy" wives in 59 per cent, "moderately happy" in 74 per cent, and "very happy" wives in 92 per cent.

Wives can live without orgasm, provided both partners accentuate the positive. If they concentrate on what both partners gain from the experience, they can get the most satisfaction out of their limited circumstances. Especially wives who focus on what they can give their husbands feel less disappointed. Sex, after all, is less important to most women anyway. Husbands are obligated to counteract this tendency. With skill and effort they can increase the wife's responsiveness and pleasure. Improved marital interaction and personal preparation increase sexual responsiveness in wives:

> My sex training and education began when I was eight. Sex was always considered a wonderful part of marriage. When my parents spoke of sex there was never any embarrassment but always an educated and healthy approach. Before I was married I had no doubts about sex being anything but right and beautiful. My education had been so complete that there were never any fears or qualms—not even momentary. As a result, when I got married we made an excellent adjustment in sex very early.

Frigidity

"Frigidity is the complete lack of sex desire with a resulting inability to respond to stimulation and arousal. On this level, frigidity is relatively infrequent. . . ." (Levine and Gilman, 1951) Such frigidity may mean inability to be sexually aroused or the negative response of vaginismus, an involuntary contraction of the vaginal muscles so tight that intromission cannot occur. Severe frigidity prevents sexual intimacy in marriage and strains the whole relationship. Often the difficulty can be traced to negative childhood conditioning:

> Josie thinks sex is disgusting, though she spends her spare time reading love stories and movie magazines. In the ten years we've been married I've had to go without intercourse as long as three months at a time, when I think I'd prefer to have it every day. Her inhibitions are so strong that she feels sex should be gotten over with as soon as possible, without any

talk. When she does relent, her attitude seems to be: "Let's pretend we didn't do it!"

Blazer's 1964 study of married virgins (wives married eight years on the average without ever having intercourse) showed the fears, disgusts, antipathies, and ignorance which trigger feminine frigidity. Fear that intercourse would cause pain, that the vagina was too small, or that the wife would get pregnant were common. (Medical examination showed that no vaginas were abnormally small.) More neurotic were fears of semen and of damaging the husband's penis. These women, however, found the male organ more disgusting than fragile. Many thought sex generally nasty or wicked. For a few, contraceptives were the source of disgust and abstinence their way of avoiding both conception and contraception.

Some women were basically hostile to men and in some cases preferred female partners. Some thought intercourse with a man implied surrender to male dominance and an admission of inferiority. Finally, a few preferred to "mother" their husbands rather than make love to them.

Searching for the cause and cure of severe frigidity is a medical responsibility. Sometimes the causes are physical, but more often there are mental blocks which may yield to psychotherapy. Even in such cases the husband can aid the patient's recovery by loving concern and tactful behavior. In milder cases, his role is even more crucial. If he accuses and blames her for being unresponsive, he will make matters worse. But patience and love and professional help will aid most wives. As Calderone put it, "There are hardly any truly frigid women. Down deep within the overwhelming majority is a sexual need and capacity for fulfillment that awaits only liberation." (1960: 176)

16 LOVE: Maintaining the Relationship

In Chapter 4, I discussed how love grows as personal relationships develop between men and women. Now I wish to analyze love within marriage and the problem of maintaining the person-to-person awareness developed to a high point during the engagement and honeymoon.

Why is maintaining the relationship a problem? Isn't it enough to choose wisely, to marry well? Won't the rest of marriage go well provided a couple get off to a good start? Can't marriage be taken for granted if it rests on a solid foundation of compatibility and love? Unfortunately the answer to these questions is "no." Nothing can be taken for granted. If it is, a marriage is headed for trouble. I will begin by describing the dangers that await marriages adrift. My purpose is to challenge the reader to make the most of his marriage. Once the urgency of the challenge becomes apparent, the value of working to maintain a growing relationship can be seen.

The Challenge to Marriage

The average marriage coasts downhill. The longer it exists, the greater the decline. Partly the loss is psychological, an ebbing enthusiasm for the partner. But it is also social in the sense that the partners become disengaged from one another. Some marriages fall apart completely. Some not only resist decay but grow and develop. In between are the bulk of marriages—superficially intact but steadily less cohesive.

Disenchantment

Most couples lose their initial enthusiasm. Although prizing the partner at first, each gradually takes the other for granted and sees him or her more prosaically. Not that marriage necessarily turns sour (save among those who get divorced). But for those who stay together, it usually cools.

Figure 16-1 shows that Detroit wives found their marriages less satisfactory as time went on (despite the gradual weeding out of the least satisfied couples through divorce). In this study 52 per cent were "very satisfied" during the first two years of marriage but only 6 per cent still were 20 years later. During the same interval the proportion of "very dissatisfied" wives jumped from zero to 21 per cent of those still married (after the loss of the divorced).

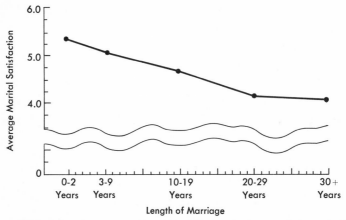

Adapted from Blood and Wolfe, 1960: 264. *Source:* Representative sample of Detroit married women, 1955.

Figure 16-1. Wife's Marital Satisfaction, by Length of Marriage

The index of marital satisfaction combines satisfaction with number of children, standard of living, and the husband's love, understanding, and companionship, weighted by the relative importance attached to each aspect of marriage. The scale ranges from zero to 10.

Gurin (1960) also found that old married couples evaluated their marriages less favorably than young ones. This might mean only that American marriages were getting better with the passing decades, since neither of the previous studies dealt with the same families over time. The acid test, however, is provided by Pineo's (1961) 20-year follow-up of Burgess and Wallin's engaged couples. Over a 20-year interval these husbands and wives declined significantly in their feeling of love for each other and in their confidence in the permanence of their marriage.

People tend to rationalize this disenchantment, saying that love doesn't matter (after it is gone). In one middle-class Syracuse sample, older couples valued sex, having children, feeling needed, and being in love less than young couples (Feldman, 1966). But this devaluation of interpersonal relationships seems to me precisely a product of disenchantment.

Two factors contribute to this waning enthusiasm: the transition from anticipation to fulfillment and the transformation of a new relationship into an old one.

FROM ANTICIPATION TO FULFILLMENT. In earlier chapters I suggested that much of the excitement of falling in love comes from anticipating new experiences. In particular, postponing sexual intimacy heightens the partners' attraction to each other. From this point of view marriage inevitably transforms an emotional relationship from fever-pitch excitement to grateful fulfillment. Competitive insecurity changes to solid security.

Many years ago, Levy and Munroe labeled it "disillusionment" and gave a classic illustration, three years after marriage:

> Mary Jane's frock for mornings at home looks a little frayed and faded. Her apron has definitely seen neither Lux nor a harsh washing soap for several days. She scrapes dispiritedly at the breakfast plates, slightly repulsive with congealed egg yolk and slimy cold bacon grease. For the fourteenth time she exhorts Junior to stop dawdling and eat his cereal. She is not at the moment enjoying her marriage very much. Why should she? Washing dishes day in and day out is not the same thing as canoeing in the moonlight with your heart's beloved. . . . She is remembering five o'clock with Jim waiting at the corner, [thinking] of dinner and dancing, of going to the movies, or a concert, or the theater, or just a long ferryboat ride. Of the difficult goodnight kiss and the ecstatic knowledge that soon she would have Jim all the time for always. She is thinking rather wryly of how entrancing, how full of promise this battered dishpan looked when it first emerged from pink tissue paper at the shower the girls gave her. She may even think, a little cynically, as she surveys the gray grease-pocked surface of her dishwater, of the foaming pans of eternally virgin suds she expected from her perusal of the advertisements. Well, she's married now. She has her own house, her own dishpan, her husband and her baby. All the time and for always. She doesn't even go to the movies any more because there's no one to stay with Junior. She speaks so crossly to the child now that his tears fall into the objectionable cereal. Why on earth won't Jim let her get Mrs. Oldacre in to stay evenings? He'll be earning more soon; Mr. Bayswater practically told him he would be put in charge of the branch office as soon as old Fuzzy retired. Five dollars a week savings—much good that does anyway. Mary Jane's thoughts about her husband become quite definitely uncharitable. "If he only had the least understanding of the kind of life I have, but all he notices is Junior's shoes are scuffed out and he wouldn't even try that Bavarian Cream I fixed yesterday. It's all very well for him to think Jimmy Junior's cute when he sneaks out of bed—he doesn't have him all day and all night and nothing but Jimmy Junior." (1945: 59-61)

Mary Jane was disillusioned because her marriage was not what she expected it to be. Naïveté about wedded bliss accentuates disenchantment.

But even hard-headed realists who don't expect marriage to be all "canoeing in the moonlight" experience a change of pace from courtship to marriage. At the very minimum, marriage is less exciting than courtship:

> This excited state of mind cannot endure the protracted association of marriage. The thrilling sexual tension which normally keeps engaged couples in a state of fervid and delighted expectation abates with frequent, satisfying intercourse. The element of uncertainty is dissipated—and there is no doubt that a goal we have not yet won is more intriguing than one which is wholly ours. We are deliciously stimulated by the desire for an object not yet obtained, but almost within our grasp. Sooner or later, when the flamboyant anticipations of betrothal give way to the sober satisfactions of marriage, we lapse back into our ordinary selves (1945: 67).

This is not to say that marriage accomplishes nothing. But whereas courtship gains intensity from its brevity, marriage loses intensity because it lasts so long. Married persons have arrived and while they thereby acquire deep satisfactions, it is less exciting than the struggle to get there.

FROM NOVELTY TO FAMILIARITY. Disenchantment takes place not only between courtship and marriage but also during marriage itself. The pre-

They're newlyweds. He just got back from putting the garbage out.   © King Features Syndicate

vious statistics involved losses between early and later marriage. They contrasted relationships that were still new with those that no longer were. Gradually the average husband treasures his partner less and takes her more for granted. At the beginning of marriage the contrast is sharp between having a wife and never having had one. Everything she does is appreciated. She is appreciated as a person. The new husband is sensitive to her presence, aware of her as a new element in his life. He misses her when he is away and looks forward to seeing her when he returns.

By contrast, after enough years elapse, the spouse becomes as familiar as a piece of furniture. Taken-for-grantedness is one way of describing the security of marriage. But it less happily means loss of appreciation. Familiarity breeds contempt not so much in the sense of downgrading the partner as in ignoring her. The husband at breakfast with his head buried in the paper is the classic symbol of disinterest.

Familiarity not only breeds contentment with the partner's virtues but sharpens awareness of his limitations and faults. Luckey (1966) found that the longer people had been married the fewer favorable qualities they saw in each other and the more negative qualities. The image tarnished. Among the virtues which faded were affection, consideration, cooperation, gratefulness, and friendliness. Instead the spouse was increasingly perceived as selfish, bitter, touchy, hard-hearted, cold, unfeeling, and always expecting others to admire him. Interestingly, Luckey's older respondents recognized more selfishness in themselves, too, but not as much more as they saw in their partners. Apparently, people become disenchanted with themselves as well as with each other. The altruism and euphoria of youth fade and the "walls," which collapsed when man and woman fell in love, begin to rise again.

Disengagement

Closely related to disenchanted feelings are disengaged practices. Cumming pointed out that old people become "disengaged" from social affairs. Aging marriages similarly involve less interaction between the partners. By aging marriages I mean not only the last few years of marriage but the whole span. Disengagement like disenchantment begins all too soon.

Within limits, I suspect, disengagement is a good thing. When I stressed the value of autonomy in marriage, I recognized that togetherness may be excessive. If husband and wife are to bloom separately, they cannot do everything together.

The trouble is, after most couples have been married very long, they do too little together. After the appropriate intimacy of the honeymoon comes the unnecessary estrangement of marriage. Instead of stopping at the right point, disengagement goes too far. We have already seen in the last chapter that couples disengage sexually faster than is physiologically necessary. A similar decline affects most kinds of marital interaction.

Pineo (1961) found that most couples spent less of their leisure together in the middle years of marriage than in early marriage. This decline is especially marked for outside activities—the dating that brought them together in the first place. If Mary Jane, three years after marriage already recalled canoeing with nostalgia, how much more regretful would she be 20 years later? In Pineo's sample almost three-fourths of the middle-aged Mary Janes confessed that "dating" had fallen off. Similarly Feldman's middle-class couples had fewer "gay times together" outside the home as they got older. Joint use of leisure declined despite the fact that relatively few couples changed their preferred activities. Most continued to like the same things, but they seldom got around to doing them together. Not only the amount but the proportion of shared to nonshared activities declined, suggesting that married couples became disengaged from each other faster than from the rest of life.

> We have not had to work very hard at loving each other in our marriage. It's been almost too easy. Things that are easy aren't as good as they might be. Each of us is being drawn into more whirling circles, separate circles—his business work, his increasing responsibilities with the advancement of the Republican party, his public speaking. In each of these he has gained confidence and in each of these he feels needed and gains satisfaction. I too have gained new confidence in my talents and skills and could easily be swept more and more into many responsibilities and friendships. So our major energies are increasingly spent apart from each other.

If disengagement occurred only outside the home, it would be less serious. Yet it happens inside as well. As time goes by, couples pay less attention to each other even when they are in the same room.

Figure 16-2 shows that the average Detroit husband reported back to his wife almost every day during the first few years of marriage. During the child-rearing years he conveyed something only a few times a week and after the children grew up less than once a week. After retirement he had understandably little to say. Up to that point the decline was not due to changes in the amount of information at his disposal so much as in his readiness to share it.

In a Syracuse middle-class sample, Feldman (1966) found that the total time spent in discussion and the frequency of discussing anything declined the longer couples were married. Topics like sex and in-laws which demanded attention at the beginning of marriage disappeared as relationships were worked out. However, some new topics partially replaced them: re-

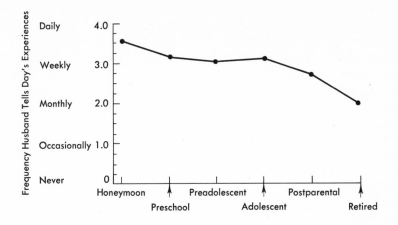

Stage in Family Life Cycle

Adapted from Blood and Wolfe, 1960: 158. *Source:* Representative cross section of Detroit married women, 1955.

Figure 16-2. Frequency Husband Tells Day's Experiences, by Family Life Cycle

pairs for aging houses, religion (for aging individuals?), and outside events —news, sports, and culture. So a qualitative shift went on behind the quantitative disengagement.

Lest it be thought that husbands are the only ones who disengage themselves, it should be acknowledged that wives do too. Blood and Wolfe found that new wives told their husbands their troubles "usually" whereas postparental wives did only half the time.

Disengagement apparently is mutual and pervasive. One cause is the boredom that comes with experience. Some activities are attractive when new but less interesting after the novelty wears off. For example, when intercourse is new, couples explore and experiment. Once they have tried everything, intercourse becomes not less satisfying but less intriguing. The incentive to engage in it diminishes. Similarly with talk. At first everything the husband encounters at work is new to the wife. But as he conveys information to her from day to day, her knowledge increases. Most of what he might say resembles what she has heard before. Maybe he should say it anyway, but the urgency wanes:

> When we were first married, Dan told me about his patients. He was just getting started in practice and every new patient was another triumph on the road to success. I heard about every operation and struggled with all the diagnostic problems. Even though I didn't understand half of what he was talking about, it was exciting to sit there and listen to him. Now I hardly hear about it even if my best friend has cancer.

However, disengagement has other causes besides familiarization: aging and the distraction of children.

THE IMPACT OF AGING. Physiological capacity declines from birth to death. Most conspicuously, energy sags. Every mother knows how strenuously preschoolers play, how exhausting the pace they maintain. Even young adults, by comparison, are sedentary. The older we become, the less energy we have for anything, the more attractive rest and passive entertainment become. As our pace slows, we do less and less, even things as effortless as talk.

THE DISTRACTION OF CHILDREN. To complicate matters, husbands and wives have children. Usually they have them on purpose. They want them, are glad to have them, wouldn't give them up for anything. Without children life would be incomplete. But children interfere with marital interaction. We have already seen in Figure 16-2 the waning reports from husband to wife after the advent of children. Taking all topics together, Feldman (1960) found the birth of the first child cut total conversation time almost in half. Whereas newly married couples averaged two hours a day, young parents managed hardly more than one. Moreover, the content of discussion shifted from themselves and their interrelationship (inner feelings and sex) to their children. In other words they became primarily parents and only secondarily marriage partners. Feldman ascribed this reorientation to having a young child in the house:

> During this period the couple's attention is focused almost constantly on the baby. They have little time and energy left over for each other. Meals are hurried and irregular and often husband and wife eat separately while one or the other performs some domestic chore. With little opportunity to go places and see people, there's less to talk about. The main topic is children. In the evening, when they finally have a few moments together, they're exhausted, physically and mentally.

When couples acquire children, the utter dependency of infancy pries them from each other's arms to respond to the baby's needs. To this extent marital disengagement is inevitably an immediate consequence of parenthood. The paradox is that when children grow less dependent and even after they leave home, few husbands and wives resume the interaction they earlier curtailed. Re-engagement, even when physically possible, seldom occurs.

Husbands and wives do so many things with their children that they are rarely alone together. The intimacy of a one-to-one relationship cannot flourish in the presence of chaperones, no matter how young. The larger the number of chaperones, the less the opportunity. According to Blood and Wolfe, husbands and wives with more than three children could not concentrate on each other enough to keep their love alive.

Love Changes

Honeymoon intensity cannot last. The transformation of love inevitably deflates the breathless excitement of new love. A good thing it is, too, suggest Levy and Munroe (p. 67):

> We can only surpass ourselves during emotional crises without seriously depleting our reserves. We can run from a bear very fast indeed, but if we made that speed habitual we would soon collapse entirely. Walking is the most practicable gait for common use, and marriage too must be paced at the rate of our usual temperament.

Nor is the change all loss. Married love gains in breadth what it loses in intensity. The reach of memory widens as husband and wife share events. Their knowledge of each other deepens as they learn to recognize barely perceptible cues to mood and desire. Symbolic of this cumulative knowledge is the increasing proportion of the husband's friends whom the wife considers her friends too (Blood and Wolfe).

Although the average couple in Pineo's 20-year study became disenchanted, there were exceptions. Among the minority of husbands whose love was still intense, 99 per cent would marry the same partner again and 97 per cent had no regrets about their marriage. The inevitable transformation of love does not mean the inevitable destruction of the feeling that marriage is basically satisfying and meaningful.

Disengagement is not inevitable. Although it may be "natural," it can be avoided. For example, 95 per cent of Pineo's "best" husbands still kissed their wives and confided in them as frequently as 20 years before. Only with respect to "dating" (sharing outside activities) did Pineo's marriages almost universally slow down.

In many areas, then, deterioration is not inevitable. To keep a relationship alive is not impossible. Some couples achieve it—but only through sustained effort.

Means of Maintaining the Relationship

What can a couple do to maintain a good marriage? Fortunately there are many things, often seemingly insignificant, and requiring small bits of effort more than major bursts. There are familiar pleasures: the kiss in the morning, coffee in the living room after dinner, or the right sauce with the broccoli. And there are unexpected ones—a cartoon clipped and brought home, a joke remembered to share, or flowers bought on a whim. Unexpected gifts demonstrate thoughtfulness and sensitivity. Expected gestures reinforce satisfying and happy memories.

Continued Interaction

In his classic analysis of primary relations, Homans (1950) suggested that "interaction produces sentiment." In Chapter 6 I noted that the sentiment of love tends to evaporate when separation prevents interaction. It evaporates just as fast when partners are together but fail to interact. When the proverbial newspaper—rather than a hundred miles—separates husband from wife, the effect is just as disastrous. Indeed, male unwillingness to interrupt reading the paper "for brief expressions of affection at the wife's approach" was one of the chief disappointments of wives interviewed by Ort (1950).

COMPANIONSHIP. Interaction involves more than laying down the newspaper. It requires doing things together, especially talking to each other and listening to what the other says. A few minutes' conversation when husband and wife meet at the end of the day is as important to keeping in touch as letters between partners half a world apart.

People change. Kelly (1955) found that between young adulthood and middle age, men and women became more religious in their values and more masculine in their interests. After 20 years, his couples had changed 52 per cent of their values, 55 per cent of their vocational interests, 69 per cent of their self-rated personality characteristics, and 92 per cent of their answers to attitude questions. These sweeping changes suggest that couples will have much to talk about if they are to grow together rather than apart.

Marriage cannot be static. If it attempts to stand still, it will regress. Rather, marriage is, in Farber's terms, a "pair of mutually contingent careers." As each career changes, couples face the challenge of what Foote (1956) calls the "matching of husband and wife in phases of development." Matching requires husbands and wives to carry on a continuing dialogue.

Interaction is more than just talk. It is also doing things together. Chapter 14 documented the key role of companionship in American marriages. Yet we have already encountered Pineo's report that this aspect of marriage fades especially fast. Effort is particularly needed to sustain joint use of leisure.

SERVICE. Love is enhanced by both partners' contributions to the division of labor as well as by their good times together. Especially when a contribution is "above and beyond the call of duty," it revitalizes the partner's appreciation:

> Whenever my husband has a special assignment, he has to get up at four A.M. The night before, I serve an early dinner and take charge of putting the children to bed so he may shower, lay out his things and turn in very early. After everyone is settled, I take the responsibility for setting two alarm clocks, one by the bed for four and one in the bathroom for four-fifteen. When the first alarm goes off, I put my feet on the floor and assume my most cheerful face—a mighty hard task for an old sack hound like me. While Fred is shaving, I fix a hearty breakfast to give him a good start. Then while he is dressing, I comb my hair and put on lipstick to give him an attractive breakfast partner. When he starts his second cup of coffee, I go out and start the car and heater and come back and lay out his coat. As he leaves, we kiss and I remind him to be careful, then stand and wave as he drives away.

Few wives could muster this much effort. But those who put themselves out are rewarded with corresponding gratitude.

A major masculine service is to give the wife time off from housework. The husband who fixes breakfast once a week or takes the kids to the park on Saturday afternoon, or takes them along on his errands will be met by an appreciative wife when he returns.

Even wives able to intersperse wall-washing with coffee at the neighbor's, or walks around the block for the baby, are still "on duty" long after the husband finishes work and may go for weeks without real breaks even at night. No prior culture left the mother alone with 24-hour care of her children and household. Always before there were arrangements for sharing the load with the extended family, servants or a close-knit community. Eventually our society will provide the facilities this situation demands: day-care centers, nursery schools, baby-sitting services in supermarkets, community training of baby sitters, prompt medical service for women with children, and so forth. Meanwhile, men must recognize that no woman can reasonably be expected to care for preschool children 24 hours a day, seven days a week, and remain a responsive wife. Resentment and fatigue will eventually take their toll. A husband can choose ways of relieving her which do not threaten his particular concept of masculinity. He may take over the screaming child, send mother off to rest, and prepare the dinner. Or he could provide a particular service regularly—the two A.M. bottle, or bathtime for the toddlers, or baseball with the older boys. Of course, the nicest break for a young mother is to leave the children with a trusted sitter, put on her favorite dress and spend the evening on a date with her husband.

New Experiences

Continued interaction enables couples to keep up with changes in each others' lives. This in itself introduces new experiences. More can be manufactured with a little effort. Because one basis of disenchantment is the replacement of novelty by familiarity, new experiences are anticorrosive.

Children from this point of view offer certain advantages. To the perceptive observer they provide an endless stream of sayings and accomplishments. As they develop, they confront parents with challenges and revive childhood memories to be shared. Beyond these intrinsic novelties, however, lie countless opportunities to be grasped or neglected, depending on the parents' ingenuity.

With children or without there are chances for travel, for making new friends, for enlarging the mind and heart in reading and service. Outside the home there are jobs to be done, organizations to be joined, new posts to be filled in old organizations and new tasks undertaken in old posts.

> Being in the sensitivity training lab has done more for our marriage than anything else in all the years we've been married. It has stimulated postmortem discussions of the lab sessions, made us see each other in a new light, made us compare ourselves with the other couples in the group. And we've started practicing on each other the human relations skills we're learning in the group.

Even separate experiences renew a marriage provided they contribute to the growth of the individual and are shared vicariously through conversation. Too many husbands and wives are bored with each other because they are bored with themselves. To invigorate their own lives through mind-stretching and feeling-stretching experiences renews their attractiveness to the partner. Love cannot thrive on the disrespect that comes with awareness that the partner's life is empty. Meaninglessness especially plagues young mothers. Tied down to routine diaper-changing at home and cut off from contact with the outside world, they get depressed. Retaining intellectual vitality and a sense of identity is difficult, but correspondingly critical.

Even mothers of young children may find time for an occasional discussion group, a hospital visit, or a phone call to a friend in trouble. Part-time employment at home may provide a stimulating diversion which can be abandoned as soon as the baby wakes up. The activity doesn't matter as long as it revitalizes the person.

Opportunities for Intimacy

That children distract their parents is inevitable. It does not, however, have to be perpetual. During the decades when they are living with children, couples need opportunities to be alone. Before marriage, privacy for quiet talk and unembarrassed affection is sought and prized. After marriage, couples may think they have privacy, but a closer look is apt to disclose the interfering presence of others, either in the flesh or on TV. The older children get, the later they stay up, whittling the private segment of parental lives. TV can be shut off but children hardly can. The only solution is to get rid of the children. Intervals of undistracted companionship require that children be shifted to someone else. Grandparents are the most convenient resource. Otherwise hired baby sitters or cooperative neighbors must be found until children grow old enough to care for themselves. The task is to get away from children and, for the wife, to get away from the house too, since it's her never-done workplace. How long parents can leave their children depends on their funds for child care and external activities. The well endowed can manage whole weekends away. The rest have to settle for occasional evenings.

Even at home, enclaves of privacy can be created in the midst of family living. Parents who feed their children early or in a separate room gain opportunities for conversation or for reading their mail together. (The parents' gain is the children's loss, and the two must be balanced against each other.) Time may be scheduled before or after dinner, centered around cocktails beforehand or coffee afterwards. The activity doesn't matter so long as it is meaningful. It need not be romantic or even recreational. Maybe the wife goes along on business trips or they circulate petitions together. The essential factor is time.

Marriage Rituals

The daily good-by and hello-again kiss is the most widespread ritual of romance. In Japan the whole family bows the husband out the door and in again at night. Farewell and welcoming rituals symbolize the daily disruption and re-establishment of personal relationships. The regularity of rituals is crucial. Bossard and Boll (1950) found that rituals added strength to relationships by providing structured opportunities for interaction.

Rituals are also elements of our culture. The culturally defined symbols of love are expected in marriage, and overladen with positive connotations derived from past history. Any ritual adds to the rooted sense of the family and its stability over the years. The more families move from one house and community to another, the more important family rituals become for adults and children. They may be the chief continuity the family experiences.

Each family can develop its own rituals. If mother always makes fruit cake for Christmas, or a fried-chicken picnic on Labor Day, or a special relish for Thanksgiving, these are anticipated from year to year, regardless of all else that has changed in the meantime.

ROMANTIC RITUALS. Love is enhanced by little extras we label "romantic"—candles on the table, flowers, gifts, dressing up. These may only be symbols of love, but they express it more visibly than words.

Romantic touches are more important to women than to men. Women notoriously remember anniversaries when husbands forget. Those in Ort's study were disappointed that their husbands failed to give them surprise gifts as tokens of affection and failed to keep as clean and tidy as they had during courtship. Since such things come less naturally to men, theirs is the challenge to convert a humdrum marriage into one spiced with romantic revivals.

A walk in the moonlight, midnight swim, or toasting marshmallows in the fireplace enable couples to rise above their everyday level, even though the next day must resume its normal course. In the words of Levy and Munroe, "Glamour in marriage cannot be continuous, but it needn't be absent. The morning after does not destroy the reality and value of the night before." Memories of the golden age when love was new are worth recalling. Wedding anniversaries are occasions to recreate old times, revisit the scenes of courtship, replay old love songs. If marriage is worth celebrating with a reception and honeymoon, it is worth re-celebrating. The original commitment of marriage can be reaffirmed but now the couple have more to celebrate than the first time—all the life they have shared since the wedding day. The whole past is worth recapturing—not only the wedding but the entire courtship. Repeating treasured experiences recalls old feelings of love. Going dancing again, to dinner or a show has added connotations if it repeats an activity that was relished in the past.

Neither romantic revivals nor family rituals are panaceas. For incompatible couples they would be a farce. But for couples whose affection is dying from lack of nourishment, they offer new resources.

Graceful Touches

The Asian tradition of submission of women does not appeal to us, but there was wisdom in admonishing women to learn the arts of pleasing men. Pleasing can go both ways. A man who controls the urge to belch in front of his wife, and she who combs her hair the first thing in the morning both contribute grace and beauty. People need not use marriage as an excuse to present their ugliest selves to each other. Each time a woman injects beauty into the household, whether by serving dinner with a freshly ironed table-cloth, or filling the house with the smell of baking bread, or wearing a special nightgown, it is a gift of love. For the man there are just as many ways of infusing grace—the courtesies of opening doors, carrying groceries, introducing and referring to his wife and whatever else contributes to her feminine feelings. The more feminine he makes her feel, the more she can help him feel like a man.

Emotional Support in Marriage

From day to day, both spouses must fulfill demanding roles. Problems and opportunities challenge their resourcefulness. Marriage provides in-creased resources as the partner stands in the wings encouraging one's role performance.

Support for Role Performance

SUPPORT FOR PARENTAL ROLES. For the first two decades of marriage, the wife's major role is raising children. Though fathers are marginally useful, their departure for work leaves the wife responsible for the children. Especially when children are not yet in school or when they are home for vacation, mothering is a full-time task. It is also a demanding task. The energy and immaturity of children require supervision, guidance, and en-tertainment. Moreover, energy is drained one way. Children depend on their mother more than she can depend on them. She must constantly give of herself and is rarely appreciated. Children are seldom satisfied. They always want more. No outside audience sees what goes on at home. Only the husband can give the support she needs to staff the home front while he is away.

How can he do this best? Working hard at his own job is one way. If she knows he is doing his best she has an impetus to hold up her end of the bargain. Teamwork in child-rearing helps too. When he is home, he can relieve her of the children. Interest in her experiences sustains her. If he listens to her day's events she senses his concern with what happens when he's not there.

Especially rewarding is applause. In the daily routines of child care, a mother's performance is rarely virtuoso enough to bring down the house. But when those occasions do occur, the husband must applaud or the wife will be disappointed. Perhaps in keeping house and in cooking there are more visible accomplishments. Occasional praise for successful mothering sustains morale even through rainy days. Mother's Day is one opportunity for recognition. And if the eight A.M. kiss wishes not only the husband but the wife well, there is a daily chance to support the wife.

SUPPORT FOR OCCUPATIONAL ROLES. With the sexes reversed, the same supportiveness applies to the husband. In some ways his work is even less visible than hers. However, promotions and salary increases are tangible and spontaneously applauded by the family. The wife may recognize accomplishments before the boss does, and from the very beginning provide encouragement:

> . . . what the wife does to help her husband in his work role is a sensitive indicator of how they feel about each other, what they mean to each other, what they do for each other. The nagging wife who undermines her husband's morale differs importantly from the appreciative wife who enhances his self-esteem. The wife's attitude and behavior in relation to the husband's chief role in life do much to shape his conception of himself, his ego-feelings. She is the mirror in which he sees himself—a mirror whose enhancing or detracting distortions become his image of himself. She is what Nelson Foote (1956) calls his "audience" when he tells of the events of his work life and who listens or turns a deaf ear (Blood and Wolfe: p. 97).

SUPPORT FOR COMMUNITY ROLES. The less routine the situation, the more useful moral support becomes. The saying about the woman behind every great man reflects the encouragement needed by those who push ahead of their peers and stick their necks out. Lesser men also need encouragement when venturing into roles new to them even though not to the world at large:

> Bob still is sometimes hesitant about meeting people or trying new ventures, but he has gained much more self-confidence. Whenever he feels incapable of meeting a situation, I bolster up his ego by pointing out to him his other successes. Somehow, when I say, "You can do it!" I can see his eyes light up in anticipation. It's very rewarding to me to build up his enthusiasm and his confidence in his own worth.

Moral support in both directions, from husband to wife as well as from wife to husband, bolsters achievement in nonmarital roles. The husband-wife relationship then becomes a source of strength for both partners.

Therapy for Emotional Stress

What if the husband doesn't get promoted? What if he gets fired instead? What if the wife's culinary masterpiece falls flat in the oven? Then what?

Frustration produces emotional stress. The natural reaction is aggression, designed to demolish the frustrating object (Dollard, 1939). But civilization inhibits this sequence. Children may be aggravating, but mothers are not supposed to beat them. When employers cause frustration, retaliation would only make matters worse. Yet adrenalin is released into the bloodstream, impelling the body toward aggressive action.

The cartoon illustrates the threat which external frustration presents to the marriage (and incidentally, to the parent-child relationship, also).

1

2

Wives, similarly, may be short-tempered with their husbands when everything has gone wrong. External stresses create crises at home which would not otherwise arise or intensify otherwise milder difficulties.

THERAPEUTIC UTILIZATION OF THE PARTNER. When emotionally upset by an external crisis, one may turn to the partner or to some other resource for help, or handle it oneself. The course taken depends on the nature of the problem and differs between the sexes.

Table 16-1 shows that a large minority of both men and women customarily reacted passively to problems. They slept them off or ate or drank

3

4

Table 16-1. Ways of Handling Worries and Unhappiness, by Sex

Way of Handling	WORRIES		UNHAPPY PERIODS	
	Men	Women	Men	Women
Passive reaction	38%	30%	26%	20%
Prayer	8	23	22	40
Informal help-seeking	22	28	19	21
Direct coping reaction	21	9	9	4
Miscellaneous	11	10	24	15
Total	100%	100%	100%	100%
Number of cases	1,077	1,383	1,077	1,383

Adapted from Gurin *et al.*, 1960: 372, 374. *Source:* National sample of adults (married and single).

them away. Or they forgot about them by watching TV, going to the movies, or engaging in other recreation. Few men and even fewer women attacked problems directly, solving them on their own. The remainder sought outside help. Women, especially, depended on other persons (or another Person).

The self-reliance of men and the dependence of women are the chief conclusions to be drawn from Table 16-1. Unfortunately we know little about the comparative effectiveness of these ways of dealing with problems, except that education increased ability to cope directly.

Where do people take their troubles? In Table 16-1, we saw that most people didn't go anywhere. Nevertheless, a minority did seek help from other people. Table 16-2 shows that informal resources were used much more than professional resources.

Table 16-2. Other Persons Utilized in Handling Worries and Unhappiness

Source of Help	Worries	Periods of Unhappiness
Informal		
Spouse	59%	19%
Parents or children	7	15
Other relatives	1	18
Friends, acquaintances	17	38
Formal		
Clergyman	4	6
Doctor	4	4
Total	99%	100%
Number of cases	689	545

Adapted from Gurin *et al.*, 1960: 368. *Source:* National sample of adults (married and single). Based on those who mentioned any source of outside help.

If men and women turned anywhere for help, they utilized their closest relationships. The spouse was a major resource for those who were married (only three-fourths of Gurin's sample), provided he was not the cause of the difficulty.

Blood and Wolfe asked married women how often they told their husbands their troubles after a bad day. Most Detroit wives told their troubles selectively. Few of them always told their husbands and few never did. Selectivity was greatest in high-status families. Telling "half-the-time" was particularly popular among college-educated wives. Perhaps the reason they were selective was not that they were so well educated but that their husbands were so busy. Business executives and professional men may be home too little and too preoccupied even then to listen to every problem.

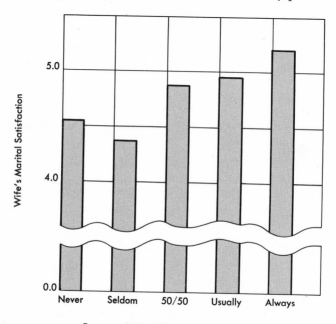

Frequency Wife Tells Her Troubles to Her Husband

Adapted from Blood, 1967: 213. *Source:* Young Detroit wives, 1955.

Figure 16-3. Wife's Marital Satisfaction, by Frequency of Telling Her Husband Her Troubles

Selectivity may be forced on high-status couples, but it doesn't make the most cohesive marriages. Figure 16-3 shows that wives who always told their troubles were most satisfied with their marriages. Nor is this just a feminine reaction. In my Tokyo sample, both sexes were most satisfied with marriages in which both always told their troubles (Blood, 1967).

To abandon selectivity about *whether* to tell one's troubles need not mean unselectivity about *when* to do so. Some times and some places are more conducive than others. Some couples listen better after dinner or over a drink. Distractions such as small children need to be out of the way. Sooner or later, though, most couples could find a time if they tried hard enough.

Floyd Mann reported that bank executives saw two values in getting their wives to talk:

> First, it is diagnostic for the listener; second it is therapeutic for the spouse. Getting the tense and nervous person to talk is a necessary first step if the listener is to decide what part, if any, he should play in the situation. The listener can learn how the other sees the situation, make his own assessment, and can then decide what course of action to take. Getting the other person to talk is therapeutic in that frustrations get formulated into words so that they are no longer free floating and tension maintaining. The very process of trying to explain what is bothering or what has happened helps the tense person to organize all of the facts of the situation and this can lead the person who is upset to see the problem in a new perspective (pp. 7–8).

When the spouse is unavailable, friends and relatives are alternatives. When stress is mild, the individual may be able to cope with it without endangering his relationship to others. Short of full-blown therapy, a sense of humor takes the edge off emotional tension and prevents it from becoming contagious:

> The first few years of our marriage, I'd come home grumpy from the office every once in a while. After a while, Joyce got so familiar with these moods that she kiddingly said I was "acting like a bear." After that all I had to do was growl and she knew I was feeling grouchy again. The bear touch was so silly it made both of us laugh instead of getting teed off at each other.

The problem is to prevent external stress from setting off displaced aggression and counteraggression. To prevent mutual recrimination, awareness of external origins is enough. Whether this information is conveyed by factual reporting, private signals, or facial expression does not matter as long as the message gets across. Once it does, the spouse can put on her proverbial kid gloves and mobilize her therapeutic responses.

THERAPEUTIC RESPONSE TO THE PARTNER'S TROUBLES. The partner's first task is to understand. This requires listening—not as easy as it sounds, especially when children are around. Husband and wife have to compete with other family members for attention. Even without children there are competing attractions—household tasks for the wife, the day's mail and the evening paper for the husband, TV for both. Yet without attention, it is impossible to respond appropriately.

Listening is intrinsically therapeutic. Emotional catharsis is a standard means of tension-reduction, requiring only an interested audience for pent-up grievances. However, to be most effective, listening demands response. The appropriate response depends on the problem. Taking all sorts of bad days together, the husbands in Blood and Wolfe's study responded as shown in Table 16-3.

Table 16-3. Comparative Effectiveness of Therapeutic Responses

Husband's Response When Wife Told Troubles	Percentage of Total Husbands	Mean Effectiveness*
Help in withdrawing from the situation	3%	3.80
Sympathy and affection	32	3.63
Advice and discussion of how wife could solve problem	23	3.53
Help in solving the problem	7	3.31
Passive listening	20	2.92
Dismissal as unimportant	8	2.79
Criticism and rejection	7	1.89
Total	100%	
Number of cases	643	

```
* Code: Wife felt much better      4 points
        A little better            3 points
        Sometimes better,
           sometimes worse         2 points
        About the same             1 point
        Worse                      zero
```

Adapted from Blood and Wolfe, 1960: 206. Source: Representative sample of Detroit wives (excluding those who never told their troubles).

The most common reactions of Detroit husbands were sympathy and advice. Passive listening is hardly a reaction yet even it was better than having the husband react negatively—brushing off her troubles or criticizing her for getting into them or for bothering him with them.

Among the positive responses, help in solving problems did not relieve the wife's feelings immediately but in the long run left her most satisfied with her husband's understanding of her problems and feelings. The most effective immediate relief came from husbands who helped her forget her troubles by taking her out to dinner or to some other distracting activity. Since bad days usually occur at home, leaving home reduces tension fast. Sympathy and affection provide pure support, whereas advice and discussion are practically oriented toward resolving the problem or preventing it from arising again.

Floyd Mann found sharp differences between the characteristic response patterns of engineers and of their wives. A man arrives home at 5:30 to confront his wife in the midst of her troubles. He must choose between taking her away from it all, helping her on the spot, advising her how to proceed, etc. If he had troubles at work, however, the wife cannot respond directly, only indirectly:

I put the dog in the basement, turn on the stereo, give a wink to the children, and after a quick dinner wait until he's ready to discuss the problem. I make sure the dinner conversation is light and casual with no complaints about anything.

Mann commented that "The wife's first task is therapy, not diagnosis. . . . she sees it as her job to establish a therapeutic environment for the husband—one in which he is enveloped, protected from further onslaughts, and one in which the natural process of recovery can function to restore his sense of well-being." (p. 22) This is not easy at a busy time of day, but many middle-class wives provide this service skillfully.

No one therapeutic method is likely to be useful under all circumstances. The two kinds of help plus advice and sympathy are alternative tools to be used as needed. Partners who provide such therapy transform external stresses into occasions for strengthening their marriage.

However, the partner must not be burdened beyond his ability to respond positively. Better not to rely on him at all than to bludgeon him into negative reactions. Once his limit is reached, outside resources may ease the load on the marriage circuit and prevent it from blowing a fuse.

Therapy for Physical Stress

We know little about the nursing care which marriage partners give each other when they are sick. The problems are analogous to those raised by emotional troubles. In fact, the two may overlap since perhaps half of all physical illnesses are psychogenic. If the husband breaks his leg skiing, it is easy for the wife to be sympathetic (provided she doesn't think he was a fool to attempt that trail). But if he wakes up with a headache and wants to be taken care of like a little boy, then what? Some wives (and husbands) believe sympathy is dangerous:

> Every once in a while, Alex refuses to get up in the morning. He mutters some excuse about his back acting up again and wants me to bring him a heating pad and serve him breakfast in bed. He exaggerates his ailments and puts on such an act that it makes me mad. I may bring him a little something but I am careful not to overdo it because I don't want to spoil him when he acts so childish.

Such behavior *is* childish. It is also, however, a transparent plea for sympathy and nurture. To withhold it only makes matters worse, creating tension between husband and wife where originally only the sick individual was tense. Paradoxical as it may seem, the patient is likely to get well faster if his illness is accepted. After he has had enough nursing, however, the time may come when he will need to be encouraged to resume his normal life.

Parsons and Fox (1952) believed that this combination of "permissive-supportive and disciplinary facets of treating illness is peculiarly difficult to maintain in the kind of situation presented by the American family." Hence professional care is often needed for physical illness. Nevertheless, even if the patient is hospitalized for primary care, the partner's sympathy or hostility will have much to do with hastening or delaying his recovery. In any case, the partner's attitude determines whether illness strengthens or weakens the marriage.

MENSTRUAL STRESS. Many couples go for years without illness, but few avoid the tensions of menstruation. "Some degree of discomfort at the time of the period is well-nigh universal." (Filler and Lief, 1963) Most men are aware that women generally have this problem. But they cannot support their wives unless they are informed when the difficulty arises. Few men can be expected to keep track of the calendar. So wives must communicate their condition. Once husbands are aware, they can provide sympathy, massage, and relief from children and can make allowances for the wife's predictable irritability. Empathy and understanding can relieve the partner's troubles, transforming them from sand in the gears of marriage to lubricating oil.

17 Conflict-Resolution in Marriage

Marriage inevitably involves conflicts. No two people can ever live together year after year without clashing—unless one of them has decided always to give in. Even then the conflict exists subliminally although the dominant partner may be unaware of it.

Marriage Breeds Conflicts

Marriage breeds more conflicts than most social situations.

The Intimacy of Marriage

People are on their best behavior in public. At home they let their hair down. The usual screens of privacy give way and the result is sometimes disgusting. Living together under the same roof, the partners are exposed to the seamy side of each other's lives. This strains the relationship they had built on the prettier aspects of life. These intimacies involve facets of life where modesty or cleanliness was learned the hard way. Acts which disgust the partner revive childhood anxieties. Unconsciously, they arouse forgotten fears of parental punishment or loss of love.

The Constancy of Marriage

Marriage tensions grow with prolonged exposure to the irritant. A child can tolerate physical irritants for limited periods, but if exposed long

349

enough he will develop an allergy. Similarly, adults can stand irritating behavior a few hours or a few days but constant exposure makes them allergic.

The Rivalry of Marriage

Sibling rivalry is most acute when two children contend for one mother. Whatever one gains is seen as the other's loss. Because the enemy is unmistakable, enmity is correspondingly focused. Marriage too is dyadic. Husband and wife have only each other to contend with and only each other to blame when they lose. They compete not for maternal affection but for other scarce resources—especially money. If there isn't enough money to meet both partners' wishes, every penny I gain is one less for you. In Chapter 11, I suggested that this implies separate allowances. However, it doesn't say how big those allowances should be. So husband and wife are inevitably pitted against each other in dividing their resources.

The Changeableness of Marriage

If a businessman had to adapt so fast to changing circumstances, he would go crazy—or bankrupt. Yet hard-won solutions to family problems obsolesce with frightening speed. While the new "firm" is still shaky, it doubles or triples in size and loses half its income. How can the "payroll" be met until the new "employees" finish their 20-year "training"? The tighter the financial strain, the tougher the decisions which will have to be made. Moreover, the original staff must do all the training alone except for occasional assistance from retired executives of the parent firm. So labor as well as capital are in perennial short supply for the crucial early decades of the new firm's existence.

No wonder the partners often quarrel over how to spend their time and money. Frictions are inevitable. Some plans must be deferred, and strategies which worked this year will have to be revised next year as the trainees' skills and outside offers increase.

Conflict-resolution, in short, is a never-ending process at best. It need not be painful. It may be effective. But it must constantly be worked at.

Obstacles to Conflict-Resolution

Every marriage has conflicts to be resolved but some circumstances complicate the task.

Immaturity

Immaturity leads insecure individuals to withhold embarrassing information. Satisfactory solutions cannot be derived from incomplete knowledge. Worse yet, secrecy destroys the trust on which a sense of mutuality rests:

> Margaret isn't always honest with me. She gets carried away by her impulses and does things she knows I won't like. Then she won't get around to telling me about it, and we get into all sorts of trouble. For instance, she will charge things at the store without telling me when we don't have enough money in the bank. How can we manage that way?

Inability to Tolerate Disagreement

Negative feelings are inevitably aroused by conflict. They may serve positive functions. Anger reveals how strongly the partner feels. Feelings are a kind of information to be communicated and read. However, some people can't stand to have anyone angry at them. They get frightened and "chicken-out":

> Chuck has quite a temper. He gets disgusted with himself more than with others but his harsh words used to make me clam up for a good long time. This was our biggest problem and we have solved it. I have learned gradually that what he says under stress is not what he really means and if I do fail him and clam up he has learned to remind me that he doesn't mean what he said.

Hostile feelings make those with sensitive consciences feel guilty and want to make up. If the need for reconciliation is too urgent, it short circuits decision-making by cutting the time devoted to searching out alternatives. This truncates the sustained dialogue and honest disagreement necessary for problem-solving to be most creative (Hoffman *et al.*, 1962). Resolving differences superficially is not likely to allocate resources satisfactorily.

Unconscious Distortions

For most couples the wife's clothing allotment can be determined by balancing the state of her wardrobe and the state of the exchequer. Unconscious needs, however, can mess up the problem. Without realizing it, the husband may find her wardrobe a threat to his need to dominate.

Every dollar seems a surrender of power, and every new dress a lure for other men. As a result, he resists the whole idea of a clothing allowance, wanting to veto every sex-appealing purchase. The more unconscious the motivation, the more unreasonable each partner's demands become. He wants a niggardly figure hardly adequate for one season. She wants a lavish amount which would wreck the budget. And with all the unconscious overtones involved, neither is willing to concede a penny.

If such couples could "understand the meaning of their difficulties in terms of their deeper needs and desires, they would then be in a position to work out an intelligent, workable compromise between their conflicting aims instead of obscurely fighting for complete satisfaction of every impulse, however contradictory and realistically impossible." (Levy and Munroe, 1945: 181)

Alcohol

By releasing inhibitions against aggressive remarks, drinking accentuates the danger that discussions will degenerate into quarrels:

> Most of our verbal conflicts come in the evening. After we've had our customary after-dinner drinks, my wife and I seem to lose all our inhibitions about what we are saying. The result is that our attacks on each other get very acrid.

The alternative need not be perennial sobriety as long as couples avoid controversial matters while under the influence of liquor.

Fatigue

Some people quarrel only when they are tired. Frayed nerves and shortened tempers make it easy to lose control. Couples who discover that their quarrels are fatigue-induced may take preventive measures. An evening curfew beyond which discussion is taboo may be a necessary precaution. Some couples take advantage of weekend leisure to tackle problems under optimum conditions:

> A few months ago we seemed incapable of settling little disputes. If one or the other of us was tired we got into trouble. We had to find some way of avoiding bringing those disputes to a head by postponing them until we were in the right mood. So I suggested that every couple of weeks we sit down over some Cokes and discuss the things that had come up between us in the interval. Now, whenever I start getting critical, all Harry has to say is, "All right, hold it until our bull-session!"

For smooth-running marriages, problems are best settled on the spot. Couples plagued by quarrelsomeness may need cooling-off periods. But postponements must not become indefinite. The promised time for resuming discussion must be respected or resentment will intensify.

Conditions for Conflict-Resolution

The conditions for effective problem-solving carry familiar names—maturity and love—plus a new one: concentration.

Maturity

Mature people are less defensive about the past, their own proposals, and the partner's counterproposals.

Nondefensiveness makes it easier to apologize for past behavior and to accept apologies from the spouse. Willingness to admit mistakes and ask forgiveness clears away resentments:

> At the first party we ever went to as husband and wife, Julian spent the whole evening talking to an old girl friend of his. It's true he hadn't seen her for years, but there I was stranded among his friends who were all strangers to me. I was so unhappy I could hardly keep from crying and I've never forgotten how thoughtless he was.

Buried resentments create barriers between husband and wife that diminish their feeling of unity. They fuel the fire of subsequent troubles, providing irrelevant gripes to sabotage the machinery of problem-solving.

No matter how ancient a resented incident, it needs resolving. The only solution is apology and forgiveness. For people who hate to admit they are wrong, apologizing is painful. For a spouse who has been badly hurt, forgiveness may be equally difficult. Whichever comes first does not matter. Logically apology precedes forgiveness. But psychologically a spouse who is forgiven first finds it easier to apologize.

Mature egos have an inner security that enables them to be more adaptable in making decisions. Less easily threatened, they can afford to be more flexible in compromising or making concessions. They are less apt to hold out for their own pet proposals, creating unbreakable deadlocks which bar the way to mutual agreement. Well-developed egos are less touchy and vulnerable. They are less inclined to misinterpret the partner's proposals as personal attacks, less apt to bog discussion down in defensive counterattacks. As a result, attention can be focused on the issue rather than distracted with emotionality.

Pickford *et al.* (1966) found happily married couples significantly more emotionally stable and objective than couples in trouble. Locke's happily married couples were significantly more mature than his divorced couples in several ways: (1) Less defensiveness in current interaction helped them *get angry less easily.* (2) Less defensiveness about the past helped them *get over anger more quickly.* (3) Less attachment to their own preferences enabled them to *"give in" more often* in arguments (not being stubborn) and to be correspondingly *less dominating;* not pressing their own ideas ruthlessly on the spouse. Locke summarized the three elements under the general heading of "adaptability." (1951)

Pickford's happy couples were less differentiated in their sex-roles than his unhappy couples. The happy husbands were less domineering and less concerned with their masculinity. Their wives were extraordinarily friendly. The net result was limited differentiation between husbands who exercised decision-making leadership and wives who specialized in integrative support. But so limited was their specialization that each could flexibly play the role of the other.

Love

The elements of love—sex, companionship, care, and affirmation—facilitate decision-making. Since unsolved problems destroy intimacy, sexual attraction is an incentive to getting problems solved. Companionship provides an interactive base for communication and multiple opportunities for expressing issues and for listening to them. Couples who spend time together because they enjoy each other, take time for decision-making, too.

Caring about the partner heightens adaptability. Mature people willingly make concessions to those they love. Caring moves beyond mere flexibility into altruism, a desire to promote the partner's welfare through generous allocation of resources. Caring promotes generosity through empathy. Less wrapped up in himself and more concerned with the partner, one who cares becomes more perceptive of the partner's wishes and eager to find solutions that will enable the partner to achieve them. If the partner is affirmed as a person, his wishes are even more likely to be accepted.

The more people love each other, the more willing they are to defer to each other in order to make the other happy. Back (1951) found that cohesive pairs of students often resolved experimental conflicts by one partner giving in all the way, whereas less cohesive pairs were forced to compromise because neither was willing to go more than halfway.

Concentration

Concentration means focusing attention on the issue until it is resolved. A common pitfall in decision-making is getting off the track, forgetting the original issue. Decision-making requires a discussion leader to keep the group focused on the issue and rap the knuckles of those who go astray. Some marriage partners are skillful discussion leaders, but self-discipline is needed from both partners to keep each issue in focus until it is resolved.

Concentration requires postponing other activities—particularly those of a distracting nature. An issue will be settled faster if the paper is laid aside, the TV turned off, and other attention-seducing devices throttled.

Having posed the problem of marital conflict and discussed conditions which affect couples' responses, I turn now to the heart of the issue: How can conflicts be resolved? Although they are not entirely distinguishable, I will divide conflicts into three types. First are individual idiosyncracies which become "tremendous trifles." Second, the system problems involved in meshing the behavior of husband and wife into reciprocal marital roles. Finally, and most elaborately, the task of allocating family resources.

Coping with Tremendous Trifles

A tremendous trifle is any irritant that is tremendously significant to the irritated party but a mere trifle to the "innocent" one. To outsiders also these often seem trifling—the cap left off the toothpaste, dirty socks on the bedroom floor, or slurped soup. They seem especially trifling to the offender if he is unaware of his behavior. Indeed sleeping habits are tremendous trifles of which awareness is impossible.

Tremendous trifles cause tremendous damage. When anxiety in the threatened partner explodes in denunciation of the offending spouse, he reciprocates defensively. Conflict and mutual recrimination become chronic if the trouble is literally an everyday affair. The fact that the issue is trifling makes it harder to deal with rationally. Major tragedies call out the best in people, but petty irritants are handled in petty ways.

Can the Leopard Change His Spots?

The indignant partner naturally wants his spouse to reform. "If only John would remember to hang up his coat when he comes in!" If a word to the wise is not sufficient, a reminder campaign is undertaken. "Don't forget to hang up your coat, John!" (said as sweetly as possible). Being a good husband, John dutifully obeys. The trouble is he doesn't necessarily get the habit. When Jane isn't around to remind him, he forgets.

Why do reform movements seldom succeed? Because habits are so ingrained that they don't respond easily to New Year's resolutions. Occasional leopards do change. The partner's reminders make him aware of his behavior. Self-consciousness makes it possible to change the disliked behavior. But crusades often backfire. The trifling nature of the issue makes it easy to accuse the spouse of being supercritical. Even if the individual reacts sympathetically, carrying out the resolve to "be a good boy" is difficult. Unconscious habits do not give way easily.

If the offensive habit persists, the crusader becomes a martyr and finally a tyrant. Gentle reminders become venomous nagging. Barbed attacks antagonize the victim. Ultimately a state of war breaks out—sporadic sniping on one side and revenge on the other. Aggression may be overt—with quarreling galore. Or it may be covert (harder to recognize but still vindictive) in sarcasm, moodiness, or sexual coldness.

Segregating Trouble

Sometimes the offense can be shoved behind closed doors—out of sight, out of mind. Separate bathrooms and separate dressing rooms solve some problems. Separate bedrooms may be needed by snoring couples. Strategically located hampers will invite dirty clothes. Separate desks or separate studies prevent husband and wife from clashing over piles of unanswered correspondence. In short, the irritation will disappear if the irritant no longer confronts the partner.

Draining Off Negative Feelings

If the situation can't be changed, then what? The next alternative is to divert the critic's resentment into harmless channels. For some couples humor provides an outlet. However, humor must be handled with care or it backfires. When the joker's motivation is hostile, humor turns into sarcasm more barbed than open criticism. Moreover, an insecure spouse may not be able to take even the mildest ribbing. Using humor to reduce tension depends on whether the couple can laugh together about their "terrible little problem," or whether the problem-spouse feels he is being laughed at.

Where even humor is too aggressive, indirect outlets are the only recourse. Traditionally, chopping wood drained off the adrenalin released by anger. The following couple devised a more psychological approach:

Dennis and I have a little scheme worked out which works wonders for us. We both have habits the other dislikes, and for a while we tried to talk each other out of them. It was no go. Then we got the idea of putting up a sheet of paper on the inside of a closet door with two columns—one for him and one for me. Then whenever he does some little thing I don't like, I go and put down a black mark under his name. And he does the same for me. There's no competition involved because we both win—it gives us both a chance to vent our bad feelings in a tangible way so that we can live together more happily.

Acquiring Immunity

Sometimes the only way out of tremendous trifles is to accept the irritating behavior. Learning to tolerate the intolerable is not easy. The reasons why trifles become tremendous in the first place bar the way to lightheartedness. Nevertheless, desensitization is sometimes possible.

The crucial step is to reduce expectations—to accept the fact that the difficulties are irremediable. Sometimes resignation comes through sheer exhaustion. Sometimes it comes through self-insight, discovering that one's sensitivity stems not so much from the grossness of the partner as from one's own anxieties learned in childhood. Similarly, one may come to understand the partner's situation—realizing it is not easy for him to change. Sometimes, love and time do the trick. Note how most mothers (and even some fathers) get used to dirty diapers. What may have been revolting at first comes to be accepted as a normal part of life.

> I will never forget how terribly embarrassed I was the first night for fear my husband would hear me in the bathroom. I turned the water in the tub on full blast before I dared use the toilet.

Some critics decide that keeping up the battle does more harm than good, so it is time to call a cease fire:

> It really gets my goat to waste electricity. For years I've been trying to get Jeanne to remember to shut off the lights when she leaves a room. Yet every time I come home the house is ablaze with light. Lately I've begun to realize that the reason Jeanne reacts so strongly to what I say is not because she doesn't want to turn off the lights but because I keep harping on it, heckling and nagging her. What's the use of causing all that trouble if it only saves a dollar a month on the electric bill? I've decided I'd pay the extra dollar.

Other critics adopt a do-it-yourself policy. With a fraction of the energy expended on this verbal barrage, all the switches in the house could have been turned off. Developing immunity doesn't necessarily require learning to live with mass illumination or mass clutter. It only requires being able to live with the spouse. If the spouse is hopeless, then the critic can take the responsibility himself.

Maturity requires accepting the inevitable, especially when the issue involves unconscious habits learned in childhood. The only way to tension-reduction may be to accept the partner as he is. Better to preserve the marriage than to destroy it jousting over a hopeless issue. Seemingly insignificant habits may be so crucial to his character and defensive structure that giving them up (whether voluntarily or under coercion) would increase his anxiety alarmingly. Recognizing this, the critic may decide to live and let live, provided the irritating behavior doesn't create too much anxiety in him!

Resolving Role Conflicts

Role conflicts emerge early in marriage from incongruent expectations. The first step in resolving them is to recognize what they are. The unconscious nature of many role conceptions makes this difficult. Discovering that the partner's discrepant behavior is not deliberately antagonistic removes much of the venom from the conflict:

> I didn't realize it when we were going together, but one of the little ways in which Anna and I differ crops up at meal times. She likes to talk a lot at meals and I don't. I know perfectly well where it came from. As far as my family was concerned, meals were a time for refueling and nothing else. Her family made meals into a big occasion where they talked about everything under the sun. So now Anna likes to chit-chat about little everyday affairs and I get through way ahead of her.

Even if the ancestry of role conflicts is not immediately apparent, to see them as system problems rather than as individual deficiencies makes them easier to tackle without defensiveness. They are system problems in the sense that they must be solved if the marriage is to operate successfully. The fault lies not in the sinfulness of either individual but in the lack of fit between the two.

Adapting Role Behavior

From the standpoint of the couple, conflict-resolution requires changes in both behavior and expectations. However, a given individual may change either his behavior or his ideas (or both in case of compromise). If my wife expects me to do more than I had originally expected, my most graceful response would be to rise to meet her extra expectations:

After we got married I found out how much Carl's folks had babied him. At first I thought it was ridiculous and I figured I'd force him to take care of himself by not doing things for him. It didn't work, though. He just got mad at me and we were both unhappy. So now I'm trying to baby him too. I figure if I just pick his clothes up off the floor and forget it we'll both be happier.

To make concessions gracefully is beneficial. To extend oneself begrudgingly only causes irritation even though the task itself gets done:

My father wanted to concentrate on his work and let my mother run the house all by herself. She has done everything ever since I can remember, but she always gripes about it to us kids. To him she keeps making remarks about how nothing ever gets done unless she does it. As a result he has given up even his few attempts to help out and developed more and more feelings of inferiority and failure in relation to her.

Smooth role changes depend not only on the maturity of the individual but on the encouragement of the partner. If my efforts to change are appreciated, I will feel less like a martyr. The following husband aided his wife in learning to enact a role they both agreed on:

When we were first married, Hugh had to adjust to the fact that I didn't previously know how to cook and that I wouldn't be a good cook for quite a while (if ever). He complimented me on my cooking (even though it wasn't very good) and thus encouraged me to learn to be a really good cook.

If, instead of accentuating the positive, this husband had criticized his wife's failures, she might have lost so much self-confidence that she would have been afraid to try anything new and would never have progressed beyond hamburgers.

Willingness to modify one's own behavior distinguished adjusted from maladjusted married couples (Buerkle, Anderson, and Badgley, 1961). For example, if a wife was bored with a party and wanted to leave but the husband was having a good time, a well-adjusted husband would tell his wife, "We'll leave, since you want to go," while she was apt to say, "I'll stay because you're enjoying yourself." Mutual deference to the other's feelings does not resolve conflict, since it doesn't specify whether they should stay or leave. But it transforms conflict from a clash of wills to an Alphonse-Gaston contest of courtesy. The willingness of both partners to please the other is appreciated no matter which solution is chosen. Moreover, if both partners are willing to modify their behavior, compromise becomes a happy medium instead of a bitter necessity.

Adapting Role Expectations

In the previous section, role conflicts were resolved by changing be-havior to meet the partner's expectations. The other possibility is that one may renounce one's claims and let the partner have his own way. This is necessary if the partner's role conceptions and/or personality needs are so firmly entrenched that they can't be changed.

> Tony makes all the ultimate decisions in our marriage. In fact he was the one who decided that I should go to work this year. It doesn't enter his head to ask what I think since he doesn't think it's any of my busi-ness to decide. I used to be very independent, but now I'm getting used to the way he tells me what to do.

This wife changed her conception of herself from independent to de-pendent and her expectations for her husband from sharing decisions to making them on his own. This resolved the discrepancy between their expectations.

It takes only one partner willing to make concessions to resolve role conflicts. Yet in the best marriages both partners stand ready to alter their expectations if necessary. In another of Buerkle's examples the wife was offered a job but the husband felt she should stay home and take care of their family of thirteen- and seventeen-year-old boys. Adjusted wives in his study said they would defer to the husband's judgment, giving up their desire to go to work, whereas adjusted husbands would typically allow her to go to work if she wanted to. By not insisting on their own preferences, both partners turned a potential conflict into an accommodation.

The first task is to harmonize conflicts that arise out of incongruent ex-pectations brought into marriage. Later role conflicts arise from new circumstances—new children, new jobs, or unemployment. Role concep-tions are rarely immutable, but gradually adapt to changing circumstances. By a process of rationalization most people come to legitimize what originally may have been simply expedient. Thus, Blood and Hamblin (1958) found that when wives worked after marriage, both partners be-came more equalitarian in their ideas than they were before marriage.

Making Joint Decisions

Decision-making is a critical skill. Most people are skillful enough to be able to concentrate on the content rather than the method of dealing with a particular problem. But clumsy couples may have to pay more attention to the process. Problem-solving requires a series of stages. Bales and Strodt-beck (1951) observed that small groups moved from problems of orientation through problems of evaluation to problems of control as they struggled to make decisions. Changing only one term, I will analyze the process in terms of orientation, evaluation, and execution.

Orientation to the Issue

When is an issue not an issue? When is a discrepancy between husband and wife better left alone? One answer is when no action is required. Husbands and wives don't have to agree on all their ideas, opinions, attitudes, and values. When they disagree, dialogue may be interesting but choice is not necessary. Moreover, in the happiest marriages, each partner maintains the illusion that agreement is greater than it actually is. Were they to make an issue of every discrepancy, the illusion of solidarity would be harder to maintain. For instance, 60 middle-class married couples in Cleveland overestimated the extent of their value consensus on their marriage goals (Levinger and Breedlove, 1966). According to the theory of cognitive dissonance, couples who want to go on living together can be expected to reduce strain by minimizing their disagreements. Better to leave well enough alone—unless practical issues must be faced.

Another time when noncommunication is preferable is when the chances of getting results are slight. For something to be worth arguing about, there must be a reasonable chance of getting a payoff. Otherwise, ignorance may be preferable:

> I know a woman whose eyes glitter with virtuous self-satisfaction every time she has had a "real heart-to-heart talk" with her husband, which means that she has spent several hours torturing him, or at best boring him to distraction, with a ruthless exposure of the deplorable status of their mutual relationship to date. She is usually so pleased with herself after these periodical inquests that she tells most of her friends, and also her coiffeur, about it. "Dick and I had such a wonderful time last evening. We made a real effort to find out the real truth about each other—or, at least, I certainly did. I honestly believe we have found a new basis of adjustment for ourselves. What a marvelous feeling that is—don't you think so?" (de Sales, 1948)

RECOGNIZING THAT AN ISSUE EXISTS. Joint decision-making requires both partners to be actively involved. Some couples have such poor communication that they are not sure whether they're in trouble or not:

> One thing I've noticed about happy couples is that they seem to understand how the other partner feels about everything. Joe has been

so reserved that I haven't known how he felt about many things. I've seldom known whether he was satisfied with things as they are, and if not, what improvements he'd like to see tried.

The responsibility for communication necessarily rested with Joe. If he was dissatisfied about something, he was the only one who could initiate the decision-making process. Rarely is silent suffering mutually beneficial. Only trifles are better endured than harped upon when there is little chance that behavior can be changed.

However, it is difficult to hold one's tongue cheerfully. It takes maturity to handle irritation, and there is danger of displacing tension into covert aggression, making matters worse instead of better. The following situation illustrates the danger that unexpressed issues will be transmuted into hidden aggression, this time in resistance to commands:

> My husband is a regular slave-driver. He believes everyone should work hard, but he is never satisfied and never appreciates what I do. Often I have a terrific urge to walk across the room and slap his face, but I don't dare. I don't really do anything to get even with him, except that I do unenthusiastically the things he asks me to do.

If grievances are severe, holding them in will hardly improve things. Tension will build up until it explodes outwardly against the partner or inwardly in ulcers or asthma. In Feldman's middle-class Syracuse marriages (1966), individuals who suppressed their responses to conflict situations were more aggressive toward the spouse. Keeping the lid on rarely works when real trouble is brewing. If the partner is perceptive, he will detect the tension. Once noticed, it is frustrating not to be able to come to grips with the issue if knowledge is deliberately withheld:

> I took to Wayne because of his calmness. It seemed to be a good balance for my excitableness. I've discovered since we've been married, though, that this means he'll go into his shell and not talk to me for a week. I never can find out the reason for his sulkiness until he finally gets over it. It's pretty exasperating to know he's got something against me but not be able to do anything about it since I don't know what it is.

Contrast the frustration in the previous case with the feeling of progress in the following:

> Both Sue and I had to learn to speak what was on our minds to each other. We had both been taught it was not right to inflict your problems on others, but we had to "unlearn" that principle so as not to shut the other partner out. We found that by talking our problems out, we not only felt better, but sometimes the problems would solve themselves when they were out in the open.

In general, then, issues are better raised with the partner than left to fester beneath the surface.

The chief danger is attacking the partner's ego. Direct criticism causes trouble. The attacked partner mobilizes his defenses and the war is on. Instead of focusing on the problem at hand, the quarrel ranges into irrelevant side issues and exaggerated innuendoes. Or the accused spouse retreats to nurse his wounded pride. In either case, the couple are no closer to dealing with their problem than before. In fact, defensiveness and despair may have stiffened their resistance.

Though criticism is liable to boomerang, the alternative need not be circuitous. The object of attack needs to be shifted from the person to the problem. The more impersonally a problem can be tackled, the easier it is to get started. Orientals are not the only ones who need to save face. Instead of saying, "I don't like the way you are treating me," an impersonal approach would be, "Something is wrong with our marriage." Even this may be dangerous for couples prone to personal vindictiveness. Even impersonal problem-posing may be taken personally. Until skill and experience have been acquired, some couples raise problems only with fear and trembling:

> Every time I start to bring up a problem my heart begins to pound and I get all jittery. I'm so afraid Newt will think I'm just griping. I suppose after we've been married longer I'll get more self-confidence about telling him when I think we need to work on something.

The converse of the responsibility for expressing issues tactfully is the partner's responsibility to take them seriously. Occasionally he will be too busy. But chronic rebuffs prevent marital understanding, no matter how legitimate the excuse:

> At the store I have to listen to the customers' troubles all day—it's part of my job. But when I get home, I don't want to hear my wife tell me everything that's gone wrong. If I just find more trouble when I get home, it's too much. I'm getting to be a nervous wreck.

Few wives can accept with equanimity the notion that they matter less than customers. Marriage is supposed to be more rewarding than business, not less. If marriage is to be a personal relationship, there may be occasions when issues are not pressed but few when overtures from the partner are rebuffed. Resistance to hearing the partner's grievances is primarily a male vice. For the wives interviewed by Terman (1938), selfishness and inconsiderateness were the most widespread criticisms of husbands, and only husbands were accused of failure to talk things over.

The counterpart of masculine imperturbability is feminine nagging. For

Terman's husbands, this was the chief complaint about wives, but they had only themselves to blame. Husbands who take issues seriously the first time, don't hear them repeated in an exasperated tone of voice. But those who dodge problems invite a barrage of needling. To prevent cycles of hopeless pestering and irritated defensiveness, moving on to the central phases of decision-making is necessary.

IDENTIFYING THE ISSUE. Like knowing that an issue exists, the nature of the problem is often obvious to all concerned. But not always. Some problems are hard to pin down because they are embarrassing. Sexual inadequacies go undefined by squeamish couples. Ignorance of sexual terminology handicaps effective communication. More often, the words are known but too emotionally loaded.

Married men at Brigham Young University were more disappointed about frequency of sexual intercourse than about any other subject. But did they say anything to their wives? Sixty-five per cent did not, preferring to "wait and see" what happened. Similarly, men disappointed with their new wife's care of the home usually said nothing, perhaps feeling this touched too closely on the wife's key role (Cutler and Dyer, 1965). Perhaps, too, these husbands felt their new brides were doing the best that could be expected, so they could reasonably hope for future improvement. Presumably, the longer a marriage has been in existence, the less appropriate it is simply to wait and see whether things will get better spontaneously. Moreover, even in this study only husbands were modally uncommunicative. Most wives broached their grievances directly.

Misleading cues are common. Symptoms often mask underlying problems. Nagging and complaining—no matter how much they are blamed for marital unhappiness—are never the root of the problem. They are attempts to cope with basic difficulties. Moreover, what may be a fundamental issue in one marriage may be a symptom in another. Sexual frigidity is sometimes basic. But sometimes it reflects the wife's dissatisfaction with her husband. Some couples say money is their problem. Yet others thrive on the same income. Locating the fundamental problem may take considerable sleuthing.

If couples know *when* their bad feelings cropped up but not exactly *how* the trouble originated, it may help to rehearse the events:

> Carol and I both love books. So when we got married, we decided to put enough money in the budget for one book a month. Last month when we went to pick out our book everything seemed to go wrong. Both of us seemed disappointed about what should have been a pleasant expedition. After we got home, I said to her, "Let's go through the whole evening again and see where we went off the track." So right there in the living room I pretended to go into the store and look around, all the while saying out loud what my thoughts had been at the time. Then

Carol did the same. It finally became clear that the crux of our problem lay in my desire to browse around and leaf through a lot of books whereas Carol wanted to find out whether they had certain books she'd already heard about, buy one, and then run home to start reading it. We haven't decided yet how to get together next time, but we're both relieved to know what the trouble was.

Soliloquizing is a technique adapted from role-playing which brings out into the open hidden assumptions and reactions.

Thinking is the best way to analyze an issue. It is promoted by leisurely *ex post facto* discussion after tempers have cooled. It requires searching for repetitive trouble spots. With the diligent use of intelligence, the puzzle should eventually be solved.

Evaluation of Alternative Solutions

Once the issue is clear, decision-making can progress from orientation to evaluation. This includes discovering what solutions are possible, evaluating them, and making a final choice among them.

PROPOSING SOLUTIONS. The chief pitfall at this stage is incompleteness. Instead of considering all possible courses of action, only a few are thought of. As a result the best solution may be overlooked.

Characteristically, each partner has a preconceived answer. The fact that other answers exist tends to be forgotten. If both partners have the same idea, they are even more likely to settle on it, regardless of its merits. If the TV announcer just made a persuasive plug for a loan company, shorthanded couples are apt to ignore less expensive alternatives. If neither partner has a ready answer, the advice of friends or relatives may be sought. There is no loss (and considerable potential gain) in outside consultation.

Couples often combine proposing with evaluating. As soon as one solution is proposed, they discuss its pros and cons. Only when a given solution looks doubtful do they begin scavenging for another. With luck this system works. For best results, special attention may need to be paid to canvassing alternatives. Couples inclined to bog down in arguments about the merits of each proposal may need to postpone evaluation until all the possibilities are out in the open. Writing down proposals guarantees that no ideas will be forgotten when evaluation begins. If evaluation is postponed, the initial order of alternatives depends simply on the accident of popping first into someone's mind. Suggesting solutions gives both partners a sense of involvement in the final decision. More importantly, it adds new items to the list of potentials.

Postponing evaluation is difficult. Each partner must curb his reactions to the other's suggestions. Spontaneous comments must be inhibited if listing is to be a separate process. Such rigidity is unnecessary for couples able to approach their problems objectively. But for high-tension couples stiff neutrality here may make the difference between successful problem-solving and just another explosion.

EVALUATING THE ALTERNATIVES. If there is only one way out of a situation, there are no alternatives to be weighed. Wherever two or more solutions are available, the first task is to measure them against the partners' values. Since value systems are hierarchical, they offer ways of ordering alternatives. After each partner has ranked them, the lists can be compared to see how much agreement exists. Low-priority items can be abandoned and attention concentrated on each partner's preferences.

Some choices have such complex ramifications that both partners feel ambivalent about the alternatives; both see gains and losses in each alternative. In such dilemmas, decision-making may be expedited by jointly listing the values involved. For example, husband and wife might evaluate a job offer in another city:

Gains	Losses
1. Higher salary	1. Moving expenses
2. More challenging job	2. Changing schools in midyear
3. Greater opportunity for promotion	3. Loss of friends for the children and for us
4. More cultural advantages	4. Leaving our home
5. Closer to relatives	5. Pulling out of organizational responsibilities
	6. Longer commuting time

In other situations, the problem may not be to choose between values but between means of achieving them. For example, husband and wife may agree that they need a new car, but have to choose among brands and models. Then evaluation may require research. Reading up on the subject, talking to others who've faced the same problem, and consulting with experts may be fruitful sources of information. First-hand experimentation sometimes yields information no amount of study could give.

Once the list of gains and losses is complete, the weighing process can begin. How likely and how important is each? Moving costs must be compared with the salary increase, the husband's job satisfaction with the wife's regret in parting with her friends, and the like. Comparing gains and losses is not easy, but the weight of various factors will gradually emerge as each partner listens to the other. Understanding the partner's feelings is even more likely if each takes the role of the other, making up arguments in favor of the other's side and against his own. Assuming the role of the other "should serve to increase empathy for the spouse and insight into one's own behavior." (Kimmel and Havens, 1966)

One pitfall is evaluating proposals as "right" and "wrong." These labels are too simple and too abstract. Calling a proposal "right" is another way of saying, "This is the answer I choose." Premature decision-making short circuits evaluation:

> Last week Ken and I were making plans for our vacation trip and he suggested that we write some of our friends and ask if we could spend the night with them. I felt pretty strongly that it wouldn't be right to do that and I told him so. He wanted to know why not, so I told him it was just the wrong thing to do.

Arguing that something isn't right because it is wrong is not only circular but too vague to be useful. Concrete effects on the wife's feelings, on the prospective hosts, or on their friendship would have contributed to evaluating this proposal.

SELECTING THE BEST ALTERNATIVE. At the end of the evaluation process may lie consensus—the partners agreeing on the best answer. If consensus is achieved, no separate decision needs to be reached. When consensus doesn't result from first-round evaluating, it may emerge by postponing the decision. As long as there is a tug of war between partners, consensus is impossible. Once the tension relaxes, agreement may unexpectedly appear. "Sleeping on it" often gives new perspective to both partners so that the next day each says, "Maybe you're right after all."

Consensus may involve one of the original alternatives. Or the differing preferences of the partners may be integrated in a creative synthesis which achieves the values of both. Not every dilemma lends itself to such creativity, but this is the most satisfying solution in situations important to both partners.

Reverting to our mobility dilemma, let us suppose that initially the husband wants to change jobs but the wife wants to stay where she is. Simple consensus would involve one partner becoming convinced that the other is right. A creative consensus might take the form of agreeing to stay in the home town but search for a new job there. If a promising opening could be found, the husband's vocational values might be achieved at the same time that the wife's domestic values were safeguarded. If both partners' values cannot be achieved through consensus, three alternatives remain: accommodation, compromise, or concession. (Voting is useless in two-person groups!)

Accommodation resembles creative consensus since it enables each partner to achieve his own goal. The difference is that consensus synthesizes separate alternatives into a mutually approved common package. Accommodation means agreeing to disagree. Both alternatives are put into effect, but each applies only to its exponent. Each individual pursues his own goal unilaterally, regretting his failure to persuade the partner to join him. Accommodation to mobility might see the husband move while wife and children remained behind. A split family illustrates the strain accommodation imposes. Less extreme (but still stressful) accommodations characterize interfaith couples who maintain their separate faiths.

A *compromise* is midway between the partners' preferences. Neither partner achieves all he wanted nor loses everything. In black and white situations no intermediate alternative may be possible, but if shades of gray are available, equalitarian couples prefer this solution. Typical interfaith compromises include Unitarianism for Jewish-Gentile couples and Episcopalianism for Catholic-Protestant couples. Contrasting with such *halfway compromises* are *sequential compromises* in which couples alternate between their preferences, achieving each partner's goal half the time. For example, they take turns going to each other's churches or spend vacations alternately at the shore and in the mountains. Compromising maintains companionship whereas accommodation separates partners. Yet in matters like religion compromise is anathema. In others it may be impossible. Moving halfway to a new job would hardly do, nor could most husbands take turns working at a new job and the old one.

When neither consensus, accommodation, nor compromise is possible, the only way out is by *concession*. One partner loses all while the other gains all. The question is, who should do the conceding? Five approaches are possible. The concession may be forced, voluntary, rational, or delegated either to outsiders or to chance.

Forced concessions strain the husband-wife relationship the most. Whether the husband threatens to beat his wife or to deprive her of money, or she badgers him verbally or deprives him of sex, the victory is costly. Force is not always physical. Stubbornness eventually forces the spouse to give in. The result is hardly worthy of being called voluntary, however:

> My husband is the stubbornest man you ever saw. I wanted to visit my folks this Christmas and he wanted to go to his. We argued for weeks about it until finally I suggested we draw straws. But he'd have none of it. He said we were going to his home or he wouldn't go anywhere. Finally, I gave up. I figured if he was going to be that pigheaded about it, I couldn't win.

Buerkle discovered that well-adjusted couples were mutually willing to make concessions. Where intermediate solutions were possible, they often compromised. Where only one-sided concession was available, both partners competed for the privilege of making the other happy. *Voluntary concessions* were based on the desire of the individual to meet the other's needs.

In equalitarian marriages the partners are equally willing to concede. In husband-dominant marriages, the wife concedes sooner than the husband. Though masculine dominance sometimes rests on force, more often it reflects deference to the husband's opinions. The wife's conceding can be just as gracious as an equalitarian couple's eagerness to please each other. If both partners are equally willing (or unwilling) to concede, other factors must be invoked. *Rational criteria* may provide an answer:

1. Are the partners equally involved in the situation? If one feels more strongly about his proposal, the nod should go to him.
2. Will both partners be equally affected by the decision? If the issue is whether to buy a tank-type or an upright vacuum cleaner, the fact that it will be used primarily by the wife means her preference should have greater weight.
3. Are both partners equally well informed on the subject? If Bill has a green thumb but Mary is a greenhorn at gardening, Bill should decide what to plant.
4. Whose turn is it to win? Taking turns works wonders among three-year-old children and may do the same for three-year-old marriages. If the wife has made the most concessions, it would be good for her morale to have her way this time (other things being equal).

If the couple remain deadlocked, can *someone else* cast a vote to break the tie? Labor and management sometimes choose an impartial arbiter; why not husband and wife? This rules out most relatives, since they're apt to be biased in favor of their own side of the family (or to lean over backwards in the opposite direction). A mutual friend may help or a professional consultant can be brought in. He may prefer reopening the evaluation process to making an out-of-hand decision. If eventually he finds it necessary to cast the deciding vote, the couple will understand the steps by which he has arrived at his suggestion.

Sometimes pros and cons are so evenly balanced that it doesn't make much difference which way the decision goes. A *flip of the coin* may be the quickest way out of the dilemma.

Regardless of the basis for concession the losing partner deserves commiseration from the winner. Small-group research shows the value of "integrative" activity (concern with hurt feelings) for restoring group solidarity after difficult decisions. Words of appreciation and sympathy will repair the marital bond.

Execution of the Decision

Evaluation is the key phase of decision-making. However, execution is not automatic.

CARRYING OUT THE DECISION. One advantage of joint decision-making is that those who participate in making a decision feel more responsible for carrying it out. Decisions arrived at by group discussion were more likely to be put into practice than concessions derived from being lectured at or otherwise externally manipulated (Lewin, 1953). No matter how a decision was reached, however, new problems may arise in carrying it out. Trouble can result from expecting immediate compliance. If deep-seated habits must be changed or complex skills acquired, individuals with the best intentions may learn only gradually. Experiments with rats show that it takes time to learn new tasks. At first, performance is poor. Only gradually does it approach perfection. Rarely is perfection itself achieved. Usually the learning curve levels off just short of perfection with random errors continuing to mar the picture. Though human beings can learn better than rats, we too are subject to lapses in memory. Much as a husband may want to remember to take out the garbage, he is likely to forget when his daily schedule is upset, he doesn't feel well, or the boss comes to dinner.

Some plans of action include alternatives to be used in emergencies. The following couple recognized that their preferred plan would not always work, and knew what to do when circumstances demanded flexibility:

> Five-thirty has been such a hectic time in our house that Cynthia and I decided something had to be done. From now on I'm supposed to relieve her of the responsibility for the children so she can concentrate on the cooking. Days when I feel too tired to cope with the chidren myself, I'll tell her and we can work out some other plan. Maybe on those days I'll do the cooking myself.

REVIEWING THE DECISION IN OPERATION. When alternative solutions are being tried in order to test their implications, reviewing comes automatically. The only problem is, how much time is a fair trial? If the trial period is clearly understood in advance, griping can be avoided:

> Leonard's family always read the Bible aloud after breakfast. In mine we preferred silent meditation. When we first got married, we agreed we'd try both methods and see which we liked best. The trouble was that we never did give my approach a sympathetic test. The very first

day Len muttered about it being "barren and unstimulating," whereas I think if he had been willing to stick it out a few days longer he would have begun to discover its value.

Even supposedly final decisions may have unanticipated consequences. Silent meditation might look good in theory, but noise from the next apartment may prove distracting.

Even more likely are changing circumstances that spoil old solutions. Children inevitably disrupt many patterns:

> Gracia and I made a big thing out of mealtimes. At dinner we'd have candlelight and silver and read to each other the letters we'd received from mutual friends. One Christmas when the mail was running heavy, we began to be vaguely aware that our reading wasn't getting across as well as it had before. Finally we realized that the baby was getting old enough to want his share of attention. We decided right then and there never to try to read mail at meals again—at least not until the children grow up and leave home.

Decision-Making in Practice

No couple's decision-making ever looks as neat as the outline I have presented. Instead of following a logical sequence, couples jump around, not finishing one stage and skipping the next. Over the years, most couples learn to solve their problems with astonishing ease. Mere awareness that a problem exists may enable an empathic spouse to alter his behavior enough to solve a problem with hardly a word spoken. Couples build up repertoires of habits, skills, and memories that are called upon when new issues arise. For partners able to read between the spoken lines, condensed versions of the decision-making process are efficient.

In Syracuse, the longer middle-class couples had been married, the less explosive their response to marital conflict became. They slammed doors less and criticized the partner less. Instead they talked more calmly or forgot about their troubles rather than pressing them (Feldman, 1966). Perhaps they learned which issues could be pursued productively and which were best left alone. Nonpunitive responses to marital conflict (calm talk and/or forgetting about troubles) were correlated with marital satisfaction and with positive feelings after discussion. Apparently this is one aspect of marriage where middle-class couples can hope to progress as they gain experience in making decisions.

Interaction that is primarily rational can absorb considerable irrationality without being undermined. Little digs, sarcasm, and innuendo may influence the partner if the marriage is solid and resilient. Subtle or not so subtle moves, such as asking leading questions or leaving newspaper clippings in strategic locations, can be taken in good humor if a couple are not already on tenterhooks.

The best indication whether problems are handled successfully is not how rigorously my outline is followed, but how the couple feel at the end. If one partner feels gypped, snubbed, insulted, or resentful, something is wrong. The right methods employed in the right spirit should leave both partners contented, no matter who "wins" or "loses."

Two Heads Are Better Than One. Small-group research by Hoffman *et al.* (1962) offered convincing evidence that shared decision-making is likely to be worth the effort. (1) If one measure of successful decision-making is creative or "integrative" solutions, experiments showed that mixed groups of men and women were better than one-sex groups even when the task was masculine-oriented. (2) Integrative solutions were also more common when no one dominated the group but all members were free to express themselves in the search for a creative solution. These findings suggest that even though husband-dominance may be the easiest method of conflict-resolution, equalitarianism is generally more creative.

Marriage Counseling—Emergency Resource

Whenever conflict is not resolved, it feeds upon itself. One quarrel leads to another, and the vicious cycle becomes difficult to break:

> We have emotional outbursts so often that something is going to have to be done or else we should call it quits. They follow a regular pattern. Julie makes a dig at me and I blow up. Since my feelings are hurt I just don't say anything to her for the next few days. She gets irritated at my coolness and then she blows up at the slightest provocation.

If conflict is chronic and the partners are powerless to stop it, outside intervention is needed to prevent the marriage from being destroyed. Living within the confines of the same house, sharing the same bed, turns love inexorably to hate once interaction becomes vindictive. When attack leads to counterattack day after day, discipline must be imported to save the situation.

The Availability of Marriage Counseling

Of all the personal problems for which people seek outside help, marriage problems are the most common. In Gurin's nationwide sample, only one person in seven had ever sought outside help, but of those who had, almost half had gone with a marriage problem. More specifically, almost eight per cent of the married individuals in his sample had sought help with a marital problem (Gurin, 1960). Since this is less than half the divorce rate, most divorces must occur without prior counseling. If we assume that counseling should always precede divorce (either to facilitate reconciliation or to improve the quality of a subsequent marriage), marriage counseling in the United States is not used as much as it is needed. Many people think about help for marriage problems but never get around to it. An additional six per cent of Gurin's married sample reported they could have used help with their marriage problems but that they never contacted a professional person when they were in trouble.

DIFFERENTIAL READINESS FOR COUNSELING. Striking differences appear between the sexes in their readiness to seek help when their marriages are in trouble. At every educational level, more women than men sought professional help with their marriage problems (Gurin). The director of the Marriage Council of Philadelphia (Mudd, 1951) suggested four factors which may account for this difference:

1. It is easier for a woman to leave her housekeeping than for a man to get time off from his job.
2. Women are less hesitant to admit that they need help.
3. Women have more role conflicts and other adjustments to make.
4. Women have more at stake in marriage when it is their only career.

The fact that women clients outnumber men means that wives often seek counseling without their husbands. Occasionally the reverse is true. Marriage counseling works best when both partners are seen. A few agencies refuse clients on any other basis. However, most work with the interested partner, hoping the other will come in later. The Marriage Council of Philadelphia reported that "In 65% of our cases, if the client has a good relationship with the counselor, the counseling is reflected on the partner so that he becomes willing to come despite his initial reluctance."

Although participation by both partners is ideal, counseling for one partner may enable her to become sufficiently objective and adaptable to restore the marital equilibrium. No individual in marital difficulty should refrain from seeking outside help because of the unwillingness of the partner to go along the first time.

Where do people take their marriage problems? Friends and relatives are the first resort. They are more accessible and infinitely less expensive than professional men.

In young middle-class white families in Washington Heights on Manhattan Island, 21 per cent of the wives were currently or had recently been in contact with professionals about their marriage problems (Mayer, 1966). Although this is higher than the national average, it is small in comparison to the number of friends and relatives they had already talked to. The average wife had shared at least some of her marriage troubles with 2.8 friends and 2.4 relatives. This means that sharing was not only widespread but utilized multiple confidantes. For most wives, one best friend stood out as the chief confidante to whom she revealed more of her troubles than to any other person—either relative or friend. For wives whose chief confidante was a relative, it was almost as often an in-law as a member of her own family. It was rarely a male relative, however. Either it was the wife's mother or mother-in-law, her sister or sister-in-law. Indeed some wives felt closer to an in-law than to anyone in their own family. Mayer suggested that the bilateral use of kin for marriage counseling in these middle-class marriages reflected the strength of the marriage bond. The closer a woman was to her husband, the closer she felt to his mother and sisters.

Unfortunately we don't know how effective these lay counselors are. They may have some difficulty being as unbiased and objective as professionals are supposed to be. But even if their success rate is low, their aggregate service must be enormous.

PROFESSIONAL RESOURCES. When the exceptional couple seek professional help, where do they go? In Washington Heights, Mayer's women went to psychiatrists (seven to psychiatrists, one to her clergyman). But New York is an unusual city and eight cases a small number. Nationwide, psychiatrists are less available.

Table 17-1 shows that clergymen were the chief resource nationally, exceeding medical men even when psychiatrists and other doctors (mostly family physicians) are put together. The pre-eminence of clergymen and family doctors reflects the on-going relationship most families have with one or both. A clergyman or doctor who is seen regularly for other pur-

Table 17-1. Source of Professional Help for Marriage Problems

Source of Help Used

Clergyman	44%
Doctor	23
Psychiatrist	12
Marriage counselor	8
Other agencies	7
Lawyer	6
Total	100%

Adapted from Gurin, 1960: 309. *Source:* National sample of 2,460 adults (married and single). Percentages based on those who ever sought professional help for marriage problems (137 cases).

poses is available when marriage crises arise. Clergymen, moreover, along with marriage counselors and lawyers, specialize in family problems. (People were more apt to take marriage problems than any other kind of personal problem to those three specialists.) Moreover, most couples were married by a clergyman which makes him a legitimate resource in time of trouble.

By contrast, psychiatrists and marriage counselors are relatively rare and seldom known to the average layman. Gurin found that these specialists depended on referrals by other professionals. People had heard of marriage counselors and considered them appropriate resources but didn't know any. Hence those interested in securing marriage counseling bulked large among those who wanted help but failed to obtain it.

MARRIAGE SPECIALISTS. Marriage counseling is a specialty practiced by increasing numbers of psychologists and social workers, some clergymen, doctors, and family sociologists, and a few lawyers. The American Association of Marriage Counselors is the only national organization concerned exclusively with marriage counseling. Standards of membership in this organization are rigorous, including specialized graduate training and supervised counseling experience. Its members are concentrated in the metropolitan and academic centers of the country. Many engage in private practice at fees which resemble those charged by other private practitioners.

More accessible are the staff members of the Family Service Association of America whose several hundred agencies are distributed throughout the urban United States. Staffed exclusively by social case-workers, Family Service societies minister to all social strata. Middle-class clients pay modest fees based on their ability to pay. Though not limited exclusively to marriage counseling, these agencies are an important source of such help. Unfortunately, they often limit their services to residents of the area covered by the United Fund or Red Feather campaign which subsidizes them.

Some reputable marriage counselors belong to neither of these national organizations, especially those whose primary professional identity is with psychiatry or clinical psychology, etc. In the 1960's several states began certifying marriage counselors who were not already certified in another clinical profession. In case of doubt about the qualifications of a particular counselor, inquiring of his fellow practitioners usually helps.

Counseling Procedures

Because marriage counselors represent many professions, their methods vary widely. Although no surveys show which methods are most popular, they range all the way from neutral, client-centered counseling to highly directive counseling such as Albert Ellis' "rational psychotherapy." (1958) Some counselors emphasize childhood personality development whereas others concentrate on the present. Some focus on inner feelings while others stress overt behavior. Some recommend spontaneity, others planfulness, and still others avoid all recommendations. In short, methods depend on the counselor's training, experience, and philosophy.

Nevertheless, some generalizations are fairly safe. A typical counselor spends much of his time listening to the client. Occasional questions stimulate self-analysis. From time to time he may interpret meanings and connections the client seems ready to understand. He may reassure the client about the value of expressing negative feelings in the interview. He may support the client in trying a new course of action. Rarely, however, does the counselor take responsibility for deciding what the client should do.

THE TIME REQUIRED. Interviews typically last a 50-minute hour, once a week. Premarital counseling may require only a single interview. Where interpersonal tensions are involved, it takes longer to overcome them. Some agencies average as little as two or three interviews per case, but this often reflects client difficulties in finding time and transportation, plus personal resistance. Five to ten interviews are more likely averages when counseling is carried through to a satisfactory conclusion. If chronic quarreling or personality disturbances are involved, correspondingly more time is needed to heal past wounds and reconstruct a marriage on a healthy footing (Mudd, 1951).

JOINT COUNSELING. Leslie (1964) noted that "most marriage counselors prefer to work with all of the significant parties to a relationship rather than to accept only one client and refer the others to different specialists." Frequently this means seeing both husband and wife together. Joint sessions allow communication between the partners and provide opportunities for mutual decision-making.

Only in extramarital triangles or predivorce cases, where one or both partners are unsure whether they wish to continue the marriage, is separate counseling preferable. If the improvement of the present marriage is the task at hand, the participation of both partners is advantageous.

Marriage counseling is handicapped by the interpersonal nature of the difficulties involved. Gurin reported that individuals with marriage problems found professional help less useful than those with other personal problems (see Table 17-2). He reasoned that marriage partners often blamed each other for their troubles and failed to seek help for their own role in the marriage. In any case, those who blamed someone else for their troubles were helped least of all, those who saw their problems as mutual somewhat more, and those who stressed their own involvement were helped the most.

The frequent ineffectiveness of marriage counseling is partly inevitable. Since marriage is a social system involving interlocking role behaviors, it

Table 17-2. Helpfulness of Therapy for Marriage Problems and Other Personal Problems

Helpfulness of Therapy	Marriage Problems	Other Personal Problems
Helped, helped a lot	52%	71%
Helped (qualified)	14	17
Did not help	34	12
Total	100%	100%
Number of cases	133	174

Adapted from Gurin, 1960: 318. Not-ascertained cases omitted. *Source:* National sample of adults.

cannot be changed as easily as an individual personality. Nevertheless, Gurin's findings have practical implications for marriage counselors and their clients. For counselors, they suggest the value of involving both partners so that change can be initiated in both members of the marital dyad simultaneously. For clients, they imply that focusing on what's wrong with the partner will hinder progress. Since the individual controls only himself, he must search for ways to improve his own behavior, confident that once he becomes a better husband or wife, the spouse is likely to respond positively.

Table 17-3. Helpfulness of Therapy, by Client's Perception of Locus of Problem

| Helpfulness of Therapy | PERCEIVED LOCUS OF PROBLEM | | |
	Self	Relationship	Other Person
Helped, helped a lot	75%	60%	52%
Helped (qualified)	15	14	16
Did not help	10	26	32
Total	100%	100%	100%
Number of cases	71	97	77

Adapted from Gurin, 1960: 318. Not-ascertained cases omitted. *Source:* National sample of adults.

Despite these handicaps, marriage counseling proves worthwhile to a substantial proportion of those who try it. Table 17-2 shows that two-thirds of those with marital problems found their professional contacts helpful.

GROUP COUNSELING. Groups of married couples may also have much to offer. As I listen to another husband argue with his wife, it may be easier to imagine what I look like to my own wife. Or as I listen to another woman complain about her husband, the message may come close to home without creating as much defensiveness as if my wife were addressing me.

Groups also widen the repertoire of behavior familiar to a couple. Mayer (1967) noted that most people knew little about anyone's marriage other than their parents'. "As married persons in the group begin to learn about the marriages of other members, they may depend less on their memories of their parents." The wider their knowledge, the more flexibly a couple can adapt to new situations.

Nor need families in trouble learn only from each other. Therapists have brought their own families together with client families for weekends or whole vacations of work and play as well as talk. Staff families could then set examples of coping with frustration, communication, and other methods of conflict resolution (Landes and Winter, 1966).

The Contributions of Marriage Counseling

Counseling offers therapeutic intervention to create the conditions of rationality, training and encouragement in rational behavior, and mediation of disputes.

THERAPEUTIC INTERVENTION. Whenever the conditions for rational decision-making are missing, counseling must begin by creating them. Insight into unconscious distortions, the development of maturity, and the restoration of love require substantial work. This is the most time-consuming form of marriage counseling, overlapping with other forms of psychotherapy. If it is successful, it may enable the couple to resolve their conflicts without further counseling.

TRAINING AND ENCOURAGEMENT. Sometimes decision-making breaks down not because of emotional difficulties but from deficiencies in technique or effort. Joint counseling enables couples to practice decision-making under the counselor's watchful eye. Like an athletic coach, the counselor can point out inadequacies in method, demonstrate better methods, and provide moral support for continuing efforts when the "players" get discouraged.

MEDIATION. Relatively rare in America but common in foreign countries like Japan is mediation for couples deadlocked over serious issues. Many American counselors shy away from giving advice or expressing opinions. However, these are often what clients want. Moreover Gurin found that advice was the most common benefit clients reported from therapy. Apparently then, professional ideology to the contrary, expert knowledge and detached judgment are major benefits available from marriage counseling. Given couples with reasonably healthy personalities and sound decision-making techniques, professional mediation might quickly resolve many husband-wife dilemmas.

18 Divorce and Remarriage

For those who fail to maintain their love or whose marriage is destructive from the very beginning, divorce and remarriage offer alternative paths to the values sought in marriage. The turning point is reached when one partner concludes that his chances of achieving those values are greater in a future marriage than in the present one, or that the present relationship costs more than it is worth.

The Incidence of Divorce

Beginning about 1875, the divorce rate in the United States began to rise (Bogue, 1959). It climbed fairly steadily for nearly 75 years, reaching a spectacular peak at the end of World War II. After a postwar return to normal, the upward trend resumed.

The main causes of the long-term rise in the American divorce rate are urbanization and industrialization. Increased anonymity and mobility have weakened social controls. These controls formerly held couples together by external pressure and provided group chaperonage to prevent them from getting involved in extramarital alliances.

Although Figure 18-1 shows that more than one-fourth of all recent marriages ended in divorce, these statistics include both first divorces and subsequent ones. Since remarriages have a higher divorce rate than first marriages, a more likely estimate of the divorce risk for first marriages is one in five. However, the risk is not distributed evenly. The higher the social status of the partners, the lower the divorce rate.

To cite only one study, Table 18-1 shows that business and professional men have only two-thirds as many divorces as the general population, whereas unskilled workers had almost double the average divorce rate. High-status families with stable, ample incomes are both skilled in personal interaction and integrated into the community through organizational participation. The result is that divorce rates among college graduates sometimes run as low as the four per cent and nine per cent reported for the Dartmouth College classes of 1929 and 1930 at their twenty-fifth reunions.

Although, in general, the more education people have, the lower their divorce rate, there are two exceptions. (1) College drop-outs had more divorces than high school graduates. Those who did not finish a course of study were less apt to finish a marriage. (2) Women who went to graduate school had more divorces than those who only finished college (although not as many as high school drop-outs). They also remarried less often after divorce (Udry, 1966). We do not know how much of this was because (a) only unusual women went to graduate school in the first place, (b) men were afraid of talented women, (c) talented women could afford to be more choosy about whether to stay married or to get remarried.

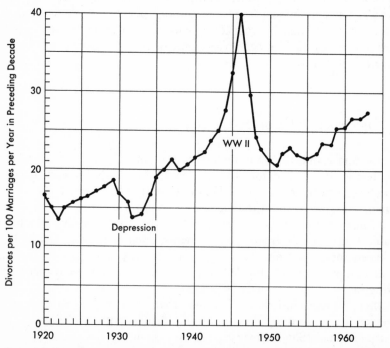

Computed from Bogue, 1959: 238–39 and from NCHS reports. For example, there were 27.8 divorces in 1963 for every 100 marriages averaged over 1953–62 inclusive.

Figure 18-1. Divorces per 100 Marriages per Year in Preceding Decade, 1920–63

Table 18-1. Index of Proneness to Divorce, by Occupation

Occupation	Ratio of Number of Divorces to Size of Occupational Category
Business and professional	0.68X
Clerical, sales, and service	0.83X
Skilled workers, foremen	0.74X
Semiskilled operatives	1.26X
Unskilled	1.80X
Total	1.00X
Number of cases	425

Adapted from Goode, 1956: 47. *Source:* Random sample of Detroit divorces, 1947–48.

These were marginal exceptions, however, to the general contribution of education to marital stability.

When Divorce Occurs

Despite jokes about the "Seven Year Itch," the worst year of marriage is the first. More marriages break up then than in any other single year (see Figure 18-2). At the very beginning the worst incompatibilities become apparent. One study in New Haven and Waterbury, Connecticut, found that over one-third of all causes of divorce appeared in the first year of marriage, even though most of those couples did not dissolve their marriages until many years later (Clark and Shulman, 1937). The alienation which eventuates in divorce often begins at the very initiation of marriage. Indeed some couples married and divorced without ever living together (Monahan, 1962). Sexual problems and personality clashes undermined the possibilities for personal relationships and led to particularly quick dissolutions (Kephart, 1954, and Goode, 1956).

Figure 18-2 shows how large a proportion of marriages that failed broke up in the first years of marriage. The process is analogous to oil-refining. The most volatile marriages crack up first and then the worst of the remainder, until after five or ten years most of the marriages still intact are capable of surviving indefinitely.

When husband and wife separate, the marriage for all practical purposes ends. Because of legal complications (including compulsory "cooling off" periods and crowded legal dockets), the interval between marriage and divorce is considerably longer. In the Philadelphia sample the median interval from marriage to separation was five years, whereas the typical divorce decree did not come through for another five years. However, Pennsylvania had notoriously belated divorces. In 1963 the total interval from marriage to divorce for 22 states was 7.5 years (N.C.H.S.).

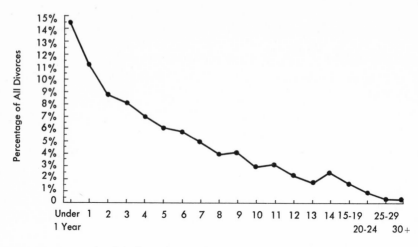

Adapted from Kephart, 1954a: 290. *Source:* Sample of divorces granted in a Philadelphia court, 1937–50.

Figure 18-2. Duration of Marriage before Predivorce Separation

Customarily, the wife sues for divorce, accusing the husband of having wrecked the marriage (though most marriages fail because of mutual in compatibility). Besides chivalrous protection of the woman's reputation, feminine law suits protect the wife's right to custody of the children. In exceptional cases (less than 29 per cent in 1962), the husband is the plaintiff. Such husbands often seek custody of their children, contending that the wife is an unfit mother. Some judges, however, will grant the divorce to the wife even if her husband was the plaintiff, and most are reluctant to take children from the mother unless she is flagrantly alcoholic, mentally ill or morally delinquent.

Divorce strikes hardest at low-status, youthful marriages in their earliest years. These factors all suggest immaturity. The sheer lapse of time involved in going through the divorce process enables some individuals to mature enough to function better in second marriages (see below).

Causes of Divorce

It is impossible to pin down the causes of divorce. The official causes (the legal grounds on which judges grant the decree) tell us little. Most divorces are granted for "cruelty," a notoriously vague term. Most of the rest are based on desertion (leaving unnoted the reason why the husband left home) or on nonsupport (which frequently overlaps with desertion).

Table 18-2. Causes of Divorce, According to Lawyers and Divorcées

IDAHO LAWYERS		DETROIT DIVORCEES	
Cause	Percentage	Cause	Percentage
Financial problems, nonsupport	20%	Consumption problems, nonsupport	21%
Adultery	19	Triangle	6
Drunkenness	18	Drinking	12
Basic incompatibility	11	Personality clashes	11
Irresponsibility	6	Lack of interest in home life	9
Immaturity	5	"Drinking, gambling, helling around"	12
Cruelty	5	Authority problems	12
Cultural differences	4	Conflicting values	8
Sexual incompatibility	4	Sexual problems	1
Desertion	3	Desertion	3
In-laws	3	Relatives	2
Miscellaneous	2	Miscellaneous	3
Total	100%		100%
Number	282		425

Adapted from Harmsworth and Minnis, 1955: 320 (Idaho) and Goode, 1956: 123 (Detroit).

It is possible to learn more about causes by asking lawyers or their clients to name them. Table 18-2 compares the opinions of Idaho lawyers about the "real" causes in cases they handled with the opinions of Detroit divorcees about the causes of their own difficulties. The latter picture is biased from the feminine point of view and underestimates the wife's own contribution to marital failure. Table 18-2 lists the lawyers' opinions in order of frequency, giving equivalent categories from Goode's study (1956). Economic problems were conspicuously prominent. Families depend so heavily on the husband's income that inadequate or wasted earnings have disastrous repercussions on family solidarity. Adultery and drinking would have ranked higher for the divorcees if what Goode calls the "complex" of drinking, gambling, and "helling around" with other women had been subdivided. Authority problems stem from attempts by husbands to dominate their wives (only roughly equivalent to cruelty). Sexual problems ranked low on both lists, leading Goode (1956) to conclude that "as every serious survey has shown, sexual problems do not form any large proportion of the 'causes' for marital disruption." Relatives, similarly, were seldom a major problem save at the very beginning of marriage.

We can illuminate these causes further by classifying them in terms of our prerequisites for personal relations: compatibility, skill, effort, commitment, and support. Compatibility is lacking in divorces involving personality clashes, authority problems, sexual incompatibility, and conflicting values. Skill, in the sense of the ability to play a responsible role in life, seems deficient in cases of immaturity, drinking, gambling, and "helling around." Lack of effort is implied by financial problems, irresponsibility, and desertion; lack of commitment in cases of adultery; and lack of support when in-laws interfere.

Adultery

Because sex is the most intimate aspect of marriage, extramarital intercourse is its most profound betrayal. For this reason churches which allow divorce on no other ground consider adultery sufficient. The varieties of adultery are endless. Sometimes it is a kind of premarital intercourse for a second marriage, the physical expression of a new love which has already superseded the old. Sometimes it is a casual fling by a traveling man who considers himself a good husband. Always, however, it threatens the solidarity of marriage socially by potential new involvements and psychologically by destroying the uniqueness of husband-wife intimacy.

Though marriage is always impaired—either as cause or effect of adultery—the relationship between adultery and divorce is not simple. Levy and Munroe were convinced that "sexual maladjustment, including infidelity, is seldom a primary cause of marital discord." Whether adultery causes divorce depends on whether it is known—40 per cent of the unfaithful wives in Kinsey's sample believed their husbands didn't suspect them (1953). Even where unfaithfulness is known, the partner does not always rush for his lawyer. In some cases, he rushes to a marriage counselor, the crisis providing an impetus for reconstructing a shaky marriage on a sounder footing.

Where divorce follows known adultery, the partner is apt to blame the unfaithfulness, especially if the offender was the wife. According to the double standard, infidelity is less forgiveable in wives than in husbands. Thus 51 per cent of the wives' known affairs were given "major" blame for divorce versus only 27 per cent of the husbands' known transgressions (Kinsey). Significantly, every offended partner attached at least some divorce-causing significance in these adultery-followed-by-divorce cases.

In short, adultery tends to destroy marriage. The recuperative prospects for a given marriage depend on the circumstances and motives:

> Infidelity may be an attack upon the wife, a refuge from her, an attempt to prove one's manliness, a revolt against childish taboos, a method of working out impulses arising from early experiences, an act of revenge either upon the other woman, the wife, or women in general, the gratification of a physical urge uninhibited by moral scruples—almost anything (Levy and Munroe, p. 92).

Kinsey estimated that half of all married men and one-fourth of all married women committed adultery sometime during their married life.

By and large the same kinds of people engage in extramarital intercourse who engage in premarital intercourse. Indeed, they are partly the *same* individuals, since premarital involvement predisposes people to extramarital involvement (see Chapter 5). People who have almost any marital inadequacy (including the global failures of marital unhappiness and divorce) are more disposed to this form of trouble, too. Who are they? The nonreligious. The emotionally immature.

Religious differences are striking—two to three times as many inactive as devoutly religious men and women were involved (Kinsey, 1948, 1953). On emotional maturity, Maslow reported that "self-actualizing" people were "relatively more monogamous than the average, and relatively less driven to love affairs outside the marriage." (1953) Generally speaking, the same factors that make for stability and success *in* marriage reduce the likelihood of involvements *outside* of marriage.

Figure 18-3 shows the usual differences between the sexes in sexual activity. Despite the fact that most extramarital partners are married too, more married men than women engaged in such affairs. A small part of this difference was accounted for by women who made themselves professionally available. The bulk, however, was due to the promiscuousness of those married women involved in adultery at all. The majority of adulterous women had sexual relations with more than one partner, manifesting greater promiscuity than premaritally intimate women (Kinsey, 1953).

College-educated men and women committed adultery more often in the

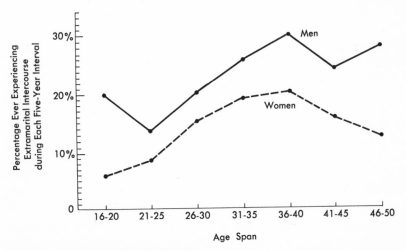

Adapted from Kinsey, 1948: 348; 1953: 440.

Figure 18-3. Experience in Extramarital Intercourse during Five-Year Age Spans for College-Educated Men and Women

middle years of marriage when disenchantment and disengagement had set in. Some middle-aged men used extramarital affairs as a substitute for divorce. The cocktail lounge of the best hotel in a West Coast city of 250,000 provided extramarital sexual contacts for business and professional men in their late thirties and forties. Most of the men were married but complained that their wives were too busy and too "cold" and that there were too many "family pressures" (which I infer means too many children). They seemed to be thoroughly disengaged from their wives, visiting the cocktail lounge ten times a week on the average and preferring such segregated sports as hunting, fishing, and golf. Other men choose divorce under such circumstances. These men did not divorce (a) because most of them were active Catholics ineligible for remarriage, and (b) because they believed in the old-fashioned with a feudalistic double standard. At home they claimed to be "good husbands and fathers" who loved their families and were loved in return. At the lounge, they satisfied their sexual needs by establishing temporary liaisons with young, good-looking, low-status single girls (many of them divorcees). For both the men and the girls, this was sex without love—it was generally understood that to become emotionally involved violated the rules of the game (Roebuck, 1967).

Adultery does not always lead to divorce. Roughly twice as many men commit adultery as get divorced. But few American women are feudal enough to accept this threat to marriage calmly. The more equalitarian and cohesive American marriages become, the more disruptive adultery is likely to become except in those rare segments of our society which have gone beyond equalitarianism to libertarianism (e.g., Lipton, 1965).

When adultery becomes a group practice, it is frequently governed by group norms which restrict its threat to marriage (Slater, 1963). Mate-swapping clubs normally discourage long-term pairings, finding safety in enforced promiscuity. In the cocktail lounge, elaborate rules governed the behavior permissible in public, limiting the development of spontaneity. Where *rendezvous* are secret, their limitation to brief times and special places prevents the development of full-blown, multifaceted personal relationships. So even when adultery is socially permitted, it is socially supervised to minimize the marital instability it would otherwise create.

One example of the tendency to segregate adultery from marriage is given in Table 18-3. The greater the marital involvement of the extramarital partners and the more marriage-like the behavior, the greater the disapproval of adultery. On the other hand, more students in both countries were prepared to tolerate adultery under noninvolving circumstances, especially when the spouse is unavailable. Moreover, the closer the students were to marriage themselves (going steady or engaged), the greater their opposition to extramarital relationships. Similarly, the more satisfied they were with their dating partner, the greater their disapproval of an extramarital relationship.

Table 18-3. Disapproval by American and Danish Students of Adultery in Varying Circumstances

Percentage Who Disapprove of Adultery for Either Sex, by Circumstance	UNIVERSITY	
	Purdue	Copenhagen
1. If a married man/woman has fallen in love with another married person	95.3%	72.3%
2. If a married man/woman has fallen in love with an unmarried person	94.2	66.5
3. If a married man/woman feels the need for sexual release (with prostitutes or others) during periods of long absence from the spouse	90.6	60.7
Number of students	277	191

Adapted from Christensen, 1962. Reciprocal percentages of students approve of marital infidelity for one or both sexes under the specified circumstances.

The Preventability of Divorce

A significant but unknown percentage of divorces could be prevented by more careful mate-selection. Better compatibility testing, courses in preparation for marriage, premarital instruction and counseling, and waiting periods prior to marriage might reduce the number of divorce-prone marriages. However, some marriages are so destined to failure that no effort by the couple or by experts could salvage them. In extreme cases (the doctor married to the stripteaser, the old man and the teenager, the rich girl and the chauffeur), everybody knows they are fools except the couples themselves.

On the borderline between unworkable marriages and compatible ones are marginal cases where divorce is not inevitable. Sometimes the period between filing for divorce and coming to trial is sufficient to produce second thoughts:

> I've been doing quite a lot of thinking, and I've decided divorce wouldn't be such a good thing. I wouldn't want to have some stranger taking care of my baby because he'd probably feel like he had two mothers. I enjoy being with him so much I'd feel pretty bad about having to go to work. I've been disappointed with Paul's low income but I'm afraid divorce would mean even less money and more expenses.

Many states require predivorce waiting periods in the hope that reconciliation will occur spontaneously. A few communities take advantage of this interval to see what can be done to engineer reconciliations. Particularly where children are involved (over half the total), referral to a marriage counselor may be mandatory. Late as it is, such counseling salvages enough marriages to warrant enthusiasm on the part of courts that have tried it.

The Value of Divorce

If marriage counseling cannot achieve a reconciliation, both partners and the counselor will recognize that continuing the marriage would only prolong the agony. If continued cohabitation only creates tension, why go on? The costs for everyone concerned (children as well as parents) are too great to allow a mutually destructive relationship to continue.

Value to the Children

In 1962, three-fifths of all U. S. divorces involved one or more children (an average of 2.14 each, the largest number on record). Were those children better off or worse off with their parents apart than if they had stayed together? Ideally their parents should have been happily married, but that option was not open. The only choice was between an unhappy home and a broken home. For students in three high schools in the State of Washington, to lose a parent was clearly preferable to living with unhappy parents.

Table 18-4 shows that children of divorce had fewer personal and family problems than children of parents unhappy enough to make divorce potentially desirable. Perhaps there should be more divorces for the sake of the children rather than so many grim marriages prolonged supposedly for their sake.

However, children of divorce had low self-esteem in certain situations: (1) The stronger the religious or ethnic taboos against divorce (as for Catholics and Jews); (2) The younger the mother when she was divorced (Rosenberg, 1965). These correlations may reflect the fact that the worst marriages broke up fastest so that the stronger the taboos, the worse a marriage had to be before it is broken. However, Rosenberg suspected that young divorcees had particularly difficult life circumstances and that young children were particularly impressionable. However, the Nye study suggested that even in these circumstances, the children might have been worse off if their parents had continued living unhappily together.

Table 18-4. Effect on Adolescent Children of Parental Unhappiness or Divorce

Adolescent Child's Characteristics	MARITAL STATUS OF PARENTS	
	Unhappy	Divorced or Separated
Child feels rejected by father	69%	40%
Child feels rejected by mother	55	44
Child rejects father	55	37
Child disagrees with father about values	53	34
Psychosomatic illness	50	31
Delinquency	48	39
Child disagrees with mother about values	47	26
Child rejects mother	42	35

Adapted from Nye, 1957. *Source:* Ninth to twelfth grade boys and girls enrolled in three Washington State high schools. One-sixth of all homes were broken by divorce but most parents were remarried by the time of the study. An equal number of homes were selected for comparison on the basis of self-rated marital unhappiness, quarreling and arguing between parents, attempted domination of each other, and lack of mutual activities or interests.

Value to the Parents

Most divorced adults say they are glad they terminated an unsatisfactory relationship. The worse the marriage, the greater the relief when it ends. Nevertheless, divorce is not a painless process. Expenses include legal fees and court costs. It is also more expensive for a broken family to operate two residences than one. Each partner loses the services the other performed in the division of labor. Hence, it takes courage to take the fateful step of filing suit. One support may be the marriage counselor whose attempt at marital rehabilitation failed and who now becomes the partners' "divorce counselor," supplementing their attorneys.

Despite the pain of getting a divorce, however, the pain of staying married would have been worse. And even pain itself may be beneficial. One divorcee felt her bitter experiences had deepened her understanding of life. Indeed she was impressed by others who had been through the same travails:

It's strange how much you can question once the structure of all the things you've taken for granted is thoroughly shaken. Personally, I find the most sensitive, tolerant, self-knowing, honest, and wide-minded people and those most loving are divorced. They are people who grew and changed over the years, often going through counseling or intensive psychotherapy in the process. They see the world differently, less innocently, but with more compassion; and they understand more of their own human nature and that of the people around them than those whose lives have traveled straighter paths.

Remarriage: Establishing a New Relationship

Divorced people are disappointed with their first marriage but rarely disillusioned with the idea of marriage. Frequently they are more eager than ever to marry before they get too old. Most Americans think a happy marriage is part of their birthright. If they didn't achieve it on the first round, they hope to the next time. (The chief exceptions are devout Catholics who believe that remarriage while the first partner is still alive is equivalent to adultery.)

The Incidence of Remarriage

In both the United States and England three-fourths of all divorced men eventually remarry and two-thirds of all divorced women (Glick, 1957). Although these rates are not as high as the proportion of the population who ever marry at all (over 92 per cent), at any particular age proportionately more divorced than single persons marry.

The picture given for women in Figure 18-4 is identical with that for men. At any age, divorced persons were the most apt to remarry and bachelors or spinsters least likely, while widows and widowers fell between. These data suggest how strongly divorced people are motivated to remarry. Widows and widowers have pleasant memories to live on, but divorced people have unpleasant memories, hopefully to be erased by remarriage.

To be sure, eligibility as well as motivation affects chances of remarriage. The younger the divorcee, the better her chances. Indeed one study showed that a divorcee's chances of remarriage remained better than fifty-fifty until she was 45 years old, whereas for widows the turning point was 33 and for spinsters 30 (P. Landis, 1950).

Eligibility for remarriage is highest for high-status people with good incomes and educations (the kind least likely to divorce in the first place). Divorcees with children need to remarry in order to solve their financial and child-rearing problems. They succeeded age for age, in doing almost as well as divorcees without children, suggesting that children were only a slight handicap (Glick, 1957).

The net effect of these motives is that if remarriage is ever to follow the first marriage, it tends to come soon. Figure 18-5 shows the interval between marriages for men and women who remarried in the early 1950's.

For postdivorce marriages the median interval was 2.7 years, for post-bereavement marriages, 3.5 years. The slower speed of the latter reflects the taboo on hasty remarriage after bereavement out of respect for the memory of the loved one. Divorced persons, by definition, have nothing to respect. Moreover, their first marriages normally ended in separation many months before the divorce decree was final. If an extramarital affair motivated the divorce, courtship for the new marriage preceded the termination of the old one. In a study of high-status Americans, Cuber and Haroff (1965) found the most frequent reason for divorce was "finding a mate who seemed better to fit the man's or the woman's needs and wants—an engaging alternative to the lackluster of one's present circumstances." Whether one wishes to call the discovery of a new partner a *reason* for divorce, it is unquestionably an *occasion* for divorce and prompt remarriage.

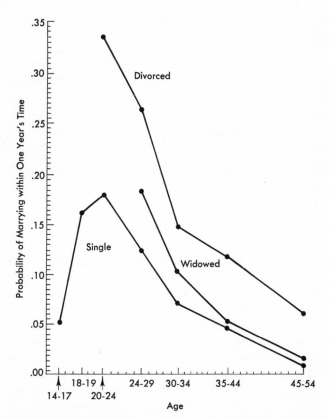

Adapted from Glick, 1957: 139. *Source:* Current Population Surveys, 1950–53.

Figure 18-4. Probability of Marrying, by Age and Marital Status, for American Women

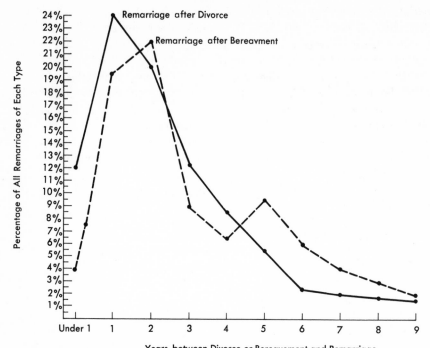

Years between Divorce or Bereavement and Remarriage

Adapted from Glick, 1957: 139. *Source:* Current Population Surveys of remarriages occurring 1950–53.

Figure 18-5. Interval between Divorce or Bereavement and Remarriage

The Success of Remarriage

There is little reason to question the success of postbereavement marriages, but the marriages of divorcees are another matter. Given the fact that 100 per cent of their first marriages failed, by sheer chance we would expect some to select better mates the next time. When we add the maturity gained in the decade between the beginning of the first marriage and the second, and the wisdom gained from previous experience, we would expect more second marriages to succeed. On the other hand, some divorced people are incapable of living with anyone. The dregs may not even try to marry again (or at least not find a willing partner). Of those who do remarry, the unfit constitute a growing proportion with successive marriages. Hence, the success rate declines when first marriages are compared with second marriages, third, and so forth.

Unfortunately, no one has followed given cohorts of the American population through their marital careers. Therefore, it is necessary to draw inferences from cross-section data about the comparative success of first marriages and remarriages. Many studies have found remarriages over-represented in the divorcing population. Figure 18-6 is based on one study in one state in the drastic years following World War II. Interpolated from Monahan's data, it shows the comparative prevalence of divorces involving remarriages (after divorce and bereavement combined), using divorces following first marriages as a base line. The larger the number of previous marriages, the greater the likelihood of divorce. Disregarding the confounding presence of the few postbereavement remarriages, this illustrates the increasing proportion of divorce-prone partners in multiple remarriages.

The percentages on the right hand side of Figure 18-6 provide a crude estimate of the probability of divorce in remarriages. If we assume that the divorce rate in first marriages in the United States was somewhere around 20 per cent, we can infer from the Iowa data that about twice as many second marriages ended in divorce, whereas close to 90 per cent did where each partner was in his third marriage. A conservative interpretation would be that a majority of second marriages succeed whereas a majority of subsequent remarriages do not. To put it another way, the average divorcing American gets a second chance for a successful marriage, but success on the third round is unlikely.

For the United States as a whole, few people ever go beyond a second marriage. Hence our main concern is with second marriages. Not only are most of them stable in the sense of avoiding another divorce, but the individuals involved are usually delighted with the contrast between the new marriage and the old. For example, 87 per cent of Goode's remarried divorced mothers found their new marriage "much better" than the first. Almost as many felt that their experience in the first marriage had made the second one easier.

CHILDREN AND REMARRIAGE. Although adults tend to be enthusiastic about their remarriages, their children are less positive. Rosenberg (1965) found that children of remarried mothers had lower self-esteem and more psychosomatic symptoms than children whose divorced mothers never remarried. Similarly Nye (1957) found that children felt closer to a mother without a partner than to one with a new partner. Apparently from the child's viewpoint, to have one's mother remarry is not to restore one's family to normalcy but to lose the remaining parent to a stranger. Bad enough to lose one parent through divorce—worse yet to lose the other by "desertion."

On the other hand, just as adoption works best with young children, the younger the child when he changes fathers, the better his adjustment to the new father. Perhaps if stepfathers courted children as effectively as they court the mother, the new family would be better integrated. Without

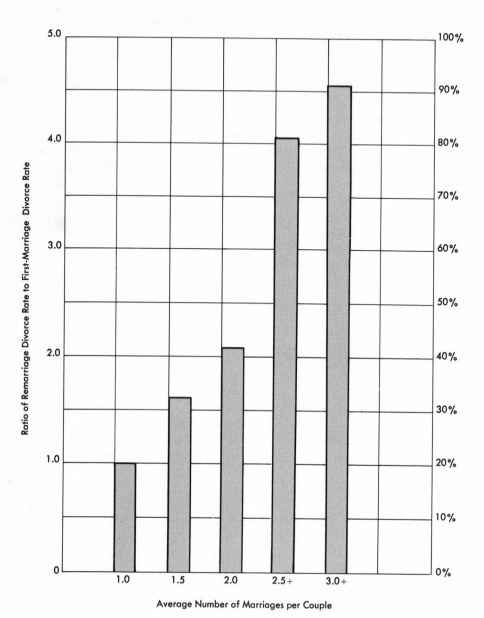

Adapted from Monahan, 1952: 287. *Source:* Statistics on number of marriages and number of divorces for state of Iowa in 1948–50, by average number of marriages for husband and wife combined.

Figure 18-6. Probability of Divorce, by Marriage Order

such effort, however, broken families are further disintegrated by the invasion of a strange man.

PREPARATION FOR REMARRIAGE. If divorced individuals are to benefit most from their previous marital experience, professional tutoring is needed. Just as children from unhappy homes need "remodeling" in preparation for marriage, graduates of unhappy marriages need remodeling, too. "Divorce counseling" can help the individual explore the reasons why his marriage failed. Realizing that he will probably remarry, the client can explore qualities to look for in a new partner and means of making remarriage work. Later on, "pre-remarital" counseling can serve the same purpose.

With life so short and the second chance likely to be the last, remarriage after divorce deserves extra preparation. Given that preparation, the chances of finding a satisfactory partner and building a rewarding second marriage are better than fifty-fifty.

PART THREE

Family Living

The remainder of this book consists of an all too brief
introduction to full-scale family living with children.
Though some couples, by conviction or lack of concern,
allow children to come when they will, most have
preferences which they seek to implement (Chapter 19). The
transition to parenthood in the nine months of pregnancy and the
addition of the first child to the family brings the wife even sharper
changes than getting married (Chapter 20).

Once a couple become parents, they assume new responsibilities for
rearing their children, divided here into closely related chapters on
the socialization and education of children (Chapters 21 and 22).
The book concludes with an analysis of life together as a family
group.

19 *Family Planning*

The desire for children is practically universal. The possibility of having them, unfortunately, is not quite so widespread. The greatest variability, however, is in the number and spacing of children born to those able to have them. Values differ about the methods and circumstances of family planning. Knowing the basic factors involved in conception and in varied patterns of child-bearing is useful for all couples, no matter what their values.

Before turning to family planning, it will be useful to review the process of human conception.

The Physiology of Conception

Conception occurs when sperm meets and fertilizes egg. This depends on many factors—knowledge of which is as pertinent to those eager to achieve conception as to those who wish to prevent it.

Female Contributions

Eggs are produced in the ovaries under the influence of hormones secreted by the anterior pituitary gland. Approximately halfway through the menstrual cycle, an egg breaks through the wall of one ovary into the body cavity. At the same time, the spot that the egg left (the follicle) enlarges into a "corpus luteum" which secretes a hormone (progesterone). Under the influence of progesterone the walls of the uterus become spongy and fill with blood in preparation for the fertilized egg. If fertilization does

399

not occur, the corpus luteum gradually dwindles and the lining of the uterus is cast off in menstruation.

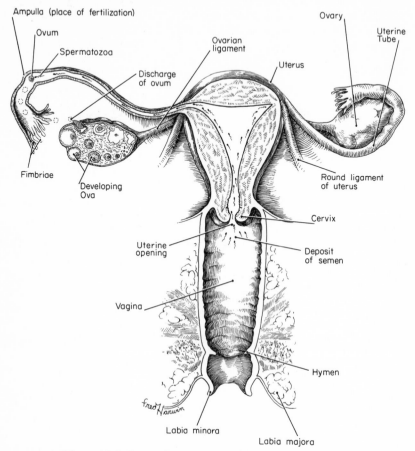

Figure 19-1. Female Reproductive Organs (Front View)

Meanwhile, the egg is attracted to the entrance of the adjacent uterine tube. It travels slowly down the four-inch tube—the entire journey from ovary to uterus requiring about a week. Fertilization normally occurs in the tube. About 20 per cent of the eggs of normal women were not capable of fertilization (though the range varied from practically zero in highly fertile women to more than 50 per cent in women of low fertility [Farris, 1950]).

Male Contributions

Whereas only one egg normally comes to maturity per month, several billion sperm are produced during the same period in a fertile man. Eggs are large enough to be barely visible, but an individual sperm is microscopic in size. Each has a small head containing the nucleus of the cell and a long, whiplash tail.

Sperm are produced in the testes—two glands in the scrotum which correspond to the female ovaries. As they are formed, they empty from each testis into its adjacent epididymis where they accumulate until ejaculation. During ejaculation sperm from both the epididymes pass through the ductus deferens, or seminal ducts (which correspond to the uterine tubes). Near the base of the bladder each duct receives secretions contributed by the seminal vesicles, the prostate gland and the bulbo-urethal glands. These contributions are indispensable to the vitality of sperm and provide them with a suitable liquid environment.

The two ducts pass through the prostate gland into the urethra at a

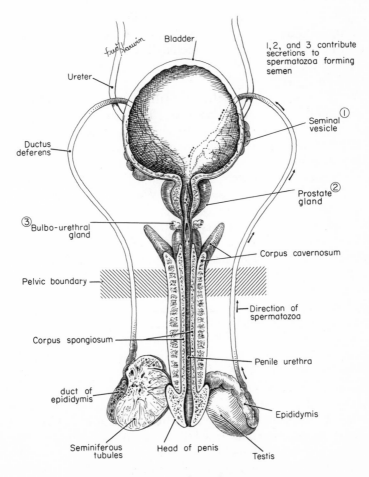

Figure 19-2. Male Reproductive Organs (Front View)

point just below the bladder. (Though the urethra serves alternately as the passage for urine and semen, it cannot do so simultaneously since the bladder outlet closes involuntarily during sexual arousal.) At the same time the numerous blood vessels of the penis become filled with blood, so that the erect, stiffened penis is capable of penetrating the vagina. Impelled by muscular contractions, at the climax, a teaspoonful of semen is ejaculated, normally including several hundred million sperm.

Fertilization

Semen is deposited at the upper end of the vagina near the entrance to the uterus. Provided the sperm are not paralyzed by too great acidity (in the vaginal secretions of some women) or prevented by mechanical contraceptives, they begin moving into the uterus, traveling one inch in eight minutes. Because the vagina is normally mildly acid, while the semen and cervical secretions are normally alkaline, the cervix provides a suitable chemical environment for the sperm. The sperm swim about randomly inside the uterus, some of them entering the tubes where fertilization may occur if an egg is present.

Within a day or two after ovulation an unfertilized egg loses its vitality. The lifespan of spermatozoa is believed to be equally short. Conception requires several factors to coincide: a normal egg; a sufficient number of vigorous spermatozoa; and proper timing of intercourse in relation to ovulation.

The average wife conceived about the fifth month of intercourse when no birth control methods were used (Westoff, 1961). Couples who had intercourse three or more times a week conceived almost twice as soon as those who had intercourse less than twice a week (Westoff, 1963). Because conception is a hit-or-miss affair, the larger the number of shots, the greater the likelihood of hitting the target. However, this is true only within limits. Successive ejaculations close together (as on the same night) declined rapidly in sperm count (Masters and Lampe, 1956). Most valuable for conception is not frequent ejaculation but ejaculation when the wife is fertile. Intentional conception need not be a purely random matter. Westoff found that couples with correct information about the fertile period conceived much sooner than those less knowledgeable.

Masters and Johnson (1966) suggested several ways in which the seminal pool could be more effectively retained intact so that the sperm would have easy access to the cervix. The pool would be most suitably located if the wife lay on her back during and after intercourse. Loss of semen would be least if the husband ceased thrusting movements after ejaculation. Ejaculation without climax for the woman and prompt withdrawal of the penis would leave the orgasmic platform as a "stopper" for the vagina, preventing the semen from running out. (Since these techniques interfere with the sexual pleasure of both partners, they will only interest couples who have had difficulty in conceiving.)

After childbirth there is usually a medically prescribed delay in resuming intercourse and a brief delay in the resumption of fertility. As a result, Freedman (1959) estimated the unplanned interval between birth of one child and conception of the next at eight months. Added to the nine months' duration of pregnancy, this means the average mother would have a child every seventeen months. Roughly every eighth conception ends in a miscarriage, reducing the total number of children who would theoretically be born to nine per family. The lower number actually born to American women reflects primarily the practice of birth control and secondarily the difficulties in conceiving that afflict a few couples.

Ability to Conceive

For some families the problem is not how to prevent conception but how to encourage it. In Freedman's national sample of white women under age 40, one-tenth of all married couples were definitely sterile (1959). Almost a fourth more had experienced some difficulty in having children.

When couples first marry, they seldom know their chances of having children. As they try and fail, they discover initial obstacles, many of which can be removed by medical treatment. Potter and Parker (1964) estimated that less than five per cent of American newlyweds are irreducibly sterile. As time passes, more couples have illnesses or operations that interfere with their ability to have children. Consequently, the proportion of couples who know they are completely or partially sterile rises steadily.

Figure 19-3 shows that by the time women under age 40 had been married 15 years or more, the proportion definitely sterile had risen to 24 per cent. An additional 8 per cent were probably sterile, and another 19 per cent had had enough difficulty conceiving to be labeled semifecund. The total of all three degrees of subfecundity reached 51 per cent. Since most couples complete their child-bearing in the first decade of marriage, much of this inability to have children comes after their desired family size has been reached.

Artificial Insemination

If the husband is the sterile partner and the wife is apparently fertile, she may be able to conceive with sperm from an anonymous donor. The physician chooses a donor of proven fertility whose physical characteristics

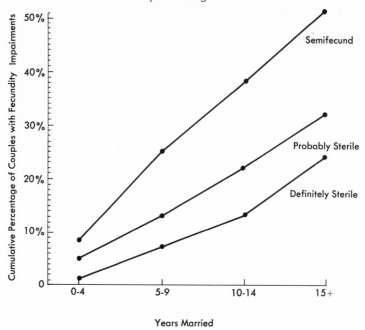

Adapted from Freedman, 1959: 42.

Figure 19-3. Cumulative Fecundity Impairments, by Length of Marriage

resemble the husband's. The physician acts as go-between in conveying semen from the donor to the patient. Behrman and Gosling (1966) reported that this procedure resulted in conception even faster than the normal five-month interval for married couples. This reflects the careful gauging of insemination to the wife's fertile period.

Artificial insemination techniques may also be applied when the husband's sperm count is low. By collecting and freeze-storing sperm from successive ejaculates, the equivalent of a highly fertile ejaculate can be secured for inseminating the wife (S. J. Behrman, M.D., in a newspaper interview, 1966).

Adoption

More common than artificial insemination is the adoption of children who are abandoned by their parents or whose parents have died or become incapacitated. Most adoptable children were conceived outside of wedlock. The adoptive procedures of social agencies are elaborate and time-consuming, designed to assure a loving home for the child and a compatible child for the parents. In recent years the definition of compatibility has relaxed, making it easier for couples to adopt children of other races.

Another innovation has been the adoption of children by fecund parents concerned to aid children who would otherwise be homeless. As the world becomes more crowded, adoption will become an increasingly attractive alternative to bearing children.

The Ethics of Planning

No aspect of family life is more controversial than family planning.

Protestant Policy

Spurred by growing concern over the worldwide population explosion as well as concern for family welfare, the National Council of the Churches of Christ in the United States issued a policy statement on "Responsible Parenthood" in 1961:

> Most of the Protestant churches hold contraception and periodic continence to be morally right when the motives are right. They believe that couples are free to use the gifts of science for conscientious family limitation, provided the means are mutually acceptable, non-injurious to health, and appropriate to the degree of effectiveness required in the specific situation. Periodic continence (the rhythm method) is suitable for some couples, but is not inherently superior from a moral point of view. The general Protestant conviction is that motives, rather than methods, form the primary moral issue. . . .

Catholic Policy

The Catholic Church agrees with the Protestant emphasis on the importance of motives but long disagreed on the unimportance of methods. The only legitimate method of family limitation was abstinence from sexual intercourse. Any mechanical, chemical, or physiological interference with the potential union of sperm and ovum, or any form of sexual activity such as masturbation or withdrawal (coitus interruptus) that deposits semen outside the vagina was prohibited as unnatural. In an Encyclical issued in 1930, Pope Pius XI stated that:

> . . . no reason, however grave, may be put forward by which anything intrinsically against nature may become conformable to nature and morally good. Since, therefore, the conjugal act is destined primarily by nature for the begetting of children, those who in exercising it deliberately

frustrate its natural power and purpose, sin against nature and commit a deed which is shameful and intrinsically vicious. . . . Any use whatsoever of matrimony exercised in such a way that the act is deliberately frustrated in its natural power to generate life is an offense against the law of God and of nature, and those who indulge in it are branded with guilt of grave sin.

However, the postwar period saw the development of controversy and diversity within the Catholic Church. Not only did individual Catholics violate the traditional ban on contraception, but some church officials began to interpret that ban more liberally. In the absence of an updated pronouncement on the subject, wide latitude arose for individual variations in interpretation and practice.

Noonan's major treatise on Catholic doctrine about contraception (1965) noted that new environmental factors such as population pressure, the education of women, and technological change stimulated this debate. As a sociologist, I assume that Catholic doctrine will respond eventually by becoming more permissive.

Methods of Family Planning

Rhythm and the oral tablets may be used either positively or negatively, either to promote or to discourage conception. The remaining methods of influencing conception are exclusively negative in effect.

Oral Tablets

By the mid-1960's, the most widespread method of contraception used by American couples was "the pill." Oral contraceptives were especially popular with college-educated women (Goldberg, 1967). Oral tablets contain hormones designed to inhibit ovulation. Most brands must be taken daily for approximately three weeks in the middle of the menstrual cycle. Several days after discontinuing the pills, menstrual bleeding occurs. One effect of the pills is to regularize the menstrual cycle. They thereby may aid the rhythm method of preventing conception or aid planned conception.

Behrman and Gosling (1966) summarized the research findings about the pill as follows:

1. It is without question the most effective method of contraception currently available, and when used correctly, the only method that is 100 per cent efficacious.

2. It reduces excessive menstrual flow in better than 63 per cent of patients.
3. Eighty per cent of women who previously had dysmenorrhea (menstrual discomfort) are relieved of this while on the medication.
4. By removing the fear of pregnancy, the enjoyment of marital relations is considerably enhanced. (pp. 403–404)

However, various unpleasant and potentially dangerous side effects made medical supervision of the use of oral tablets essential. Many women experienced such symptoms of pregnancy as nausea and weight gain, especially during the first few months before they became acclimated to the dosage. Certain illnesses may have been caused or masked by the use of hormones. This method was therefore inappropriate for women with certain physical problems.

Because new scientific and technological developments occur frequently, printed information rapidly becomes outdated. Couples desiring the latest information about this and other methods of family planning should consult their doctor or Planned Parenthood Clinic.

Intrauterine Devices

Various objects made of plastic, in a variety of shapes (coils, bows, loops, etc.) may be inserted by a medical specialist into the uterus and left there indefinitely. This does not prevent conception but prevents the fertilized egg from becoming implanted in the uterine wall. The mechanism is not entirely clear but was reported by Dr. John Gosling to be an alteration of normal muscular functions so that the egg is propelled through the tube and uterus faster than usual. Unfortunately, the intensification of muscular functioning sometimes expels the device as well as the egg or causes painful uterine contractions during menstruation and excessive menstrual bleeding (especially the first few months).

Next to oral tablets, the intrauterine devices were the most effective contraceptive method available at this writing. However, they were not 100 per cent effective. Occasional pregnancies occurred with the device in place but were not harmed by its presence. The method had the advantage of being inexpensive and requiring no attention as long as the device remains in place.

Diaphragm

The vagina contains few nerve endings. Hence, use of a rubber diaphragm by the wife does not interfere with her enjoyment of intercourse.

Moreover, the diaphragm may be applied before going to bed so that it doesn't interrupt the sex act itself. The diaphragm is a flexible rubber dome roughly two inches in diameter (the exact size determined through fitting by a physician). It is coated with spermicidal jelly, cream, or foam for added protection and inserted along the upper wall of the vagina to cover the cervix. It should be left in place eight hours following intercourse and therefore does not disrupt relaxation.

The fact that the diaphragm is worn internally is both asset and liability. It does not interfere with husband-wife intimacy but the wife must learn how to insert it properly, and both partners may doubt her proficiency. For neurotic wives with negative attitudes toward sex, any vaginal insertion was disgusting (Rainwater). A technical problem is that some women's internal anatomy is unsuitable to holding the diaphragm in position (Johnson and Masters, 1962).

Jelly, Cream, or Aerosol Foam

The contraceptive jelly or cream used to coat the diaphragm may also be used separately. Inserted in the vagina a quarter of an hour prior to intercourse, it is intended to coat the surfaces of the vagina and cervix with a spermicidal chemical lasting six hours. However, Johnson and Masters (1962) found that some jellies and creams failed to distribute themselves evenly and may not be effective with early ejaculation. Jellies and creams were disliked by many women because they were messy. Aerosol foams were the least messy of these three substances.

Condom

The condom is a sheath made of rubber or animal membrane which fits over the penis during intercourse, retaining the ejaculated sperm. Provided condoms are properly manufactured (they should be tested by inflating before use), this method is fairly reliable.

A condom decreases the husband's pleasurable sensations during intercourse and can be applied only to the erect penis, disrupting the spontaneity of foreplay. For husbands who wish to delay their climax, dulled sensitivity is an asset rather than a liability.

The condom requires the husband to assume contraceptive responsibility. For neurotic wives averse to sex generally, to handling their own genitals, or to contact with the husband's penis and semen, the condom was attractive. Its visibility as an external device meant few fears about whether it was properly in place (in contrast to a diaphragm). Psychologically, however, it seemed to those who used it the most "unnatural" of mechanical methods, impairing the sense of intimacy in sexual union. As one of Rainwater's male respondents put it, it's "like going swimming with your clothes on." (1960)

Even for the wife, Chesser (1957) found that "male methods" interfered with the enjoyment of intercourse more than "female methods." Hence, to minimize interference with the sexual relationship, most couples prefer other methods.

Withdrawal

Withdrawal or coitus interruptus is another method for which the male is responsible. It interferes with intercourse more than any other method because it requires the man to withdraw prior to ejaculation. It is therefore unacceptable on psychological grounds. Although its contraceptive adequacy was high in one study portrayed in Figure 19-5, Gosling said that study was exceptional and noted that ordinarily this method is unreliable. Although better than no method, it breaks down due to leakage of semen prior to ejaculation and to failure to withdraw soon enough.

Foams and Suppositories

Foam tablets and suppositories are inserted into the vagina and dissolve in contact with body heat and moisture. Many brands present timing problems, requiring insertion some minutes prior to intercourse and offering protection of such limited duration that another application must be made if intercourse is delayed an hour or more. Johnson and Masters (1962) found that tablets did not foam properly in some women until ejaculation provided additional liquid (which might be too late for contraceptive purposes). Also some women experienced unpleasant sensations from the foaming action. Suppositories had some of the same disadvantages as jellies and creams—uneven interior distribution and unpleasant external dripping.

Douche

Douching involves washing sperm out of the vagina immediately after intercourse with a mildly acid solution intended to kill any remaining sperm. The necessity of getting out of bed immediately after the husband's ejaculation is psychologically unfortunate. Physically, the method provides no guarantee against sperm entering the cervix where they are beyond reach of the douche. Its chief attraction was for wives with negative reactions to sex who felt "cleaner" after they had washed themselves out (Rainwater). Because of its unreliability, it is not medically recommended.

Rhythm

"Rhythm" normally refers to periodic abstinence from intercourse in order to reduce the likelihood of conception. In reverse, it may be used to increase the likelihood of conception by scheduling intercourse when the wife is fertile. In both cases the crucial problem is to discover when ovulation occurs.

Farris (1956) found that fluctuations in the woman's bodily temperature were an unreliable indication of ovulation. However, the "rat test" (in which urine from the woman is injected into young female rats, producing an ovarian reaction if the woman is ovulating) makes it possible to determine ovulation more accurately. From this information, Farris derived the following formula: ovulation is most likely to occur on the second day prior to the midpoint of the menstrual cycle (the cycle is defined as beginning with the onset of menstruation). Using this formula as a guide to experimentation with artificial insemination and with once-a-month coitus, Farris charted the dates when conceptions occurred in several hundred couples.

Figure 19-4 shows the point in the menstrual cycle when semen was implanted in the wife resulting in conception. It can be seen that conceptions tended to cluster around the date of ovulation predicted from the formula. However, due to variability in length of the menstrual cycle as well as in the viability of sperm and ovum, conceptions were dispersed over several days in the "fertile" interval.

Farris' research involved the positive use of rhythm to facilitate conception. When used for family limitation purposes, Figure 19-3 suggests that unintended conceptions will be minimized if couples abstain from sexual relations for an eight-day period surrounding the midpoint of the woman's average menstrual cycle.

Irregular cycles make the prediction of ovulation difficult. The same pills which serve as contraceptives may also be used to regularize the menstrual cycle and thereby to increase the effectiveness of the rhythm method. However, stabilization of the basic cycle does not prevent delays in ovulation occasioned by emotional stress or illness.

Rhythm places heavy demands on the self-discipline and mental alertness of those employing it. When the eight-day fertile period is combined with the menstrual period, intercourse is unavailable up to a dozen days a month. Were sexual desire and favorable circumstances easily relegated to the remaining days, the problem would be easier. But the husband's desire and the wife's readiness for intercourse cannot be expected to be so considerate.

Contraception in Practice

How widely have these family-limitation methods been used and how effectively did they prevent conception?

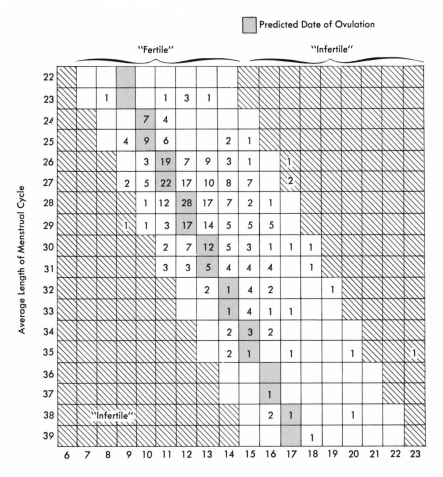

Figure 19-4. Date of Conception, by Length of Menstrual Cycle

Day of Menstrual Cycle

Adapted from Farris, 1956: 103. Figures show the number of conceptions resulting from artificial insemination on the specified day of the menstrual cycle.

The Use of Contraceptive Methods

Family planning of some sort—with rhythm or some other method—is almost universal in the United States. The methods chosen and the schedule used depend on the couple's desire and ability to have children, the number already born, and their religious values and education. Contraception is discontinued by couples who discover that they have fertility problems. Conversely, it is used most widely and most diligently by those who have proven their ability to bear children.

LIMITING FAMILY SIZE. American families use contraception more to control the number than the timing of children. Especially with the first child, many let nature take its course. Because they are either unsure of their ability to have children or eager to have one as soon as possible, they postpone contraception until after the first child is born.

As of 1960 four-fifths of all American wives in the child-bearing ages had used some method of contraception (Whelpton). Freedman's 1959 study showed that only half the population attempted to delay the birth of their first child. Most of the remainder began using birth control after that, but a few waited until they reached their desired family size. Almost 100 per cent of fecund couples took precautions by the time they completed their preferred family size.

RELIGIOUS VALUES AND CONTRACEPTIVE METHODS. Catholics and non-Catholics differed less in the extent to which they attempted to limit their reproduction than in the methods used. To be sure, Catholics usually wanted larger families. Hence they did not begin to shut down their reproduction as soon. Nevertheless, most Catholics eventually used rhythm and/or other methods to end their child-bearing long before the potential nine children.

Table 19-1 shows that Catholic couples used rhythm more and other methods less than non-Catholics. However, more than one-third of these Catholics had already used methods other than rhythm by the time they were interviewed and still more were likely to do so prior to menopause. Some Catholic couples began with rhythm but switched to other methods as their preferred quota filled up (Freedman).

Table 19-1 shows that interfaith couples tended to compromise on contraception. Since wives generally take religion more seriously and are more involved in child-bearing and child-rearing, they influenced the choice of contraceptive methods more than their husbands.

For unmixed Catholic couples, the more often the wife went to church, the more she adhered to the norm of the Church. Those who attended

Table 19-1. Actual or Expected Use of Rhythm and Other Methods of Contraception, by Religion of Husband and Wife

Percentage using contraception	Wife: Husband:	Catholic Catholic	Catholic Protestant	Protestant Catholic	Protestant Protestant	Jewish Jewish
Rhythm only used		35%	27%	11%	6%	2%
Other methods used		35	46	70	80	87
Ever had used or ever expected to use any method		77	81	89	90	89

Adapted from Freedman, 1959: 105, 185. Source: National sample of white women under age 40. Reciprocal percentages had not used (and/or did not expect to use) the specified methods.

413

regularly used rhythm more than disapproved methods. However, nominally Catholic wives who seldom or never attended Mass paid less attention to Church teachings about contraception (Freedman).

The Effectiveness of Contraceptive Methods

The various methods differ appreciably in their ability to prevent conception. However, the greatest source of unintended pregnancies is disuse or misuse of the methods. Few couples use any method consistently, so human factors are more important than technical factors in contraceptive failure.

THE HUMAN FACTOR IN CONTRACEPTIVE FAILURE. Rainwater (1960) found that willingness to practice contraception at all, as well as to practice it consistently, was closely correlated with sexual feelings. Couples who were neither afraid of sex nor disgusted by it but treated it matter of factly and discussed it openly used contraception more consistently. Babchuck and LaCognata (1960) similarly found that unwanted pregnancies happened most to those Planned Parenthood Clinic patients with sexual problems or with multiple marital problems, whereas those with few or no problems used the same methods more successfully. The ability to practice contraception depends on having a stable personality and a stable marriage.

Many couples who otherwise practice birth control faithfully take chances when they run out of contraceptive materials or don't want to be bothered. Especially after drinking too much, their normal controls against indiscretions are weakened. Though most couples "get away" with it the first time, the probabilities of conception are predictable. Hence, a substantial proportion of so-called "accidental" pregnancies are not accidents in the technical sense but the inevitable consequence of taking too many chances.

Table 19-2 shows that the chief source of unintended pregnancies was taking chances by discontinuing contraception. In coitus interruptus the husband failed to withdraw soon enough. Taking chances with rhythm meant narrowing the fertile interval until the period was no longer "safe." Human failures were most common with contraceptive methods that required precautions "late in the game" of intercourse. But no matter what the method, chance-taking introduced a high margin of error.

TECHNICAL DIFFICULTIES IN CONTRACEPTIVE EFFECTIVENESS. In Table 19-2 rhythm had a high rate of technical failure. Ovulatory variability is so great that couples often got caught in unintended conceptions when they thought they were safe.

Table 19-2. Cause of Unintended Pregnancies, by Method of Contraception

Cause of unintended pregnancy	METHOD OF CONTRACEPTION				
	Withdrawal	Douche	Condom	Diaphragm	Rhythm
Method not used at time of conception	75%	69%	57%	56%	46%
Method failed	25	31	43	44	54
Total	100%	100%	100%	100%	100%

Adapted from Freedman, 1959: 209. Source: Unintended pregnancies after first use of specified method by those who used only that method.

Figure 19-5 shows that douching and rhythm produced similarly high rates of failure when the results of various field studies are compared. These unintended pregnancies resulted from the combined effects of technical and human weaknesses. Oral tablets and intrauterine devices were markedly more effective than other methods.

Some accidents bring children sooner than intended. Relatively few result in "surplus" children, that is, in families larger than the parents say they preferred. In Detroit, for example, only eight per cent of wives interviewed in 1955 said they already had or expected to have more than their ideal number (Blood and Wolfe). In retrospect, some couples revised their expectations upward to accommodate unexpected arrivals. Others, however, secured illegal induced abortions to cope with contraceptive failures, especially when their preferred family size had already been reached (Gebhard, 1958).

SUCCESS IN FAMILY PLANNING. When these human and technical factors

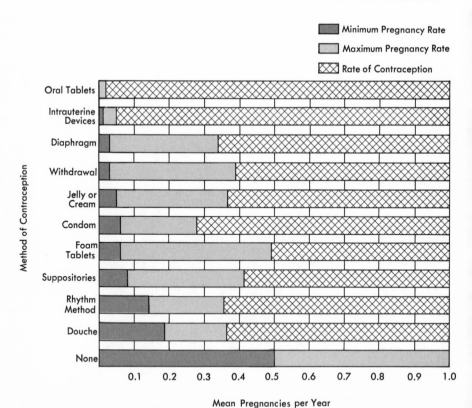

Mean Pregnancies per Year

Adapted from Behrman and Gosling, 1966: 407. *Source:* Best and worst pregnancy rates per year in various studies.

Figure 19-5. Annual Pregnancy Rate, by Method of Contraception

are put together, relatively few American families succeed in having just the number of children they want when they want them, though others profess not to care. Few couples are rational enough to plan successfully both the number and spacing of children. As of the 1950's, hardly more than a fourth of all college-educated American wives achieved this. Another fourth had fewer children than they wished because of fecundity impairments. Most of the rest either had "wanted" children at the wrong time or made no attempt to space their children. Few confessed to having more children than they really wanted. Since that time, technical improvements may have increased ability to plan successfully.

Child-Spacing

Child-spacing involves both the interval between marriage and the birth of the first child, and the interval between successive children. The actual pattern of child-spacing by American families is shown in Table 19-3.

Table 19-3. Child-Spacing, by Wife's Religion

Average Interval in Months	Protestant	Catholic
Marriage to first birth	24	22
First to second birth	34	30
Second to third birth	34	34
Third to fourth birth	32	28

Adapted from Whelpton, 1966: 321.

Because of fewer attempts at child-spacing and less effective methods, Catholics have slightly briefer intervals between children than do Protestants. Nevertheless, the basic pattern is essentially the same—two years from marriage to birth of the first child, then three years to each succeeding child except in families with more than three children. The latter have shorter intervals both because they wish to have more children and because they include fecund nonplanners who control neither the spacing nor the size of their families. Conversely, the greater the wife's education and the higher the husband's income the longer couples postpone the birth of their first child.

Readiness for Child-Bearing

The next chapter describes in detail the impact of children on parents. Here we need to preview the marital, financial, and emotional prerequisites for the transition from marriage to parenthood.

MARITAL READINESS. No matter how wealthy or well adjusted a man and woman may be, they are rarely ready to have children when they first get married. Learning how to be a good husband and wife is job enough for the first year without adding the complexities of parenthood. Living together provides a smooth transition from premarital activities. It also gives poorly matched couples a testing period in which to find out whether they can make a go of marriage. Otherwise, young parents may get trapped in unworkable marriages:

> I've been trying to get away ever since I got married, but I've never succeeded. The children started coming too soon, and now I feel I have to stick it out for their sakes until they're grown up. If it hadn't been for them, I would have divorced Hank long ago.

For most couples the question is not whether marriage will work but how soon they will be ready for pregnancy and parenthood. There is no set answer but a minimum of one year prior to conception is often suggested as a rule of thumb. In two American communities the longer the delay from marriage to first birth, the lower the divorce rate. Christensen (1962) believed this reflected greater readiness for parenthood and a lower proportion of unwanted pregnancies.

Women who marry late enough in life to be threatened by menopause wish to start having children sooner. Moreover, infant mortality rose sharply in children born to mothers past age 35 (N.C.H.S., 1965). On the other hand, couples who foresee a coming separation may be well advised to postpone children until the husband returns.

> When I came back from overseas, the son I'd never seen was almost two years old. Of course, he didn't know who I was. My wife and he had come to depend on each other so much that I felt like an intruder. It didn't make coming home any easier to have to break into that charmed circle of theirs.

The first pregnancy and first child are such significant experiences that few husbands want to miss the opportunity to share them and few wives to miss the husband's emotional support.

FINANCIAL READINESS. How much does it cost to have a baby—and to keep it? Delivery and hospitalization expenses may be covered by insurance. Otherwise the former reflects the patient's ability to pay, and the latter depends on the number of days in the hospital. In addition there are the costs of prenatal and postnatal care. Medical expenses will total hundreds of dollars if they have to be paid out of pocket.

Once the baby arrives, his impact on the budget is felt gradually. As he grows older, his food and clothes cost more. If the husband's income rises correspondingly, increased costs may be taken in stride. If not, long-range planning may be required. Couples struggling for upward social mobility tended to postpone their first child while they concentrated on training and equipping the husband for his career (Tien, 1961).

More critical than the cost of a child is the loss of the wife's income. Couples who have geared their standard of living to two incomes must cope with reduced income and increased expenses simultaneously.

EMOTIONAL READINESS. Those mature enough to be ready for marriage are usually mature enough two years later to be ready for parenthood. However, some couples marry prematurely, and others, skilled enough for marital interaction, are not ready for the complexities of child-bearing and child-rearing. The emotional strain on the mother depends on how rapidly the children are born. Sears (1957) found that young mothers with several children felt overwhelmed and took out their frustration on their children by treating them coldly.

One sign of readiness is wanting to have children. The desire for children is almost universal, but not quite. Some women don't want to be bothered. Those wrapped up in themselves or embittered by their own distraught mothers may be afraid to have children:

> Shelly flatly told Sam that she would never under any circumstances have children and that if he would be unhappy without them, the wedding would be canceled. He thought her mind would change so the wedding ceremony was performed. They have been married six years, but to his great unhappiness she has not changed her feelings. In addition to thoroughly disliking children as such, Shelly takes great pride in her appearance and abhors the thought of losing her slim figure during and after pregnancy. She spends her days figure-skating and playing tennis which she is loath to give up. She steadfastly maintains that having children is to end all independence.

Shelly may find herself short of tennis partners as other wives become mothers. Being left out of conversations about discipline and diapers could change her mind.

But whatever the reason a woman doesn't want children, she is wise to avoid them. To bear a child is no guarantee that she will love it. No figure is more tragic than an unwanted child except, perhaps, his guilt-laden mother.

Hardly less important is the husband's readiness. A man's impact on his children is almost as influential as his wife's. And his help is important to her when the going gets tough.

Most girls look forward to becoming mothers from the time they play with dolls. Boys less often anticipate their role as fathers. Hence, the transition from readiness for marriage to readiness for parenthood is in some respects sharper for the man:

> When I fell in love with Adrienne I was very anxious to get married— and we did after a whirlwind courtship. We got along real well with each other and had a wonderful time that first year. Then Adrienne began to hint about wanting a baby. To tell the truth, I'd never thought much about it before. I'd had very little contact with kids and always felt a bit embarrassed when I had to deal with them because I didn't know how to behave. So it took me a while to get used to the idea. Eventually I came around.

Comparing three aspects of readiness for parenthood, Westoff (1961) found the largest number of couples unready financially (41 per cent), whereas 26 per cent wished they had had more time to enjoy things together, and 19 per cent felt they didn't have time to get adjusted to each other. Though most wives were satisfied with the timing of their first birth, twice as many felt it came too soon as too late and the most enthusiastic wives were those who waited the longest—two to three years.

Readiness for parenthood benefits the child as well as the parent. Morgan (1962) found that children born into families which began childbearing prematurely ended up with less education than those born to parents of similar education, income, etc., who had their children later. Educational impairment was particularly severe when the first child was born while the father was still a teenager. This suggests the value of postponing the birth of the first child at least two years after marriage. The earlier a couple marry, the more urgent this delay.

Spacing Subsequent Children

Table 19-3 showed that American families typically had their second and third children at three-year intervals. Was this spacing ideal? Westoff's young respondents were most enthusiastic about second children born only two to two-and-a-half years after the first. The problem, as they saw it, was to balance their desire to provide a playmate for the first child against their desire to avoid having too many small children at once. With the third child, the playmate problem presumably figures less than the need to limit the burden of child-care.

In any case, ideal intervals to third and fourth births are clearly longer than between the first and second. In general, of course, the farther apart children are born, the smaller the proportion who are born too soon. In four-child Detroit families, the minimum interval between second and fourth children necessary to reduce born-too-soon children to less than 0.5 per family was seven years (Freedman and Coombs, 1966). From this standpoint, the minimum preferred spacing between children was two years from first to second child, three years from second to third, and four years between the third and fourth children.

HOUSEKEEPING ADVANTAGES. Young mothers recognize that child-care is easier when children are spaced farther apart. Confirmation comes from a study by Wiegand and Gross (1958) of fatigue among mothers of young children. Tiredness increased (a) the younger the child and (b) the larger the number of children. When these factors combine in a large number of preschool children, housekeeping and child-care become difficult. Mothers of closely spaced children cannot perform either their housekeeping, their child-rearing, or their marital roles as adequately as those whose children are spaced farther apart. The energy saved by spacing children an extra year or two apart more than offsets the lessened vitality of the mother because she is older. Aging is a gradual process but the difference between a two-year and a four-year interval between children is drastic.

CHILD-REARING ADVANTAGES. Overtired mothers cannot give children the attention they deserve. Fatigue is probably one reason why mothers showed less warmth and affection toward children bunched close together, not only while they were infants but as much as five years afterward (Sears, 1957). Sears also suggested that mothers still protectively attached to one child may have found it difficult to respond warmly to a new baby who arrived too soon. For mothers as well as for prior children, a rapid succession of children creates more resistance than leisurely timing.

Since maternal warmth is indispensable to the successful socialization of children (Chapter 21), any gain in warmth from wider child-spacing is valuable to the child. Widely spaced children also gain more attention to their educational potentialities. Conversely, when too many children are born too close together to an immature mother, she can hardly give them the attention they need if they are to be motivated to achieve.

Rosen (1961) found that when as many as three children were born to working-class mothers still in their early twenties, the children's achievement motivation was conspicuously low. He suggested this may have been caused by the inability of older children to help care for younger ones when they were bunched too close together (since all were young simultaneously):

> In this case the young mother, particularly if she is lower class and unable to obtain help, may simply be overwhelmed. She will have little time or energy for the supervision and complex training in achievement that the development of achievement motivation requires (p. 584).

Although middle-class mothers in Rosen's study managed despite these handicaps to motivate their children to achieve, we can infer that the faster children are born, the more likely they are to suffer or, conversely, the more strenuously the parents will have to extend themselves to meet the children's needs.

Sears suggested still another advantage in spacing—lessened sibling rivalry. A two year old's language skills are too weak for him to be able to understand why he is being displaced. By three or four, sex education and loving orientation could help him anticipate the birth of the baby, reducing his resentment. What the naïve young mothers of infant second children in Westoff's sample didn't realize is that closeness in age makes sibling rivalry more likely at the same time that it makes companionship more possible. The problem is to space children far enough apart to minimize competitiveness without making companionship impossible. Three or four years apart is probably better than briefer intervals.

FINANCIAL ADVANTAGES. Having children "thick and fast" concentrates them early in the father's career when his income is low. Spreading them out delays the expense of later children until income has risen. The farther apart children are spread, the greater the family's opportunity to accumulate financial assets: a home, car, savings, investments, and insurance. For example, Detroit families with four children born in the first five years after marriage averaged only $4,000 in assets, whereas those who spaced the same number of children over 12 years or more accumulated almost $11,000 (Freedman and Coombs, 1966).

The burdens of child-bunching intensify when children go to college. I noted in Chapter 11 that many families found it difficult to meet college expenses. Most depended on current income for this purpose. If more than one child is in college at the same time, this is much more difficult. From this point of view, a four-year interval between children is ideal.

Family Size

The number of children born per family declined steadily in the United States to a low ebb of 2.4 per married woman during the Depression (Freedman, 1959). The postwar baby boom pushed family sizes back to pre-World War I levels. In 1965, the expected number of children born to married women in the United States averaged 3.3. No decline in family size was yet in sight (Goldberg, 1967). Though some of this increase represented a revival in the popularity of four-child families, even more resulted from the disappearance of voluntary childlessness and single-childness. At the same time, very large families went out of style. So, most families had from two to four children. Families with less than two or more than four usually couldn't help it—suffering either fecundity handicaps or fecundity accidents.

Preferred Family Sizes

College-educated women typically preferred three children. Blood and Wolfe interpreted their narrow range of preferences as follows:

> In practically eliminating subnormal preferences, education provides women with husbands sufficiently prosperous to release the more or less universal American desire to have one child for the sake of the parents and at least one more for the sake of the first. In reducing preferences for outsize families, education creates in women more interests outside the home, not at the expense of having any children but certainly at the expense of being tied down by a long string of them. Educated women are also familiar with child psychology and its emphasis on giving more love and affection to each child. The easiest way a mother can give more attention to each child is to have fewer of them. By and large, most Americans say that they want fewer children because they love them so much, not because they like them so little. Children are not nuisances to be avoided, but individuals who deserve a fair deal within the limits of the parents' ability to provide for them (pp. 122–23).

COMPETING VALUES. One reason why few college alumnae preferred more than four children is that they had outside interests. Career-oriented wives similarly preferred to limit their child-bearing.

Table 19-4 shows how profoundly the family-size preferences of women in three mid-Western cities were affected by their internal/external orientation.

Table 19-4. Middle-Class Wives' Desired Family Size, by Personal Orientation

Percentage of wives with desired family size	PERSONAL ORIENTATION		
	External Companion *	Equal	Domestic †
Small family	63%	20%	7%
Medium family ‡	16	45	21
Large family	21	35	72
Total	100%	100%	100%
Number of wives	19	20	14

* Solely oriented to outside interests or to husband as companion.
† Solely oriented to children and home.
‡ A medium-sized family for Protestants was three children and for Catholics four.
Adapted from Rainwater, 1965: 191. *Source:* Married women, mostly in Chicago, some in Cincinnati and Oklahoma City.

Both husband and wife may have alternative uses to which they wish to devote their time and money. Some occupations and avocations are difficult to integrate with parenthood. The economic choices involved in having children are apparent. Analysis by Lucille Ketchum of the 1960–61 Survey of Consumer Expenditures showed that each child cost between $15,000 and $27,000 to raise to age 18. The larger the number of children, the less spent per child. (In this restricted sense, they come "cheaper by the dozen.") The aggregate cost to the family, however, rose with the number of children.

For devout Catholics, preferred family sizes run large. Even when carefully matched on socioeconomic characteristics, Catholic couples differed significantly from Protestant and Jewish couples, preferring 3.7, 2.8, and 2.6 children respectively (Freedman, 1961). Given the same income, the average Catholic family preferred one child extra. Even for Catholics, however, the choice was still confined largely to the usual two-to-four limits, the difference resulting chiefly from higher preferences within that range.

"A Boy for You, a Girl for Me." Because children come in two sexes, child-bearing preferences are based on assumptions about the number of sons and daughters. Americans strongly prefer having both sexes so that families unlucky enough to have only one frequently raise their sights in hopes of breaking the spell. Especially when all the children were girls, parents extended themselves to have a boy, but the tendency was almost as strong the other way (Westoff, 1961).

The Consequences of Family Size

Blood and Wolfe found that Detroit wives with three children were the most satisfied with their marriages, but I am not sure whether this was a cause-and-effect relationship. Perhaps it was. Perhaps beyond a certain number children interfere with the ability of the partners to communicate with each other, to spend their leisure together—in short to maintain a personal relationship with each other. Perhaps three is ideal for most Americans.

Reed found (1947) that marital adjustment increased with success in controlling fertility according to the couple's own desires. To have more than three children *may* have negative repercussions for the average marriage but surely does for those who want only three. Generalizations about ideal family size may be precarious, but the value of achieving one's own ideal is clear.

The consequences of family size must be considered not only for the parents but for the children. Children benefit in some ways from siblings but suffer in others. For example, studies in many nations have shown that the larger the family, the lower the average I.Q. of the children (Lipset and Bendix, 1960). At least part of this intellectual impairment results from the inability of parents to stimulate and educate adequately large numbers of children. Similarly, the larger the number of children, the less the education they received even when differences in parental education, income, etc., were controlled (Morgan *et al.*, 1962). These differences were especially great for girls since their education is considered less necessary.

Achievement motivation declines as the individual family gets larger. All families start out small, but some last-born children must contend with larger families than others. The larger the number of siblings ahead of them in line, the less attention they receive. Consequently, last-born children in large families have fewer chances of acquiring the motivation, the education, and the financial wherewithal to enter top-flight graduate and professional schools. (In the University of Michigan Medical School, last-born children in two-child families were represented in the student body only two-thirds as often as their elder siblings, in three-child families one-third as often as their eldest siblings, and in families of four or more children one-tenth as often [Cobb and French, 1966].)

Most mothers gradually tire of having children. As a result they were less likely to breastfeed each succeeding child, more severe in weaning it, and clamped down more on the noise children made (Sears *et al.*, 1957). This suggests that the larger the number of children, the less apt each succeeding child is to be adequately mothered. For the children, then, as well as for the father and mother, family size must be limited.

Finally, the consequences of family size must be considered for the world at large. An average of 2.2 children per family produces a stable population. Each extra child intensifies the worldwide population explosion.

20 The Advent of Children

The arrival of the first baby revolutionizes family life. In some ways, the transition to parenthood is like the transition to marriage. Conception is like getting engaged; the nine months of pregnancy, the engagement period; childbirth, the rite of passage into parenthood; and the hospital sojourn, the honeymoon for mother and child.

Pregnancy

Women are not aware of pregnancy until several weeks after conception. The fertilized egg moves slowly down the tube to the uterus whose walls have become enriched with blood under the influence of two hormones, progesterone and estrogen. The embryo becomes embedded in the spongy tissues of the uterine wall. A week or two later the woman misses most or all of her menstrual flow because a hormone produced by the embryo retains the lining of the uterus. This hormone also inhibits the ripening of other eggs in the ovaries. Within five weeks, a hormone is produced in sufficient quantities to be detectable when urine specimens are injected into experimental rabbits, mice, or frogs. By the sixth week, the cervix has deepened in color enough to provide further evidence of pregnancy to the physician.

Symptoms that *may* indicate pregnancy are skipped menstrual periods, feelings of nausea or excessive fatigue, tenderness, tingling, or enlargement of the breasts, or more frequent urination. Each of these may have causes other than pregnancy, and some of them (especially nausea) are not universally present. Nevertheless, the more signs there are, the greater the chances that the woman is pregnant.

426

Growth of the Fetus

At the end of the first month the embryo is still so small that it may not be recognized even on autopsy. In the fourth month the heartbeat becomes audible through the obstetrician's stethoscope, and in the fifth the mother can feel the baby's kicking and stretching movements.

Table 20-1. Average Size of Fetus, by Monthly Intervals

Age	Length	Weight
One month	¼ inch	Tiny fraction of an ounce
Two months	1¼ inches	$\frac{1}{14}$ ounce
Three months	3 inches	1 ounce
Four months	6–8 inches	5–6 ounces
Five months	10–12 inches	1 pound
Six months	14 inches	2 pounds
Seven months	16 inches	3 pounds
Eight months	18 inches	5 pounds
Nine months	20 inches	7–8 pounds

Adapted from Bowman, 1960: 403–05.

FETAL DEATHS. Pregnancies which terminate in death of the fetus prior to birth are referred to popularly as stillbirths, technically as fetal deaths or antenatal deaths. Just as divorces come early in marriage, so fetal deaths occur early in pregnancy, declining steadily in successive time intervals. In a comprehensive study on the island of Kauai in the State of Hawaii, almost one-fourth of all pregnancies detected at four weeks after the last menstrual period subsequently ended in fetal death (Bierman *et al.*, 1965). Figure 20-1 shows how the chances of surviving to a live birth rise, the longer the fetus survives in the uterus.

Most fetal deaths are less tragic than they seem. They usually involve defective germ plasm incapable of normal development. For example, Guttmacher (1957) reported that more than two-thirds of all spontaneously aborted fetuses were observably malformed. The tragic cases involve women who have trouble carrying any pregnancy through to successful completion. Medical treatment with hormones, vitamins, and bed rest may enable them to retain a fetus long enough to improve its chances of survival at birth.

PREMATURE BIRTHS. We have already seen in Figure 20-1 that the period of gestation is measured from the first day of the last menstruation (since this is more easily ascertained than the date of ovulation and conception roughly two weeks later). The American College of Obstetricians and Gynecologists arbitrarily defined the beginning of "viability" as 28 weeks of gestation. It defined prematurity on the basis of the weight of the fetus

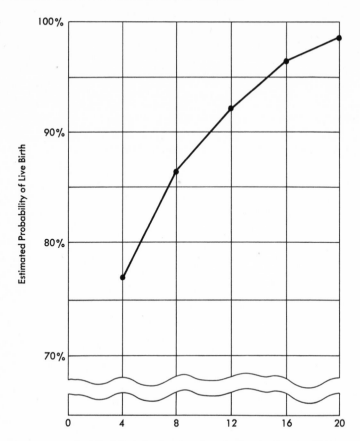

Length of Gestation (number of weeks since last menstruation)

Adapted from Bierman *et al.*, 1965: 38. *Source:* Kauai pregnancy study.

Figure 20-1. Estimated Probability of Live Birth, by Length of Gestation

(under 2500 grams or about five and one-half pounds). Actually, both the size and age of the fetus determine its chances of survival (see Table 20-2). Prematurity is clearly a relative matter. Any definition is arbitrary. In

Table 20-2. First Year Deaths, by Length of Gestation and Birth Weight

	LENGTH OF GESTATION	
Weight	Under 37 Weeks	37 or More
Under 5½ pounds	22.0%	5.4%
5½ pounds or more	2.6%	0.9%

Adapted from Bierman *et al.*, 1965: 39. Reciprocal percentages of live-born infants survived to age one year. Length of gestation was calculated from the beginning of last menstruation. *Source:* 1,922 live births on the island of Kauai in Hawaii.

Kauai, most of the technically premature underweight babies were so clinically mature that the attending physicians allowed them to go home promptly without any special care. The doctors' good judgment was attested by the survival of every one of those normal tiny babies at least to age two years.

CONGENITAL HANDICAPS. Not counting underweight babies requiring no special treatment, almost 11 per cent of the Kauai babies were born with handicaps. These fell into four fairly equal categories.

1. Premature children requiring special care but who matured into normal children by age two.
2. Children with minor physical defects and disorders which could be easily corrected.
3. Children with more serious disorders such as a hernia or strabismus ("cross-eyes") which could be corrected with short-term, specialized care as by a major operation.
4. Children with handicaps requiring long-term specialized medical, educational or custodial care.

Typical among these last were congenital heart defects, severe mental deficiency (I.Q. below 70), or combinations of physical and mental handicaps. Bierman (1965) commented that "Even with the best of care most of these children will be permanently handicapped in some degree."

Handicaps are not always detectable at birth. Many are noted only as the child begins to mature or if he receives special diagnostic study. Parents who have already had a normal child can tolerate an abnormal one more easily. But an abnormal first child produces not only unrelieved disappointment but anxiety about future children:

> We knew as soon as Mary was born that she wasn't normal physically, but it was only gradually that we realized that she was also mentally retarded. We could not love any baby more than we love her—normal or not. She is ours and when I feed her, stay up with her at night, and hold her tight, I'm sure I feel no different than a parent of any normal child. Yet there is no future in our relationship—she does not know either of us.
>
> When she was seven months old and we were quite sure she was retarded, we had long visits with my gynecologist. He assured us that Mary's condition is extremely rare and not hereditary and encouraged us to have another child. It was not the easiest pregnancy in the world, however, as I had many fears about the normality of the child I was carrying. I had seen so many abnormalities in Children's Hospital that I never knew existed. Even though I kept myself as busy as possible, it was a tremendous relief when the nine months of waiting were over and we finally had a healthy, normal baby in our house.

Changes in the Mother

While the embryo is still too small to be felt in the abdomen, the mother's body chemistry is transformed to nurture it.

PHYSICAL CHANGES. The woman's body is marvelously adaptable to the size and needs of her growing child. Pregnancy is a natural state, not an illness or a medical "problem." Most expectant mothers experience no change in their general health. However, three times as many mothers in one study said their health improved as said it deteriorated (Landis, 1950). Some women's complexions bloom during pregnancy so that they look prettier than ever. On the other hand, occasional nausea was typical, especially during the first three months (Poffenberger, 1952). Some women reacted to pregnancy as though it were an illness, worrying about their changing body, emphasizing the pain and suffering, feeling that they should be excused from normal duties, and relying on their doctor to help them "return to normal." Women who were unhappy or insecure were more apt to assume this "sick" role during pregnancy (for example, women married to less-well-educated husbands or whose husbands were downward mobile). Moreover, negative reactions were intensified when pregnancy conflicted with other values (for example, aspirations for material things such as a home and furniture or the opportunity to continue working in a high-status job). In other words, how a pregnant woman felt depended on her personal and marital resources and on the place of familistic values in her philosophy of life (Rosengren, 1961).

The interaction of cultural and physical factors was apparent in McCammon's report (1951) that nausea among American Indians was confined to those who had learned to speak English (that is, who were marginal women between Indian and American society). Within American society Robertson (1946) found nausea associated with disturbed sexual functioning, including lack of orgasm and dislike of intercourse. This applied especially to women with persistent, severe nausea and vomiting, illustrating the profound repercussions of social and psychological factors on physical well-being during the rapid changes of pregnancy.

Even for women whose health is better than ever, periodic visits to the obstetrician are recommended, especially in the first pregnancy. This is a precaution against anything going wrong and a means of guaranteeing optimum conditions for mother and child.

Many pregnant women have trouble keeping their weight down to the normal gain of 18–20 pounds. The doctor may restrict starches and sweets, since excess weight makes childbirth more difficult. Even if the weight gain is not excessive, the growing baby presses inward on the intestines and bladder so that constipation and frequent urination plague the last weeks of pregnancy.

MENTAL CHANGES. Most women have looked forward to pregnancy and childbirth so that they bring a sense of fulfilling their destiny. At worst, they are necessary evils prerequisite to having children. They are seldom resented wholeheartedly, except when conception itself was unwanted. Even then, Newton (1955) found that negative reactions were strongest when pregnancy was first discovered. As time progressed, most expectant mothers became reconciled to the prospect of having a child.

The first pregnancy is exciting. Not that dramatic things happen all the time, but the whole sequence is new. The first discovery that the wife is pregnant, the bodily changes, the first fluttering movements of the baby inside the body—these are extraordinary events that have long been anticipated.

Despite euphoria and elation, there are negative aspects. During the last few weeks, the nine months seem like they will never end. When it's uncomfortable to sit, stand, walk, or sleep, anyone could be pardoned for looking forward impatiently to childbirth.

The Marriage Relationship During Pregnancy

Much of the wife's reaction to pregnancy depends on her husband's reaction (and his on hers). If he is happy about the pregnancy, sympathizes with her problems, and does not regret her change of figure, her morale will be reinforced. Except for insecure husbands married to narcissistic wives and jealous of the coming baby, most couples adapt well.

In one study of obstetrical patients, actions didn't change much, but the partners' feelings toward each other notably improved. Half the couples said their love became deeper, and nearly two-thirds said the prospective baby drew them closer together. Wives especially felt more appreciated and better understood (Stott, 1952).

If the husband fails to respond to the wife's need for love and sympathy, she feels lonely and deserted. Faced with a new and perhaps terrifying experience, her loneliness is intensified by losing contact with her colleagues when she quits work. Fear of childbirth and anxiety about the health and normality of the fetus are so widespread (63 per cent and 41 per cent of Poffenberger's student wives) that the husband has a crucial supportive role during pregnancy.

SEXUAL CHANGES. During the first few months, the embryo is too small to be noticeable. However, physiological changes affect the wife's sexual responsiveness. Masters and Johnson (1966) found that increased breast size during the first pregnancy was sometimes painfully intensified by vaso-congestion under sexual stimulation. Nausea, sleepiness, and chronic fatigue also depressed the sexual interest of more than three-fourths of their first-pregnancy women during the first trimester. However, most women experienced none of these sexual handicaps in subsequent pregnancies.

During the middle trimester, the concentrated blood supply to the growing fetus accentuated vasocongestive responses to sexual stimulation of the genital area. As a result, many women were more sexually responsive and more interested in having intercourse than at any other time in life. During the last trimester, husbands and wives lost interest in having sexual relations with each other as the fetus became more of an obstacle. The last six weeks, most doctors prohibited intercourse for fear of infection. However, Masters and Johnson suggested that antibiotics made infection so easily curable that this risk was no longer significant. They recognized, however, that uterine contractions during orgasm may precipitate premature delivery by women with a history of miscarriages.

For a man to lose interest in having intercourse with his wife or to be forbidden to do so by the obstetrician does not mean he will lose his sexual feelings. In Masters and Johnson's college-educated sample, almost one-fourth of the husbands resorted to extramarital sexual intercourse during the months just before and after childbirth when their wives were unavailable. For the sake of the marriage, Masters and Johnson advocated shortening the interval when intercourse is prohibited.

OCCUPATIONAL CHANGES. Chapter 11 described the financial repercussions of losing the wife's income. Not only from the financial standpoint but for psychological reasons, there are advantages in continuing to work during pregnancy. Just as long engagements are hard to endure, so are inactive pregnancies. Once the wife quits work, time can be devoted to preparing for childbirth. Exercise classes, prenatal classes, baby showers, and conversations with young mothers help the mother physically and psychologically. Time can be allotted to preparing the nursery and layette. But hardly nine months. The more active the wife is, the less arduous the waiting.

Childbirth

Pregnancies vary greatly in length. The average date of delivery is calculated at 280 days from the last menstruation. However, the date of conception is not a fixed interval following menstruation, nor is the interval from conception to delivery standardized. Hence, considerable latitude must be allowed in predicting the date of childbirth.

Figure 20-2 shows that only one birthdate out of 25 was predicted correctly. The middle 50 per cent fell within a two-week interval, but the remainder were more than a week off and 10 per cent as much as three weeks early or late.

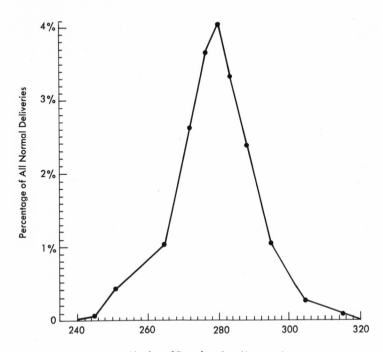

Number of Days from Last Menstruation

Adapted from Eastman, 1950: 198.

Figure 20-2. Duration of Pregnancy (from last menstruation)

Onset of Labor

Labor usually begins gradually—especially for women who have never had a baby before. Sometimes the "bag of waters" surrounding the baby breaks first, precipitating labor. Sometimes the first sign is a thick, mucous, bloody discharge from the vagina. More often the muscular contractions of the uterus begin first. Since there may be false starts, the usual procedure is to keep track of the decreasing interval between contractions. When they come regularly as often as every ten minutes, the chances are that "this is it," so the mother goes to the hospital.

The first stage of labor involves dilation of the mouth of the uterus until it is open wide enough for the baby to pass through. The cervix consists of a band of circular muscles that have been contracted throughout the life of the woman up to this point. These muscles are potentially elastic, capable of stretching until the head (usually the first and always the largest part of the baby) is ready to pass through (see Figure 20-3).

Relaxation is the circular muscles' natural response to being nudged by the baby when the longitudinal muscles of the uterine walls begin to contract. If the mother is tense and fearful, her circular muscles tighten, blocking the egress of the baby and causing pain. The mother's task during this stage is to relax. Between contractions she may chat with her husband in the hospital room, read, or otherwise busy herself. When a contraction comes, lying back and consciously relaxing helps the dilation. Deep, slow abdominal breathing helps the baby rotate into position for passing out through the pelvic opening.

The average duration of labor was twice as long the first time (12 hours) as in subsequent births because the first dilation is the hardest (ACOG, 1965). "Natural childbirth" emphasizes advance preparation of the mother for dilation. Dr. Grantley Dick Read (1944) believed that fear of the unknown tenses the uterine circular muscles. Such fear is reduced by education and training for parenthood, giving the expectant mother confidence about the experience she is undergoing. Trained mothers deliver faster than

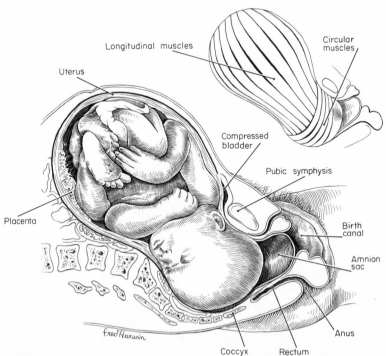

Figure 20-3. Fetus at Full Term and Uterine Muscles Involved in Birth

untrained ones. The time span from onset of labor to completion of delivery was 19 per cent shorter for first deliveries given the benefit of training (Thoms, 1950). Similarly, for all women subsequent deliveries tend to be easier after their muscles have once been stretched.

Even mothers and doctors philosophically committed to natural childbirth may use drugs to relieve pain and ease tension during dilation, especially for the first baby. During delivery itself, gas may be inhaled continuously or intermittently during contractions to ease the pain. Hypnosis has been used by some doctors with responsive patients to achieve similar results. Frequently the doctor aids the egress of the child by surgically widening the cervical opening (episiotomy) or using forceps to pull the baby out.

Delivery

While the cervix is dilating, the baby begins moving through the vagina or "birth canal" (see Figure 20-4). Rhythmic contractions of the longitudinal uterine muscles force the baby out, a push at a time. The mother may aid this process by gently "bearing down," voluntarily reinforcing the uterine contraction. During each contraction she can take several deep breaths and hold her breath at the peak of the contraction. Active cooperation with the birth process is hard work, but speeds up the delivery and gives the mother a sense of participation. Where medical authorities permit the husband to be present, the wife may appreciate his support and the husband no longer feels literally left out (Bradley, 1965).

Movement of the baby through the birth canal stretches the vulva. Panting like a puppy during emergence of the head prevents pushing at this time and insures a gentler delivery. If the mother has not had too much anesthesia, the baby emerges wide awake, and his spontaneous crying enables his lungs to fill with air and start breathing.

THE AFTERBIRTH. Discharge of the placenta along with the umbilical cord and membranes is called the "afterbirth." This occurs five to 15 minutes after the baby is born. Usually the mother is so busy holding or looking at her baby and discussing her experience that the afterbirth occurs spontaneously. If help is needed, the mother can contract her longitudinal muscles as in the second stage of labor.

CHILDBIRTH IN RETROSPECT. Mothers who remain conscious during childbirth often describe it as one of the most significant experiences of their lives. Mothers generally viewed it in retrospect as less painful than they had anticipated (Poffenberger, 1952).

Following childbirth, some women suffer a postpartum depression so

Figure 20-4. The Birth Process (photos copyrighted by the Cleveland Health Museum, reproduced by permission).

severe that they have to be hospitalized. Jacobs (1943) reported that this psychosis accounted for more than five per cent of all female admissions to mental hospitals. A mild depression in the form of a "blue day" is a common postpartum experience. However, the termination of the long period of expectancy and fascination with a child of one's own give most mothers a honeymoon-type of euphoria.

Hospitalization

Mothers are encouraged to get out of bed within 24 hours after delivery. By that time they have slept off much of their fatigue from the exertions of labor and delivery. Physical activity revitalizes muscular tone and physical energy, making it possible for most mothers to go home in three to seven days.

Most American hospitals assign mother and child to separate rooms. The baby is placed in a central nursery which only the nursing staff enters. Much of the responsibility for the baby is therefore assumed by the nurses, relieving the mother of full-time responsibility. This is an asset to overtired veteran mothers but deprives novices of the opportunity to learn how to care for their infants.

Some hospitals have "rooming-in" arrangements, placing the baby where the mother can see it and have easy access to it. Sometimes the baby is in a bassinette beside the mother's bed. Sometimes a tiny nursery is next to each hospital room so the mother can observe her child and get him at will. Rooming-in helps new mothers gain self-confidence. If the mother carries the responsibility for the child from the beginning (with the instruction and help of the nurses as needed), she gains skill in interpreting the child's needs.

If the baby has the full-time attention of its mother instead of sharing one nurse with the other inhabitants of the nursery, it is more likely to get attention when it needs it. The mother is able to feed, change, or cuddle the baby when necessary. This gives the baby a more comfortable transition from the uterine environment where its needs were met continuously. The mother is reassured to know that her baby's needs are not being neglected by harried nurses. Also, Thoms (1950) found that breast feeding gets off to a better start since the baby is fed when it is hungriest.

The Birth Crisis

The advent of the child must also be considered from the standpoint of what it means to the child to emerge from the uterus into the outside world. The prenatal environment is warm, secure, mobile, and sustaining. Casler

(1961) suggested that each of these characteristics has implications for infant care if the birth of the child is to be less traumatic. Warmth may be provided by contact with other human bodies. (Infant monkeys prefer warm mother substitutes to cold ones.) Babies enjoy being carried about on the mother's back or in her arms, sleeping beside her, etc. Security can be provided by holding the baby. Petting and caressing him also provide tactile stimulation similar to the uterine environment. The kinesthetic stimulation of the prenatal environment suggests the advantages of a cradle and rocking chair as nursery equipment. Carrying the child also has this effect. Finally, the continuous feeding of the umbilical cord is approximated by demand feeding after birth. Presumably the transition from uterus to nursery is difficult at best. But such efforts will minimize the birth trauma.

From Marriage to Family Living

As soon as the first child arrives, life at home changes so sharply that this is properly labeled a crisis, especially for the mother. These changes are not necessarily resented, but they are more drastic than at any other turning point in life, not excluding marriage.

The stronger the marriage, the less severe the impact of the first child. Dyer (1963) found that only brittle marriages were seriously endangered by the child. Similarly the impact was less severe for couples who (1) had prepared for marriage by taking courses in family life education, (2) had been married several years, and (3) had successfully planned the child so that it was wanted. Nevertheless, almost all of Dyer's middle-class couples, no matter how well prepared, found life harder than they expected after the child was born.

From Dyad to Triad

"Two's company, three's a crowd" symbolizes the difference between a pair able to give their attention to each other and a trio whose attention must be divided. Since a newborn infant is helpless and the mother is responsible for him, this trio lacks the symmetry of marriage. The child alters the power structure, the division of labor, and the interpersonal relationship generally of the parents.

REVISED POWER STRUCTURE. With the wife's withdrawal from the labor force, she becomes more dependent on her husband. The younger she is and the more rapidly she acquires children, the more the husband dominates:

> As the mother of a new baby, she gives up her job and is confined to her home by the heavy demands of child-care. Not only is she cut off from contact with her fellow workers but even the opportunity to participate in recreational activities and organizational meetings is impaired by her baby-sitting responsibilities. Under these circumstances, parenthood brings a sudden loss of resources to the wife combined with increased need for husbandly support. It is no wonder, therefore, that the wife's dependence increases (Blood and Wolfe, p. 43).

REVISED DIVISION OF LABOR. Shifting from full-time work outside the home to full-time housekeeping brings corresponding changes in the allocation of domestic tasks. When the mother has just given birth to her first child and is learning how to care for it, she needs her husband's help. However, once she recovers her strength and masters new skills, the division of labor becomes sharper. The husband does less housework now that his wife is a full-time domestic. The couple share fewer tasks and role specialization increases (Blood and Wolfe). For years afterward the husband is the only wage-earner, the wife the "chief cook and bottle-washer."

REVISED PERSONAL RELATIONSHIPS. Once children arrive, the honeymoon is over. No longer can husband and wife enjoy each other's unlimited companionship, especially outside the home. In Great Britain, ". . . before they had children, all couples had had far more joint activities, especially in the form of shared recreation outside the home. After their children were born, the activities of all couples had become more sharply differentiated and they had had to cut down on joint external participation." (Bott, 1957)

A baby inevitably alters the husband-wife relationship. Where before the two could focus on each other, now there is a distraction. Or perhaps it should be called an attraction. Both parents' attention is diverted to the child. His needs and interests compete with those of the partner. As more children arrive, each family member's slice of attention gets thinner. Never again, however, is the change as drastic as with the first child.

Objectively, the husband is inevitably "neglected" by the wife. Half of Dyer's new fathers recognized that they were sometimes neglected and 12 per cent more felt that they were "often" neglected in favor of the child. The more immature the husband, the more resentful he feels:

> Fred got pretty pouty when our first baby was born. I suppose he really was jealous of the attention I had to give Sally. If I had to get up from the table to do something for her, he'd make a crack about having to eat all alone. If I didn't have his dinner ready on time because of a

five o'clock feeding, he'd be irritable. I think his resentment has made him hard and demanding on Sally ever since.

While some ambivalence about parenthood is natural, most husbands release their wives to their children without protest. They recognize that this is one of the costs of having children. But if the husband does act like a sibling rival to the baby, strategy is called for:

> I think I've handled Irving's jealous streak pretty intelligently. While he's away at work, I lavish attention on the kids—playing games with them, answering their questions, telling them stories. Then when he gets home at night they're content to play by themselves, and I can listen to his report of the day's work just as though the kids weren't around.

Responsibilities of Parenthood

The trouble with infants is that they are helpless. In time they will become domesticated and eventually self-sufficient. But their initial impact is critical precisely because they make such total demands. Since these responsibilities fall primarily on the wife, it will simplify our discussion if we focus on what happens to her.

Loss of Mobility. A newborn infant can never be left alone and for some purposes not even entrusted to someone else. Most young parents have so little money that they can hire correspondingly few mother-substitutes. Substitutes can stay with the sleeping baby and feed him too (provided he's on the bottle instead of the breast). If the cost of sitters comes too high, time-out must be fitted to his majesty's schedule or his grandmother's: "I can't come then because he'll be asleep. . . . I'm sorry but that's when he's liable to need feeding. . . . I'll have to see whether I can get a baby sitter. . . . It depends on whether Steve can be home that night. . . ."

Sometimes the baby can go out too—sleeping peacefully in his bassinette or breaking into the middle of the party with demands for attention. The problem may be solved by grandmother's willingness to help (if she lives in the same town and enjoys *her* new role). Or husband and wife take turns sitting for the neighbors, replacing funds with barter.

Nevertheless, the fact remains that social life is curtailed, though the change has some compensations. The very fact of having a baby is a new activity—a kind of recreation as well as work. It is no accident that parents are often described as "proud." A baby represents not only a task but an achievement. He is "flesh of our flesh." Every development is an event for co-parent to hear about (and friends and relatives too). The first smile, first tooth, and first step highlight what is often a wearing but seldom a dull existence. If husband and wife go out less, they have more to stay in for. Instead of saying that social life is restricted, better to say it is revised (except for those to whom bright lights are indispensable):

> Now that Eileen is tied down more at home, I've about decided to give up Sunday morning golf. I'll miss it—especially at first when the boys call up and put the pressure on. But it will give me more of a chance to get acquainted with the baby. And I think Eileen will appreciate it too.

I have assumed that the baby also inhibits external employment. Nor is it just a question of his physical welfare. As we shall see in the next chapter, socialization depends on the child's emotional dependence established in infancy by the mother's devoted service. Not until well past infancy is extensive separation of mother and child advisable.

> We used to go out quite a bit but the money we spent that way goes to the baby's expenses now. I miss my job, too, though I wouldn't want to go back and have to leave the baby with someone. Just once in the two months since the baby came a neighbor offered to come in and we went out to the movies. Today I took the baby in the car and went to visit an old girl friend—it made me feel good to get a change of scenery.

No matter how interesting a child may be, adult companionship and outside stimulation are missed. For women who work right up to the last months of pregnancy, the change to constant staying at home is especially sudden. By inviting neighbors to drop in, taking the baby out in his carriage, having the husband take over in the evening so the wife can go out, feminine morale can be bolstered, enabling the wife to return to her chores with renewed vigor.

DISRUPTION OF ROUTINES. In the uterus the baby was fed continuously, 24 hours a day, and slept when he felt like it, unaware of day or night. Getting adjusted to the routines of the adult world takes time. In the meantime most babies are irregular and unpredictable. Only a lucky few are "good" babies who wake up, take their feeding, and promptly go back to sleep. But for every one of those, several ordinary babies want a middle-of-the-night feeding, fuss at odd hours, and change their "schedule" every few days. Worse yet are those whose "three-month colic" doesn't yield to treatment.

The average mother finds her sleep disrupted and her meals disturbed just when she is recuperating from the labors of childbirth. As a result, she is apt to feel chronically tired. In a Houston sample of college-educated couples, Dyer (1963) found the most widespread problems were tiredness, exhaustion, and loss of sleep, especially during the first two months. These complaints came from 87 per cent of the new mothers.

EXPANSION OF TASKS. At the same time that her duties become unpredictable, they balloon in scope. Whereas the last weeks of pregnancy there was hardly enough to do, suddenly there is too much. Now, the time required by the family jumps to the highest it will ever be (save when subsequent infants are equally young).

Figure 20-5 shows that infants doubled the hours required for housekeeping. In later years the burden eased as the youngest child became responsible for his own affairs and spent more time away from home.

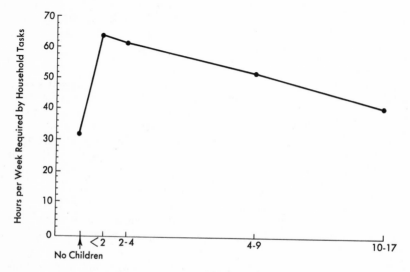

Adapted from Wiegand, 1954: 18.

Figure 20-5. Amount of Housework, by Age of Youngest Child

The key new task is feeding. To be sure, childless wives have themselves and their husbands to feed, but the complexities of feeding infants make adult requirements seem simple. Freudians believe that oral gratification is crucial to the child's early adjustment. Some experts advocate breast-feeding, self-demand scheduling (or lack of scheduling), and cuddling the baby during feeding. Although there may be values in each of these, Brody found that going through the motions of any one of them did not automatically provide the child with the intended satisfactions:

> Breast-feeding did not insure gentle procedures, intimacy or restfulness.
> . . . The endorsement of self-demand schedules was poorly related to
> satisfactory feeding experiences for either mother or infant. . . . Hold-

ing an infant did not necessarily enhance his comfort during feeding, and often it meant being held awkwardly or uncomfortably. . . . It appears that a mother may choose to breast feed, may try to give good physical support to her infant and may try to feed on a demand schedule —all . . . important criteria for adequate feeding—and yet she may unknowingly offer little satisfaction to her infant in the process (1956: 319–21).

This does not mean that methods of infant care do not matter but that the mother's feelings are at least as important as her methods.

In breast feeding, the infant's sucking is sexually stimulating, sometimes to the point of orgasm (M/J, 1965). Also the reduced tension in the breast as the milk supply is consumed is indirectly satisfying. Psychophysiologically, then, breast-feeding may be a pleasurable experience. Some women, however, resent being reduced to the status of a cow. Although bottle-feeding may be just as time-consuming, the responsibility can be shared with willing husbands and paid servants. Mothers who find themselves exhausted at two A.M. or who don't want to cart their suckling wherever they go, prefer bottle-feeding.

Experimental studies with infant monkeys suggest that the baby benefits primarily from being held during feeding, regardless of whether he is breast-fed or bottle-fed (Harlow and Harlow, 1966). One danger with bottle-feeding is that the mother may provide the baby with an inanimate bottle-holder rather than holding the baby herself.

Most babies settle down to fairly even schedules. Even so, they sometimes wake up ahead of schedule and scream for their milk. At other times they don't wake up when they are supposed to eat. For a few babies schedules never fit. Some infants need to eat oftener than others—and the mother can best determine this by observation (with clues from the doctor about what to look for). Just as adults occasionally feel hungry earlier or later than usual, it is natural for babies to vary from their usual pattern. Consequently, the rule of thumb is "when he is hungry." For both child and parent this is more comfortable.

Such complexities make infant care time-consuming. But long hours and difficulties do not mean that mothers feel unrewarded:

> Let's be realistic, a baby is a helpless, uncivilized, and demanding creature. He requires a lot of work, acceptance and patience on the part of mom. You're not exactly smiling after you change an active, husky baby's diaper, containing a special present, and he proudly grabs a handful and smears everything within reach. And what about the times when he burps curdled milk? You can brush your dress off, but the sour smell remains. And how long can you tolerate a baby's crying all night when he is teething, knowing there is nothing to stop him? And how much patience do you have or can you develop for the child who is a

very slow eater and spits out every other spoonful? Then, what about toilet training the little boy who thinks it much more convenient to wet and then has the exceptional talent of missing the deflector every time? And when you realize you are stuck for 24 hours every day, the picture looks pretty hectic. However, it is not all black. A tender smile can be very rewarding as well as the experience of watching a baby develop physically and mentally. Also, there is something about babies which is hard to define but makes them just something wonderful to have around.

ANXIETY ABOUT THE CHILD'S WELFARE. The heaviest responsibility of parenthood is not the time and money that must be invested but knowing what to do. Even experienced baby sitters never have the ultimate responsibility for a helpless infant that mothers face with their first child. In Houston, more than half the new mothers reported feeling inadequate and uncertain about whether they would be a good mother (Dyer, 1963).

The problem is intensified by the child's inability to talk. When he cries it could be hunger, wet diapers, diaper rash, too many blankets, wanting to be cuddled, or half a dozen other things. Worse yet is the panicky fear that he is seriously ill. One function of the pediatrician is to provide support and reassurance to new mothers. A more accessible source of encouragement is Dr. Spock's *Pocket Book of Baby and Child Care:*

> We know for a fact that the natural loving care that kindly parents give to their children is a hundred times more valuable than their knowing how to pin a diaper on just right, or making a formula expertly. Every time you pick your baby up, even if you do it a little awkwardly at first, every time you change him, bathe him, feed him, smile at him, he's getting a feeling that he belongs to you and you belong to him. Nobody else in the world, no matter how skillful, can give that to him (1946:3).

Yet even the best support from doctor, husband, mother, or married sister only partially allays anxiety. Brody found new mothers "conspicuously active but also erratic in their attentiveness, efficiency and sensitivity. They quite sedulously governed their infants' actions by stimulating, restricting, or instructing them. . . ." (p. 266) Even though ". . . experience itself did not necessarily provide mothers with sensitivity or consistency, experience was likely to increase the assurance, competence, and predictability of maternal behavior." (p. 271) Experienced mothers were not always *better* than inexperienced ones, but they were usually more relaxed.

Unfortunately, maternal anxiety can be felt by the child, creating a vicious cycle—the mother's tension increases the child's tension, producing symptoms that aggravate the mother's anxiety, and so forth. Mussen and Conger (1956) noted that many research projects have found more nervous symptoms in first-born children than in later-born ones. One of the worst infant symptoms is colic:

> Attacks of colic usually begin suddenly with an agonizing, loud and more-or-less continuous cry. . . . The abdomen is distended with legs flexed on the chest. Fists are clenched. The paroxysms end abruptly after minutes or hours, sometimes only to begin again (Lakin, 1957:7).

While colic was not confined to firstborn children, it was definitely associated with maternal anxiety:

> Mothers of colicky babies . . . more often cited feelings of nervousness and tension in response to the infant's crying. They expressed greater inadequacy in attempts to interpret the demand or need which was the source of the crying. They also more often complained of feeling ill at ease in handling their babies (Lakin, p. 29).

When mothers find themselves in such a quandary, they need external support. In Lakin's study mothers who had the most trouble with their infants got the least help from their husbands and mothers. Perhaps if they received more support, the vicious cycle could be broken.

The demands of children not only test the maturity of parents but promote it too. When all is said and done, the advent of children—taxing as it is—is primarily a joyous occasion. After the child-rearing years have passed, couples look back with nostalgia as much as relief. So despite the complications, children are welcomed.

21 *Parental Roles in Socializing Children*

The child-rearing responsibilities of parents have so many facets that this chapter and the next can hardly do them justice. On the other hand, there is some virtue in simplicity. This chapter focuses on socialization, the next on education. The distinction is arbitrary, for the terms are often used interchangeably. But there is a difference between teaching self-control and teaching anything else. Self-control has a negative emphasis--keeping oneself from antisocial behavior. The remaining goals of child-rearing are positive—skills and knowledge that enrich the life of the individual and society. Many basic principles of learning and teaching underlie both socialization and education. Nevertheless, the practical implications are sufficiently different to justify separate treatment.

The Importance of Socialization

Children are born with abundant potentialities but begin their lives undeveloped. The newborn child previously knew no distinction between himself and his warm, nourishing environment. Despite the birth trauma, he still considers himself the center of the universe. He is not aware that other people exist separately. Only gradually and painfully does the "Copernican revolution" dawn. First he discovers that his mother is not part of himself, then that his father is distinguishable from his mother. Later he discovers they have needs of their own and other roles besides mothering and fathering him. Finally, he learns that his role is not simply to receive but to give, and that he must temper his impulses to meet the needs of others. Only then is he fully human.

This humanization is socially significant because the child graduates from the family into the outside world. If he has been properly humanized, society will not have to defend itself from his aggressive impulses and can depend on him to conform to social norms. The fabric of society would soon crumble were more than a few of its new recruits unsocialized. The machinery of justice can cope with a few criminals, but society relies on the inner controls of the vast majority.

To the family the stress of coping with an unsocialized creature comes early. Long before society encounters what the family produces, parents must live with what nature brings. No matter how great their generosity, their tolerance, or even their masochistic urge to be martyrs, parents must curb their "little monster" if he is not to destroy their domestic tranquility. Every child is a potential "Dennis-the-menace." Although socialization sometimes occurs so swiftly that the threat is never apparent, its success is just as crucial to the family as to society.

To a child, being allowed to run wild seems delightful at first. But wild men end up in cages—either prisons or mental hospitals. The fact that society cannot tolerate unsocialized adults means that children who fail to learn conformity face a tragic future. For the child perhaps most pointedly, socialization is indispensable.

The Provision of Love

Paradoxically, socialization begins with gratifying the infant's needs. Later he must learn to limit his demands, but first he must learn to depend on his parents. Dependency is created as the parents provide food, clothing, shelter, warmth, and affection.

By and large, the nuclear family effectively creates dependency. Whenever a child depends on a single source of gratification—his mother—a strong bond develops between them. In societies with more complex family systems, a given child may be cared for by many women—aunts, grandmother, and older sisters as well as mother. In some societies he indiscriminately calls them all "mother." And so his dependency is correspondingly diffuse.

Few American infants are subjected to multiple mothering. Those who grow up in large families may be, especially if they are the youngest child. Those whose mothers leave them to numerous baby sitters may be too. By and large, however, in the crucial years of infancy American children have only one mother to depend on, so they cling to her with a vengeance. The relationship thus established is "primary." It differs, however, from the normal criteria for personal relationships since it is one-sided. The child at first is pure parasite, using the mother as means to the end of his own gratification.

Creating a selfish relationship seems like a back-handed way to socialize a child. Nevertheless, research and psychological theory suggest that gratification prepares for socialization in two ways: it provides the child with a sense of emotional security and it provides the mother with leverage to make him into whatever she wants.

The value of security is self-evident. The idea of leverage, however, deserves comment. Insofar as the mother gratifies the child's needs, she acquires by conditioning a secondary reward value. Having learned that she is the source of so many good things, the child is gladdened by the mere sight of her. Just as Pavlov's dog learned to salivate when a bell rang, the child learns to smile when his mother approaches. He wants to please her, not only to keep from alienating the giver of all good things, but to reward the person who means so much to him.

Once the child reaches this point, he is ready to be influenced even at the expense of needs that originally created the relationship. Once his attachment to his mother *for herself* becomes strong enough, she can frustrate his needs and he will sacrifice them for her sake. This does not happen without conflict. Nevertheless, if the parent-child relationship is close enough the transition can be made.

What is the evidence that dependency is the first step in socialization? One criterion for successful socialization is the absence of antisocial behavior (such as delinquency) due not simply to fear of punishment but to belief in social norms. Three major research projects dealt with each criterion. Bandura and Walters (1959) and Glueck and Glueck (1950) compared adolescent boys who were respectively aggressive versus nonaggressive and delinquent versus nondelinquent. Sears, Maccoby, and Levin (1957) compared five-year-old children with high and low consciences. From the previous discussion, we should expect dependency to be concentrated among nonaggressive, nondelinquent boys and high-conscience children.

For five-year-olds of both sexes conscience development was greater among dependent children (see Table 21-1). Moreover, conscience was accentuated when the dependent behavior of the child resulted from warm, accepting behavior by the mother. Sometimes children of this age are over-

Table 21-1. Conscience Development, in Relation to the Child's Dependency and the Mother's Acceptance

Mother's Acceptance of the Child	PERCENTAGE OF CHILDREN WITH HIGH CONSCIENCE	
	Less Dependent Children	More Dependent Children
Rejecting	13%	23%
Accepting	29	35

Adapted from Sears, 1957: 383. Reciprocal percentages of each cell had low conscience—e.g., 87% of the 47 less dependent, rejected children. The number of cases on which each percentage was based are as follows:

	47	53
	118	101

dependent in a desperate attempt to cling to mothers who basically reject them. Under these circumstances conscience development is impeded. Only when dependency springs naturally from a positive mother-child relationship does conscience develop successfully.

These processes apply primarily to boys. For little girls conscience development is smoother. Their tie to their mothers is more often accepted by the mother and respected by the father, leaving little to interfere with the socialization process. For boys, on the other hand, depending on the mother may be rebuffed by the parents as sissified. Fathers unsure of their own masculinity rush their sons into independence and punish them for childish dependence. These circumstances develop dependency-anxiety; that is, they become afraid of depending on anyone because of the punishment it brought in the past. With their dependency needs throttled, they fail to follow the parents' example. Though the parents hardly intended it, frustrating the dependency wishes of their children alienates them and leaves them at the mercy of their delinquent impulses.

For Bandura and Walters' teenage boys the pattern was similar. Their normal boys sought help, companionship, and praise from parents, teachers, and peers, showing that they were not afraid to establish close personal relationships. These dependency relationships had their origin in childhood when their mothers and especially their fathers were warmer toward them. Their fathers also spent more time in affectional interaction with them.

On the other hand, boys who later became aggressive were punished for seeking help from their parents until they learned to resist both their help and their companionship. They felt rejected by both their fathers and their mothers. To be sure, once a boy becomes aggressive, a vicious cycle of aggression and rejection is set in motion. However, the researchers concluded that ". . . the parents' retrospective accounts of their handling of their sons in early childhood and their descriptions of early parent-child relationships gave considerable support to the hypothesis that parental rejection and lack of nurturance are determinants of aggression." (p. 69)

Table 21-2 shows a similar pattern when the criterion for successful socialization is the prevention of delinquency. Dependency-producing warmth was provided by the successful parents, especially the fathers. From mothers the chief danger was not too little warmth but too little discipline. Many mothers of delinquent boys were warm enough but indulgent to the point of laxity, allowing them to run wild without interference.

The Imposition of Discipline

Besides love there must be discipline. If parents always gratified a child, he would grow up a parasite. If he always had free rein to do whatever he

Table 21.2 Non-Delinquency Rate, by Parental Love and Discipline

Percentage Not Delinquent, by Parental Relationship to Son	Father	Mother
Affection		
Warm	66%	57%
Indifferent	27	14
Hostile	16	13
Supervision		
Suitable	—	90
Fair	—	43
Unsuitable	—	17
Discipline		
Firm but kindly	91	94
Erratic	30	38
Lax	40	17
Overstrict	25	27

Adapted from Glueck and Glueck, 1950: 113–31. Reciprocal percentages were delinquent. *Source:* 500 matched pairs of delinquent and non-delinquent boys, ages eleven to sixteen, Boston area, 1940. For the total group of 1,000 boys, the delinquency rate was *ipso facto* 50% (much higher than the community-wide rate).

wished, he would never mature. To be socialized, restraints must be imposed. Bad behavior must be discouraged and good behavior encouraged. Rather than being allowed to grow up "naturally," the child must be trained to grow up socially.

The word "discipline" is often used interchangeably with "punishment," but that is a corruption of its root meaning of *instruction*. The goal of disciplinary intervention is to produce an individual capable of self-control through conscience and reason.

Setting Standards

To learn to conform to social norms, a child must know what those norms are. The parents' first task is to inform him. This happens in several ways. Parents are living demonstrations of adult behavior, models the child observes in action day after day. Secondly, parents verbally instruct the child about what behavior is expected. Lastly, they intervene in the child's behavior to point out which acts are desirable and which are undesirable.

Research by Bandura (1964) suggests that the parents' own example is probably a more powerful influence than either what they say or what they reward. Setting an example is particularly useful when parents wish to teach their children something new. Unfortunately, most parents are unaware of how their behavior looks to their children and concentrate on verbal and disciplinary teaching methods instead of on modeling.

CLARITY. If a norm is to work, it must be understood. Clarity requires consistency. If a norm is presented consistently over a long period of time not only by the parents but also by others, the lesson will be clear. Conversely, a norm is blurred if a parent is not consistent with himself but says one thing and does another or wobbles in his behavior from time to time. Confusion arises if the parents advocate contradictory norms, one strict, the other permissive or vacillating. If parents with different norms are not consistently present, standards will fluctuate with their comings and goings:

> While my father was gone, my mother had to rely on herself and she was always afraid she was making mistakes. She'd be very permissive for a time and then suddenly become very restrictive. Because we didn't know exactly what was expected, we became more unruly. We beat up the house and each other but couldn't look to mother for justice. We could persuade her into most anything relatively easily. Whoever could talk fastest and most convincingly won out. When my father was home, our family was in a confused permissive-authoritarian atmosphere. We knew he demanded obedience, so on the rare occasions he told us to do something, we were afraid to talk back. But mother usually let us do as we pleased, although on certain occasions she also was irrationally firm.

Peck (1958) found that consistent parental control produced a stronger ego (emotional maturity), a stronger conscience, and willingness to conform to social norms. Bandura and Walters found that mothers of aggressive boys did not consistently expect obedience:

> The mothers of the aggressive boys made fewer demands for obedience and were more inclined to overlook non-compliance. Consequently, their sons had become inclined to ignore their mothers and to obey only at times when extra pressure had been brought to bear. The mothers' mounting anger usually served as the cue that they expected compliance and that they would brook no further delay (p. 205).

Consistency here involved not *what* standard of behavior was advocated but *whether* the standard was to be taken seriously. Clarity requires consistency in both senses: a single standard and certainty that the parents mean what they say.

Consistent support from other people helped parents socialize their children (Zimmerman and Cervantes, 1960). Surrounding children with relatives and friends who shared the same social norms reinforced those norms. Conversely, conflicting neighborhoods and social circles undermined parental teaching through cross-pressures from different directions. The child in such circumstances became a "marginal man," not sure where he belonged or what was expected of him.

FEASIBILITY. The goal of socialization is to produce a mature adult. This can't be done overnight. Expecting too much is just as fatal as expecting too little. When standards are low, the child is not encouraged to progress. When they are high, he becomes discouraged because he cannot attain them. Standards should therefore be tailored to the child's age and readiness to learn. This is more easily said than done. Expectations must constantly be revised upward as the child grows older. As he attains each goal, a higher one must be set. Moreover, what is appropriate for one child may not fit a sibling of the opposite sex or of different ability or temperament. Appropriate standards stimulate each child to move ahead as fast as he is able.

Reasoning

There are two possible ways of imposing standards: authoritatively or rationally. A child naturally responds to new norms with the question "Why?" Why must he abandon his childish ways? Why must he curb his impulses? Why must he act differently? The easy answer is, "Because I said so." It is short and swift. It requires no thought. And it allows no room for argument. Yet research proves that taking the trouble to reason with the child pays off in the long run. Bandura and Walters' socialized teenagers were reasoned with significantly more than their aggressive boys. Reasoning promoted conscience development among both their teenagers and Sears' kindergarten-age children.

How does this happen? How do reasons make demands more palatable?

Authority creates a power struggle between parent and child. At first the contest is uneven. A young child is at the mercy of his parents. Nevertheless, he instinctively rebels, and the older he gets the more successful the rebellion. By adolescence, rebels do the opposite of what their parents demand, just because they demand it.

Parental authority also fails because it is external. It depends on the parents' say-so. When they are not around, the child has no basis for controlling his own behavior. Parents are not portable. But portable standards are precisely what every child needs. If he is to function independently, he must control his own behavior. Nothing external can do that for him. He needs something internal.

Reasoning takes the emphasis off parental coercion and puts it on the intrinsic features of the situation. Reasoning describes the circumstances in which particular actions are appropriate. It shifts the child's attention to the thoughts and feelings of those around him. It develops empathy, sensitivity, awareness of the needs of others. It helps him understand how he would feel if he were in their shoes.

When parents take the trouble to discuss issues, the child realizes that demands are not being imposed as punishment or because the parents are mean. When his why's are answered, he senses that his parents respect him; so their ideas deserve respectful consideration in turn. By contrast, how would you feel if your parents stretched their authority beyond the bounds of truth?

CHILD: Mother, why can't I go out and play?
MOTHER: It's raining, dear, and I don't want you to catch cold.
CHILD (looks out the window): But it *isn't* raining, mummy. It just stopped.
FATHER (overhearing interchange): Young lad, if your mother says it's raining, it's raining.

(Sears, p. 353)

For socialization to be successful, standards set by parents must be adopted by the child as his own. They must be internalized so that the child no longer conforms because his parents tell him to or because they will punish him if he doesn't or reward him if he does, but because he feels that he should. Given good reasons, that will happen sooner.

Reasoning involves the interpretation of values. It describes the values to be gained by adhering to norms. As values are interpreted, they make more sense and are eventually adopted by the child as his own philosophy of life.

Rewarding Conformity

Learning theory suggests that responses must be rewarded if they are to be reinforced. Some rewards come automatically. When a child imitates his parents' behavior, he feels grown-up, "like Daddy or Mommy." When he responds to requests, he can anticipate their pleasure (which makes him feel good). When he responds to reasoning, he has already been rewarded by their attention as they discuss the problem with him.

Nevertheless, how parents respond is vital to speedy socialization. If they pay no attention to how he behaves, his incentive to learn is weakened. If they treat him the same no matter whether he tries or not, why try? It is not enough to set standards and give reasons. Parents must find out whether the child performs as requested, and they must alter their behavior depending on how well he does. The better their response fits his performance, the more rapidly he will learn.

SUPERVISION AND TRUST. The first job is to gather information. If he was supposed to make his bed, mother must take the trouble to inspect it, or she must be sure he reports back when he has finished. One way or another, she must learn whether he did it or not. Table 21-2 showed that the better the mother's supervision, the more successful the socialization.

This is a delicate matter. Supervision can backfire. Checking up too much gives the impression that the child isn't really expected to do his job. By contrast, trust creates an expectation the child tends to live up to. Not wanting to let his parents down is a powerful incentive to good behavior. (Peck found mutual trust and approval between parents and children even more important than consistency in producing socially conforming behavior.)

> My parents let me believe that I was doing something because I wanted to, not because I had to. I was never allowed to stay out exceptionally late at night. I had to be in at a certain time, but I hated to have my parents tell me when I had to be in, each time that I went out. At first, they did. But soon they did not say anything more about what time I should be in when I left to go someplace. I knew what time I should be home, according to where I was going (which they always knew), and I was home on time. If I hadn't they would have immediately stepped in. In other words, I still came home at the appropriate hour (which wasn't always the time I would have chosen), but I felt more like an adult because they had not told me.

Supervision is important, but it must be carried out in such a way that it doesn't undermine the child's sense that he is expected to succeed.

REWARD VERSUS PUNISHMENT. If the child does well, he needs to be rewarded. Rewards increase his sense of accomplishment, compensate him for his trouble, and make him more likely to repeat the act.

The parents must react differentially according to the child's performance, to gauge the reward to the accomplishment. If he behaves poorly, he should be rewarded less—provided that the cause was lack of effort. Where performance is poor despite earnest effort, parents may have expected too much, and may need to coach him in how to proceed.

If the problem is not the standard but the child, if his failure stems from laziness or disobedience, if he is deliberately bad, is nonreward enough, or should he be punished? The answer is "no," at least as a general practice. Sears found that conscience developed slowest when punishments were frequent. Bandura and Walters' aggressive boys, similarly, came from families who used punishments of all sorts, especially taking away privileges, punishing physically (in early childhood), and nagging, scolding and ridicule. In general, punishment makes matters worse. Why?

1. Punishment hurts the child (either physically or psychologically) and creates resentment. This resentment interferes with the mutual confidence and trust essential to socialization.
2. It undermines the child's self-confidence, lowering his ego strength so that he feels discouraged and hopeless. At worst, he thinks of himself as a bad boy, unable to do right, expected to misbehave.
3. Punishment is perceived by the child as aggression. Especially physical punishment. When parents use their hands in dealing with him, he learns to use his fists. Becker (1962) found that physical punishment produced children with more conduct problems generally and who were aggressive both at home and elsewhere. Sears found that severely punished children responded with counteraggression directed against their parents or displaced onto others.
4. From the standpoint of learning theory, punishment is a poor way to teach desired behavior. Sears recognized that in certain circumstances, punishment (or the threat of it) is the quickest way to halt undesirable behavior. But "action control" is not the same as motivating future good behavior:

> The permanent elimination of changeworthy behavior, and its replacement by more desirable and mature forms, i.e., the control of learning, offers a different problem. To effect elimination of a response requires that it no longer be rewarded, i.e., that it not be followed by a satisfying state of affairs. The strengthening of desirable behavior can occur only when a satisfying state of affairs does follow. It has been found that the introduction of punishment into the *learning* process (as distinct from action control) creates some difficulty, for punishment *after* an undesirable performance breaks up the child's activity but does not give direction toward any specific new behavior, and may produce an emotional state that interferes with the learning of the desired substitute behavior. Usually, punishment provides a fairly inefficient means of nonrewarding the changeworthy actions, and offers a strong sanction that tends to impel some new (but not specified) kind of action, perhaps mainly an avoidance of the punisher (Sears, p. 318).

PHYSICAL VERSUS VERBAL SANCTIONS. Both rewards and punishments may be subdivided into physical and nonphysical categories. Physical rewards include pay and gifts. The commonest physical punishment is spanking. Praise is a verbal reward, ridicule a verbal punishment. Earlier we saw that reasoning aids socialization by facilitating the internalization of standards. The same principle applies here. Verbal sanctions promote socialization more than physical sanctions since the latter are external.

Figure 21-1 is not a statistical table but a diagram of the theoretical relationships between the two variables I have discussed: rewards versus punishments and physical versus verbal sanctions. It suggests that verbal

rewards are the most effective and physical punishments the least effective
(or perhaps even the most harmful) sanctions.

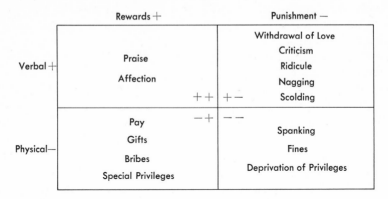

	Rewards +	Punishment −
Verbal +	Praise Affection + +	Withdrawal of Love Criticism Ridicule Nagging + − Scolding
Physical −	Pay Gifts Bribes Special Privileges − +	− − Spanking Fines Deprivation of Privileges

Figure 21-1. Socialization Effectiveness of Various Methods of
Discipline

Conscience—the Goal of Discipline

The goal of discipline is not conformity to norms in order to be rewarded by the parents but internalization. Internalized norms operate
via anxiety and guilt.

ANXIETY. After a child has internalized a parent-imposed norm (for
example, against stealing), his anxiety is aroused whenever he is tempted
to misbehave. Unconsciously, he feels a negative emotional reaction which
is the legacy of previous experiences of parental disapproval. He no longer
thinks of his parents but only of the wrongness of stealing. As a result,
his temptation is overruled and the act inhibited.

Anxiety prevents individuals from engaging in antisocial behavior. Lack
of enough anxiety to inhibit delinquent behavior was one deficiency in
Bandura and Walters' aggressive boys. They lacked anxiety particularly in
the sexual area where they were blasé.

For a few neurotic people, anxiety is excessive, preventing not only antisocial behavior but ordinary social interaction. It is possible to "oversocialize" a child, especially when parents fail to use enough reasoning to
enable the child to understand the difference between tabooed and proper
behavior. However, the chief danger in contemporary America is too little
anxiety rather than too much.

GUILT. Closely related to anxiety is guilt. If conscience is not strong
enough to prevent antisocial behavior in the first place, it may create guilt

feelings afterward. Guilt feelings have two uses: (1) they make the individual less likely to repeat his behavior; (2) they encourage him to undo his "crime." Guilt feelings are a form of self-punishment which makes deviant behavior less rewarding and less likely to recur. If restitution is possible, a guilt-ridden individual will attempt it even if no one knows what he has done.

Poorly socialized children feel less guilty than well-socialized ones, even though the former's crimes are far more gross than the latter's. Bandura and Walters' well-socialized teenagers felt guilty and ashamed in the few instances when they were aggressive toward parents, peers, or teachers or after they committed minor delinquencies. On the other hand, their aggressive boys felt little guilt even after flagrant misdemeanors.

Guilt, like anxiety, causes trouble when it is excessive. Some people need psychotherapy to reduce their anxiety and guilt. However, where parents fail to inculcate a strong enough conscience to produce anxiety and guilt, psychotherapy can accomplish relatively little. In appropriate amounts, guilt and anxiety are signs of successful conscience development.

Behavior Control—Pending the Growth of Conscience

"What to do until the conscience comes" is one of the problems faced by those who try to salvage conscience-less children (paraphrasing Redl and Wineman, 1951). The same problem faces all parents when children are young. In some respects the latter problem is worse because a toddler lacks not only a conscience but speech. Hence verbal methods of reasoning and praise are ineffective.

An infant is no problem, because he can't get into trouble. Once he begins to crawl, however, and especially after he learns to walk, he can create serious trouble for himself and others. How can he be handled during the period between walking and talking?

DISTRACTION. A child doesn't learn anything when he is distracted. He simply turns from one activity to another. If the distraction is skillful, he may not even realize that anything was wrong with his behavior. For a very young child, incapable of understanding or learning, distraction is the easiest way to get him to shift from undesirable to desirable behavior. The only danger is that the latter may reward the former so that he learns to repeat precisely what he wasn't supposed to do! After language is acquired, distraction becomes obsolete. Henceforth, parent and children confront issues head-on, rather than bypass them.

ISOLATION. Sending Johnny to his room may have either a punitive or therapeutic intent—with correspondingly different effects. As punishment, isolation comes close to rejection. The child feels unloved and excluded from the family circle. His natural response is to kick and scream, or weep and mope. His objection to confinement testifies to his need to re-establish contact with the family. If his desperation increases his parents' determination to isolate him, a vicious cycle ensues.

But some children need isolation at certain times. Those who are nervous and high-strung get overstimulated in groups. They talk louder and act more wildly until they lose control. When a child gets "high," removal from the group provides a chance for calming down. If parents recognize what is happening, they may be able to intervene before they lose their temper. Firmly but calmly, they may be able to get across to the child the feeling: "This is not punishment but a good move—an opportunity for you to recover your equilibrium." Communication is enhanced by going with him, explaining what is being done and why. Brevity reduces the chances of making matters worse by slipping into an argument. Though he may not respond immediately, interesting playthings may sooner or later distract him from thinking about the group he has left. In such ways the point may be made that isolation is not rejection.

In families who use isolation therapeutically, children learn to appreciate their need for cooling-off. As they grow older, they recognize their oversensitivity and retreat to solitude when groups threaten their equanimity.

SPANKING. While distraction and isolation may be useful solutions to problems that have already arisen, some situations are so dangerous that they must be prevented in advance (or when they almost happen, prevented from ever happening again). Physical safety is the main problem—how to keep children away from fire, water, and moving automobiles. Sears found that most parents relied on environmental controls for this purpose. They put up fences, locked doors, hid matches and poisons. They supplemented preventive measures with constant vigilance, since the most innocent-appearing situations are exploited by youthful ingenuity in unexpected ways. Some hazards, however, cannot be removed. Hot stoves are the traditional example. To teach a preverbal child to avoid such hazards, spanking has dramatic value. Like distraction, however, spanking obsolesces with the advent of speech.

Sons and Daughters

So far I have ignored the fact that children come in two sexes. Bronfenbrenner's research (1961) suggested that boys and girls need to be treated differently for best results. The chief danger for boys is that they will be undersocialized, but many middle-class families oversocialize their daughters. To avoid these dangers, parents need to give their sons more affection and discipline than their daughters. They need to limit the extent to which they reject their daughters when they misbehave (since girls are so sensitive that "a little rejection goes a long way—and very soon too far").

These prescriptions run counter to the usual tendencies. Most parents are free and cool with their sons, but strict and warm with their daughters. Yet the aggressiveness and independence of boys requires more vigorous discipline and warmer affection if they are to be socialized adequately.

Father Role and Mother Role

Two parents are better than one, and the fact that parents come in both sexes makes their duality even more valuable. Nevertheless, more fundamental than the differences are the similarities in the tasks of fathers and mothers.

Similarity

The main socialization tasks for parents are providing love and imposing discipline. Historically these tasks were assigned to different parents—love to the mother and discipline to the father. Research by Moulton (1966) suggested that such differentiation reduces the influence of parents over children. The father's discipline becomes coercive and the mother's love seductive. Only discipline from a loving parent can be accepted and internalized by the child. Only parents concerned with the child's progress toward maturity can avoid infantilizing him with their love. Hence, fathers and mothers ideally play similar roles, uniting love and discipline. The quality of their behavior cannot differ greatly if the child-rearing is to be effective.

Differentiation

The chief difference between fathers and mothers is in the time devoted to child-rearing. Mothers who are home full-time have far more contact with children than husbands can.

MOTHER ROLE. Most mothers prefer not to work while their children are young. Though they like to get out occasionally, even half-time work would be too much. That can wait until the children are in school. Meanwhile, motherhood is a career in itself.

What does it mean to make a career of mothering? For one thing it means taking time to play with the child. At first he appreciates being cuddled, rocked, sung to, and talked to. Not that he understands the monologue, but out of such attention grow feelings of warmth and acceptance. Later he wants stories read to him, games played with him, and chances to "help" with the housework.

Career-mothers take advantage of opportunities to increase their knowledge. They read *Parents'* magazine, go to child-study clubs, and attend lectures by child psychologists. How much does one have to know to be a good mother? Some women with little education but deep emotional resources do a superb job. Nevertheless, knowledge paves the way to understanding—particularly in unusual situations.

Career-mothers work to provide better facilities and programs for children. By organizing cooperative nursery schools, teaching Sunday School, and helping with the PTA, they help their own children as well as others.

Finally, career-mothers are prepared to turn elsewhere for help. When a child needs special help, they take advantage of professional resources. They use community facilities not only to help their children but to improve their own functioning.

A word of warning is in order to career-mothers. Any career can become too absorbing at the expense of other interests, jeopardizing the balance on which mental health depends—especially motherhood. Other careers have the safety valve of time at home, away from the job. Even doctors who spend their evenings reading medical journals change settings from office to home. For mothers home is where the job is. When children go to bed, there are still dishes to be done and piles of pressing.

Some mothers can forget their work only by escaping from the house. Others can more philosophically let the housework slide while they relax with husband, TV, or reading. Some relief is indispensable for maintaining resiliency.

Taking motherhood too seriously hurts both mother and child. From this source comes "smother love" corroding children's spontaneity and initiative. Wise mothers know when to stop mothering and let their children roam. Remembering their other roles as wives and individuals is the easiest way to rediscover perspective.

FATHER ROLE. That fathering is a part-time role is taken for granted. Most fathers come to their tasks unprepared. Confronted with their first child, they feel all thumbs. The arts of pinning on diapers, supporting a baby's neck, and burping him after his bottle have to be learned. But these tasks are rewarded by the responsiveness of the child and the appreciation of the wife. Some husbands spend as much time as their wives doing things with their children (since wives are preoccupied with housekeeping). Reuben Hill describes children as "mother deaf"—they hear her preach so much that they ignore what she says. The father's unique contribution is his freshness. This gives his words special authority and enables him to mediate in mother-child conflicts. Children feel able to confide in him, and he can interpret his wife's needs to the younger generation.

For such reasons fathers play crucial parts in children's socialization. For example, Peterson (1961) found that maladjustment among kindergarten children was caused at least as much by fathers as by mothers. Inadequate fathers were weak and ineffectual or cold and excessively strict.

For boys in particular, fathers are indispensable. Growing up to be a man requires a masculine model with which to identify. Children need warm, effective parents of their own sex to emulate. Those who lose their sex-role model through death, divorce, or long-term separation are handicapped. For families blessed with both sons and daughters, parents of both sexes are much to be preferred.

Collaboration

Dual parents are advantageous not only to children but to the parents themselves, as those who bear the burden alone know all too well. A second parent provides support, consultation, and relief for the first.

SUPPORT. The confusion for children when parents hold different standards has already been mentioned. Solo parents are better off than those who disagree over disciplinary methods and standards. Battles are easy because children raise so many issues. Indeed when their children are preadolescents and adolescents, parents quarrel over children even more than over money.

When parents speak with a single voice, two parents are better than one. If only one takes a stand, it can be dismissed as a parental quirk. When two parents say the same thing, the message is more impressive.

CONSULTATION. Parents don't always know what stand to take. When situations are new, complex, and baffling, a consultant in the home is a welcome resource. To be able to talk the situation over with someone who knows the situation equally well provides perspective.

Perhaps mothers provided with effective consultation, support and relief would find their anxiety about child-rearing reduced. Becker (1962) found that high maternal anxiety had a devastating effect on children, making them aggressive toward others. One can easily imagine a mother and child trapped in a vicious cycle of mutually reactive anxiety and aggressiveness, a cycle disruptable only by collaborative intervention from the father.

RELIEF. For mothers saddled with children all day, the greatest value of the partner is for relief. When the husband comes home, she has "held the fort" all day. Five P.M. is characteristically the mother's most fatiguing time of day (Wiegand and Gross, 1958). Just when fathers arrive, mothers have to prepare dinner. To be sure, fathers can be tired too, but the change of scene makes children a relief instead of work.

> I used to think we had a regular jinx in our house the way Jan always burned the steak the few times we could afford it. I criticized her pretty ruthlessly for her carelessness. Recently though, I've realized she gets distracted by the children while she's doing the cooking. They get fidgety at that time of day. So the next time I bring some expensive meat home I'll see whether taking over the kids myself solves the problem.

Parents generally come to each other's rescue when the energy of one ebbs and patience wears thin. Since children have more energy than adults, they need two parents to keep up with them. Being a good parent means being sensitive not only to the child's needs but to the partner's. Especially when one parent is having difficulty imposing discipline on a recalcitrant child, the other can make a fresh approach.

Living with Children

Important as discipline is in handling critical situations, it would be a mistake to think of it as the chief way parents guide their children. The time devoted to discipline is a small fraction of the total. More often parents and children interact spontaneously with no thought of methods or goals. Most of the time children simply live as members of a family, inevitably but unconsciously influenced by the behavior of father and mother.

The parents' example and their activities with the child are far more influential than their occasional disciplinary intervention. As long as the underlying tone of the parent-child relationship is positive, he automatically absorbs their way of living, their values, and their philosophy of life. The largely automatic nature of this process reduces the pressure on parents. They don't have to shape their children deliberately all the time. They can have faith in the future. If they are emotionally mature, their children will grow to maturity too, through the guidance that human beings spontaneously give each other.

22 *Parental Roles in Educating Children*

As civilization becomes more complex, the task of parents enlarges. No longer is it enough for children simply to avoid misbehavior. The opportunities of modern life are too rich to be missed. Yet missed they will be unless children are introduced to them and motivated to take advantage of them. This chapter focuses on the parents' opportunity to teach children what they know and to motivate them to learn even more.

Parental Aspirations and Children's Potentialities

Just as parents set standards for behavior, they set goals for learning. If children are to achieve their full potential, goals must be high (else they are not goals), but not so high as to discourage effort. Parents may betray a child in either direction—by underestimating or overestimating his ability. If they underestimate it, he will be satisfied with less than his best. If they overestimate it, he may not try because they will be disappointed.

The task is to encourage the child to do his best. This is easier to express in attitudes—of conscientiousness, diligence, and ambition—than in concrete goals. Nevertheless, goals are more tangible than attitudes, so as he grows older, parents must suggest goals as well: learning to typewrite, making first chair in orchestra, going to college or, more specifically, going to a first-rate college.

Achievement motivation is one consequence of successful socialization. Rosen and d'Andrade (1959) found that parents of highly motivated boys were more interested in their sons' performance and set higher goals for them. Without that goal-setting, their motivation would have been weaker.

Only among aristocrats can children take their status for granted and rest on their parents' (or grandparents') laurels. Among those near the top but not quite at it, the motivation to move upward is strongest. (Rosen and d'Andrade found achievement motivation in sons of lower-middle-class parents even higher than in upper-middle- and upper-class families.)

Achievement motivation is more characteristic of males because parental aspirations are higher for sons than daughters. For instance, parents stressed college training more for sons—higher education was "nice" for girls but indispensable to male occupational advancement (Aberle and Naegele, 1952).

Respect for the Child

We have already mentioned the danger of overestimating a child's ability. Morrow and Wilson (1961) found a similar distinction between "encouraging" and "pressuring" with respect to achievement. High-school boys did better in school when their parents encouraged achievement but didn't "overinsist" on it. The distinction is subtle but important. If parents push too hard, the child is miserable. If they are always "harping on" his grades and insisting that he study, he is more apt to rebel than achieve.

Parents who overinsist are usually self-centered. They want the child to fulfill their own dreams, to accomplish what they didn't, to become someone they can be proud of. Rosen and d'Andrade found that it was particularly easy for *fathers* to crush their sons. Mothers were less dangerous, perhaps because they were more apt to be affectionate than authoritarian, or to combine pressure with love.

Parents need to encourage their children to do well. But in the last analysis, the child must do the achieving. He is not likely to try very hard unless he chooses the courses, avocations, and vocation where he is to invest himself. Parents must respect the child's autonomy—his existence as a separate person—at the same time that they express high hopes for him and support his efforts to fulfill them.

Parental Responsiveness

One of the saving graces in children is that they have their own drives. They are not clay, dependent on the potter to be fashioned. They are alive and growing. Children are blessed with boundless curiosity. Especially little children. As soon as they can talk, they want to know what makes things tick. They ask so many questions that parents tire of answering. They jabber so much that mothers close their ears in self-defense.

The Cultivation of Curiosity

Children are curious because they know so little. They haven't learned yet not to ask questions. When parents tell children to stop pestering them or when they pay no attention to questions asked, children learn all too soon that it doesn't pay to be curious—it gets you into trouble or it wastes your breath. Curiosity is a priceless asset, worth more than all the encyclopedias, atlases, and dictionaries a family could buy. Home equipment will never be used if the spark of curiosity is quenched with parental cold water.

The best way to cultivate curiosity is to reward it—which means taking the trouble to answer every question. With examples from religious education, here are several principles designed to keep curiosity alive:

NONPOSTPONABILITY. How seriously parents take each question determines whether a child will come back for more. If he doesn't get a proper response, he may turn to playmates for answers, inadequate as they may be. Or he may decide that asking questions is fruitless and lose that eagerness to learn which is essential to mental growth. Hence, when Johnny asks, "Where is God?" it pays to take time to answer.

Sometimes parents are so busy they can't spare the time. But they should give their reasons for not answering. Provided their excuses are genuine and rebuffs do not come too often, curiosity should survive. To some extent parents can count on questions coming up again if they're not answered now. But only partially. Those who want the best for their children must seize every opportunity for discussion. It's too easy to say, "I'm busy now—come back later." Later may never come. Not only may the child hesitate to ask again, but his attention-span is so short and his distractability so great that he can hardly be relied upon to use a raincheck.

APPROPRIATENESS. Answers must be geared to the child's ability to understand. This is partly a problem of vocabulary. Children are capable of learning complicated concepts, but new words must be defined as they are used. It doesn't do much good to talk about "salvation" without explaining what it means. Sometimes a shorter word does just as well and saves time.

HONESTY. Does appropriateness mean that religion must be brought down to the child's level? Must God be depicted as a bearded patriarch so children can "picture" Him? Not unless that is the parents' conception. Settling for anything less than the parents' own beliefs is distracting in the same way the birds and bees distract in sex education. Parents should give what they believe to be the truth, no matter how difficult it seems. As time goes on, the child's understanding will grow, provided he has been started on the right track.

Take, for example, the question, "Where is heaven?" If parents believe heaven is not a place but a divine-human relationship, it may take awhile to convey the difference. Yet parental attempts to explain their point of view are appreciated by the child, no matter how little he understands at the moment. Honest efforts leave the way open for growth in understanding.

Parental Elusiveness

Sometimes the problem is not the complexity of the subject but its unpleasant aspects. For instance, race or death or sex.

Racial questions are toughest for Negro parents because they reflect a dawning awareness of being an outcast. Hence parents try to avoid the problem by putting off answers or waiting until the child is "old enough." Even then Goodman (1952) found parents tongue-tied over how to explain, confused over the terminology to use, and unwilling to use certain words at all.

Negro parents in a prejudiced community know their child is going to discover eventually that he is a second-class citizen. On the theory that well-balanced individuals can take a lot of punishment, some try to postpone the day of disillusionment:

> So far my four-year-old boy doesn't know that he's a Negro but I'm afraid he's going to find out awfully soon. Last week when we went shopping downtown he dashed into the first elevator he saw and I had a tough time explaining why we should change to the freight elevator without confessing the real reason.

This boy will soon discover segregation. Then, he'll ply his parents with questions excruciatingly difficult to answer. Beyond admitting the facts of prejudice and discrimination, they can reassure him of their love and appreciation. Moreover, they can share their understanding of the causes of prejudice and help him see "the man" as a human being like himself.

These tasks are difficult but not impossible. Parents who take a growing child into their confidence establish a we-feeling that can hardly be equaled as a base of operations in a bewildering world.

Negro parents would have fewer problems if more white parents discussed human relations with their children:

> I told my boys very early (two years on) that the world has many countries in it besides our own. Each country has its own people. There

are people of various colors of skin, hair, eyes, and so forth. They speak many languages and differ in their dress and ideas about things, but certain things are common to all people and important to everyone on earth—being treated kindly, having enough to eat, enough money for necessary things for each family, roads, schools, homes, and care for the sick.

We've had hundreds of short discussions in the evenings about aspects of these topics and talked about the importance of the different countries and peoples learning to get along without bombing each other. By the time the boys reached school age they both had an orientation to their place in the world and some of the crucial issues of our day—war and peace, racial discrimination, population problems, and conservation issues. I didn't use big words. We talked about things in daily life that relate to the big problems—neighborhood quarrels, Negro schoolmates, overcrowded city streets and polluted rivers not safe for swimming. Talking about these things has given the boys ideas of which kinds of work they may want to take up, which problems they'll want to attack.

How about death? Some parents try to protect their children from knowing about the death of a neighbor or pet. Yet the fact of death is no more avoidable than the "facts of life." Better for parent and child to discuss death openly than for the child to feel something is hush-hush, too terrible to mention.

No matter what happens in the world around, children who are loved feel secure. Studies in Great Britain during World War II showed that those who stayed in bombed-out London with their parents were less afraid and upset than those evacuated to country estates away from their families (Freud and Burlingham, 1943). As children hear of war, crime, and death, they want to know how their parents feel about these strange events. Precisely how parents interpret these troubles counts less than the child's sense that "we're in this together." This sense of security provides a basis for living in a world where one can never be entirely sure what the next minute will bring.

WHAT PARENTS ACTUALLY DO AND DON'T DO. Faced with embarrassing questions, most parents find excuses for not answering. Sears summarized parental policies toward five-year-olds' sex questions under the heading of "information control." Parents generally believed in *not* satisfying their children's curiosity:

Some mothers were clearly antagonistic to what they called the "modern doctrines" that they felt were advocated in some child-training books and newspaper columns. . . . When a mother was opposed to giving any sex information to children, however, she had to be able to give the child some other explanation when a younger sibling was born. One said to her son, "Gee I'm getting fat. I guess I'll have to go away for a week or so and go on a diet. . . ." Others spoke of "putting in an order for a baby at the hospital."

Most of the mothers were willing to tell their children a little more than that about the reproductive process, however. At least, they described the presence of the new baby inside the mother. Mothers who had tried to be completely free and open in their information-giving usually found, however, that there was a point beyond which they were unwilling to go in answering the child's questions. . . .

It is safe to say that not one family in our sample was completely free and open in the discussion of sex with their young children (Sears, 1957: 190–92).

Closely related to parents' unwillingness to answer embarrassing questions was their tendency to avoid sexual terms. Sears called this "avoiding labels." This policy limited the answers parents gave and limited even more their educational initiative:

Many families got along without any names for the genital area, using vague terms of reference like "it" or "there." . . . When communication was necessary between parent and child, one of the babyish toileting terms current in the family was used, as in a child's "Mommy, my wee-wee hurts." . . . Despite the absence of explicit language, however, mothers and children seemed to be able to communicate with each other fairly effectively about some events in the intellectual shadowland of sex, as was illustrated in the following interchange between mother and son:

The mother saw the boy rubbing his penis. She said:

"Johnny, what are you doing?"

"Nothing, Mummy."

"Well, stop it, then."

"O.K." and he stopped.

While some parents avoided any sort of labeling in the area of sex, some did provide their children with names for the genital parts of the body. We did not encounter anyone, however, who helped the children to identify the *emotional* states related to sex. Many mothers said to a child something like: "You're angry and upset now. We'll talk about it when you're calmer." But none, as far as we could tell, said: "You're feeling sexy, that's why you're acting like that." (Sears, pp. 189–90)

Information control and nonlabeling were part of a pattern of avoiding the issue. Sears' parents also used (1) distraction rather than discipline to curb unwanted sexual behavior and (2) indirect, nonsexual arguments for conforming to sexual norms (for example, telling the child he would catch cold if he didn't get dressed when the real issue was nudity). Sex education—whether intellectual or practical—was restricted in most families.

Middle-class parents—despite their general emphasis on education—are no freer than lower-class parents. (In one Iowa sample, less than half the parents at either social level gave full and frank replies to sex questions from their daughters [Burchinal, 1960].)

Table 22-1. Major Sources of Sex Information for Boys and Girls

Source	Boys	Girls
Mother	25%	71%
Father	23	5
Companions	40	43
Teachers	41	47
Reading	36	44
Total	165%	210%
Number of cases	234	218

Adapted from Lee, 1952: 471. *Source:* Oregon high-school students. Totals add to more than 100% because some students had more than one source.

Daughters were better off than sons. Table 22-1 shows that most Oregon mothers told their daughters at least something (even if only to forewarn them about menstruation). Many sons, however, got no sex education from either parent, even though fathers communicated with sons more than with daughters. The fathers were so reticent that the sons were just as apt to be informed by their mothers as by their fathers (in spite of the fact that parents normally take more responsibility for a same-sex child). Because of parental failure, many boys received their *only* sex education from companions or teachers, whereas for most girls these were supplementary sources. Lee believed that in many parts of the United States parents and teachers gave even less sex education than in Oregon, making companions elsewhere even more important.

Some subjects are more embarrassing than others. One study showed that mothers told their daughters about "where babies come from" and about menstruation. However, girl friends were the chief source of knowledge about touchier subjects like intercourse and contraception (Angelino, 1958).

Kingsley Davis (1940) suggested that intercourse would always be a difficult topic between parent and child since it impinges on the incest taboo (the ban on sexual relations between parents and children). He cited the observation of Malinowski that "Even among the essentially 'unrepressed' Trobrianders the parent is never the confidant in matters of sex." (1927: 36) One cannot expect either parents or children (especially adolescents) to find sex as easy to talk about as other topics. Nevertheless, the question remains: how much *should* parents respond to their children's sexual curiosity?

Responsive Sex Education

Some parents are less reticent. Generally speaking, responsive parents are good socializers in other respects. Parents with the happiest marriages were more apt to tell the truth about sex, whereas unhappily married parents often brushed off their children's questions and even more often responded with untruths (Chesser). Similarly, a permissive approach to the sexual problems of preschool children was used by mothers who were emotionally warm and seldom spanked their children (Sears).

Children who receive their sex education from their parents conform more closely to social norms than those whose parents fail them. Table 22-2 shows that parent-educated British women were more restrained pre-maritally and had the happiest marriages (another proof of successful socialization). On both counts, reading was next best, followed by other adults, leaving companions the worst source of sex education. Similarly, unwed mothers of illegitimate children especially often received their sex information from companions rather than from either mothers or teachers. (Vincent, 1961). Moreover, they generally had less sex information and more negative attitudes toward sex than other girls.

Table 22-2. Consequences of Alternative Sources of Sex Education

| | MAIN SOURCE OF EARLY SEX EDUCATION | | | |
	Parents	Reading	Other Adults	Companions
Proportion without premarital intercourse	70%	61%	60%	54%
Proportion with exceptionally or very happy marriages	77	69	62	53
Number of cases	325	136	245	436

Adapted from Chesser, 1957: 175. Source: Married women patients of British physicians. Reciprocal percentages had premarital intercourse or less happy marriages, respectively.

Sex education may be difficult for parents, but it pays off in better socialization than any other source. Parents who wonder whether sex information stimulates sexual promiscuity can see in Chesser's data quite the opposite. Presumably those parents inculcated their values along with factual answers. By contrast, children whose curiosity is not satisfied by their parents are likely to find that companions (especially male peers) "teach" quite differently, actively encouraging promiscuity.

Because parents often feel tongue-tied, it may be useful to illustrate possible responses to sex questions. For a child the question, "Where did I come from?" is innocent enough. He is oblivious to the connotations stirred up in his mother's mind. All he wants is the answer to another question—like the one he just received to "Where did this book come from?" The most useful answers are simple and direct. There is no one "best" answer as long as it satisfies the child and is accurate.

The following answers to typical questions are not prescriptions but samples:

Q.: Where did I come from?
A.: You grew inside of me.
Q.: Where? (*One question leads to another—sooner or later.*)
A.: In a special place called the uterus. (*References to tummy or stomach are apt to create images of being eaten.*)
Q.: Where is the uterus?
A.: Inside here. (*At this point a simple diagram of female internal anatomy may help. If the mother is not an artist, she may use an encyclopedia or a biology book.*)
Q.: How did I get there?
A.: Mommy had a tiny egg which joined with a tiny sperm from Daddy and grew into a baby.

More drawing may be needed to show where the egg came from, and so forth. Some parents wonder how soon the male role should be introduced. Describing reproduction is difficult enough without having to discuss intercourse! Yet this is another of those eventual discoveries that can be taken in stride most easily when the issue first arises. Most children are satisfied with brief answers and pursue the question further only at intervals. On the other hand, a concentrated barrage of questions probably signifies an inquiring mind more than morbid preoccupation.

No age is too young for the facts of life. If a child is old enough to ask questions, he is old enough to be answered. The answers, however, should fit the questions. One about reproduction need touch off no more detailed a lecture than one about automobile production. Yet neither lecture involves much danger of "overdosing" the child. As soon as he is tired, he will turn his attention elsewhere. Answers too complex to be understood do not harm him. They just waste the parents' energy.

Parental Stimulation

Curiosity is not entirely innate. Parents can supplement inborn motivation in at least two ways: by their own example and by exposing children to other educational influences.

The Family Environment

Parental stimulation begins the day the child is born. Research on child development suggests the value of stimulating all the senses: seeing, hearing, tasting, smelling, and feeling (Casler, 1961). Culturally deprived children experience too few of these stimuli to develop adequately. As the infant gets older, he needs freedom of movement, and toys which he can manipulate. These experiences enable him to learn with his body. Finally, social stimulation is important. Both parents and peers contribute to growth.

One caution, however. It is possible for a child to be so overstimulated that he withdraws in self-defense. Human beings need rest as well as exercise.

Parents set a persuasive example for their children. If parents enjoy hiking in the woods, children become aware of wildflowers, birds, and sunsets. If they go to the ball game, sports become salient. If classical music is played on FM or stereo, children not only observe their parents' enjoyment but acquire a musical repertoire by osmosis. Most home learning is automatic. It does not require instruction but is an environmental by-product.

Schramm noted a similar process with television tastes:

> . . . if a parent views educational television, then the child is almost sure to do so; and if neither parent does view educational television, then the child is almost sure *not* to do so. This is a very potent kind of influence. We venture to say also that if parents use the Sunday press conferences and discussions, then the children are almost sure to do so when they come to be old enough. Example is the best persuader. . . . (1961: 182).

Another aspect of the home is toys and play equipment. Perceptiveness and creativity develop as children experiment with paper, cardboard, building blocks, crayons, paint, paste, clay, and tape for assembling them.

Parental Initiative

Although most of what children learn at home is accidental, learning can be intentional. Parents concerned to enrich their children's lives can involve their children in educational activities at home and expose them to educational resources outside the home.

EDUCATION AT HOME. Bossard and Boll (1960) stressed the impact of family conversations on children who sit around the dinner table day after day, year after year. They suggested that "in many respects, family table talk may be likened to a university seminar on family culture that continues for a number of semesters." During the meal, parents may ask about school, discuss the day's news, conduct quiz games, share family mail. These conversations transmit the family culture from generation to generation.

Parents must take the initiative in discussing sex if the child does not. Responsiveness is fine as far as it goes, but it must be replaced by responsibility when questions cease. Religious parents take this responsibility especially seriously. (Chesser found that the more religious parents were, the more apt they were to be the main source of sex education for their children.)

Sex teaching must be done by precept rather than example. The sexual side of marriage is private, so sex education cannot rely on interpreting the meaning of events but must be undertaken deliberately.

As puberty approaches, information about menstruation and other physiological changes is needed by both boys and girls. The problem is not simply one of biological information. Parents can assist adolescent emotional and sexual adjustment. Growing up can be interpreted as challenging and rewarding. The menstrual cycle can be described as an aspect of reproduction, rather than as an illness or "curse."

Parents are also important to adolescent boys in coping with sexual feelings which surge to a peak at that age. Most of all, adolescents need help in deciding between right and wrong in relations between the sexes. When parents have the respect and confidence of their children, their ideas are welcomed.

Teaching about marriage has a place too. Seldom is this instruction given systematically. Yet parents who want their children to be well prepared communicate their philosophy and techniques of married living. When their children are in a receptive mood, some parents talk about the importance of unselfishness and forgiveness in marriage. Others comment about domestic events. When everyone has a good time raking leaves, a word about the satisfactions of cooperative work helps children realize why the afternoon has been fun. When parents have a scrap, children profit from observing the process of reconciliation and being told how the trouble developed in the first place. By taking children into their confidence, parents help them understand how people get into and out of difficulty. Such knowledge is worth a dozen wedding presents.

Parental initiative requires not only exposing children to desirable influences but shielding them from undesirable ones. For example, children need both positive and protective intervention in their televiewing. I found (1961) that high-status parents encouraged their children to watch educational programs (even beyond their usual bedtime) and controlled the types of programs watched. Crime and violence were especially forbidden. Middle-class parents also censor the movies their children attend and other influences to which their children are exposed—inside and outside the home.

I have often noted how children imitate their parents. Bandura (1963) found that they also imitate actors and even cartoon figures portrayed on film.

Table 22-3. Imitative Aggressive Behavior of Children in Response to Portrayals of Aggression

Ratio of Stimulated/Unstimulated Aggression by Sex	PORTRAYAL OF AGGRESSION			
	None	Cartoons	Filmed Actors	Live Actors
Boys	1.0X	4.1X	6.1X	7.3X
Girls	1.0X	4.3X	5.0X	7.9X

Adapted from Bandura, Ross and Ross, 1963: 6. *Source:* 96 children enrolled in the Stanford University Nursery School, all of whom were subjected to a common frustrating situation before being observed for aggressive behavior imitative of what they had seen.

Table 22-3 shows that although live actors stimulated aggressive behavior the most, film actors came a close second. Even cartoon portrayals of an aggressive cat significantly increased children's aggressiveness in comparison to a nonstimulated control group. The authors noted that most parents of these children "were quick to discourage their children's overt imitation of television characters by prohibiting certain programs or by labeling the imitative behavior in a disapproving manner." Without such parental controls, television would be a more destructive influence.

Perhaps the chief trouble with televised violence is not its brutality (which, after all, is censored) but its casualness. Children are not harmed by tragedy presented with real feeling. But they become calloused when injury and death are committed remotely and impersonally on the television screen. In this sense, perhaps, children need to be encouraged to take televised violence more seriously, not less so. They need to sense the pain suffered by the victim.

Berkowitz (1964) believed that filmed violence affected the viewer differently depending on whether the victim was seen as deserving his fate. "Crime does not pay" portrayals of victims getting their just deserts were likely to provoke the viewer to behave aggressively. Berkowitz believes that films of justified aggression lower the viewer's inhibitions against behaving violently.

These findings indicate that filmed violence affects children variously. They raise doubts about the idea that fictional violence provides cathartic release of aggressive impulses. Rather it provides a contagious model of aggressiveness.

EXTERNAL RESOURCES. Many community resources are optional and depend on parental initiative: concerts, plays, museums, libraries, travel. Another resource is extracurricular schools and lessons—religious schools, music lessons, art lessons, and so forth.

How much initiative should parents take? With formal schooling, parents don't wait for the child to express interest but insist that he attend. The fact that school is compulsory makes it more acceptable.

In optional areas parents must exert stronger pressure. Having lived longer, parents know what is good for the child. When they insist that he take music lessons, they are doing him a favor (which in the long run he will probably appreciate). To be sure, they cannot force him to be educated against his will. They must make learning as attractive and as rewarding as possible. Nevertheless, their initiative legitimately includes extracurricular learning.

Parental Structuring of Learning

Homework and practicing cause friction in many families. Friction can be reduced by minimizing distractions, providing encouragement, and rewarding achievement.

Minimizing Distractions

Parents must safeguard the child's opportunity to study. For efficient studying, peace and quiet are necessary. To find them, there may have to be special places for study or times when younger siblings and even parents are not allowed to make distracting noises (even if those noises are labeled "music").

TV is a powerful distractor. Televiewing and studying cannot go on in the same room at the same time. Nevertheless, well-socialized adolescents have enough self-control to shift voluntarily from screen to print. Schramm classified those who read a lot and watched seldom as "reality-oriented":

> In the sixth grade the reality-oriented group is very small, but by the tenth grade it has grown a great deal. When we studied children in this group we found that they are different from others in that they have internalized the social norm of self-betterment, deferred gratification, and activity which is considered, in our culture, to be typical of the upward mobile middle class (1961: 172).

Parents who endow their child with achievement motivation can leave the rest to him. He will disdain ordinary television and prefer reading.

Nevertheless, in borderline cases and on borderline occasions, parents may still have to protect wavering resolves from undue temptation.

Temptation comes not only on the screen but in the flesh. The attractions of the opposite sex can pre-empt study time too. While a book on marriage is not likely to oppose dating flatly, work and play must be kept in balance. Parents may have to forbid dating on school nights if homework is to be completed.

Encouraging Practice

Getting started is easier when it is ritualized. If homework always comes right after dinner, less struggle is necessary. Routine scheduling from day to day and week to week provides another framework (besides physical quiet) within which lessons get done more easily.

Except for providing suitable conditions, parents must beware of taking too much responsibility. It is easy for parents to nag about getting started. For children as much as for anyone else nagging stiffens resistance. When other activities interfere with the usual schedule, parents may ask the child when he plans to do it instead. This gives him a choice and yet commits him to a specific objective.

By and large homework is a solitary business. Sometimes collaborators are needed and parents can help coach. When an exam is pending, parents can ask review questions. When the child is stumped, they can help him find his way through unfamiliar problems. But only sometimes. The farther he advances, the harder it is for parents to keep up. Perhaps both generations can search together. As long as the child shares in the learning process and doesn't have work done *for* him, he learns along with the parents.

Music-practicing benefits more than homework from regular collaboration. Even in studying the piano, four-hand duets are sociable. If neither parent can play, one is still a welcome companion on the bench. For any other instrument, accompanists are valuable. Few instruments except the piano sound pleasant alone the first year or two. Stringed instruments sound awful at first. Parents can make the early stages more satisfying by surrounding the child's feeble instrumentation with supporting chords and melodies.

Rewarding Achievement

When parent and child practice together, learning is intrinsically rewarding. Children relish the companionship of a parent almost any time.

Of course, the parent will have to hold his tongue when tempted to criticize. He must be supportive if he is to be helpful.

Regardless of whether the parent actively helps, the previous chapter suggests the importance of rewarding the child if he is to continue trying. To sustain a high level of motivation, parents must be interested in what he does. As he progresses, they must reward his achievements with warmth and approval. For example, when the orchestra gives a concert, parents must be in the audience. When a project is brought home from school, they must take the trouble to look at it. When the Scouts hold a Court of Honor, they must attend. Whatever talent they want to encourage, they must invest themselves as well as their money. Teacher-approval is not enough, for teachers seldom have a close relationship to students. How parents react—whether indifferently or attentively—determines whether the child's interest will be sustained and encouraged.

23 *Family Life*

A family is not only an instrument for rearing children. It is a group of people living together. It must maintain its equilibrium—a task complicated by the continually changing ages of the members. The task is eased by a suitable environment—inside and outside the home.

Facilities for Family Living

Physical facilities in house and equipment plus social facilities in neighborhood, school, church, and recreational sites form the family's environment.

Housing the Family

Studies of consumer preferences have revealed the kind of house the average American family hoped to buy:

> It is a new six-room, three-bedroom house with basement and garage. It is of "modified contemporary-traditional" style with a lot at least 70 by 100 feet, on a curving street with full-grown trees. It is set amidst houses different from, and somewhat more pretentious than, itself. The house contains three bedrooms, a quiet living room, a fully equipped kitchen large enough to eat in, a dining or "family" room, and 1½ baths with colored tile walls and separate tub and shower facilities. Preferably it has a porch or flagstone patio, and an extra den or guest room. It is inexpensive to heat and easy to maintain (Foote *et al.*, 1960: 103).

478

The home either encourages or limits joint activities. The amount of space, the allocation of rooms, and the kind of furniture affect family behavior. Needs for space and furniture change over the life cycle. Newly-weds tend to buy furniture that is comfortable for themselves and stylish for their friends. Inspired by *House Beautiful,* they install wall-to-wall carpeting, soft upholstery, and fragile lamps. For a year or two they enjoy beauty and comfort. Then comes the baby. He dumps food on the carpet, knocks over the lamps, and scars the furniture—not because he is vicious, but because he is young, clumsy, and adventurous.

CHILD-PROOFING THE HOME. Wear and tear can be decreased by child-proofing a home. Given a child of specified age and vigor, the damage wreaked depends on the vulnerability of his environment. Washable paints and scrubbable wallpaper can protect the walls. Smart upholstery may be covered by washable slipcovers to catch spilled food and grimy fingerprints, or replaced by plastic or leather. Coiled springs in easy chairs and sofas are notorious invitations to bouncing when mother isn't looking. Foam rubber cushions are more durable. When the baby pulls himself up to a standing position, he fingerprints white drapes or tears lace curtain but not rugged, figured materials.

Even the wooden surfaces of tables and chairs are vulnerable. Polished dark wood shows scars and dents from weapon-wielding hands. I found that parents with "traditional" child-rearing philosophies preferred mahogany furniture, but that "developmental" parents preferred the lighter woods and rougher finish of colonial furniture. As one mother expressed it, "The more beat up our pine coffee table gets, the more lived-with it looks" (Blood, 1952).

Loose articles in prechild living rooms may be stored away "for the duration." Bric-à-brac sometimes frequent the flat surfaces accessible to climbing youngsters: potteryware, glassware, and other smashables. Two-year-olds cannot be expected to leave such objects alone or handle them safely. A few years on the shelf leaves children and parents less worried and the breakables intact for the day when the children will be old enough to live with them.

Anyone can store away decorative objects, but few families can afford to replace their furniture when children come. Hence, couples need to anticipate the consequences for themselves, the furniture, and their children when they embark on interior decorating. As one parent stuck with handsome but impractical furniture said, "If I had only known then what I know now about children!"

> At first my fiancé and I were not planning our home around the children we are hoping to have. We had been thinking about a French Provincial house with a recreation room in the basement for the kids. I never

stopped to think that the children won't want to be in the basement all the time and would be hard on the kind of living room we had planned. Now, however, we are planning somewhat more sturdy furniture for the first part of our married life, and perhaps when our children are old enough, we can have our French Provincial.

Picture windows can't be stored away, but anxiety about baseballs can be alleviated by insuring them. No matter how heavily insured or how indestructible the house, parents must teach their children to respect property, not to spill food, not to write on walls. The purpose of child-proofing is not to eliminate the need for property-socialization but to minimize the consequences of the inevitable failures.

Parents don't want to live in a gymnasium. They have needs, too. Hence, one room of even a small house may be reserved for parental hobbies, relaxation, and homework. Also, common rooms may contain concessions to adult comfort and grace that limit childish boisterousness.

INSULATING COMPETING ACTIVITIES. Child-proofing is designed to cope with the temporary destructiveness of unsocialized toddlers. The need for environmental durability diminishes as the last child becomes old enough to be taught. However, as long as multiple family members share the same house, they are liable to come into conflict. Conflicts can be minimized by strategic architecture, room-use planning, and equipment acquisition:

> Conflict in the American home often centers around use of scarce physical facilities. The current trends to a second car, a second television set, and a second telephone result . . . in decreased tension for family personnel who can now use parallel facilities simultaneously instead of having to compete for control of single channels. Similarly, the newfangled recreation room provides the rest of the family with a retreat when daughter decides to throw a party in the living room, taking the tension off competition for "the only room in the house where I can entertain my friends." (Blood, 1960)

Some conflicts intensify as children get older. They result not from failures in socialization but from the development of adolescent interests. A 1957 survey of adolescent girls by the Gilbert Youth Research Company found that conflict over the telephone was almost universal if only one line was available. Since the average teenager used the phone more than an hour a day, the demand on facilities outran the supply when the whole family was home. The larger the family, the larger the number of bottlenecks, with bathrooms at 7:30 A.M. another prime example.

Conflicts may be reduced by zones of privacy within the house. Noises that would antagonize a father reading the newspaper or a daughter doing her homework are tolerable when muffled by closed doors. Contrary to the theory that "open planning" creates sociability, kitchens without walls and rooms that "flow" into one another often create irritability. The din of kitchen machinery (dishwasher, disposal, washer and dryer) needs to be segregated by walls and closed doors from the rest of the house. The sound of music needs segregation too. If family members want to practice the piano and listen to television simultaneously, equipment must be dispersed in separate rooms. A "music room" equipped with record player, radio, television, and piano is fine for a bachelor but prevents parallel musical activities for families of more than one.

SPACE ENOUGH FOR GROUP ACTIVITIES. Where family members need to be in the same place at the same time, conflict is reduced by allowing ample space. Although the living room is an obvious example, the kitchen is more apt to be skimped. Some experts recommend a so-called "efficiency" kitchen in which stove, refrigerator, and sink are placed close together to save steps for the cook. The trouble is that children like to play there and families to eat their ordinary meals there. An efficiency kitchen either makes multiple-person activities impossible or frays nerves as people literally bump into one another. Foote (1960) found that almost no one (with the possible exception of newlyweds in small apartments) preferred small kitchens, and most people who criticized their kitchens wanted more space for preparing and/or eating meals.

Choice of Neighborhood

Neighborhood interaction is so intense that choosing neighbors is almost like choosing a marriage partner. Social classes, nationality groups, religious groups, and races tend to be segregated. Just as mixed marriages create extra problems, so do mixed neighborhoods.

Rosenberg (1965) found that it made little difference whether children lived in a completely homogeneous neighborhood or in a balanced neighborhood. For example, Protestant children in half-Protestant neighborhoods had just as much self-esteem and just as few psychosomatic symptoms as those who lived in all-Protestant neighborhoods. But Figure 23-1 shows that when children were a minority (25% or less) in a "foreign" neighborhood, their emotional health suffered.

One reason why children in alien neighborhoods suffered more psychosomatic symptoms and lowered self-esteem was that they were more often teased, left out of things, or called names by other children. However, active discrimination wasn't the only consequence of living in a dissonant religious context:

What is also probably involved is the insecurity which stems from lack of integration in a group, issuing from a feeling of social isolation, a sense of being "different," an absence of "belongingness." (Rosenberg, 1965: 72)

Ideally, then, parents will choose a neighborhood where their children will have enough support from their peers to feel socially accepted.

As bad as uncongenial friends, however, are no friends at all. Neighborhoods go through cycles in age composition. New subdivisions swarm with preschool children who don't have enough baby sitters to take care of them. Ten years later there is a surplus of baby sitters (Henry, 1953). A decade more and the teenagers are gone, leaving middle-aged parents behind. If

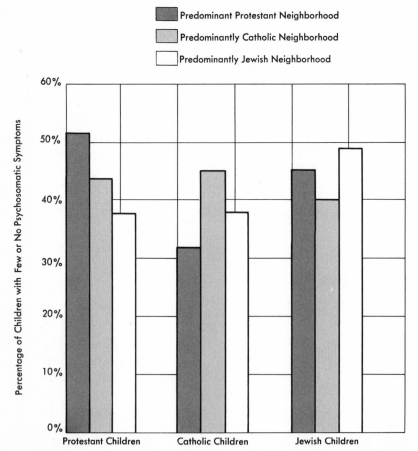

Adapted from Rosenberg, 1965: 67 and 73. *Source:* Random sample of 5,024 juniors and seniors in New York State public high schools.

Figure 23-1. Psychosomatic Health of Children, by Predominant Religion of Neighborhood

a family with young children moves in at this point, there may be scarcely a playmate for blocks around. Choosing a house entails choosing playmates and schools for the children. Parents therefore must look beyond the four walls of a prospective house.

Family Problem-Solving

Although problems can be reduced by appropriate facilities, an occasional clash of wills is inevitable. The intimacy and emotional intensity of family relationships make conflict more likely than in casual groups. Mixed sexes and ages complicate the task of solving problems.

Large families in small houses have the most conflicts. The more permissive the parents, the more noise and clutter per square foot (Blood, 1953). No one "issue" is most troublesome, but little frictions pile up into emotional tautness. The mother interacts with her children at the same time that she tries to keep up with the washing, pressing, cleaning, cooking, and dishwashing. Explosions come when so many demands coincide that not all can be met:

> Last night Dan came home late to supper. The kids were hollering for their dessert and he wanted his supper, so I felt like an automat. He wanted me to sit down and hear about his troubles, but I had to tell him we'd talk about it later. He said, "I can see that you're not one bit interested in me. All you think of is the kids!" Then I blew up and told him off. I told him that if he had to go through everything I had, he wouldn't feel like listening to someone else's troubles either.

Parental tension infects children too, making them quarrelsome and irritable. Family crises are common on that bane of every mother's existence: rainy days. Mothers long for the end of school vacations, house-confining colds, and dreary weather so children can leave them for a while.

Resolving Conflict over Scarce Facilities

Where facilities cannot be enlarged, families may establish priority systems:

> If the bone of contention is the television set, a schedule for the whole week, born of a major showdown, may take the place of petty conflict "every hour on the hour." If the scarcity has been financial, the record of decisions takes the form of a budget. Here the mutual recriminations sparked by overdrawn bank accounts can be obviated by advance planning about where the money is to be spent (Blood, 1960).

Priority systems determine which family member has precedence. For example, the hardest working member of the family should have his choice of recreational activities, the rarest viewer of television the chance to watch what he wishes, the newest swimmer the choice of lakes to learn in. Taking turns may be fairest when competing interests are equally strong. Even for interests that are unpredictable, systematic solutions are sometimes available. For example, answering the next phone call may be the job of whoever received the last one. Whatever the problem, systems end personal conflict once they are agreed on.

ADULT PRIORITY. Historically, the problem of family living was solved by a caste system. Parents were the privileged caste. "Little children should be seen and not heard." Children were expected to conform to adult wishes, work hard, and beware of bothering busy parents. As long as everybody practiced adult priority, the caste system worked well. Any system works best when it is taken for granted. That is no longer the case with adult priority.

Today family patterns differ. Parents who seek to perpetuate their priority must contend with their own and their children's knowledge that the rights of parents have gone the way of the "divine right of kings." Aware of competing democratic ideas, parents cannot wield authority arbitrarily without misgivings. Sensitive to possible criticism by others, they can no longer issue orders with equanimity.

Meanwhile, children have discovered that they have rights too. Hence, parental authoritarianism is at least resented if not resisted:

> Mother and I had a showdown last week because she insisted on reading my letters from Dave. She maintains that no matter how old a girl is— whether 21 or 31—she should still confide everything to her mother. She *is* my mother, and I don't want to flout her. But I'd feel more like confiding in her if she didn't insist on everything.

THE CHILD IS KING. As often happens in history, the pendulum moved from one extreme to the other. Rebellious children resolved to do better by *their* children and sensitive experts defended the "rights of infants."

If parents were not at the same time persons, breadwinners or housekeepers, and husbands or wives, they could devote themselves exclusively to serving their children. But since parents have other roles, the "children-first" motto gets people into trouble. Children's demands are often insatiable:

> The children always want something different from what they get—it's most frustrating and I have no patience with them. I hate people who swear, but I say under my breath, "Damn those kids!" One busy day

last week Jane wanted me to wash her doll's clothes. That wasn't so bad, but next the clothes had to be pressed just so. After that she insisted that I sit down and mend a frayed hem on the doll's dress. At that, my patience just gave out.

When parents abandon their own interests and responsibilities to their children's desires, trouble results. When a child becomes a tyrant, his mother feels like a martyr. The more time and energy she spends on her children, the more she begrudges the sacrifice of her own interests. Her grudge is nursed during moments of despair and wielded against her children in moments of anger: "Look at all I've done for you—and you don't appreciate it!" Such diatribes confuse the child after what seemed to be enjoyable times together. The end result is the parent-child tension Della Cyrus (1946) caricatured so well:

> Actually the intense, mutually exhausting emotional and physical relationships which develop between mothers and preschool children in the typical urban family lead inevitably to that worst of all maternal sins, overmothering with undercurrents of hostility, and that most fatal of all child responses, overdependence with undercurrents of resentment.

Substituting tyrannical children for authoritarian parents does not improve the situation. However, priorities for adults or children are not always carried to the extremes we have portrayed. In moderation they reflect differing values with less disastrous consequences.

THE PERSON-CENTERED FAMILY. Priority need not be assigned to either generation. Every family member can be important. This means that childish interests are limited by parental interests (and vice versa). For example, a happy medium can be found between the child's desire to keep his parents home at night and the parents' enjoyment of social life. In adult-centered families parents go out whenever they want, limited only by their baby-sitter budget. In child-centered families parents feel it is their duty to stay home. If they do go out, they feel shame-faced and the children resentful. Compromise lies somewhere between—not so much in a fixed quota of nights as in a working balance between the parents' and children's wishes. With no customary priority for either generation, families must find other bases for resolving intergenerational conflicts.

SIBLING RIVALRY OVER PARENTAL AFFECTION. The toughest conflicts are not between generations but between siblings. Jealousy is almost universal. In families where it is not apparent on the surface, it often crops up in fantasies and dreams. Jealousy originates in a young child's resentment at being displaced by a new baby. Previously (if he was the only child) he was the center of attention, but now an intruder gets the attention. "Losing" his mother makes him bitter. Sears (1957) found that first-born children were unusually aggressive toward their parents. Younger siblings, in turn, attacked the next oldest child. In each case rivalry focused on the adjacent child as chief competitor.

Sibling rivalry cannot be entirely prevented. However, the traumatic consequences of sharing one's parents with a stranger can be minimized. Children who are informed of the impending arrival have time to get used to the idea and may become eager for his delivery. Parents can give a displaced child extra doses of time and affection to allay his fear of losing their love.

Every child needs to feel loved and accepted as much as his brothers and sisters. Many an emotionally disturbed person was slighted by parents who favored another. The best parents are occasionally accused of favoritism, but they can do much to make this accusation undeserved. Most important is unreserved affection for all their children. Beyond this is fairness and appropriateness in handling each child.

Because siblings differ in age, equality is not always appropriate. Suppose a six-year-old would like to be able to stay up like his nine-year-old sister. He can be assured that he too will be able to stay up when he's nine. In practice, however, older children often "run interference" for younger siblings in securing age-graded privileges. Parental resistance weakens by the time later children come along. Such changes are often begrudged by the older child:

> When Paul and I were both in our teens, he would often go to my parents saying, "You never let me do that when I was his age." I know it is true that I was allowed to do more things at an earlier age than he was. However, I did not like him to say such things to my parents. We always got along best when they were not at home, for when they were not around we were not vying for their attention.

Some parents tighten up with subsequent children, feeling they learned a lesson from earlier permissiveness. Whichever way they change, the child who is treated more strictly is likely to complain. If parents communicate to each child that they care even though they cannot satisfy every demand, conflict diminishes. By adolescence it may even vanish:

> Our parents' methods of dealing with us have varied with the individual and his apparent needs. This has resulted in three siblings who love and respect each other and their parents, and yet who are as different as three kids in the same family can be—interest-wise. Each of us has been encouraged in areas of our own interests and abilities instead of made to feel that we had to keep up with each other.

Perhaps siblings accept each other in adolescence because they pair off *against* their parents. In any case, parents should know that rivalry is more or less inevitable. Like any conflict, sibling rivalry provides opportunities for learning how to resolve friction, to share—in short, to get along with other people. This goal cannot be reached in "one easy lesson." But when parents handle their children with fairness, flexibility, and understanding, lessons in human relations are learned from sibling squabbles.

Family Decision-Making

Chapter 17 dealt with decision-making processes in marriage. With children added, everything becomes more complicated. Decision-making becomes a family affair.

When children are small, they can be taught how to make decisions by being given choices between alternatives which are equally acceptable to the parent. For example, they might choose between a red or yellow shirt to go with black shorts, any of the canned soups on the kitchen shelf for lunch, or any piece of penny candy in the store.

As children grow older, they want more say in family decisions. Many parents consult children before making family decisions and give them a voice in the decision-weighing itself. Some families organize a formal council, with regular meeting times and perhaps a constitution and by-laws. Families thrive on internal communication, regardless of whether the channels are ritualized or spontaneous.

Discussible questions are almost limitless. Important are those that affect the whole group: where to go on vacation, which house to take, whether to buy a new car or build a garage for the old one. More routine are raising the children's allowances, when they should go to bed, or where to drive on Sunday afternoon.

> Our family was quite democratic. When problems came up or decisions had to be made, we sat down and decided things together. When our neighborhood began to change and our whole block became almost entirely Negro, we all sat down and discussed whether we should move. My parents felt that the decision should be mainly made by my sister and me. We felt that we didn't want to move and so we didn't.

The preceding case might more accurately be labeled child-priority than complete democracy. It illustrates the variability and flexibility that alter democratic decision-making under differing circumstances.

Bossard (1950a) believed that decisions based on everyone's point of view are wiser, more enthusiastically supported, and contribute more to family solidarity. Group discussion trains children in problem-solving methods they will use when they become parents. Meanwhile, children appreciate having their views considered and tend to rebel less against their parents.

Despite the advantages of democratic decision-making, it is rarely applied to family finances. One study showed that "high-school students on the whole did not participate in the money-management process of the family," nor did they seem to want to:

> They seemed to trust their parents' judgment and considered their decisions as final. . . . They were given allowances which they apparently considered adequate to cover their needs. Beyond that, only those discussions over money matters that directly affected them held their interest (Moore, 1953).

Perhaps that is as it should be. Perhaps family democracy does not require universal participation in every decision, but only the right to be heard when one wishes. If so, decision-making methods should vary with the circumstances. Rather than group decision-making, perhaps flexibility should be the hallmark of family democracy. Family councils serve some purposes well but not all. They need not be a bottleneck through which all decisions must be funneled.

The Division of Labor

We have seen that adding a child to the family doubles the mother's housework. As children grow older, they learn to take care of themselves, at least to the point of making their beds and picking up their toys. How much they help with the housework depends on the mother's philosophy. At first, clumsiness and irresponsibility make children more nuisance than help. Yet their natural desire to help (like their desire to know) is an asset worth cultivating. When children want to cook or paint or mow the lawn, they should be encouraged to learn how and given the necessary instruction. Even though the immediate task is delayed or botched, this motivation is too valuable to rebuff.

When children don't volunteer to work, should they be forced? Task-training and home chores are now optional, designed more to benefit the child than to relieve the parent. They are intended either to prepare him for marriage roles or to benefit his character. On the latter score there is some doubt. Harris (1954) did not find that assigning more tasks made children any more responsible. On the other hand, responsible children regularly did a few tasks: boys emptied the garbage, girls helped with the dishes and prepared food for cooking, and both sexes kept their rooms neat.

The greatest danger for modern families is not that children will be spoiled by too few tasks but angered by too many. When parents give children the tasks they dislike themselves, negative reactions are predictable:

> Such chores are not shared by parents and children working together, but are forced on children as essentially persons of less significance or privilege than adults . . . consequently, children come to dislike them, do them only under pressure, and evade them whenever possible (Women's News Service, 7/20/60).

Perhaps such circumstances lie back of the discovery that Waterloo, Iowa, high school girls fought their parents over housework more than any other issue (Women's News Service, 2/6/57).

If children are to help around the house, parents must motivate them more skillfully and rely less on dictation. Children respond positively in emergencies (as when the mother is ill) or when help is necessitated by family size. Under ordinary circumstances they enjoy companionship in work as much as in music. Family "work parties" to weed the vegetable garden or rake the lawn are fun. When children work well, parents must recognize and reward their accomplishments with appreciation and perhaps compensation. Fundamentally, however, urban parents cannot expect children to take as responsible an attitude toward housework as they will be forced to when they become adults. The technical know-how learned from chores is less important than their basic socialization in achievement motivation through other channels.

Family Recreation

Weekends are family times for special projects, picnicking, swimming or skating, and visiting friends and relatives.

Rituals

Families develop patterned ways of doing things which give continuity to family living. Bossard's study of autobiographies disclosed that recreational rituals were the most common form (Bossard and Boll, 1950).

For students at San Diego State College the most important family rituals were dinner together at Christmas, Thanksgiving, Easter, and other holidays; opening Christmas presents and decorating the tree; and gifts, cards, or parties to celebrate birthdays, Mother's Day and Father's Day (Klapp, 1959).

Other recreational rituals include the Wednesday night television program everyone anticipates, the family night at gym or swimming pool. Many families develop bedtime rituals:

> When Larry was three, he always wanted the same songs in the same order: "Little Boy Blue," "Twinkle, Twinkle Little Star," and "Rockabye Baby," while Alan prescribed fifteen kisses and one bear hug.

Sundays may involve unfailing visits to grandparents or dinner guests after church. Summer vacations may become ritualized pilgrimages to the family cottage.

Rituals sometimes arise spontaneously. A few are consciously engineered. More are handed down from generation to generation. Bossard believed that the ritual-produced piling up of happy memories contributes to family integration and to family pride. Klapp found solidarity highest in families with the most rituals.

Companionship

Family rituals require the participation of every family member. But families contain too many ages and sexes to make community of interest always possible. Subgroups can have a special closeness the whole group seldom achieves:

> I'll never forget the time Dad came to visit me at Wellesley. He'd bought a new suit and overcoat which was very unusual for him. He was a real Dad to me and we had a fabulous time. The girls in the dorm just loved him. He took several of us to a cabin in the mountains for the weekend with no idea of the money involved. We went on hikes and played cards and stayed up all hours. I wish he'd done that sort of thing more often when I was growing up.

Among Tallahassee teenagers, swimming, movies, fishing, and picnics were enjoyed by many combinations of family members. Ball games and hunting were for fathers and sons only, while mothers and daughters enjoyed going shopping together or cooking special dishes (Connor, 1955). When children are strung out in age, some activities appeal to only the younger ones, while others are too mature for them. Again, flexibility is the answer.

Balance

Some families wear themselves out trying to do too much. Especially when children are old enough to participate in outside activities, the demands on the mother for chauffeuring are notoriously heavy. Hawkins and Walters (1952) found that families with the most family recreation also entertained most, attended the most social functions, and engaged in the most activities away from home. Perhaps because they overdid things, they reported the most family tensions.

> I never see my children any more. They're out for something every night in the week. Monday is Scout night, Tuesday HI-Y, Wednesday the band rehearses, and Thursday the senior play. Of course, on Friday and Saturday there are social activities, and Sundays their youth group meets. It's gotten so we don't have any family life any more.

In some communities organizational competition for family time becomes so overwhelming that one night in the week is set aside as a meetingless "Family Night." Even without community support individual families can reserve their own regular family occasions.

Parents cannot expect growing children to spend all or most of their time at home. Even ritualized family times need escape clauses. Many adolescent crises are caused by insistence on participation in a routinized family activity.

The Cycle of Family Living

Family relationships change as each child grows older. At first a baby is helplessly dependent. As he learns to walk and talk, he begins asserting his identity, culminating in the two-and-a-half-year-old's delight in discovering that he can say, "no." During the preschool years, family interaction is at its peak, children spend most of their time at home and participate in everything. This is when family rituals are most often innovated—partly for fun, partly as crystallized solutions to harried mothers' needs for order in the midst of chaos (Bossard and Boll, 1950).

The Grade-School Years

When the oldest child leaves proudly or reluctantly for school, his family enters a new era, less involved internally, more involved with the school and other community agencies.

Most middle-class families cooperate closely with the school. Parents and teacher form a united front. They cooperate not only in crises but through routine participation in PTA, classroom visits, and dinner invitations to the teacher. Regular contact makes problems easier to deal with. In every family problems crop up occasionally. Teacher personalities differ so that the same child may love school one year and loathe it the next.

The classroom seldom has the same rules as the home. Strict parents may be disturbed by the flexibility of a progressive classroom. Or permissive parents may wonder how their child can accept school routines. Though the temptation may be great, parents can rarely reform the teacher. Her methods reflect her personality, training, and experience. Discrepancies between home and school seldom disturb children as much as parents fear. A well-adjusted child usually adapts to the situation. He sees what is expected and acts accordingly. The same child may delight in freedom at home, yet conform nicely at school (or vice versa).

One reason children adapt well to school is their admiration for the teacher. Whatever she says is law. When Miss O'Piela says children should brush their teeth *before* breakfast, nothing father and mother can say could persuade Junior to wait till afterward. Parents may be irked when teacher's views differ from theirs, and may be jealous even when they coincide, but respect and affection for the teacher are assets in learning.

Parents should rarely precipitate a showdown, even over important issues —the child may become the victim. A teacher under fire unconsciously tends to "take it out" on the child. Acquiescence is not the only alternative, however. Discussion with the teacher may secure the desired results.

When a child is having difficulty, parents can often supply information that makes it easier for the teacher. A few comments may help her see in kindergarten restlessness Mary's eagerness to learn to read and write like her big sister. She will want to know that Jonny's inattentiveness resulted from worrying about the illness of his father.

Since children spend more time at school than anywhere else, good home-school relations have far-reaching benefits. They are worth more time than the average mother and (especially) father give. Mary and Lawrence K. Frank suggested that even parent-teacher conferences are not enough:

> Individual conferences between parents and teacher do not take the place of the parents' visit to their child's class. It gives a child a warm, comfortable feeling to know that his father (when he can get away from his work) and mother want to see for themselves what his class is like, what he does in school, how he gets along with the other children. It helps his parents, too, to see his teacher in relation to the class, to see the school program in action. School visits thus enrich not only the parents' understanding of their child's school situation but also the entire relationship between parent and child (1954: 885).

Adolescence

In the grade-school years children begin making friends outside the family. Yet their parents remain special people with whom they enjoy doing things. With adolescence, however, parents lose prestige as the discrepancy narrows between their status as adults and the adolescent's as a "near-adult."

ADOLESCENT AMBIVALENCE. Adolescents are halfway between the dependence of childhood and the independence of adulthood. Adolescents are caught. Although they long for independence, they fear it. They waver between resentment of parental controls and fear of losing their parents' love. Often they are dissatisfied with their parents, no matter what they do:

> When I finished high school I was lost in a world of freedom and completely unable to cope with the situation myself. My parents suggested a trip to South America, but I interpreted the offer as a ruse to try to run my life. I refused and became secretive, evasive, and quite remote from the folks. They tried to reason with me but it did no good. Then they decided that to put me on my own would help, so they said I would have to straighten myself out. This idea filled me with resentment and I stubbornly took the challenge and set off for New York where I lived according to my own dictates, and only succeeded in making matters worse. I went from one job to another and from one trouble to another.

When children resent both freedom and control, parents are baffled. One moment the teenager wants protection, while the next he wants to be "treated like an adult." Mood swings are sudden and unpredictable. Worse yet, he often doesn't know what he wants or has contradictory desires. Faced with this dilemma, many parents don't know what to do. Especially with daughters, panic sometimes leads them to reinstate long-abandoned controls:

> It seems, as I look back on that not-too-far-removed time, that I could do nothing to please my parents—everything was wrong and there was much open conflict between them and me. It seemed as if my parents were reverting to my childhood days again in being extremely overprotective and not allowing me to do anything.

How much freedom daughters can have varies with the community. In some urban neighborhoods, it isn't safe for a woman to be alone on the streets at night (much less a girl). In smaller communities such threats do not exist, and teenage girls have more freedom:

Since the age of nine, we have lived in a small town in Northern Ohio (population 2,000). My parents did not have to worry about me if I walked to a girl friend's house in the evening or if they left me alone at home. The undesirable people who are often seen wandering around city streets at night were not present in our small town.

PARENTAL AMBIVALENCE. Parents have their own mixed feelings which make it hard to be objective. They are proud of the increased skill of their fast-growing offspring. However, they mistrust his judgment and remember the tragedies that befell other adolescents—the auto accidents, premarital pregnancies, and drug addictions. It is difficult to be permissive when tragedy may ensue. Moreover, releasing control means cutting back the mother's main role. And some parents have frustrated ambitions they would like to realize through their children.

These motives lead some parents to override children's wishes and map out their lives. Such parents choose careers for their sons and husbands for their daughters. This "guidance" is rationalized as interest in the children's welfare, but parental welfare often outweighs the child's.

ADOLESCENT REBELLION. When parents apply such pressures, they intensify the adolescent's dilemma. They increase his need to rebel. But their attitude makes rebellion tantamount to betrayal. Caught between powerful desires, he fears rebelling because of the bitterness it will create, yet fears conforming when it frustrates his deepest desires.

While revolution makes parents feel rejected, it may pave the way to better parent-child relations. Going away to college provides an opportunity for emancipation:

> When I transferred to State my parents were far enough away so that they couldn't dominate me as easily. I was much happier since I could be independent and express myself as an individual. I deliberately stayed away from home for a whole year, and they gradually got used to the idea that I loved independence. After that, we grew closer as a family but on a new plane. All along I basically loved both my parents but I could not accept them under the conditions they imposed. This made me feel guilty. Under the new conditions, however, we could again become friends and I was much relieved. My parents were proud of my achievements, yet they felt left out and were worried about the breach. Our new level of acceptance was different than before. It was a mutual respect and a realization of each other's needs. My father began to ask my advice on family and business matters, and I began to take them into my confidence about my aspirations and goals. My parents and I are now very close.

Rebellion does not always have a happy ending, and the process is painful for both generations. Can it be avoided? Seldom entirely. But much can be done to smooth the process of emancipation.

FAMILY FLEXIBILITY. Sensitive parents can keep up with changes in their children's needs and capacities. Long before adolescence, family consultation builds self-confidence. As children grow older, their ability to participate in decisions develops with use.

Adolescents are in training for adulthood. This does not mean that they *are* adults. They can be expected to make mistakes and come crying home. They will sometimes be bewildered by the choices they have to make; hence, eager for guidance. When the going gets rough, they may enjoy being babied a bit. Nevertheless, as trainees they need opportunities to gain experience under supervision.

What is needed therefore is flexibility—a combination of support and release:

> My parents have always treated me as an individual and considered me a mature person in accordance with my age. They are always willing to listen to my side of the issue. They never close their minds to my viewpoints and they do not draw conclusions irrationally, but reason things out with me. If I am right they will admit it as readily as I will admit being wrong. They have never been overly strict with me but allowed me to date as soon as I felt I was ready to. They never told me who not to date but felt that I was the best judge of the type of person I would like. They never gave me a curfew as they felt I had enough sense to know what was a reasonable time to be home. But if, due to unexpected circumstances, I found I would be home so late that they might worry, I would call home and tell them. This way I was given a certain amount of responsibility, but I did not abuse it. I therefore justified my parents' opinions of my capabilities and gained their respect.

A flexible approach lessens intergenerational conflict. In a study of high school seniors in the state of Washington, Landis and Stone (1952) found that "democratic" parents handled their teenagers quite differently than "authoritarian" parents. Democratic parents

1. Allowed their children to go out as many evenings as they wished.
2. Never criticized where they went on dates.
3. Were "fairly generous" with allowance money.
4. Usually gave reasons for requests.
5. Discussed family problems with their children.
6. Respected their opinions and judgment "at least half the time."

Democratic families can be permissive because their children have internalized appropriate standards of conduct. Free rein is good for teenagers who are ready for it. More basic, however, to smooth-running family living is discussion which enables parents to communicate their own standards at the same time that they find out their children's views.

Table 23-1 shows that democratic families had appreciably fewer problems. Conflict with parents occurred less often and rebellious wishes to leave home were reduced even more. Generally girls had more complaints than boys, perhaps because parental controls over daughters were tighter.

Table 23-1. Adolescent Difficulties, by Family Authority Pattern and by Sex

		FAMILY AUTHORITY PATTERN		
Problem	Sex	Democratic	Intermediate	Authoritarian
"Trouble getting along with my parents"	Boys	6%	11%	17%
	Girls	8	11	24
"I want to leave home"	Boys	2	2	9
	Girls	3	3	12
Number of cases	Boys	769	735	396
	Girls	537	1340	533

Adapted from Landis and Stone, 1952: 24–25. *Source:* High school seniors in Washington State, 1947. Reciprocal percentages of students in each category did not have the specified problem.

Most middle-class parents in both the United States and Canada treat their adolescents reasonably flexibly. Landis and Stone classified only one-fifth of their families as "authoritarian" whereas twice as many were "democratic." In a Montreal suburb, Elkin and Westley (1955) found parent-adolescent relationships so harmonious that they labeled their report "The Myth of Adolescent Culture." In most families, they asserted, the generations shared a common culture. In short, the socialization processes of love and discipline described in Chapter 21 can produce adolescents so self-disciplined that parents can trust them to abide by family norms—except under the severest provocation.

PARENTS AND PEERS. No matter how homogeneous the neighborhood, there are times when adolescents are torn between parental teachings and their friends. To the parents, the peer group often seems pernicious, undermining the standards they try so hard to teach.

Psychologists have long since proven that cliques contribute to social development. The family provides interaction with siblings of varying ages and with parents from an older generation. The peer group provides experience with equals in age, strength, and skill. Like families, it gives a sense of security. It is a special group among the hundreds of fellow students. Identification with this group reduces emotional dependence on parents. The emancipation essential to readiness for marriage is assisted by this shift in loyalties from parents to peers.

Children raised in a loving family can usually be trusted to abide by family standards. However, counterpressures from the clique sometimes require parental intervention. The child's problem is rarely solved by demanding permanent withdrawal from the group. Enforced severing of group ties is traumatic.

Because the group is important, the best approach is to change the group itself. This may seem an insuperable task, and *is* for a single parent. However, other parents may have the same desires. When children are young, consultation among parents often suffices to change the situation. By adolescence, joint meetings of both generations offer an opportunity to talk over problems and search for neighborhood solutions. If the problem is late hours, a common curfew may be agreed on. Change is always easier if everyone changes together.

In that middle-class suburb of Montreal, parents controlled peer-group activities by organizing adolescent activities, sponsoring family activities and jointly setting standards of conduct for the teenager:

> Typically on school days, he spends his out-of-school hours doing about two hours of homework, helping in household activities, and participating in school organizations, directed sports, or church activities. . . . Thus, much of the adolescent's activity has a productive or educative orientation. . . . In many areas no sharp distinction is made in the family between parental and adolescent activity. . . . The protectiveness of the setting is perhaps evident in the joint actions of parents regarding the social activities of their adolescent children. Many instances were reported in which parents, in collusion, decided how much allowances should be, the number of dates permitted per week, and the required hour of return from dates (Westley and Elkin, 1957: 245).

In exceptional cases, parents and peers clash over major issues. One circumstance is where parents represent an old-fashioned ethnic way of life whereas peers are Americanized. For example, conflicting pressures undermined parental efforts to "keep kosher" in communities where Jews were a small minority (Rosen, 1955). In general, where peers and parents disagree, adolescents take the easy way out, especially when the dominant pattern is easier. Only when parents provide a homogeneous external environment do cross-pressures disappear. This is comparatively easy for the majority group. For minority groups it is seldom possible except in rural isolation, in urban ghettos, or when peer groups form along ethnic lines. Otherwise adolescents caught between parents and peers often change their values, or else they have to change groups. To be caught in the middle is too hard for ambivalent adolescents to endure for long. The need for group security is too great to be easily resisted:

> I felt that I had to do everything my friends did. I had to dress exactly like the other girls and had a terrific argument with my mother because she felt that I was too thin to wear the straight skirts that *everyone* else wore. If my mother or father would say they would rather I didn't do

something the other kids were doing, it was enough to send me into tears for an hour.

Fortunately, crises are not the general pattern of adolescence. When parents tolerate the idiosyncrasies of the group or collaborate to control them, teenagers don't have to choose: "The protective environment is effective in Suburban Town because it has become the accepted pattern of life and because it is so completely accepted by the adolescents themselves." (Westley and Elkin, p. 246)

Terminal Stages

Families enter the "empty nest" stage when their children leave home. For parents absorbed in their children this is like bereavement. Life turns barren and meaningless. Such parents subtly block their children's marriages and turn into meddlesome in-laws.

Mature parents make the transition more easily. Watching their children get married punctuates their lives too, but the tears shed at the wedding are partly tears of joy. Launching young adults into the world is as much an accomplishment as completing a business venture:

> We know that our children don't need us as much any more, now that they are grown up and have families of their own. It makes us feel old now, and that our work is accomplished. This is a somewhat sad feeling but it is mitigated by the gratification of knowing that we have given to society three fine young citizens who are well adjusted and useful.

Launching seldom means cutting family ties altogether. Visiting and correspondence maintain the ties of friendship. When families live close enough together, there are chances to baby-sit and help in other ways.

But the home now contains only the two people who began family life many years before. In some ways this is a relief—an emancipation from responsibility that many parents looked forward to during the child-rearing years (Deutscher, 1959). Not since the days of courtship and early marriage have they been so carefree, able to do whatever they want without the impediments of children. The occasion may well call for a second honeymoon. There is more opportunity now for summer travel and February in Florida. Friends can be entertained without fear of waking the children. Gone are the days when the expense of evenings out was doubled by baby-sitting fees. Husband and wife can chat at dinner without competition from eager youngsters.

Old age is sad in some ways, but it brings compensating advantages. Typically this new relationship lasts a decade or two before widowhood and the end of marriage.

References

ABERLE, DAVID F., and KASPAR D. NAEGELE. 1952. "Middle-Class Fathers' Occupational Role and Attitudes toward Children," *American Journal of Orthopsychiatry*, 22:366–78.

ADORNO, T. W., E. FRENKEL-BRUNSWIK, D. J. LEVINSON, and R. W. SANFORD. 1950. *The Authoritarian Personality*. New York: Harper.

AMERICAN COLLEGE OF OBSTETRICIANS AND GYNECOLOGISTS. 1965. *Manual of Standards in Obstetric-Gynecologic Practice* (Second Edition). Chicago: A.C.O.G.

ANDERS, SARAH F. 1955. "Religious Behavior of Church Families," *Marriage and Family Living*, 17:54–57.

ANGELINO, H., E. EDMONDS, and E. MECH. 1958. "Sex-expressed 'First' Sources of Sex Information," *Psychological Newsletter*, 9:268–69.

BABCHUK, NICHOLAS, and ANGELO LA COGNATA. 1960. "Crises and the Effective Utilization of Contraception," *Marriage and Family Living*, 22:254–58.

———. 1965. "Primary Friends and Kin: A Study of the Associations of Middle Class Couples," *Social Forces*, 43:483–93.

———, HARRY J. CROCKETT, JR., and JOHN A. BALLWEG. 1967. "Change in Religious Affiliation and Family Stability," *Social Forces*, 45:551–55.

BACK, KURT W. 1951. "Influence through Social Communication," *Journal of Abnormal and Social Psychology*, 46:9–23. Cited in George C. Homans, *Social Behavior*, New York: Harcourt, Brace & World, 1961, pp. 90–93.

BALES, R. F., and FRED STRODTBECK. 1951. "Phases in Group Problem Solving," *Journal of Abnormal and Social Psychology*, 46:485–95.

BANDURA, ALBERT, and RICHARD H. WALTERS. 1959. *Adolescent Aggression: A Study of the Influence of Child-Training Practices and Family Interrelations*. New York: Ronald.

———, DOROTHEA ROSS, and SHEILA A. ROSS. 1963. "Imitation of Film-Mediated Aggressive Models," *Journal of Abnormal and Social Psychology*, 66:3–11.

* Multiple works by the same first author are listed chronologically by year of publication. Multiple works in the same year are listed alphabetically by title.

499

————. 1964. "Behavioral Modification Through Modeling Procedures" in L. Krasner and L. P. Ullman, eds., *Research in Behavior Modification*, New York: Holt, Rinehart and Winston.

BARRON, MILTON L. 1946. "The Incidence of Jewish Intermarriage in Europe and America," *American Sociological Review*, 11:6–13.

BATES, ALAN. 1942. "Parental Roles in Courtship," *Social Forces*, 20:483–86.

BATES, JEROME E., and EDWARD S. ZAWADZKI. 1964. *Criminal Abortion: A Study in Medical Sociology*. Springfield, Illinois: Charles C. Thomas.

BECKER, WESLEY C., DONALD R. PETERSON, ZELLA LURIA, DONALD J. SHOE-MAKER, and LEO A. HELLMER. 1962. "Relations of Factors Derived from Parent-Interview Ratings to Behavior Problems of Five-Year-Olds," *Child Development*, 33:509–36.

BEHRMAN, SAMUEL J., and JOHN R. G. GOSLING. 1966. *Fundamentals of Gynecology* (Second Edition). New York: Oxford University Press.

BELL, ROBERT R., and LEONARD BLUMBERG. 1960. "Courtship Stages and Intimacy Attitudes," *Family Life Coordinator*, 8:61–63.

————, and JACK V. BUERKLE. 1962. "The Daughter's Role During the 'Launching Stage,'" *Marriage and Family Living*, 24:384–88.

BENSON, PURNELL. 1955. "The Common Interests Myth in Marriage," *Social Problems*, 3:27–34.

BERKOWITZ, LEONARD. 1964. "The Effects of Observing Violence," *Scientific American*, 210:35–41.

BESANCENEY, PAUL H. 1962. "Unbroken Protestant-Catholic Marriages Among Whites in the Detroit Area," *American Catholic Sociological Review*, 23:3–20.

BIERMAN, JESSIE M., EARL SIEGEL, FERN E. FRENCH, and KENNETH SIMONIAN. 1965. "Analysis of the Outcome of All Pregnancies in a Community," *American Journal of Obstetrics and Gynecology*, 80:37–45.

BIGMAN, STANLEY. 1957. *The Jewish Population of Greater Washington in 1956*. Washington: The Jewish Community Council of Greater Washington. Cited in Gordon, 1964.

BLAZER, JOHN A. 1964. "Married Virgins—A Study of Unconsummated Marriages," *Journal of Marriage and the Family*, 26:213–14.

BLOOD, ROBERT O., JR. 1952. "Developmental and Traditional Child-Rearing Philosophies and Their Family Situational Consequences," unpublished Ph.D. dissertation. Chapel Hill: University of North Carolina.

————. 1953. "Consequences of Permissiveness for Parents of Young Children," *Marriage and Family Living*, 15:209–12.

————, and MORRIS AXELROD. 1955. Unpublished data from Detroit Area Study and my companion rural research project.

————. 1956. "Uniformities and Diversities in Campus Dating Preferences," *Marriage and Family Living*, 18:37–45.

————, and ROBERT L. HAMBLIN. 1958. "The Effect of the Wife's Employment on the Family Power Structure," *Social Forces*, 36:347–52.

————. 1960. "Resolving Family Conflicts," *Conflict Resolution*, 4:209–19.

————, and DONALD M. WOLFE. 1960. *Husbands and Wives: The Dynamics of Married Living*. Glencoe, Illinois: Free Press.

————. 1961. "Social Class and Family Control of Television Viewing,"

Merrill-Palmer Quarterly, 7:205–22.

———. 1963. "The Husband-Wife Relationship," in F. Ivan Nye and Lois W. Hoffman, eds., *The Employed Mother in America.* Chicago: Rand McNally, pp. 282–305.

———. 1967. *Love Match and Arranged Marriage: A Tokyo-Detroit Comparison.* New York: Free Press.

———. Forthcoming. "Kinship Interaction and Marital Solidarity," *Merrill-Palmer Quarterly*, in press.

BOGUE, DONALD J. 1959. *Population of the United States.* New York: Free Press.

BOLTON, CHARLES D. 1961. "Mate-Selection as the Development of a Relationship," *Marriage and Family Living*, 23:234–40.

BOSSARD, JAMES H. S., and ELEANOR S. BOLL. 1950. *Ritual in Family Living.* Philadelphia: University of Pennsylvania Press.

———, ELEANOR S. BOLL, and WINOGENE P. SANGER. 1950a. "Some Neglected Areas in Family Life Study," *The Annals of the American Academy of Political and Social Science*, 272:68–76.

———, ———. 1960. *The Sociology of Child Development.* New York: Harper.

BOTT, ELIZABETH. 1957. *Family and Social Network.* London: Tavistock.

BOWMAN, HENRY A. 1960. *Marriage for Moderns.* New York: McGraw-Hill.

BRADLEY, ROBERT A. 1965. *Husband-Coached Childbirth.* New York: Harper.

BRAV, STANLEY. 1947. "Note on Honeymoons," *Marriage and Family Living*, 9:60.

BRESLER, JACK R. 1961. "The Relation of Population Fertility Levels to Ethnic Group Backgrounds," *Eugenics Quarterly*, 8:12–22.

BRODY, SYLVIA. 1956. *Patterns of Mothering.* New York: International Universities Press.

BRONFENBRENNER, URIE. 1961. "Toward a Theoretical Model for the Analysis of Parent-Child Relationships in a Social Context," in John C. Glidewell, editor, *Parental Attitudes and Child Behavior*, Springfield, Illinois: Charles C. Thomas, pp. 90–109.

BUBER, MARTIN. 1958. *I and Thou.* New York: Scribner.

BUERKLE, JACK V., THEODORE R. ANDERSON, and ROBIN F. BADGLEY. 1961. "Altruism, Role Conflict, and Marital Adjustment: A Factor Analysis of Marital Interaction," *Marriage and Family Living*, 23:20–26.

BURCHINAL, LEE G. 1957. "Marital Satisfaction and Religious Behavior," *American Sociological Review*, 22:306–10.

———. 1960. "Sources and Adequacy of Sex Knowledge Among Iowa High School Girls," *Marriage and Family Living*, 22:268–69.

———, and LOREN E. CHANCELLOR. 1963. "Survival Rates Among Religiously Homogamous and Interreligious Marriages," *Social Forces*, 41:353–62.

BURGESS, ERNEST W., and LEONARD S. COTTRELL, JR. 1939. *Predicting Success or Failure in Marriage.* New York: Prentice-Hall.

———, and PAUL WALLIN. 1953. *Engagement and Marriage.* Chicago: Lippincott.

CALDERONE, MARY S. 1960. *Release from Sexual Tensions.* New York: Random House.

CAMPISI, PAUL J. 1948. "The Italian Family in the United States," *American Journal of Sociology*, 53:443–49.

CASLER, LAWRENCE. 1961 *Maternal Deprivation: A Critical Review of the Literature*. Child Development Monograph #80.

CAVAN, RUTH S. 1959. "Unemployment: Crisis of the Common Man," *Marriage and Family Living*, 21:139–46.

CHAMBLISS, WILLIAM J. 1965. "The Selection of Friends," *Social Forces*, 43:370–80.

CHANCELLOR, LOREN E., and THOMAS P. MONAHAN. 1955. "Religious Preference and Interreligious Mixtures in Marriages and Divorces in Iowa," *American Journal of Sociology*, 61:233–39.

————, and LEE D. BURCHINAL. 1962. "Relations Among Migratory Marriages and Civil Weddings in Iowa," *Eugenics Quarterly*, 9:75–83.

CHESSER, EUSTACE. 1957. *The Sexual, Marital and Family Relationships of the English Woman*. New York: Roy.

CHILMAN, CATHERINE S., and DONALD L. MEYER. 1962. "Educational Achievement of Undergraduate Married Students as Compared to Undergraduate Unmarried Students, with Analysis of Certain Associated Variables," Cooperative Research Project No. 961, Syracuse University, Syracuse, New York. Cited in Marshall and King, 1966.

CHRISTENSEN, HAROLD T. 1952. "Dating Behavior as Evaluated by High School Students," *American Journal of Sociology*, 57:580–86.

————, and ROBERT E. PHILBRICK. 1952. "Family Size as a Factor in the Marital Adjustment of College Couples," *American Sociological Review*, 17:306–12.

————, and HANNA H. MEISSNER. 1953. "Studies in Child-Spacing: III. Premarital Pregnancy as a Factor in Divorce," *American Sociological Review*, 18:641–44.

————. 1962. "A Cross-Cultural Comparison of Attitudes Towards Marital Infidelity," *International Journal of Comparative Sociology*, 3:124–37.

————, and GEORGE R. CARPENTER. 1962. "Value-Behavior Discrepancies Regarding Premarital Coitus," *American Sociological Review*, 27:66–74.

————. 1963. "Timing of First Pregnancy as a Factor in Divorce: A Cross-Cultural Analysis," *Eugenics Quarterly*, 10:119–30.

CHRISTOPHERSON, VICTOR A., JOSEPH S. VANDIVER, and MARIE N. KRUEGER. 1960. "The Married College Student, 1959," *Marriage and Family Living*, 22:122–28.

CLARK, CHARLES E., and HARRY SHULMAN. 1937. *A Study of Law Administration in Connecticut*. New Haven: Yale University Press. Cited in Monahan, 1962.

COBB, SIDNEY, and JOHN R. P. FRENCH, JR. 1966. "Birth Order Among Medical Students," *Journal of the American Medical Association*, 195:172–73.

COHEN, DAVID B., F. J. KING, and WILLARD H. NELSON. 1963. "Academic Achievement of College Students Before and After Marriage," *Marriage and Family Living*, 25:98–99.

CONNOR, RUTH, and EDITH FLINN HALL. 1952. "The Dating Behavior of College Freshmen and Sophomores," *Journal of Home Economics*, 44:278–81.

————, THEODORE B. JOHANNIS, JR., and JAMES WALTERS. 1955. "Family Recreation in Relation to Role Conceptions of Family Members," *Marriage and Family Living,* 17:306–309.

CONVERSE, PHILIP E. 1966. Data from a national survey conducted by the Survey Research Center of the Institute of Social Research of the University of Michigan, Ann Arbor.

COOMBS, ROBERT H. 1962. "Reinforcement of Values in the Parental Home as a Factor in Mate Selection," *Marriage and Family Living,* 24:155–57.

————. 1966. "Value Consensus and Partner Satisfaction Among Dating Couples," *Journal of Marriage and the Family,* 28:167–73.

————, and WILLIAM F. KENKEL. 1966. "Sex Differences in Dating Aspirations and Satisfaction with Computer-Selected Partners," *Journal of Marriage and the Family,* 28:62–66.

CUBER, JOHN F., and PEGGY B. HARROFF. 1965. *The Significant Americans: a Study of Sexual Behavior Among the Affluent.* New York: Appleton-Century-Crofts.

CUMMING, ELAINE, LOIS R. DEAN, DAVIS S. NEWELL, and ISABEL MCCAFFREY. 1960. "Disengagement: a Tentative Theory of Aging," *Sociometry,* 23:23–35.

CYRUS, DELLA. 1946. "What's Wrong with the Family?" *Atlantic Monthly,* 178:67–73.

DAVIS, KINGSLEY. 1940. "The Sociology of Parent-Youth Conflict," *American Sociological Review,* 5:523–34.

DAVIS, MAXINE. 1956. *The Sexual Responsibility of Woman.* New York: Dial.

DENTLER, ROBERT A., and PETER PINEO. 1960. "Sexual Adjustment, Marital Adjustment and Personal Growth of Husbands: A Panel Analysis," *Marriage and Family Living,* 22:45–48.

DE SALES, RAOUL DE ROUSSY. 1948. "Love in America," in Henry Steele Commager, editor, *America in Perspective,* New York: Mentor, pp. 194–204.

DESCHIN, CELIA S. 1961. *Teen-agers and Venereal Disease.* Atlanta: United States Public Health Service.

DETROIT AREA STUDY. *A Social Profile of Detroit.* Ann Arbor, Michigan: Institute for Social Research. An annual series of research reports.

DEUTSCHER, IRWIN. 1959. *Married Life in the Middle Years: A Study of the Middle Class Urban Postparental Couple.* Kansas City, Missouri: Community Studies, Inc.

DEWEES, LOVETT. 1947. "Premarital Physical Examination," in Morris Fishbein and Ernest W. Burgess, editors, *Successful Marriage.* Garden City, New York: Doubleday.

DICKINSON, ROBERT L. 1957. "Anatomy and Physiology of the Sex Organs," in Morris Fishbein and Ruby Jo Reeves Kennedy, editors, *Modern Marriage and Family Living,* New York: Oxford University Press.

DINKEL, ROBERT M. 1943. "Parent-Child Conflict in Minnesota Families," *American Sociological Review,* 8:412–19.

DOLLARD, JOHN, L. W. DOOB, N. E. MILLER, D. H. MOWRER, and R. R. SEARS. 1939. *Frustration and Aggression.* New Haven: Yale University Press.

DOUGLAS, WILLIAM. 1965. *Ministers' Wives.* New York: Harper.

DOUVAN, ELIZABETH. 1963. "Employment and the Adolescent," in Nye and Hoffman, pp. 142–64.

————, and JOSEPH ADELSON. 1966. *The Adolescent Experience.* New York: Wiley.

DUVALL, EVELYN. 1954. *In-Laws: Pro and Con.* New York: Association Press.

DYER, EVERETT D. 1963. "Parenthood as Crisis: a Restudy," *Marriage and Family Living,* 25:196–201.

EASTMAN, NICHOLSON J. 1950. *Williams' Obstetrics* (Tenth Edition). New York: Appleton-Century-Crofts.

EHRMANN, WINSTON W. 1952. "Student Cooperation in a Study of Dating Behavior," *Marriage and Family Living,* 14:322–26.

————. 1955. "Influence of Comparative Social Class of Companion upon Premarital Heterosexual Behavior," *Marriage and Family Living,* 17:48–53.

————. 1959. *Premarital Dating Behavior.* New York: Holt, Rinehart and Winston.

ELKIN, FREDERICK, and WILLIAM A. WESTLEY. 1955. "The Myth of Adolescent Culture," *American Sociological Review,* 20:680–84.

ELLIS, ALBERT. 1949. "A Study of Human Love Relationships," *Journal of Genetic Psychology,* 75:61–71.

————. 1958. "Rational Psychotherapy," *Journal of General Psychology,* 59:35–49.

ELLIS, EVELYN. 1952. "Upward Social Mobility Among Unmarried Career Women," *American Sociological Review,* 17:559–63.

ESHLEMAN, J. ROSS, and CHESTER L. HUNT. 1967. "Social Class Influences on Family Adjustment Patterns of Married College Students," *Journal of Marriage and the Family,* 29:485–91.

FAIRCHILD, ROY W., and JOHN CHARLES WYNN. 1961. *Families in the Church: a Protestant Survey.* New York: Association Press.

FARBER, BERNARD. 1964. *Family: Organization and Interaction.* San Francisco: Chandler.

FARRIS, EDMOND J. 1950. *Human Fertility and the Problems of the Male.* New York: Author's Press.

————. 1956. *Human Ovulation and Fertility.* Philadelphia: Lippincott.

FELDMAN, HAROLD. 1960. Preliminary research report entitled "Why Husbands and Wives Can't Talk to Each Other," written by John Kord Lagemann, *Redbook,* December 1960.

————. 1966. *Development of the Husband-Wife Relationship: A Research Report,* mimeographed. Ithaca: Cornell University.

FILLER, WILLIAM, and HAROLD I. LIEF. 1963. "A Psychologic Approach to the Gynecologic Patient," in Harold, Victor and Nina Lief, editors, *The Psychological Basis of Medical Practice.* New York: Hoeber, pp. 449–60.

FOOTE, NELSON. 1956. "Matching of Husband and Wife on Phases of Development," *Transactions of the Third World Congress of Sociology,* 4:24–34. London: International Sociological Association.

————, JANET ABU-LUGHOD, MARY M. FOLEY, and LOUIS WINNICK. 1960. *Housing Choices and Housing Constraints.* New York: McGraw-Hill.

FORD, CLELAND S., and FRANK A. BEACH. 1951. *Patterns of Sexual Behavior.* New York: Harper and Paul S. Hoeber.

FOREMAN, CLYDE M. 1957. "Levels of Aspiration and Marital Status on the College Campus." Unpublished Ph.D. dissertation, University of Washington. Cited in Marshall and King, 1966.

FRANK, MARY, and LAWRENCE K. FRANK. 1954. "Helping Your Child at School," in Sidonie M. Gruenberg, editor, *The Encyclopedia of Child Care and Guidance*, Garden City: Doubleday.

FREEDMAN, MERVIN B. 1965. "The Sexual Behavior of American College Women: An Empirical Study and an Historical Survey," *Merrill-Palmer Quarterly*, 11:33–47

FREEDMAN, RONALD, PASCAL K. WHELPTON, and ARTHUR A. CAMPBELL. 1959. *Family Planning, Sterility, and Population Growth*. New York: McGraw-Hill.

——, ——, and JOHN W. SMIT. 1961. "Socio-economic Factors in Religious Differentials in Fertility," *American Sociological Review*, 26:608–14.

——, and LOLAGENE COOMBS. 1966. "Childspacing and Family Economic Position," *American Sociological Review*, 31:631–48.

FREEMAN, HARROP A., and RUTH S. FREEMAN. 1966. "Dating Behavior Between American and Foreign College Students," *Journal of Sex Research*, 2:207–13.

FREEMAN, LINTON. 1955. "Homogamy in Interethnic Mate Selection," *Sociology and Social Research*, 39:369–77.

FREUD, ANNA, and DOROTHY BURLINGAME. 1943. *War and Children*. New York: International Universities.

FROMM, ERICH. 1956. *The Art of Loving*. New York: Harper.

GEBHARD, PAUL E. 1966. "Factors in Marital Orgasm," *Journal of Social Issues*, 22:88–95.

GEBHARD, PAUL H., WARDELL B. POMEROY, CLYDE E. MARTIN, and CORNELIA V. CHRISTENSON. 1958. *Pregnancy, Birth and Abortion*. New York: Harper and Paul B. Hoeber.

GEIGER, KENT. 1955. "Deprivation and Solidarity in the Soviet Urban Family," *American Sociological Review*, 20:57–68.

GIBRAN, KAHLIL. 1923. *The Prophet*. New York: Knopf.

GLICK, PAUL C. 1955. "The Life Cycle of the Family," *Marriage and Family Living*, 17:3–9.

——. 1957. *American Families*. New York: Wiley.

——, and HUGH CARTER. 1958. "Marriage Pattern and Educational Level," *American Sociological Review*, 23:294–300.

——. 1960. "Intermarriage and Fertility Patterns Among Persons in Major Religious Groups," *Eugenics Quarterly*, 7:31–38.

GLUECK, SHELDON, and ELEANOR GLUECK. 1950. *Unraveling Juvenile Delinquency*. Cambridge: Harvard University Press.

GOLD, MARTIN. 1961. *A Social-Psychology of Delinquent Boys*. Ann Arbor, Michigan: Institute for Social Research. Data reprinted in Hoffman, 1963: 195.

GOLDBERG, DAVID. 1967. "Our Falling Birth Rate: Fact and Fiction," a paper presented at the meeting of Planned Parenthood/World Population in Denver, May 5, 1967.

GOLDSEN, ROSE K., MORRIS ROSENBERG, ROBIN M. WILLIAMS, JR., and EDWARD A. SUCHMAN. 1960. *What College Students Think*. Princeton: Van Nostrand.

GOLDSTEIN, SIDNEY, and CALVIN GOLDSCHEIDER. 1966. "Social and Demographic Aspects of Jewish Intermarriages," *Social Problems*, 13:386–99.

GOODE, WILLIAM J. 1956. *After Divorce*. Glencoe, Illinois: Free Press.

————. 1959. "The Theoretical Importance of Love," *American Sociological Review*, 24:38–47.

GOODMAN, MARY ELLEN. 1952. *Race Awareness in Young Children*. Cambridge, Mass.: Addison-Wesley.

GORDON, ALBERT I. 1964. *Intermarriage: Interfaith, Interracial, Interethnic*. Boston: Beacon.

GREENBLATT, BERNARD R. 1957. *A Doctor's Marital Guide for Patients*. Chicago: Budlong.

GROSS, EDWARD. 1953. "Some Functional Consequences of Primary Controls in Formal Work Organizations," *American Sociological Review*, 18:368–73.

GROSS, NEAL, WARD S. MASON, and ALEXANDER W. McEACHERN. 1958. *Explorations in Role Analysis*. New York: Wiley

GURIN, GERALD, JOSEPH VEROFF, and SHEILA FELD. 1960. *Americans View Their Mental Health*. New York: Basic Books.

GUTTMACHER, ALAN F. 1957. "Abortions," in Morris Fishbein and Ruby Jo Reeves Kennedy, editors, *Modern Marriage and Family Living*. New York: Oxford University Press, pp. 401–13.

HAFSTROM, JEANNE L., and MARILYN M. DUNSING. 1965. "A Comparison of Economic Choices of One-Earner and Two-Earner Families," *Journal of Marriage and the Family*, 27:403–409.

HAMILTON, G. V. 1929. *A Research in Marriage*. New York: Boni.

HARLOW, M. K., and H. F. HARLOW. 1966. "Affection in Primates," *Discovery*, January, 1966.

HARMSWORTH, HARRY C., and MHYRA S. MINNIS. 1955. "Nonstatutory Causes of Divorce: The Lawyer's Point of View," *Marriage and Family Living*, 17:316–21.

HARRIS, DALE B., KENNETH E. CLARK, ARNOLD M. ROSE, and FRANCES VALASEK. 1954. "The Relationship of Children's Home Duties to an Attitude of Responsibility," *Child Development*, 25:29–33.

HAWKINS, HAROLD, and JAMES WALTERS. 1952. "Family Recreation Activities," *Journal of Home Economics*, 44:623–26.

HEISS, JEROLD S. 1960. "Premarital Characteristics of the Religiously Intermarried in an Urban Area," *American Sociological Review*, 25:47–55.

————. 1961. "Interfaith Marriage and Marital Outcome," *Marriage and Family Living*, 23:228–33.

————. 1962. "Degree of Intimacy and Male-Female Interaction," *Sociometry*, 25:197–208.

HENRY, ANDREW F. 1953. "Residential Turnover and Family Composition of Home Owners in Four Subdivisions in Natick, Massachusetts," *Social Forces*, 31:355–60.

HENRY, WILLIAM E. 1949. "The Business Executive: A Study in the Psychodynamics of a Social Role," *American Journal of Sociology*, 54:286–91.

HERMAN, ROBERT D. 1955. "The 'Going Steady' Complex: A Re-examination," *Marriage and Family Living*, 17:36–40.

HILL, REUBEN. 1949. *Families Under Stress*. New York: Harper.

————. 1963. "Judgment and Consumership in the Management of Family Resources," *Sociology and Social Research*, 47:446–60.

HOBART, CHARLES W. 1956. "Disagreement and Non-Empathy During Court-ship," *Marriage and Family Living*, 18:317–22.

HOFFMAN, LOIS W. 1961. "Effects of Maternal Employment on the Child," *Child Development*, 32:187–97.

———. 1963. "Effects on the Children: Summary and Discussion," in Nye and Hoffman, pp. 190–212.

HOFFMAN, L. RICHARD, ERNEST HARBURG, and NORMAN R. F. MAIER. 1962. "Differences and Disagreement as Factors in Creative Group Problem Solv-ing," *Journal of Abnormal and Social Psychology*, 64:206–14.

HOLLINGSHEAD, AUGUST B. 1952. "Marital Status and Wedding Behavior," *Marriage and Family Living*, 14:308–11.

HOMANS, GEORGE C. 1950. *The Human Group*. New York: Harcourt, Brace and World.

HUNT, CHESTER L., and RICHARD W. COLLER. 1957. "Intermarriage and Cultural Change: A Study of Philippine-American Marriages," *Social Forces*, 35:223–30.

HUNTER, JOYCE TURNER. 1959. "Scholastic Achievement of Married Women Students," *Marriage and Family Living*, 21:110.

HUNTINGTON, EMILY H. 1957. *Spending of Middle-Income Families*. Berkeley: University of California Press.

ILLSLEY, RAYMOND, and BARBARA THOMPSON. 1961. "Women from Problem Homes," *The Sociological Review* (England), 9:27–54.

JACOBS, BETTY. 1943. "Aetiological Factors and Reaction Types in Psychoses Following Childbirth," *Journal of Mental Science*, 89:242. Cited in Newton, 1955:30.

JACOBSON, ALVER H. 1952. "Conflict of Attitudes Toward the Roles of the Husband and Wife in Marriage," *American Sociological Review*, 17:146–50.

JOHNSON, VIRGINIA E., and WILLIAM H. MASTERS. 1961. "Treatment of the Sexually Incompatible Family Unit," *Minnesota Medicine*, 466–71.

———, ———. 1962. "Intravaginal Contraceptive Study: Phase I. Anatomy," *Western Journal of Surgery, Obstetrics and Gynecology*, 70:202–207.

KANIN, EUGENE J., and DAVID H. HOWARD. 1958. "Postmarital Consequences of Premarital Sex Adjustments," *American Sociological Review*, 23:556–62.

KAREN, ROBERT L. 1959. "Some Variables Affecting Sexual Attitudes, Be-havior, and Consistency," *Marriage and Family Living*, 21:235–39.

KARPF, MAURICE J. 1951. "Marriage Counseling and Psychotherapy: A Case," *Marriage and Family Living*, 13:169–78.

KATZ, ALVIN, and REUBEN HILL. 1958. "Residential Propinquity and Marital Selection," *Marriage and Family Living*, 20(1958):27–35.

KELLY, E. LOWELL. 1955. "Consistency of the Adult Personality," *American Psychologist*, 10:659–81.

KEMPER, THEODORE D. 1966. "Mate Selection and Marital Satisfaction Ac-cording to Sibling Type of Husband and Wife," *Journal of Marriage and the Family*, 28:346–49.

KEPHART, WILLIAM M. 1954. "The Duration of Marriage," *American Socio-logical Review*, 19:287–95.

———. 1954. "Some Variables in Cases of Reported Sexual Maladjustment," *Marriage and Family Living*, 16:241–43.

KERCKHOFF, ALAN C., and KEITH E. DAVIS. 1962. "Value Consensus and Need Complementarity in Mate Selection," *American Sociological Review,* 27:295–303.

———. 1964. "Patterns of Homogamy and the Field of Eligibles," *Social Forces,* 42:289–97.

KIMMEL, PAUL R., and JOHN W. HAVENS. 1966. "Game Theory Versus Mutual Identification: Two Criteria for Assessing Marital Relationships," *Journal of Marriage and the Family,* 28:460–65.

KIMURA, YUKIKO. 1957. "War Brides in Hawaii and Their In-Laws," *American Journal of Sociology,* 63:70–79.

KING, FRANCIS P. 1954. *Financing the College Education of Faculty Children.* New York: Holt.

KINSEY, ALFRED C., WARDELL B. POMEROY, and CLYDE E. MARTIN. 1949. *Sexual Behavior in the Human Male.* Philadelphia: Saunders.

———, ———, ———, and PAUL H. GEBHARD. 1953. *Sexual Behavior in the Human Female.* Philadelphia: Saunders.

KIRKENDALL, LESTER A. 1955. "A Concept of Interrelationships Applied to Premarital Behavior," unpublished manuscript.

———. 1956. "Premarital Sex Relations: The Problem and Its Implications," *Pastoral Psychology,* 7:46–53.

———. 1960. "Circumstances Associated with Teenage Boys' Use of Prostitution," *Marriage and Family Living,* 22:145–49.

———. 1961. *Premarital Intercourse and Interpersonal Relationships.* New York: Julian.

———. 1961a. "Sex Drive," in Albert Ellis and Albert Abarbanel, editors, *The Encyclopedia of Sexual Behavior,* New York: Hawthorn, pp. 939–48.

KIRKPATRICK, CLIFFORD, and THEODORE CAPLOW. 1945. "Courtship in a Group of Minnesota Students," *American Journal of Sociology,* 50:114–25.

———, and CHARLES HOBART. 1954. "Disagreement, Disagreement Estimate, and Nonempathetic Imputations for Intimacy Groups Varying from Favorite Date to Married," *American Sociological Review,* 19:10–19.

———, and EUGENE KANIN. 1957. "Male Sex Aggression on a University Campus," *American Sociological Review,* 22:52–58.

KLAPP, ORRIN E. 1959. "Ritual and Family Solidarity," *Social Forces,* 37:212–14.

KOLLER, MARVIN R. 1951. "Some Changes in Courtship Behavior in Three Generations of Ohio Women," *American Sociological Review,* 16:366–70.

KRAIN, MARK. 1966. "A Conceptual Exposition of Heterosexual Interaction," unpublished graduate term paper. Ann Arbor: University of Michigan, Department of Sociology.

KYRK, HAZEL. 1953. *The Family in the American Economy.* Chicago: University of Chicago Press.

LAKIN, MARTIN. 1957. "Personality Factors in Mothers of Excessively Crying (Colicky) Infants," Monographs of the Society for Research in Child Development #22.

LANDES, JUDAH, and WILLIAM WINTER. 1966. "A New Strategy for Treating Disintegrating Families," *Family Process,* 5:1–20.

Landis, Judson T. 1947. "Adjustments after Marriage," *Marriage and Family Living*, 9:32–34.

——, Thomas Poffenberger, and Shirley Poffenberger. 1950. "The Effects of First Pregnancy Upon the Sexual Adjustment of 212 Couples," *American Sociological Review*, 15:766–72.

——, and Mary G. 1958. *Building a Successful Marriage* (Third Edition). Englewood Cliffs, New Jersey: Prentice-Hall.

——. 1960. "Religiousness, Family Relationships and Family Values in Protestant, Catholic, and Jewish Families," *Marriage and Family Living*, 22:341–47.

Landis, Paul H. 1950. "Sequential Marriage," *Journal of Home Economics*, 42:625–28.

——, and Carol L. Stone. 1952. *The Relationship of Parental Authority Patterns to Teenage Adjustments*. Pullman: Washington Agricultural Experiment Station.

Lang, Richard D. 1932. "A Study of the Degree of Happiness or Unhappiness in Marriage as Rated by Acquaintances of the Married Couples," Chicago: University of Chicago, unpublished M.A. thesis. Cited in Burgess and Cottrell, 1939: 140.

Lansing, John B., and James N. Morgan. 1955. "Consumer Finances over the Life Cycle," in Lincoln H. Clark, editor, *Consumer Behavior*, Volume II, "The Life Cycle and Consumer Behavior," New York: New York University Press, pp. 36–51.

——, Thomas Lorimer, and Chikashi Moriguchi. 1960. *How People Pay for College*. Ann Arbor: Institute for Social Research, University of Michigan.

Leavitt, John A., and Carl O. Hanson. 1950. *Personal Finance*. New York: McGraw-Hill.

Lee, Margie Robinson. 1952. "Background Factors Related to Sex Information and Attitudes," *Journal of Educational Psychology*, 43:467–85.

LeMasters, E. E. 1954. "Social Class Mobility and Family Integration," *Marriage and Family Living*, 16:226–32.

——. 1957. *Modern Courtship and Marriage*. New York: Macmillan.

Lenski, Gerhard. 1961. *The Religious Factor*. Garden City, New York: Doubleday.

Leslie, Gerald R. 1964. "The Field of Marriage Counseling," in Harold T. Christensen, editor, *Handbook of Marriage and the Family*. Chicago: Rand McNally, pp. 912–43.

Levine, Lena, and Mildred Gilman. 1951. *Frigidity*. New York: Planned Parenthood Federation of America.

Levinger, George. 1966. "Systematic Distortion in Spouses' Reports of Preferred and Actual Sexual Behavior," *Sociometry*, 29:291–99.

——, and James Breedlove. 1966. "Interpersonal Attraction and Agreement: A Study of Marriage Partners," *Journal of Personality and Social Psychology*, 3:367–72.

Levy, John, and Ruth Munroe. 1945. *The Happy Family*. New York: Knopf.

Levy, Marion J., Jr. 1949. *The Family Revolution in Modern China*. Cambridge: Harvard University Press.

LEWIN, KURT. 1953. "Studies in Group Decision," in Dorwin Cartwright and Alvin Zander, eds., *Group Dynamics*. Evanston: Row, Peterson, pp. 287–301.

LIND, ANDREW W. 1964. "Interracial Marriage as Affecting Divorce in Hawaii," *Sociology and Social Research*, 49:17–26.

LINDENFELD, FRANK. 1960. "A Note on Social Mobility, Religiosity, and Students' Attitudes Toward Premarital Sexual Relations," *American Sociological Review*, 25:81–84.

LINTON, RALPH. 1936. *The Study of Man*. New York: Appleton-Century-Crofts.

LIPSET, SEYMOUR M., and REINHARD BENDIX. 1960. *Social Mobility in Industrial Society*. Berkeley: University of California Press.

LIPTON, LAWRENCE. 1965. *The Erotic Revolution*. Los Angeles: Sherbourne.

LOCKE, HARVEY J. 1951. *Predicting Adjustment in Marriage: A Comparison of a Divorced and a Happily Married Group*. New York: Holt, Rinehart and Winston.

———, GEORGES SABAGH, and MARY MARGARET THOMES. 1957. "Interfaith Marriages," *Social Problems*, 4:329–33.

LOWRIE, SAMUEL H. 1951. "Dating Theories and Student Responses," *American Sociological Review*, 16:334–40.

LU, YI-CHUANG. 1952. "Predicting Roles in Marriage," *American Journal of Sociology*, 58:51–55.

LUCKEY, ELEANORE B. 1961. "Perceptual Congruence of Self and Family Concepts as Related to Marital Interaction," *Sociometry*, 24:234–50.

———. 1966. "Number of Years Married as Related to Personality Perception and Marital Satisfaction," *Journal of Marriage and the Family*, 28:44–48.

MAIER, JOSEPH, and WILLIAM SPINRAD. 1958. "Comparison of Religious Beliefs and Practices of Jewish, Catholic, and Protestant Students," *The Phylon Quarterly*, 18:355–60. Cited in Gordon, 1964:47.

MALINOWSKI, BRONISLAW. 1927. *Sex and Repression in Savage Society*. London. Cited in Davis, 1940.

MANN, FLOYD C. No date. "The Handling of Job Tensions," unpublished manuscript, Ann Arbor: University of Michigan Survey Research Center.

MARSHALL, WILLIAM H., and MARCIA P. KING. 1966. "Undergraduate Student Marriage: A Compilation of Research Findings," *Journal of Marriage and the Family*, 28:350–59.

MASLOW, A. H. 1953. "Love in Healthy People," in Ashley Montagu, editor, *The Meaning of Love*. New York: Julian Press, pp. 57–93.

———. 1954. *Motivation and Personality*. New York: Harper.

MASTERS, WILLIAM H., and E. H. LAMPE. 1956. "Problems of Male Infertility, II. The Effect of Frequent Ejaculation," *Fertility and Sterility*, 7:123–27.

———, and VIRGINIA E. JOHNSON. 1966. *Human Sexual Response*. Boston: Little, Brown.

MAYER, JOHN E. 1957. "The Self-Restraint of Friends: A Mechanism in Family Transition," *Social Forces*, 35:230–38.

———. 1961. *Jewish-Gentile Courtships*. New York: Free Press.

———. 1966. *The Disclosure of Marital Problems: An Exploratory Study of Lower and Middle Class Wives*. New York: Community Service Society.

———. 1967. "The Invisibility of Married Life," *New Society*, February 26, 1967.

McCammon, C. S. 1951. "A Study of Four Hundred Seventy-five Pregnancies in American Indian Women," *American Journal of Obstetrics and Gynecology,* 61:1159. Cited in Newton, 1955:25.

McGinnis, Robert. 1958. "Campus Values in Mate Selection: A Repeat Study," *Social Forces,* 36:368–73.

McGuire, Carson. 1950. "Social Stratification and Mobility Patterns," *American Sociological Review,* 15:195–204.

McLean, Norman. 1953. "A Study of Catholic-Protestant Marriages," a paper presented at the Groves Conference on Marriage and the Family, Ohio State University.

Metropolitan Life Insurance Company. 1963. "The Changing Economic Role of Women," reprinted from their *Business Economics* house organ.

Monahan, Thomas P. 1952. "How Stable Are Remarriages?" *American Journal of Sociology,* 58:280–88.

———. 1953. "Does Age at Marriage Matter in Divorce?" *Social Forces,* 32: 81–87.

———. 1962. "When Married Couples Part: Statistical Trends and Relationships in Divorce," *American Sociological Review,* 27:625–33.

Moore, Denise Francq. 1953. "Sharing in Family Financial Management by High-School Students," *Marriage and Family Living,* 15:319–21.

Morgan, James N. 1955. *Consumer Economics.* Englewood Cliffs, New Jersey: Prentice-Hall.

———, Martin H. David, Wilbur J. Cohen, and Harvey E. Brazer. 1962. *Income and Welfare in the United States.* New York: McGraw-Hill.

———. 1965. "A Pilot Study of Economic Decision Making in the Family," *Research Forum* of the Institute of Life Insurance, 3:5–30.

Morrow, William R., and Robert C. Wilson. 1961. "Family Relations of Bright High-Achieving and Under-Achieving High School Students," *Child Development,* 32:501–10.

Mott, Paul E., Floyd C. Mann, Quin McLoughlin, and Donald P. Warwick. 1965. *Shift Work: The Social, Psychological, and Physical Consequences.* Ann Arbor: University of Michigan Press.

Moulton, Robert W., Eugene Burnstein, Paul G. Liberty, Jr., and Nathan Altucher. 1966. "Patterning of Parental Affection and Disciplinary Dominance as a Determinant of Guilt and Sex Typing," *Journal of Personality and Social Psychology,* 4:356–63.

Mudd, Emily H. 1951. *The Practice of Marriage Counseling.* New York: Association Press.

Murphy, Robert C., Jr. 1963. *Freedom, Love and Innocence,* unpublished manuscript.

Mussen, Paul H., and John J. Conger. 1956. *Child Development and Personality.* New York: Harper.

National Center for Health Statistics. *Vital and Health Statistics.* Washington: U.S. Department of Health, Education and Welfare.

Newcomb, Theodore M. 1961. *The Acquaintance Process.* New York: Holt, Rinehart and Winston.

Newton, Niles. 1955. *Maternal Emotions: A Study of Women's Feelings To-*

ward Menstruation, Pregnancy, Childbirth, Breast Feeding, Infant Care, and Other Aspects of Their Femininity. New York: Paul B. Hoeber.

NOONAN, JOHN T., JR. 1965. *Contraception: A History of Its Treatment by the Catholic Theologians and Canonists.* Cambridge: Belknap.

NYE, F. IVAN. 1957. "Child Adjustment in Broken and in Unhappy Unbroken Homes," *Marriage and Family Living,* 19:356–61.

————, and LOIS W. HOFFMAN. 1963. *The Employed Mother in America.* Chicago: Rand McNally.

ORT, ROBERT S. 1950. "A Study of Role-Conflicts as Related to Happiness in Marriage," *Journal of Abnormal and Social Psychology,* 45:691–99.

PARSONS, TALCOTT, and RENÉE C. FOX. 1952. "Illness, Therapy, and the Modern Urban American Family," *Journal of Social Issues,* 13, 4:31–44.

————, and ROBERT F. BALES. 1955. *Family, Socialization and Interaction Process.* Glencoe, Illinois: Free Press.

————. 1959. "The Social Structure of the Family," pp. 241–274 in Ruth Nanda Anshen, editor, *The Family: Its Function and Destiny.* New York: Harper.

PECK, ROBERT F. 1958. "Family Patterns Correlated with Adolescent Personality Structure," *Journal of Abnormal and Social Psychology,* 57:347–50.

PETERSON, DONALD R., WESLEY C. BECKER, DONALD J. SHOEMAKER, ZELLA LURIA, and LEO A. HELLMER. 1961. "Child Behavior Problems and Parental Attitudes," *Child Development,* 32:151–62.

PICKFORD, JOHN H., EDRO I. SIGNORI, and HENRY REMPEL. 1966. "The Intensity of Personality Traits in Relation to Marital Happiness," *Journal of Marriage and the Family,* 28:458–59.

PINEO, PETER C. 1961. "Disenchantment in the Later Years of Marriage," *Marriage and Family Living,* 23:3–11.

PIUS XI, POPE. 1930. "On Christian Marriage," Encyclical Letter.

POFFENBERGER, SHIRLEY, THOMAS POFFENBERGER, and JUDSON T. LANDIS. 1952. "Intent Toward Conception and the Pregnancy Experience," *American Sociological Review,* 17:616–20.

POTTER, R. G., and M. P. PARKER. 1964. "Predicting the Time Required to Conceive," *Population Studies,* 18:99–116.

PRATT, WILLIAM P. 1965. *A Study of Marriages Involving Premarital Pregnancies,* unpublished Ph.D. dissertation. Ann Arbor: University of Michigan.

PRINCE, ALFRED J. 1961. "Factors in Mate Selection," *Family Life Coordinator,* 10:55–58.

RAINWATER, LEE, RICHARD P. COLEMAN, and GERALD HANDEL. 1959. *Workingman's Wife.* New York: Oceana Publications.

————. 1960. *And the Poor Get Children.* Chicago: Quadrangle Books.

————. 1965. *Family Design: Marital Sexuality, Family Size, and Contraception.* Chicago: Aldine.

RAPOPORT, RHONA, and ROBERT N. RAPOPORT. 1964. "New Light on the Honeymoon," *Human Relations,* 17:33–56.

READ, GRANTLEY DICK. 1944. *Childbirth Without Fear.* New York: Harper.

REDL, FRITZ, and DAVID WINEMAN. 1951. *Children Who Hate.* Glencoe, Illinois: Free Press.

REED, ROBERT B. 1947. "The Interrelationship of Marital Adjustment, Fertility Control, and Size of Family," *Milbank Memorial Fund Quarterly,* 25: 383–425.

REISS, IRA L. 1960. *Premarital Sexual Standards in America.* New York: Free Press.

———. 1965. "Social Class and Campus Dating," *Social Problems,* 13:193–205.

———. 1967. *The Social Context of Premarital Sexual Permissiveness.* New York: Holt, Rinehart and Winston.

RIESMAN, DAVID. 1954. *The Lonely Crowd.* Garden City, New York: Doubleday Anchor.

ROBERTSON, G. G. 1947. "Nausea and Vomiting in Pregnancy," *Lancet,* 2:336. Cited in Newton, 1955:25.

RODMAN, HYMAN. 1965. "The Textbook World of Family Sociology," *Social Problems,* 12:445–57.

ROEBUCK, JULIAN. 1967. "The Cocktail Lounge: A Study of Heterosexual Relations in a Public Organization," *American Journal of Sociology,* 72:388–95.

ROPER, ELMER and ASSOCIATES. 1960. "Parents' College Plans Study," The Education Program of the Ford Foundation.

ROSEN, BERNARD C. 1955. "Conflicting Group Membership: A Study of Parent-Peer Group Cross-Pressures," *American Sociological Review,* 20:155–61.

———, and ROY D'ANDRADE. 1959. "The Psychosocial Origins of Achievement Motivation," *Sociometry,* 22:185–218.

———. 1961. "Family Structure and Achievement Motivation," *American Sociological Review,* 26:574–84.

ROSENBERG, MORRIS. 1965. *Society and the Adolescent Self-Image.* Princeton: Princeton University Press.

ROSENGREN, WILLIAM R. 1961. "Social Sources of Pregnancy as Illness or Normality," *Social Forces,* 39:260–67.

ROTH, JULIUS, and ROBERT F. PECK. 1951. "Social Class and Social Mobility Factors Related to Marital Adjustment," *American Sociological Review,* 16:478–87.

ROY, PRODIPTO. 1961. "Adolescent Roles: Rural-Urban Differentials," *Marriage and Family Living,* 23:240–349. Reprinted in Nye and Hoffman, 1963: 165–81.

RUBENSTEIN, RICHARD L. 1963. "Intermarriage and Conversion on the American College Campus," in Werner J. Cahnman, editor, *Intermarriage and Jewish Life.* New York: Herzl, pp. 122–42.

RUBIN, ISADORE. 1965. *Sexual Life After Sixty.* New York: Basic Books.

SCANZONI, JOHN. 1965. "Resolution of Occupational-Conjugal Role Conflict in Clergy Marriages," *Journal of Marriage and the Family,* 27:396–402.

SCHEINFELD, AMRAM. 1943. *Women and Men.* New York: Harcourt, Brace and World.

SCHNEPP, GERALD J., and AGNES MASAKO YUI. 1955. "Cultural and Marital Adjustment of Japanese War Brides," *American Journal of Sociology,* 61: 48–50.

SCHOFIELD, MICHAEL. 1965. *The Sexual Behaviour of Young People.* London: Longmans, Green.

SCHRAMM, WILBUR, JACK LYLE, and EDWIN B. PARKER. 1961. *Television in the Lives of Our Children.* Stanford: Stanford University Press.

SCHRODER, RALPH. 1963. "Academic Achievement of the Male College Student," *Marriage and Family Living*, 25:420–23.

SCOTT, JOHN FINLEY. 1965. "The American College Sorority: Its Role in Class and Ethnic Endogamy," *American Sociological Review*, 30:514–27.

SEARS, ROBERT R., ELEANOR E. MACCOBY, and HARRY LEVIN. 1957. *Patterns of Child-Rearing*. Evanston, Illinois: Row, Peterson.

SHAFFER, JAMES D. 1963. *Financial Aspects of Undergraduate Student Life at Michigan State University, 1961–62*. East Lansing: Office of Institutional Research, Michigan State University. Cited in Marshall and King, 1966.

SHUTTLEWORTH, FRANK K. 1959. "A Biosocial and Developmental Theory of Male and Female Sexuality," *Marriage and Family Living*, 21:163–70.

SIDDIQUI, H. R. 1962. "Patterns of Help at the Time of Crisis," unpublished paper analyzing data from the Detroit Area Study under Professors Ronald Freedman and David Goldberg. Ann Arbor: University of Michigan Department of Sociology.

SIEGEL, ALBERTA E., LOIS M. STOLZ, ETHEL A. HITCHCOCK, and JEAN ADAMSON. 1959. "Dependence and Independence in the Children of Working Mothers," *Child Development*, 30:533–46. Abridged in Nye and Hoffman, 1963:67–81.

SKIPPER, JAMES K., JR., and GILBERT NASS. 1966. "Dating Behavior: A Framework for Analysis and an Illustration," *Journal of Marriage and the Family*, 28:412–20.

SLATER, ELIOT, and MOYA WOODSIDE. 1951. *Patterns of Marriage: A Study of Marriage Relationships in the Urban Working Classes*. London: Cassell.

SLATER, PHILIP E. 1963. "On Social Regression," *American Sociological Review*, 28:339–64.

SMITH, CHARLES E. 1966. "Negro-White Intermarriage: Forbidden Sexual Union," *Journal of Sex Research*, 2:169–77.

SOLOMON, PHILIP. 1955. "Love: A Clinical Definition," *New England Journal of Medicine*, 252:345–51.

SPIEGEL, JOHN P. 1957. "The Resolution of Role Conflict Within the Family," *Psychiatry*, 20:1–16.

SPOCK, BENJAMIN, M.D. 1946. *The Pocket Book of Baby and Child Care*. New York: Pocket Books.

STOTT, LELAND. 1952. Report on pregnancy research project at the Merrill-Palmer Institute, presented at the annual meeting of the National Council on Family Relations.

STRAUSS, ANSELM. 1954. "Strain and Harmony in American-Japanese War-Bride Marriages," *Marriage and Family Living*, 16:99–106.

STRYKER, SHELDON. 1955. "The Adjustment of Married Offspring to Their Parents," *American Sociological Review*, 20:149–54.

SUSSMAN, MARVIN B. 1953. "The Help Pattern in the Middle-Class Family," *American Sociological Review*, 18:22–28.

———. 1953. "Parental Participation in Mate Selection and Its Effects upon Family Continuity," *Social Forces*, 32:76–81.

———. 1959. "The Isolated Nuclear Family: Fact or Fiction," *Social Problems*, 6:333–40.

TAEUBER, CONRAD, and IRENE B. TAEUBER. 1958. *The Changing Population of the United States*. New York: Wiley.

TALMON, YONINA. 1964. "Mate Selection in Collective Settlements," *American Sociological Review*, 29:491–508.

TERMAN, LEWIS M. 1938. *Psychological Factors in Marital Happiness*. New York: McGraw-Hill.

THOMAS, JOHN L. 1951. "The Factor of Religion in the Selection of Marriage Mates," *American Sociological Review*, 16:487–91.

———. 1956. *The American Catholic Family*. Englewood Cliffs, New Jersey: Prentice-Hall.

THOMASON, BRUCE. 1955. "Marital Sexual Behavior and Total Marital Adjustment: a Research Report." in *Sexual Behavior in American Society*, Jerome Himelhoch and Sylvia Fava, editors. New York: W. W. Norton.

THOMS, HERBERT. 1950. *Training for Childbirth*. New York: McGraw-Hill.

THORPE, ALICE C. 1951. "How Married College Students Manage," *Marriage and Family Living*, 13:104–105, 130.

TIEN, H. YUAN. 1961. "The Social Mobility/Fertility Hypothesis Reconsidered: An Empirical Study," *American Sociological Review*, 26:247–57.

TOMAN, WALTER. 1961. *Family Constellation*. New York: Springer.

UDRY, J. RICHARD. 1966. "Marital Instability by Race, Sex, Education and Occupation Using 1960 Census Data," *American Journal of Sociology*, 72: 203–209.

U. S. BUREAU OF LABOR STATISTICS. 1957. *Study of Consumer Expenditures, Incomes and Savings*, 18 volumes. Philadelphia: University of Pennsylvania Press.

———. 1959. *How American Buying Habits Change*. Washington, D.C.: U. S. Department of Labor.

VERNON, GLENN M., and ROBERT L. STEWART. 1957. "Empathy as a Process in the Dating Situation," *American Sociological Review*, 22:48–52.

VINCENT, CLARK. 1961. *Unmarried Mothers*. New York: Free Press.

WALLACE, KARL. 1960. "Factors Hindering Mate Selection," *Sociology and Social Research*, 44:317–25.

WALLER, WILLARD. 1937. "The Rating and Dating Complex," *American Sociological Review*, 2:727–34.

———. 1938. *The Family: A Dynamic Interpretation*. New York: Cordon.

———, and REUBEN HILL. 1951. *The Family: A Dynamic Interpretation*. New York: Dryden.

WALLIN, PAUL. 1950. "Cultural Contradictions and Sex Roles: A Repeat Study," *American Sociological Review*, 15:288–93.

———. 1957. "Religiosity, Sexual Gratification, and Marital Satisfaction," *American Sociological Review*, 22:300–305.

WESTLEY, WILLIAM A., and FREDERICK ELKIN. 1957. "The Protective Environment and Adolescent Socialization," *Social Forces*, 35:243–49.

WESTHOFF, CHARLES F., LEE F. HERRERA, and P. K. WHELPTON. 1953. "The Use, Effectiveness, and Acceptability of Methods of Fertility Control," *Milbank Memorial Fund Quarterly*, 31:291–357.

———, ROBERT G. POTTER, JR., PHILIP C. SAGI, and ELLIOT G. MISHLER.

1961. *Family Growth in Metropolitan America.* Princeton: Princeton University Press.

——, ——, ——. 1963. *The Third Child: A Study in the Prediction of Fertility.* Princeton: Princeton University Press.

WHELPTON, PASCAL K., ARTHUR A. CAMPBELL, and JOHN E. PATTERSON. 1966. *Fertility and Family Planning in the United States.* Princeton: Princeton University Press.

WHYTE, WILLIAM F. 1955. *Street Corner Society.* Chicago: University of Chicago Press.

WHYTE, WILLIAM H., JR. 1951. "The Corporation of the Wife," *Fortune,* November, 1951.

——. 1952. "The Wife Problem," *Life,* January 7, 1952:32–48.

——. 1954. "The Web of Word of Mouth," *Fortune,* November, 1954.

——. 1957. *The Organization Man.* Garden City, New York: Doubleday Anchor.

WIEGAND, ELIZABETH. 1954. *Use of Time by Full-time and Part-time Homemakers in Relation to Home Management.* Ithaca: Cornell University Agricultural Experiment Station.

——, and IRMA H. GROSS. 1958. *Fatigue of Homemakers with Young Children.* East Lansing: Michigan State University Agricultural Experiment Station.

WILLMOTT, PETER, and MICHAEL YOUNG. 1960. *Family and Class in a London Suburb.* London: Routledge and Kegan Paul.

WINCH, ROBERT F. 1958. *Mate Selection.* New York: Harper.

WOMEN'S BUREAU. 1962. *Fifteen Years After College.* Washington, D.C.: U. S. Department of Labor.

YOUNG, T. R. 1964. "Recreation and Family Stress: an Essay in Institutional Conflicts," *Journal of Marriage and the Family,* 26:95–96.

ZIMMERMAN, CARLE C., and LUCIUS F. CERVANTES. 1960. *Successful American Families.* New York: Pageant.

Author Index

517

Subject Index